CULTURES OF THE MEDIEVAL KINGDOM OF JERUSALEM

A volume in the series

Medieval Societies, Religions, and Cultures
Edited by M. Cecilia Gaposchkin and Anne E. Lester

A list of titles in this series is available at cornellpress.cornell.edu

CULTURES OF THE MEDIEVAL KINGDOM OF JERUSALEM

FRONTIER INVENTIVENESS IN THE AGE OF THE CRUSADES

BENJAMIN Z. KEDAR

CORNELL UNIVERSITY PRESS
Ithaca and London

First published 2025 by Cornell University Press

Library of Congress Cataloging-in-Publication Data
Names: Kedar, B. Z., author.
Title: Cultures of the medieval kingdom of Jerusalem : frontier inventiveness in the age of the Crusades / Benjamin Z. Kedar.
Description: Ithaca : Cornell University Press, 2025. | Series: Medieval societies, religions, and cultures | Includes bibliographical references and index.
Identifiers: LCCN 2024048427 (print) | LCCN 2024048428 (ebook) | ISBN 9781501781704 (hardcover) | ISBN 9781501781711 (pdf) | ISBN 9781501781728 (epub)
Subjects: LCSH: Franks—Jerusalem (Latin Kingdom) | Crusades—Influence. | Civilization, Medieval. | Jerusalem—History—Latin Kingdom, 1099-1244. | Jerusalem—History—Latin Kingdom, 1099-1244—Civilization.
Classification: LCC D182 .K44 2025 (print) | LCC D182 (ebook) | DDC 956/.014—dc23/eng/20241213
LC record available at https://lccn.loc.gov/2024048427
LC ebook record available at https://lccn.loc.gov/2024048428

In memoriam
Nurith Kenaan-Kedar (1938–2015)
Hans Eberhard Mayer (1932–2023)
Jonathan Riley-Smith (1938–2016)

Contents

Introduction
The Cultural Inventiveness of Frankish Jerusalem

The large number of books that tell and retell the history of the crusades—with a focus on that undertaking of epic dimensions known as the First Crusade, which between 1096 and 1099 swept many tens of thousands of men and a number of women all the way from western Europe to Jerusalem—attests to the incessant fascination this topic evokes among nonspecialist readers; in recent decades, its popularity has been enhanced by the injection of the crusade motif into present-day political discourse. The evolution of the medieval crusade idea and the political, military, and ecclesiastical history of the states that came into being in the wake of the First Crusade along the littoral of the eastern Mediterranean are dealt with in far less numerous books, read mainly by professional historians. And only one book-length study, the cultural/civilizational history of the crusades by Hans Prutz, published in Berlin in 1883, has explicitly focused on the culture of the people who lived in those states.[1] It is a culture worthwhile of study, because it stands out for a pervasive—though often overlooked—inventiveness. In the present book I intend to deal with various manifestations of this singular culture, from the particularities of everyday life to the spiritual and intellectual endeavors that evolved in this faraway periphery of medieval Europe.

The book offers a series of new departures. I attempt to integrate the discoveries, insights, and conclusions of many friends and colleagues, of my students, and of myself—but, beyond integration, much of what follows is original research. Also, I have decided to call attention to some underlying problematical attitudes of some historians working in this field. And, after a lifelong grappling with the topic at hand, I experiment with a novel nomenclature.

Let me now introduce the main features of the approach here advocated.

From Eurocentric to Franko-centric

In 1806, the Institut de France offered a prize for the best historical work that would "examine the influence of the crusades on the civil liberty of the peoples of Europe, on their civilization, and on the progress of the Enlightenment, commerce and industry."[2] The offer reveals an outlook that would be characterized today as Eurocentric: the Institut was not interested in the impact of the crusades on the political history of the lands of the eastern Mediterranean, or on Muslim perceptions of and attitudes toward crusaders or European Christians. It called for an assessment of the influence of the crusades on Europe, and more specifically, on European developments consonant with Enlightenment ideals.

For a long time, similar Eurocentric outlooks dominated the study of the culture that evolved in the four Frankish states established by the First Crusaders, namely, the Kingdom of Jerusalem, the Principality of Antioch, and the Counties of Edessa and Tripoli.[3] This is true of Prutz's book of 1883. Nowadays all too rarely consulted, it is an outstanding work, based on a painstaking utilization of the sources available at the time; I shall repeatedly acknowledge my indebtment to it. Yet its basic argument is flawed. Prutz contended that the crusades bestowed on Western culture an abundance of stimuli and innovations that paved the way for the Italian Renaissance. This abundance was not brought West by returning crusaders, but by the Westerners who settled in the East, and whom the indigenous called "Franks." They were those who absorbed and transformed components of Arabic culture and then transmitted them, in modified form, to the West. Having overcome their initial aversion to the language and literature of the infidel, the Franks played the role of mediators and became the West's teachers.[4] However, Prutz was not able to document such modification, transmission, and teaching.

Later historians took an increasingly darker view of the influence of the crusades on Western culture. Ernest James Passant contributed to the fifth volume of the *Cambridge Medieval History*, published in 1926, a chapter on "The Effects of the Crusades upon Western Europe"; evidently it revisits the issue that the Institut de France called to examine 120 years earlier. Passant did not believe that the crusades affected Western thought much, did not mention the possibility that elements of Arabic culture reached Europe via the Frankish East, and tentatively reverted to the view, criticized by Prutz, that some *returning crusaders* may have come back with fresh ideas. "The coincidence of the thirteenth-century [*sic*] 'Renaissance' with the period of the Crusades is striking," wrote Passant, "and it would be rash to deny any share in the outburst of intellectual energy which marks the thirteenth century to the new ideas and broadened outlook of those who, having gone on crusade, had seen the world of men and things in a way to which the society of the tenth and eleventh centuries was unaccustomed. But it must be admitted," he added, almost qualifying his previous statement out of existence, "that a man may travel much and yet see little, may preserve intact the narrowness of vision with which he set out."[5]

About the same time, Charles Homer Haskins dedicated a few pages of his 1924 book, *Studies in the History of Mediaeval Science*, to the "Translators in Syria during the Crusades." The opening sentences convey what has become the consensual view:

> The influence of the Crusades upon the intellectual life of Europe has been variously judged. Once considered the great channel for the westward flow of Arabic culture, the estimate of their importance has greatly diminished with the clearer apprehension of the manifold contacts established with the East through Spain, Africa, Sicily and the Byzantine Empire. It has even been denied that the Crusades had any direct effect upon the diffusion of Arabic learning. . . . Plainly the crusaders were men of action rather than men of learning, and there was little occasion for western scholars to seek by long journeys to Syria that which they could find nearer home in Spain. Nevertheless, intellectual relations with the Arabs of Syria were not wholly lacking.[6]

Steven Runciman (d. 2000), the author of the most influential history of the crusades written in the twentieth century, devoted fewer than four pages of his three-volume opus, *A History of the Crusades* (1951–54), to "Intellectual Life in Outremer" (Beyond-the-Sea, a term often used to designate the Frankish East). The Eurocentric outlook comes to the fore in the concluding sentence, where he asserts that the absence of "real centres of study where native and neighbouring learning could have been absorbed . . . made the cultural contribution of the Crusades to western Europe so disappointingly small." Frankish culture remained an import from the West, with rare contacts with indigenous culture, except in the arts. The contrast with the intellectual interaction with the Muslim world that took place in Sicily or Spain was striking.[7]

Joshua Prawer (d. 1990), who shared Runciman's perception of the Frankish entity as a colony, presented his view of Frankish culture in his 1972 book, *The Latin Kingdom of Jerusalem: European Colonialism in the Middle Ages*. He believed that the Franks espoused a policy of nonintegration, of apartheid, vis-à-vis their Muslim, Eastern Christian, and Jewish subjects, and that this attitude "was probably one of the major factors responsible for the failure of the crusader kingdom to become an intermediary between the Moslem East and Christian Europe." The Franks, "non-receptive" to the intellectual riches of the people they conquered and lacking centers of intellectual activity of their own, played a negligible role as cultural mediators between East and West.[8]

In more recent decades, historians have shifted increasingly from this Eurocentric perspective to what may be called a Franko-centric one. Instead of focusing on the question whether the Franks contributed to the westward flow of cultural influences, historians tend nowadays to concentrate on Frankish culture as such. In other words, the various cultural activities that took place in Europe's newly conquered lands in the East are now deemed worthy of study for their own sake.[9] Within this perspective, cultural interactions between the Franks and the West constitute of course an important topic—but by no means the only one.

Present-day studies of Frankish culture—not always announced as such—do not restrict themselves to intellectual attainments. They deal with monumental and domestic architecture; with food and attire as well as with liturgy, the administration of relics, and the evolution of a distinct dialect; with the innovative "mingling of knighthood with religion" and the running of bathhouses and hospitals; with the aggrandizing of secondary holy places as well as with the differential use of ceramics and the introduction of gold coinage; with military tactics, the patronage of art and historical writing, the construction of distinctive foci of religiosity, and much more.[10]

These studies are conducted in numerous subfields that are largely isolated one from another. It is the purpose of the present book to sum up and integrate their results, and to augment them with those of my own research.

Crusaders and Franks

The term "crusader" is used rather loosely in current studies, with "Crusader Castles," "Crusader Cities," "Crusader Institutions," "Crusader Coinage," "Crusader Art," "Crusader States," and so forth, figuring repeatedly in titles of books and articles.[11] Yet the castles and cities were not inhabited by crusaders, nor were the institutions, coins, or artworks fashioned by them. Crusaders were European Christians who made the vow to go on crusade for the liberation and defense of Jerusalem and the Holy Land; the cross fixed on their clothing served as a palpable sign of the vow; typically, they stayed in the East for a short time. After the conquest of Jerusalem in 1099 some crusaders settled in the East, but the majority returned to the West. The few who remained were joined later by Europeans who chose to migrate to the newly conquered territories, and they and their descendants came to be known primarily as Franks. Thus, the Frankish phenomenon is part and parcel of the history of the crusades, but the Franks as such were not crusaders: this is proven, for instance, by the testimony of Jacques of Vitry, bishop of Acre, that on the eve of the Fifth Crusade (1217–21) he gave the sign of the cross to Frankish inhabitants of Acre, Tyre, and Beirut, urging them to make ready arms for the defense of the Holy Land.[12]

True, the term "crusader" is a historian's construct: it did not exist in the twelfth century. Neither were the Westerners who settled in the East known exclusively as "Franks": they appear also as "Latins," "Jerusalemites," "Antiochenes," and so forth.[13] Moreover, Muslims and other indigenous Easterners referred to Franks, crusaders, and indeed to all Westerners, as *al-Ifranj* (the Franks, in Arabic). Yet a historian's vocabulary, far from slavishly reflecting bygone terms, should first and foremost serve for the examination of the reality s/he is studying. The adoption of the terms "crusaders" and "Franks" effectively draws attention to the difference between two distinct groups of Westerners who came East: short-term warriors and permanent settlers. These groups were not mutually exclusive: crusaders could stay in the East and become part of the Frankish population, while Franks could take the cross. Both groups professed Christianity in its Roman Catholic form and shared basic values, the memory of the First Crusade, and much more. Nevertheless, they were two different though interrelated entities, with tensions occasionally arising between them from the aftermath of the Second Crusade (1147–49) onward.

Therefore, to present all inhabitants of the Kingdom of Jerusalem as crusaders, and speak, for instance, of "crusader masons" at work in mid-twelfth-century Jerusalem, does not do justice to reality.[14] Neither is it helpful when a historian uses a term like "crusader castles" as shorthand for castles erected in the East by people of Western origin during the period of the crusades. The term may confuse the uninitiated nonspecialist. Reading about, say, the "crusader castle of Bethgibelin," s/he understandably assumes that just as the French Fort Carillon (nowadays Fort Ticonderoga in New York State) was constructed by the French, Bethgibelin was built by crusaders—which is not true. It was constructed, in 1136, by "all the people of the kingdom called together," that is, by Franks, not by crusaders temporarily in the East.[15]

In sum, it is appropriate to abstain from speaking of "crusader art," "crusader institutions," "crusader coinage," and so forth. If we wish, we may speak of artworks created and institutions established in the states founded by the First Crusaders, and of coins struck in them. But it is simpler to call a spade a spade and refer to "Frankish art," "Frankish institutions," "Frankish coinage." Of course, I know that spades often give way to pennies, and a book with "Crusader" in its title has a better chance on the market.

Just as we ought to be more precise with regard to crusaders and Franks, the Franks' personal names deserve a more accurate rendition. Present-day convention requires a historian to convey them in the forms they assume in the modern language in which s/he happens to be writing. This convention—which, of course, is not limited to studies of the Franks—distorts the appellations by which the persons concerned were known in their own time and erects a needless barrier between them and the present-day reader. I believe that we should aim at giving back the Franks their genuine names, reproducing them in the manner in which they were probably pronounced at the time. In appendix 1 I discuss the clues that may allow us to do so, and in the book itself I experiment with the proposed way of rendering Frankish names. Readers may find it helpful to look up appendix 1 before encountering the names used in the book itself.

Also, wishing to aid readers in placing past historians in time, I have indicated their date of death following their first in-text citation. I have forgone any notation for historians active at present.

The Kingdom of Jerusalem (1099–1187) and the Kingdom of Acre (1191–1291)

When, about forty years ago, I started work on what was to become the present book, I planned to deal with the cultural history of all four Frankish states founded by the First Crusaders throughout their existence, that is, down to the fall of Acre in 1291. Leading experts advised me at the time that this culture was either not worthwhile of a book-length study, or that the available sources could not sustain it. But as my work proceeded, and as my conception of culture widened, the sources became ever more abundant. Also, I was lucky to discover some unknown texts: vestiges of the works of Gerard of Nazareth (fl. 1140–61), the most notable of which deals with "Men of God," hermits who chose to go East and to live in seclusion in the Holy Land (*Terra Sancta*, in Latin); the descriptions by Ḍiyā᾿ al-Dīn al-Maqdisī (1173–1245) of Muslim holy people—thirteen men and one woman—active in villages of the Holy Land (*al-arḍ al-muqaddasa*, in Arabic) under Frankish and early Ayyubid rule; a letter of Patriarch Eraclius of Jerusalem sent to the West a few days before Ṣalāḥ al-Dīn started his siege of the city on 20 September 1187.[16] From a Vatican codex that belonged originally to the Frankish church of Sidon, I reedited the canons of the Council of Nablus (1120), the only extant body of ecclesiastical legislation promulgated in the Kingdom of Jerusalem in the twelfth century. I also edited an account about the Jerusalem Hospital, probably written in the later part of the twelfth century, and reedited a description of the "Holy Jerusalemite Land" dating from the years 1168–87. As sources accumulated, I decided to limit my study to the Kingdom of Jerusalem and its successor, the Kingdom of Acre, with only a few intrusions to the other Frankish states.

Later, I decided to concentrate on the Kingdom of Jerusalem in the years 1099 to 1187, that is, between the conquest of Jerusalem by the First Crusaders and its reconquest by Ṣalāḥ al-Dīn. This entity, sometimes called the First Kingdom of Jerusalem, differs on many counts from the Second Kingdom of the years 1191–1291, often called the Kingdom of Acre after its capital; the culture of this Second Kingdom, notably differing from that of its twelfth-century predecessor, calls for a separate book-length examination.[17] In the meantime, I attempt to delineate its main characteristics in the last chapter of the present book.

This notwithstanding, I deal with the entire period of 1099–1291 in chapter 1, which surveys the population of the Frankish Kingdom, and in chapter 2, which looks at everyday life there. The nature of the sources on which these chapters are based renders it difficult to treat the Kingdom of Jerusalem and the Kingdom of Acre separately.

Why a Sociocultural Approach?

One cannot study a culture without understanding the society in which it came into being. Neither should one assume that all strata of a society share the selfsame culture. Surely such sharing did not occur in the Frankish Kingdom of Jerusalem, where disparate indigenous groups—Muslim, Eastern Christian, and Jewish, all subordinated to the dominant Frankish stratum—clung to their distinct cultural traditions, as we shall see in chapter 8. Yet the Franks themselves must not be considered as uniformly and fully sharing one and the same culture. Of course, all Franks adhered to Roman Catholic Christianity and were conscious of their common origin in the West, but it is worthwhile to look for variances in cultural outlook between Franks of different social standing.

Let me exemplify what I mean by cultural variances between different classes of the same society by drawing attention to an arresting, extreme disparity in outlook between knights and clerics in the medieval West. The *Voyage of Charlemagne to Jerusalem and Constantinople*, a poem that oscillates between knightly epic and a parody of it, and whose author apparently visited Jerusalem in about 1135, highlights the boast of Olivier, one of Charlemagne's twelve peers, to "have" the daughter of Constantinople's emperor a hundred times during a single night. Divine will sustains Olivier, who stops at thirty yet persuades the princess to report that he made good his boast in full.[18] A similar fantasy appears in a poem by William IX of Aquitaine (1071–1127), the early troubadour and First Crusader, who employs a verb far more coarse and cites a number almost twice as high, albeit spread over several days.[19] But even as erotic bragging and sexual prowess were celebrated in these knightly works despite the ongoing Christianization of the chivalrous ethos, clerical authors, all sworn to celibacy, adopted a diametrically opposed attitude, conspicuously manifested in their anti-Islamic polemics. The traditions that ascribed the virility of thirty or forty men to the Prophet roused their abhorrence; in their eyes, the Islamic belief that God bestowed on Muḥammad such extraordinary prowess was scandalous, a compelling proof that he was no true prophet.[20] In short, we have here a novel juxtaposition of *Mohammed and Charlemagne*:[21] in a knightly work, divine will grants stupendous sexual potency to the emperor's paladin; clerical treatises brand as outrageous the belief in its divine grant to the Prophet.

In an attempt to pinpoint cultural orientations characteristic of different components of Frankish society, chapters 3 to 6 examine the cultural activities and attitudes of Frankish clerics and knights, as well as those that took place at Jerusalem's royal court. Chapter 7 endeavors to find out whether, despite the dearth of direct sources, it is possible to sketch some cultural features characteristic of Frankish burgesses.

It is important to emphasize that the present quest for cultural variances between different strata of Frankish society is by no means rooted in a belief that different social classes develop totally different cultures. Surely values produced by one group can be embraced by another: for instance, the foci of religiosity devised by Frankish clerics were venerated by all Franks. Intergroup cultural overlaps may be more common than contrasts, and yet typical group orientations may differ.

Asymmetrical Comparisons

The concentration of one's studies solely on the culture/s of the Frankish East may lead to intrinsically valid conclusions that ignore, however, the wider context. For instance, William of Tyre (ca. 1130–ca. 1186) has been acclaimed for openly relying on an Arabic chronicle written by a tenth-century Eastern Christian author; yet, as long as we focus exclusively on the Frankish East, the fact that he did not rely on an Arabic book composed by a *Muslim* tends to escape our attention; at least, I do not recall that the fact has been noted. But when we remember that in William's own time a Muslim scholar, Muḥammad al-Idrīsī, prepared a work of geography and a world map for King Roger II of Sicily (1130–54), the limits of William's openness to Arabic-written works become apparent. In short, to understand William in his proper context, we ought to lift our eyes sometimes to Sicily, sometimes to Iberia, sometimes to Westerners who studied in the schools of France and Bologna in about the same time as he did, and so on. In general, we should compare cultural developments in the Frankish East with relevant analogues in Europe and in the Islamicate realm.[22]

This may be considered a tall, even unrealistic order. A historian studying some facet of the history of the Frankish East may retort that the research literature on the subject is growing at so rapid a pace that to take all of it into account becomes ever more difficult; to compare the facet in question with relevant phenomena in other areas is just impossible. The argument is persuasive; and even when we remember that Claude Cahen (d. 1991)—perhaps the most perceptive twentieth-century historian to deal with the crusades—wrote, back in 1983, that the quality of the publications on the subject is too often inverse to their quantity, one still must spend considerable time separating the wheat from the chaff.[23]

Yet there is a way out of this quandary: the asymmetrical comparison proposed by Jürgen Kocka, the eminent social historian. Kocka urges us to aim at a better understanding of the particular case that is our chief concern by contrasting it with other cases that are merely sketched, not systematically compared. He is aware of the pitfalls of this skewed procedure, such as deriving the sketches from secondary literature and consequently falling victim to sundry modes of distortion. Yet he believes that these dangers are more than offset by the advantages of the approach: it widens historians' horizons by providing them with a comparative perspective that does not require a minute knowledge of all the cases compared, and it is capable of leading to otherwise unsuspected questions and answers. In short, Kocka presents asymmetrical comparison as a high-powered, low-cost tool.[24] I employ this method repeatedly, with the compared cases sketched in varying degrees of roughness.

An Octogenarian Historian's Credo

More than the average historical investigation, studies of the crusades tend to betray an emotional involvement or partisanship—manifest or latent—on the part of their authors. This may take the form of a naïve statement like "*Unfortunately*, this did not prevent [the Hospitallers] being ambushed before regaining Acre."[25] But often it is possible to discern what I propose to call a sanctimonial (not to be confused with sanctimonious!) approach to crusading that treats the phenomenon with reverence, admiration, and even glorification. Sometimes such attitude comes openly to the fore, like when my late friend Jean Richard (d. 2021), a leading historian and first president of the Society for the Study of the Crusades and the Latin East (SSCLE), asserted that "the crusade appears to us as the touchstone of a Christian faith whose vivacity and profoundness hold moving lessons for the Christian of today."[26]

In other instances, such perception seeps through a casual remark, like when my late friend Jonathan Riley-Smith (d. 2016), another prominent historian and second president of SSCLE, referred, in a bibliographical list, to a volume as containing "the Hebrew sources on the pogroms that *marred* the First and Second Crusades."[27] In other words, the pogroms damaged or disfigured an endeavor otherwise purportedly virtuous. And on one occasion I witnessed an acute blurring of the divide between faith and research: the conference on the military orders held in September 1996 in London opened with a Latin oration by Father Bernhard Demel, OT, who addressed the assembled scholars as "Fratres et Sorores in Domino nostro Jesu Christo!" and wished them that the memory of His sacramental Cross and Resurrection render them ready "for the eternal meal in His Kingdom, at which all still-extant problems will find their solutions."[28]

True, a historian of integrity knows to repress underlying inclinations and uphold unequivocally what s/he considers to be the truth. Such conduct is eloquently exemplified by one of Riley-Smith's articles on the First Crusade. Having shown that the peasants who perpetrated the 1096 pogroms in the Rhineland were led by a considerable number of knights, he concludes with the revealing statement: "It is not possible, therefore, to adhere to the *comforting* view that the massacres were perpetrated by gangs of peasants."[29] In other words, while a dichotomy between virtuous knights and murderous peasants might be more to one's liking, professional integrity demands rejecting it. However, the problem is that we are not always aware of our susceptibility to comforting views.

Among Israeli scholars, identification with the fate of the crusaders and Franks, and an exaltation of the crusade idea, is occasionally evident. The late Joshua Prawer, my first teacher in medieval studies, fumed—in the original Hebrew version of his history of the Kingdom of Jerusalem—against the Italian city-states who allegedly "competed with one another in the systematic destruction of the crusader state," and indignantly condemned the commutation of the crusade vow, by which "the greatness of the [crusade] idea and its religious splendor were totally abused."[30] In his last book he repeatedly referred to the decisive battle of 4 July 1187 as "the disaster of Hattin."[31] And the late Ronnie Ellenblum (d. 2021), my student and friend, confessed to a reading of the crusades "as part of my own country, and to a certain degree, as part of my own history."[32]

I beg to differ from these fine historians and personal friends. Precisely because of the emotions the subject at hand is capable of stirring, I suggest that we do our best to steer clear of partisanship, identification, glorification, apologetics, and condemnation: they may befog our perceptions and lead us astray. Surely a historian must endeavor to understand the men and women s/he is studying, even to try putting oneself in their shoes. Yet this attempt at understanding should engulf all actors at play—in our case, crusaders, Franks, Muslims, Byzantines, Genoese, Venetians, Eastern Christians, Jews, Samaritans, and so on. As for the history of this country, Sultan Ṣalāḥ al-Dīn (1137–93) is part of it no less than King Amaurry (1136–74); I regard as a highlight of my career the rediscovery of the scant remnants of the Dome of Victory, which Ṣalāḥ al-Dīn erected on the southern of the two Horns of Ḥaṭṭīn after his triumph over the Franks on 4 July 1187.[33]

I know well that this approach may perturb some historians. Back in 1990, at the conference organized in Madrid by the Comité International des Sciences Historiques, a leading French medievalist asked me what I was working on at the time. When told that it was an article on the Battle of Ḥaṭṭīn, he exclaimed: "Ah, the disaster of Hattin." I still remember his incredulous stare when I responded: "The disaster? Why not: the victory?"

I believe that, within crusade studies, a useful antidote against undue involvement and partisanship may be the scrutiny of works on the subject written in earlier times. The noxious impact of passion or prejudice becomes almost effortlessly perceptible once we turn our attention to such writings.[34] These may sensitize us to notice more readily such flaws in works of our contemporaries—and, hopefully, in our own as well.

As for the presentation of historical arguments, I prefer to proffer bits of evidence one after another without long-winded commentaries, sometimes without explicitly spelling out my conclusion: ideally, readers should arrive at it on their own. Evidently, a reader who does not specialize in the history of the crusades sometimes needs explanations that a crusade historian can dispense with, but I prefer to supply such explications sparingly, remembering that "the secret of being boring is to say everything."[35] Indeed, instead of time after time restating the well-known, we should respect the reader's time constraints and concentrate on new sources, explanations, insights. Also, I believe in displaying portraiture whenever offered by the sources, and in presenting protagonists' stories in their own words, limiting my interpretation as much as feasible. And, following in the footsteps of Eileen Power (d. 1940) and her unforgettable Carolingian peasant Bodo, I indulge at one point in the writing of "faction"—fiction based on historical facts.[36]

Alas, the facts known about the Frankish Kingdoms of Jerusalem and Acre are scanty, and very many of the questions we would like to pose—starting with the size of the kingdom's population—are unanswerable or allow, at best, for conjectures. Of course, documentation always reflects only a part of reality: this is true even in our own age, in which countless people are capable of publicizing their thoughts and feelings. Still, the scarcity of documentation about the Kingdoms of Jerusalem and Acre, realms that ended in defeat and the loss of archives and libraries, is more acute than elsewhere. Therefore, we should always beware of equating documentation with reality: for instance, the fact that only the *qāḍī* (judge) of Jabala is mentioned in our sources should not be taken as evidence that no other *qāḍī*s were active under Frankish rule. Absence of evidence is not evidence of absence. Following in the footsteps of Jean Richard, we should always be aware of the fragmentary state of the documentation that has come down to us. We should be ready to develop protocols for the formulation of permissible conjectures that may help us to venture beyond the available documentation. Yet we should also constantly aspire to broaden that documentation by the discovery of new written sources in various languages and by the harnessing of new data, especially those emerging from archaeological research.

Is there a recipe for making a discovery? Yes, there is, prescribed by no less a discoverer than Louis Pasteur (d. 1895). In an address delivered in 1854, he observed in a side remark—in print it appears within parentheses—that "chance favors only the prepared minds."[37] In other words, we should always be ready to expect some discovery lurking behind the corner. If we train ourselves to so expect, it is likely that we shall spot the discovery on sight, even as researchers with minds unprepared will inattentively trudge on.

Map 1. The Frankish Kingdom of Jerusalem

CHAPTER 1

A Tiny Kingdom of Diverse Peoples

Compared with the contemporary kingdoms of Europe, the Kingdom of Jerusalem was tiny; a well-informed author stated that since it was so small, he chose to call it a barony.[1] But its population was heterogeneous to an extent that had no counterpart anywhere in the West of that period.

The dominant, Frankish stratum came into being out of the turmoil of the First Crusade. While most crusaders returned home after having conquered the city on 15 July 1099, a small number—in 1100 we hear of three hundred knights and three hundred foot soldiers—chose to remain in the nascent kingdom; these Founding Fathers were joined in subsequent decades by later arrivals, Westerners eager to live close to the Holy Places or attracted by the opportunities the new kingdom offered.[2]

Were eagerness and attraction mutually exclusive for those who chose to stay after Jerusalem's conquest and for those who joined them later? Modern studies have tended to present crusader motivation as either predominantly material or spiritual, and of late, the pendulum has swung decisively toward an emphasis on the latter possibility. Crusaders, we have been told, sought remission of their sins by participating in a penitential war-pilgrimage; the dispatch of a crusader required considerable material support by his family, proffered because it shared his idealism; influential monks soon presented the crusade as a nomadic military monastery on the move.[3] This reasoning is crucial to the sanctimonial approach toward the crusades.

As I see it, the promise of Pope Urban II, in 1095, to grant penance to those who were to go to Jerusalem to liberate the Church of God was indeed the critical event in the genesis of crusading; but the clue for comprehending the spectacular response of Western knights to his promise is found in a neglected eighteenth-century remark. This is Voltaire's astute observation that the pope offered to the knights the remission of all sins "by imposing on them, as penance, the pursuit of their greatest passion—the waging of war."[4] In other words, the ingeniousness of Urban II's offer lay in proposing to the knights a mode of penance that overlapped with their foremost predilection, and it was this papal stroke of genius that launched a myriad of hoofs (and, in later crusades, hundreds of ships) to what eventually turned out to be a shore too far. As for the portrayal of the crusade as a monastery on the move, the historian Hans Eberhard Mayer (d. 2023) wittily observed that this would have been a jolly, abbot-less monastery, where a man could live with his wife and continue to enjoy his riches.[5] And as for the hypothesis that the dispatch of a crusader was a costly affair, willingly shouldered by a family that shared his idealism, one may argue that while this might have been the case in many instances, in numerous other cases the family might have been eager to see him depart, especially if he was unruly, and would have considered the expenditure a reasonable investment, seeing that he stood a chance to attain benefits—material, spiritual, or both—in the East.

That attaining material benefits was high in the mind of many a crusader (and not only of those crusade leaders who chose to establish their rule over Antioch or Edessa and abstained from marching to Jerusalem, the expedition's goal) is revealed by a largely overlooked statement by Raymond of Aguilers, the eyewitness chronicler of the First Crusade who usually tends to highlight the expedition's spiritual aims. Raymond relates that when the First Crusaders drew close to Jerusalem in June 1099, many left camp at midnight and rushed to take possession of castles and villages in the mountainous region around the city as well as in the Jordan Valley; the custom was, Raymond explains, that he who placed his sign on a castle or a village ensured thereby his ownership thereof. The other crusaders continued barefoot to Jerusalem, exasperated by this contempt for God's word; yet none of them attempted to stop his comrade or friend from partaking in the scramble for possessions.[6]

Does this mean that those scramblers were animated solely by worldly motives? No. They might have yearned to do penance for their sins; they might have wished to save Eastern Christian brethren from Saracen (that is, Muslim) oppression as instructed by the pope; but at the same time, they were evidently eager to secure worldly gains. Raymond does not tell us whether, having acquired them, they rejoined their comrades in the siege of Jerusalem; it stands to reason that they did.

In sum, we should recognize that spiritual motivation was far from being the sole or paramount impulse, and that the same man may have been differently motivated at various points in time.[7] We should also remember that the crusade's spiritual dimension could be variously interpreted: Abbot Guibert of Nogent, an astute observer, wrote in 1109 that "those who saw Jerusalem and the Sepulcher, believed that thereafter they may fearlessly stick fast to crime."[8] Even more importantly, we should desist from giving pride of place to spiritual motivation and from presenting it—consciously or not—as admirable and uplifting, while concurrently dismissing material motivation as reprehensible. In studying the crusades—as in studying any other phenomenon—we should strive to understand human behavior, not to rank it according to our personal values. Also, we should remember that according to Honorius Augustodunensis (ca. 1080–1150) a pilgrim might have left for his destination out of piety, or curiosity, or wishing to attain glory—and here, too, the various urges must not have been mutually exclusive.[9]

European Migrants to the Kingdom of Jerusalem

Let us now focus on the motivations of the Westerners who migrated to the Kingdom of Jerusalem after its establishment in 1099 and gradually augmented its initially tiny dominant stratum. The spectrum of motivations is broad and variegated. At one end we find hermits who chose to live in seclusion near holy places; at the other extremity we see sinners of various stripes who were sentenced to migrate to Jerusalem.

Hermits

Awareness of hermits who chose to live in the Frankish Levant arose from the publication, in 1983, of the biographical notices about twenty-six of them, which Gerard of Nazareth, later bishop of Laodicea, wrote in the mid-twelfth century, and which have come down to us in the form of summaries printed by the Lutheran Centuriators of Magdeburg in the sixteenth century.[10] In subsequent years further information about these recluses, culled from various sources, has enhanced our knowledge of Frankish eremitism.[11] If we may believe the *Life* of St. Bonfilius of Foligno (ca. 1040–1115), he was a First Crusader who remained in the East and became a hermit, spending several years in a desert cave before returning to Italy; yet this *Life* was written more than a century after his death.[12] Other hermits arrived after the First Crusade. Some of them—including two women—lived in cells within the walls of Jerusalem, probably considering themselves the city's spiritual shield. Others lived in Nazareth, on Mount Tabor, on the banks of the Jordan, and on the Black Mountain near Antioch. Some shunned all human contact. Renunciation of meat and wine, scant and rough clothing, bare feet, uncombed hair, and unwashed limbs as well as self-flagellation recur time and again in Gerard of Nazareth's portrayals of these enthusiasts. Many of his "Men of God Living in the Holy Land" resemble the New Hermits active in the eleventh and twelfth centuries, mainly in Italy and France, who strove to practice asceticism in remote places yet formed eremitical communities.[13] Gerard mentions such communities in Palmaria on the shore of the Sea of Galilee and in Jubin and Machanath on the Black Mountain. Bernard of Blois, the rigorous ascetic who became prior of Machanath, in 1123 preached the Christian faith to Nūr al-Dawla Balak, the Turcoman captor of King Baldwin II of Jerusalem.[14] In Jerusalem, Bernard publicly censured the king for some "immense offenses," which unfortunately remain unspecified.[15] Possibly some of the hermits who fled Galilee and Jerusalem when these came under Muslim rule in 1187 chose to make their abode on Mount Carmel, which in 1191 became part of the rump Frankish Kingdom of Acre, and that early in the thirteenth century some of them became the nucleus of the Carmelite order.[16] The most spectacular of the twelfth-century enthusiasts is Ranieri Scacceri (1117–60), whose spiritual progress is recorded in the astonishing *Life*, written by Ranieri's disciple Benincasa shortly after his death.

The fond-of-good-living, lyre-playing son of a wealthy Pisan merchant, young Ranieri undergoes an intense conversion that leaves him temporarily blind, and then adopts a life of severe austerity. While still a merchant, he sails to the Kingdom of Jerusalem with some fellow Pisans and has a vision of God, who tells him to give away his possessions and strip himself naked on the day he, the Lord, was stripped naked at Calvary. Portents and visions follow swiftly one after another. In the church of Tyre, Ranieri hears the bishop declare on Christmas

1138 that God "is now among us and has assumed the flesh of one of you for the salvation of all Christians," and the eyes of the many Pisans present come to rest on him. On Good Friday he distributes his clothes to the poor of Jerusalem and offers his hairshirt and psalter on the altar at Calvary. The priest returns both to him, and Ranieri spends the following night in the Lord's Temple—that is, in the Christianized Dome of the Rock. Soon its priest learns through a vision that "God who stripped at Calvary is now stripped in the Temple for the salvation of the Christian people." For Ranieri, what the bishop hinted at in Tyre, the Temple's priest now spells out. He hides among the recluses atop the walls of Jerusalem until his fellow Pisans leave town and then returns to the Church of the Holy Sepulcher for incessant vigils and prayers. While reciting the verse of the psalter, "You made Man little less than the angels" (Psalm 8.6), his voice is stifled until the fragrance of incense comes out of his mouth and with it a resonant voice, much different from his own, that reveals to him: "I made myself less than my angels, I crowned you with glory and honor, and I made you master over all creatures." Soon afterward the voice tells him: "Glory to the Father in you, glory to the Son in you, glory to the Holy Spirit in you." Subsequently, God tells Ranieri that he has been chosen to lead the Christian people and that the Virgin, the angels, the patriarchs, the prophets, Peter and Paul, the martyrs and the confessors, all should adore God in him, Ranieri. Later, he is told to do penance for the Christian people, which he does for seven years. The most startling revelation takes place when God tells him: "I have made you like me; as I made myself the son of the [Jewish] people for the salvation of the human race, assuming flesh of my maid, and as I carried that flesh to heaven, where it is now with me, so I am made now the son of my Christian people, for its salvation, by putting on your flesh. And I shall make this flesh remain on earth, to be adored by all the peoples that are on it." What had been alluded to before, God now proclaims in so many words: Ranieri is nothing less than God's second incarnation! In 1154, Ranieri returns to Pisa and there performs numerous miracles; still more miracles occur at his tomb after his death in 1160; and he becomes the patron saint of his hometown.[17]

Sinners and Delinquents

The hermits seeking to arrive at perfection in solitude saturated with biblical reminiscences occupy one edge of the motivational spectrum;

the other extremity is populated by sinners sentenced to go to Jerusalem.[18] Twenty years after the city's conquest, the 1119 Council of Reims, presided by Pope Calixtus II, laid down that whosoever violates the Truce of God by assaulting and killing a person, and whosoever perpetrates arson at any time, must become—if unmarried—a monk, or go to Jerusalem; the decision's wording suggests that he had to stay there for good.[19] Later councils, proscribing solely arson, imposed on the culprit the penance of staying in Jerusalem or in Spain for an entire year "in the service of God," that is, fighting the Muslims.[20] The practice also features prominently in the *Tale of Renart the Fox* (*Roman de Renart*), a cycle of fables that reached a huge public in the West. When—in a part of the cycle dated to ca. 1180—the wicked and cunning Renart is condemned to death by hanging, he offers, "in the name of holy penance," to take the cross and go, with God's help, "beyond the sea." King Noble the Lion assents, on the condition that Renart is to remain there for good. He supposes that were Renart the Fox to return, he would become still wickeder, "because"—he explains—"they all have this habit: those who go there as good men return as bad ones."[21] Two generations later, Eudes of Châteauroux (ca. 1190–1273), in one of his sermons, observed likewise that many of those who go beyond the sea find there more opportunities to sin than at home.[22]

The most famous case of banishment to Jerusalem in retribution for a crime is that of the four barons who murdered Thomas Becket in 1170: they were sentenced to fight there, within the Templar order, for fourteen years against the "pagans," that is, the Muslims.[23] However, Roger of Howden (d. 1202), the chronicler who relates that they were buried "before the door of the Temple"—presumably in the cemetery around Jerusalem's Golden Gate—reports also that Pope Alexander III (1159–81) imposed on them to do penance on the Black Mountain, and Romuald of Salerno spells out that he enjoined on them to depart for the East barefoot and wearing haircloth, to make the rounds of Jerusalem's holy places, then to hurry to the Black Mountain in order to spend there the remainder of their lives as hermits.[24] Evidently, the two extremities of the motivational spectrum could occasionally converge.

In another case, Pope Alexander III, keen on preventing undesirables from reaching Jerusalem, averted a sinner's departure. A Flemish woman, who murdered her infant son after her lover had denied fatherhood, was banished by the count of Flanders from his lands for seven years, unless the pope were to rule otherwise. When the woman appeared before Alexander III and declared that she had taken the cross and was ready to set out for Jerusalem, he barred her from doing so, "seeing that her presence in those regions cannot be advantageous, but indeed destructive." He instructed the bishop of Tournai to induce the woman to enter a monastery and, should she refuse to do so, to permit her to marry, in order to make her "cleave to just one man rather than to many."[25]

A far less famous but probably more ingenious outcast than Becket's murderers was the unnamed Englishman who, permanently banished from England on account of unspecified misdeeds, made his way to Acre, where he managed to lose all his possessions by gambling at games. Wearing just a shirt of sackcloth and a haircloth cap, he then trudged through the wintry countryside, hungry, weak, tonsured like a buffoon, and emitting inarticulate sounds like a mute. In this manner he passed freely through many countries, enjoying the hospitality of benevolent people, until he reached the land of the Chaldeans, where he remained for some time and taught himself several languages. He came to the attention of the Mongols, who employed him as translator and envoy. After the Mongol defeat at Wiener Neustadt in 1241, he was captured, discovered by Duke Frederick II of Austria, and henceforth began to supply information about the Mongols to his captors.[26]

The relocation of delinquents to the Kingdom of Jerusalem led some observers to defame it as a refuge of Europe's criminals. Writing a few months after the fall of Jerusalem in October 1187, the English chronicler and biblical commentator Ralph Niger asserted that the Latin populace of Palestine (*Palestina*) consisted of crime-polluted men who chose to flee thence from the West; with the crimes of all countries coagulating in their land, transgressions went on there unrestrained.[27] In the same vein, the chronicler William of Newburgh claimed about a decade later that villainous and lustful people, drunkards, buffoons, and jugglers of all Christian nations flocked together in the Holy Land as if it were a cesspool, befouling it with their obscene practices.[28] In 1238, Pope Gregory IX wrote to Patriarch Gérold of Jerusalem that, because of the refuge wicked people find in the Hospitaller, Templar, and Teutonic orders, many homicides and much wrongdoing take place with impunity.[29] And in 1283–85 Burchard of Mount Sion decried the murderers, bandits, thieves, and adulterers who came from Europe to do penance in the Holy Land or fled there to escape punishment.[30] This presentation of the Frankish East as a penal colony of sorts is tendentious, often put forward to explain why God allowed it to succumb to the Saracens.[31] Nevertheless, remembering the decree of the Council of Reims in 1119, we may assume that indeed there lived in the kingdom people who had good reason to conceal that Reims had been their place of birth and chose to present themselves as citizens of Tyre—though not because of the lofty reason given in Foucher of Chartres's famous passage, namely, that God had transferred the West into the East, Occidentals had been turned into Orientals, and he who was a citizen of Reims had been made a citizen of Tyre. . . .[32]

Yet was the influx of such delinquents necessarily detrimental to the Frankish East? Those of us who are not latter-day moralizers, or addicted to the sanctimonial approach to crusading, may argue that nonconformist, strong-willed, aggressive individuals who deviate from the norms governing a long-established society may be an asset for a new entity that struggles to survive in challenging frontier circumstances. Indeed, no less a personage than Bernard of Clairvaux (1090–1153) comprehended these dynamics when he observed, some time before 1129, that those who flock together in Jerusalem had been mostly crime-polluted robbers, homicides, perjurers, and adulterers, and that their relocation caused a twofold joy: in the West, for getting rid of them; in the East, for providing much-needed assistance.[33]

Heretics

In the thirteenth century, members of a further category of sinners—heretics—were sentenced to depart to the Frankish East. In 1238, Pope Gregory IX laid down that, lest heretics sent to the Holy Land to do penance should contaminate there true believers with their errors, the patriarchs of Antioch and Jerusalem and their suffragans must compel them to wear some differentiating sign.[34] In 1246, the Council of Béziers went much further and prescribed the exact size, position, and color of the crosses that the various categories of penitent heretics had to wear on their way to the East and back; while in the Holy Land they were—contrary to Pope Gregory's injunction—exempt from doing so, but they had to present to the patriarch of Jerusalem or to some ultramarine bishop the letters that stated the reason for their passage and obtain an attestation that their pilgrimage came to a laudable conclusion.[35] In 1247, on the eve of King Louis IX's first crusade, Pope Innocent IV decreed that condemned heretics might be allowed to take the cross for the defense of the Holy Land.[36] Some such people may have become active crusaders. Olivier of Termes, one of the most prominent *faidits*—outlawed seigneurs who lost their lands and castles because of their sympathy for the Cathar heresy—played a prominent role in the *faidits'* last attempt to reconquer their ancestral lands in 1240 and was excommunicated. Later he submitted to King Louis IX. In 1247 he took the cross, saw action at Damietta and Bāniyās (ancient Paneas, called by the Franks Belinas), and returned to France in 1255. Yet in 1264, 1267, and 1273 he sailed East again, and from 1269 onward commanded the royal French contingent in Acre.[37]

Some heretics may have disseminated their tenets in the Frankish Kingdom. On 21 February 1290—fifteen months before the fall of Acre—Pope Nicholas IV wrote to the patriarch of Jerusalem that since numerous heretics were attempting to subvert the faithful in the region under his jurisdiction, he orders him to appoint inquisitors commissioned to eradicate this depravity.[38] It remains unknown whether an inquisition office did come into being in Acre.

Those Fleeing Difficult Situations

In addition to the Westerners sentenced to go to the Holy Land, some chose to do so on their own in order to extricate themselves from a knotty situation, merging the solution to a personal quandary with a demonstration of piety. Several of these people were well-known clerics. Abbot Gerhard of Schaffhausen, mistreated and nearly expelled by his monks, joined the First Crusade, served as custodian of the Holy Sepulcher, and died in Nazareth.[39] Pontius of Melgueil, abbot of Cluny from 1109, came into conflict with the bishops of Lyon and Mâcon; many of his own monks opposed him as well; therefore Pontius laid down his office in 1122 and left for Jerusalem, intending—so relates Petrus Venerabilis (ca. 1092–1156), his rival and successor—to stay there for good.[40] He made the rounds of the Holy Places, was greatly esteemed "in Judea" for his piety, and carried the Holy Lance in a battle against the Saracens.[41] Yet after about two years he returned to the West, tried in vain to regain the abbacy of Cluny, was excommunicated as a schismatic, and died in 1126 in a papal prison.[42]

Bishop Pontius II of Le Puy went to Jerusalem and Antioch for two and a half years after having clashed with his townspeople; he died soon upon his return in 1128.[43] Foucher of Angoulême, abbot of the house of canons regular at Celles, sided with Innocent II after the contested papal election of 1130; his bishop, who supported Anacletus II, harassed him to the point that he decided to leave for Jerusalem "for the sake of prayer." He became first a canon of the Church of the Holy Sepulcher, then archbishop of Tyre, and finally, in 1145, patriarch of Jerusalem.[44] And when during the schism of 1159 King Valdemar I of Denmark and the clergy of his country sided with Antipope Victor IV, whereas Archbishop Askil of Lund supported Pope Alexander III, tensions ran so high that a castle held by Askil's followers came under siege and had to surrender to the king. Askil decided to make up with the king, but "wishing to steer clear of any taint of schism, he undertook a pilgrimage to Jerusalem, thinking it better to suffer exile from his home than to be out of sympathy with the Church of Rome and be banned from its doors." Six years later, in 1167, Askil reappeared in Denmark, a long beard attesting to his pilgrimage.[45]

In 1168, Étienne du Perche, chancellor of Sicily and bishop-elect of Palermo, became the victim of a baronial conspiracy and fled to the Kingdom of Jerusalem with a small retinue. He fell ill and died shortly after his arrival.[46] And clerics unable to obtain ordination by their bishops in the West "either on account of their lack of knowledge or because of their dissolute life, on account of a faulty title or because of inadequate age," went East and were ordained there. The practice is attested—and condemned—in a decision appended to those of the Third Lateran Council of 1179.[47]

There were also lay Westerners for whom a pilgrimage or move to the Holy Land amounted to a virtuous escape from a sticky situation. Count Rodrigo Pérez of Traba, a Galician magnate who in 1137 supported the Portuguese invasion of his region, was subsequently banished from the court of King Alfonso VII of Castile-León; in the wake of this rupture he chose to make a pilgrimage to Jerusalem with a small retinue; a charter drawn up at the Church of the Holy Sepulcher in 1138 records that he donated a village to it.[48] Another magnate who fell from King Alfonso's favor in 1137 was Count Rodrigo González de Lara, an erstwhile governor of Toledo. He too chose to go to Jerusalem, fought there repeatedly against the Saracens, and constructed the castle Toron de los Caballeros (present-day Laṭrūn), which he secured with knights, foot soldiers, and provisions and handed over to the Knights Templar. Later the count returned to Iberia, though not to his native Castile, and after 1143 went again to Jerusalem "in order to pray," remaining there until his death.[49] In 1168, Gui of Lusignan killed Patrick, earl of Salisbury and governor of Poitou on behalf of King Henry II of England (1154–89), while the earl was returning from a pilgrimage to Santiago de Compostela. The king banished Gui from Poitou, and Gui took the cross and sailed to the East, ultimately becoming king of Jerusalem in 1186.[50] And, alongside these men, there were also women who chose to join a crusade in order to extricate themselves from difficult situations.[51]

Yet not all those who found it expedient to leave for the East when facing complications at home were people of much importance. For instance, the monk and master-mason Johan, having become a bone of contention between Bishop Hildebert of Le Mans (r. 1096–1125) who wanted him to work in his service and Abbot Geoffroy of La Trinité de Vendôme who was about to excommunicate him for having left the monastery, chose to go to Jerusalem, then returned to Le Mans in about 1108; Geoffroy saw fit to complain about the matter to Pope Paschal II (1099–1118) and, toward the end of Paschal's pontificate, formally excommunicated the recalcitrant mason.[52] In 1141 the knight Gosselin, known by the ominous nickname *Malus Vicinus* (bad neighbor), fell ill and requested to become a monk of the Abbey of St.-Aubin in Angers. Later he decided to forsake monasticism, a step that must have placed him in a quandary. Therefore he chose to go to Jerusalem but died some time later, presumably under way.[53] In about 1150, the shoemaker Constantin of Châlons-sur-Marne, irritated by the demands of his bishop's underlings to pay dues, set out for Jerusalem. The bishop later came to Jerusalem on pilgrimage. Constantin persuaded the bishop to grant him the right to engage in his trade freely and returned home.[54] And Archdeacon William of Le Mans, accused in about 1185 of having engineered there the murder of a woman, went East and in 1190 attested a deed as "William, dean of Acre and archdeacon of Le Mans." Already a year later he was back in Le Mans.[55]

It is possible that the nickname by which the Poulains—that is, the Franks born in the East—referred to newcomers from Europe, namely, "the sons of Hernaud" (*filii Hernaudii*), expresses a disparagement of their motivation. Jacques of Vitry, bishop of Acre in the years 1216–25, asserts that the Poulains used this nickname on account of the newcomers' light-mindedness, intemperance, and silliness.[56] The nickname sounds enigmatic, until one encounters it in a slightly different form in the chronicle of Otto Morena (d. after 1174)—where it has, however, a social connotation. Describing Emperor Frederick I's siege of Crema—southeast of Milan—in 1159, Otto writes that the city was initially assaulted by a large company composed solely of poor and indigent men, scornfully called *filii Arnaldi* (sons of Arnald).[57] Thus, the nickname may have originated with Poulains who looked down on poor Westerners, believed to have come East to better their station in life.

Coming to the Kingdom's Defense

Moving still further toward the center of the motivational spectrum, we encounter the very many Westerners who departed for the East in order to defend the Kingdom of Jerusalem. Most of them probably joined the military orders of the Knights Templar and Knights Hospitaller and, after 1198, the Teutonic Knights. Others became mercenaries.[58] And there were knights who joined a crusade and then decided to stay in the East. For instance, of the crusaders who came to fight on the second, Syro-Palestinian, front of the Fourth Crusade of 1204 rather than to join the main force that conquered Byzantine Constantinople, three are known to have settled down in the Frankish East and to have married into the kingdom's high nobility.[59] Among the Westerners who went East to defend the kingdom were also some women. Margaret of Beverley in September 1187 actively participated in the defense of Jerusalem against Ṣalāḥ al-Dīn: protected by a cooking pot instead of a helmet, she feigned to be a warrior, kept watch on the city walls, and brought drinks to the exhausted defenders until a millstone-sized rock wounded her.[60]

Seekers of New Opportunities

Then there were those who came East in the hope of securing the patronage of prominent personages to whom they were related. The careers of the numerous new men, some of them Angevin, who arrived there after Count Fulk V of Anjou had become King Fulk of Jerusalem in 1131, and the resentment they caused among some old-timers, have been studied in detail, yet we may assume that the expectation of patronage by a blood-related Frankish magnate, or even a middle-level noble, emboldened aspirants to migrate to the kingdom.[61] Similar mechanisms probably facilitated demographic growth in the autonomous merchant quarters that the Genoese, Venetians, and Pisans established in the kingdom's main harbors.

Lower on the social rungs, artisans and peasants may have wished to move East in search of new opportunities. The wish is alluded to in a letter Pope Innocent III sent in 1200 to the archbishop of Canterbury, warning him that of the craftsmen and husbandmen who had taken the crusade vow only a limited number could gain a livelihood in the Holy Land, as both land and population were scarce there.[62] Although we have no documentary proof as of now, it is plausible to assume that some serfs succeeded in making their way to the Kingdom of Jerusalem, where they, regarded as Franks, would enjoy free status. And at the bottom of the social ladder were the poor, whose wish to go East, on crusade or otherwise, met with the disapproval of men of authority. For instance, in 1267 Patriarch William of Jerusalem instructed Amaurry of La Roche, the Templar Provincial Master of France, to urge the pope and the legates of France and Sicily to prevent poor or old people, or such who were unfit to bear arms, from crossing the sea. But surely some poor and old did make it to the East, for the patriarch complains that they tend to fall into the hands of the Saracens, are killed by them, or abjure their Christian faith.[63]

A New Society

Out of the disparate constituents, discussed above, a new, vigorous society sprang up. It transformed by and by the country's appearance. Even al-Qāḍī al-Fāḍil (1135–1200)—the head of Ṣalāḥ al-Dīn's chancellery and a bitter foe of the Franks—wrote appreciatively, after Jerusalem's reconquest in 1187, that "the Muslims regained possession of a place that, when they last saw it, was almost devoid of inhabitants, but that had been so well-attended to by the infidels that it turned into a garden of paradise."[64]

At the apex of this new society was a new royal house—established by members of Europe's higher nobility, not by occupants of or claimants to a European throne. Yet the resonance of the title "King of Jerusalem" was such that its bearer came to rank highly in the imagination of many a European. For instance, *The Play of Antichrist*, probably written in about 1160 by a Bavarian monk, seats just five rulers on the stage, dominated by the Lord's Temple: The king of Jerusalem, the Roman emperor, and the kings of the Franks (French), Greeks (Byzantines), and Babylon (the Muslims).[65] There arose a new clergy, marked by peculiar, idiosyncratic interests, contributing—as we shall see—a new if hitherto disregarded component to the Renaissance of the Twelfth Century. A new nobility, initially composed of knights of modest or obscure background, gradually rose to predominance.[66] There emerged the new military orders, one of the most important innovations the Kingdom of Jerusalem contributed to European civilization. In the main harbors, the Genoese, Venetian, and Pisan "communes," or quarters, stood out, fiercely guarding their autonomy while vying against one another for commercial predominance. And there were the kingdom's commoners, or burgesses, all of whom enjoyed free status.[67]

Women and the Gender Imbalance

A critical but little documented facet of this Frankish society is its initially skewed gender ratio and its social consequences.[68] Women did participate in the First Crusade and occasionally played a role in battle,[69] but they constituted a minor segment in a predominantly male expedition. Of the six dukes and forty-four counts listed in Riley-Smith's pioneering study as having "certainly, or nearly so" taken the cross in the years 1096–1103, only one—Raymond IV of St. Gilles, count of Toulouse—is known to have traveled East with his wife; of the other 406 lay First Crusaders appearing in the list, only six are recorded as having been accompanied by their wives.[70] It is probable that in later years, when crusaders, pilgrims, and would-be settlers increasingly chose the less arduous sea passage to the East, the gender imbalance became less severe.[71] We have just one document that amounts to a passenger list of those times. This is a verdict of 1250, which lists the passengers of the ship *St. Victor* that carried crusaders to King Louis IX's camp and settlers to the parts of Egypt he hoped to conquer, and which reveals that 411 men and 42 women were on board. Thus, women constituted 9.3 percent of the total; among the 342 commoner passengers their percentage was slightly higher, 12.3. It is noteworthy that of these forty-two women, fifteen (or seventeen) traveled with their husbands and three with a father or brother, while no fewer than twenty-two appear to have had no male chaperon.[72] Yet there is no way to know to what extent the gender ratio on the *St. Victor* was typical.

Jacques of Vitry relates that because of the small number of women who had come East with the First Crusade, the Franks were constrained to fetch wives mainly from Apulia, the closest Latin region, and therefore their descendants were known as Poulains.[73] This amounts to a late, blurred memory of an initially acute gender imbalance, with Western women in short supply. Indeed, in the early decades of the kingdom, the pressure single male Franks exerted on the restricted marriage market was boosted by married Franks who chose to surreptitiously remarry; presumably they left their wives in Europe and remarried in the East.

The Canons of Nablus of 1120 punished such bigamists with expulsion, while allowing their innocent, deceived spouses to stay.[74] A later Frankish law attempted to deal with the problem by requiring the future groom and two witnesses to swear on the saints that he had no living wife, and the future spouse to swear likewise.[75] A handy solution to the Frankish gender imbalance was to marry local women or cohabit with them. Foucher of Chartres, in his famous piece of propaganda promoting immigration to the kingdom in the 1120s, speaks of Franks who married Syrian or Armenian women, and occasionally even a baptized Saracen one.[76] In his idyllic tableau, Foucher insinuates that such converted Muslim women consented to marry Frankish men out of their own free will, but when we remember, on the one hand, the severity with which the Canons of Nablus attempted to curb the rape of Muslim women by Franks and, on the other hand, the age-old willingness of the church to recognize forcible baptisms as valid, we may assume that some such unions were enforced.[77] At any rate, the documentation confirms that interethnic marriages did indeed occur.

The first two kings of Jerusalem, Baldwin I and II, married Armenian noblewomen, and so did Joscelin I of Courtenay, the third count of Edessa. In Antioch, Riso, the chaplain of Princes Bohemond I and II, refers in 1138 to a slave whom he "drew forth from infidelity to the grace of baptism," and a Frank named Barutellus is mentioned in 1149 alongside "his Saracen wife."[78] The Syrian emir and man of letters Usāma ibn Munqidh (1095–1188) relates that in Nablus he met the son of a Muslim woman who was married to a Frank—and killed him.[79] In 1193 Pope Celestine III instructed Bishop Theobald of Acre that a Saracen who killed a Christian in battle and then converted to Christianity might marry the dead man's widow, and a Christian might marry the converted widow of the Saracen he slew.[80] Thus, there is some evidence for Frankish-Muslim intermarriage; sexual relations between Frankish men and Muslim women, as well as between Muslim men and Frankish women, were sternly prohibited by the Council of Nablus, with transgressors punishable with castration or nasoctomy—yet a prohibition always attests to the existence of the behavior outlawed.[81]

However, one statement in the research literature about Frankish-Muslim intermarriage must be quashed once and for all. It is the assertion of Steven Runciman, in the most influential of twentieth-century crusade histories, that "intermarriage with Moslems was allowed. In 1114 the Patriarch Arnulf [of Jerusalem] was severely scolded by Pope

Paschal [II] for having performed a marriage ceremony between a Christian and a Moslem lady."[82] Runciman bases his statement on the succinct but accurate summary of Pope Paschal's bull by Reinhold Röhricht (d. 1905)—a summary that by no stretch of imagination can be interpreted as referring to a Christian-Muslim marriage.[83] In reality, in the bull of 19 July 1117 by which Paschal reinstates Arnoul (Arnulf) as patriarch, he divulges that Arnoul was accused of having had sexual intercourse with the wife of one Gerard and with a Saracen woman who gave birth to his son.[84] Clearly, Runciman transubstantiated Arnoul's alleged sexual relations with two women, a Christian and a Muslim, into Arnoul's presiding over a marriage between a Christian man and a Muslim woman—and then went on to comment: "[By scolding Arnoul] Pope Paschal showed once again his misunderstanding of the East. For if the Franks were to survive there, they must not remain an alien minority but must become part of the local world." Evidently, Runciman's strongly held conviction that only the adoption of Eastern customs and a readiness to blend into the Eastern environment might have conferred permanence to the Frankish experiment, led him to misconstrue the pope's bull so awkwardly. A powerful warning to all of us to beware of reading texts through the lenses of our fixed ideas.[85]

The at least initially skewed gender ratio within the Frankish population was partly balanced by the large number of Frankish men who fell in battle or were captured by the Muslims. In a passionate call for help that Patriarch Amaurry of Jerusalem (1157–80) dispatched in 1166 to all Christians of the West, he claimed that the number of captured and fallen exceeds "once, twice, thrice, far more often" the number of Christians who resided in the Kingdom of Jerusalem at that time.[86] This is rhetorical exaggeration; but surely the attrition of men was considerable.[87] Consequently—unlike in the West—Frankish widows were expected to, and did, remarry. As James Brundage (d. 2021) facetiously put it, the women of the kingdom amounted to a "knighthood of the bedchamber" (*militia cubiculi*).[88]

Pope Innocent III's letter of 1200 and Patriarch William's instruction of 1267 each attest, alongside other texts, that numerous Westerners were eager to move to the Kingdom of Jerusalem even after it had lost most of its territory to the Muslims. The written documentation provides few clues to the ratio between such newcomers and Franks born in the East, but, in the future, data of a new nature may provide more trustworthy answers.[89] Thus, the isotope analysis of the tooth enamel of twenty individuals buried in the Frankish coastal city of Caesarea, and of two individuals interred in the inland Frankish village of Le Petit Gerin, suggests that thirteen of the Caesarea individuals probably spent their childhood in the West, and six others may have done so as well; only the teeth of one Caesarean, and of the two individuals of Le Petit Gerin, yielded values consistent with a childhood passed in the East.[90] On the other hand, a team that examined the ancient DNA from skeletal remains of nine males buried together in thirteenth-century pits near the castle of Sidon concluded that four were locals, three of European ancestry, while two were of mixed descent, possibly having had a European father and a local mother.[91] These are early results from which it would be foolhardy to generalize; but the techniques, if further developed and applied to the large Frankish cemetery at ʿAtlīt and to Franks buried elsewhere, hold the promise of generating evidence on the newcomer/old-timer ratio and on Frankish/Easterner genetic admixture.[92]

Muslims in the Kingdom of Jerusalem

Our discussion of the dominant, Frankish population of the Latin East's society started with the questions: Who went East, and why? When we turn to the subjected Muslim population the main question is: Who remained after the crusader conquest and why?[93]

The mode of crusader takeover largely determined the fate of the Muslim population in each place:

(1) When a town was besieged and taken by assault, many Muslim and Jewish inhabitants were massacred or enslaved. The best-known example is Jerusalem, stormed on 15 July 1099, where—uniquely—the desire to put an end to infidel desecration of the Holy Places prompted the prohibition of Muslim and Jewish residence in the city.[94] Caesarea, stormed in 1101, similarly lost its Muslim population: forty years later, in 1141, the traveling traditionalist ʿAbd al-Karīm b. Muḥammad al-Samʿānī found there just one Muslim family.[95]

(2) Fear of massacre led some Muslims to flee for safety even before the advent of the crusaders. The two regional capitals of Ramla and Tiberias were deserted when the crusaders entered them, but probably some of the refugees returned after the consolidation of Frankish rule.

(3) A takeover that followed a formal act of surrender was equally bloodless and did not entail Muslim dislocation. Nablus, whose inhabitants promised to hand over the town if the crusaders were to conquer Jerusalem, was the earliest instance of this kind.
(4) Siege culminating in negotiated surrender was another mode of Frankish takeover. The terms of surrender varied: in some cases, Muslims were permitted to leave for Muslim-ruled territory, in others they were given the choice between going into exile and remaining under Frankish rule.[96]

The crusader conquest had a dramatic impact on the elite of the local Muslim population. Jerusalem, which a few years before the crusader conquest could boast of twenty-eight Muslim study circles and two *madrasas* (institutions teaching Islamic law), became an exclusively Christian city.[97] Elsewhere, members of the Muslim leading strata chose to go into exile. Some of these later engaged in intellectual activities; their works, especially inasmuch as they refer to the Franks, amount to an indirect offshoot of the Frankish East and will be discussed below.

In precrusade times, most Muslims of the region were Sunnis, but in some parts Shiʿi presence was considerable. Nāser-e Khosraw, the Persian civil administrator turned pilgrim and traveler who passed through the region in 1047, observed that Tyre's inhabitants were mostly Shiʿi and so were the people south of Tiberias, whereas Ibn al-ʿArabī of Seville (1075–1148), who spent some time in the country in the 1090s, encountered Shiʿis in Ascalon and Acre.[98] Inasmuch as Shiʿis believed that the struggle against Sunnis must precede that against the infidel, they may have had a special reason for staying under Frankish rule.[99]

It is certain that the mass of the Muslim peasant population stuck to the land. Until several decades ago, not much was known about its fate under Frankish rule. Ibn Jubayr (1145–1217), the Muslim traveler from Granada who briefly passed through a part of Frankish-ruled Galilee in 1184, observed that the Muslim peasants he encountered on his way lived prosperously under the Franks, owned their houses and other possessions, faring better and enjoying sounder justice than their brethren under Muslim rule.[100] This oft-quoted observation should, however, be read alongside the remark of Gautier, chancellor of Antioch in the first half of the twelfth century, that Frankish rule was "more intolerable" for the local population than that of their Byzantine and Turkish predecessors.[101] The report of an anonymous continuator of William of Tyre, that when the Templars bought the island of Cyprus in 1191, they intended to treat the Cypriots as if they were the inhabitants of a *casal* (village) in the Kingdom of Jerusalem, that is, to beat and maltreat them, points in the same direction.[102] Indeed, the Templar Rule spells out that, without receiving permission from his superior, a member of the order may beat a (usually Muslim) slave with a leather belt as long as he takes care not to cripple him.[103] The meager documentation at our disposal suggests that the treatment of Muslim subjects was far from uniform throughout the Frankish East.[104]

In a seminal article of 1967, Emmanuel Sivan (d. 2024) drew attention to documentation about some Muslim peasants who lived under Frankish rule in the vicinity of Nablus. These peasants were followers of a Ḥanbalī *imām*, Aḥmad ibn Muḥammad ibn Qudāma (1098–1163), who lived in the village of Jammāʿīl (today known as Jammāʿīn). The Frankish lord of the area was harsher than others, levying a tax four times higher than usual and mutilating the peasants' legs. (Apparently he was not the only one to do so: when Robert of Retest decided in 1158 to mark the boundary between his fields and those of the Church of the Holy Sepulcher, and his rustic—a hoary, knowledgeable Saracen nicknamed "Twisted Leg"—was to verify it, Robert threatened that if he were to lie about the field boundaries, his remaining good leg would be cut short.)[105] When Jammāʿīl's Frankish lord learned that Aḥmad ibn Qudāma's Friday sermons drew peasants from several villages and diverted them from work, he decided to have him killed. However, one of his subordinates alerted Aḥmad, who fled to Damascus—the year was 1156—and soon thereafter ordered his relatives and disciples to follow him, implying that emigration from infidel territory was their religious duty. In all, some 140 men, women, and children came to Damascus between 1156 and 1173, and founded the suburb of al-Ṣāliḥiyya on the slopes of Mount Qāsyūn. Fortunately, Ḍiyāʾ al-Dīn al-Maqdisī, Aḥmad's grandson, wrote an account of this exodus and listed its participants—a unique document that allows inter alia a reconstruction of the considerable size of the families of several Muslim peasants and a study of the patterns of name-giving among them.[106] It also reveals that the flight to Damascus was not necessarily final: some participants in the exodus chose later to return to their native villages.[107]

Ḍiyāʾ al-Dīn also wrote a tract titled "The Wondrous Doings of the Shaykhs of the Holy Land." Its extant part contains descriptions of fourteen shaykhs, that is, local holy persons, most of whom were active in villages of the Nablus region; one of them was a woman. These descriptions brim with scenes of everyday life that serve as a backdrop to the shaykhs' wondrous deeds: here a small child cries out in the evening, craving for roasted meat; there a woman insists that her husband—one of the shaykhs—reveal why he suddenly burst into laughter, wonders loudly whether he was laughing at her, and finally succeeds in making the reluctant husband disclose a surprisingly risqué story; people go to their vineyards or trespass at night on other people's vineyards, draw water from a well, reap harvests.

The shaykhs are portrayed as standing out for piety and asceticism, being closer to God than the simple believers whom they lead to repentance and on whose behalf they intercede and perform miracles—from the multiplication of food to the reading of thoughts.[108] While earlier studies revealed that the local peasant communities were led by a *raʾīs*, or village headman, who apparently acted also as the representative of the Frankish lord, Ḍiyāʾ al-Dīn's work brings to light a different, spiritual sort of leadership that existed in several villages, that of the shaykh.[109]

In one instance we are able to observe the clear-cut supremacy of the latter sort of leadership. Shaykh ʿAbd Allāh of Funduq, a village six miles southwest of Nablus, tells the local *raʾīs*:

> "O So-and-so, I would like you to go to Nablus to buy me a water-jug for ablutions." The *raʾīs* asked: "Don't you need anything but the purchase of the water-jug?" The shaykh said: "No," and the *raʾīs* set off. I think he said it was in the afternoon, so he went quickly. He kept saying to himself: "The shaykh has sent me just for a water-jug. I may make it to town before they close the shops." He arrived and found one shop still open. He bought the jug and said to himself: "I shall spend the night in the Friday mosque and not go to anyone, until I leave tomorrow morning."
>
> He sat down in the western side of the Gharbī Friday mosque. There were three *fuqarāʾ* (poor men, or Sufis) there, and he sat with them. Since nobody came to bring them anything, he went to the market and spent there a *dīnār* he had with him, to buy them bread and something to go with it. He came back and said, "Eat and pray for me," and they ate. When morning came, he went back to the village, to the shaykh, who said: "O So-and-so, I know that you had tired yourself and that on your way you were wondering why I had bothered you only for a water-jug. However, I had sent you

because of the three men for whom you spent the *dīnār* and bought bread. I have chosen you for that. Those three are of the people who uphold the earth," or something to this effect. The *ra'īs* was gladdened and kissed the shaykh's hand.[110]

The references to Franks in Ḍiyā' al-Dīn's work allude to Frankish violence and Muslim fear of it.[111] Yet we have to remember that the author grew up in a refugee community intensely hostile to the Franks and that he wrote down his stories after their flight from the Nablus region. The very many Muslims who did not follow Aḥmad ibn Qudāma's call to emigrate to Damascus appear to have adopted a more compliant attitude toward their Frankish rulers. Indeed, Ḍiyā' al-Dīn relates that when Aḥmad's relatives decided to abide by his call and flee to Damascus, they kept their plan a secret from the other villagers of Jammā'īl, but these found them out and, unable to deter them, alerted the Franks, who tried unsuccessfully to ambush the emigrants at the River Jordan.[112] The villagers may have had various reasons for attempting to thwart the tiny exodus, but in any case, they obviously chose to cooperate with the Franks. Certainly they enjoyed religious freedom and apparently could go on pilgrimage to Mecca.[113] Ṣalāḥ al-Dīn's secretary 'Imād al-Dīn (1125–1201) stated, after the 1187 reconquest, that the Franks did not change "a single law or cult practice" of the Muslims of the Nablus region and permitted them "to maintain their customs as regards their laws, their statutes, their shrines and their mosques."[114] Elsewhere, speaking of Muslim children who "were brought up under Frankish rule and so were accustomed to it," he admits that some Muslim compliance had taken place; but he goes on to claim that "because they were afraid of them [the Franks], they concealed their love for us," insinuating that compliance was superficial.[115]

The dividing line between the Frankish and Muslim societies was traversable by change of religion. The evidence for Muslim conversion in the Kingdom of Jerusalem is considerable. Latin chronicles tell of Muslim converts who entered the service of Godefrid of Bouillon (1099–1100) and Baldwin I (1100–18), the kingdom's first two rulers. We have seen that Foucher of Chartres, in the 1120s, mentions that some Franks married baptized Saracen women. Ḍiyā' al-Dīn relates that a Muslim (apparently a muezzin) "entered a church and became a Christian." Some baptized Muslims fought alongside the Franks, risking execution should they fall into Muslim hands. In 1193, Pope Celestine III replied to queries by Bishop Theobald of Acre about Muslim conversion, and in 1201, writing to a bishop of Tiberias, Pope Innocent III proclaimed the validity of consanguineous marriage between converts and the inadmissibility of polygamy among them. In letters of 1237–38 Pope Gregory IX dealt with the vexed issue of slave conversion. The "custom of the land" promised manumission to a baptized slave—for which reason many slaves sought baptism, and therefore many Frankish lords forbade them to attend sermons and be baptized. In his letters, Gregory IX endorsed an ingenious compromise between faith and mammon: the lords must allow their slaves to accept baptism; the baptized slaves must remain in bondage. In 1264 Pope Urban IV wrote to the patriarch of Jerusalem that the poor Muslims and Jews coming to Acre to be converted should be provided sustenance while receiving Christian instruction. And accords drawn up between the Mamluks and various Frankish rulers in the years 1267–83 refer repeatedly to Muslims fleeing from Mamluk to Frankish territory and converting there, and vice versa. Manifestly, sources of various types point to conversions among the kingdom's Muslims, mostly from the lower strata.[116]

There were also cases of conversion to Islam. Latin and Arabic chronicles relate repeatedly that Christian warriors who could not withstand the hardships of battle crossed the lines and converted to Islam. Such cases occurred during the Second Crusade of 1147–49 as well as in Ṣalāḥ al-Dīn's time and during the Fifth Crusade. Also, many Frankish prisoners chose to convert.[117] But not all cases of conversion to Islam occurred in the thick of battle or in its aftermath. An early law attributed to King Baldwin II (1118–31) lays down that a son might disinherit his father and mother if they left for the land of the Saracens in order to abandon their Christian faith, or became Jews or Saracens.[118] An archbishop of Tyre wrote to Pope Alexander III that in his province frequently a husband or wife passed to Muslim territory, whether of their free will or by force, converted to Islam, and raised there a new family.[119] And the *Book for the King*, the Frankish juridical treatise dating from the years 1197–1205, deals with the case of a knight who went to the land of the Saracens in order to embrace the religion of *Mahoumet*.[120]

"Cultural commuting"—this is how Thomas Glick calls the passing back and forth between Christian and Islamic societies in Iberia—occurred also in the Frankish East.[121] Usāma ibn Munqidh recounts that a Frank by the name of Ra'ul (Raoul), who was captured by the men of Shayzar, converted to Islam and learned the craft of marble carving. He seemed so sincere in his prayers and fasting that the ruler of Shayzar, Usāma's father, married him to the daughter of a pious family; she bore him two sons. When the boys were six or seven years old, Raʾul moved with his Muslim family and possessions to Apamea in the Principality of Antioch, where he reverted to Christianity with his children.[122] In 1193, in his letter to Bishop Theobald of Acre, Pope Celestine III dealt with the similar case of a Christian who left his faith and wife and according to Gentile rites took a pagan woman for wife, who in due time bore him a number of sons. The abandoned Christian wife, with the consent of her archdeacon, married another man and bore him children. The bishop asked what should be done if the renegade decides to return to Christianity and, after the death of his first wife, wishes to marry the pagan wife "who on his account converted to our faith together with her children." Pope Celestine ruled that revert and convert may marry and their children be considered legitimate.[123] However, Celestine's approval of the archdeacon's decision to let the abandoned Christian wife remarry deviated from the traditional view, and six years later, in 1199, Pope Innocent III abrogated it.[124]

Eastern Christians under Frankish Rule

Of the indigenous inhabitants of the kingdom, the closest to the Franks were the Eastern Christians. Their proportion within the population at large is a moot point. Most likely they were a majority in some parts of the country, such as in the vicinity of Jerusalem, whereas Muslims formed the bulk of the native population in the region of Nablus and in parts of Galilee.[125] William of Tyre mentions Bethlehem and Thecua as localities inhabited solely by Eastern Christians, yet these two were not the only ones.[126] Ronnie Ellenblum has shown, on the basis of archaeological surveys and charter evidence, that the kingdom's indigenous villages tended to be mono-religious—that is, either Eastern Christian or Muslim. His study suggests also that the Franks chose to found their rural settlements in areas populated by Eastern Christians and abstained from doing so in regions in which Muslims predominated.[127] But, as frequently happens in research, here too a historian's conclusion, based on painstaking examination of the evidence, is prefigured in a contemporary's statement. Writing in 1109, Guibert of Nogent relates that after the conquest of Caesarea in 1101, the conquerors established there a colony of Franks (*Francorum colonia*). Later, he adds, many other towns were captured, "but as they were so embedded within that savage paganism, few of our people considered it safe to set up colonies there."[128]

Eastern Christian inhabitants who were expelled from Jerusalem by the Fatimids at the onset of the crusader siege in June 1099 returned after the crusader conquest. King Baldwin I, eager to enlarge the population of his capital, arranged in about 1115 a migration of Christian peasants from Transjordan to Jerusalem; an Arabic source reveals that they settled in the city's eastern part and that some of them followed the Melkite (Greek Orthodox) rite.[129] We have no clue as to the share of the Eastern Christians in the city's population, but it is possible to estimate the proportion of Eastern Christian churches: A comprehensive survey indicates that of Jerusalem's eighty-nine ecclesiastical buildings, forty-nine were Latin and twenty-five Greek Orthodox, while fifteen belonged to other Eastern Christian groups. Thus, in the capital of the Frankish Kingdom, Eastern Christian churches made up about 45 percent of the total.[130]

The Armenians and Jacobites—Miaphysites branded by Rome as heretics—gained from the advent of Frankish rule, whereas the Greek Orthodox—considered by Rome to be schismatics who nevertheless basically belong to the one true church—were adversely affected by it. The kingdom's major sanctuaries and their properties passed from Greek Orthodox to Latin hands, and Greek prelates were replaced by Latin ones. Yet Frankish religious discord with the Greek-speaking Orthodox clergy and monks and the Syrians (*Suriani*), that is, the mass of Orthodox believers who spoke Arabic and used Greek or Syriac as their liturgical language, was tempered by the dependence of the Frankish clergy on Greek Orthodox knowhow and by the reliance of Frankish kings on Byzantine support and on the military service of the Syrians.[131] Franko/Eastern Christian intermarriages took place, especially between Frankish men and Eastern Christian women, and some Eastern Christians gained access into Frankish society: a Petrus Armenus is listed in a document of 1163 among the knights of the city of Jerusalem, and a Jacobus Surianus appears in about 1170 among the city's burgesses.[132] In twelfth-century Acre, Ebu'l Fazl (Abū al-Faḍl), an Eastern Christian who adopted the Latin rite, founded a church and memorialized his deed by a still existing Latin inscription.[133]

On the local level, Franks and Eastern Christians sometimes used the same church, but the evidence for their interrelations is too scanty to allow for generalizations.[134] In ʿAyn Kārim, west of Jerusalem, where such common use appears to have taken place, the relations were marked by constant friction—not about theological questions, but solely about ritual issues like cutting the beard, or whether the Eucharist should be celebrated with leavened or unleavened bread.[135] In the Church of St. George above Tiberias, Syrians as well as Latins were baptized, married, and buried until 1178, when Bishop Gerald of Tiberias and Abbot Johan of St. Mary in the Valley of Josaphat laid down that henceforth Latins were to be barred from doing so.[136] But did the place constitute, before 1178, a joint Frankish/Syrian parish?[137] Possibly, but not necessarily. The Church of St. George was granted to the Abbey of St. Mary in the Valley of Josaphat as early as 1109, which suggests that it was a pre-existing Greek Orthodox institution that served an Eastern Christian community.[138] In the coming years, Frankish monks ran the place, which continued to serve the religious needs of the Syrians as well as those of the monks' servants. Apparently, the monks succeeded in attracting some Frankish parishioners of nearby Tiberias, possibly by offering them lower fees for baptism, marriage, and burial there than in the city's cathedral.[139] The 1178 accord put an end to this situation, coercing the Franks to use the services of the church of Tiberias. Still, the accord reveals that some Franks were willing to be baptized, married, and buried alongside Syrians, and that this willingness was stifled because the Frankish prelates insisted on the rights of the city's bishop. On the other hand, in 1186, a Frankish couple in Jerusalem was forbidden, by the Hospitaller Master Roger of Moulins, to sell the house they bought to "Syrians and other people who are not obedient to the Church of Rome."[140] Here the animus against the Syrians is unmistakable.

Frankish ambivalence toward Eastern Christians is perhaps best epitomized by a detail of the story of King Gui of Lusignan's release from Ṣalāḥ al-Dīn's captivity in the summer of 1188. A continuator of William of Tyre's chronicle relates that the sultan allowed him to choose ten knights who would be released with him. Gui chose nine knights—and a scribe. "And this was regarded a greatly wicked and impudent deed, for he left a knight [to linger in prison] because of a Syrian."[141] Thus, the king prefers a scribe to a knight, and to make things still worse, the scribe is a *Surien*.

No counterpart to Gerard of Nazareth or to Ḍiyāʾ al-Dīn al-Maqdisī is known to have arisen among the Frankish Kingdom's Eastern Christians, and therefore we have no twelfth-century account about the little-known individuals of this large and heterogeneous group. The closest to a portrayal of such an Eastern Christian emerges from a will drawn up in Acre on 16 September 1264. The testator's name is Saliba, and he dictates his will as he lies sick in the Acre Hospital of the Order of the Knights Hospitaller.[142] The will presents him as a burgess of Acre and reveals that he is a wealthy man.

The will also affords a glimpse of his household: he lays down that his slaves Amet (Aḥmad) and Sophia should be manumitted and goes on to *order* them to be Christian; he leaves forty bezants to "Maria, my baptized one," that is, his converted slave (of whom he appears to have been quite fond, for he bequeathed just twenty bezants to each of his nephews and nieces); and Marinetus, his "baptized one," is one of the will's witnesses.[143] Evidently, Saliba is surrounded by two converts and two future converts, but the will does not divulge his household's total size. Since it mentions his daughter and stepdaughter, but not his wife, we may deduce that he is a widower.

Saliba was of Eastern Christian origin: his name means "Cross" or "Crucified" in Syriac.[144] Yet he conducts himself like a consummate Latin Christian. He is a confrère of the Military Order of the Hospital, requests to be laid to rest in Hospitaller attire, and appoints Etienne of Meses, Grand Preceptor of the order, to be his heir as well as one of the three executors of his will, the two others being a Pisan and a Genoese.[145] He leaves thirty-six bezants for a chaplain who is to say Mass for a year for the salvation of his soul and the remission of his sins in Acre's Genoese church. That church will receive five bezants for its paving; the city of Acre will get five times as much for its defenses. Acre's Dominican, Franciscan, and Carmelite houses are bequeathed five bezants each, St. Lazarus of the Knights six, and eight other Latin institutions either two or three, while Acre's Eastern Christian churches go unmentioned.[146]

The testament, which lists several members of Saliba's extended family, reveals that acculturation on the onomastic level occurred mainly in the younger generation. Saliba had a sister named Nayma (Nāʿima, pleasant in Arabic) and a sister-in-law known as Settedar (Sitt al-Dār, Arabic for mistress of the house). Two other persons who appear to have belonged to Saliba's generation were called Bedera (Bādir, moon in Arabic) and Sarquisius (Sarkis, the Armenian form of Sergius). The younger generation, on the other hand, bears mostly names that were also current among Franks. Saliba's daughter was called Katelina, his stepdaughter Isabella, his nephews Leonardus, Thomasinus, Georgius, Dominicus, Nicholaus, Bonaventura, Leonardinus, and Isabellonus. The names of his two nieces—Vista and Caolfa—do not sound Western.

The same is true of the name of his daughter Haternia. Saliba totally ignored her in his will, and she and her husband Pierre attempted to challenge the appointment of Etienne of Meses as Saliba's heir, but on 15 June 1267 they had to concede defeat, in the presence of the patriarch of Jerusalem, William of Agen.[147] By that time Etienne was no longer alive—he fell in an ambush near Acre in October 1266.[148]

In the act of 1267 Saliba is not presented as a burgess of Acre and confrère of the hospital, but simply as a Syrian: his identification with the Church of Rome, so conspicuously demonstrated by his will, did not suffice to obliterate his otherness.

Each of the Muslim and Eastern Christian groups living in the Kingdom of Jerusalem amounted to a distinct sociocultural entity that believed in its own superiority; the same was true of the Jews and Samaritans, much smaller in number. From the Frankish point of view, however, there prevailed a hierarchy, with the Franks on the top, the Muslims at the bottom, and the Eastern Christians in the middle; among the latter, the Armenians, who enjoyed the highest status, were followed by the Maronites, then by the Greek Orthodox.[149] The paramount Frankish position was bluntly proclaimed by the royal title "King of Jerusalem of the Latins" (*rex Ierusalem Latinorum*)—a title poles apart from "the Emperor, Lord of [the adherents of] the Two Faiths," which Alfonso VI of León and Castile, conqueror of Toledo in 1085, apparently used in Arabic-written letters to Muslim rulers.[150] In the Kingdom of Jerusalem, the "Latins"—adherents of the Christian faith in its Roman Catholic version—were the only ones the king deemed fit to mention in his title. They were not just the upper social stratum: they were the body politic. In Greek history, the period of post-1204 Frankish rule over lands formerly belonging to the Byzantine Empire is known as *Frankokratía*; the character of the regime the First Crusaders imposed on the lands they conquered may be duly highlighted by calling it "Frankocracy."

Chapter 2

Everyday Life in the Kingdom of Jerusalem

Around the middle of the twelfth century, Nikulás Bergsson, future abbot of the monastery of Munkaþverá in northern Iceland, set out on a pilgrimage to the Holy Land. Upon his return, he dictated—in what is known today as Old Icelandic—an account of what must have been the longest voyage of a Westerner of those times: from Iceland to Norway and Denmark, and thence via Germany, Italy, and Cyprus to "*Acrs-borg* [Acre] which lies in *Iorsala-land* [the land of Jerusalem] and was formerly called *þolomaida* [Ptolemais]."[1]

His description of the country is terse, just 538 words long. And yet it is informative in several ways. Since Nikulás reports that in *Iorsala-borg* (Jerusalem) "there lies the church where the Lord's grave is, and that place where the Lord's cross stood," he must have visited the shrine after 1149, when the new Frankish church, incorporating the Rotunda around the Tomb and the hill of Golgotha, was inaugurated; and since he remarks that "*Askalon* lies in *Serkland* [the land of the Saracens] and is heathen," he must have left the country before the Frankish conquest of that last Fatimid stronghold in August 1153. The description reveals also that our Icelander must have encountered serious problems in understanding locals and fellow pilgrims. For him, the Church of the Holy Sepulcher is *Pulkro kirkia*, a designation that implies an amusing miscomprehension of the shrine's Latin name. Also, describing his progress southward to *Iorsala-borg*, Nikulás notes: "Next comes *Nepl* [Nablus], a large town. Then a town called *Casal*"—whereby he divulges that he considers the Frankish generic term *casale* (village) to be the name of a specific location. (Nikulás probably had in mind the Casale Sancti Egidii, today Sinjil, thirteen miles south of Nablus.)[2] And he continues: "Next comes *Maka Maria*"—another misunderstanding, this time concerning Mahumeria, the large Frankish new town founded by the canons of the Holy Sepulcher (today al-Bīra, nine miles north of Jerusalem).[3]

In addition, some of Nikulás's references to sacred history are rather unconventional, for instance when he relates that at "the mountain *Querencium* [Quarantena] God fasted and the Devil tempted him." On the other hand, Nikulás makes an observation that has no counterpart in the vast, multisecular corpus of itineraries to the Holy Land.[4] Having mentioned the traditional site of Christ's baptism near Jericho, he continues: "If a man out at the Jordan lies on his back on level ground and raises his knee and sets his fist on it and stretches his thumb out from the fist, then the polestar is to be seen above it [the thumb], just so high and no higher." Clearly this is evidence of Nikulás's interest in celestial navigation—and of his dexterity at it. Indeed, when I followed his instructions at the latitude of Jericho, the North Star duly appeared just above my thumb, but when I did so in southern Sinai and in Cambridge, the outcome did not recur.

Evidently, the future abbot of Munkaþverá was a man of acute observation, and not only of stars: as he trudged through Tuscany on his way to Rome, he noted that in Siena the women were very good looking.[5] Surely, he made many observations while in the Kingdom of Jerusalem, yet he did not see fit to mention them in his account. I take the liberty of paying homage to this exceptional pilgrim by conjuring up some of the experiences he may have had in *Acrs-borg*. But, to save him from flawed observations of the *Casal* and *Maka Maria* brand, he must visit the city alongside a more knowledgeable companion who speaks his language. Can we plausibly make up such a travel mate? Well, Nikulás's last stop before Acre was at Paphos on the western coast of Cyprus, then under Byzantine rule, and Nikulás is the only author to mention that in *Baffa* (as he calls the town) is stationed a garrison of the Varangian Guard—that is, of the elite Byzantine unit composed of Scandinavians and Anglo-Saxons.[6] Let us assume that the garrison's commander time after time sends one of his Varangians to Acre on some hush-hush errand; that this man is a Swede by the name of Ragnvald, who has picked up enough words of the languages spoken in Acre to be able to communicate with locals; and that Ragnvald and Nikulás become friends and sail together from *Baffa* to *Acrs-borg*. The subsequent account is admittedly imaginary, but its components are not: almost all reflect, in one way or another, some contemporary evidence on acculturation in various spheres. There are two reasons why I chose to embark upon this mental experiment. First, I wish to avoid the tedious prose into which impersonal accounts of everyday life tend to slip. Second, I subscribe to the view of my unforgettable master, Roberto Sabatino Lopez (d. 1986), that "the supreme goal [of a historian], rarely reached but never to be forgotten as an ideal, is a work of art constructed of authentic materials."[7] I do not pretend to have attained that goal, but the attempt has been rewarding for me—and hopefully it will be so for some readers.

As the ship on which Nikulás and Ragnvald are sailing is about to glide into *Acrs-borg*'s harbor, the city's bells start to ring, and Ragnvald explains that they are sounded to signal welcome to pilgrims arriving from beyond the sea.[8] A moved Nikulás turns his attention to the massive iron chain strung between the two towers at the harbor's entrance. He knows the story about Harald Hardrada, who about a century earlier escaped from *Miklagarð*, the "Great City" commonly known as Constantinople, by making his ship ride over the chain, but now he encounters for the first time this age-old but relatively rare Mediterranean device.[9] He immediately understands that the chain can be hauled up during hostilities to thwart an attack, and at nightfall to prevent a ship from stealthily entering the harbor. Ragnvald explains that, under the *Serkir*—that is, the Saracens—*Acrs-borg*'s harbor was defended by this chain for centuries; when the Franks conquered the city, they promptly learned how to operate it, and a few years later fended off a Muslim naval attack with its help.[10]

Disembarking, Nikulás is irritated by foul smells that are particularly intense around the harbor; Ragnvald tells him that locals call the area "Lordemer," that is, "the filthy sea."[11] As they make their way into the city, Nikulás is surprised to see that all the houses, even the poorest, are built of stone, their roofs flat—so different from Iceland's turf houses.[12] Coming closer to the city's churches he discovers that they, too, are flat-roofed, devoid of the gabled tops to which he is accustomed. Neither do the transepts protrude beyond the northern and southern walls, and therefore the churches do not exhibit the cross shape he had encountered time and again while traversing Europe from Aalborg to Bari.[13] Ragnvald explains that the layout of most Frankish houses of worship is influenced by that of local, much earlier, churches.

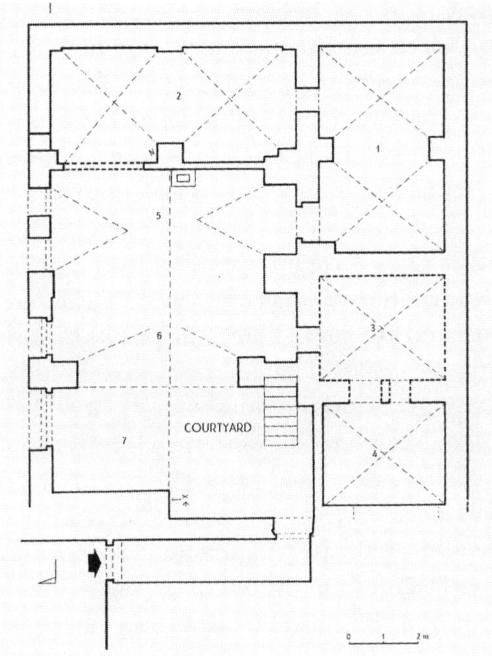

FIGURE 1. Acre: Plan of a courtyard house. Boas, *Domestic Settings*, 272, fig. 69. By permission of Boas and Brill Academic Publishers.

Ragnvald asks Nikulás whether he wishes to lodge with a Christian widow or stay in a hospice.[14] The monk expresses a preference for the latter, and Ragnvald leads the way to a new hospice in which—so he explains to his friend—pilgrims are fleeced less callously than elsewhere.[15] The hospice, bordering on the vacant land in *Acrs-borg*'s northeastern part, is a sturdy two-story house.[16] The two northerners approach it from the street through an arched doorway that gives way to a high, narrow, vaulted passageway. At its end they must turn at a right angle and face a closed door: This, explains Ragnvald, is the indirect entrance typical of Eastern domestic buildings, which the Franks tend to adopt in their urban dwellings.

The two knock on the door, and a slave admits them to an interior courtyard open to the sky, on two sides of which are the hospice's rooms.[17] Soon they are welcomed by the elderly Frankish owner, Pierre, and his young wife; Ragnvald whispers to Nikulás that she had been Pierre's Serk slave, whom, upon the birth of their first son, he baptized, manumitted, and married, changing her name from Fāṭima to Stefania.[18] She shows them the available rooms on the ground level, then takes them to the upper story via the staircase near the courtyard's entrance. Nikulás is surprised to see that the rooms are totally devoid of wooden or any other heavy furniture; instead, they are full of assorted textiles that invite one to sit or recline upon them: mattresses, round and long cushions of different colors, pillows, mosquito nets, carpets, and curtains used for decoration or hung across the room to divide it and provide privacy.[19]

When asked, Ragnvald credits this decidedly Eastern character of the rooms to Fāṭima-Stefania and comments: "The interior is the wife's domain. The husband provides a home, the wife its furnishings. He takes care of the shelter; she makes it habitable."[20] Nikulás concurs: "As we say, 'The wife runs things within the threshold.'"[21] Only the furthest room on the upper floor, set aside for Western pilgrims averse to novelties, has bedsteads, chairs, a table, and some chests, and Ragnvald explains: "Timber is scarce in *Iorsala-land*—as it is in your country."

As they descend the staircase, Nikulás notes that the last room on the ground floor is walled off from the rest of the hospice and has a separate entrance. In front of it three men are slouching on a bench, apparently expecting to enter. When he looks sideways at Ragnvald, the Varangian shrugs his shoulders: "Yes, they are waiting to visit the daughters of joy." Later, with Ragnvald attempting to translate, Nikulás asks Pierre why he is renting to harlots a part of a hospice frequented by devout Christian pilgrims. Pierre retorts: "In this city," he says, "even members of the clergy rent out lodgings to prostitutes, so why should I not do so? Besides, they pay more than pilgrims!"[22]

After a brief rest in the textile-abounding room that has been assigned to them, the two northerners leave for the Church of the Holy Cross, the city's cathedral. While Ragnvald is explaining that before the Frankish conquest the edifice served as the principal mosque of the Saracens, Nikulás is surprised to see half a dozen of them prostrating themselves in a remote part of it. "Yes," Ragnvald tells him, "this section has remained in Saracen hands, and they are permitted to pray there near the tomb of some saint of theirs."[23] Having said their own prayers in front of the church's main altar the two northerners leave for their next destination—the bathhouse of the Venetian Quarter.

Nikulás heard often how keen Scandinavians were on enjoying the baths of *Miklagarð*, so much more complex than the hot tubs of the Far North.[24] He is now eager to enter one in person, "according to the custom of the Orientals."[25] On drawing close to the bathhouse, the dense smoke emanating from its furnace irritates the two visitors, but once they enter the building the nuisance is over.[26] The bathhouse keeper demands two *deniers* (silver pennies) from each of them, and Ragnvald explodes: "Aren't you ashamed to fleece this pilgrim who has come from the far end of the world? I know that locals pay just one-half of a *denier*!"[27] The keeper gives in, takes just one *denier* and leads them to an undressing hall with a cold-water basin in its middle.[28] The two use the latrines nearby, undress, and relax for a while on one of the cushion-covered benches that run along the hall's walls. The keeper offers them towels to wear about their waists, but they prefer to bathe in the nude.[29] Through a narrow door they enter the bath proper, passing slowly from the cool to the warm room, and finally to the hot one, paved with marble floor tiles.[30] Nikulás is amazed to see that light enters the room through green, purple, and blue glass windowpanes installed in the dome above.[31] Having sweated there to their hearts' content, they retrace their steps to the undressing hall, where they are offered rose water and apple juice.[32] An attendant doubling up as a barber proposes to shave them.[33] Ragnvald lets him do so, but Nikulás, intent to return home with a long beard attesting to his pilgrimage, declines.[34]

Shortly after leaving the bathhouse, they see many Frankish men and women, forming two lines in front of the entrance to a stately house. Trumpets and flutes play merrily. The door opens and a young woman emerges, with two men holding her from right and left. She is stylishly garbed in a beautiful dress from which trails a long train of gold-interwoven silk. On her head she wears a golden diadem covered by a net of woven gold, and a similar composition adorns her breasts. Soon a procession is formed, with the musicians in the lead, followed by the city's notables in their finest clothing, their trains falling behind them. Then comes the woman, walking with little steps of half a span, recalling a dove or a wisp of cloud. Behind her parade the women, proudly exhibiting their richest apparel and ornaments. Ragnvald explains, "This is a nuptial procession," and he and Nikulás join the Frankish and Serkir onlookers who form two ranks along the route, gazing at the spectacle as the bride is led to the groom's house.[35]

Later the two northerners pass a vault under which a small group of men stands around a scribe who sits on a carpet-covered stone bench, a small table in front of him. The scribe listens to the men, dips his quill-pen into an ebony inkstand to record their statements, and writes them down on a thin material that Nikulás has never seen, but which definitely is not the parchment he knows so well, made of skins of domestic animals.[36] Ragnvald explains: "This is a Genoese notary, drawing up some contract; he writes on a flimsy material made of linen rags—an innovation taken over from the Serkir, I think. Its name is paper."[37]

Finally, on the way back to the hospice, they cross the section of the main market in which locally grown foodstuffs are sold. Nikulás is dazed by the smells and colors of fruit he has never seen before: oranges, lemons, dates, figs, bananas, pomegranates, and much more.[38] One merchant dangles before him a bit of high-grade sugar, but Nikulás does not comprehend what the man is trying to tell him by calling it first *sukkar an-nabāt* and then *sucre nabet*.[39] Another trader pushes into his hands a slice of bread with *ṭaḥīne* spread on it.[40] Nikulás's attention is, however, drawn to a nearby shop where a customer is handing the merchant a small yellowish object in return for a bag of pepper—and he realizes with a jolt that he is seeing for the first time a gold coin. Then his attention turns to a Serk merchant who briskly shows different lengths of linen to a young Frankish woman chaperoned by a matron, and Nikulás smiles at the merchant's excited comportment, which gives away his infatuation with the beautiful customer.[41]

The next morning Ragnvald leads Nikulás to *Acrs-borg*'s eastern gate, from which he will start his pilgrimage on foot to *Iorsala-borg*. Ragnvald enjoins him to drink water regularly whenever the heat becomes scorching, even though in this country "a small drop is obtained at a high price."[42] He warns him also to beware of the country's wild animals: lions, panthers, bears, and especially hyenas, far more frightening than the rest.[43] The two northerners embrace, and Nikulás sets off on his way to *Nazaret*, *Nepl*, *Casal*, and *Maka Maria*, in a group of Westerners and local Franks whose language he does not comprehend. His pilgrimage is solemnized by an involuntary, contemplation-inspiring quietness.

The Frankish Dialect of Medieval French

What were the characteristics of the language the Franks spoke, the language our Icelandic pilgrim could barely understand, if at all? One promising starting point for dealing with this knotty issue is a study of the names by which the Franks designated some of the kingdom's localities.

Latin chronicles and charters of the twelfth century tend to refer to towns mentioned in the Bible by the names appearing in its Latin translation, the Vulgate. For instance, the harbor town of Jaffa, occupied by the crusaders in June 1099, is routinely designated as *Ioppe*.[44] It is therefore of considerable import that Benincasa, in his *Life* of Ranieri of Pisa, writes: "*Ioppe*, which is now generally called *Iaffa*."[45] Now, *Yāfā* is the Arabic name of the town, and Benincasa's remark indicates that this was the name used in everyday parlance.

Jaffa was not exceptional. Saewulf, the Anglo-Saxon pilgrim who arrived in the kingdom on 12 October 1102,[46] writes that on his return voyage he sailed past the coastal cities "Sur and Saegete, which are Tyre and Sidon."[47] Now, *Ṣūr* is the Arabic name of Tyre, whereas Saegete—which appears elsewhere as Sagitta, Saget, Saiette, Sayette, Seete, or Saeta—goes back to a corruption of Sidon's Arabic name in medieval times, *Ṣaydā*.[48]

How common was it to refer to Tyre by its Arabic name and to Sidon by a derivation of it? The anonymous author of *The Deeds of the Franks*, describing the advance of the First Crusade toward Jerusalem, relates, "Thence we came to another city called Sagitta, and so to another called Sur," obliging the modern editor to explain that ancient Sidon and Tyre are meant thereby.[49] Raymond of Aguilers, another participant in that advance, explains that *Tyrus* is now commonly called *Sur*.[50] Foucher of Chartres, the erudite author of the earliest chronicle of the Kingdom of Jerusalem, consistently refers to Sidon and Tyre by their Latin names, but on their first occurrence explains that the inhabitants of the region now call the one Sagitta, the other Sur.[51] And the well-informed if enigmatic Albert of Aachen, whose chronicle starts with the First Crusade and ends with a Frankish defeat in 1119, mentions Tyre twenty-three times: in twelve he refers to the city solely as Sur, in seven he explains that Sur is Tyre, and only four times does he refer to it only by its Latin name, Tyrus.[52] The breakdown of his twenty-two references to Sidon is similar. In later years, some notarial acts drawn up in Tyre in Latin fluctuated between the Latin and Arabic names of the city.[53] The thirteenth-century works written in Old French—which may be considered as coming close to the Franks' spoken language—refer routinely to Tyre as Sur and to Sidon as Saiete. And even a tomb inscription announces:

ICI GIST MESSIRE BERTHELME CHAYN CH[evalie]R DE SUR.[54]

Tiberias—mentioned in the New Testament—appears in Albert of Aachen's chronicle twenty-four times, but always as Tabaria, thus replicating the city's Arabic name, Ṭabariyyā![55] Nor does Albert mention Tabaria's biblical name.[56] Later, Old French works habitually called the city Tabarie or Tabarié[57]—with the second variant indicating that the Franks adopted the pronunciation current in the local Arabic dialect, namely, Ṭabariyye.[58]

In Frankish documentary sources, the kingdom's indigenous villages appear under their Arabic names, roughly transcribed into Latin letters: for example, Qalansuwa became Calansue, and Bīr Māʿīn became Bermenayn.[59] (The Latin transcriptions reveal that some twelfth-century localities still retained their pre-Arabic names, whether Aramaic or Greek.)[60] The newly erected Frankish castles and villages bore Old French names like Belvoir and Casal Imbert, yet in at least one case a castle was given Latin and Old French names that simply translated an Arabic one: this was the Templar castle of Faba / La Fève (the bean) in the Jezreel Valley, which supplanted the indigenous village al-Fūla (the bean, in Arabic).[61] Elsewhere, local designations were taken over with minor changes. The important castle in Transjordan, founded by Paien the Butler in 1142, was given the name Crac, which echoes the Arabic Karak.[62] The first castle of the Hospitaller order was called Bethgibelin, and William of Tyre, who erroneously—but probably on the basis of a local tradition—identifies the place with biblical Beersheba, explains that it is known in Arabic as Bethgebrin, which means "the House of Gabriel."[63] His explanation is almost correct: the Arabic place-name oscillates between Bayt Jibrīn (which goes back to the Aramaic Beth Gabra) and Bayt Jibrīl (the House of Gabriel).[64] Consequently, William presents the first Arabic variant as bearing the meaning of the second. Again, speaking of a castle south of Gaza that King Amaurry founded in about 1165, William explains that according to local tradition a Greek monastery had existed there in the past, and therefore the castle is known as Darum, which in Latin means *Domus Grecorum* (the House of the Greeks).[65] He reveals thereby that he knows that the Arabic name of the locality was Dār al-Rūm (the House of the Greeks, or Byzantines, here fused into Darum).

These and other explanations indicate that William had some basic grasp of spoken Arabic—a grasp superior, incidentally, to that of many Western crusade historians of our time.[66] Thus, William speaks of a place east of the Sea of Galilee known as Ras el Me and explains correctly that the Latin translation of the Arabic words is *Caput Aque* (Head of Water).[67] But the editors of William's *History*—from Jacques Bongars in 1611 to Auguste-Arthur Beugnot and Auguste Le Prévost in 1844 to Robert Huygens in 1986—deciphered erroneously the third part of the Arabic name, *me* (a vernacular form of *mā'*, water), as *ine*, and consequently transcribed the place-name as *Raseline* or *Ras el Ine*.[68] An editor with a rudimentary knowledge of Arabic could not have committed this mistake, especially having been told that the letters to be deciphered amount to the Arabic equivalent of *aque* ("of water").

The discovery that the Franks consistently used to refer to Tyre, the seat of the kingdom's major archbishopric, and to Tiberias, the capital of its foremost principality, by their Arabic names suggests that they had little or no compunction about using terms of Arabic origin in their daily parlance. How many of these were absorbed into their spoken language? Since that language has been extinct for centuries, we must turn to the testimony of the Latin and Old French sources written in the Kingdom of Jerusalem. In 1972, Prawer culled from these sources only thirty-six terms of Arabic origin. In 2012, Laura Minervini authoritatively discussed seventy-two such terms; to these one may add the sixteen that appear in Prawer's list but not in hers. On the basis of his findings, Prawer concluded that the few loans, made over a period of two hundred years, point to a limited impact of the local language, an impact definitely more restricted than that of Arabic on Spanish or Italian.[69] As the *arabismos* (loanwords from Arabic) in present-day Spanish are very numerous, Prawer would hardly have changed his conclusion had he been able to read Minervini's study.

Yet the testimony of the written sources—chronicles, charters, the customs tariffs of Acre, and the like—is problematic, as these texts focus on politics, administration, warfare, and commerce, and thus echo the spoken language only partially. Hence, the terms in the Prawer/Minervini lists refer to officeholders, local geographical features, arms, money and measure units, transportation, agricultural, and manufactured goods, but the household and domestic life, for instance, are barely represented. We must turn to the Old French/Arabic phrase book—probably composed in Acre before 1258 for the benefit of Coptic pilgrims and merchants, and in which the Old French words are transcribed in Coptic letters—to learn that the Franks borrowed the Arabic word *shubbāk* (window), pronounced it *chubbec*, and integrated it into their parlance with the specific meaning of "window balcony."[70] And if it were not for an Old French translation of the Bible made in thirteenth-century Acre, we would not know that the Franks called a midwife *daye*, which is evidently the *dāye* (midwife) of the local Arabic dialect down to this day.[71] The term's adoption suggests that the Franks employed native midwives.[72] In any case, we may take for granted that the Franks' spoken language contained considerably more terms of Arabic—and possibly also of Greek—origin than the written sources, skewed as they are toward politics and commerce, suggest.[73] Also, we may assume that the absorption of these terms was gradual, their presence far more conspicuous, say, in the 1280s, than in the 1120s.

And what about the purported contrast between the impact of Arabic on Franks and Spaniards? Well, I believe this is a faulty comparison, which sets side by side the multitude of *arabismos* in present-day *spoken* Spanish, and the few loanwords from Arabic appearing in works *written* in the Kingdom of Jerusalem.[74] The proper procedure calls for comparing the Prawer/Minervini lists with the terms of Arabic origin appearing in works *written* in medieval Iberia. Such a procedure is feasible thanks to the painstaking study by Eero Neuvonen (d. 1981) of the *arabismos* in Spanish works written before 1300. Not surprisingly, the comparison reveals that the topics to which most *arabismos* pertain are largely identical with the subjects around which the Arabic-derived terms of the Frankish East cluster, yet the Iberian sources also contain some words that refer to abstract ideas and science.[75] Neuvonen concluded that the total number of *arabismos* in the pre-1300 written sources was about three hundred.[76] Since by the end of the thirteenth century Christian-Muslim interaction in Iberia had lasted about three times as long as in the Kingdom of Jerusalem, the ratio 300:88 between the findings by Neuvonen and by Prawer/Minervini points to a basically similar dynamic in the two regions.

Finally, what did the French spoken in the Kingdom of Jerusalem sound like? Thanks to a brilliant study by Cyril Aslanov, who resuscitated the vocal features of the Old French words transcribed into Coptic letters in the Old French/Arabic phrase book by analyzing their transcriptions, we now have an answer: the phonetics of the French spoken in the Kingdom of Jerusalem exhibit a marked predominance of the Walloon and Lotharingian dialects, but also of the Picard and Burgundian ones, and their amalgam produced a new, Jerusalemite standard parlance.[77] This finding, Aslanov observes, is consistent with the origin of Jerusalem's first three rulers in areas of the Walloon and Lotharingian dialects; one may add that it is also in step with Alan Murray's conclusion that men from Flanders, Picardy, and Lotharingia were preponderant in the kingdom's early nobility.[78] Yet this standard parlance, which presumably emerged from the blend of several northern French dialects in the kingdom's early days, was still predominant in the language spoken in Acre in the mid-thirteenth century—despite the influx of immigrants from other regions in the intervening decades, such as the arrival of Angevins in the wake of Count Fulk V of Anjou's elevation to the throne of Jerusalem in 1131.[79] Apparently, as often happens, the founding stratum of the new society established what was to become the normative pronunciation of subsequent generations of more variegated origin.[80] Also, the new standard parlance absorbed terms from Italo-Romance, Occitan, and Arabic.[81] A Frankish word could be pronounced in an Arabic fashion: in 1282 in Acre, the translator Johan of Antioch mentioned people who say *hosbital* instead of *hospital*.[82] In addition, some habitual Old French words acquired in the Frankish East a new meaning, occasioned by the local reality: for instance, *bain* (bath) came to denote a bathhouse, a *ḥammām*; *jardin* (garden), an orchard; *rue* (street) came to mean also "a quarter."[83] Hence the hybrid French spoken in the Kingdom of Jerusalem differed on several counts from the vernaculars spoken in the home country. We may well consider it the Frankish dialect of medieval French—and regard the Old French/Arabic phrase book as a Frankish/Arabic one.[84]

And what about Frankish words making their way into Arabic? Hartwig Derenbourg (d. 1908), the discoverer of the only manuscript of Usāma ibn Munqidh's *Book of Contemplation*, listed the ten words of the "language of the Franks" that Usāma used in his work. Most of these referred to components of Frankish society and army—*burjāsī* (from *burgensis*, burgess); *turkubūlī* (Turcopole, explained as "Frankish archer"); *sirjandī* (serjeant)—and to Frankish titles such as *barūns* (baron, Old French *barouns*), *al-biskund* (viscount), *dāmā* (dame).[85] Another Frankish title, *qumis* (*comes*, i.e., count), appears in a Judeo-Arabic letter from the Kingdom of Jerusalem that made its way into the Geniza, that vast collection of documents and fragments originally kept in the storeroom of an Old Cairo synagogue.[86] Other titles may be encountered, for instance, in the Frankish-Mamluk truce treaties of the years 1265–85: *ibrins* (prince); *al-māstir* (Master) of the *bayt al-isbitār* (House of the Hospital); *sinjāl* (*sénéchal*, seneschal); *ifrayr* (*frère*, brother); and so on.[87] And at least two Frankish toponyms appear to have survived to this day: The twelfth-century Templar road station east of ʿAtlīt, called in Latin *Districtum* and in Old French *Destreiz*, is known today in Arabic as Khirbet Dusṭrī.[88] The name of the Arab village Sinjil, between Jerusalem and Nablus, may go back to St.-Gilles, the vernacular form of Casale Sancti Egidii—apparently the village Nikulás presented as "a town called Casal."[89]

Yet not all Frankish words that made their way into Arabic pertain to titles and toponyms. An Arabic inscription from 1210, found in the mosque of the small village of Farkhah, northwest of Jerusalem—a village under Frankish rule only until 1187—mentions the endowment of the mosque from the *faṣal* paid by the villagers. Evidently this term, derived from "vassal," entered Arabic already in the twelfth century. It remained in use for a long time: al-Nuwayrī, an administrator in Mamluk service in Syria who died in 1333, speaks of *mafṣūlah*-land in certain districts of Syria and remarks that *mafṣūlah* is derived from *faṣal*, "a Frankish word that continued to be used in the coastal areas that had been repossessed from the hands of the Franks." It is not clear which aspect of vassalage the Arabicized term *faṣal* denoted; obviously, it underwent transformation after passing into the Islamic ambit.[90] Similarly, *anklīs*, denoting "eel" in some medieval Arabic sources, may have been derived from Old French *anguile* or Latin *anguilla*.[91] Cedric Norman Johns (d. 1992), the archaeologist, believed that when in about 1930 a local Arab mason recognized a vault of the thirteenth-century bathhouse of ʿAtlīt as a *tirs*, he was using an Arabic derivation of *tiers* (third part).[92] And Meron Benvenisti (d. 2020) argued that the term *babriyyah*, which appears at least ten times in modern maps or name-lists of Palestine and always refers to remnants of Frankish buildings, derived from Old French *boverie* (ox barn).[93] Probably the spoken Arabic of the Franks' local subjects comprised more such terms, but these either did not impact the written language at all or entered it only fleetingly.

Varieties of Adaptation and Hybridization

Having mentioned that Prince Bohemond III of Antioch dispatched a carrier pigeon during the German Crusade of 1197, Arnold of Lübeck (d. 1214) goes on to observe in general on the adoption of Muslim devices by the Franks: "Because the Gentiles [here: the Muslims] are wiser in their generation than the sons of light [here: the Franks], they contrive [or: invent] many things with which our people were not acquainted, unless they learned [them] perchance from them."[94] It is noteworthy that this candid, possibly unique, acknowledgement of Muslim knowhow being adopted by the Franks appears in a chronicle written in northern Europe.

Such transfer of know-how surely occurred in other instances, yet it was not expressly stated in writing as in the case of the carrier pigeons. Let us examine some such occurrences, starting with those for which the evidence is visible and compelling.

Bathhouses

The lure of eastern Mediterranean bathhouses appears to have mesmerized many Europeans long before the crusades. In the Frankish Kingdom of Jerusalem, the Venetians, the Genoese, and the Pisans insisted on obtaining the right to possess a bathhouse in their quarters, but there were also many bathhouses elsewhere.[95] The written sources mention bathhouses in the palace of the prince of Antioch, in the towns of Beirut, Tyre, Acre, Belinas, Jerusalem, Jaffa, and Ascalon in the Kingdom of Jerusalem, as well as in Latakia and Maʿarrat al-Nuʿmān in the Principality of Antioch and in Rafaniyyah in the County of Tripoli.[96] The military orders, too, owned bathhouses. Indeed, even Franks who decided to live in a newly established village were not willing to deny themselves the pleasures of a bath. William Marçais (d. 1956) famously claimed that the bathhouse (*ḥammām*) was one of the three essential features of a Muslim town, alongside the Friday mosque and the market. Apparently, the bathhouse fulfilled a similar function in Frankish towns. The thirteenth-century Frankish/Arabic phrase book contains five calls to go to specific destinations. One of them is *bōsthibinirōpain* (that is: *vuels tu venir au bain?*, do you want to go to the bathhouse?), rendered in Arabic as *qūm narūh al-ḥammām* (get up, let us go to the *ḥammām*). The four other sentences call to go to the market, the orchard, the church, and the town.

As of now, a single well-preserved Frankish bathhouse has come to light, the one unearthed in the early 1930s by Cedric Norman Johns in the faubourg underneath the huge Templar castle Château Pèlerin (ʿAtlīt). Johns assiduously described this bathhouse; but as no studies of contemporary Islamicate bathhouses were available at the time, he was unable to compare it to them. Nowadays such a comparison is feasible, and when we place Johns's plan of the ʿAtlīt bathhouse alongside the plans, drawn to the same scale, of the Damascene *ḥammām*s of Sūq al-Bzūriyyeh (constructed between 1154 and 1172) and al-Surūjī (erected before the end of the twelfth century), and of the Bustān Nassīf bathhouse in Baalbek, Lebanon (dated to the Ayyubid period), the similarities of layout are instantly recognizable.

Whereas the physical setup of the Frankish bathhouse was virtually identical with, and clearly derived from, the Islamicate *ḥammām*, its functioning differed in some critical respects. While the twelfth-century author ʿAbd al-Raḥmān b. Naṣr al-Shayzarī prescribed that the owner of a *ḥammām* "must have some bathrobes to hire out or lend to the people, because strangers and poor people need this," and called on the *muḥtasib* (supervisor) to chastise both those who reveal their nakedness and those who witness it, the Muslim bathhouse-keeper at Maʿarrat al-Nuʿmān told Usāma ibn Munqidh that the Franks disapprove of people who in the bathhouse wear a towel about their waist—in other words, they preferred to bathe in the nude. The story ties in with evidence from medieval Europe of nude or seminude bathing. And while the mixed bathing of men and women was anathema to Muslims, Frankish Tyre had—according to a charter of 1190—bathhouses in which men and women bathed together. Was this a Frankish innovation imported from the West, where the church struggled against mixed bathing in the eleventh century and later? On the other hand, while the widely read Arabic treatise *Sirr al-asrār* (Secret of Secrets) recommends that the bather, having had his drink, should "stretch himself a little while looking at some beautiful picture, well fashioned, or if possible, at some beautiful human being, which is better still," and a private bath in thirteenth-century Baghdad had on its floor depictions of such human beings, kissing and embracing in various postures so as to arouse a male beholder's lust for a male or female partner, Filippo of Tripoli's Latin translation of this treatise recommends only that the bather should stretch himself a little, and omits the sensuous sequel altogether! Behavior in the bathhouse, according to Filippo, should conform to Western norms.

Coinage

Like the *ḥammām*, gold coins were a novelty for the conquerors and immigrants from western Europe, accustomed as they were to a coinage system based on silver.[97] They called the gold coins "bezants," although the leading gold coin in use in the Kingdom of Jerusalem in its early years was the Fatimid dīnār, predominant in the region before the crusader conquest.[98]

At an unknown date, the Franks started to mint imitation Fatimid dīnārs (see fig. 2). The imitated gold coins were known as *bizancii saracenati* (saracenate bezants, i.e., Islamicized Byzantine coins). The term appears for the first time in the documentation of the Kingdom of Jerusalem in the Frankish-Venetian agreement of 1124, but since this term appears also in Venetian notarial acts drawn up in Damietta and Alexandria in which it refers to genuine Fatimid dīnārs, the 1124 agreement may have referred to them as well.[99] The earliest unequivocal mention of saracenate bezants minted within the Kingdom of Jerusalem appears in a notarial act drawn up in July 1142 in Venice, which refers to "good golden *bizancii saracenati* of the king of that country [that is, the Kingdom of Jerusalem], of the weight according to the custom of that country."[100] Variants of this formula appear in Venetian acts of the years 1161–1211.[101] Evidently, the Frankish imitation dīnārs became

FIGURE 2. A Fatimid gold coin and its Frankish imitation. *Left*: Dīnār of Caliph al-Amīr bi-Aḥkām Allah, minted at Alexandria in AH 499/AD 1105–6, excavated at Ascalon, 2009. Reverse. Photo: Clara Amit IAA 145448, B-435745-050209141565. *Right*: Frankish Bezant, excavated at Vadum Jacob in 1997. Reverse. Photo: Dafna Gazit IAA 107776, B-990825-0201075131344121.

an important means of payment for large commercial transactions in the kingdom.[102] In other words, the Franks embarked on a major act of transcultural borrowing in order to conform to the monetary practices of the region.[103] (The royal-controlled production of imitated gold coins in the Kingdom of Jerusalem, which recalls the control of gold minting by the rulers of the Fatimid and Byzantine Empires, may have been a further such act of borrowing.[104]) It is noteworthy that although the Fatimid dīnār was imitated, the imitation went by the name "saracenate *bezant*." Why this misnaming? Was it the early encounter of the First Crusaders with gold coinage that occurred in Byzantium and in northern Syria?[105] The concern lest a Frankish gold dīnār be confused with a Western silver *denarius*/*denier* (penny)? Or a reluctance to state openly that the Franks were imitating a Muslim coin?

The Frankish imitation dīnārs have Arabic inscriptions on them, or inscriptions that at first glance look as if they were written in Arabic but on closer inspection are often illegible. Like their Shiʿi Fatimid prototypes, the imitated inscriptions bear Islamic contents—the names of the Prophet Muḥammad, of ʿAlī (the Shiʿis' first *imām*, or community leader) as well as of Fatimid caliphs[106]—and state the year of the Islamic era. Why did the Franks make recourse to inscriptions that must have struck those who were aware of their contents as blatantly sacrilegious? The question becomes even knottier when we remember that in the twelfth century the Franks also issued petty silver coins, cut-gold fragments, and lead tokens bearing *Latin* inscriptions, and that in the thirteenth century they minted imitations of Ayyubid full-weight silver dirhams, engraving Arabic inscriptions on them.

As for silver versus gold minting in the twelfth century, one may argue that in each case the Franks chose to assimilate their coins to a prevailing norm: their silver *deniers* were modeled on the silver and billon (silver-copper alloy) coinage of western Europe with its Latin inscriptions, while their gold coins imitated the widely circulating Fatimid dīnārs with their Arabic legends. Consequently, the appearance of the newly minted *deniers*, recalling those of France in layout, iconography, and inscription, must have looked familiar to the Frankish inhabitants of the kingdom and to newcomers from the West.[107] The new imitation gold coins may perhaps have passed initially for the genuine Islamic articles, with Franks, merchants arriving from Genoa and Venice, or indigenous people unable to read Arabic accepting them at parity with the Fatimid dīnārs. However, since the weight and fineness of the saracenate bezants were lower than that of the dīnārs, and their Arabic or Arabicate inscriptions often garbled, people in the know must have noticed pretty soon the disparity between the original and its imitation and began to treat them as two distinct, separate currencies. In Arabic, the Frankish imitation came to be known as "the dīnār of Tyre" (*dīnār ṣūrī*) and was quite often used among Muslims.[108] Thus, by conforming outwardly to the dominant norm both in design and in the use of Arabic inscriptions, the Frankish imitation dīnār attempted to blend into the regional network of gold coinage.[109] Yet the attempt was not totally successful: ʿAbd al-Raḥmān b. Naṣr al-Shayzarī laid down that it is not permitted to sell Egyptian dīnārs for those from Tyre.[110]

Let us now turn to the cut-gold fragments, lead tokens, and imitation silver dirhams. The cut-gold fragments that served the Fatimids for small transactions were adopted by the Franks for the same purpose and became an important means of payment in the Kingdom of Jerusalem.[111] As these gold fragments appear in very many sizes, their value could not have been established visually. They had to be weighed for each monetary transaction, as did the Islamic cut pieces—with which the Frankish pieces repeatedly occur in the same assemblage. The indispensable weighing may have entailed the marking of Latin inscriptions on the Frankish gold fragments: since only weighing established value, disguising the Frankish pieces under an Arabicate garb would not have rendered them more acceptable.

The cast lead token, on the other hand, was a Western practice with no counterparts in the Islamicate East; in fact, some tokens openly imitated the French *deniers*. These lead pieces served as unofficial, substitute money for small transactions within the limits of a Frankish town, castle, or village, and therefore they were free to flaunt their Western character, whether by prominently displaying a cross, a Latin inscription, or a fleur-de-lis (lily flower, a common heraldic emblem).[112]

The Frankish imitation of Ayyubid silver coins in the thirteenth century resulted from Ṣalāḥ al-Dīn's introduction of full-weight good silver dirhams and the subsequent spread of full silver coinage in western Asia.[113] In the wake of this reemergence of silver as an additional standard means of payment in substantial transactions, the Franks started to mint imitation Ayyubid dirhams. Unlike the saracenate gold bezants, which came to be treated as a separate currency, the imitation silver dirhams were—until about 1245—visually almost indistinguishable from their models, with their silver content about the same and their Arabic inscriptions legible, and therefore they succeeded in circulating alongside Ayyubid dirhams.[114] Several studies have shown that the Franks used Frankish as well as Islamic coins.[115] On the other hand, Frankish and European money circulated after 1192 in Ayyubid-ruled parts of Palestine, and the remains of a hoard discovered in Fayyūm, Egypt, in 1950 contain 306 genuine Islamic silver dirhams as well as thirty-one Frankish imitation dirhams.[116] In sum, considerations of acceptability dictated the use of Arabic or Latin on Frankish coinage.

The mention of the Prophet and of the Islamic era in the Arabic legends of the Frankish imitation gold and silver coins scandalized Eudes of Châteauroux, papal legate to the Frankish East from 1249 to 1254, who excommunicated those who would in the future engrave on them "the name of *Machometh* and the number of years [that passed] since his birth." (Evidently the legate did not know that the Islamic era started with the Prophet's migration to Medina.) Eudes alerted Pope Innocent IV, who on 12 February 1253 endorsed his legate's order, declaring that "to commit such a blasphemous name to so solemn a remembrance is not only shameful but abominable." But already two years before the pope buttressed Eudes's ruling with his authority, the Franks complied, possibly prodded by King Louis IX of France who was then fortifying Acre and other places.[117] The Islamic components of the inscriptions were suppressed and replaced, from 1251 onward, with explicitly Christian texts and dates, which may have aimed also at proselytizing.[118] For instance, the new imitation gold dīnār displayed a large cross at its center, and the surrounding outer and inner circular inscriptions proclaimed: "We are glorified by the Cross of our Lord Jesus the Messiah, in whom is our salvation and our life and our resurrection, and in whom is our deliverance and pardon."[119] Similar texts appeared on the new imitation silver dirhams. The latter, despite their Christian messages, appear to have circulated freely in Ayyubid Egypt: nineteen of them form part of the remains of the Fayyūm hoard.[120] Yet all these Christian texts were engraved on the new coins—in Arabic! Obviously, the Franks responsible for the new, imitation dīnārs and dirhams—and apparently the papal legate as well—believed that only coins with Arabic inscriptions stood a chance of being accepted in the region at large.

They were right. The Frankish Kingdom, or what remained of it by 1251, was a relatively minor player in the region's economy. True, a text attributed to Matthew Paris (ca. 1200–59) recounts that Richard of Cornwall learned from Templars and Hospitallers—evidently during his sojourn in the kingdom in 1240–41—that Acre brought in fifty thousand pounds sterling annually to its lord.[121] Since the English Crown's annual cash incomes averaged between 1241 and 1245 only about 36,500 pounds a year, modern crusade historians are inclined to regard Acre's income as huge.[122] Yet the statement about Acre ascribed to Matthew Paris should be read alongside the subsequent assertion that Damascus brought in to its lord a yearly income equivalent to 182,500 pounds sterling—that is, more than three times as much as Acre.[123]

A relatively minor player felt that he must conform to the region's conventions. Not so a major economic power. In 1252, a year after the Franks issued their new coins with their Arabic-written Christian texts, Genoa minted its first gold coin, the *januinus*. A large cross took up its center, and the inscriptions, as on Genoa's customary silver coins, were in Latin.[124]

Paper

As is well known, paper—a Chinese invention—entered the realm of Islam via Central Asia around the mid-eighth century, gradually replacing papyrus and curtailing the use of parchment.[125] By the time the crusaders reached the eastern Mediterranean, paper was serving the Muslims, Eastern Christians, and Jews there as normal writing material, also for the copying of books of religious content. In Syria-Palestine, centers of paper production existed in Tiberias, Damascus, and Tripoli, and there is evidence for trade in paper in Tyre, Jerusalem, and Ramla in the mid-eleventh century. Accordingly, the Franks found themselves living in an environment well supplied with paper. Their native subjects continued to use paper. Almost all the Geniza letters by Jews who lived under Frankish rule are written on paper, and we may assume that Muslim, Eastern Christian, and Samaritan subjects likewise used paper for that purpose.

To what extent did the Franks adopt the use of paper? As of now, we have just one specimen of material evidence. During the works at the Aqṣā Mosque in the 1920s, a small piece of paper was discovered between two stones of a pillar. It is the only Latin document of the period of the crusades ever discovered in what had been the Frankish East; it is apparently also the earliest letter on paper in the Latin sphere to come down to us. It was written between 1179 and 1184 by Gerard of Ridefort, seneschal of the Templar order, who reports on the action taken against an aberrant brother. The letter, now on display in the Islamic Museum on Jerusalem's Ḥaram, reveals that the scribe used most sparingly the paper on which he wrote, a thriftiness suggesting that paper was rather expensive (see fig. 3).

Now here, too, documentation must not be equated with reality, and the fact that we have only this single piece of evidence should be taken as indication neither that the Franks barely used paper all along nor that it was in the late twelfth century that they started to use it. We may assume that they did so, possibly already earlier, for short-term purposes—letters, orders, receipts, administrative records—even as they were writing their charters, considered of enduring value, on parchment. The Frankish notaries of Acre may have used paper, as did their colleagues in Genoa and the Genoese notaries active in the Frankish East. And it stands to reason that the Franks, who learned from the Muslims the use of carrier pigeons, emulated their practice of writing pigeon-conveyed messages on the light and small-size "bird paper."

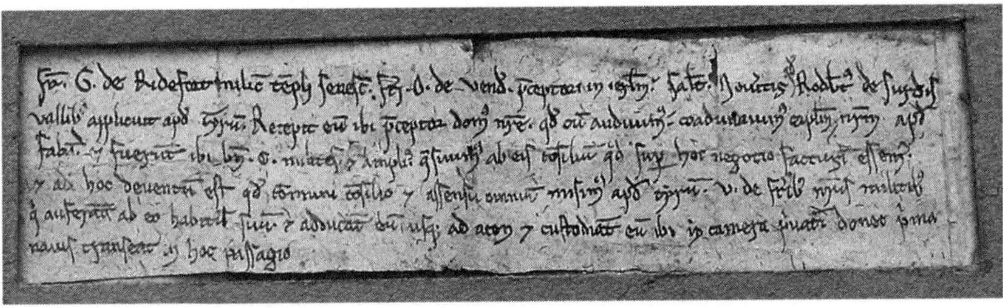

FIGURE 3. Unique Frankish letter on paper, 1179/84. Islamic Museum, al-Ḥaram al-Sharīf/Temple Mount, Jerusalem. Photo: courtesy Dr. Nazmi al-Ju'beh

For the thirteenth century, we have hard evidence that the Franks used paper for the composition of wills. The Frankish *Book of the Assizes of the Court of Burgesses* lays down that a will is valid whether written on parchment, *paupier* (paper), or wax-coated tablets, and it is plausible to assume that binding documents of a similar nature, pledges for instance, could also have been written on paper. The distinctiveness of the stipulation in the *Book of the Assizes* becomes apparent when we compare it with contemporary legislation in the West. In 1231 Emperor Frederick II ordered that (a) public instruments and documents spelling out obligations must be written on parchment; (b) documents written on paper—with the exception of attestations to the payment of a debt—would no longer be considered as binding; and (c) documents written on paper must be transcribed onto parchment. The reason given for this rejection of paper was its short-lived durability. Similar legislation is attested in Padua and Castile, while in southern France and eastern Iberia paper appears to have been restricted to writings regarded as of secondary importance, such as notaries' minutes and administrative registers. Therefore, the *Book of the Assizes* stands out for a considerably more favorable attitude toward the use of paper—probably revealing the impact of the surrounding paper-centered culture.

On the other hand, there is no evidence for the manufacture of paper in the Kingdom of Jerusalem. Things were different in the West. A paper mill at Albarells, northwest of Barcelona, figures in an act drawn up in February 1193; in Genoa, the production of paper is mentioned in a contract of 1235; after King Jaume I of Aragon conquered in 1244 Játiva, famous for its paper manufacture, he encouraged the newly subjected Muslims to continue production. Why, then, did the Franks, who—as we presently shall see, learned to produce sugar from the subjected indigenous population—dispense with manufacturing paper? Was their demand for it too limited? Was the supply from Damascus—where two paper manufactories outside the city walls are casually mentioned in about 1167—sufficient? In any case, Frankish production of paper is not attested, nor is paper listed in the customs tariffs of Acre compiled in the thirteenth century, while it figures in the 1222 toll of Barcelona and elsewhere.

In the thirteenth-century West, paper was slowly gaining ground as the material used for writing books. Yet the Frankish East—implanted in the midst of a civilization that had been writing books on paper for centuries—remained, for all we know, unaffected by this trend. All surviving Frankish codices are on parchment; and this is true also of the illuminated manuscripts of Acre, which rightly occupy prime space in all exhibitions of "Crusader Art." Indeed, the very idea that these illuminations could have been made on paper strikes one as outlandish—until one realizes that during the period in which they were executed on parchment, the outstanding illuminations of a Coptic-Arabic Gospel were drawn, in 1249/50 in Cairo, on paper.

Why this reluctance to adopt paper for the writing of books, while wills written on *paupier* were considered binding? Could it be that Frankish clerics, responsible for much of the copying of books, refused to adopt the writing material prevalent among the Muslim foe and, by clinging to parchment, demonstrated an observance of Western tradition that was stricter than in the Western homeland? Such purported animosity to paper may be compared to the long-standing Ottoman aversion to printing, considered a "Christian invention"; when finally, in 1727, Sultan Ahmed III authorized the establishment of an imperial printery, he explicitly prohibited the printing of books of religious content. Consequently, the differential adoption of paper in the Frankish East may exemplify a dependence of transcultural borrowing in various sectors of society on the beliefs and norms that govern them.

The House and Its Furnishings

The houses of the Franks, both urban and rural, display varying degrees of hybridization. In the towns, the Franks took possession of houses that had belonged to slain or departed Muslims and Jews; and, having come to appreciate their suitability to the region's climate, they set out to build houses of similar design. Yet they were constructed with Western methods and displayed features of variegated origin. The trailblazer of Frankish domestic architecture studies, Adrian Boas, shows how such diverse elements may coexist in a single building: "For example," he writes, "in an urban house in the Genoese quarter of Acre we come across the Eastern 'courtyard-house' layout together with the use of Western construction techniques such as diagonal tooling and masons' marks, Eastern-type interlocking joggled voussoirs in an arched window and a wall chimney that was possibly an adaptation from the regions under Byzantine rule."[126] Another Eastern feature appears in Wilbrand of Oldenburg's description of Antioch's houses and palaces: the German envoy, who visited the city in 1211, observes that while they exhibit a muddy appearance on the outside, the inside is golden and delightful.[127] In the Genoese and Venetian quarters of Acre, and probably of Tyre as well, stood Italian-type *palazzi*; but unlike the family palaces in Genoa and Venice, their Eastern variants were communally owned, multistoried apartment houses, erected and maintained for the benefit of visiting merchants, with ground floors serving as shops and warehouses.[128] Also, thirteenth-century Acre could boast of an elaborate network of waste removal through covered tunnels, probably influenced by Fatimid precedents.[129]

In the new settlements that the Franks established in the twelfth century in the countryside, they made use of the linear street-village layout, then common in western Europe's planned "new settlements" (*villae novae*), whether villages or towns. Elongated houses of almost uniform design, mostly two stories high, formed rows on each side of the single street, with every house sharing a side wall with the adjacent houses.[130] But, unlike their Western counterparts, these humble village houses were always built of stone and—unlike contemporaneous rural houses in the East—many of them had wall chimneys. The rear walls of the houses, which formed a continuous line, provided some protection against marauders.[131] The little-studied indigenous villages of the kingdom, which appear to have lacked a regular layout and to have extended centrifugally from an original nucleus, do not appear to have influenced the design of the new Frankish settlements.[132]

The archaeological evidence for the Frankish use of tables comes, as of now, from just two sites: the refectory of the Hospitaller castle of Bethgibelin, where tables formed from ancient marble columns cut in half served the brothers, and a farmhouse at Har Ḥozevim (northern Jerusalem), where a limestone table came to light during excavations.[133] The chronicle that goes by the name of Ernoul relates that the coronation ceremonies of a Frankish king concluded with a banquet in the Temple of Solomon (the Christianized Aqṣā Mosque), where the new king and his barons sat down to dine at tables;[134] and people dining at tables appear in illuminated manuscripts of thirteenth-century Acre.[135] On the other hand, eating on the ground was a punishment imposed on Templars who fled battle or otherwise seriously misbehaved.[136] Nevertheless, it would be rash to conclude that the recourse to tables was habitual among all Franks. This is because Jehan of Joinville (1224–1317), describing the fortification of Caesarea in 1251–52 by King Louis IX of France, remarks that when the king placed fifty knights under his—Jehan's—command, ten of them ate at his table with him and with his own ten knights, while the others "ate facing one another, as is the custom of the country, seated on mats on the ground."[137] Furthermore, illuminations painted in Acre in the 1270s and 1280s depict two Frankish rulers, Raymond of Antioch and Joscelin of Edessa, playing chess while sitting cross-legged on the ground.[138]

There is no archeological evidence for beds, but the written sources often mention them. The German pilgrim Theoderich, who visited Jerusalem in about 1172, writes that he saw in the Jerusalem Hospital more than a thousand beds.[139] The anonymous author who left behind a treatise on the functioning of this hospital describes these beds as beautifully wrought and covered with feather-stuffed quilts. The brothers of the Hospitaller order, too, slept on beds; during an emergency, they lay on the floor, having given up their beds to the sick. Ailing women occupied a separate building, equally equipped with beds.[140] As for the Templars, in 1182 Bishop Eudes of Beirut decreed that they must provide a bed, a hearth, and water to the poor of a hospital they were to administer.[141] In 1187, when the Franks had to leave Jerusalem after its conquest by Ṣalāḥ al-Dīn, bedsteads were among the objects they had to leave behind, so ʿImād al-Dīn reports.[142] The *Book for the King* lists a "furnished bed" among a knight's possessions.[143] Joinville mentions having had a bed when he stayed in the house of a priest in Acre, and later in his tent in King Louis IX's camp at Caesarea.[144] In 1252–53, while in Jaffa, the king provided the local Franciscan house with beds.[145] The chronicler, poet, and jurist Phelippe of Novara (ca. 1200–late 1260s) mentions his bed and the screen above it.[146] Also, bedsteads appear in miniatures painted in Acre.[147] However, most of the above-mentioned sources refer to beds in institutions geared to the needs of people who came from Europe, or to beds of nobles, and do not shed light on bedding arrangements in the houses of Frankish commoners.

Neither do we have information on seating and bedding habits in the homes of the indigenous population. Yet we may claim to have a fair idea about them. This is so because Shelomo Dov Goitein (d. 1985), in one of the most important historical works of the twentieth century, reconstructed in great detail the contemporaneous house, and its furnishings, in the southeastern Mediterranean. Having meticulously analyzed the documentation and especially the trousseau lists deposited in the Cairo Geniza, he concluded that tables and chairs were unknown and that bedsteads, still mentioned occasionally in the tenth and eleventh centuries, totally disappeared later on; he linked this phenomenon to the scarcity of wood and to the abundance of textiles. Hence carpets, mattresses, sofa sections, cushions, bolsters, and pillows served for seating and bedding.[148] Some of the documentation that allowed for Goitein's reconstruction originated in precrusade Palestine, and this is a further reason to suppose that the domestic furnishings of the Frankish Kingdom's indigenous population resembled those mentioned in the Geniza documents at large.[149] One may assume that the interior of some Frankish houses, especially of mixed couples where the husband was a Frank and the woman an Eastern Christian or a Christianized Muslim, was of a similar nature.[150]

The furnishings about which our knowledge is steadily expanding are the pottery vessels for the storing, cooking, and serving of food. This is because every new excavation brings to light substantial quantities of pottery shards, and methods developed over the past few decades enable the examination of their composition and the pinpointing of the provenience of the vessels of which they formed part.

The growing body of ceramics studies suggests that various processes of adoption and hybridization were at work.[151] In Beirut, the glazed cooking vessels known from the Fatimid period continued to be manufactured, with some changes, under Frankish rule. The large quantity of these vessels excavated in Acre indicates that Franks chose to use cooking pots and baking dishes of a local, traditional type.[152] In various places in the Principality of Antioch and in Cilician Armenia, glazed pottery of several types was produced in the thirteenth century. The best-known of these is known as Port St. Symeon ware, after the harbor of Frankish Antioch, the present-day al-Mina. The form of this ware followed Islamic models, but its decoration was hybrid, mingling Islamic, Eastern Christian, and Frankish motifs—the latter including triangular shield designs. These vessels made their way to Anatolia, Cyprus, and Egypt—and to the Frankish Kingdom of Jerusalem; in Acre, remnants of seventy-eight shards were excavated, three of them with what look like pseudo-Arabic letters.[153] In addition to Beirut and Port St. Symeon wares, pottery from Cyprus as well as from the central and western Mediterranean was imported to Acre;[154] among the latter the exquisite polychrome glaze-painted Proto-Maiolica ware from southern Italy and Sicily stands out.[155] Still other fine vessels, some of them decorated with pseudo-Arabic script, were imported from Muslim-ruled parts of central Syria.[156] The latter are probably identical with the "the pottery goods that are brought from Pagandom [the realm of Islam] to Acre," mentioned in the customs tariffs of Acre.[157] Pottery, like coinage, passed between Muslim- and Frankish-ruled regions.

But Acre, in addition to importing various vessels from so many regions, was also a new production center for plain, unglazed pottery that arose under Frankish rule. Some of its wares—for instance, jugs—exhibit European characteristics, while others resemble contemporary Islamicate vessels.[158] Possibly Frankish potters were working alongside indigenous ones, but it is also conceivable that the same potters produced diversely inspired vessels for different clienteles.

Food

Albert of Aachen relates that when in May 1099 the crusaders camped near Tripoli, they "sucked there little honey-sweet reeds called *zucra*, found abundantly throughout the plains; they enjoyed the reeds' salubrious juice and—because of its sweetness—once having tasted it they could scarcely get sated. The cultivation of this plant requires the peasants' hardest work every year. At harvest time the indigenous crush the ripe crop in small mortars and store the cleansed juice in their vessels until it coagulates and hardens with the appearance of snow or white salt."[159]

This detailed description leaves little doubt that sugar was an exciting, exotic novelty for the crusaders. Its consumption soon came to be deemed important. In 1108 King Baldwin I looted a caravan that was making its way from Egypt to Syria and sent to Jerusalem eleven camels laden with *zucra* and twenty-one with other goods, and—so remarks Albert of Aachen—this abundant supply relieved the entire region.[160] In 1116 a Frankish-owned sugarcane plantation appears for the first time in our documentation; the plantation was situated near Mont-Pèlerin in the County of Tripoli.[161] Then, after a hiatus in the records that does not necessarily reflect real life, such plantations and the sugar they yielded are repeatedly mentioned from 1160 onward.[162] Archaeological work has revealed that, unlike the manual reed-crushing described by Albert, the Franks harnessed water power to do so, at least in some cases: one water mill, fitted for the preparation of sugar, is known to have functioned in the twelfth century near Jericho, while another was active in the thirteenth century at Manueth, northeast of Acre.[163] Sugar, a lucrative cash crop, became one of the assets of the Frankish Kingdom's economy.[164] Benjamin of Tudela and William of Tyre concur in attesting to its extensive export from Tyre.[165] Indeed, when in 1239 Emperor Frederick II attempted to revitalize Sicily's waning sugar production, he instructed his legate in Tyre "to find [in the Frankish East] two men who know well to make sugar," and send them to Palermo, where they were to produce sugar and teach locals how to do so.[166]

Thus, for the Franks sugar was a novel commodity they learned to mass produce and market. But there were many other unfamiliar crops they encountered in the East and for which they acquired a taste. The anonymous visitor from the West who described in his treatise the Kingdom of Jerusalem as it looked between 1168 and 1187—and to whom I shall refer henceforth as the Western Visitor—observed that in addition to the trees common in Europe, the country has date palms, "trees of paradise" (undoubtedly bananas), lemons, "Adam's apples," sugar canes, cotton, "Pharaoh figs," and maritime fruit-bearing cedars.[167] Jacques of Vitry, who between 1216 and 1224 substantially elaborated on this description, noted that the fruit of those cedars is known as citron, and that the fruits of a similar tree are called by the indigenous *poma orenges*—that is, orange apples (consequently the term *orenge*, borrowed from the Arabic *nāranj*, may be added to the Prawer/Minervini lists).[168] He also mentioned huge cucumbers, melons and gourds whose size exceeds a donkey's head, silk produced by worms, and a species of palatable thorns called *sparee*.[169] And the customs tariffs of Acre list, among the goods brought to the city from the countryside, *tahine*—that is, *ṭaḥīne*, the paste made of ground sesame, a prominent feature of the regional cuisine down to the present day, which the Franks evidently learned to relish.[170] The same tariffs also list a number of spices; and, indeed, the safe conveyance of Far Eastern spices via Iraq to Acre and Tyre as a result of a greater stability in the Caliphate appears to have allowed Venetian and Genoese trade with the Kingdom of Acre to surpass that with Egypt in the first quarter of the thirteenth century.[171]

Exposed and attracted to the East's novelties as they were, the Franks did not give up the penchant for wine and pork so typical of the West. They intensified grape cultivation and wine production, combining Western and local usages: for instance, they constructed wine presses that conformed to the Roman-Byzantine pattern, yet located them—like in the West—under the roofs of their buildings.[172] Pigs, pigsties, and a tax on the butchering of a pig are mentioned in the Frankish documentation, and the import of bacon and pigs from Sicily is attested in Norman and Angevin sources.[173] Archaeological excavations have disclosed that pigs, rare in the pre- and postcrusade periods, were important in Frankish animal husbandry, though their salience appears to have varied by place and situation.[174]

However, at least one Frank chose to abstain from pork altogether, evidently influenced by Islamic cuisine. Usāma ibn Munqidh famously relates that one of his men was invited in Antioch to dine at the table of an old Frankish knight who had come East many years ago. When the knight saw that the Muslim guest was hesitant, he assured him that pork never entered his house and that he refrained from Frankish food, eating only what his Egyptian female cooks prepared. But Usāma hastens to point out that such Franks, "who have been acclimatized and frequent the company of Muslims," are the exception.[175]

Yet there was also some Frankish influence on Eastern cuisine. A culinary treatise that appears to date from Ayyubid times contains a recipe for the baking of a bread "which the Franks and the Armenians prepare"; the anonymous author comments: "This recipe is excellent."[176]

Appearance and Attire

In the latter part of the eleventh century, Westerners used to shave their beards. The clash between the crusaders and the Muslims during the First Crusade was therefore also a confrontation between shaved and hirsute males.[177] First Crusaders who let their beards grow put their safety at risk. Guibert of Nogent relates that when during the siege of Antioch in 1098 many fatigued crusaders neglected to shave their beards, Bishop Adhémar of Le Puy, the papal legate, urged them to do so, lest in the thick of battle Christians were to attack other Christians, taking them by mistake for Turks "because of the likeness of their beards."[178]

The Franks followed the First Crusaders in this respect. The Western Visitor observed that, of its many peoples, only the Franks shave their beards.[179] His observation is corroborated by an episode related by Bahā᾽al-Dīn ibn Shaddād (1145–1234), Ṣalāḥ al-Dīn's biographer. When in 1190 the Franks were besieging Muslim-held Acre on land and sea, and a boat from Muslim Beirut attempted to cross the Christian naval cordon around Acre and convey much-needed supplies to the besieged city, a number of Muslims on board "dressed up as Franks, even shaving their beards. They also placed pigs on the deck, so that they could be seen from a distance, and flew crosses." When the boat arrived among the Christian galleys, some of the Muslims, pretending to be Franks, talked with the Christians—which indicates that they were capable of uttering some sentences in the Frankish dialect without an immediately recognizable accent. The ruse worked, and the boat sailed into Acre's harbor safely.[180] Later, Bahā᾽ al-Dīn relates that at the signing of the agreement between King Richard I of England and Ṣalāḥ al-Dīn in September 1192 he saw the Frankish noble Onfroi IV of Toron—the first husband of Isabella, daughter of King Amaurry—who struck him as "a handsome young man, although clean-shaven according to their [the Franks'] distinguishing feature."[181]

Yet Frankish beardlessness was not general. In 1113 members of the papal curia at Benevento were astonished to see that the canon Pons and the legate Roland of the Antiochene church, envoys of Prince Roger and Patriarch Bernard of Antioch, displayed head hair and beards grown together.[182] Apparently, just fifteen years after the conquest of Antioch some Latin clerics saw fit to imitate the Eastern clergy's appearance in this respect.

Among Frankish laymen, with whom shaving was not required as with the clergy but merely customary, beards were not unusual.[183] Pilgrims grew beards—remember Archbishop Askil's long beard that attested to his pilgrimage. So did many hermits. Four of Jerusalem's twelfth-century kings—the first three Baldwins and Amaurry—are known to have had beards, unlike many of their Western counterparts, but like Count Geoffroy Plantagenet of Anjou and Maine (1113–51), half brother of Kings Baldwin III and Amaurry, whose dark-brown beard appears on his contemporary effigy now in the Musée de Tessé in Le Mans.[184] Herbertus-with-a-Beard is a burgess of Jerusalem who attests to a charter of 1130/33; he may be identical with Humbertus-with-a-Beard, who attests in 1138.[185] In 1156 a burgess of the Frankish new town of Mahumeria (al-Bīra), situated north of Jerusalem, was called Arnaldus-with-a-Beard.[186] By the 1180s, beards must have become a characteristic feature of many Poulains, because an account of the Battle of Ḥaṭṭīn refers to "the *Poleins* with all their beards."[187] We do not know how common this trait was among them, but clearly beards ceased to be a characteristic that consistently distinguished between Franks and non-Franks.[188] Indeed, the anonymous author of the Old French adaptation of William of Tyre's chronicle, who was writing in the first third of the thirteenth century,[189] believed that, a century earlier, a thin, long beard had been customary in the Kingdom of Jerusalem.[190]

For one group of Franks the beard served as a marker of membership: the Knights Templar who, unlike the clean-shaven Knights Hospitaller, habitually grew beards. According to their statutes, a brother who wished to shave his beard had to ask permission of the Master or his stand-in.[191] Muslims were aware of the Templar beards' salience. An old Muslim, who knew the Franks well, purportedly criticized Ṣalāḥ al-Dīn for having massacred his Templar prisoners after the Battle of Ḥaṭṭīn, telling him: "Do you think that you have put an end to your war? I must tell you that the Templars will be born with all their beards."[192] Similarly,

Jacques of Vitry relates that the Saracens assumed that a bearded and bald Christian must be a Templar.[193] The Templars' beards may have advertised the nonclerical nature of their order, but at the same time they brought the appearance of their bearers closer to that of Easterners of various stripes.[194]

Franks may have adopted beards, but they refrained from wearing Eastern clothes. An Antiochene copper coin showing the bust of a bearded Tancred allegedly presented him as wearing a turban, and historians interpreted this as an early instance of assimilation to Eastern customs; "but"—as Michael Metcalf (d. 2018), the leading expert on Frankish numismatics, noted—"well-struck specimens [of the coin] suggest that the turban is a figment of the imagination."[195] Of the five heads figuring on corbels of the twelfth-century Frankish dome of the Church of the Holy Sepulcher, three are bearded and one wears a turban-like headdress. These may be self-representations of the sculptors—yet they may have been local, Eastern Christians.[196] The Franks' basic attitude toward Eastern dress was one of aversion. This is expressly stated by the chronicler Ibn al-Athīr (1160–1233), who relates that when Henri of Champagne, ruler of the rump Kingdom of Acre in the years 1192–97, asked Ṣalāḥ al-Dīn to bestow a robe of honor on him, he pointed out that the wearing of the *qabāʾ* (a sort of cassock, open at the front) and *sharbūsh* (a tall triangular birretta) is considered a disgrace among the Franks but that he, Henri, would wear them nonetheless, as a mark of respect for the sultan.[197] Archaeology, too, implies that the Franks adhered to Western fashion: the many buckles excavated in Frankish sites have close parallels in the West and differ from those unearthed in Islamic contexts.[198]

Yet even as the Franks stuck to Western dress habits, they took a liking to precious Eastern textiles: while the cut of their garments remained Western, the cloth was often Eastern.[199] Hence, their appearance could strike Westerners not only as different but also as loathsome: the Poulains, fulminates Jacques of Vitry, the fiery bishop of Acre, wear soft garments according to the custom of women.[200] Similarly, the recourse to Eastern fragrances could evoke revulsion. When Patriarch Eraclius of Jerusalem came to Europe in 1184 to plead the cause of the endangered kingdom, Ralph Niger was scandalized by the sweet smells his garments diffused, and by much else.[201] Eraclius, born in the Auvergne and educated in Bologna, came to Jerusalem in about 1168; sixteen years later his comportment was perceived by Ralph as markedly deviating from that of the West's prelates and princes.

While Franks shunned Eastern garments, some non-Frankish inhabitants of the Kingdom of Jerusalem were keen to adopt the dress of their rulers, and therefore in 1120 the Council of Nablus saw fit to lay down that a Saracen man or woman who wears Frankish dress should be seized on behalf of the fisc.[202] What caused these Muslims to "go Frankish" as far as clothing was concerned? It is difficult to believe that they hoped to trick Franks into sexual relations, as some historians have assumed, because even though wearing Frankish dress their speech would easily have revealed their identity: it is one thing to utter a few sentences at sea off Acre in 1190, and quite another to initiate a conversation that aims at intimacy. Neither is it plausible to assume that they wished to mount surprise attacks on Franks while wearing their clothes; had this been the case, the Nablus decision would hardly have banned the wearing of Frankish dress by Saracen *women*. The ban rather implies that some Muslims acquiesced in Frankish supremacy: as Ibn Khaldūn (1332–1406) was to remark, the vanquished imitates the victor's dress or his other distinctive marks, as he wishes to assimilate with those to whom he is subservient.[203] Yet the Frankish leaders who convened in 1120, clerics and laymen, opted for separation.

As for Eastern Christians, there is one piece of evidence suggesting that they, or some of them, were able to cross the dress barrier. Ya'qūb ibn Siqlāb was a Jerusalemite who studied and practiced medicine in his natal city. Ibn Abī Uṣaybi'a (ca. 1200–1270), the well-informed author of an encyclopedia of prominent physicians, recounts that Ya'qūb arrived in Damascus as a young man in about 1188 and came to a meeting with a renowned Christian court physician while wearing a *kūfiyyah* (headdress), a light turban, and a tight-fitting blue coat, "the usual dress of Frankish physicians." The court physician gave his young colleague some practical advice: "These clothes you are wearing," he said, "will not help you to practice medicine among the Muslims in this country. It would serve your interest to change your attire. You would do better to dress like the local physicians."[204] Evidently, Ya'qūb dressed in Jerusalem like his Frankish colleagues without causing offense. In Damascus he experienced an aversion to Frankish dress that amounted to a mirror image of the Frankish view that the wearing of Muslim garments was a disgrace.

Just like some Frankish dishes entered Eastern cuisine, at least one Frankish ornament came to be worn by some Muslim women. The Persian poet Sa'dī (d. ca. 1291)—once taken prisoner by Franks and forced to dig a trench in Tripoli—sings the praises of a ravishing beauty whose "Frankish necklet is not to be compared to her curly locks."[205]

Hybridity, Identity, Stigmatization

The use of carrier pigeons may have been a rare case in which the Franks adopted a local element in its entirety, yet even here we cannot be sure that they did so without some modification. However, in many instances the adoption was partial: for example, the bathhouses, where an indigenous physical layout served as a backdrop for home country behavior; the documents in which a Latin place-name alternated with its Arabic equivalent; the gold coins imitating the form of Fatimid dīnārs but not their weight and fineness.

More frequently a novel creation arose from the amalgam of disparate components: for instance, the street-village, established according to European pattern, whose houses were, however, built of stone and equipped with a chimney; the urban abode based on the Eastern courtyard-house layout yet constructed with Western techniques; the Port St. Symeon glazed pottery, whose form followed Islamic models yet whose decoration combined Islamic, Eastern Christian, and Frankish motifs; and, last but not least, the Frankish dialect that attests to the impact of northern French vernaculars, Occitan, Italo-Romance, and Arabic.

From a present-day vantage point, these varieties of hybridity—far from being superficial or fleeting—reveal that the Franks, having started a new life in a country not only distant thousands of miles from their places of origin but also differing in climate, landscape, natural resources, practices, and customs, exhibited an impressive capacity to adjust and innovate, and evolved a creativity that allowed them to cope with their new surroundings and progressively develop a new, distinct identity.[206] And this identity, taking shape through processes of adjustment and acculturation, presumably also had profounder layers, like elation at inhabiting and defending a country perceived as uniquely sacred. Yet from the vantage point of contemporary Westerners, the Franks' acclimatization and innovativeness rendered them increasingly odd and disconcerting, and their predilection for, say, bathhouses and delicate garments led to their stigmatization as an inferior offshoot of Latin Christendom.[207] The censure was boosted by pilgrims and crusaders who felt that the Franks were defrauding them while providing lodging and food.[208] One Westerner, William of Newburgh, writing in the 1190s, went so far as to assert that the Poulains, "spoiled by their proximity to the Saracens, do not differ much from them in faith and customs, and are considered as being neither Christians nor Saracens."[209] At least a generation later, Frankish leaders were well aware of their bad reputation among many Westerners. Describing the confrontation in 1228 between Emperor Frederick II and Johan of Ibelin (1200/1205–36), the "Old Lord of Beirut" and leader of the Frankish nobility, Phelippe of Novara has Johan proclaim that he wants to prevent the spread, throughout Christendom, of the accusation that he and his family, "the treacherous of Outremer, who love the Saracens more than the Christians," wrecked the emperor's crusade.[210]

The assumption that Frankish acculturation led necessarily to social assimilation, that is, to a narrowing of the distance between rulers and ruled, is unwarranted: as Thomas Glick has rightly pointed out, cultural borrowing does not by necessity flatten a social cleavage.[211] And, indeed, even as some Westerners disparaged the Poulains for purportedly resembling the Muslims, the latter looked down at them as rude and uncivilized. It is well known that Usāma ibn Munqidh derided Frankish jurisprudence by ridiculing a judicial duel he witnessed in Nablus; a century later the Egyptian jurist al-Qarāfī (1228–85), too, adduced a duel, this time held in Acre, in order to pour scorn on Christian justice.[212]

Did the Franks develop a sense of pride in their vilified distinctiveness? We can only guess. However, Phelippe of Novara penned a sentence that exudes affection for their country. When in August 1225 the thirteen-year-old Queen Isabella II of Jerusalem was about to sail from Tyre to Brindisi in order to marry Emperor Frederick II, Phelippe has her gaze at the land she was leaving and sigh: "I commend you to God, *douce Surie* [sweet Syria], which I shall never see again."[213] The *dulce France* (sweet France) of the *Song of Roland* found its peer along the eastern shores of the Mediterranean.

But even as Phelippe, the knight, has the young queen gazing at sweet Syria (not at "the sweet Holy Land!"), Jacques of Vitry, the cleric, extols the many devout pilgrims who flocked to the Holy Land (*ad Terram sanctam*) attracted by the pleasant odor of the holy places, and lauds the hermits of Mount Carmel who, "like bees of the Lord, made a honey of spiritual sweetness."[214]

Chapter 3

An Intellectual Backwater?

The Frankish Kingdom of Jerusalem that lasted from 1099 to 1187, and the Frankish East of those years, existed in the age in which the Latin West witnessed the revival of Roman law and the application of dialectic to canon law, the assimilation of scientific and philosophical knowledge translated from Arabic or Greek, and a dramatic intensification in the study of the Latin classics, in the writing of history, in theological and philosophical speculation, and much more. This upsurge in cultural activity, habitually labeled the Renaissance of the Twelfth Century, was largely initiated and shouldered by members of western Europe's clergy.

Seen from this perspective, the clerics of the Kingdom of Jerusalem were a sorry lot. They did not engage in philosophy, theology, or canon law, and despite their proximity to Muslims and Greeks did not translate philosophical or scientific works written in Arabic or Greek; the writing of chronicles was the one field in which some of them engaged. As Bernard Hamilton, the leading historian of the Frankish church put it, "at a time when the west was experiencing the great intellectual awakening commonly called the twelfth-century renaissance, Frankish Syria was an academic backwater."[1] Other prominent crusade historians were no less brusque: Prawer described the Frankish East as a "provincial and marginal" appendage of Latin Europe's culture, while Riley-Smith described the Frankish church as "of low quality and provincial" and agreed with Prawer that "the low educational level in the Latin settlements" explains why the Frankish East did not play a major role in the transmission of Arabic learning to Europe.[2] And Christopher Tyerman asserted that "certain elements of Latin Outremer culture and society reflected western life, notably in the church, language and law, but overlaid with a profound provincialism. The radical intellectual, artistic, and legal developments in western Europe in the twelfth century found only a thin echo in the east. . . . Academically, Outremer existed in a backwater, distanced alike from west and east."[3]

The Problem: Frankish Jerusalem and the Twelfth-Century Renaissance

How should one explain this lack of interest of the Frankish clergy in most of the new intellectual ventures in the West, from which they or their progenitors had come? Let us examine the evidence in some detail.

To begin with, the Frankish Kingdom did not lack cathedral schools. Already by 1102–3 there was in the Church of the Holy Sepulcher in Jerusalem a schoolmaster, whose annual prebend of three hundred bezants amounted to twice as much as that of a regular canon.[4] By 1136 Johannes the Pisan, who in later years was to attain the rank of cardinal of the Church of Rome, taught there the "little clerks" (*clericuli*).[5] Hans Eberhard Mayer has persuasively argued that Johannes was preceded as schoolmaster at the Church of the Holy Sepulcher by master Robert, and that in 1160 the post was held by master Achilles. There is also evidence for the existence of schools at other cathedrals. In Beirut a "teacher of clerics" is mentioned in 1133; in Acre in 1175, both the bishop and the Order of the Hospital maintained schools; an act drawn up in Antioch in 1184 mentions among the patriarch's counsellors the schoolmaster Leonard as well as one master Hugo. And it is plausible that masters William of Sidon, Anschetinus of Ramla, Gerard of Tyre, and Hugo of Hebron, who appear in acts of 1152, 1160, 1161, and 1163, were schoolmasters as well.[6] Given the modest amount of documentation that has come down, the information on grammar schools gleanable from it is substantial. We may assume that with regard to such schools the Frankish East did not differ from the West.

There is also evidence for libraries. A remark Foucher of Chartres makes in his chronicle some time before 1127 reveals that he was able to use a library in Jerusalem.[7] A priest by the name of Hugo, who styles himself "librarian of the church of Bethlehem," draws up an act in 1129.[8] William of Tyre mentions that he deposited books in the archive of his cathedral; another of his remarks indicates that many churches possessed archives.[9] Also, one catalog of a Frankish library has come down to us: it lists the books owned by the canons of the cathedral of Nazareth and appears on the last folio of one of these books, which made its way into the Amplonian Library of Erfurt.[10] As we shall see, the catalog, datable to the late twelfth century, tells a complex story; it is worthwhile to examine it at some length and compare it to contemporary library catalogs in the West.

The Nazareth catalog refers to a hundred volumes but contains just seventy-two titles. The reason for this discrepancy is that in several instances the Nazareth library possessed a number of copies of the same work: for instance, five copies of Prosper, the fifth-century Aquitanian author; three of Prudentius, the fourth-century Spanish poet; three of Boethius; two of Ovid's letters; and so forth. Therefore, the number of titles is smaller than that of volumes.[11] Yet it is well-nigh certain that the number of titles was larger, possibly much larger, than the seventy-two listed in the catalog. This is so because we can examine one volume that belonged to the Nazareth library and compare its actual content with the way the catalog represents it. This volume is, of course, the one that made its way to Erfurt. An examination of the volume's content reveals that it contains nine different works, but only the titles of the two longest of them are spelled out in the catalog.[12] In other words, the library of the canons of the cathedral of Nazareth possessed seven additional works that go unmentioned in the catalog; and we may assume that such underreporting of titles affected other Nazareth volumes as well. The phenomenon is well known to students of medieval catalogs: evidently, the clerics who drew them up aimed primarily at identifying the volumes possessed by their libraries, not at exhaustively listing the titles of the works they contained.[13]

We do not know how many of the hundred volumes reached Nazareth from Europe or from other places in the Kingdom of Jerusalem, and whether some were copied on the spot. Nor do we know whether some originated in bequests or gifts to the library.[14] All the catalog divulges is that two volumes, containing works of Augustine of Hippo, were on loan with the bishop of Sidon—a unique piece of evidence for the circulation of books within the kingdom.

Now, how do the hundred volumes of the Nazareth catalog compare with the number of volumes possessed by contemporaneous western

European cathedrals? I have been able to locate only four complete catalogs from the later twelfth century that list the books possessed by such cathedrals; these are the catalogs of Novara in northwestern Italy, Rouen in Normandy, and Durham and Lincoln in England.[15] It should be noted that of these, only Rouen was—like Nazareth—the seat of an archbishop. A comparison of the Nazareth catalog with its European counterparts reveals that the latter contain numerous liturgical books, whereas the Nazareth catalog does not list a single specifically liturgical book, even though the cathedral of Nazareth must have possessed some.

A meaningful comparison of the Nazareth catalog with the European ones must therefore juxtapose the hundred Nazareth volumes, all nonliturgical, to the nonliturgical volumes listed in Novara, Rouen, Durham, and Lincoln. The comparison reveals that Nazareth could boast of about twice as many nonliturgical volumes as Novara, which had just fifty-three such books, and surpassed Lincoln and Rouen, which owned ninety and sixty, respectively. On the other hand, Durham Cathedral had a much larger library than Nazareth: its catalog lists 522 nonliturgical volumes. Durham Cathedral was, however, the home of a Benedictine monastic community that inherited the books of several abbeys.[16]

Notes in the margin of the Nazareth catalog divide it into two categories: *de divinitate*, that is, theology, and *de gram[m]atica*, that is, language and literature. The dividing line is not clear-cut. Two of the volumes listed above the line deal with mostly profane subjects.[17] The works of four late antique Christian authors—Prudentius, Sedulius, Prosper, and Maximianus—appear below it, suggesting that they were appreciated mainly for their literary form. When we transfer the two profane works from the first to the second category, we arrive at forty-three volumes treating religious subjects and fifty-nine dealing with literature and other profane topics, a ratio of 0.73:1.[18] When we apply the same criteria to the European catalogs, we arrive at a ratio of 5.6:1 for Novara (45 religious, 8 profane); 4.8:1 for Rouen (58 religious, 12 profane); 7.2:1 for Lincoln (79 religious, 11 profane); and 1.5:1 for Durham (317 religious, 205 profane).[19] Consequently, the Nazareth catalog stands out as the only one of the group in which nontheological volumes constitute the majority. Nazareth stands out also for the availability of several nontheological works in two or more copies. For instance, while Novara, Rouen, and Lincoln had no copy of the works of Prosper or Prudentius, and Durham had two of each, Nazareth—as we have seen—possessed five copies of Prosper and three of Prudentius. It is plausible to assume that some of the works available in Nazareth in more than one copy served for teaching purposes. Also, Julian Yolles has shown that of the twenty-one authors who made up the contemporary canon according to Konrad of Hirsau (d. ca. 1150), no less than fifteen are listed in the Nazareth catalog, and all but one of Konrad's classical authors appear in it.[20] Thus, the catalog leaves little doubt that Nazareth's library was well-equipped for the study of the Latin language and classics, and could also serve for the study of other liberal arts.[21] It is perhaps not coincidental that two of the Frankish Kingdom's authors are known as "of Nazareth": Rorgo Fretellus, the chancellor of the lord of Galilee in 1119 who at some later date became archdeacon of Antioch and wrote a description of the Holy Places, and Gerard, later bishop of Laodicea, the author of several treatises.[22]

At the same time, the Nazareth catalog, datable to the late twelfth century, lists none of the major attainments of the preceding decades. The most recent works figuring in it are *Cur Deus Homo* (Why God Became Man), which Archbishop Anselm of Canterbury completed in 1098; the vastly popular theological treatise *Elucidarium* written by Honorius Augustodunensis about 1100; and the letters of Bishop Ivo of Chartres, the prominent canonist (d. 1115).[23] Does this absence of works dating from subsequent years testify to a lack of interest in the intellectual revitalization that was taking place in the West?[24] The question calls for a careful weighing of the evidence because, as James Stuart Beddie observed back in 1929, the works of many leading twelfth-century writers are seldom listed in contemporary catalogs and therefore the latter cannot be taken to record intellectual advances adequately.[25] Still, a comparison with our four European catalogs allows for a definite answer. The most recent work appearing in the Novara catalog of 1175 is the commentary on the Psalms by Anselm of Lucca (d. 1086), but the catalog also records the presence of Justinian's *Codex* and *Novellae*, and it attests thereby to an interest in the revived Roman law. The Rouen catalog does not include works of major figures of the Twelfth-Century Renaissance, yet it does list the relatively recent books written by a prominent local author, Hugues of Amiens, archbishop of Rouen in the years 1130–64.[26] The two other catalogs, those of Lincoln and Durham, testify unequivocally to an interest in recent advances. Both libraries owned the Psalms commentary of Gilbert de la Porrée (d. 1154) and the *Book of Sentences* of his opponent Petrus Lombardus (d. 1160). The Lincoln library, which had two copies of Gilbert's commentary, also owned Petrus Comestor's *Historia scholastica* of ca. 1170 and seven volumes by Ralph Niger (ca. 1143–before 1199), well-known for his criticism of crusading.[27] Durham also had the *Decretum* (Gratian's authoritative canon law collection), works by Bernard of Clairvaux, Roger of Salerno's book on surgery compiled in about 1180, and much more.

It follows that the absence of recent works from the Nazareth catalog is meaningful. Consequently, the Nazareth library allows for two divergent conclusions about the attitude of its owners to the phenomenon we call the Renaissance of the Twelfth Century: they shared the enthusiasm for the study of the Latin language and classics, yet were indifferent to, or estranged from, the renaissance's attainments in further areas. In other words, the catalog illustrates the problem we set out to elucidate, but renders it more baffling, since in some important respects the catalog outstrips its Western counterparts and by no means attests to a motionless backwater.

An examination of the educational level of the Frankish clergy leads to similar conclusions. We have seen that this level has been appraised as low. Indeed, Runciman went so far as to depict Eraclius, the last Frankish patriarch to reside in Jerusalem, as "a barely literate priest."[28] Yet Runciman was not aware of the letter in which Étienne of Tournai (1128–1203), the decretist and theologian, mentions that he and Eraclius studied together at the nascent University of Bologna; neither did he take into consideration two patriarchal deeds drawn up in Jerusalem in 1167/68 that present Eraclius as a *magister* (master).[29] Of course, in the twelfth as in any later century, attendance at a university did not vouchsafe intellectual eminence, but a Bologna-trained master could not have been, comparatively speaking, a man of little learning, much less a barely literate one. Neither was Eraclius the Frankish East's only *magister*. Far from it: forty-two of them are mentioned in the years 1126–85, their number rising from the 1150s onward.[30] This upsurge parallels the growth, in the contemporary West, in the number of men who bore the title "master" after having acquired some kind of special learning. Indeed, it is possible to hypothesize that this growth occurred in the Frankish East about a decade earlier than in the northwestern part of the German Empire, though probably somewhat later than in France and England.[31] Also, the rise in the number of law-trained masters in Jerusalem's royal chancery parallels the one that took place in chanceries in the West, like that of Emperor Frederick I Barbarossa.[32] And the influx of notaries from the West ensured that the changes in document design then taking place in Europe were taken up in Jerusalem's royal chancery without a notable lag.[33]

Let us now retrace our steps from Eraclius (1180–91) to Arnoul of Chocques (1099; 1112–18), that is, from the last to the first Frankish patriarch of Jerusalem. Posterity has not been kind to either of them; both were accused, inter alia, of transgressions in the sexual sphere. Yet Arnoul, like Eraclius, was far from being barely literate. Before going on the First Crusade he served as tutor to Cecilia, daughter of William the Conqueror, and as teacher to Raoul of Caen, who later, in Jerusalem, asked him to edit his *Deeds of Tancred*.[34] Even Guibert of Nogent, who criticizes Arnoul severely, grudgingly admits his knowledge of dialectic and grammar, while Orderic Vitalis, the contemporary Anglo-Norman chronicler, unambiguously characterizes him as "a most learned man."[35] And in early twelfth-century Jerusalem resided other men of letters beside Arnoul. Foucher, who came from Chartres, one of the centers of the Twelfth-Century Renaissance, became the kingdom's first chronicler. True, Guibert of Nogent dismissed Foucher's style as rough and bombastic, yet a meticulous study of his chronicle has revealed that he shared many theological and historiographical notions with major contemporary thinkers in the West, Guibert included; that his views on the relationship between church and state as well as on other fundamental issues betray the influence of Bishop Ivo of Chartres; and that his interest in natural phenomena and his stress on the human role in historical causation resemble the somewhat later, systematic reflections of Thierry of Chartres.[36] Acardus of Arrouaise, prior of the Lord's Temple in Jerusalem in the years 1112–36, had been a hermit who became schoolmaster of Arras and archdeacon of Thérouanne; in Jerusalem he wrote a work of poetry that marks him a man of considerable learning.[37] Anseau, cantor of the Church of the Holy Sepulcher, was educated at Notre-Dame of Paris where he served until 1096, when he went East with the First Crusade; in 1120, in a letter sent from Jerusalem to his erstwhile Parisian confrères, he confides that during the many years since his departure he tried to learn about their doings by questioning newcomers from the Paris area, and that in his dreams he often partook in their worship.[38] In about 1115 all four clerics—Arnoul, Foucher, Acardus, and Anseau—lived in Jerusalem, still sparsely populated at that time, and could engage in a scholarly give-and-take had they so wished, but neither they nor their successors are known to have contributed to the intellectual upsurge in the contemporary West. So the educational level of the Frankish clergy, too, does not elucidate the enigma of its abstention from most of the scholarly activities typical of the Renaissance of the Twelfth Century.

Jerusalem vs. Europe's Marches

But perhaps there is in reality no enigma, no problem calling for elucidation? To follow one way of thinking, we should compare the Frankish Kingdom with the European marches rather than with central France.[39] If so, the Frankish clergy's abstention ceases being problematic: examined in its purportedly appropriate, geographically peripheral framework, it turns out to be typical of Latin Europe's marches and does not require a specific explanation.

Yet the Frankish Kingdom of Jerusalem was much more than one of Latin Europe's marches. What with Jerusalem's role in scripture, liturgy, and pilgrimage, what with the high drama of the First Crusade and the subsequent eruptions of sanctified warfare, the Frankish Kingdom occupied a singular place in Europe's consciousness, and the interest it stimulated far surpassed that of any other periphery. Suffice it to recall that in about 1125 Ari the Wise knew in faraway Iceland that Baldvini, king of Jórsala (King Baldwin I of Jerusalem), and Arnaldus, patriarch in Híerúsalem (Arnoul of Chocques), died in 1118, as did Iceland's Bishop Gizurr, Pope Paschal II, King Philip of Sweden, and Alexíus, king of the Greeks; or that—as John of Salisbury reports—in 1170 Archbishop Frederic of Tyre served as intermediary between King Henry II of England and King Louis VII of France, with Henry designating "his paternal uncle the king of Jerusalem"—that is, King Amaurry—the primary pledge of his willingness to reconcile with Thomas Becket.[40] None of Latin Europe's other outlying areas came close to attaining such salience. Also, some of the most prominent thinkers of the age passed some time in the kingdom: Bishop Otto of Freising (ca. 1114–58), author of *The History of the Two Cities*, the major historico-philosophical work, participated in the Second Crusade; Joachim of Fiore (1135–1202), the Calabrian mystic and theologian whose vision of a peaceful Age of the Holy Spirit had a long-lasting impact, made a pilgrimage to Jerusalem in his youth—and valiantly withstood there the temptations of the widow in whose house he lodged.[41]

There was also an influx of clerics from Latin Europe's heartland. Some came as pilgrims and chose or were persuaded to stay; others were invited by relatives and friends who had settled in the East.[42] Still others sought—as we have seen—a temporary or permanent refuge from a precarious situation in the West. Consequently, the Frankish church was largely manned by immigrants. All twelfth-century patriarchs of Jerusalem came from the West: thirteen from France, one from Italy.

As for the pre-1187 episcopate, a quantitative study mainly based on the examination of geographical bynames suggests that twenty-nine prelates originated in France, six in Italy, three in the German Empire, three in England, and one in Iberia, whereas only two—one certainly and one presumably—were born in the Frankish East.[43] Even in the lower clergy locals appear to have been outstripped by immigrants. An examination of the canons of the Church of the Holy Sepulcher who attested to documents in the years 1128–78 and bore geographical bynames indicates that the share of local-born canons did not rise with the progress of time, while the salience of the European-born ones remained constant or increased:

Table 3.1 Canons of the Church of the Holy Sepulcher with geographical bynames, 1128–1178

ORIGIN	1128–1144	1145–1161	1162–1178
Frankish East	4	4	1
France	7	6	5
Iberia	2	2	1
Italy	-	2	1
England	1	-	1
Undetermined	1	-	-
	15	14	9[a]

Source: Cart St Sép, 79–80, 84, 108, 161, 163, 166–67, 215, 222, 235, 236, 245, 250, 251, 309, 315, 354, 356, nos. 22, 24, 38, 66, 67, 69, 97, 102, 114, 115, 121, 123, 124, 158, 162, app. 4, app. 5.

[a] On the sharp decline in the number of canons after 1160 and its possible explanation, see Bresc-Bautier, "Les effectifs du chapitre du Saint-Sépulcre de Jérusalem," 408–9

This preponderance of Western-born clerics, many of whom came from regions in which the higher studies of the Twelfth-Century Renaissance flourished, renders still more puzzling the Frankish clergy's evident lack of interest in the new, exciting intellectual departures of the age. Consequently, the Kingdom of Jerusalem's geographical peripherality, too, fails to offer a satisfactory solution to the problem under consideration.

Chapter 4

The Clergy and the Establishment of Cores of Devotion

Let us now choose a different approach and focus on the Frankish clerics and the activities in which they engaged. A closer look at them and their attainments, starting with an examination of three major cores of devotion they established, the True Cross, the Miraculous Fire, and the Holy Resurrection, may provide a clue to their remoteness from the new intellectual trends that burgeoned in the contemporary West.

The True Cross

The most concise contemporary documentation of the Frankish Kingdom of Jerusalem consists of just twenty-two, mostly single-line, entries written in a crude Latin. Canons of the Church of the Holy Sepulcher whose names remain unknown jotted them down in some liturgical books on various occasions. The entries, occupying in their fullest form a single page of a manuscript preserved in the Church of the Holy Sepulcher at Barletta, Apulia,[1] do not reveal new facts about the kingdom's history and therefore have not attracted much attention since their publication in 1901. And yet two of them shed stark light on a major constituent of Frankish religiosity. Following one upon another, they describe two battles of the late 1170s:

> On 28 November 1177, Baldwin, sixth king of Jerusalem, contended in battle with *Salahadinus* and an infinite multitude of Turks at Montgisard; and although the Christian army was very small, it subdued, defeated, and overcame the Turks, by God's victory and the presence of the vivifying Cross.
>
> In 1179 the said King Baldwin contended in battle with *Salahadinus* in a place called Margelion [Marj 'Ayyūn, present-day southern Lebanon] and it did not turn out well for our men. The Master of the Templars and many other barons and knights were captured, killed, and defeated. This came about, we believe, because the Holy Cross, which the king ordered to be conveyed in support of the entire army, was left behind at Tiberias. Since they put their trust more in their own vigor than in the Holy Cross, they did not fare well.[2]

Evidently, the author or authors of these entries presumed that victory in 1177 was secured by the presence of the Holy or True Cross, and defeat in 1179 ensued from its absence.[3] This piece of wood, believed to have formed part of the cross on which Jesus suffered in agony, served as a tangible link between Christ and the Christians who fought to defend the country sanctified by his ministry and passion. It visualized Christian Holy War, a war in which Christ himself leads his followers to victory over his enemies, far more dramatically than the crosses Pope Urban II told the crusaders in 1095 to sew on their clothes. It was the culmination of an age-long process, starting with Emperor Constantine's Standard of the Cross and enhanced from the tenth century onward with ecclesiastically blessed banners carried into battle, by which the idea of Holy War became decisively entrenched in the realm of symbols.[4]

It was allegedly Empress Helena, the mother of Emperor Constantine, who found the True Cross during her pilgrimage to Jerusalem in 326. She divided it into two parts, sending one to her son in Constantinople and leaving the other in Jerusalem.[5] The Persians carried the latter away upon their conquest of Jerusalem in 614; Emperor Heraclius triumphantly brought it back in 631.[6] Its fate under Muslim rule is not clear, but soon after the crusader conquest of Jerusalem on 15 July 1099 it acquired a crucial role. Arnoul of Chocques, the chaplain of Duke Robert of Normandy who was elected first Latin patriarch of Jerusalem on 1 August 1099, knew that the True Cross had been previously worshiped by pilgrims and immediately set out to question local Eastern Christians about its whereabouts. Initially pretending not to know the hiding place, they were soon coerced to disclose it and to dig up the relic. On 5 August, Arnoul was in possession of the True Cross.[7]

Its authenticity was never questioned. This was in stark contrast to the doubts that engulfed the Holy Lance upon its discovery a year earlier, when the First Crusaders were in dire straits in Antioch. The contrast was not accidental. It was Arnoul who led the party that decried the Lance as a fraud and ultimately made its discoverer submit to an ordeal by fire.[8] But Arnoul, an able if defamed orator and organizer, must have sensed the crusaders' need for an arousing sacred emblem, for he persuaded them to forge a golden image of Christ around which they would rally on their way from northern Syria to Jerusalem like the Israelites of old had done around the Tabernacle. By engineering the rediscovery of the True Cross right upon his election as patriarch, Arnoul bestowed on the crusaders a still more potent replacement of the Lance.[9]

On 12 August 1099, a week after its rediscovery, the True Cross made its first appearance on the battlefield. A large Egyptian army that arrived in Ascalon threatened to crush the Franks, and the crusading leaders Godefrid of Bouillon, his brother Eustache, Count Robert of Flanders, and Tancred the Norman from Apulia urged all other princes to join them in the impending crucial battle. They also told Peter (probably known as Pedron) the Hermit and Arnoul to bring along "the wood of the Lord." This is what Albert of Aachen, who represents the viewpoint of Godefrid and his Lotharingians, relates in his chronicle; yet it may have been Arnoul who endeavored to boost the crusaders' morale by bringing the holy relic into camp.[10] Albert also recounts that during the march to Ascalon the former Muslim ruler of Ramla—now Godefrid's ally—marveled at the crusaders' joyful progress to a battle in which they might meet their death. Godefrid gave him at length the reasons for their confidence, one of them being the certitude that by "this wood of the Holy Cross" they had been redeemed from death and hell.[11] The battle ended in a resounding crusader victory.

Two years later the Holy Cross worked its first miracle. On 7 September 1101, a ferocious battle raged near Ramla between King Baldwin I of Jerusalem and his men, and a huge Egyptian army. Four of the king's formations were destroyed one after another. Then the fifth, and last, "in which the wood of the holy and venerable Cross was carried before the king and his comrades," set forth. An Egyptian emir charged at the prelate who held the Cross and was about to behead him, but divine vengeance stopped the attacker and he choked to death. The king killed the other emir, and the Franks emerged victorious. Albert of Aachen, who relates the story, points out that it demonstrates the power of the True Cross.[12]

In May 1102, King Baldwin waged two battles against the Egyptians. The first ended with a crushing Frankish defeat; the second, in which the Holy Cross was present, concluded with a resounding Frankish victory. Describing these two battles, Foucher of Chartres observed that it was fitting for the Franks, protected by the Holy Cross, to gain victory over its enemies; had the Holy Cross been carried into the earlier battle, surely God would have been propitious to his people—but the Franks trusted their vigor more than the Lord, and lost.[13] The belief that the presence of the Holy Cross bestowed victory and its absence resulted in defeat made its first recorded appearance.

Carrying the True Cross to the battlefield soon became habitual. Describing another battle with the Egyptians that took place in 1105 at Ramla, Foucher reported that the patriarch held in his hands the Lord's Cross, "which it was customary to convey in such circumstances."[14] Indeed, our sources mention thirty-three instances from the years 1099–1187 in which the True Cross was carried into battle or siege—and once, in 1122, in an advance against Tripoli's Frankish count.[15] During a march or a battle, the True Cross—mounted within a much larger wooden cross—probably also served as a rallying point, indicating to all warriors the army's center.[16]

A prelate could do more than just carry the True Cross into combat and uplift it in prayer.[17] When the Franks were hard-pressed in a battle that took place on 14 August 1119 in the region of Antioch, Archbishop Evremar of Caesarea directed the Cross at the Turks and—so reports Gautier, chancellor of Antioch—exclaimed: "You most abominable ones, be cursed through the holiest power of this Cross! May divine vengeance make you run away and scatter! Perish right away!" (Somewhat uneasily, Gautier's editor—Heinrich Hagenmeyer—commented in 1896: "The archbishop may have, after all, cried out such words at the enemy; they attest to a rather rude though courageous character. To all appearances, they render in a somewhat more polished manner a crude curse probably uttered in French dialect.") Accordingly, the way in which the True Cross was wielded on the battlefield appears to have depended on the temperament of the prelate who carried it—or perhaps of his chronicler. At any rate, Evremar's curse was soon followed by action: King Baldwin II, calling upon the True Cross to protect and help, charged at the Turks and drove them away.[18]

Though it was normally the patriarch of Jerusalem who carried the True Cross to the battlefield, on a number of occasions he entrusted it to an archbishop or bishop.[19] The commander of the Knights Templar in the city of Jerusalem and ten of his men were assigned to guard it day and night throughout a campaign's duration.[20] The relic's safe return to Jerusalem occasioned a festive welcome.[21] When in Jerusalem, it was in the custody of the canons of the Church of the Holy Sepulcher. It became, alongside the Sepulcher, the goal of the Jerusalem pilgrimage: the *Voyage of Charlemagne to Jerusalem and Constantinople*, probably dating from the mid-twelfth century, presents Charlemagne as desiring to adore in Jerusalem "the Cross and the Sepulcher."[22] For some worshipers the Cross may have overshadowed the Sepulcher: King Konrad III of Germany wrote in 1149, upon returning from his unsuccessful crusade, that in Jerusalem he adored "the trace of the vivifying and salvatory cross"; the Sepulcher goes unmentioned.[23]

The canons of the Church of the Holy Sepulcher were normally entitled to the offerings that worshipers presented to the True Cross. But the act of 1114, by which Patriarch Arnoul imposed the Augustinian rule on the canons, sets down that they were not to receive these offerings on Good Friday or whenever the patriarch had to carry the Cross with him—"on a military expedition," spells out an act of 1169 issued by Patriarch Amaurry.[24] On such occasions the offerings went to the patriarch, who might have chosen therefore to prolong his voyage to and from the battlefield and stop in various towns for a number of days; consequently, the canons obtained a papal ruling that assigned them the offerings given to the Cross after the second day of the patriarch's arrival in a certain town.[25] It is therefore likely that when in June 1120 Jerusalem's clerics were reluctant to let King Baldwin II take the True Cross on an expedition to faraway Antioch, they feared not only its possible capture by the Turks—as Foucher of Chartres, probably a canon of the Church of the Holy Sepulcher by that time, relates—but also the certain loss of offerings during the relic's protracted absence from Jerusalem.[26] Yet the king, who a year earlier had escaped harm near Antioch by virtue of the True Cross that he and the count of Tripoli "carried—like slaves their mistress—into battle," insisted that he did not dare to go to Antioch's rescue without the relic, and ultimately the clerics gave way.[27] Still, the True Cross is not known to have accompanied the Franks on any of their expeditions into Egypt. King Amaurry, who led these expeditions, had to content himself with a fragment of the True Cross that dangled from his neck.[28]

Believers all over the Christian West were eager to obtain some piece of the True Cross. As early as 1101 Patriarch Daibert of Jerusalem—erstwhile archbishop of the mercantile town of Pisa—was accused of sacrilegiously reducing a part of the wood of the Holy Cross to fragments and dispersing them.[29] Though Daibert was deposed soon thereafter, fragments of the relic continued to be disseminated throughout the existence of the Kingdom of Jerusalem and beyond. Kings and patriarchs bestowed some pieces on crusade leaders and dispatched others to personages and churches in the West they held in special esteem; and some crusaders and pilgrims obtained fragments and brought them West.[30]

Some of the clerics who served in the Church of the Holy Sepulcher came into the possession of fragments. Abbot Gerhard of Schaffhausen, guardian of that church's treasure, allegedly acquired the fragment that made its way to Zwiefalten in southern Germany.[31] Adam, a canon of the Sepulcher who originated in the diocese of Le Mans, entrusted two of his erstwhile countrymen with a cross that contained two pieces of the True Cross; in 1116 Bishop Hildebert of Le Mans solemnly placed the gift in his cathedral.[32] Anseau, the cleric of Notre-Dame of Paris who became cantor of the Church of the Holy Sepulcher, desired to send a piece of the True Cross to his erstwhile confrères in Paris. Unwilling or unable to obtain a fragment of the relic kept in his church, he bought another fragment from the widow of King David of Georgia, abbess of Jerusalem's impoverished Georgian convent, and dispatched it in 1120 to Paris, where it soon became one of Notre-Dame's most cherished possessions. Fortunately, Anseau saw fit to send his Parisian friends a letter in which he explained how he acquired the relic, and when they asked for more details about its provenance, he sent them a fuller account. The two letters reveal that Anseau was keenly interested in the history of the True Cross under Muslim rule and invested considerable effort to piece it together. After the death of Emperor Heraclius, he writes, the infidel burned a part of the Sepulcher and intended to burn the True Cross, but Jerusalem's Christians succeeded in hiding it, though many were killed on this account. To prevent the Cross from falling into infidel hands, the Christians decided to divide it into many parts. These were sent to various places, and consequently there are three fragments in Constantinople, two in Cyprus, one in Crete, three in Antioch, and one each in Edessa, Alexandria, Ascalon, and Damascus. The patriarch of Georgia has a fragment; the one that had belonged to the Georgian king is now in Paris. In Jerusalem there are four pieces: the Syrians have one, the Greeks of St. Sabas (Mār Sābā) have another, the monks in the Valley of

Josaphat have the third, and the Latins at the Church of the Holy Sepulcher have the fourth. Anseau gives the dimensions of the latter, Frankish, True Cross: it is one palm and a half long and one thumb broad. Significantly, Anseau points out that he derived his information from Greek and Syrian writings and from talks with leading Syrians; "the Greeks own many things that the Latins do not," he comments.[33] For him, the True Cross was part of Eastern Christendom's heritage, and the wood that came into Frankish possession in 1099 was just one of numerous fragments revered by Greeks, Syrians, and other Easterners.

At least one fragment of the Frankish Holy Cross was sent to the West to stimulate donations for the Church of the Holy Sepulcher. Patriarch Foucher of Jerusalem (1145–57) dispatched one of his canons to Germany, entrusting him with a cross that contained a fragment of the Holy Cross and other relics. This cross was to serve as a proxy sanctuary and as an authenticated repository for donations by believers whom sickness or poverty prevented from fulfilling their vow of pilgrimage to the Holy Sepulcher. The cross was forcibly seized while under way, apparently at the instigation of Duke Konrad II of Dachau, and the canons of the Sepulcher were unable to recover it. In the early 1180s Duke Konrad III of Dachau made a pilgrimage to Jerusalem and begged Patriarch Eraclius to allow him to possess the relic. The patriarch agreed, imposing on the duke to recover other misappropriated possessions of the Sepulcher. The relic, encased in its reliquary, became the property of Scheyern, an abbey the dukes of Dachau patronized. It is venerated there to this day.[34]

Studies of Frankish art reveal that the Scheyern reliquary has several close counterparts. All are True Cross reliquaries. One, originally in the cloister of the Holy Sepulcher at Denkendorf, is now in a Stuttgart museum; another, now in an Augsburg collection, belonged to the Cistercian monastery in Kaisheim; a third is in the Church of the Holy Sepulcher in Barletta; the remains of a fourth form part of a portable altar of the cathedral of Agrigento, Sicily; the fifth is in Conques, the sixth in the Louvre, the seventh in Angers, the eighth, originally in the Galician abbey of Carboeiro, is now in Santiago de Compostela, the ninth made its way to the Cleveland Museum of Art; and three others were discovered in Anglesola (Catalonia), Castel Sant'Elia (near Viterbo), and Troia (near Foggia). Since all these reliquaries exhibit striking similarities and contain, or contained, fragments of the True Cross, it is likely that they were produced in Jerusalem. Recurring, identical stamp impressions and a very simple filigree work indicate that they were swiftly manufactured, and therefore we may assume that the surviving reliquaries formed part of a larger group. Byzantine in style and in their technical features, Western in the iconography of their medallions, the reliquaries may be ascribed to Western goldsmiths imitating Byzantine models. The dozen goldsmiths who appear as witnesses in various acts of the Church of the Holy Sepulcher possibly point to the existence of a goldsmith workshop in its vicinity or employ.[35]

Hence, the centrality of the True Cross for the Franks can hardly be exaggerated. It afforded protection and assured victory against the longest odds. A proven talisman as well as a supreme symbol of holy warfare waged in defense of the Holy Places, it attested time and again to the power of the Christian faith. It was a major repository of donations. Its custody had to be regulated, its liturgy had to be established, its history had to be written; the most important chronicle of the kingdom, that by William of Tyre, mentions it on its very first page.[36] Its fragments were the most sacred objects a Frankish king or prelate could bestow, and to which a pilgrim or crusader could aspire; the production of their reliquaries became a substantial enterprise. And we may assume that with each new victory attained with the True Cross present on the battlefield, the belief in its power deepened.

By the 1180s at the latest, some Muslims gained an accurate idea of the importance of the True Cross for the Franks. ʿImād al-Dīn has the Franks exclaim: "The Messiah is for us, the Cross is with us!" He also has King Gui of Lusignan declare before the Battle of Ḥaṭṭīn: "I shall erect the True Cross; no Christian will push back from it." ʿImād al-Dīn knows that the Franks believe it to consist of the wood on which Jesus was crucified, that they have bedecked it with pure gold, pearls, and precious stones, and that their priests carry it to the battlefield. This Cross, he writes, "was their divinity: in front of it they soiled their foreheads in the dust . . . they gave for it their blood, beseeched it for solace." Therefore, when the Muslims captured the True Cross during the collapse of the Frankish army at the Horns of Ḥaṭṭīn, the Franks, he relates, were struck with the worst catastrophe possible, more painful than the capture of their king, Gui of Lusignan.[37] ʿImād al-Dīn's observation is corroborated by Frankish sources. When Patriarch Eraclius wrote in September 1187 to Pope Urban III about the defeat at Ḥaṭṭīn, he mentioned first the loss of "the sacrosanct and vivifying Cross, the sole and singular means of our salvation," then the fate of the two bishops who carried it on the battlefield, and only thereafter the capture of the king and the destruction of the army.[38] Similarly, the anonymous canon of the Church of the Holy Sepulcher whose sad fate it was to record the defeat at Ḥaṭṭīn in the liturgical book in which his confrères had registered so many victories wrote: "On 1 May 1187 the Master of the Hospital was killed and on 4 July there took place the loss of the Holy Cross and the annihilation of the Franks by *Salahadinus* near Saphorie and on 11 July Acre surrendered to him and on 4 September Ascalon surrendered to him and on 2 October the city of Jerusalem surrendered to him. On that day there was an eclipse of the sun."[39]

Was this entry written by the canon who trusted that the presence of the relic on the battlefield made the difference between victory in 1177 and setback in 1179? If so, how did he come to terms with the shocking certainty that, despite the presence of the True Cross at Ḥaṭṭīn, Ṣalāḥ al-Dīn gained the decisive victory that spelled the end of the Frankish Kingdom of Jerusalem and that—still worse—the Cross itself was captured by the infidel? We do not know.

Yet people confronted with a belief-shattering catastrophe are capable of contriving odd solutions in their quest to come to terms with the new situation. Pierre of Blois, the noted man of letters who went on crusade in 1189, relates that *Saladinus* displayed the captured True Cross to his Frankish captives in order to break their will, yet the presence of the relic fortified them to persevere in their Christian faith: the loss of the relic on the battlefield paved the way to a victory of the spirit in the dungeon.[40] Similarly, the anonymous author of the account of the Frankish Kingdom's downfall has the people of Jerusalem exclaim, at the beginning of Ṣalāḥ al-Dīn's siege in September 1187: "O Holy True Cross, and Sepulcher of the Resurrection of Jesus Christ, protect the city of Jerusalem with its inhabitants!"[41] Evidently the relic, though in Muslim hands, did not lose its supernatural powers.

The Miraculous Fire

Like the True Cross, the Miracle of the Easter Fire was originally Eastern Christian.[42] It was a local, Jerusalemite event. While in churches throughout Christendom the New Fire blessed on Holy Saturday is produced by the striking of flint, in the Church of the Holy Sepulcher in Jerusalem the fire was believed to descend from heaven on the Tomb of Christ in its midst. The annually recurrent miracle was probably contrived after the Arab conquest of 638 and aimed at fortifying the faith of Christians who lived now under infidel rule. It is mentioned for the first time by the monk Bernard, who pilgrimaged to Jerusalem in about 868.

Thus, by the time of the Frankish conquest in 1099, the Miracle of the Holy Fire had a history of some 250 years or more. Now it was to occur for the first time in a Christian-controlled Jerusalem. Yet on 31 March 1100, the first Holy Saturday under Frankish rule, the Fire caused much grief by going out some time after its descent, but after a while, by God's mercy, it reappeared: so reported the anonymous chronicler of St.-Maixent, a monastery in southwestern France, who was well informed of events in the Frankish East and particularly interested in the Holy Fire. Still worse was to come on 20 April 1101, the second Holy Saturday celebrated in Frankish Jerusalem: this time the miracle did not occur at all.

The stunning debacle triggered a frenzied consternation. There were professions of penance, and a shattered Daibert, believing that his sins offended God, abdicated the patriarchal office. Some Franks became so disheartened that they contemplated returning to the West. On the morning of Easter Sunday, a devastated King Baldwin I threw himself to the ground before the doors of the Sepulcher and was about to remove his diadem and step down but was dissuaded from doing so. Then it was decided to march in procession to the Lord's Temple, remembering that King Solomon had beseeched God there to forgive the sins of a repentant people. The Frankish clerics, many laymen, Baldwin, and his barons marched barefoot to the sanctuary. In the meantime, the Greeks, Syrians, and Armenians, who remained in the Church of the Holy Sepulcher, went in procession around the aedicule; ululating in anguish, they plucked at their cheeks and beards "according to the custom of that people."

When the Franks returned from the Lord's Temple, they were overjoyed to hear that the Holy Fire was burning in one of the lamps in front of the Tomb. Its reddish glow could be observed through the Tomb's small windows. There was a tremendous outburst of jubilation, all crying *Kyrie eleison* (Lord, have mercy), applauding, singing, kindling thousands of candles with the Holy Fire, celebrating the Easter Mass. Daibert was reinstated as patriarch, and King Baldwin, crowned and wearing royal garments, threw a banquet in his palace. While the banquet was in progress, two additional lamps were divinely ignited in the Church of the Holy Sepulcher. The Holy Fire did ultimately descend on Frankish Jerusalem, albeit a day later than usual.

As the miracle took place with only the Eastern Christians present in the Church of the Holy Sepulcher, we may assume that the Easterners, and especially the Greeks who had been forced to cede their predominant position there to the Frankish clerics, hoped to redress some of their grievances by temporarily withholding the miracle. According to this scenario, the delay on 31 March 1100 was a warning; the debacle on 20 April 1101 heralded an all-out confrontation. In any case, one may rule out the possibility that the Greek clerics were momentarily incapable of bringing about the miracle that they had so deftly handled for centuries and that they continue to allow regularly to recur down to the present.

Henceforward the miracle resumed its customary appearance and soon became a major attribute of Frankish Jerusalem. For Bishop Baudri of Bourgueil, writing in about 1110, it was God's annual miracle, with the lamps rekindled by divine radiance; in his version of Urban II's Clermont Address of 1095 that launched the First Crusade, he makes the pope extol it. For Albert of Aachen, a heavenly fire rekindles, by the grace of God, the flame in the oil lamp standing in the Lord's Sepulcher; the miracle serves "to corroborate faith in the Lord's Resurrection"; in 1119, about seven hundred pilgrims witnessed it.

There is evidence for changes in the ceremony over the years. While in 1101 it was Patriarch Daibert who entered the aedicule of the Tomb and emerged thence carrying the Fire, a liturgical book that describes practices established by Patriarch Foucher in the mid-twelfth century entrusts with this task some local worshiper of high repute or a similarly qualified pilgrim, "in order to repress the irresolution of the incredulous and strengthen the faith." This man, together with two or three others, is told to circle the Tomb, barefoot, three or four times, with the True Cross in his hands. But Theoderich relates in about 1172 that it was the patriarch and the clergy who circled the Tomb with the True Cross. He also mentions that the Fire may appear at various hours, either in the Church of the Holy Sepulcher or in the Temple of the Lord or in the Hospitaller Church of St. John. Thus, the originally Eastern Christian miracle was by now firmly in Frankish hands, to be produced at will at one of the major Frankish shrines of Jerusalem. Westerners were keen to experience it. In 1137, Bishop Zdík/Heinricus of Olomouc (Moravia) was delayed in Constantinople and could not reach Jerusalem before Holy Saturday; therefore, he decided to remain there and wait for the following Paschal Feast. At Eastertime 1178, Count Philip of Flanders hurried from Antioch to Jerusalem "on account of the sight of the Holy Fire."

A Latin poem probably composed for the anniversary of the crusader conquest of Jerusalem on 15 July 1099, which glories in the town's preeminence with an exuberance that marks its author a Jerusalemite Frank, devotes to the Holy Fire one of its six stanzas:

Urbs insignis	ad quam ignis	venit annis singulis
quo monstratur	quod amatur	omnibus in seculis
honoranda,	frequentanda,	regibus et populis.[43]

(City eminent, to which the Fire comes in each successive year,
Showing that it is beloved in all and every time,
To be honored and frequented by kings and peoples.)

Yet the most eloquent acclamation of the Holy Fire was penned by a man who never set foot in the Frankish Kingdom. This was Petrus Venerabilis, abbot of Cluny in the years 1122–56 and one of the most influential churchmen of his age. In a sermon in praise of the Lord's Sepulcher, Petrus presents the Fire as the ultimate testimony of the Tomb's glory, coming as it does not from earth or men but from heaven and God. A Christian merely hears about the miracles of the prophets, the apostles, the Savior himself; but he is able to bodily see with his eyes the miraculous, celestial yet corporeal Fire that corroborates the miracles of old. Its descent on the Tomb and on Holy Saturday, rather than on other places or anniversaries of Christ's ministry, is not accidental: it appears at the place and day of Christ's repose in his burial chamber so as to proclaim that only his death could have brought about human salvation. Then Petrus proceeds to accord the Holy Fire a still more exalted place in sacred history: just as God put aflame Abel's offering but not that of Cain, that of Elijah but not that of the priests of Baal, so at this time the Holy Fire demonstrates his pleasure with Christian worship and vexation with that of Jews and Gentiles. Moreover, as Christ's enemies scorn especially his death, the heavenly light that descends on his burial place manifests that what the stupid infidel regards as most ignominious is indeed most glorious.[44] (Possibly the latter reasoning triggered the original contrivance of the miracle at some point after the Muslim conquest of Jerusalem in 638.) Petrus dwells on the Holy Fire also in his polemical treatise against the Jews. Here he presents it as an undeniable miracle, attested by Gentiles and Saracens of the entire East and South.[45]

Petrus would have been dismayed to learn that the one Muslim of his times who left a record of his view of the Holy Fire was far from considering it an incontrovertible miracle. This was the ascetic, pilgrim, preacher, and poet ʿAlī al-Harawī, who visited Jerusalem in 1173 and observed acidly: "As for the descent of light [there], I resided in Jerusalem for a time during the Frankish era long enough that I was able to determine how it was done."[46]

The miracle apparently aroused the skepticism of some Franks, too. Caffaro, the Genoese witness of the debacle of 1101, relates: The Holy Fire not coming down, Patriarch Daibert explained to the people that since Jerusalem had come under Christian rule, the miracle—destined to attract nonbelievers to the faith—was no longer necessary. Nevertheless, he prayed that the Fire come down, "because we believe that many amongst you are feeble in their Christian faith and incredulous."[47] The wish "to repress the irresolution of the incredulous," noted in the liturgical book of the Church of the Holy Sepulcher, may also have aimed at overcoming skepticism. Yet the most eloquent proof of incredulity is indirect. William of Tyre, a native of Jerusalem who was undoubtedly aware of the centrality of the Holy Fire in the local celebration of Easter, does not mention it at all throughout his extensive chronicle! And this is by no means accidental. Foucher of Chartres, William's source for the events of 1101, mentions the arrival of a Genoese fleet in Jaffa, the ascent of the Genoese to Jerusalem to celebrate Easter there, the confusion occasioned by the nonappearance of the Fire, the departure of the king to Jaffa, and the agreement he made with the fleet's consuls. William duly paraphrases these observations—but chooses to skip altogether the reference to the Fire![48] We may conclude that, like his younger contemporary ʿAlī al-Harawī, William comprehended how the descent of the Fire was done.

However, incredulity was a minority attitude. The common view was expressed by the knight-troubadour Bertran of Born who, after the Frankish defeat at Ḥaṭṭīn, exclaimed that the True Cross and the king were captured

E-l sepolcres ha de socors fraichura,
Don tuit crezem ab lial fe segura
Qe lo saintz focs i deissen, q'om o ve,
Per qe no fai nul esfortz qui so cre.[49]

(And in need of help is the Sepulcher,
Where we all believe with loyal assured faith
That the Holy Fire descends; since one sees it,
To believe it, no effort is needed.)

The Third Crusade of 1189–92, which Bertran promoted, failed in reconquering Jerusalem, and so it came about that at Easter 1192 it was Ṣalāḥ al-Dīn who came to the Sepulcher to observe the Fire's descent. The Norman poet Ambroise relates that when the "spiritual fire" materialized in the lamp, the Saracens asked whether this happened by enchantment, and *Salahadins*, wishing to put the occurrence to a test, ordered to extinguish the lamp, which however reignited. *Salahadins* ordered to extinguish it once again, but the Lord, wishing the truth to be manifested, relit it again. An impressed *Salahadins* told his Turks that he would die soon, and this is what happened.[50] On the other hand, the preacher and chronicler Sibṭ ibn al-Jawzī (1185–1276) recounts much later that Ṣalāḥ al-Dīn, suspecting a fraud, wished to see the miracle with his own eyes, but the (by now, Greek) patriarch dissuaded him from doing so, arguing that by disclosing the secret the sultan would lose income.[51]

In 1229, in the wake of the agreement between Emperor Frederick II and al-Malik al-Kāmil, the Frankish clergy returned to the Church of the Holy Sepulcher. Sibṭ ibn al-Jawzī, who lectured and preached in Frankish Jerusalem in subsequent years, relates that he found out how the clerics produced the descent. He adds that the fire was carried to Acre, Tyre, and all other Frankish cities down to Rome, to be venerated there.[52] During the second, brief, Frankish rule in Jerusalem the Holy Fire became tangible in the West.

But, as we shall see, not for long. Half a century after the True Cross was captured by Ṣalāḥ al-Dīn, the Holy Fire was branded by a pope as a fraud. The "incredulous" were, at long last, vindicated.

The Holy Resurrection

The Frankish clerics got hold of the True Cross just three weeks after the conquest of Jerusalem, and a few months thereafter they attempted to preside over the descent of the Holy Fire. On the other hand, what was to become the third distinctive hallmark of Frankish devotion—the pronounced emphasis on the Holy Resurrection—emerged only much later. Its genesis and significance call for a broader examination.

The liberation of the Church of the Holy Sepulcher was the goal of the First Crusade: the crusade itself came to be known as *via sancti sepulchri*, "the road of the Holy Sepulcher."[53] It was the Church of the Holy Sepulcher to which the First Crusaders hurried to give thanks to their God upon the conquest of Jerusalem. It was the Church of the Holy Sepulcher in which they deposited the True Cross and in which they awaited the descent of the miraculous Fire. It was in the Church of the Holy Sepulcher that the Frankish patriarchs officiated and the Frankish kings were, from 1118 onward, crowned and, since 1143, buried.[54] On the early patriarchal seals we see an angel who shows the empty Tomb to the three Holy Women—Mary Magdalene, Mary the mother of James the Less, and Salome, according to Mark 16:1—and the legend encircling this scene reads: "The Sepulcher of Our Lord Jesus Christ."

All this is not surprising: in Latin Europe, Jerusalem's main shrine had been known for centuries as the Church of the Holy Sepulcher, or the Church of the Lord's Sepulcher. Yet in the 1130s Frankish documents start to designate the shrine by a new name, which comes to be used ever more frequently: "the Church of the Lord's Resurrection."[55] The new designation appears in three charters of 1137 (or 1138) that record grants to the church, or its chapter; in two of these the new name appears alongside the old.[56] Both designations figure also in a charter King Fulk issued in 1138, but here the new name appears in a more elaborate version: "the Church of the Lord's Glorious Passion and Resurrection."[57] In later charters, too, the new name does not supplant the traditional one altogether: some mention both, others only the old or only the new.

In one area, however, the new designation became exclusive: in the intitulation of Jerusalem's patriarchs. While the earlier heads of the Frankish ecclesiastical hierarchy presented themselves, in charters and seals, simply as patriarchs of Jerusalem,[58] Patriarch Foucher styled himself in his charters as "Patriarch of the Church of the Sacrosanct (or sometimes: Holy) Resurrection of Christ Our God," and on his seals as "Patriarch of the Church of the Holy Resurrection."[59] Foucher's two successors who were to reside in Frankish Jerusalem, Amaurry and Eraclius, used the new title both in their charters and on their seals.[60] This patriarchal emphasis on holiness may have triggered an extension of the royal appellation: the earlier "king of Jerusalem" was replaced with "king of the holy city of Jerusalem," regularly attested between 1144 and 1191.[61]

As Patriarch Foucher was the first to use the new title, and as it was under his aegis that the renovated Church of the Holy Sepulcher was dedicated on 15 July 1149, one may assume that the new name was related to the construction of the new complex, which brought under a single roof the site of the crucifixion at Calvary, the spacious, originally Byzantine Rotunda with Christ's Tomb in its midst, and the new Choir of the Canons. True, the new name appears already about a dozen years before the 1149 dedication, but the planning and execution of so vast a building project must have been going on for years; it has been suggested that the planning took place already in the 1130s.[62] Now, could it be that the new name designated the entire complex, while the term "Sepulcher" continued to refer persistently to the Tomb and/or its Rotunda? No: William of Tyre, who worked between 1170 and 1184 on his chronicle of the Frankish Kingdom, refers to the shrine as "the Church of the Holy (or the Lord's) Resurrection" even when speaking of events that took place before the crusader conquest of Jerusalem; indeed, in his version of Urban II's Clermont Address of 1095, William has the pope call for the liberation of the Church of the Holy Resurrection! Also, in his description of Jerusalem on the eve of the crusader conquest, he remarks that the Church of the Holy Resurrection (not the Holy Sepulcher!) has a rotund shape.[63] Moreover, the juxtaposition of two passages shows him actually replacing the old name with the new one: Reproducing a letter Patriarch Daibert sent in 1100, he copies the sentence that maintains that Godefrid of Bouillon gave one-fourth of Jaffa to the Church of the Holy Sepulcher; but while paraphrasing that sentence he writes that one-fourth of Jaffa was given to the Church of the Holy Resurrection.[64] All this proves beyond doubt that the original Rotunda with the Tomb at its center, traditionally designated by Latins as the Church of the Holy Sepulcher, came to be known—by itself, or together with Calvary and the new Canons' Choir—as the Church of the Holy Resurrection.[65]

But what made the Frankish patriarchs adopt the new appellation? What was its significance? One may distinguish between several layers of meaning. Evidently, the new name attests to local, Eastern Christian influence. In Greek, the shrine was known as the *Anastasis*, that is, the Resurrection; Arabic-speaking Christians called it *al-qiyāma*, which means the same (Muslims gleefully took recourse to the insulting pun *al-qumāma*, the dunghill).[66] Indeed, on the obverse side of the seals of Patriarchs Foucher, Amaurry, and Eraclius there appears, in Greek letters, the Greek name of the shrine, "H ANACTACIC [The Resurrection]."[67] Like the True Cross and the Miraculous Fire, the Holy Resurrection originally formed part of the local Christian heritage.

The new designation points to a shift in emphasis. The term "Holy Sepulcher" could, and can, be understood to connote that the Tomb was sacred because it served as the temporary abode for Christ's body after its deposition from the cross: the Armenian chronicler Matthew of Edessa (d. 1144) speaks bluntly of "the Holy Sepulcher which contained God."[68] Of course, all believers held that the burial was followed by the Resurrection, and that the empty Tomb was one of its proofs, and yet before the 1130s the church built around the Tomb was not known in Latin as "of the Resurrection." Similarly, in Christian art the Resurrection was not depicted directly, with Christ rising from the Tomb, but through scenes like that in which an angel shows the empty Tomb to the Three Women. But whereas the term "Holy Sepulcher" connotes the Resurrection, the term "Resurrection" points to it directly. And the new designation also expresses a shift from tangible to spiritual sanctity.

Yet the adoption of the new name exposes a still more profound intention. "Resurrection" denotes Christ's own rising as well as his raising of the dead, and the Frankish clerics chose to stress this raising. The seals of Foucher, Amaurry, and Eraclius show Christ striding with the cross in his left hand and with his right hand dragging a small crouching figure upward. This is the scene known in modern literature as Christ's Descent into Hell, or as Christ's Harrowing of Hell. It depicts Christ rising from the underworld kingdom of the dead and rescuing Adam and others who were held captive there.

Just like the new name of the church demonstrates Eastern Christian inspiration, so does the scene on these seals testify to an

FIGURE 4. Seals of Greek and Frankish Patriarchs of Jerusalem. Above: Seal of Patriarch Sophronios II (post 1036–1076/83). Winchester, Assize Courts South 253 (in the care of Hampshire Cultural Trust). © Copyright Winchester Excavations Committee. Not to be reproduced without written permission. Below: Seal of Patriarch Eraclius (after 1180). Bayerisches Hauptstaatsarchiv München, KU Scheyern 10

influence of the seals of the pre-1099 Greek patriarchs of Jerusalem (see figs. 4a–d). Because of the overspecialization that so often mars our investigations, the seals of the Greek patriarchs and their Frankish successors have not been studied conjointly; but once set side by side, it transpires that the scene of Christ rising from the kingdom of the dead and rescuing Adam appears on Greek patriarchal seals of the tenth and eleventh centuries and that the seals of Foucher and his successors are modeled on them.[69]

This scene has also been ingeniously identified as a miniature version of the lost mosaic that had adorned the apse above the main altar of the new, Frankish-built Choir of the Canons, an altar that—so Johann of Würzburg, who made his pilgrimage in the mid- or late 1160s,[70] informs us—was dedicated to the Anastasis, "that is, the Holy Resurrection." The mosaic showed a rising Christ who shattered the gates of the underworld and was pulling Adam upwards. Theoderich, who visited the shrine a few years later, writes that Christ carried the cross in his left hand, held Adam in his right, and was striding toward heaven, with the Virgin, the Baptist, and all the apostles around him. One Latin inscription called on the beholders to adore him who arises from death; the other, rendering verse 4:8 of the Epistle to the Ephesians, read: "Ascending on high, He led captivity captive: He gave gifts to men."[71] The lost mosaic stressed in image as well as in word the two aspects of the Resurrection and alluded also to the promise of redemption for all.[72]

The shift from Holy Sepulcher to Holy Resurrection allowed for, or coincided with, a boost in the ecclesiastical authority the patriarchs of Jerusalem claimed for themselves. In the urgent call for help that Amaurry, "patriarch of the most Holy Resurrection of the Lord," dispatched to all Christians early in 1166, he promised eternal life to all those who wished to *visit* the Lord's Sepulcher "because of the pressing exigency," and either completed their journey or died underway.[73] And he made this promise, which—when understood literally—extends the crusade indulgence to mere pilgrims to Jerusalem, "by the authority of the Lord's Passion and Resurrection."[74] Just a few months earlier, on 14 July 1165, Pope Alexander III promulgated a bull in which he offered *crusaders*, by the authority of omnipotent God and St. Peter, the remission of and absolution from sins, and "the fruit of everlasting recompense."[75] But while Alexander III emphasized that his offer replicated that of his predecessors, Popes Urban II and Eugenius III, Patriarch Amaurry, in his slightly later call for help, did not mention the papacy at all. He evidently believed that the custody of the site of the Resurrection bestowed on him an exalted status that empowered him to make a promise exceeding those of the successors of St. Peter.[76] It was a truly stunning, if hitherto little noticed, shot at ecclesiastical preeminence.

Neither did Amaurry believe that his writ ran only in the Kingdom of Jerusalem. In 1169/70 Bishop Raoul of Sebaste called on all the faithful in the West to help complete his cathedral, and informed them that Patriarch Amaurry, "by the authority invested in him by the Omnipotent," absolves those who were to pilgrimage to Santiago de Compostela from going there, on condition that they give the church of Sebaste one-half of the expenses they would have incurred by making the pilgrimage. In addition, Amaurry grants them all the remissions they would have obtained by it. This commutation of pilgrimage markedly differs from its few Western precedents, offered to the faithful of definite areas, or limited to instances in which the would-be pilgrim could adduce compelling reasons for his wish to have his pilgrimage commuted.[77] Contrary to these precedents, the commutation offered in the Sebaste appeal was to be given unconditionally to all the faithful.[78] The patriarch reveals thereby an assuredness in the amplitude of his power that renders him—at least with regard to this particular issue—the direct superior of believers throughout Latin Christendom.[79] Such a lofty self-perception ties in with the view of the Western Visitor, who presents the patriarch of Jerusalem as "father of the faith and of the Christians, and vicar of Jesus Christ."[80]

Frankish clerics may have known that some opponents of the papal claim to supremacy chose to downplay Rome's importance by emphasizing Jerusalem's superior sanctity. In the West, the so-called Norman Anonymous forcefully argued in about 1100 for Jerusalem's precedence over Rome, mentioning inter alia that Peter always stood in awe of James, Jerusalem's bishop, and honored him as his master. Similarly, the Byzantine theologian Niketas Seides (d. after 1117) claimed that if primacy depends on greater age, then Jerusalem, in which James was ordained by Christ himself, precedes the sees of Antioch and Rome founded by Peter; Emperor Manuel Komnenos of Byzantium (1143–80) is said to have used almost the same argument in discussion with several cardinals.[81] Frankish prelates certainly knew that in 1130 and again in 1159, when the church was split by struggles between two competing popes, the support of the patriarchs of Jerusalem and Antioch was regarded as especially weighty, and by some even as crucial, inasmuch as they were—like the pope—incumbents of apostolic sees, the first founded by James, the second by Peter.[82] Accordingly, Amaurry's belief in the authority he derived from the custody of the Church of the Lord's Resurrection may have been reinforced also by notions from without.

Two patriarchs of Antioch, Bernard of Valence and Raoul of Domfront, went so far as to reject out of hand the popes' claim to supremacy. Bernard is said to have declared that he was the pope's equal and to have expelled his legates; in 1128 he was sternly rebuked by the papal legate, Bishop Gilo of Tusculum, who reminded him that Antioch owed to Rome its liberation from Muslim oppression.[83] Raoul is reported to have claimed that the churches of both Antioch and Rome were founded by Peter, with Antioch being the earlier and therefore the more distinguished of the two.[84] As far as we know, the patriarchs of Jerusalem never made such claims. Patriarch Amaurry unequivocally acknowledged the pope's superiority: when in 1160 he announced to Alexander III that he and his suffragans recognized him as pope and repudiated his rival, he explicitly acclaimed him as "temporal lord and spiritual father," addressing him as "the universal pope of the Roman and apostolic church" while presenting himself as the "humble minister of the Church of the Holy Resurrection."[85] And yet this humble minister, by his call for help in early 1166, disclosed his confidence of being authorized to extend the crusade indulgence to mere pilgrims.

The papal response to this extension is truly surprising. One would have expected Alexander III, the great lawyer-pope, to condemn it as a brazen arrogation of power. In reality, he adopted a diametrically opposed course. In his subsequent crusade bull, issued on 29 June 1166, he first closely paraphrased, and occasionally reproduced verbatim, Amaurry's account of the military setbacks the Franks suffered as well as his announcement that the Master of the Hospital, Gilbert of Assailly, was sent to the West to muster help.[86] Then Alexander issued a call for a crusade, offered once more the crusaders the remission of sins that Urban II and Eugenius III had instituted, and "confiding in God's mercy and in the merits of St. Peter and St. Paul," promised differential remission according to the length of military service in the East. Finally, he granted to all those who wished to *visit* the Lord's Sepulcher "because of the pressing needs" that their journey, whether completed or interrupted by death, should serve as "penance and obedience and remission of all sins and that, after the prisons of the flesh, they should deservedly gain eternal life."[87] So Alexander made Amaurry's promise his own, copying almost literally the patriarch's wording! Far from contesting "the authority of the Resurrection," Rome's pontiff tacitly followed Jerusalem's patriarch on a matter of no little import. Neither was this a one-time lapse: the passage originally penned by Amaurry reappeared in Alexander's subsequent calls for a crusade, issued in 1169 and 1181.[88]

Still, the grasp for authority, implied by the patriarchal title introduced in the 1140s and forcefully expressed by Amaurry's letter of 1166, must have caused concern at the papal court. In none of his letters did Alexander address, or refer to, Amaurry as "patriarch of the Church of the Holy Resurrection": for him, he was, and remained, merely "patriarch of Jerusalem," whom he treated as a subordinate, like when he forbade him to encroach upon the rights of the canons of the Holy Sepulcher.[89] In 1162 Alexander appointed Archbishop Syrus of Genoa and his successors as papal legates to the lands beyond the sea, laying down that the legate was to go there once every eight years, accompanied by a member of the college of cardinals; thus, a short time after Amaurry acknowledged him as pope, Alexander devised a periodic inspection of the Frankish East's ecclesiastical affairs.[90] And when Alexander emerged victorious from his struggle with Emperor Frederick I and convened in March 1179 the Third Lateran Council, the opening address dealt precisely with the issue of the relative standing of the five patriarchal sees, Rome, Antioch, Alexandria, Constantinople, and Jerusalem. Bishop Rufinus of Assisi, the noted professor of canon law, delivered the address, which amounts to a rousing hymn on Rome's absolute, irrefutable supremacy.

The other patriarchal sees, Rufinus explained, depend on human authority and synodal statutes: only the Roman see came into being by divine word, and therefore differs in essence, not merely in rank, from the other four. Rome is the mother, teacher, and ruler of all, and the pope is the supreme patriarch.[91] Among the three hundred prelates who had to listen to this vigorous exposition of Roman superiority and the implicit rejection of patriarchal pretensions, were Archbishop William of Tyre, Archbishop Eraclius of Caesarea (the future patriarch of Jerusalem), and six other leading clerics from the Frankish East. But this was not the only snub the Frankish prelates had to take. Appended to the council's decisions was an unequivocal annulment of ordinations that were bestowed in the Frankish East on Western clerics who had been deemed unworthy of preferment in the ecclesiastical provinces from which they originated.[92] And immediately after the council, on 9 April 1179, Alexander notified the patriarchs of Jerusalem and Antioch that he appointed once again Genoa's archbishop as his legate beyond the sea and ordered the patriarchs and their clergy to honorably receive and humbly obey him.[93]

It is against this background that one may read William of Tyre's account of the genesis of the First Crusade, apparently revised a few years after the Lateran Council of 1179.[94] The account, which gives pride of place to Petrus the Hermit and to Jerusalem's Greek patriarch, depends heavily on Albert of Aachen's chronicle.[95] William's decision to follow Albert rather than the other accounts at his disposal is significant. Indeed, William goes beyond Albert and spells out that Pope Urban II delivered his Clermont Address "at the Hermit's instigation."[96] The intention to deflate the role of the papacy is evident. And we should hardly be surprised to notice that, while Albert lets the Hermit have a vision of Christ in the Holy Sepulcher, William places it in the Church of the Lord's Resurrection.

The True Cross, the Miraculous Fire, and the Holy Resurrection were effectively appropriated by the Frankish clergy from the Eastern Christians and turned into foci of a fresh, distinctive religiosity. The Fire was scarcely affected by its passage into Frankish custody; the Cross and the Resurrection, on the other hand, assumed new roles, the first in battle against the Muslims, the second in the pursuit of authority within the Western church. The three were main foci of sanctity whose worship had to be shaped and administered by the Frankish clerics. These had to cope also with additional manifestations of sanctity, now to be discussed.

CHAPTER 5

The Husbanding of Sanctity

In their role as custodians of the Holy Places, Frankish clerics faced numerous problems. They had to cohabit in some of their main shrines with local, Eastern Christians. They had to make their choice among the usages of the various European regions from which they originated and decide whether to add some local ones. They had to design the celebration of Christendom's primordial events at the very locations where they were believed to have occurred. They had to conceive a fitting commemoration of the crusader conquest of 1099 and, later, of the dedication of the Church of the Holy Resurrection in 1149. In Jerusalem, they had to strike a balance between the city's two major sacred compounds. Throughout the country, they had to articulate the particular message of the site at which they lived, gain recognition for that message, and raise funds for the construction of an appropriate place of worship. The two-way flow of believers to relics and of relics to believers had to be regulated.

Granting Access to Shrines, Disputing Customs

No documents shed light on the ways by which the Frankish clerics came to grant access to the Church of the Holy Sepulcher—and presumably also to other major shrines—to Eastern Christians whom Rome regarded as schismatics or heretics. But this unprecedented and, from a Western point of view, scandalous cohabitation undoubtedly took place right from the establishment of the Frankish Kingdom.[1] The chronicler Ekkehard of Aura, who was in Jerusalem in 1101, mentions that, in the Church of the Holy Sepulcher, first the Latins and then the Syrians celebrated Mass; and the accounts of the troubled descent of the Holy Fire in that year show Frankish and Greek clerics praying side by side for its belated coming.[2] Theoderich proffers the most detailed evidence on the sharing of the Church of the Holy Sepulcher with non-Latins. A substantial altar at the entrance of the new Canons' Choir was reserved for Syrian service, and each day, when the Frankish clerics concluded celebrating the divine office, the Syrians chanted their hymns there, or at one of several smaller ones they possessed elsewhere in the church. Theoderich also reports that Latins, Syrians, Armenians, Greeks, Jacobites, and Nubians (presumably Copts) held their services there; the Armenians owned a chapel dedicated to the Virgin, and the Syrians had a chapel in which they guarded their portion of the True Cross.[3] And in about 1161—in the same decade in which Catholic and Cathar leaders bitterly clashed at an assembly near Albi—the canons of the Church of the Holy Sepulcher and the monks of the monastery of St. Mary Magdalene peacefully settled a dispute about two pieces of land, and the deed of settlement coolly designates the canons as Latins and the monks as Jacobites, and goes on to present this accord between true believers and heretics as attained by divine grace![4] As for the Greeks, one of the Latin calendars of the Church of the Holy Sepulcher spells out the dates on which spring and summer begin according to the Greek and the Western traditions.[5] The close political ties between Byzantium and Jerusalem, established in the late 1150s, probably improved the standing of the Greek canons at the Church of the Holy Sepulcher.[6] And there can be little doubt that Greek clerics were present in the Church of the Nativity in Bethlehem in about 1169, when it was redecorated under joint Frankish-Byzantine patronage.

It is noteworthy that explicit references to the cohabitation in the Church of the Holy Sepulcher appear in pilgrims' accounts, not in Frankish sources.[7] Probably the Frankish clerics—the chroniclers Foucher of Chartres and William of Tyre included—chose to leave unmentioned these extraordinary arrangements, alien to their Western heritage. They might have been imperative in a country in which Eastern Christians were numerous, yet to broadcast the celebration of heretical or schismatic rites in Jerusalem's main sanctuary would have been detrimental to the Frankish image in the West. Neither must we assume that these arrangements were established at one fell swoop, or consistently heeded. It is rather likely that, like in post-Frankish times down to the present, Christian sects were maneuvering to improve their positions, trying to make the best of the reign of an Armenian-born queen, or of an improvement in Franko-Byzantine relations.

It is hardly surprising that the Frankish clerics, coexisting with non-Latins in their main shrine within Jerusalem, accepted the existence, outside of Jerusalem, of the ritual center of a non-Christian religion. This was the sacred place on Mount Gerizim south of Nablus, to which Samaritans were allowed to come each year "from the land of Egypt and from the land of Damascus and from all the pagan [that is, Muslim] realm" in order to perform the Passover sacrifice there.[8]

Also, Frankish clerics allowed Muslims to pray in or immediately near Christian sanctuaries: in the crypt of John the Baptist at Sebaste, at the tomb of the prophet Ṣāliḥ in Acre's main mosque that had become a Frankish church, and even near the Lord's Temple, the erstwhile Dome of the Rock that became one of the most important shrines of Frankish Jerusalem.[9] Moreover, a piece of evidence hitherto unnoticed by crusade historians reveals that Muslims were allowed, upon paying an entrance fee, to pray even *inside* the Lord's Temple. The Sufi shaykh Rabīʿ of Mārdīn (d. 1205) relates that when he was making his living in Frankish Jerusalem by working as a laborer, he used some of his wages to visit repeatedly the Dome of the Rock, giving each time a small coin to the man at the entrance responsible for collecting the fee from Muslims. Once when Rabīʿ arrived empty-handed, the man nevertheless let him in, and when other Franks reproached him for doing so, he explained: "That is because he pays whatever he pays from the bottom of his heart. If he had anything, he would use it to pay. That is why I allowed him in."[10] Rabīʿ's account allows us to comprehend Maimonides's hitherto enigmatic statement: "I entered the Great and Holy House and I prayed in it on Thursday, the sixth day of Marḥeshvan [4926]," that is, 14 October 1165.[11] Similarly, entrance fees were collected from Muslim visitors to John the Baptist's tomb in Sebaste, and from Jewish and Muslim visitors to the Cave of the Patriarchs in Hebron.[12]

Local Christians were the Franks' mentors with regard to traditions pertaining to the Holy Places. Saewulf, who visited Jerusalem in 1102–3, refers to the testimony of local Syrians no less than five times.[13] Local Christians, we have seen, disclosed the hiding place of the True Cross, and the cantor Anseau learned about its history from Greeks and Syrians. A Greek monk of the Sinai Monastery and a Syrian priest told another Frankish cleric about an unsuccessful attempt to find the relics of the patriarchs Abraham, Isaac, and Jacob.[14] Rorgo Fretellus, in his description of the country's sacred places, mentions two Syrian traditions.[15] A Syrian monk buttressed the belief of Jacques of Vitry that John the Baptist did not subsist on locusts as written in Matthew 3:4, by telling him that the Baptist consumed an herb called *langusta*, which grows abundantly near the Jordan and which the monks of his monastery used to eat.[16] But encounters with local Christians could also weaken a Westerner's confidence in the veracity of his tradition: this is what happened to Johann of Würzburg when confronted with the Jacobite arguments for the distinction between Mary of Bethany and Mary Magdalene, regarded in the West as one and the same person.[17] Also, since nine or ten out of the twenty-five Canons of Nablus, the earliest Frankish legislation, have markedly close counterparts in Byzantine law collections of the eighth to tenth centuries, it stands to reason that some Frankish clerics came to know these Byzantine laws through Greek Orthodox confrères; the adaptation of the Byzantine laws on adultery and "sodomy" amounted to an innovation with no parallels in the contemporary West.[18] One may wonder in which language such exchanges between Franks and local Christians took place. William of Tyre presents, twice, just one cleric as fluent in Greek: Abbot Gaufridus of the Lord's Temple, whom Kings Fulk and Baldwin III sent as envoy to the Byzantine court in 1142 and 1158.[19] But there may have been others who, with more limited skills, were capable of communicating with the locals; and some of the latter may have acquired a passable command of the Franks' vernacular. Also, it is conceivable that some Eastern Christians embraced the Latin rite. The anonymous Armenian scribe who—apparently in the 1140s—wrote a Latin missal of the Church of the Holy Sepulcher and used Armenian numerals to number his quires, with his Latin letters recalling Armenian script by their strong vertical strokes, may have been one of them.[20]

Besides being the Franks' mentors with regard to various local traditions, many Eastern Christians came to side with them in the struggle against the Muslims: for instance, during a crucial Frankish-Egyptian battle in 1123, Franks, Greeks, and Syrians held processions in Jerusalem, and a year later, when the Frankish army was besieging Tyre, and Jerusalem—denuded of most of its defenders—came under Ascalonite attack, Frankish and Syrian Jerusalemites joined forces to repel the Muslims.[21]

What with Frankish and Eastern Christian clerics officiating alongside one another in the Church of the Holy Sepulcher and probably elsewhere, some of the differences between them came to be debated. As early as 1107 Pope Paschal II, in a letter to the clergy of Jerusalem, voiced concern over Eastern Christian ridicule of Latin custom.[22] About the same time, Joannes VIII, the Greek Orthodox patriarch of Jerusalem, complained that the Latins ridicule the Greeks on account of their use of leavened bread in the Eucharist.[23] The encounters led to an accumulation of Latin knowledge about Eastern Christian customs and beliefs. The Western Visitor dwells on the characteristic external appearances of Franks, Greeks, Syrians, and Georgians, mentions the bitter animosity between Greeks and Armenians, correctly points out that the Greeks believe in the procession of the Holy Spirit solely from the Father and that the Nestorians regard Mary only as the mother of the man Jesus, and spells out the alphabet used by each sect.[24] Also, some formal examinations of religious tenets took place: William of Tyre relates that at the Council of Jerusalem in 1141, the articles of faith that divide Armenians from Catholics were reviewed in the presence of a papal legate and the head of the Armenian church, and that in 1181 Patriarch Aimery of Antioch succeeded in making the Maronite patriarch and his followers abjure their errors and observe the Roman rite.[25] No such overtures took place toward the Muslims: no twelfth-century Frankish cleric is known to have entered into a dialogue with Muslims, or to have attempted to convert them. The fiery hermit Bernard of Blois was the only one to endeavor, in 1123, to preach the Christian faith to a Muslim ruler of Aleppo—thereby antedating by more than a century Francis of Assisi's famous preaching of Christianity to Sultan al-Kāmil of Egypt.[26] But Bernard's was an isolated, hardly noticed attempt.

Just one Frankish polemical treatise on a religious issue has survived, albeit in a much later summary.[27] This is Gerard of Nazareth's *On the Single Magdalene, against the Greeks*, which Matthias Flacius Illyricus and his fellow Centuriators of Magdeburg recapitulated in 1569.[28]

Gerard, who from ca. 1140 to ca. 1161 served as bishop of Laodicaea in the Principality of Antioch, chose to tackle a marginal issue. Ever since Pope Gregory the Great (590–604), the Latin Church generally identifies Mary Magdalene with Mary of Bethany as well as with the repentant sinner of Luke 7:36–50, whereas the Greek Orthodox Church, following Origen, regards them as three distinct persons. Paschasius Radbertus (d. ca. 860) was the last Latin to discuss the issue at any length, with later Western writers assuming the identity as a matter of course, or limiting their reservations to a few, lapidary remarks.[29] For Gerard, however, the issue must have been of concrete interest, since Laodicea had a considerable Greek population that would honor Mary of Bethany on 4 June and Mary Magdalene on 22 July.[30] Also, Gerard is known to have maintained ties with the Latin nuns of Bethany, and these may have raised questions about the Orthodox feast of Mary of Bethany, probably taking place at the sanctuary under their custody.[31] In any case, Gerard chose to dedicate a full-length treatise to the issue, the only Latin to do so before Jacques Lefèvre d'Étaples was to trigger a lengthy debate with his *On Mary Magdalene* of 1518.[32]

Gerard quotes passages from Ambrose, Augustine, Jerome, Gregory the Great, and Bede, and is aware of the views of Origen and Anselm. This assembly of authorities attests to a remarkable learning: in the High Middle Ages only Thomas Aquinas (ca. 1225–74) was to match Gerard in his breadth of reading—though not in the length of his discourse—on the subject. In his exposition, Gerard deals perceptively with his authorities, noting for instance Ambrose's vacillation on the issue and attempting to harmonize the views of Jerome and Augustine. Yet there is nothing to indicate that he attempted to find a recent Greek text that would bolster up his case. Had he done so, he might have discovered that the eleventh-century Byzantine chronicler Cedrenus considered Mary Magdalene to have been the sister of Lazarus, that is, he posited—like the Latins—an identity of the two Marys. Possibly Gerard's knowledge of Greek was not sufficient for the task. At any rate, he concludes on the conciliatory note that a Christian may believe either in the unity or in the diversity of the two Marys without great peril to his soul; yet it is preferable to adhere to the view more true or likely.

Gerard reverted to the issue in another work, *Against Sala the Priest*. This Sala—probably a Greek Orthodox—came to Laodicea, read Gerard's work, and attacked it, whereupon Gerard saw himself constrained to refute his arguments. The Centuriators, who print a lengthy summary of Gerard's *On the Single Magdalene*, chose to quote just one sentence from its sequel: "As necessity coerces me to read the work of this Sala, I feel as if, chewing pitch or a gluey substance with clogged-up teeth, I were barely capable of gulping it down. As it is written in the book of Job: 'Is it possible to eat tasteless food, unseasoned with salt?'"[33] It transpires that Gerard was a quite formidable polemicist and a wit as well: with *sal* being the Latin word for "salt," Gerard implies that Sala did not do justice to his name.[34]

Gerard's learned treatise deals with an issue of negligible theological import though of some consequence for the liturgical calendar. We have seen that Patriarch Joannes VIII dealt with the question of leavened vs. unleavened bread—an issue of ritual, not theology. However, the capacity of differences in ritual to serve as a trigger for conflict should not be underestimated. As Andrew Jotischky has rightly observed, ritual and theology were equally rooted in the underlying issue of ecclesiastical authority and could equally spark friction between Latins and Greeks.[35] Still, no Frankish cleric composed a treatise dealing with fundamental issues. On these, interested Frankish clerics had to rely on Western authors. Petrus Venerabilis, abbot of Cluny, authored the articulate discussion of Jerusalem's Holy Fire. In about 1176, Patriarch Aimery of Antioch was delighted to receive from the Pisan, Constantinople-based theologian Hugo Etherianus his treatise on the procession of the Holy Spirit.[36] And a Frankish patriarch of Jerusalem purportedly asked the Parisian theologian Petrus Comestor (d. ca. 1179) for arguments justifying warfare against the pagans.[37]

An issue about which the twelfth-century documents are silent is the way in which clerics dealt with infiltration of Eastern customs into Frankish popular religious practice. One such custom took place at the conclusion of some Frankish nuptial ceremonies: a cleric of the church in which the wedding ceremony took place would carry blessed water and five lit candles to the couple's abode, place the candles under the feet of the groom and bride, and receive a remuneration. On 6 August 1254, at Acre, the zealous papal legate Eudes of Châteauroux was to sternly prohibit this "abominable and horrible" custom, which he branded as witchcraft.[38] But how did Frankish churchmen of earlier times regard this custom, in which a cleric played the central role? Did they permit it, or did they turn a blind eye?

While Frankish clerics maintained variegated contacts with their Eastern Christian counterparts, no such interaction with non-Christian ones are mentioned in written accounts. But, here as elsewhere, documentation must not be equated with reality. A page from the Cairo Geniza hints at the possibility that some Frankish clerics exhibited an interest, perhaps very limited, in non-Christian lore. On one side of this page appears the beginning of the commentary of Rav Saʿadya Gaon (882, Fayyūm - 942, Sūrā) on the book of Isaiah. What renders the page exceptional are three Latin words, *[inter]pretacio esaye prophete* (commentary on the Prophet Isaiah), in a handwriting typical of the second half of the eleventh century (see fig. 5).

FIGURE 5. Three Latin words inscribed on a Jewish commentary on the book of Isaiah. To render the Latin words more easily readable, the lower side of the page has here been turned upside down. Cambridge University Library, T.-S. 12.722

The words are situated in the bottom right-hand corner of the page: the western European cleric who wrote them, used as he was to reading and writing from left to right, evidently held the volume upside down as if it were Latin-written, and took the page's bottom for its top. The three words leave little doubt that he was curious about the contents of the book and that some Jew divulged them to him. We know that about 350 Hebrew manuscripts captured by the crusaders at the conquest of Jerusalem in 1099 were later ransomed; the page in question may have belonged to one of these or came into crusader hands during the conquest of another Palestinian town. In any case, the Latin words bear silent witness to some verbal exchange between a Western cleric and a Jew, pertaining to Jewish learning.[39]

Devising a Liturgy

The list of saints venerated in the Church of the Holy Sepulcher illustrates how the Frankish clerics went about devising their liturgy. While most of the list conforms to Roman usage, it includes also ten Palestinian saints (the patriarchs Abraham, Isaac, and Jacob, six early bishops of Jerusalem, and a local martyr); St. Paulinus and St. Lambert who were venerated throughout the West; St. Cataldo, bishop of Taranto; and eighteen saints whose cultic centers were in France, mostly in its central and northern regions.[40] This prominence of French saints is not surprising: as we have seen, Frenchmen constituted the largest group among the clerics who settled in the Kingdom of Jerusalem.[41]

The combination of various traditions was a relatively easy task; so was the replacement, in a Mass, of the customary reference to "enemies" with "pagans"—the Frankish Kingdom's Muslim foes.[42] On the other hand, the observance of the Annunciation in Nazareth, of Christmas in Bethlehem, or of Easter in Jerusalem demanded much more inventiveness.

The manner by which the Franks endeavored to celebrate the events of Easter at the site at which they had presumably taken place is quite well documented. One climax of the celebration was an enactment of the encounter of the Holy Women with two angels at the empty Tomb on Easter Sunday. Three young clerics dressed up behind the altar as women and, carrying vessels of gold or silver filled with ointment, would approach the Tomb at the center of the Church of the Holy Sepulcher's Rotunda; two clerics impersonating angels by wearing amices over their heads would stand near the Tomb's entrance with candles in their hands. Then the following exchange would take place:

> WOMEN [*repeating thrice*]: O God! Who shall roll <us away the stone from the Tomb's door>?
> ANGELS: For whom do you look?
> WOMEN: For Jesus of Nazareth.
> ANGELS: He is not here, he has risen.
> WOMEN [*enter the Tomb and, after a brief prayer there, walk to the middle of the choir and announce, chanting in high-pitched voice*]: Hallelujah, the Lord has arisen![43]

By the time the crusaders conquered Jerusalem, a rudimentary Easter Play did exist in the West, but its elaborate enactment at Christ's Tomb itself, designed by the Frankish clerics, must have had an extraordinary effect. Yet the Ordinals of the Church of the Holy Sepulcher, reflecting twelfth-century practice, reveal that the designers were constrained at some later juncture to modify the enactment: the young clerics were no longer dressed up as women, "because of the multitude of pilgrims standing around."[44] Did the tumultuous crush of worshipers converging on the actors really render the change of dress impossible, or perhaps—less probably—the pilgrims considered it inappropriate?[45] Fortunately, the compilers of the Ordinals chose to mention the suppressed part of the enactment, perhaps hoping that it may be reversed one day.

Even as the Easter enactment was modified, the scene of the Holy Women at the empty Tomb was permanently rendered, in mosaic, above the entry to the Tomb's edicule.[46] Moreover, it came to be prominently displayed, probably also in mosaic, at the very entrance of the sanctuary, above and between the two doors of the main, southern façade where it must have attracted the attention of all comers. The scene chosen was much bolder than the one whose reenactment had been suppressed. Instead of the Holy Women conversing with two angels, it showed Christ, just risen from the dead, appearing to Mary Magdalene, lying prostrate at his feet but not touching them. Christ held to her a scroll on which the following verses, based on the Gospel according to John 20:15–17, were inscribed in Latin:

QUID, MULIER, PLORAS?	Woman why are you weeping?
IAMIAM QUEM QUERIS ADORAS.	You worship now the one you are seeking.
ME DIGNUM RECOLI	Me—worthy of devotion,
IAM VIVUM TANGERE NOLI.[47]	alive already—do not touch.

This no longer existing depiction of the resurrected Christ appeared but rarely in monumental decoration designs in the Byzantine sphere or in the contemporaneous West.[48] Its prominent location at the façade's center proclaimed to all comers that they were entering the Church of the Holy Resurrection rather than that of the Holy Sepulcher. It is possible that the conspicuous placement in Jerusalem's main sanctuary paved the way for positioning the encounter between the risen Christ and the Magdalene at the center of subsequent Western versions of the Easter Play.[49] The oldest manuscript that contains this addition dates from the late twelfth or early thirteenth century, several decades after returning pilgrims could first have brought to the West the news about the Jerusalem image.

In the Easter service in the Church of the Holy Resurrection, the correspondence of liturgy and site was brought home in a further way. When the deacon reads the Gospel on Easter Sunday—so writes a Frankish chronicler—he turns toward Calvary as he utters the word "crucified"; then he turns back toward the Tomb and says, "He has risen again, he is not here," and pointing at it with his finger, he adds, "Here is the place where they laid him," whereafter he resumes his plain reading from the book.[50] In the eyes of the chronicler, the correspondence warranted its inclusion in his description of Frankish Jerusalem.[51]

A far more ambitious dramatization took place on Palm Sunday, with the clerics and people of Jerusalem enacting Christ's entry into the city. Before sunrise, the patriarch, the prior of the Church of Mount Sion, as well as the canons of the Church of the Mount of Olives, and the monks of the Abbey of St. Mary in the Valley of Josaphat—that is, the congregations of two major shrines situated outside Jerusalem's walls—would walk to Bethany, about two miles east of the city. They would pray there at the place where Jesus raised Lazarus from the dead, and then slowly return to Jerusalem along the route Jesus and his disciples are said to have taken on the original Palm Sunday. The True Cross, carried on this occasion by the patriarch, would represent Christ. The procession would descend from the Mount of Olives westward into the deep ravine of the Valley of Josaphat.

At the same time, the canons of the Church of the Holy Sepulcher, the brothers of the Hospital of St. John, the monks of St. Mary the Latin—that is, members of three congregations of Jerusalem proper—and the canons of the Church of Mount Sion would assemble, together with the city's populace, in the esplanade that surrounds the Lord's Temple.[52] Here a bishop, or the prior of the Holy Sepulcher, would bless the palm flowers and olive branches held by the celebrants, and then all would leave the city and descend eastward into the Valley of Josaphat.

At the bottom of the valley, the group representing Christ and his disciples and the group representing the inhabitants of Jerusalem would face one another. Four or five of the Jerusalemites, led by the cantor, would intone the antiphon "Hail Our King," and the entire group would genuflect before the True Cross and the patriarch. This would be repeated twice. Then four or five of those coming from Bethany would chant the same antiphon, facing the Sepulcher and the Temple, and the members of their group would genuflect. Subsequently, both groups would chant together, then one would chant and the other genuflect. Next, the deacon and subdeacon, followed by the patriarch, the king, and other leading personages, would ascend an elevated site to be seen by all. The cantor would intone the antiphon "The Crowds Go out to Meet the Redeemer with Flowers and Palms," then the account in Matthew 21 of Christ's entry to Jerusalem would be recited, and finally the patriarch would deliver a sermon. Thereupon all would ascend, chanting, to the otherwise closed Golden Gate and enter Jerusalem from the east. The succentor, the schoolmaster, and the boys' choir would await them atop the gate.[53] The placing of the boys above the gate recalls a miniature of a sixth-century codex of Eastern provenance, in which children observe Christ's entry into Jerusalem from windows above the city's gate.[54] Possibly the reenactment of scripture blended here with the enactment of a Byzantine tradition.[55]

Once all celebrants assembled on the gate's inner side, the succentor, the boys, and the crowd would chant alternately the verses of the hymn "All Glory, Praise, and Honor to Thee, King Christ Redeemer." The boys or the patriarch would intone the antiphon "As the Lord Was Entering the Holy City"; the crowd would form a procession, enter the esplanade of the Lord's Temple, descend to the Temple of Solomon by one flight of stairs, and ascend by another to the southern door of the Lord's Temple, where the final prayers would be said.[56] But for the ass and the foal, the features of the Gospel account were enacted step by step, with narrative coinciding with or slightly anticipating gesture, and with the entire populace given a chance to participate. The choice of the southern door of the Lord's Temple as the site of the final station may have been motivated by a wish to underscore that the days of Muslim rule were over: by facing the southern door of the erstwhile Islamic shrine, the Frankish celebrants were turning their backs to Mecca, while looking at a Latin inscription that must have gladdened Jerusalemites in particular: "Blessed are they who dwell in Thy House, O Lord, they will praise Thee for ever and ever."[57]

It was in fourth-century Jerusalem that historical commemoration became central in Christian liturgy, and it was from there that it spread all over Christendom. Yet only in Jerusalem could an event involving motion, like Christ's triumphal entry, be commemorated by itinerant worship at a sequence of genuine locations.[58] In devising the celebration of Palm Sunday in Jerusalem, the Frankish clerics exhibited considerable inventiveness: not only did they graft the symbolic on the real by intoning the traditional Latin ritual in the very locale to which it refers, but they also utilized the landscape's dramatic potential more astutely than their fourth-century predecessors. Egeria, who made her pilgrimage in the 380s, reports that on Palm Sunday all Jerusalemites ascended to the Mount of Olives and then slowly returned into town and dispersed at the Church of the Holy Sepulcher (which she denotes by its Greek name, Anastasis).[59] The Franks, on the other hand, let two processions, each impersonating a different group, confront one another across the valley where the Last Judgment was to take place, and then ascend together through the Golden Gate, topped for the occasion with a boys' choir, to the site where the Temple stood in Jesus's days.[60] Surely this reenactment resonated of the original event more powerfully than the one of Byzantine times.

In devising their Palm Sunday ceremony, the Frankish clerics could build upon rites prevalent in the West.[61] In designing the commemoration of the crusader conquest of Jerusalem on 15 July 1099—a commemoration inaugurated shortly thereafter, and probably becoming by the early 1130s, alongside Christmas and Easter, one of Jerusalem's major feasts—they had to innovate, drawing on existing liturgical schemes.[62] A highpoint of the commemoration was the procession that made its way from the Church of the Holy Sepulcher to the Lord's Temple (where the crowd would—once again—stop at the southern door) and thence to the spot where the First Crusaders scaled the city wall in 1099. There a sermon would be delivered to the people. A fragment of one such sermon has survived: it contains numerous quotations from Foucher of Chartres's account of the First Crusade.[63] After hearing the sermon the celebrants would return to the Tomb and disperse. Thus, the procession broadcast that the spot symbolizing the First Crusade had become part of Jerusalem's holy geography.[64] The liturgy for the feast presented the city's conquest by the First Crusaders as an act of liberation, a crucial point in the history of salvation as foretold by the prophets of Israel, and the entreaty that the celebrants of earthly Jerusalem's conquest attain the joys of its heavenly counterpart was repeatedly intoned.[65]

This feast, too, underwent a radical modification. On 15 July 1149, on the fiftieth anniversary of the city's conquest or liberation, the new, expanded Church of the Holy Sepulcher was rededicated, and henceforward the commemoration of the 1099 crusader conquest was eclipsed by that of the 1149 dedication of the principal Frankish sanctuary. Patriarch Foucher, under whom the new shrine was consecrated, ordered that the festivities of 15 July should primarily celebrate the latter event; the conquest was to be commemorated thereafter merely by the Matins Mass and the procession.[66] Once again in Jerusalem's long history, a Solomonic temple outshone a Davidic conquest.

The modification of the 15 July celebration was just one component of Foucher's profound liturgical reform that set Jerusalem's practice apart from the Western one. This reform focused the entire liturgy on Christ's Resurrection by celebrating it time and again throughout the year, by inserting Easter motifs into non-Easter feasts, and even by starting the liturgical year not with Advent Sunday as in the West but with a pre-Advent Commemoration of the Resurrection.[67] The reform may be regarded as the liturgical facet of the attempt to present the Church of the Holy Sepulcher as the Church of the Lord's Resurrection and to broadcast the unique, exalted status of the shrine and its chief custodian.

We are quite well informed about the efforts of the clergy of the Church of the Holy Sepulcher to devise, adjust, and revise the liturgy for the commemoration of events that had taken place, or were believed to have taken place, within the church and the city. But we may assume that the Frankish clerics who served in the very many churches of the kingdom, erected on sites figuring in Christian sacred history, similarly evolved rituals aimed at reminding parishioners and pilgrims of the specific events and messages linked to the Holy Places under their custody. The Latin inscriptions on the walls of various churches in Jerusalem and of Bethlehem's Church of the Nativity, which Johann of Würzburg and Theoderich assiduously copied into their pilgrimage accounts, hint at this probably pervasive if virtually undocumented commemorative enterprise.[68]

The intense liturgical activities of the Frankish clergy left some mark on the West; it is a subject not yet systematically studied. Some elements were taken over disjointedly: Bishop Zdík/Heinricus of Olomouc, who stayed in Jerusalem in 1137–38, introduced—upon his return home—the Jerusalemite rituals of ordination; the liturgy evolved in the Church of the Holy Sepulcher for the annual commemoration, on 15 July, of the crusader conquest influenced the feasts held on that date in Autun, Bourges, and Laon; a distych engraved at the tomb of the Virgin in the Valley of Josaphat reappears (but for a slight change) in the Church of Ste.-Marie de Cornellà de Conflent (Pyrenées Orientales); the Mass against the Pagans enjoyed wide diffusion in the early fourteenth century.[69] But there were also cases of wholesale reception: the Knights Templar, the Knights Hospitaller, and the Carmelite order all adopted the liturgy of the canons of the Holy Sepulcher.[70]

Commissioning Works of Art

More than 330 Latin ecclesiastical edifices were constructed or reconstructed in the Frankish Kingdom of Jerusalem and its successor, the Kingdom of Acre, during the less than two hundred years of their existence.[71] As this intensive building activity took place in a realm that at the height of its territorial expansion covered an area only slightly larger than modern Belgium or South Carolina, one may assume that the ratio of Frankish churches constructed per year and per area was one of the highest in the Latin world of that age.[72] It was an activity noted even by an anonymous Jewish poet who, somewhere in Germany before 1147, complained that Jerusalem's Christian rulers "have built houses of idolatry" and "defiled unclean entrances with carved images."[73] After Ṣalāḥ al-Dīn's reconquest of Jerusalem in 1187, al-Qāḍī al-Fāḍil more respectfully observed that the Franks "placed their churches there . . . adorning them with every type of wonderful marble . . . and columns resembling trees, covered with the leaves of plants."[74]

The Frankish clerics, as well as the Frankish rulers and the military orders, commissioned these edifices, all erected in what Oleg Grabar (d. 2011) appositely characterized as "an artistically underdeveloped area."[75] Their surviving remnants have fascinated scholars from the mid-nineteenth century onward: the earliest systematic study appeared back in 1860, and today research on the subject is intensive and wide-ranging.[76] Most studies refer to it as "Crusader Art," but—as pointed out in the introduction—it is more appropriate to call it Frankish.[77]

The character of this art has been much disputed. While earlier scholars regarded it as a derivation of contemporary Western art and attempted to ascertain which Western school influenced a specific Frankish object, in the past half century the pendulum has swung to a highlighting of the interplay between local, Western, Byzantine, and other Eastern influences.[78] There is indeed some clear-cut evidence for the participation of Eastern artists and masons. At the Church of the Nativity in Bethlehem, redecorated in about 1169 under the joint patronage of Emperor Manuel of Byzantium, King Amaurry of Jerusalem, and Bishop Raoul of Bethlehem, at least two Easterners were at work. The Latin and Greek inscriptions on the lower part of the bema spell out that the monk, painter of historical subjects, and mosaicist Effrem (in Latin) and Efraìm (in Greek) completed the artwork; this proclamation of the Eastern artist's role, with no parallels in the Byzantine or Eastern Christian orbit, looks Western-inspired.[79] Another bilingual inscription gives the name of a second Eastern artist: in Latin, he is presented as BASILIUS PICTOR (Basil the Painter), whereas in Syriac he appears as *Bāsīl* the deacon.[80] The Byzantine-style mosaic works of Effrem and Basil may point to their origin in Byzantium; alternatively, they may attest to a survival of Byzantine traditions in pre-1099 Palestine and their utilization under the Franks.[81] Again, Armenian letters were found on two stones of the Frankish Church of the Annunciation in Nazareth: on the first appears the name Hagop (Jacob) and on the second what looks like Vardan.[82] The male with a turban-like headdress, moustache, and beard, depicted next to a mason's mallet on one of the little-known corbels that decorate the Frankish dome of the Church of the Holy Sepulcher, may be the self-representation of such an Eastern craftsman.[83] And, as Gil Fishhof has recently argued, designers of Frankish monumental figurative cycles may often have aimed at their simultaneous, differential comprehension by Frankish and Eastern Christian spectators;[84] for him, this is just one manifestation of the "model of flexibility" that purportedly characterized Frankish art, by addressing diverse audiences and by allowing for complementary or contradictory interpretations by each of them.

The Bethlehem inscriptions are the only ones to document the names of artists responsible for a work commissioned in the Kingdom of Jerusalem. But even without the Eastern names divulged by these inscriptions, art-historical examination of the work itself reveals the presence of Eastern, Byzantine topics and motifs alongside the Western ones. As John H. Elliott (d. 2022) observed, art historians teach us that "an image or object is itself a form of document. Historical evidence is not confined to the written word."[85] Yet an art historian's "reading" of an object depends far more on his idiosyncratic perception, imagination, and speculation-proneness than a historian's reading of a written text. Hence, interpretations proffered by art historians often diverge radically.[86]

Nevertheless, there prevails today a broad agreement about the basic characteristics of twelfth-century Frankish art. It is a new, distinct art engendered by multicultural impulses, displaying the impact of Western, Byzantine, Eastern Christian, and Islamic traditions—all partially rooted in classical art—and the influence of local models. For example, while the foliated acanthus capitals, prominent in the monumental Romanesque stone sculpture in the West, were fashioned in various regions of France and Italy according to locally found classical models, in the Frankish East they replicated a variety of local capitals dating from late antique, early Christian, Byzantine, and Umayyad times, all ultimately deriving from classical archetypes. Hence, Frankish acanthus capitals—al-Qāḍī al-Fāḍil's "columns resembling trees, covered with the leaves of plants"—translate a Romanesque motif into local idiom. Likewise, the Frankish double portal of the Church of the Holy Sepulcher recalls the Late Byzantine or Umayyad Golden Gate with its two entryways, and the octagonal Frankish Church of the Ascension on the Mount of Olives, a sacred stone at its center, may have harked back to a much earlier local octagonal edifice, likewise centered on a holy stone—the Dome of the Rock.[87]

Like the Frankish dialect of medieval French, Frankish art reflects the multicultural setting in which it arose, but while the Frankish dialect left few if any traces in Western languages, thirteenth-century Frankish icons—inspired by Byzantine models yet exhibiting original, innovative features—appear to have transmitted Byzantine artistic ideas to the West, especially to Tuscany.[88]

Christianizing the Dome of the Rock

The two Islamic shrines on the erstwhile Jewish Temple Mount—the Dome of the Rock and the Aqṣā Mosque—posed a problem for the Franks. They could have turned the Mount back into the heap of ruins it had been in pre-Islamic times—an act that would have commemorated not only the destruction of the Jewish Temple, as it did in Byzantine times, but also Christianity's recent victory over Islam. However, the Franks are not known to have contemplated this option. Instead, like the contemporaneous Latin conquerors in Sicily and Iberia, they Christianized the Muslim shrines, turning the Aqṣā Mosque into the Temple of Solomon and the Dome of the Rock into the Lord's Temple, with the Temple of Solomon evoking the first Jewish temple and the Lord's Temple relating to the second Jewish temple that figures repeatedly in the life of Jesus.[89] The form of the shrines—the first, basilical, the second, a central structure—probably facilitated their adoption, as some crusaders must have recognized their resemblance to Western ecclesiastical buildings.[90] Consequently, under Frankish rule Christian Jerusalem possessed, for the first and only time in its history, two sacred foci: the Church of the Holy Sepulcher and the Lord's Temple. Before 1099, the rivalry between the two was open, with the Islamic dome above the Rock erected expressly to outshine the Christian dome above the Sepulcher. After 1099, with both shrines in Christian hands, the tension between them obviously diminished.[91]

This bifocality of the sacred came into being in the early years of the Kingdom of Jerusalem.[92] The anonymous author of *The Deeds of the Franks* and Raymond of Aguilers both relate soon after the conquest of 1099 that, when the fighting ended, the victorious Franks came to pray in the Church of the Holy Sepulcher.[93] Yet already a few years afterward Foucher of Chartres, writing in Jerusalem, asserts that the conquerors went "to the Lord's Sepulcher and His glorious Temple," and when the True Cross was found a few weeks later, the Franks went to the Sepulcher and thence to the Temple, singing psalms and thanking God.[94] The bifocality was institutionalized in the liturgy that the Frankish clergy developed: for instance, on the feast of the Purification of the Virgin the procession would start at the Sepulcher and proceed to the southern door of the Temple, while on Palm Sunday four or five of the celebrants who came from Bethany would chant while facing the Sepulcher and the Temple.[95] The two shrines also played central roles in the coronation ceremonies of Jerusalem's Frankish rulers.[96] And the seals of King Baldwin I and his successors showed the Tower of David in the center, flanked by the Sepulcher and the Temple.[97]

Of the two shrines, the Sepulcher had the full force of tradition on its side, while the Lord's Temple had to be established from scratch as a Christian shrine. Acardus of Arrouaise, the Temple's prior in the years 1112–36, left behind a long poem in which he attempted to do just that.[98] He surveys the site's history in considerable detail, from David and Solomon down to Vespasian and Titus. Then he proceeds abruptly to present the shrine of his own days as the work of some Byzantine emperor—Justinian or Heraclius—or of Helena, the mother of Constantine; its erection by Caliph ʿAbd al-Malik in 691/92 is blotted out of existence.[99] Acardus does not tackle the question of why a Christian ruler should have rebuilt the Temple whose destruction Jesus had foretold; evidently he either did not know, or chose to disregard, that Adso of Montier-en-Der (d. 992) had foreseen in his influential eschatological treatise that, toward the Last Days, the *Antichrist* would restore the ruined Temple and reside in it.[100] Acardus notes that the three dedications of the Temple—by King Solomon, by the Jews returning from the Babylonian Captivity, and by Judas Maccabeus—had taken place, respectively, in autumn, spring, and winter. A future, fourth dedication, he declares, will take place in the summer. The first to be undertaken not by Jews but by Christians, this dedication will also be the last, to be commemorated forever.

Acardus is aware of the Muslim occupancy of the Temple before the crusader conquest, and in one important respect, he looks back to it with envy. The infidel, he writes, although not knowing the Lord of the Temple, kept its property intact and used its income to adorn the building with mosaics and marble within and without, whereas Christians, who ought to have venerated the Temple much more, looted its belongings upon the conquest of Jerusalem. These plunderers claim to be defenders of the Faith, but behave like enemies of the Lord; he, Acardus, knows them by name and appeals to King Baldwin to force them to restore the property they had seized.[101] As Acardus celebrates the king as "the most invincible knight," he was probably addressing Baldwin I rather than Baldwin II, who lingered in Muslim captivity both before and after his accession to the throne.[102] Acardus's wish to get back the pillaged property may have affected his account of the shrine's history, for if it had been built and endowed by a Christian ruler, as he claims, the present Frankish custodians could legitimately claim its pre-1099 possessions. But the main reason for Acardus's ascribing of the construction to a Christian was probably different: the unwillingness to acknowledge that his last, Fourth Temple was erected by a Muslim.

The shrine was dedicated on 1 April 1141 by the papal legate Cardinal-Bishop Alberic of Ostia, Patriarch William of Jerusalem, and several bishops.[103] Acardus died about five years earlier; his wish that the dedication take place in the summer was not honored. His successor Gaufridus dealt in his works at great length with the history of the Temple under the Hasmonaeans and Romans, implanted diatribes against simony, but totally dispensed with discussing the origin of the contemporary shrine. In his presentation, the continuity between the biblical Temple and the Frankish shrine is self-evident.[104]

Baldwin I bestowed some property on the Lord's Temple and so did, in later years, various lay and ecclesiastical benefactors, most notably Queen Melisende (r. 1131–52).[105] Yet the Temple's property was considerably smaller than that of the Sepulcher: while a list apparently dating from the mid-1180s stipulates that the chapter of the Sepulcher must raise five hundred sergeants during a military emergency, the Lord's Temple is required to supply merely fifty.[106] Still, the Temple had sufficient resources at its disposal to undertake works that gradually altered the shrine's original appearance and rendered it ever more church-like. According to Foucher of Chartres, for the first fifteen years after the conquest the Rock remained exposed; but because it disfigured the building, it was then covered over and paved in marble. By the time he wrote in the 1120s, an altar had been placed over it and a choir fitted out for the canons. Ibn al-Athīr later reported that a Frankish king had ordered the Rock to be covered because the Frankish priests used to break off fragments of it to sell to pilgrims. It is possible that the wrought-iron grill with which the Franks enclosed the Rock—first mentioned in an Icelandic account ca. 1150—served for its protection, besides acting as a chancel screen. Images decorated the walls, numerous Latin mosaic inscriptions covered the building's exterior and interior, and a large golden cross was placed on its top. Johann of Würzburg provides a thorough description of the building and the sites in and around it, quoting the inscriptions to be seen there. Inscriptions recorded by Theoderich suggest that the work of Christianizing and embellishing the Lord's Temple went on almost continuously.[107] Yet the Frankish canons of the shrine left its original Qur'anic inscriptions untouched, even though the oldest of these rejected the Trinity and Jesus as the Son of God, and extolled Muḥammad as God's Messenger and the Muslims' intercessor at the Last Judgment. But, as Hannes Möhring rightly remarked, one should not regard this Frankish inaction as an indication of religious tolerance but as a manifestation of an almost incredible ignorance.[108] Only a present-day observer is able to savor the silent confrontation that had taken place—on the outer side of the edifice facing the Sepulcher—between the original, still extant Qur'anic inscription proclaiming that Allah has not taken to himself offspring, and the Frankish one that hailed the Lord as the Eternal Father.[109]

The Christianization of the Dome of the Rock did not involve only its physical space. Saewulf asserts that it was in the Lord's Temple that Jacob saw the heavenly ladder, betraying thereby the influence of an Islamic tradition.[110] Johann of Würzburg was shown the imprint left by Jesus's foot in the Rock when he was expelling the merchants from the Temple—evidently a Christian takeover of what Islamic tradition sees as the imprint of Muḥammad's foot during his ascension to heaven.[111] The bulk of the shrine's new Christian content, however, derived directly from the Bible—from the identification of the Rock in the shrine's center with the Holy of Holies of the Solomonic Temple, to that of the nearby crypt as the location of Christ's encounter with the adulterous woman.[112] Mosaic inscriptions in Latin, added to the shrine's exterior, mostly reproduced biblical passages exalting the Temple as the House of the Lord, and aimed at imbuing the literate visitor with the certainty that he was indeed facing the rebuilt Temple.[113] Acardus's poem and the mosaic inscriptions broadcast the same message.

If Acardus believed that his poem would effectively obliterate the memory of the shrine's Islamic origin, he was to be proven wrong. Jerusalem's Eastern Christians must have known the true facts all along. The Russian pilgrim Daniel, who visited Jerusalem in 1105/6, relates that the shrine was built "by a Saracen chieftain called Amor," evidently a distortion of ʿUmar.[114] Some Latins, too, had an inkling, or more, of the truth. In 1137, Rorgo Fretellus, probably sharing the same source with Acardus, mentions that the shrine, which he, too, presents as the Fourth Temple, was built either by Helena or by Heraclius or Justinian. He adds, however, that some believed the builder to have been an

Ammyrator (emir) of Memphis in Egypt, who erected it "in honor of *Allachiber* [probably an attempt at transcribing the Arabic words *Allāh kabīr*], that is to say, God most high." He remarks that this last possibility was the more likely one, since an Arabic inscription supported it.[115] Yet he does not appear to have been certain on this point, or perhaps found it troublesome. In a second redaction of his work, he no longer declared the greater likelihood of the last possibility and omitted the reference to the Arabic inscription.[116]

Johann of Würzburg copied Rorgo Fretellus's second, diluted redaction almost verbatim, thus presenting the four candidates—three Christian, one Muslim—as equally likely.[117] Theoderich resembles Acardus in ignoring the possibility of a Muslim builder; unlike Acardus, he is certain that it was Helena and Constantine who erected the shrine.[118] William of Tyre also has no doubts about the shrine's builder; for him, however, it is not Helena, but the caliph ʿUmar, Jerusalem's Arab conqueror. He claims to make this statement on the basis of Arabic mosaic inscriptions on the shrine's interior and exterior, which spell out the builder's name, the dates of the beginning and completion of the edifice, as well the expenses it entailed.[119] In reality, the relevant—still existing—inscription mentions the ʿAbbasid caliph al-Maʾmūn (813–33), who ordered the name of the shrine's true builder, the Umayyad caliph ʿAbd al-Malik, to be replaced with his own, but neglected to have the original year, 72 according to the Islamic era (that is, AD 691/92), supplanted as well. The cost of the edifice and the date of the beginning of its construction go unmentioned there. Consequently, William's assertion exposes his inability to read inscriptions and casts doubt on his knowledge of literary Arabic; but, from the present point of view, he stands out for unequivocally stating that a Muslim had built the shrine.[120] Yet there was more than one layer in William's perception of the shrine. In his version of Pope Urban II's call for the crusade at Clermont in 1095, William makes the pope lament that "the Lord's Temple, from which the Lord in his zeal drove out those who were selling and buying lest the House of his Father turn into a robbers' cave, has become the abode of demons. The same Temple fired the zeal of the high priest Mattathias, the progenitor of the holy Maccabees."[121] Here the present-day Temple is—or amounts to—a latter-day embodiment of the Temple of old. William's Urban speaks the language of Acardus.

Against the background of this whirlpool of Frankish perceptions of the shrine's origin, it is noteworthy that the Damascene mystic, theologian, and poet ʿAbd al-Ghanī al-Nābulusī (1641–1731)—a descendant of the Banū Qudāma who fled their homes in the Frankish-ruled area around Nablus and settled in Damascus—assumed that the Dome of the Rock had been erected by the Franks! Al-Nābulusī, who visited Jerusalem in 1690, believed that the Rock was miraculously suspended between heaven and earth and that the Franks built the Dome in order to conceal this wonder that testifies to the distinction of Islam and the power of God. "Especially since what is widely known among people had reached [the Franks]—that when our Prophet Muḥammad, may God's prayer and salutation be upon him, ascended to heaven from the Rock on the night of Ascension, the Rock ascended behind him, but was held back by the angels and so remained hanging between heaven and earth."

Al-Nābulusī explained that upon Ṣalāḥ al-Dīn's reconquest of Jerusalem the Muslims thought that the Frankish-built edifice had been there originally and therefore did not demolish it. And he concluded that in the final analysis it was God who made the Franks conceal the miracle of the Rock.[122] Similarly to Rorgo Fretellus half a millennium earlier, al-Nābulusī envisaged the probability that infidels had erected a principal shrine of the one and only true religion.

Aggrandizing Secondary Holy Places: Hebron versus Sebaste

At Hebron it is possible to observe in some detail how local Frankish clerics went about propagating the distinction of their shrine. For Sebaste, there is some documentation on the development of the local cult and on the fundraising for the construction of the cathedral.

The Herodian shrine above the Cave of Machpela in Hebron became a mosque after the Arab conquest; upon the arrival of the Franks it was pillaged by Pierre of Narbonne, bishop of Albara (northern Syria), probably in 1102/3.[123] The Augustinian canons who subsequently settled in Hebron, turning the shrine into their convent and the mosque into a church, were eager to discover the Cave itself and unearth the remains of Abraham, Isaac, and Jacob. The comprehensive account documenting their efforts, written by an anonymous author not too long after 1128, recalls Acardus's poem insofar as it mentions respectfully the former Muslim custodians of the shrine who, "although infidels," erected in it an "oratory" marvelously decorated with gold, silver, and silk.[124] But, unlike in the poem, the Frankish pillage is not explicitly contrasted with the Muslim stewardship, nor is restitution of the looted possessions demanded. The account underscores that Latins succeeded in finding the remains that eluded one hundred earlier generations.[125] It then goes on to describe the canons' excavation vividly, amounting to an archaeological report of sorts.[126]

It is a hot June day of the year 1119.[127] After noontime, the canons are asleep on their beds, according to custom. The chapter's scribe seeks to evade the heat, enters the church, and lies down on the stone floor near the cenotaph of Isaac. Before long he becomes aware of a puff of cool air coming up through a crack between two large stones of the pavement. He throws down small stones, hears them landing far below and concludes that there must be some cistern or cave underneath. He then fetches a rod, ties a long rope to its tip, and fastens a piece of lead to the rope's end, then lowers the rope through the crack and establishes that the hollow is eleven cubits—that is, about 6.3 meters—deep.[128] He chooses to divulge his discovery only after his fellow canons arise to celebrate Nones. Therewith the anonymous scribe disappears from our story. He may have fared better had he, less truthfully but more conventionally, claimed to have fallen asleep while at prayer in the church and to have had a vision of the patriarch Abraham divulging to him the relics' location. This, indeed, is how a later author, probably writing in the West, retold the story: here the anonymous canon, said to have originated from the region of Tours, is the main protagonist, alongside a repeatedly intervening Abraham.[129]

The original account is different. Utterly devoid of dreams, visions, apparitions, or some other form of supernatural guidance, it tells realistically of prayers, determination, and hard work—and has been remarkably corroborated by an archaeological examination. Let us return to it.

As the prior, Rainier, is away on business in Jerusalem, the canons decide to wait two or three days.[130] In the meantime, they beseech God to let them find the Patriarchs' Cave; also, they prepare the iron tools needed to cut the pavement's large stones.

Then, having obtained the permission of Hebron's castellan, Baldwin, they set to work, with priests celebrating Mass, clerics reading Psalms, and laymen praying. After working hard for several days, they manage to cut an aperture in the floor. The oldest priest of the chapter, Eudes, is lowered through it by rope to the hollow's dark bottom but, unable to find any passage, he begs to be hauled up.

On the following day the canons lower down the next-ranking priest, Arnoul, who is to become our story's hero and, alongside Eudes, an informant of the unnamed author who wrote it down. Equipped with a light, Arnoul discovers walls built so well they appear to consist of a

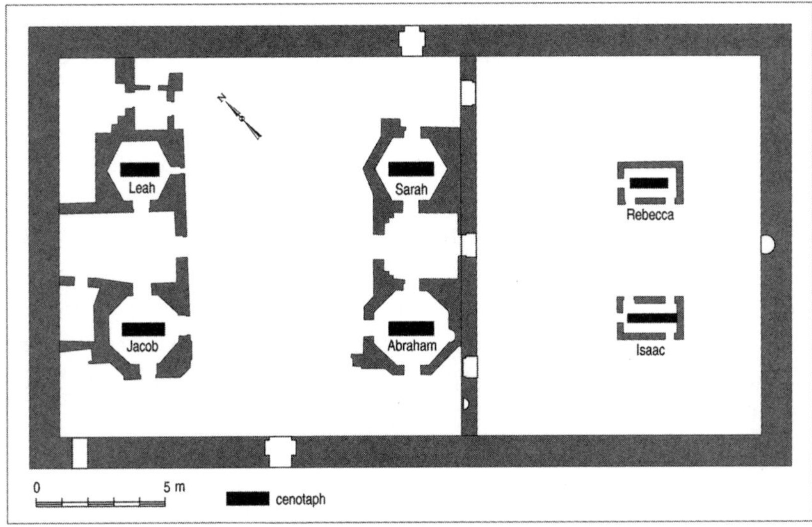

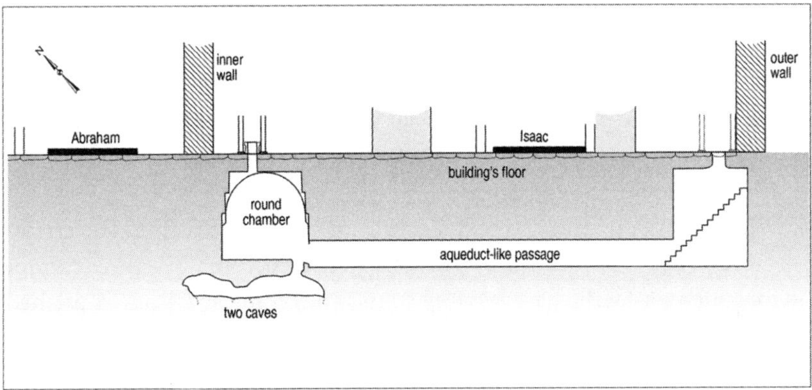

FIGURES 6a and 6b. Frankish Church of St. Abraham, Hebron (Cave of Machpela; al-Ḥaram al-Ibrāhīmī). *Above*: Church of St. Abraham (after Vincent, Mackay, and Abel, *Hébron*). *Below*: The subterranean passage, round chamber, and caves (after Yeivin, "The Machpela Cave Subterranean Complex," and Chen, "Measuring the Cave of Abraham").

single stone. Unable to locate any opening, his spirits flag; but after a while he plucks up courage, asks for an iron hammer, and strikes the walls with it, hoping to hear a hollow sound that would point to a cavity on the far side. At the western wall he meets with success and orders several men to descend the rope. They toil for about four days to dislodge the large stone at the far side of which Arnoul presumed a cavity; and indeed, upon the removal of that stone, there appears a dry, aqueduct-like passage two cubits high, one cubit wide, and twenty-eight cubits long, whose walls and ceiling consist of square, smooth stones.

The entrance to that passage had been blocked several centuries before our own age, and historians familiar with Arnoul's story could only guess its whereabouts.[131] But in 1981, an Israeli archaeological team, led by Ze'ev Yeivin (d. 2015) and accompanied by officials of the Muslim *waqf*, was able to follow in Arnoul's footsteps. Thereafter the entrance was sealed once again. However, the archaeologists measured and photographed the passage and some other underground structures and prepared a plan (see figs. 6a–b). We know now that the passage is 1.06 m high, 0.59 m wide, and 17.60 m long—and these measures closely match those given in the anonymous account and suggest that the canons' cubit amounted to 0.57 m.[132] The plan also allows an understanding of Arnoul's progress.

The aqueduct-like passage Arnoul has discovered appears to lead nowhere, and a great sadness falls on the canons. But Arnoul, with his hammer, saves the situation once again when he locates another stone that promises to conceal a cavity. After another four days of hard work a hole is cut, and a round, subterranean structure, large enough to accommodate thirty people, becomes visible. The canons, sure that they are about to find the patriarchs' relics within, give glory to God but, as their prior has not yet returned from Jerusalem, refrain from removing the stone that blocks the entrance.

When the prior finally returns, the canons resolve to enter the chamber after their afternoon sleep: evidently the customary repose cannot be forgone even with the discovery so near at hand. The stone is pushed aside, the canons marvel at the round, subterranean edifice, but once again there is no sign of the patriarchs' cave. Arnoul resumes his probing. Closely examining the area near the chamber's entrance, he discovers a medium-sized, wedged-shaped stone inserted in the natural rock. He orders it to be removed, and the entrance to the patriarchs' burial cave becomes at long last visible. The date is 25 June 1119.

Prior Rainier entreats Arnoul to be the first to enter the cave, since his share in the effort has been the largest. Arnoul fears that Baldwin, Hebron's castellan, may claim that a treasure of gold or silver has been found and insists therefore that he accompany him. Holding a candle in each hand, making the sign of the cross, and chanting *Kyrie eleison*, Arnoul enters the cave, with Baldwin at his heels. However, Baldwin is overcome by fear and recoils in a hurry, and Arnoul remains in the cave alone. (Our anonymous author evidently enjoys depicting Arnoul the cleric as braver than Baldwin the knight, and his designation of Baldwin, a few lines earlier, as Hebron's defender acquires a somewhat farcical quality.) But Arnoul finds in the cave nothing but earth that appears to be spattered by blood. Once again, a great sadness falls upon the brothers.

The next day the prior urges Arnoul to examine the cave more thoroughly. His second entry is less ceremonious; but with the stick he is carrying he pokes the ground and soon comes upon a skeleton whose bones he gathers into a heap. Near the skeleton's head he discerns the blocked entrance to another cave. He forces it open and finds there the marked body of Abraham, with the bones of Isaac at his feet.[133] He now comprehends that the skeleton he had found in the first, outer cave was that of Jacob.

When Arnoul emerges from the double cave and announces that he has found the patriarchs' relics, his jubilant confrères burst out in hymns glorifying God. Arnoul washes the bones with water and wine and places them on wooden boards; the prior seals the cave's entrance. A day later, some brothers who wish to pray in the cave notice on the right side of the entrance some letters carved on a stone, but neither they nor others are capable of deciphering them. They remove the stone but find nothing behind it. A month later, on 27 July, they decide to pierce the wall opposite the letters and find behind it fifteen earthenware vessels full of bones. Our anonymous author assumes that these are the remains of some leaders of the Children of Israel.[134]

Exultation is soon followed by disappointment, yet our author, so remarkably meticulous in describing the discovery of the patriarchs' relics, becomes close-lipped in his account of the ensuing setback. Prior Rainier, he writes, traveled to Jerusalem to announce the discovery to Patriarch Warmund and to ask him to preside at the ceremony at which the relics were to be transferred from the cave to the church above it. The patriarch gladly agreed to come to Hebron, but then "made use of a counsel that was not good" and went back on his promise. Consequently, the prior decided to perform the ceremony on his own on 6 October, more than three months after the discovery. In the presence of a multitude of people from Jerusalem and elsewhere, with the canons chanting the *Te Deum*, Rainier brought the relics up to the festively illuminated cloister for all to see, and the Franks joyfully kissed the bones that no people before them were privileged even to behold. After the ceremony, the relics were placed in the church.

They were not to stay there. Two years later Patriarch Warmund ordered that they be returned to the cave (see fig. 7). The only explanation the anonymous author chooses to proffer for this blow to the

FIGURE 7. The name ABRAHAM, in twelfth-century Latin letters, on a stone within the cave. The inscription was discovered during the brief inspection of the cave by Israeli archaeologists and Waqf officials, 9 November 1981. The substandard photo, taken in haste during the inspection, is the only one in existence. Photo: courtesy of the late Dr. Ze'ev Yeivin

Hebron chapter is that "since it is the habit of the bad to regard with envy the successes of the good, some people came up to the patriarch and incited him" to issue that order. Rainier, sad but obedient, complied.[135]

Thus, the attempt of the Hebron canons to turn their church into a major shrine in which the relics of the three patriarchs were to be prominently displayed was nipped in the bud. Possibly some influential prelates persuaded Patriarch Warmund that an enhancement of Hebron was premature. Perhaps he himself decided that it was not conducive to his interests, seeing that in 1119 Jerusalem itself was still in desperate need of manpower and aid; about the same time, Warmund beseeched Archbishop Diego Galmírez of Compostela for help, writing that nobody dared to leave Jerusalem's walls without an armed escort since Saracen raids were reaching the city's gates.[136]

If the anonymous account about the discovery intended to reverse Warmund's decision, as the case well may have been, it did not attain its aim. Benjamin of Tudela, ʿAlī al-Harawī, and Petaḥya of Regensburg, who visited Hebron between 1170 and 1180, relate that the patriarchs' relics were in the cave.[137] Also, Hebron—a bishopric only since 1168—appears to have been inadequately endowed.[138] Count Henri the Liberal of Champagne, who visited the place in 1179, was struck by the poverty of the bishop and the canons.[139] The modest extent of the bishop's possessions is attested also by the list that stipulates that during a military emergency the bishops of Bethlehem and Lydda must raise 200 sergeants each, the bishop of Acre 150, the bishops of Tiberias and Sebaste 100 each, whereas the bishops of St. Abraham (that is, Hebron) and Sidon are required to raise merely 50 each.[140] Still, 6 October—the day on which Prior Rainier raised the relics from the cave to his church—became, in the Kingdom of Jerusalem, the feast day of Abraham, Isaac, and Jacob.[141]

While Hebron illustrates a largely ineffective attempt at boosting the attraction of a local shrine, Sebaste tells a success story. According to tradition, it was at Sebaste that John the Baptist was buried, but a Frankish bishop is attested there only from 1129 onward, and a remark by Usāma ibn Munqidh indicates that at the time of his visit between 1141 and 1143 the local cathedral was a small structure that had not yet encompassed the Baptist's tomb.[142] Pope Innocent II took the church of Sebaste under papal protection sometime between 1130 and 1143, but its fortunes took a real turn for the better in 1145, with the discovery of a silver casket that contained relics of the Baptist, the prophets Elisha and Obadiah, "and many prophets and patriarchs."[143]

Unlike their ill-starred counterparts in Hebron, the clerics of Sebaste succeeded in obtaining the active support of the patriarch of Jerusalem at that time, William, who announced the discovery to the prelates and all faithful in the West, claiming that he, as well as his archbishops and bishops, "and many others," found the relics. Evidently the true discoverers—presumably, some local clerics—astutely let the patriarch and other leading prelates uncover the relics, even though it obscured their own role. Their gambit paid off: while Arnoul, Eudes, and Rainier of Hebron gained some fame, the self-effacing discoverers of the Sebaste relics secured high-level endorsement.

In his letter, Patriarch William proclaims that he has established an annual feast to commemorate the discovery, and that he is granting a forty days' remission of penance to all those who visit Sebaste on that feast, as well as on the days of the Baptist's nativity (that is, 24 June) and decollation (29 August), and contribute to the restoration of the church. The proclamation was effective. ʿImād al-Dīn reports some forty years later that the Baptist's tomb, bedecked with veils and ornaments of silver and gold, became one of the Franks' principal sanctuaries, the goal of a yearly pilgrimage.[144] And the list that stipulates that the bishop of Hebron must raise fifty sergeants in an emergency requires the bishop of Sebaste to raise twice as many.[145]

By promising remission of penance to contributors to the restoration of Sebaste's church, Patriarch William gave his support to an ambitious building program. A later bishop of Sebaste, Raoul, wrote that the new church was constructed "of the best stone"—and indeed it is one of the few Frankish buildings that consists entirely of costly, high-quality masonry.[146] But the donations of the faithful, and the sums exacted from Muslims wishing to visit the Baptist's tomb, did not suffice to bring the project to its conclusion, and therefore Raoul launched in 1169/70 a further appeal to the faithful in the West. The patriarch of Jerusalem, Amaurry, supported his initiative.

While Patriarch William's appeal, promising as it did remission of penance in return for visits on feast days and contributions, had been in the mainstream of Western tradition, Raoul's appeal stands out for its sophistication and innovation.[147] First, the bishop announces that he is sending West some canons who carry relics of the Baptist and of the prophets Elisha and Obadiah. Sending relics on a fund-raising campaign was a scheme repeatedly employed in the West since the mid-eleventh century.[148] Raoul's originality in this respect lies in the ambiguous sentence that can be understood not only as a call to the addressees to offer shelter to the relics and their bearers and give them alms, but also as an invitation to admit for good the relics-bearing canons into a landed property in the West—as was indeed to happen. Second, Raoul solemnly announces that the patriarch of Jerusalem is offering the remission of one year of penance for major offenses to all those willing to provide the funds sufficient to recompense two men working in the church's construction, and the remission of one-half of a year to those paying for one such worker. He also promises a remission of forty days to all who are to transmit some funds according to their ability. It is probable that this sliding scale imitates the one proffered by Pope Alexander III, who in his crusading bulls of 29 June 1166 and 29 July 1169 promised a full remission of penance to those who were to fight in the East for two years, and a partial remission to those who were to do so for just one year.[149] Thirdly, the patriarch proclaims—as we have already seen—that those who intended to make a pilgrimage to Santiago de Compostela, whether in order to fulfil a vow or to do penance, are absolved from going there, on condition that they contribute to the church of Sebaste one-half of the expenses they would have incurred by making the pilgrimage. The patriarch grants them also all the remissions they would have obtained. Fourthly, all benefactors of the church of Sebaste are granted pardon for all minor offenses committed in the past, and perpetual participation in prayers offered throughout the holy city of Jerusalem.

Thus, having succeeded in securing the patriarch's support, Raoul devised an original if canonically questionable package of fund-raising schemes. He did not establish, though, a confraternity of donors for the cathedral's reconstruction—probably his parishioners were too few to warrant such an initiative.

Raoul's appeal met with considerable success (see figs. 8a–b). On 28 August 1170, King Louis VII, who had visited Sebaste during the Second Crusade and had been impressed by the canons' piety, donated to its church "and to the brothers who were sent thence to [him]," the annual rent of twenty pounds from the income of Château Landon, and confirmed to those brothers the possession of alms that the faithful had given them. On 24 December 1170, Archbishop William of Sens, the king's brother-in-law, gave the churches of Nemours and Ormesson with all their appurtenances to Sebaste, on the condition that two canons from Sebaste should serve permanently in the church of Nemours; later he added the church of Treuzy to his donation. Apparently, the canons from Sebaste, with most of the relics they brought, settled down in Nemours. The archbishop's sister, Elizabeth, whose husband was buried in the church of Sebaste, had promised its canons an annual gift back in 1168; the archbishop's brother, Count Henri the Liberal of Champagne, granted them an annual revenue of ten pounds during his stay in Sebaste in 1179. Similarities between the cathedrals of Sens and Sebaste—especially, a support system in which cruciform engaged pillars alternate with double columns, and the employment of a sexpartite vaulting in the nave and of quadripartite rib-vaultings in the aisles—render it plausible that Archbishop William was not only one of Sebaste's main benefactors but also saw to it that a headmaster acquainted with his cathedral should be responsible for Sebaste's overall design.[150]

While only Sebaste provides evidence for the methods used to raise the funds needed for the erection of its cathedral, we may assume that other Frankish bishops and abbots invested energy in devising ways to finance the construction of the kingdom's numerous ecclesiastical edifices. Raoul's remark, in his appeal, that he is sending West some relics-bearing canons on the advice of his fellow prelates, implies that by 1170 this fund-raising practice had become common. And the comparison of Hebron with Sebaste demonstrates the importance of winning a patriarch's goodwill.

Alongside the guardianship of age-old shrines, whether Christian or Christianized, the Frankish clerics had to pay attention also to recently created sites of veneration. The main sources on the kingdom's history in the twelfth century are silent about such sites, but the vestiges of Gerard of Nazareth's biographies of the "Men of God Living in the Holy Land" reveal that after the death in 1142 of one such Man of God, the hermit

FIGURES 8a and 8b. Sebaste, Cathedral of St. John the Baptist. Central apse (from the east). *Above*: Drawing of the apse, in Léon de Laborde, *Voyage au Levant* (Paris, 1847). *Below*: Daguerreotype of the apse, by Joseph-Philibert Girault de Prangey in 1844. https://gallica.bnf.fr/ark:/12148/btv1b6903034k.r=btv1b6903034k.?rk=21459;2. The apse was demolished in about 1892, when a mosque was built in the eastern part of the ruined cathedral: Pringle, *Churches*, 2:288.

Radulf, many sick believers flocked to his tomb in Tripoli and regained their health.[151] Similarly, a thirteenth-century guide to the holy places relates that believers afflicted with cold and hot flashes were cured after visiting the tomb of "Seint Guilleme/Guillame" in the cemetery of Acre, close to the fountain he set up there.[152] Riley-Smith plausibly suggested that this was the tomb of Bishop William of Acre (ca. 1166–72), who, having been mortally wounded by a priest of his retinue, asked to spare him, and was apparently regarded as a martyr.[153] There is no reason to suppose that these were the only sites of this kind. Also, it is plausible to assume that, even as tombs of Muslims regarded as martyrs of the anti-Frankish *jihād* became sites of pilgrimage and prayer, graves of crusaders and Franks believed to have attained martyrdom while fighting the Muslims served similar purposes.[154]

Administering Relics

Before the Latin conquest of Constantinople in 1204, Westerners longing to own physical vestiges of the Crucifixion, or of other crucial events in sacred history, turned their eyes to the Kingdom of Jerusalem. Some dispatched requests to Frankish clerics of their acquaintance; for instance, a monk of St. Amand somewhat clumsily entreated his uncle, Archbishop Evremar of Caesarea, to send him, through a trusted emissary, relics of the Lord's Passion and of the saints "who are sleeping in your places next to you."[155] Other Westerners who arrived in the kingdom as crusaders or pilgrims took advantage of their stay to acquire relics; for instance, Bishop Zdík/Heinricus of Olomouc, who made his second pilgrimage in 1137, attests that he received from Patriarch William of Jerusalem a fragment of "that Holiest Cross that he himself carries in his hands in procession and against the pagans."[156] Indeed, it is possible to consider relics as valuable material resources, in effect luxury goods, that Westerners could gain in the Frankish Kingdom.[157]

A letter of Bishop Frederic of Acre, written in about 1150, allows for following in some detail how a Frankish prelate dealt with a request for relics.[158] Frederic, grandson of Count Albert III of Namur and formerly archdeacon of St. Lambert of Liège, was asked by the canons of the Church of St. John the Evangelist of that city to obtain for them some of the relics of the Baptist that had "recently"—that is, in 1145—been discovered at Sebaste. Frederic delayed acting upon this request until a reliable messenger who could be entrusted with conveying the relics to Flanders became available. Some time later he found him in Master Bovo, with whom he conversed in Jerusalem and who asked him to obtain some of the Baptist's relics for the abbey of Florennes, southwest of Liège. On the Vigil of the Baptist's feast, Frederic went with Bovo to Sebaste, spent a night there, and celebrated Mass on the following day. Then he put his request to the bishop and to the canons, "at one time to each of them separately, at another to them all," and ultimately succeeded in overcoming their objections. Bovo conveyed the relics to

Florennes and Liège alongside a letter in which Frederic recounted the story and assured the recipients of the relics' authenticity. Subtly, he let them also realize that he did well in the Kingdom of Jerusalem: he made Bovo remark that he, Frederic, was highly regarded by the patriarch, the archbishops, bishops, the king (that is, Baldwin III), and the queen-mother (that is, Melisende)—a statement that allows dating the letter to between 1149 and 1152.[159] Its seal, like those appended to letters of other bishops of Acre, shows a patriarchal cross with the legend: THIS SIGN WILL BE IN HEAVEN.[160] The bishops of Acre, a town of no biblical distinction, had to fall back on an all-Christian symbol; likewise, Acre's cathedral bore the name of the Holy Cross. Frederic did not specify the nature of the relics he dispatched, but a seventeenth-century author who venerated those that reached Florennes wrote that they consisted of a piece of the Baptist's head, a molar tooth, and fragments of dress and hair.[161]

Ten letters of authentication, all given to Maurice II, lord of Craon in northwestern France, shed light on the way Frankish prelates meted out relics to visitors from the West.[162] As one of the letters was issued by "Amaurry, patriarch of the Church of the Holy Resurrection of Christ" on 20 March 1169, and as a later document mentions a vow Maurice had made "in Egypt," it follows that he participated in King Amaurry's Egyptian expedition of that year.[163] The king—the only layman among the ten authenticators—sent him a fragment of the True Cross, becomingly encased in cruciform crystal.

The ten letters reveal that Maurice made the round of Jerusalem's main churches and traveled also to Bethlehem, Hebron, and Sebaste. In most places the prelates gave him relics distinctive of the shrine under their custody: the abbot of the Lord's Temple, a relic of the Presentation of Jesus; the bishop of Bethlehem, of Jesus's crib; the bishop of Hebron, of the three patriarchs; and so forth. However, most donors gave more than one relic, and the additional fragments were often unconnected to their shrines. The abbot of the Lord's Temple gave Maurice fragments of the Holy Sepulcher and of Calvary, whereas the bishop of Bethlehem gave him a nail with which Christ was crucified, a fragment of the hammer that Joseph of Arimathea used to take Christ's body down from the cross, some of the ashes of the Baptist, and slivers of his skull. Between them, the ten donors gave Maurice twenty-six relics, four of them fragments of the True Cross. Evidently, Frankish prelates managed to have at their disposal collections of relics on which they would draw when approached by worthy believers from beyond the sea.

Did the nobleman Maurice—whom the abbot of Mount Sion hailed as "the strongest of most strong knights"—stand out for the number of relics he gathered?[164] Not really. In the same decade, Gui, an otherwise unknown monk of the abbey of Grandmont who claims to have been on friendly terms with Jerusalem's patriarch, also obtained twenty-six relics, though from fifteen donors.[165] A comparison of the relics the knight and the monk gathered suggests that Frankish prelates tended to bestow on different people the same objects, evocative of their particular shrines. But Gui was less lucky than Maurice: on his way home, thieves stole all the sealed authentications he was given, and therefore he had to compose a letter that lists the donations and the fellow-pilgrims capable of attesting their bestowal.

Frankish clerics could also offer a composite relic, consisting of fragments originating in several holy objects. Already in 1116 Bishop Hildebert of Le Mans received from Adam, a canon of the Church of the Holy Sepulcher who originated in his diocese, a cross that contained two fragments of the True Cross as well as stones from the site of the Ascension on the Mount of Olives and from Gethsemane, Gabatha, Calvary, and the Sepulcher.[166] The cross that Patriarch Foucher sent to Germany, and that can be marveled at today at Scheyern, contained a fragment of the True Cross, as well as fragments of the Church of the Nativity and Jesus's crib in Bethlehem, the site of the Presentation in the Lord's Temple, Gethsemane, Calvary, the Holy Sepulcher, the site of the Ascension, the bed of the Virgin on Mount Sion, and her tomb in the Valley of Josaphat.[167] Similarly, a miter-shaped reliquary found in 1893 in Jerusalem contains fragments of the True Cross, relics of John the Baptist, Peter, and fifteen other saints, all identified by Latin inscriptions.[168]

While Frankish clerics bestowed relics on pilgrims or dispatched them to the West, they did not encourage visitors to deposit *ex votos* in their churches. No source mentions such deposition, while a story in *The Miracles of Our Lady of Rocamadour*, a collection dating from 1172, has a knight who returned from Jerusalem observe that waxen images pierced by various weapons—that is, *ex voto* offerings that commemorate miraculous cures of battle wounds—are missing altogether in the Tomb of the Virgin in the Valley of Josaphat, the Church of the Assumption on Mount Sion, and the many other churches dedicated to the Virgin in the vicinity of Jerusalem.[169] Another story in that collection implies that one should not expect a miraculous cure because of a pilgrimage to the Church of the Holy Sepulcher.[170] Apparently, the custodians of the country's major shrines saw no need to prop up their reputation by accounts of miracles that occurred to specific individuals. The wish to see the sites in which the ministry of Christ had taken place, to obtain the remission of one's sins, to procure relics of Christianity's main personages and places, or to die at the gate of the heavenly fatherland—these were the motives that propelled pilgrims toward Jerusalem. For a miraculous cure, believers would turn to a local healing shrine, within easy reach of a person in pain.[171]

Neither did the Frankish church of the Kingdom of Jerusalem produce even one single local saint in the twelfth century, despite the many Christians who fell in battle against the infidel foe and, regarded as martyrs, could have been worthy candidates for canonization. Possibly the Frankish clerics supposed that the sanctity-permeated country was in no need of further, potentially competing, foci of devotion.[172] Only a Westerner presented a Frank as a saint: this was Pierre of Blois (ca. 1130–ca. 1204), the theologian, poet, and crusade propagandist, who cast in that role none other than Renaud of Châtillon, the tempestuous lord of Transjordan whose breach of the truce with Ṣalāḥ al-Dīn triggered the downfall of the Kingdom of Jerusalem in 1187.[173]

In addition to bestowing relics of religious import, Frankish prelates gave to Western confrères exotic items that held the promise of successful medical cure. Thus, in 1104, Patriarch Evremar of Jerusalem sent to his former bishop, Lambert of Arras, "with the blessing of the Holy Sepulcher," two small crystal flasks filled with balsam, and an archbishop of Mamistra in the Principality of Antioch dispatched "a flask full of well-proven theriac" to his friend Étienne of Tournai; sending it later to Archbishop Absalon of Lund, Étienne described it as "a humble but useful gift."[174] A secular ruler could bestow a still more unusual gift: in 1102 King Baldwin I sent to the Byzantine emperor Alexios Komnenos a pair of tame lions.[175]

Sacralization and Its Perils

"Looking back" and "efflorescence" are two major characteristics of a renaissance, but—as Jack Goody has justly observed—they need not necessarily happen together.[176] The Franks' evocation of the country's biblical past may be regarded as one instance of looking back that did not trigger a major efflorescence.

There were several facets to this evocation. The Franks were the first since biblical times to make Jerusalem their kingdom's capital. The seal of their kings, from Baldwin I onward, proclaimed it to be CIVITAS

REGIS REGUM OMNIUM (City of the King of all Kings), conjuring the biblical references to Jerusalem as City of God (Psalms 46:4 and 48:1) and to Christ as King of Kings (Revelation 17:14 and 19:16). The seals of Frankish prelates highlight the biblical event commemorated in the church over which they presided. The seal of the archbishop of Nazareth shows the praying Virgin faced by the angel Gabriel, and the legend repeats his greeting to her, HAIL MARY, MOST FAVORED ONE, THE LORD IS WITH YOU. The seal of the bishop of Bethlehem features the infant Jesus lying in a crib between the ox and the ass, whereas that of the bishop of Tiberias shows Peter and Andrew casting a net from a small boat. The abbot of the Benedictine monastery on Mount Tabor chose to depict the Transfiguration; the abbess of the convent of Bethany, the resuscitation of Lazarus; the archbishop of Caesarea, a nimbate Peter baptizing a bearded centurion Cornelius; the bishop of Hebron, the three patriarchs Abraham, Isaac and Jacob; and the bishop of Sebaste, John baptizing Christ.[177]

The evocation of the biblical past permeates the description of the country by Rorgo Fretellus, preserved in a large number of manuscripts.[178] The author states at the outset that he will deal with "the sacred places of the Kingdom of David," as well as of Arabia, Syria, and Phoenicia, but it soon transpires that he considers that kingdom to be in existence at his time, for he relates that King Baldwin I erected the castle of Montreal beyond the Jordan "in order to protect the Kingdom of David."[179] The Frankish Kingdom of Jerusalem is the revived Kingdom of David, and the Franks the second Israel.[180]

Unlike earlier Latin pilgrimage accounts that tend to concentrate on Jerusalem's New Testament sites, especially those relating to the Passion, Rorgo Fretellus deals about equally with Old and New Testament traditions and devotes a relatively limited space to Jerusalem and the Passion.[181] He aims at situating sundry biblical events on the ground: Beth Horon is the place unto which Joshua pursued the Amorite kings, on the walls of Beth Shean was the head (*sic*) of Saul displayed, at Ger near Megiddo did King Jehu of Israel strike King Ahaziah of Judah, Jericho is the town of the prostitute Rahab, of the boys who jeered at Elisha, of the blind man whom Jesus healed.[182] He locates also scenes whose protagonists are hardly exemplary: from Jezreel, he writes, came the impious Queen Jezebel who seized Naboth's vineyard; at the foot of Caymont (*Kaym mons*), Lamech slew his ancestor Cain.[183] In sum, Rorgo Fretellus's Kingdom of David is the Land of Holy Scripture. Indeed, in the early part of the treatise he presents the sites not according to geographical sequence but according to the order in which they occur in biblical history.[184]

By listing so large a number of "sacred places of the Kingdom of David," Rorgo Fretellus comes close to presenting the country itself as sacred. Yet he stops short of calling it the "Holy Land." The term *Terra Sancta* came into vogue soon after the crusader conquest, though, possibly because the various Holy Places were for the first time included in a separate Christian entity.[185] Foucher of Chartres uses the term in describing events of 1101 and 1105; Ekkehard makes Baldwin I use it in his exhortation before the First Battle of Ramleh, 1101; Emperor Henry IV takes recourse to it in a letter of 1106 to Abbot Hugues of Cluny; Baudri of Bourgueil has Urban II use it in his version of the Clermont Address.[186] In 1138 it appears in a charter of King Fulk, and in about 1146 in the Clermont Address as rendered in the chronicle that his son, young King Baldwin III, commissioned.[187] The Western Visitor observed that "the Land of Jerusalem is holy and solemn in its entirety" and that the Old and New Testaments disclose that "there is no mountain, no valley, no plain, no river, no fountain, no pool that has not been visited by the prophets and the apostles or [that has not witnessed] the miracles of Christ himself."[188]

And this holy land was ever more perceived as being at the center of the world. The notion goes back to the prophet Ezekiel, who has God say: "This is Jerusalem, which I have set in the center of the nations, with countries all around her"; it reappears in various Christian writings, from Jerome onward.[189] But it is only after the crusader conquest in 1099 that European maps started to show Jerusalem at their center.[190] They were echoed by the Western Visitor, who began his report asserting that "the Land of Jerusalem is situated in the center of the world."[191]

But when an entire country comes to be perceived as incomparably holy, disappointment with its inhabitants' tenor of life cannot be far behind. This is so because the relationship between sacredness and space depends on the physical dimensions of the space in question. When that space is relatively small—a tomb, a church—sacredness may pervade it all, with the space in its entirety set apart from ordinary life and with all activity in its boundaries limited to dealings with the sacred. Under such circumstances, it is possible to ensure that well-nigh all behavior on the premises follows religious precepts. How different the situation when the sacred space encompasses an entire country! Within the boundaries of so extensive a space, sanctity must necessarily coexist with ordinary life and with its many deviations from those precepts. For a Western pilgrim habituated to small sacred areas, the coexistence of sacred and profane in a land proclaimed to be holy would come as a shock; the profane activities within the country would strike him as bewildering, repugnant; an innkeeper's display of greed that he may have shrugged off at home as irritating but commonplace, in the land considered holy would strike him as outrageously scandalous. This tension between expected sanctity and experienced ordinariness is a constant, observable in various periods. William of Tyre may have been aware of the perils inherent in the country's presentation as *Terra Sancta*, for he abstained from using the term throughout his chronicle.

The Frankish Clerics: A Sancterranean Fragment of Western Clergy

All the above-discussed activities of the Frankish clergy attest to a sweeping preoccupation with objects and places believed to be pervaded by an incomparably unique sanctity.

In the early days of the Kingdom of Jerusalem, the Frankish clerics—whatever their original inclinations may have been—were obliged to focus on the many problems posed by their ministry at the holy places. The Western clerics who joined them in later years do not look like a representative sample of the Western clergy of their day, a microcosm consisting of the same elements that made up the European whole. They appear to have been just a fragment of that whole—a fragment characterized by an urge to live in the Holy Land, in the Holy City, to cling to Holy Places.[192] Not satisfied with symbolic renderings, replicas, miniatures, even relics, theirs was a tactile religiosity that yearned for direct, physical contact with sacredness. Western churchmen, whose conception of the sacred was spiritual rather than object- or place-bound, rebuked them sometimes for their wish to live at the Holy Places, but the persistent stream of incoming clerics reveals that such reprimands did not thwart the attraction of tangible sanctity.[193]

The Western clerics who played leading roles in the shaping of the Twelfth-Century Renaissance did not share this urge to cling to the sacred. It is symptomatic that Abelard (ca. 1079–1142), the towering luminary of that renaissance, far from expressing a wish to live in Jerusalem or merely to pilgrimage to it, once contemplated the possibility of living under Muslim rule. As a young man, he surely witnessed the elation that swept the West after the triumph of the First Crusaders in 1099, and he may have watched, in 1120, the festive arrival in Paris of the fragment of the True Cross dispatched by Anseau. Yet in his autobiography Abelard divulges that—when persecuted in the 1120s on account of his teachings—he often saw no other way out but to take refuge among the heathen (that is, the Muslims), knowing that he would have to pay a tribute in order to live quietly in a Christian spirit amidst those enemies of Christ. He even went so far as to ruminate that they, considering his flight a result of shaky Christian faith, would kindly receive him, hoping to win him over to their "sect."[194]

Many Frankish clerics appear to have shared the new interest in the study of Latin classics. Yet they harnessed it almost exclusively to their principal concern, whether by devising and modifying the liturgy at the holy places, or by glorifying them through works like the rhymed histories of the Lord's Temple by Acardus and Gaufridus or the account of the 1119 Invention of Abraham, Isaac, and Jacob. Rorgo Fretellus composed the treatise that describes "the sacred places of the Kingdom of David"; Gerard of Nazareth wrote the biographies of the "Men of God Living in the Holy Land"; chronicles written by Frankish clerics deal with the Crusader conquest of the Holy Land and its subsequent defense against Saracen attacks. And the solitary (hitherto unnoticed) contribution of a Frankish cleric to contemporary theological debate in the West pertains to this defense. Discussing the ecclesiastical ban on the use of the crossbow, Petrus Cantor (d. 1197), the influential teacher of theology in Paris, observed that the bishop of St. George claimed that crossbowmen should not be given communion, "unless they [use the crossbow in] fight against the Saracens or in a just war."[195] The title "of St. George" was borne by the Frankish bishops of Lydda.[196]

Therefore, the Frankish clerics may be characterized as "sancterranean" not only because they lived in the Holy Land, but—first and foremost—because they were preoccupied with the celebration, propagation, and day-to-day husbanding of its sacred treasures.[197] In doing so they exhibited considerable creativity and innovativeness; the extant remains of their writings suggest a notable sanctity-related output of which probably mere vestiges have come down to us. Indeed, these clerics may be considered as an outlying variant of the Twelfth-Century Renaissance. Rodney Thomson has drawn attention to the variegated "cultural cartography" of this renaissance, with scholasticism flourishing in northern France and England, secular studies developing in southern France and northern Italy, non-Christian lore impacting on Iberia, southern Italy, and Sicily, and with the German-speaking lands intensifying the teaching of liberal arts, partially receptive to scholasticism without contributing to its development.[198] From this point of view, the Western clerics who moved to the Kingdom of Jerusalem and created a Latin sacred center on Europe's far-off periphery added a further tint to this many-hued upsurge in cultural activities.

And they—or many of them—also dramatically moved up the social and perceptual ladder. A Western cleric of intrinsic mediocrity who became bishop of Bethlehem, archbishop of Nazareth, or patriarch of Jerusalem enjoyed an exceptional standing and resonance throughout Latin Christendom: a charisma of the title—distinct from Max Weber's charisma of the office (*Amtscharisma*)—was here at work.

In addition, such a cleric could expect that his oeuvre, unimpressive or worse by Western standards, was capable of bestowing on him outstanding acclaim in the Frankish East. The reception of Foucher of Chartres's chronicle illustrates this West/East differential. As Julian Yolles has recently shown, the content and style of the chronicle's early version were devastatingly censured by Guibert of Nogent, and the style was harshly criticized by an anonymous Western author, whereas in Jerusalem the chronicle became a canonical text. Readings from it were the only nonscriptural passages to figure in the liturgy for the feast of the Liberation of Jerusalem, several quotes from it appear in a sermon delivered on that date, and it served a major source for the account of the First Crusade and the Kingdom of Jerusalem sponsored by young King Baldwin III in 1146. Largely overlooked in the West, it enjoyed remarkable success in the East.[199]

A further reason may be adduced for the sanctity-centered output of the Frankish authors active in the Kingdom of Jerusalem. Muslim Toledo was hailed as "the Kingdom of Science"; several decades after King Alfonso VI of Castile conquered the city in 1085, numerous scientific and philosophical treatises were translated there from Arabic into Latin.[200] If Muslim Jerusalem had similarly stood out for the fostering of the sciences or philosophy, and if some Muslims and Jews had been permitted to live in the city after the 1099 conquest, some Western clerics interested in these disciplines may have chosen to move there and temper the one-sidedness of the Frankish clergy. But neither Jerusalem nor any other city conquered by the crusaders was a center of Islamicate secular studies.[201] Nor were the native inhabitants of these cities fluent in both Arabic and some Romance vernacular. The bilinguality so crucial for Iberian Arabic-to-Latin translations was absent.

Pre-1099 Jerusalem stood out for vibrant discussions of Islamic theology and law. Ibn al-ʿArabī of Seville, who stayed in the city for a number of years in the early 1090s, found there Muslim study circles and *madrasas*, and attended several lessons as well as debates between scholars of various Muslim factions. Although the Palestinian Academy (*yeshīva*) had left Jerusalem for Tyre in 1073, there were still learned Jews in the city with whom Muslims debated matters of faith, and so were Christian and Samaritan sages.[202]

Thus, neither before nor after 1099 was Jerusalem a center of secular studies. Is this a mere coincidence, or may we hypothesize that, at least in the three monotheistic religions, there prevails an elective affinity (*Wahlverwandschaft*) between sacred space and sacredness-centered, sacredness-related cultural activities, and therefore a city perceived as holy is not conducive to the advancement of secular studies? The flourishing of sciences and philosophy in Baghdad rather than in Mecca during the classical Islamic era, in Florence more than in Rome during the Italian Renaissance, appears to support this hypothesis.

It is also supported by the fact that the one city of the Frankish East in which, in the twelfth century, scientific treatises were translated from Arabic into Latin was situated far to the north of Jerusalem and its kingdom. This city was Antioch, mentioned in the New Testament and an important center of early Christianity, yet whose role in sacred history was no match to that of Jerusalem; Western pilgrims usually did not include it in their itinerary.[203] It was here that Stephanus Philosophus of Pisa, probably treasurer of the Antiochene monastery of St. Paul and nephew of Antioch's patriarch, translated in the 1120s *The Royal Book on Medicine* by ʿAlī ibn al-ʿAbbās al-Majūsī (d. ca. 994), supplementing it with a Greek-Latin-Arabic glossary of medical terms, the first of its kind. Stephanus also translated, under the title *Liber Mamonis*, the cosmological work *On the Configuration of the World* by Ibn al-Haytham (d. after 1040), inserting numerous comments of his own. And a translation of Ptolemy's *Almagest*, from the Arabic, appears to have been prepared in Stephanus's milieu.[204] Similarly, the prominent lay scholar Adelard of Bath (ca. 1080–ca. 1152) who translated numerous scientific treatises from Arabic and Greek, spent several years in the Principality of Antioch—but is not known to have visited Jerusalem.[205]

Stephanus of Antioch eloquently expresses his admiration for lore stored in Arabic and repeatedly dwells on its superiority to knowledge accessible to Westerners and on the desirability of its absorption by them. Toward the end of his prologue to the translation of *The Royal Book of Medicine*, he announces that "all the secrets of philosophy" are hidden within the Arabic language, and to these he intends to devote his skills once adequately refined.[206] In the prefaces to the four books of the *Liber Mamonis* Stephanus does not mince words while describing what he regards as the sorry state of Western knowledge: "Europe, who could have been in the almost full possession of the arts, seems now inferior to any other people"; later he observes that, with regard to astronomy, "*Latinitas* [Latinity; the Latin realm] possesses only little certain knowledge and most of it is obscured by the darkness of error." To change this state of things Stephanus intends "to deliver to Latin stock secrets unknown to the ears of our people" and provide "geometrical proofs of which Latinity is ignorant, and therefore has tumbled about greatly in widespread error for a long time."[207] Stephanus announces that in the present work he mostly follows "a certain Arab," and thus leaves no doubt that the superior lore he is about to transmit to Latinity originated in the Islamicate realm.[208]

Significantly, none of the clerics of the Kingdom of Jerusalem shared Stephanus's high regard for Arabic-written works of philosophy and science; indeed, none of them appears to have been conscious of their existence. Likewise, they did not exhibit the interest in rhetorical theory and the emphasis on rhetorical skill for which some of their Antiochene counterparts stood out, nor did they share with them a serious engagement with non-Latin intellectual traditions.[209] It is also significant that Stephanus Philosophus and his original outlook go unmentioned in some major histories of the crusades and the Frankish East.[210]

William of Tyre (ca. 1130 – ca. 1186), on the other hand, is the Frankish cleric conspicuously dealt with in each and every study of the twelfth-century Frankish East. Let us take now a close look at him.

Chapter 6

A Candid Portrait of William of Tyre, the Kingdom's Most Erudite Cleric

Ernoul, who wrote his chronicle a short time after the Battle of Ḥaṭṭīn, relates that Archbishop William of Tyre, born in Jerusalem, was the best *clerc* in all of Christendom of his times—and *clerc* in those days meant not only "cleric," but also "a man of learning."[1] Modern historians are hardly less appreciative. For Charles Homer Haskins, in 1927, William's chronicle was "one of the chief [historical] works of the age," its author the only Jerusalemite to make the pages of *The Renaissance of the Twelfth Century*. For Max Manitius, in 1931, the chronicle was "the greatest achievement in the field of crusade histories," its interpretation and style "superb," with William "looking always for a logical connexion." For Runciman, in 1952, William was "one of the greatest of medieval historians," who "understood the sequence of cause and effect in history," while for Peter W. Edbury and John Gordon Rowe, in 1988, William's narrative "possesses an intellectual integrity whose grandeur is not to be belittled, and he is thus entitled to his place among the foremost historians of the Middle Ages."[2]

William's *History*, his only work to have come down to us, does indeed stand out for a number of singular achievements, of which the following may be the most remarkable. First, it places the crusader capture of Jerusalem and the establishment of Frankish states along the Levantine littoral within a multisecular context in which

Muslim conquest is offset by Christian reconquest: (Byzantine) Christians lose the region to the Muslims in the seventh century; Muslims rule Jerusalem and the region, often oppressing its Christian inhabitants; (European) Christians wrest away a considerable part of the region during the First Crusade, reestablish Christian rule, and repulse Muslim attacks time and again. Second, the *History* rationally diagnoses some crucial political developments, especially the unification of Egypt and Syria under Ṣalāḥ al-Dīn and its repercussions for the Kingdom of Jerusalem. Third, the early chapters of the *History* are based on Arabic chronicles written by Eastern Christians—an unprecedented feat in the Frankish East.[3] Fourth, the *History* presents the Muslim adversary more realistically than other chronicles. William never refers to the Muslims as pagans, is the first Westerner who attempts to explain the difference between Sunni and Shiʿi Muslims, differentiates between Muslim contingents according to their commanders' ethnic origins, and is one of the first Franks to exhibit an ethnographer's curiosity about alien populaces.[4] Muslims and Franks are presented repeatedly as fighting for the very same reasons: to defend their wives and children, and to uphold their liberty.[5] Fifth, the *History* contains several subtle portraits—physical as well as mental—of Frankish rulers and prelates, as well as of Ṣalāḥ al-Dīn's uncle Shīrkūh.[6] Sixth, William repeatedly tells his readers how he gathered the information or reached his conclusions.[7] Also, as we have seen, he chooses to ignore the recurrent, miraculous descent of the Holy Fire.

Beyond all that, William is a skillful storyteller. As far as we know, he never experienced battle at first hand. We look in vain in his chronicle for confessions like that of Foucher of Chartres, who discloses that he and his companions, surrounded by the enemy, "feigned courage but feared death," and who—writing about a battle in the midst of which he found himself—candidly reports: "I saw war with my eyes, my mind swayed to and fro, I was afraid of being struck."[8] And yet William, the armchair historian, is able to transform combatants' oral reports, conveyed to him in the vernacular, into gripping accounts of warfare composed in ornate Latin. This is, for instance, how he describes a scene of the return march of the Frankish army from Bosra (Buṣrā, nowadays in southern Syria) in the summer of 1147, evidently on the basis of stories he heard some two decades later from veterans of that ill-starred expedition:

> All that area was full of low thorn-bushes and shrubs, dry thistles and lots of wild mustard, old stubble, and crops already ripe. The

> enemy set all this on fire, and the wind blowing against our men heaped tinder on them. Doubly harassed—by the blast of nearby flames and by the dense cloud of smoke—all our people turned shouting and wailing to that venerable man, Lord Robert, archbishop of Nazareth, who was carrying the Lord's Cross, and tearfully beseeched him: "Pray for us, Father, and through the wood of the Vivifying Cross that you bear in your hands and upon which we believe that the originator of our salvation hung, rescue us from these calamities, for we cannot withstand them any longer!" The wind-driven soot discolored the people's faces and bodies, rendering them black like smiths working at furnaces, and the summer's heat, redoubled by that of the flames, and the extreme thirst, made them suffer beyond their powers. The shouts of the groaning people greatly aroused the compassion of the man worthy of God's love, who—contrite in heart and soul—raised the Salutary Wood against the flames that were rushing at him in all ferocity, and invoked help from above. Immediately divine power was at hand, the winds whirled instantly round into the opposite direction and tossed the flames, as well as the dark foul smoke, at the enemy that preceded our army; they saw the harm they had contrived for us wheeling round to their destruction. The enemy were stunned by the miracle's rareness, regarding as matchless the faith of the Christians, which so quickly can obtain, through prayers, support from their Lord God.[9]

Forty years later, during the Battle of Ḥaṭṭīn, with the Franks on the march to relieve Tiberias, the Muslims employed the same stratagem, starting scrub fires on several occasions. But William of Tyre was no longer around, and we must depend on our imagination to envisage the blackened faces of thirsty Franks beset by flames and smoke, yearning that the True Cross might rescue them. But the Cross, far from bringing about a miracle, was captured by Ṣalāḥ al-Dīn's men, never to return into Christian hands.

Yet even as William's *History* is justly conspicuous for a number of reasons, its merits should not be exaggerated. Yes, William comprehends in 1174 that the Frankish East was weakened by Ṣalāḥ al-Dīn's unification of all the Muslim territories surrounding it—but even as we draw attention to this realistic insight, we should remember that William posits it as merely the *third* reason for the loss of Christian superiority. The first two are the alleged monstrous sinfulness of the Frankish generation of his time, and the purported shortage of military experience of the peace-enjoying Muslims who had faced the trained warriors of the First Crusade three generations earlier, a shortage (this is how William's reasoning should be completed) that has given way to abundant skill in more recent years.[10] Of these reasons, the first betrays conventional thinking, and the second amounts to a tendentious rewriting of history; only the third reveals a rational appraisal. Moreover, William is capable of interpreting military events in strictly conventional terms. When in November 1177 a small Frankish force succeeded in defeating Ṣalāḥ al-Dīn's army at Montgisard, William maintains that God let the few prevail over the many in order to proclaim that divine grace, not human might, brought about the victory.[11] Again, when in August 1179 a large Frankish army, reinforced by many French crusaders, failed to prevent Ṣalāḥ al-Dīn's conquest of the Templar castle of Vadum Jacob, William muses that God may have deprived the Christians of a victory they might have attributed to the huge force they amassed, not to divine grace.[12] William is far more a child of his age than some of his modern admirers assume.

Neither does William always attempt to integrate the facts he recounts. This is especially so when he deals with events that took place in his own days. For instance, writing about what happened in 1168, William states: "Hardly anything worthy of remembrance occurred in the kingdom in that year, except the regulating around Lent of two churches in the kingdom, and the institution of bishops in them." Having given a few details about the new ecclesiastical sees of Petra and Hebron, and having spelled out the names of the prelates in charge of them, William goes on to report that in the following summer Étienne du Perche, chancellor of Sicily and bishop-elect of Palermo, escaped to Jerusalem, fell sick, died, and was buried in the chapter hall of the Lord's Temple. Then he relates that about the same time Count William of Nevers came to Jerusalem at the head of many knights in order to fight the enemies of the Christian faith, but soon succumbed to illness and died.[13] In sum, his account for that year, as well as for several others, amounts to a string of annalistic entries. And—as Mayer observed—William is often sloppy with his facts.[14]

Again, while William definitely presents the Muslims in a more knowledgeable, differentiated, and realistic manner than other crusade chroniclers, his understanding of the motivation that in his days stimulated much of the Muslim struggle against the Franks appears to have been limited. He repeatedly presents Muslim fighting as rooted in the wish to protect wives and children and preserve liberty, while the term *jihād*, and the idea behind it, although increasingly reverberating in the Muslim world of his day, go unmentioned and un-alluded to throughout his 257,783 words-strong chronicle.[15] Yet he knows to characterize accurately the *Mameluc* (i.e., Mamluks) or to distinguish between the *Toassin* (i.e., *tawāshī*), and the *Caragolam* (i.e., *qaraghulām*), that is, between the upper and lower ranks of Ṣalāḥ al-Dīn's regular troops.[16] Only once, while describing a Frankish-Muslim battle in northern Syria in 1125, does William remark that warfare between coreligionists is less ferocious than that between combatants adhering to different faiths, "because even if there is no other cause for hatred, the lack of agreement on articles of faith suffices to entail continuous strife and perpetual quarrels."[17]

This general observation, appearing also more succinctly in William's discussion of Fatimid-Abbasid and Byzantine-Turkish relations, is, however, a far cry from an awareness of the power of the *jihād* idea.[18] William's silence about it starkly contrasts with the accurate depiction of crusader motivation by his Muslim contemporaries and fellow-chroniclers ʿImād al-Dīn al-Iṣfahānī, Bahāʾ al-Dīn ibn Shaddād, and Ibn al-Athīr. Indeed, already in 1105 the Damascene preacher ʿAlī ibn Ṭāhir al-Sulamī maintained that the Franks, having taken Jerusalem and eager to conquer ever more territory, were "fighting the *jihād* against the Muslims"; al-Qāḍī al-Fāḍil, Ṣalāḥ al-Dīn's secretary and adviser, referred to the Christian warfare as a *jihād* of impure intent; and the geographer Yāqūt (d. 1229) presented the Templars as "a group of Franks who have consecrated themselves to waging *jihād* against the Muslims."[19] We are left to wonder whether Muslims were really more interested in crusader motivation than crusaders and Franks in theirs, and whether William was indeed unaware of the *jihād* idea and propaganda, or chose to leave them unmentioned. It is noteworthy in this context that William presents Nūr al-Dīn (1118–74), the Franks' foremost enemy in Syria, as a just ruler—and *al-ʿādil* (the just) was indeed the sultan's most important title. Did he really not know that Nūr al-Dīn's second most common epithet was *mujāhid* (engaged in *jihād*)?[20]

Neither does William exhibit true understanding of the importance of Jerusalem for Muslims. He does mention that in 1152 the descendants of the Turkish family that had ruled Jerusalem before the crusader conquest raised a large army, led it to the Mount of Olives, and gazed thence at the city, "and especially at the Lord's Temple, which they hold in uppermost and exceptional respect," before the Frankish inhabitants, invoking help from heaven, repulsed them.[21] A reader relying only on

William may conclude that only the descendants of Jerusalem's erstwhile rulers felt so deeply for the Dome of the Rock, captive in Christian hands. To learn that, under Frankish rule, many Muslims used to pray near the Christianized Dome, and that Muslims, pained by the sight of the cross the Franks had affixed at its top, offered much gold to have it removed, we must turn to Johann of Würzburg.[22]

Similarly, William, who dwells at great length on the history of the city of Tyre of which he was archbishop from 1175 onward, does not mention that several mosques functioned in it—we learn about this from Ibn Jubayr, who stayed there briefly in September 1184.[23] And even as William reproduces five letters concerning the status of the archbishopric of Tyre that Pope Innocent II issued in 1139, he does not see fit to mention the condolence letter Ṣalāḥ al-Dīn sent in 1174 to King Baldwin IV, calling him "the Guardian of Jerusalem" (*Ḥāfiẓ Bayt al-Maqdis*) and expressing grief over the death of his father Amaurry—a letter of which William, chancellor of the realm at the time, must have known.[24]

While we cannot be sure that William was really unaware of the *jihād*, he certainly chose to downplay the recurrent crossings of the Christian-Muslim religious divide, so amply documented in other sources.[25] Also, he avoided incorporating into his *History* references to Frankish-Muslim sexual relationships that he must have encountered in his sources. For instance, while closely following Albert of Aachen's account of the crusader conquest of Nicaea in 1097, William skips altogether Albert's story about the nun from Trier who, upon her liberation from Turkish captivity, "complained that she underwent a filthy and abominable intermingling with a certain Turk and some others, with scarcely a pause," was granted forgiveness by Bishop Adhémar because the acts took place against her will—and then, when the Turk, "inflamed by passion for her inestimable beauty," beseeched her to return to him, the nun did so, "for no other reason than because her lust was too much to bear."[26] Elsewhere, William mentions the "filthy" conduct of Patriarch Arnoul of Jerusalem, relates that it led to his deposition by a papal legate, but chooses to abstain from specifying the nature of Arnoul's transgressions. However, Pope Paschal II, in the bull of 19 July 1117 by which he quashed the deposition and reinstated Arnoul, divulged (as we have seen) that he had been accused of illicit relations with two women, the one Christian, the other a Saracen.[27] Once again, William—whose references to Arnoul are hostile all along, and who has no qualms about hinting that the pope acquitted him in return for a bribe—refrains from mentioning a purported sexual relationship between a Frankish man and a Muslim woman; and although he reproduces verbatim five bulls of Paschal II, that of 19 July 1117 goes unmentioned.[28] This squashing of references to sexual relationships between crusaders (or Franks) and Muslims is not rooted in a sense of decorum that dictates an all-out abstention from mentioning such relations: William has no qualms to write that the wife of Firuz, Bohemond's confidant at Antioch, was "joined in an illicit bond of the flesh" with a Turkish chief.[29]

William's silence on topics he must have been familiar with is not restricted to issues concerning Muslims. For instance, he mentions Jerusalem's Church of the Holy Sepulcher about forty times, and he must have been well aware of its daily routine—but, had our knowledge about that shrine depended solely on him, we would have never known that under Frankish rule numerous non-Latin groups celebrated the divine office in it. It is from Theoderich that we learn about this.[30] And while William relates that King Amaurry asked him to tutor his son—the future King Baldwin IV, the Leper—in liberal studies and spells out that the boy became an excellent horseman, "most apt, far more than his forefathers, at letting horses go and at controlling them," he does not mention who the leprous boy's instructor in horsemanship was.[31] It is Ibn Abī Uṣaybiʿa, the author of an encyclopedia of physicians, who spells out the instructor's identity: he was Abū al-Khayr, a son of the Eastern Christian physician Abū Sulaymān Dāwūd.[32] Again, while William mentions the town of Nablus twenty-four times, he does not mention that the Samaritans own there a sacred place at which they offer their paschal sacrifice; we owe this information to Ernoul.[33]

William's chronicle exhibits a penchant for venomously attacking people he loathed. Patriarch Arnoul of Chocques is branded as "the firstborn of Satan, the son of perdition" (the only other personage whom William characterizes as the firstborn of Satan is the Prophet *Mahumet*!).[34] Arnoul is also described as a man who stands out for his delight in stirring up scandals; his excessive incontinence during the First Crusade made him the butt of lascivious songs.[35] Milo of Plancy, a relative of King Amaurry who became his seneschal, is depicted as noble according to the flesh but of degenerate morals—a shameless, noisy, disparaging, quarrelsome, vile, exceedingly incautious, haughty, and arrogant man, who indulged in hurtful language and had a far too good opinion of himself.[36] Agnes of Courtenay, King Amaurry's first wife, is characterized as "thoroughly hateful to God, and harsh at wrenching out [money from people]," whereas Aliénor of Aquitaine, one of the most remarkable personages of William's age, is brushed off as "one of the silly women."[37] William presumably detested Agnes because she blocked his election to the patriarchal see of Jerusalem.[38] The reasons for his hostility toward Milo and Aliénor are open to conjecture; in any case, the attacks lay bare William's fiery temper.

Now, what do we know about William's intellectual evolution, and to what extent does it throw light on the emphases and silences in his *History*?

The Education of a *Clerc*

William was born in Jerusalem in about 1130 to a family he would have defined as belonging to the "second class" (*secunda classis*) of Frankish society; contemporaries called members of that class *burgenses*, that is, burgesses. William does not reveal his social origins; they were detected in 1883 by Prutz, who noted that in the list of witnesses to an act of 18 December 1175 there appears, among the burgesses of Jerusalem, "Radulfus, brother of the archbishop of Tyre."[39] Neither does William disclose from which Western country his parents or grandparents came to Jerusalem. His description of the city—starting with Mount Sion, then moving to the Tower of David, then to the Church of the Holy Sepulcher that stands on the slope of the city's western ridge, which, he says, is higher than the church and renders it shadowy—suggests that his family lived in the southwestern part of Jerusalem, and that the sight of the church in the early evening imprinted itself on his memory.[40]

Young William must have learned to read and write in the school attached to the Church of the Holy Sepulcher, whose existence is attested as early as 1102–3.[41] By 1136 Johannes the Pisan was teaching there the "little clerks," and William, then about six years old, must have been one of them. Johannes, a man interested in theological questions and especially in the controversy between the Roman and Byzantine churches, went on to have a distinguished ecclesiastical career, becoming archdeacon of Tyre by 1146 and cardinal by 1152. Yet he unmade his career by repeatedly betting on wrong horses: in 1159 he engineered the election of the ill-starred antipope Victor IV, and in 1164 he was the driving force behind the election of another antipope, Paschal III, both of whom were challenging Pope Alexander III. Shortly thereafter Johannes fell from a horse and died. In his chronicle, William speaks of him twice, both times favorably.[42] Evidently, he continued to cherish the memory of his first teacher even after Alexander's victory cast him among the losers.[43]

In 1962, Robert Huygens (d. 2022) published the lost autobiographical chapter of William's chronicle—one of the most spectacular discoveries in twentieth-century medieval studies.[44] William relates there that he studied for about twenty years in the schools of France and Italy, and Huygens assumed that the studies lasted from 1146 to 1165. We do not know how it came about that William departed for Europe. Perhaps it was his burgess family that sent him West; in Europe of those years some such families let their sons study in Bologna, hoping to attain thereby honor and advantages.[45] Again, it is possible that some Frankish prelates saw fit to send promising "little clerks" to the West to obtain there an education unattainable in the East. Perhaps it was Johannes the Pisan who effected William's departure and, later as cardinal, watched over his progress, planning for him an ecclesiastical career under the auspices of the antipopes he supported. Maybe it is not coincidental that Johannes died in 1164 and William sailed back to the Kingdom of Jerusalem in 1165, the year in which Alexander III returned to Rome, his victory imminent.[46]

William's autobiographical chapter is an amazing document. Possibly it is the only text in world history by which a historian, while relating a country's past, deems fit to acquaint readers in detail with his own personal education—and to do so not in an introduction or a postscript, but by interrupting the general narrative. The chapter struck some contemporaries as out of place: Of the ten manuscripts containing William's chronicle that have come down to us, two do not mention the chapter at all; seven include its heading but omit the text; just one manuscript—BAV, Vat. lat. 2002, dating from about 1200—contains both heading and text.[47] Neither does the text recur in the sixty-four extant manuscripts of the Old French adaptation of William's chronicle, dating from the first third of the thirteenth century.

In the autobiographical chapter, William mentions by name the sixteen teachers under whom he studied in France and Italy for about twenty years—in all likelihood one of the longest spans of time devoted to studies by a scholar of those days.[48] First, he studied for about ten years the liberal arts under ten masters, eight of whom are known to have taught in Paris, and an analysis of William's statements suggests that the two remaining ones also taught there.[49] He then studied theology under two masters who are likewise known to have taught in Paris. In Bologna, William tells us, he studied civil law under four masters. In addition, he studied classics under Hilarius of Orléans, probably in that city, and geometry under William of Soissons, in a place difficult to ascertain. In a general statement that precedes the listing of these masters William mentions canon law among the subjects he studied, yet none of the masters listed was known as a canonist.

William's list of his masters includes some of the most illustrious names of the age, especially Petrus Lombardus, author of the *Book of Sentences* that was to become the standard textbook of theology at the universities, and the Four Doctors of Bologna—that is, the highly influential jurists Hugo (called by William: Hugolinus) de Porta Ravennate, Bulgarus, Martinus, and Jacobus. R. C. "Otto" Smail (d. 1986), a founding father of rigorous British studies of crusading, once remarked in conversation that William's assertion that he studied theology and law under these masters resembles a twentieth-century person bragging to have studied physics under Albert Einstein and psychoanalysis under Sigmund Freud; and he went so far as to question whether William's statements should be taken at face value. The comparison to Einstein and Freud is appropriate, as it effectively brings home to present-day readers how towering William's teachers were in their time; but the skepticism is out of place, for other contemporary students followed a scholarly itinerary similar to that of William. This is especially true of Pierre of Blois, who studied in Paris, Tours, and Bologna.[50]

William's account stands out for the extravagant praise he heaps on his masters. He starts with three teachers of liberal arts—Bernardus Brito, Petrus Helie, and Ivo of Chartres—whom he presents as "extraordinary doctors, venerable men worthy of pious remembrance, repositories of knowledge, treasure-vaults of the branches of study"; all three were disciples of "the most lettered" Thierry of Chartres, while Ivo profited also from the teaching of Gilbert de la Porrée, bishop of Poitiers.[51] His seven other liberal arts teachers are described—in words recalling Genesis 1:16—as *maiora luminaria*, "greater lights."[52] Petrus Lombardus, his main teacher in theology, is characterized as matchless in that branch of knowledge: "a multitude of prudent men embrace with highest respect and cultivate with reverence the extant works of the man whose sound teaching is commendable in every manner." Of his four Bolognese teachers, Hugolinus de Porta Ravennate and Bulgarus are "men of supreme authority," whereas Martinus and Jacobus exhibit an "extraordinary skill in law"; together they resemble "four firm-shafted columns set up to sustain the Temple of Justice."[53] None of the sixteen masters as depicted by William displays even the slightest intellectual shortcoming. William of Soissons, he says, suffered from an impediment of speech; but this sole negative comment, referring to a physical weakness, is immediately evened out by highlighting William's sharp mind and subtle thinking. (William appears to have been sensitive to difficulties in talking: he reports that King Amaurry had a slight impediment of speech, and remarks that his son and successor Baldwin IV shared that predicament.)[54] Moreover, four of William's masters were disciples of Abelard, but Abelard's name goes unmentioned. William states that he studied under a disciple of Gilbert de la Porrée, but he does not even hint at Gilbert's purported heretical propositions on the Trinity, attacked by William's teacher Petrus Lombardus and partially condemned in 1148. William evidently chooses to restrict himself to conferring on his masters a garland of superlatives.

This garland becomes still more remarkable when compared to two other contemporary descriptions of leading scholars. In his *Metalogicon*, William's older contemporary John of Salisbury (ca. 1115–80) discusses the twelve masters under whom he studied from 1136 to 1148. Of these twelve, four—Petrus Helie, Albericus de Monte, Robert of Melun, and Adam of the Petit Pont—were also William's teachers about a decade later.[55] But what a disparity between William's blanket adulation and John's discriminating, repeatedly critical appraisals! For instance, all William has to say about Albericus and Robert is that they were two of the "greater lights." John, on the other hand, presents Albericus as the most bitter opponent of the nominalist sect, then goes on to juxtapose him to Robert. Albericus, "exact in every respect, found arguments to question at every turn, no surface—however polished—being in his eyes without roughness, nor any bullrush without knots, as the saying goes. For there too he would point to a knot that needed untying." Robert, in contrast, "was invariably ready with a reply, never declining a proposed subject in order to make an escape but opting for the other side of a contradiction, or by determining that an utterance had manifold meanings, showing that there was no single response. The former therefore was subtle and expansive in his questioning, while the latter was penetrating, succinct, and pertinent in his responses." Then John shifts to criticism: "And I think that they would have attained the highest eminence and distinction in the study of philosophy had they supported themselves on a broad foundation of literature, and had they followed in the footsteps of their predecessors to the same extent as they applauded their own discoveries." John's criticism is not restricted to these two dialecticians. Adam of the Petit Pont, whom John lauds for his wide reading, is presented as a man "considered to suffer from the affliction of envy," whereas another teacher, the theologian Simon of Poissy, is characterized as "a trustworthy lecturer yet more dull as a disputant."[56] Similarly, the anonymous author of the *Metamorphosis of Bishop Golias*, writing in 1142/43, describes thirteen masters as taking part in a poetic gathering. They are depicted favorably, with the exception of Adam of the Petit Pont, who "disputed with fingers that split an iota, and regarded as self-evident everything he asserted," and the monk Reginaldus, who contradicted everybody and suspended in a noose "our Porphirius"—presumably Abelard.[57]

John of Salisbury's differentiating appraisal of his teachers forms part of his plea for a thorough grounding in the liberal arts; the author of the *Metamorphosis* aims primarily at pitting the followers of Abelard against his attackers. But what may have been William's aim when he interrupted his account of the history of the Kingdom of Jerusalem by inserting a chapter about his lengthy studies?[58]

Peter Edbury and John Gordon Rowe have convincingly argued that William revised his *History* upon his return from the Third Lateran Council of 1179 and that the new version, addressed to the prelates of the West, many of whom he had met there, aimed at convincing them that the Franks in the East were worthy of assistance. The revision took place in the early 1180s; since Huygens, the discoverer of the autobiographical chapter that lists William's masters, cogently contended that it was composed in 1181–82, it may be regarded as a part of the revised text aimed at a learned Western readership.[59]

What, then, could have been William's purpose in highlighting his studies in so unusual a manner? The emphasis on his many years of study and on the boundless excellence of his many masters apparently intended to convince the prelates of the West, many of whom studied in Paris or Bologna, that he, William, author of the book they were about to read, was at least equal and probably superior to most of them. His mentioning that, of the three hundred prelates who participated in the Third Lateran Council, it was he who was entrusted with writing down the council's decisions, apparently aimed at making the same point.[60]

And yet the very need to underscore his learning so curiously marks William as a provincial outsider: No insider who truly formed part and parcel of the Western elite of those times saw fit to parade his belonging by so spectacular a departure from the conventions of historical writing. Moreover, William's verbose litany of his illustrious masters, loaded with grandiloquent superlatives and devoid of any matter-of-fact differentiation, denotes him as an outsider who, even as he proudly proclaims that he studied under the best of the West's teachers, unwittingly reveals that he either did not grasp the tensions among them or regarded them as irrelevant to his objective. For William, the essential fact to broadcast was that he, a man from Latin Christendom's distant periphery, made it to the West's foremost schools.

William's Literary Style, Body of Knowledge, and Prejudices

William's *History* attests in several ways to his extensive, variegated though somewhat flawed knowledge. The general prologue, the preface to book 23, and the descriptions of cities stand out for a large number of direct quotations from classical and later authors, which caused two historians to comment that William "did indulge [there] in some self-conscious erudition."[61] Far more frequently William uses expressions that closely or loosely echo biblical or classical phrases, and it is difficult to decide whether he is deliberately referring or subconsciously alluding to them.[62] He definitely exhibits a predilection for proverbs, sayings, and similes. Several times he presents lines from classical authors as proverbs, which makes one wonder whether he knew from where they came.[63] In two cases he introduces as a proverb the phrase: "It is difficult for things to close with a good end when they started with a bad beginning"—which virtually repeats a sentence of Pope Leo the Great.[64] Some sayings may amount to a translation from the vernacular: thus, *male orat qui sui obliviscitur* (he who is forgetful of himself prays badly) appears in a collection of French proverbs as *mal prie qui s'oblie*.[65] As for similes, William reveals a penchant for medicine and animals: no less than four times he likens a maltreated host to a man with a serpent in his lap and to a sack of grain gobbled by a rat.[66] And the computer discloses that the range of William's knowledge and associations was even wider than that which emerges from the outstanding apparatus in the 1986 edition of the *History* provided by Huygens. Thus, the phrase "delaying made desire swell" (*dilatione votum creverat*), which William quotes twice, is taken from *Epitalamica*, an Easter sequence presumably penned by Abelard or a poetess who lived in the Abbey of Paraclet and imitated his style; in both instances William couples it with a quotation from Sallust (which he presents as a proverb).[67] The maxim "It is wrong to keep faith with one who tries to act against the agreements" (*iniquum est ei fidem servari, qui contra pacta nititur versari*), which William quotes three times—always with regard to a Byzantine emperor, always proclaiming that it is congruous with the law of treaties[68]—appears to reformulate in a more elegant Latin a statement of the *Summa Trecensis*, the earliest compendium on the

Codex of Justinian.[69] This work was presumably written around 1140 by Géraud, a master active in the Midi who was influenced by Irnerius, the teacher of the Four Doctors of Bologna.[70] The Roman Law expression *boni viri arbitratu* (by arbitration of a good man, that is, of an impartial expert) appears twice—in both cases referring to a settlement concerning a Muslim ruler.[71] The above examples also illustrate William's tendency to use the same saying several times, and a computer-aided study of his chronicle reveals many more instances of this kind.[72] Moreover, a close scrutiny brings to light a tendency to describe events of the same category in a strikingly similar way: for instance, there is a word-for-word resemblance between his accounts of the entries into Antioch of the Byzantine emperor Ioannes Komnenos in 1138, and of his son and heir Manuel in 1159.[73] Likewise, he uses the same words to describe the public humiliations, in Aleppo, of the captured prince of Antioch, Renaud of Châtillon, in 1160, and of the captured count of Tripoli, Raymond III, and other Frankish nobles, in 1164.[74]

Rigidity marks William's references to his countrymen: he calls them "our people," "Christians," "Latins" (*nostri, Christiani, Latini*)—but not *Franci* (there is just one exception: William copies the term as it appears in a charter he reproduced verbatim). He reserves the term *Franci* for people from the Kingdom of France, even though Foucher of Chartres, his source for the history of the kingdom's early decades, repeatedly refers to its ruling stratum as "Franks."[75] Now, it is understandable that the royal chancery decided to present the Frankish rulers of Jerusalem as "Latin kings," because styling such a ruler *rex Francorum* (King of the Franks) would have caused diplomatic difficulties with the Kingdom of France, whose rulers had borne that title for centuries.[76] Yet even the royal chancery used the title *rex Francorum* on at least one occasion, and outside the chancery it is attested repeatedly in charters of the chapter of the Church of the Holy Sepulcher and the Knights Hospitaller, as well as in a charter of a lord of Caesarea.[77] William, on the other hand, throughout his narration avoids the term *Franci* when referring to his fellow countrymen.

William displays his erudition by employing a Latin that aims at classical purity and by having recourse to archaic, anachronistic terms.[78] For instance, speaking of twelfth-century armies he uses the words "legion" and "cohort" 188 and 58 times, respectively. Yet there is a gap between William's intent and performance. Huygens's meticulous investigation of William's language has revealed that, while his sentences resemble classical Latin in length and complexity, he tends to resort to stereotypical formulae and recurring phrases, and to repeat—in literally hundreds of cases—the same words in close proximity to one another, sometimes in a truly awkward way.[79] In many other instances, a noun in the singular is followed by a verb in the plural; when commanders and their troops are dealt with, verbs may jump from the singular to the plural and vice versa; often the subject or object of a sentence hangs in the air, with the reader left to guess which person is being referred to.[80] And there are various types of deviation, some of them surprising, from the rules of classical Latin, as well as sundry inconsistencies in their use.[81]

A contemporary reader familiar with, say, the lucid Latin of Otto of Freising, might have found William's language stilted and flawed. Well, Otto—far from being, like William, a scion of society's "second class"—was the grandson of Emperor Henry IV, half brother of King Konrad III, and uncle of Emperor Frederick Barbarossa, and evidently saw no need to mention, in his writings, the names of the teachers under whom he studied in Paris, or even the very fact that he had studied there. In the epistle to Emperor Frederick at the beginning of his *Chronicle or History of the Two Cities*, Otto styled himself as "by the grace of God that what he is [*id quod est*] of the church of Freising"—gracefully avoiding thereby having to spell out his episcopal rank—and abstained thereafter from any reference to his ecclesiastical career.[82] Similarly, William informs his readers at the outset of the *History* that he is "by God's patience the undeserving minister of the holy church of Tyre," but sees fit to mention later his appointments as canon of Acre and archdeacon of Tyre, and even to specify the date—8 June 1175—of his consecration as archbishop of that city.[83] In the same vein, he recounts in detail his diplomatic activities.[84] It is symptomatic that William refers to Otto as bishop of Freising and brother of King Konrad, and calls him a "lettered man."[85] At the same time, none of the many chroniclers and writers active in the West deems it appropriate to even mention William's name.[86]

William reveals his classicist taste also by favoring a hypercorrect, well-nigh pedantic orthography that leans toward obsolete forms. However, when dealing with Eastern terms he resorts to an orthographic innovation, transliterating the Arabic ش (nowadays rendered as *sh*) by a doubling of the Latin letter *s*: for instance, Shiʿa appears as *Ssia*, the town Rashīd in the Nile Delta as *Ressith*.[87] Yet this minor adjustment to Eastern reality contrasts with a critical attitude toward, or a downright shunning of, Latin neologisms routinely utilized in the Frankish Kingdom. William's limited recourse to the term *casale* is a case in point. In the Kingdom of Jerusalem, *casale* meant "village." Since the term had that meaning in precrusade Norman Italy but not elsewhere in Europe, and as it makes its earliest appearance in the documentation of the Kingdom of Jerusalem in a grant of 1100/1101 by Tancred, the Norman leader from southern Italy, it stands to reason that the Jerusalemite adoption of the term *casale* in the sense of "village" was inspired by Italo-Norman usage.[88] However, the equation *casale* = village, limited as it was to Norman Italy and the Frankish East, had to be explained to readers living in other areas. Hence, Hugo Falcandus, writing in the mid-twelfth century his *History of the Kingdom of Sicily*, deemed it appropriate to explain that villages (*villae*) are called by Sicilians *casalia*.[89] Similarly William, who as chancellor of the Frankish Kingdom issued documents in which the term *casale* appeared habitually, sees fit to elucidate its meaning for his readers; yet unlike Hugo Falcandus, he does not do so by equating it with a *villa*—probably because in classical Latin *villa* normally designated a country house—but by equating it with a "suburban locality." In his account he uses the term four times, reiterating in each instance that the suburban localities in question are called *casalia*.[90] Elsewhere he avoids the term altogether and refers to villages as "suburban places" or simply as *suburbana*.[91] Only when *casale* occurs in an official document that William is transcribing does he cite it without explanation.[92] Is this consistent avoidance of the term, throughout William's own account, rooted merely in his awareness that, with the exception of Norman Italy, it was unknown in the West? No. The term *burgensis* (burgess) was very well known throughout the West. Nonetheless, William never uses it in his own account, speaking instead of members of "the second class" (*secunda classis*).[93] Only in transcribing official documents does he cite the term *burgensis*.[94] Evidently, William's avoidance of this word originates in a reluctance to use a nonclassical term.[95]

To comprehend better this reluctance, it is worthwhile to have a closer look at the expressions *vulgo* and *vulgari appellatione*. These recur frequently in William's chronicle—to be precise, forty-two and thirty-five times. On the face of it, they may be—and have been—translated as "commonly" and "commonly known."[96] But there is more to it. William presents as "vulgar" place-names that originate in Arabic, such as Arsur, Beitenuble, Bussereth, and La Boquea, or in Romance vernacular, such as Blanche Guarda and Forbelet; terms that amount to medieval Latin neologisms such as *galea* (galley), *casale* (village), *feodum* (fief), and *tallia* (tallage); or impeccable Latin appellations such as Brachium Sancti Georgii (Sea-arm of St. George), Portus Sancti Symeonis (Harbor of St. Simeon), Terra Montis Regalis (Land of Montreal), and Pons Ferri (Iron

Bridge).[97] All these have in common that they are not attested in classical Latin literature or in the Vulgate. Wherever possible, William, the linguistic purist, adduces first the classical or biblical term—which he evidently regards as the proper one—and then adds the "vulgar" counterpart. However, as a good Latinist, William surely knew that in classical Latin *vulgus* could mean "rabble," and one may indeed detect an air of condescension in many of his references to terms explained as *vulgo* or *vulgari appellatione*.[98]

This attitude occasionally breaks out into the open. For instance, William notes four times that the town of Antarados is now known, "by vulgar appellation," as Tortosa, but on the fifth occasion he discloses that, in his view, the town is now so known "by corrupt naming."[99] Similarly, while in a chapter heading he announces the construction of the castle of Alexandrium, known "by vulgar appellation" as Scandalium, in the chapter itself he explains that the place had been established by Alexander the Great during his siege of Tyre, but nowadays the common people call it, "by corrupt appellation," Scandalium; the equation of "vulgar" with "corrupt" is unmistakable. He goes on to explain that in Arabic Alexander is known as Scandar and Alexandrium as Scandarium, and that the (Frankish) *vulgares*, transforming "r" into "l," call the place Scandalium.[100] In another instance, however, he prefers an Arabic name to a wrongly used classical one: this is the capital of Egypt, called *vulgo* "Babilonia," but in the Arabic language "Macer."[101] The correction attests also to William's distance from literary Arabic, for he reproduces the city's (and country's) name in a way that closely echoes *Maṣr*, which is the local pronunciation, and not in a way close to *Miṣr*, which is how the name appears in the literary language (indeed, one may add to William's many attainments this early if inadvertent documentation of Egyptian Arabic).[102] And at one point, William brusquely reveals his contempt for his compatriots' blanket ignorance of the historical names of the country's localities. Speaking of Caesarea Philippi, he observes that the town was known also as Paneas, "but our Latins [*nostri Latini*], corrupting its name like the names of almost all towns, call it Belinas."[103] The Jerusalemite who made good at the West's finest schools and proudly displays the learning he gained there looks down condescendingly at "our Latins," his ignorant countrymen.[104]

But not only at them. William's appraisal of the learning of the Frankish patriarchs of his day is similarly condescending. He expresses this attitude by spelling out the stature of each of them as a *litteratus* (lettered)—a term that denotes not only literacy in Latin but also command of the liberal arts.[105] Aimery of Limoges, patriarch of Antioch in the years 1142–96, is disparaged as an unlettered man of disreputable conduct.[106] Each of the two patriarchs of Jerusalem, William of Messines (1130–45) and Foucher of Angoulême (1145–57), is characterized as "slightly lettered"; Patriarch Amaurry of Nesle, while "suitably lettered," is written off as exceedingly simple and almost useless; and Eraclius of Gévaudan, who studied in Bologna and in 1180 defeated William in the contest for the patriarchal throne, is mentioned without any reference to his learning.[107] Of the other contemporary prelates, Frederic the Lotharingian, William's immediate predecessor as archbishop of Tyre (1164–75) with whom he had some unspecified conflict, is described as slightly lettered and excessively warlike, while Bishop Raoul of Bethlehem, William's predecessor as chancellor of the realm, is presented as undoubtedly lettered but too worldly.[108]

Only Eudes, whom William—in his capacity as archbishop of Tyre—consecrated as bishop of Beirut, is described in unreservedly positive terms as "a respectable man and lettered master."[109] Now, William's characterizations should be taken with more than a single grain of salt: we know from other sources that Patriarch Aimery of Antioch had wide-ranging theological interests.[110] But a reader dependent only on William's *History*, awestruck by the account of his extensive studies in Paris and Bologna and impressed by the vast learning displayed in his book, must have reached the conclusion that William was head and shoulders above the Frankish patriarchs of his time, and had no peer among the other prelates of the Frankish East. Our putative reader would also have concluded that the pope who reigned at the time William was completing his chronicle did not measure up to him: Lucius III (1181–85) is described by William as "slightly lettered."[111]

Frankish prelates of former times emerge from William's *History* as more learned. Of the early patriarchs of Jerusalem, Daibert of Pisa (1099–1101) is presented as "lettered," and the same is true of Arnoul of Chocques, a foremost villain of William's chronicle, while Patriarch Étienne of Chartres (1128–30) is said to have been "suitably" instructed in the liberal arts in his youth.[112] In Antioch, Patriarch Raoul of Domfront (1135–40), whom William decries, is just "moderately lettered," while two of his victims, Arnulf and Lambert, are characterized as "lettered."[113] Among Westerners, Thierry of Chartres, the master of three of William's teachers, is described as "most lettered," the papal legate Egidius of Tusculum as "very lettered," and Antipope Guibert of Ravenna (1080–1100), Pope Gelasius II (1118–19), and Bishop Otto of

Freising as "lettered."[114] We may conclude that William considers the learning of the ecclesiastical leadership of the Frankish East in its early days as superior to that of his contemporaries. Possibly he includes the latter among "our Latins," whose ignorance he derides. However, William's criticism of his contemporaries is not limited to their lack of learnedness. Far from it. In his already mentioned appraisal of the state of the Frankish East in 1174, he denounces his countrymen as utterly lost sinners, betrayers of the Christian faith, whose monstrous practices are prone to elicit satire rather than historical narration.[115]

William's Blinding Love of the Kingdom of Jerusalem

William keenly differentiates between his contemporary countrymen and the country itself. He is deeply attached to Christendom's "new plantation," as he refers to it twice; elsewhere, he underscores his belonging to his country by referring to "our Syria," "our province, Palestine," "our Orient," and even "our Mediterranean Sea."[116] In the prologue to the chronicle, he professes to be motivated by the "most insistent love of the fatherland," "the sweetness of natal soil"—in other words, by a precocious sense of patriotism.[117] In his rendition of Urban II's Clermont Address, he has the pope describing Jerusalem as "the City of the King of All Kings," a phrase that appears on the seals of the kings of Jerusalem and, through its Christological allusion, proclaims Jerusalem's unrivalled eminence in Christendom.[118] In William's account of the First Crusade, miraculous episodes occur only at Jerusalem.[119] It is a city he repeatedly presents as *civitas* or *urbs sancta* (holy city or town).[120] At one point, William goes so far as to half-quote a text in a way that must have led uninformed readers to exaggerate Jerusalem's importance. Quoting a decision of the First Council of Nicaea of 325, William asserts that it lays down that "the bishop of Aelia [that is, Jerusalem of Roman-Byzantine times] should be honored by all, et cetera."[121] His "et cetera" conceals that the decision goes on to state that the honor due to Jerusalem's bishop must not diminish the rights (or dignity) he owes to his Metropolitan—who evidently outranks him. Here it is again worthwhile to compare William with Otto of Freising. Otto quotes *both* parts of the decision and discusses whether the phrase "without violating the Metropolitan's rights" refers to the rights of the archbishop of Caesarea—the metropolis of Palestine in Roman and Byzantine times—or whether it maintains that the bishop of Jerusalem should be honored as a Metropolitan, but not as highly as the pope. One way or another, Otto concludes that it is evident that, at the time of the Council of Nicaea in 325, Jerusalem had not yet attained patriarchal status.[122] (It was granted only at the Council of Chalcedon in 451.)[123] Otto's dispassionate discussion is a far cry from William's "et cetera" twisting.[124]

William evidently intends to portray his beloved fatherland as an essentially Latin entity, hence worthy of continued Western support.[125] This was probably the reason for his choice to take no notice of matters his Western readers would have considered outlandish, or aberrant—such as the celebration of the divine office by schismatics and heretics in the Church of the Holy Resurrection; the prayer of Muslims near the Lord's Temple; or the toleration of the Samaritan cultic center. For the same reason William may have played down instances of cooperation or conjoint action between the kingdom's Latin and non-Latin Christians. His decision to ignore Abū al-Khayr, the Eastern Christian instructor in horsemanship of the future King Baldwin IV, is a case in point. Yet it is not the only one, as a comparison between some of William's statements and those of Foucher of Chartres, his main source for the early decades of the kingdom, demonstrates. Describing the funeral of Baldwin I in 1118, Foucher relates that the king's coffin reached the Valley of Josaphat on Palm Sunday, even as the customary procession carrying palm branches descended there from the Mount of Olives, and when the people saw the coffin, "the Franks wept aloud, the Syrians lamented, and so did the Saracens who saw it." William follows Foucher in reporting that the king's body reached Jerusalem through the Valley of Josaphat while people converged there to celebrate Palm Sunday, but he chooses to omit the statement about the mourning Franks, Syrians, and Saracens.[126]

Similarly, while Foucher relates that when the Franks and Egyptians fought a battle near Ibelin in 1123, those who remained in Jerusalem—Latins, Greeks, and Syrians alike—prayed, bestowed alms, and went barefoot in processions to all the city's churches, William, who relies on Foucher for his description of the battle, does not mention these processions at all.[127] And when a year later, while the Frankish army and the Venetian fleet were besieging Tyre, the Fatimid Ascalonites attacked Jerusalem, "our Franks and the Syrians came forth and boldly opposed them." This is what Foucher relates. But William, who closely follows Foucher's account of the Ascalonite attack and its repulse, ascribes the successful resistance to Jerusalem's citizens, who, "though few in number but glowing with faith, afire with the most righteous zeal for their fatherland, children, and wives, snatched up their arms and came out of the city, rushing against the enemy as of one mind."[128]

A typically Williamesque scene, richly embroidering Foucher's terse statement—yet Foucher's Syrians vanish into thin air.

While one may interpret William's depiction of these scenes as deriving from a wish to exclude the non-Frankish subjects of the kingdom from his narrative, an alternative explanation should also be considered. Julian Yolles has shown that in the early part of his chronicle William refers both to the Christians of pre-1099 Jerusalem and to the First Crusaders as the "People of God" (*populus Dei, plebs Dei*); he goes on to hypothesize that after the crusader conquest, these two peoples of God coalesced into one.[129] If so, William may have chosen to present to his Western readers, say, the defenders of Jerusalem in 1124, as "citizens" of a unified People of God rather than as "Franks and Syrians." The omission of Foucher's references to the Syrians would be motivated accordingly by a wish to include them in the new, divinely elected entity.[130]

Yet while it is unclear whether William aimed in the above instances at exclusion or inclusion, his unmistakably negative opinion about the Syrians comes occasionally into view. Thus, relating that the Muslims conquered in 1182 the rock-fortress of Ḥabīs Jaldak beyond the Jordan, William quotes a report according to which the stronghold was betrayed by its commanders, "Syrians, who are considered by us effeminate and weak."[131]

William is also apt to censor and leave out condemnatory statements about the first generation of the kingdom's Frankish population. A comparison of the earliest legislation of the kingdom promulgated in 1120 at the Council of Nablus, with William's rendition of it, exposes this tendency. The introduction to the twenty-five canons approved by that council states that they aim at the admonishment of the fallen people that seeks to attain all declivities of pleasure, and at imposing some bridles of righteousness on the sins of this tottering populace. None of these harsh expressions reappears in William's rendering: he mentions merely the people's sins, errors, and excesses. The original introduction concludes with the names of the sixteen leading ecclesiastical and lay personages who attended the council, and William reproduces these names conscientiously one by one. But surprisingly, he does not copy the twenty-five canons decreed at the council, explaining that there is no need to do so as they are easily accessible in the archives of many of the kingdom's churches.[132] This is a weak explanation, because the introduction to the canons and the list of participants were equally available there, yet William chose to summarize the first and copy the second. Moreover, elsewhere in his *History*, William sees fit to present the full text of a much more recent and therefore still more easily accessible document—namely, the decree of 1183 that imposed a general tax on the kingdom.[133] Possibly he included the decree because its character is basically Western, modeled on the English and French 1166 taxes for the relief of the Kingdom of Jerusalem, and because it assigns to him, as archbishop of Tyre, and to his rival, the patriarch Eraclius, identical roles in the collection of this tax.[134]

A scrutiny of the twenty-five canons allows for a more satisfactory explanation. Four of them deal with homosexuality, four others with sexual relations between Christians and Muslims, three with bigamy, one with a cleric's intercourse with a Frankish woman—in other words, their inclusion in the *History* could have raised, among Western readers, disturbing questions about the early Frankish settlers' morals, which might have invalidated William's claim that the ethical stature of that first generation was vastly superior to that of his own contemporaries.

It is quite clear that William wished to persuade his readers that the kingdom was part and parcel of the Latin world. Yet his temperament undermined, at least to some extent, his intent: he shot himself in the foot by condescendingly referring to the ignorance of "our Latins."

Chapter 7

King Amaurry of Jerusalem, a Twelfth-Century Renaissance Ruler

Twenty-seven years old at his coronation in 1163, thirty-eight at his death in 1174, King Amaurry of Jerusalem was a remarkably active ruler. He led his army into Egypt on five occasions, succeeded once in installing a Frankish commissioner and Frankish guards in Cairo, waged five campaigns elsewhere, established an alliance with Byzantium and paid a state visit to Constantinople, and in the Kingdom of Jerusalem, introduced several crucial pieces of legislation and curtailed the privileges of the Genoese and the Pisans. At one point he is said to have contemplated a radical transformation of the kingdom by expelling all Muslim peasants and replacing them with Armenians. His Muslim enemies considered him the greatest of the Frankish kings, in courage as well as in cunning.[1]

His cultural interests single him out as a hitherto neglected ruler-figure of the Twelfth-Century Renaissance: more multifaceted than his half nephew Henry II of England, he rather resembles his older contemporary, King Roger II of Sicily (1095–1154). In any case, his interests provide further evidence that Frankish Jerusalem was not the intellectual backwater decried by leading modern historians.

William of Tyre was King Amaurry's protégé. In his chronicle, William described in considerable—and quite astounding—detail the discords in the king's physique and comportment. Of medium stature, with glittering eyes and aquiline nose standing out in a comely, bearded face, Amaurry was excessively fat, with breasts drooping to his waist in womanly fashion, yet otherwise his limbs were notable for their good looks; despite his corpulence, he was not bothered much by cold and heat. A taciturn man who—stricken with a slight impediment of speech—shunned conviviality, he could also erupt in convulsive laughter. He used to hear Mass every day; a *vir evangelicus* (committed to the message of the Gospels) in this respect, he ordered tithes be provided to the church without reservation; yet he vehemently assailed the liberty of the kingdom's churches, draining their patrimonies by frequent exactions. Likewise, he made frequent inroads into his subjects' wealth. Moderate in eating and drinking, and utterly abstaining from wine, "he suffered ungovernably, it was said, from the lewdness of the flesh and—may the Lord pardon him with forbearance—was said to encroach upon the marriages of others." William does not mention that Amaurry strove to curb such encroachments when perpetrated by his subjects: one of his assizes laid down that a husband who finds in his house "another man lying on his wife" may kill both of them.[2] *Quod licet regi, non licet gregi* (What is permissible for the king, is not permissible for the crowd).

As for Amaurry's mental caliber, William draws a far brighter picture. He asserts that the king's modest Latin learning was more than offset by his intellect and memory, and stresses his exceptional knowledge of customary law and interest in history. Immersed in serious matters, he wasted no time on entertainers or games of chance, yet delighted in watching hawks in their chase. His predilection for conversing with people familiar with foreign countries, his frequent interrogations, his delight at the solutions proffered to his queries, all point to an uncommon curiosity.[3] During his visit to Constantinople in 1171 he constantly questioned his guides about the purpose and origin of the many churches, monasteries, columns, trophies, and triumphal arches he was shown. Later he sailed to the Black Sea to see for himself the spot where the Bosphorus starts and "made the circuit of unknown places," so writes William, "like an inquisitive man in search of causes."[4]

But Amaurry was not only inquisitive; he also tended to rely on his own judgment in areas that more conventional spirits considered the domain of learned clerics. This unorthodox trait is revealed in a remark by William that the modestly learned Raymond III of Tripoli endeavored, *like King Amaurry*, his cousin, to grasp the meaning of the scriptures "through the liveliness of his innate mind"—that is, by personal reaction to the sacred text rather than by subscribing to an authoritative interpretation.[5] William does not reveal whether so nonconformist an approach was limited to the two cousins. Neither does he spell out to what extent was exceptional their contemporary, Gui of Scandalium, whom he characterizes as "most experienced in warfare, but of little faith and utterly not knowing God."[6] Hence one should not rule out the possibility that more members of the knightly class held views apt to perturb a mainstream cleric.

King Amaurry's Query about the Resurrection of the Flesh

Once, when Amaurry had fallen ill in the citadel of Tyre, he summoned William—archdeacon of that town since 1167—to discuss several questions. Unfortunately, William chose to record in detail only one of the questions the king raised. Yet a telling question it is, suggestive of Amaurry's unconventional interests and, quite probably, of the impact some unorthodox notions made on him.

In a lucid interval between bouts of fever, the king asked whether it was possible to devise—apart from Christ's teaching that he, Amaurry, did not doubt—a reasoning that would prove the resurrection by compelling arguments. The subsequent exchange between the two men clarifies that Amaurry had in mind the resurrection of the flesh, the *carnis resurrectionem* of the Christian credo.[7] William relates that he was perturbed by the novelty and strangeness of the query, inasmuch as it implied that this orthodox king born of orthodox parents might harbor doubts with regard to a basic article of faith that ought not be discussed.[8] William's agitation may well betray the influence of Petrus Lombardus, the foremost Latin theologian of the age, under whom he had studied in Paris. For Petrus, almost literally quoting Augustine, laid down in his *Book of Sentences* that a Christian must in no way doubt the future resurrection of all flesh.[9] Western consensus on this issue must have been broad indeed, for even Abelard, that maverick philosopher and theologian who infuriated conformist contemporaries on so many counts, is not known to have questioned the resurrection of the body: the closest he came to this issue was to ask whether those who had risen from the dead at the time of Christ's resurrection did then die again—a relatively harmless question.[10] Only heretics—specifically, the Cathars—denied bodily resurrection or, like the Amauricians in the early thirteenth century, were accused of such a denial.[11] A few twelfth-century authors endeavored on occasion to spiritualize the resurrected body, but they contradicted themselves by perceiving it elsewhere in their writings in a patently material manner, and at any rate their spiritualizing tendency did not become the focus of a major debate.[12] It is understandable, therefore, that to William of Tyre, the king's question sounded startlingly, perhaps even dangerously, odd.

However, had William studied in the schools of Cairo or Damascus rather than in those of Paris and Bologna, he would hardly have been surprised. For he would have learned there that, in the realm of Islam, bodily resurrection and the possibility of denying it by rational, philosophic reasoning had long been an issue. Already in the tenth century, discussion of the resurrection had been presented as of utmost importance by the Brethren of Purity (Ikhwān al-ṣafāʾ), a secret confraternity based in Baṣra that compiled a philosophical and religious encyclopedia consisting of fifty-two epistles; this encyclopedia is a basic Ismāʿīlī text that also had a considerable influence on many orthodox Muslim philosophers. Now, in the thirty-seventh epistle, the Brethren taught that women and street boys, the ignorant and the masses, regard man as being mere flesh and bones, and the resurrection as being the reconstitution of the decayed body, followed by recompense for its erstwhile deeds, good and bad; the more knowledgeable believe the body to be associated with a nobler substance—that is, with the spirit or the soul—and that at the resurrection this soul or spirit returns to the original body or to a surrogate one, whereupon both are recompensed for their deeds; and finally, that men possessing the highest intellectual capacities look upon this-worldly life with disdain and therefore consider the resurrection to be the separation of the soul from the body, so that it might lead an independent existence.[13] This cautious formulation does not obscure the Brethren's conviction that resurrection, in reality, amounts not to a reunification of the soul with the body, but to the soul's detachment from it.

Other Muslim thinkers were more outspoken. Abū Yaʿqūb al-Sijistānī, a prominent Ismāʿīlī of the mid-tenth century, categorically denied the resurrection of the body. At death, he declared, the body dissolves, and the soul starts a separate, spiritual existence; at the end of time, God will resurrect the souls, not the bodies. Al-Sijistānī understood the Qur'anic descriptions of paradise's corporeal delights and hell's corporeal punishments as intended for simple folk who experience merely sensual pleasure or pain, whereas the People of Truth, of whom he was one, know better. Paradise is spiritual, and only the soul—a spiritual substance—is able to attain its true reward: rational knowledge, which the soul obtains in paradise in proportion to the knowledge it acquired during its lifetime.[14]

Ibn Sīnā (980–1037), the philosopher-physician-statesman who came to be known in the Latin West as Avicenna, dealt on a number of occasions with life in the hereafter and with resurrection, without transgressing the boundaries of Islamic orthodoxy. But he also put forward views that recall those of al-Sijistānī. In his daring *Epistle on the Return*, probably written in 1014/15, he unequivocally denied the resurrection of the body, arguing inter alia that the quantity of matter available in this world would not suffice for the reconstitution of the bodies of all the people who had died, and that the soul cannot return to its original body at the resurrection, since that body had turned first into dust and then into nourishment for subsequent human bodies. Only the souls, Ibn Sīnā maintained, will be resurrected, with the perfect among them attaining absolute bliss, contemplating the essence of the Supreme Ruler. Presumably, they will experience the corporeal Qur'anic hereafter, with its fire and gardens, merely through their imagination.[15]

This denial of bodily resurrection was emphatically denounced by the theologian and mystic al-Ghazālī (1058–1111), known in the Latin West as Algazel, who sojourned in Jerusalem in the summer of 1096, visiting the Dome of the Rock every day, and who wrote for the city's ordinary people his *Letter for Jerusalem*.[16] In his *Incoherence of the Philosophers*, written around 1095, he first fairly recapitulated and clarified many of the arguments Ibn Sīnā had made in the *Epistle on the Return*, then set out to refute them. Ibn Sīnā's assertion that the available, finite matter will not suffice to reproduce bodies for all souls is—he claimed—based on the false and un-Islamic assumption that the world is eternal and the number of souls infinite; besides, even if the number of souls were to exceed the number of bodies reproducible from available matter, God could create new matter so as to allow the bodily resurrection of all. As for the impossibility of the soul returning to its original body, al-Ghazālī explained that since it is the soul, not the body, that really distinguishes an individual, it is possible to effect resurrection "by returning [the soul] to the body, whatever body this might be, whether [composed] of the matter of the first body [or from that] of another, or from matter whose creation commences anew." In other words, it is not important whether the resurrected body will be identical with the original one. In sum, al-Ghazālī maintained that he who denies bodily resurrection and repudiates the explicit Qur'anic announcements of a corporeal hereafter is guilty of flagrant blasphemy.[17]

The issue was not laid to rest with this clear-cut condemnation. Ibn Rushd (1126–98), the theologian and philosopher of the Islamic

West who came to be known in Latin Europe as Averroes, expressed, in different works, diverse views on bodily resurrection. In his *Incoherence of the Incoherence*, written between 1174 and 1180, he pointed out that al-Ghazālī wavered, from one book to another, on the question whether the belief in a purely spiritual resurrection was heretical or not. Ibn Rushd himself maintained that the original, earthly bodies will not be resurrected but only their simulacra, and asserted that the belief "that the bodies which arise are identical with those that perished cannot be true."[18]

In the Muslim East, the spiritualization of the resurrection was actualized by the Assassins, the radical Ismāʿīlī sect whose strongholds were in northern Persia and western Syria. Ḥasan II, Grand Master of the Assassins, solemnly announced to his Persian followers on 17 Ramadan 559 / 8 August 1164 that the *sharīʿa* (Islamic law) was abrogated and that they were "brought to the Resurrection." This resurrection, as well as paradise and hell, were perceived as purely spiritual. It was the state in which "men shall come to God and the mysteries and truths of all Creation be revealed, and acts of obedience abolished"; evidently Ḥasan's followers were supposed to have attained that state while still living. Ḥasan invited them to break the Ramadan fast then and there, and ritually violate the abrogated law by the enjoyment of diverse pleasures. Henceforth the seventeenth day of Ramadan became the Festival of the Resurrection and Ḥasan, the Lord of the Resurrection.[19] Shortly thereafter Rashīd al-Dīn Sinān, the Master of the Syrian Assassins—known among the Franks as the Old Man of the Mountain—proclaimed the new era in Syria. The subsequent antinomian practices of his followers—such as drinking wine, eating pork, and practicing incest—were noted with scorn by Muslim and Latin authors.[20]

Ṣalāḥ al-Dīn, the champion of Muslim orthodoxy—who in 1169 emerged victorious from the struggle with King Amaurry for the control of Egypt and in the mid-1170s survived two Assassin attempts to murder him—"believed in the resurrection of the body and that the righteous would be rewarded with Paradise and the evil-doers with Hellfire." So wrote Bahāʾ al-Dīn, the *qāḍī* of Ṣalāḥ al-Dīn's army and his biographer. He went on to relate that Ṣalāḥ al-Dīn detested philosophers and other adversaries of Islamic orthodoxy, and ordered his son, the ruler of Aleppo, to execute "a young man called Suhrawardī" who had been accused of heresy.[21] This man, Shihāb al-Dīn Yaḥyā al-Suhrawardī (1154–91), one of the most original philosophers of medieval Islam, endeavored to design a new scientific system; however, unlike Ibn Sīnā, al-

Ghazālī, and Ibn Rushd, he came to be known in the West only in modern times. He was thirty-seven years old when Ṣalāḥ al-Dīn had him put to death in Aleppo on 29 July 1191, just two weeks after the Third Crusaders reconquered Acre. This major philosopher, commonly known as "the Master of Illumination," wrote in about 1186, in a discussion of Qur'anic verses concerning the resurrection, that the verse "Now have ye come unto Us solitary" (6:95) means: "Your immaterial souls, such as they are in themselves, will accomplish their Return all alone, separated from the organs of the physical body; as it is said in another [Qur'anic] verse: 'And each one of them will come unto Him on the Day of Resurrection, alone' (19:95). This 'aloneness' refers to the monadic essence, the soul, which is the only one to possess consciousness and knowledge."[22] In short, the soul will be resurrected, not the body.

The issue of bodily resurrection came to be discussed also among Jews. And with much vehemence. Maimonides (1138–1204), the greatest Jewish thinker of the age, who at one point declined to become King Amaurry's physician, dealt with the issue at some length in his Hebrew-written *Code*, on which he was working even as Amaurry asked his disturbing question.[23] Maimonides asserted there that in the World to Come there will be no corporeal bodies, and the bodiless souls of the righteous will bask in the radiance of the Divine Presence like the ministering angels. He went on to clarify that this soul, not in need of a body, would amount to the "soul's form," which is the knowledge that the Creator allowed it to acquire.[24] The similarity to the views of al-Sijistānī, Ibn Sīnā, and Suhrawardī is striking, with Maimonides lashing out at people who, like "the foolish, ignorant Arabs, immersed in lechery," imagine a hereafter in which one eats and drinks well, copulates with beautiful forms, wears choice garments, and so forth.[25]

This negation of bodily existence in the world to come triggered an uproar among Jews, from Yemen to Baghdad, and the head of the Babylonian Academy (*yeshīva*) in Baghdad, Shmuel ben ʿEli, composed a treatise attacking Maimonides's views on the resurrection.[26] Yosef ibn Shimʿon, Maimonides's favorite disciple, wrote in response a *Silencing Epistle Concerning the Resurrection of the Dead*.[27] He explains at considerable length that the resurrection of decayed bodies, although not called for on rational grounds, must be believed since it is foretold in holy scripture. All biblical passages dealing with bodily resurrection refer, however, to the *Messianic age*. On the other hand, a perusal of the Bible reveals that none of the passages dealing with reward and punishment in the *world to come* mentions the resurrection of the body, and a Talmudic passage indicates that none of the physical activities necessary for the body's existence will take place in the world to come. Yosef therefore concludes by squarely denying the return of the soul to the body in the world to come.[28]

In 1191 Maimonides decided to join the fray and defend his position by writing his *Treatise on the Resurrection*. ʿAbd al-Laṭīf al-Baghdādī (1162–1231), who met Maimonides in Egypt, was impressed by his great learning, but opined that he was "overcome with the adulation of authority and service to those who occupied important positions."[29] It is conceivable that he worried lest his foes denounce him before the orthodox Ṣalāḥ al-Dīn—even as he was writing, Suhrawardī was languishing in Aleppo's prison. At any rate, in his Arabic-written *Treatise*, Maimonides presents a clear-cut two-stage scenario that goes beyond the vague notions of Yosef ibn Shimʿon. First, he envisages a physical resurrection: the revived individuals whose souls have returned to their bodies will eat, drink, copulate, and procreate—but ultimately will die again after enjoying the long life characteristic of the Messianic era. Second, he envisages a world to come in which life will not be followed by death; but this everlasting existence will be that of bodiless, angel-like souls.[30] Consequently, by positing a resurrection followed by death, Maimonides disconnects resurrection and immortality and attributes the latter to the soul alone.[31] The two-stage scenario, which may be regarded as an attempt to harmonize Maimonides's earlier affirmation of a spiritual existence in the world to come with scriptural references to the resurrection of the dead, has some antecedents and parallels in Jewish and Islamic thought.[32] Yet Maimonides's argumentation did not put an end to the controversy. It continued to agitate Jewry for many decades.[33]

The issue of bodily resurrection was also discussed in contemporary Byzantium by Michael Glykas Sikidites (ca. 1130–ca. 1200), a secretary at the court of Emperor Manuel and versatile author.[34] In his *Theological Chapters on the Problems of the Holy Scripture*, he rejected the view that the resurrected body will be identical with the flesh that perished, contending that it would constitute a superior, spiritualized version of it. Resurrected human beings will not need food, drink, or clothes, nor be prone to decay; they will not exhibit age or gender differentiation; and yet they will be able to recognize each other. In short, the resurrected bodies will resemble the body of Adam before the Fall.[35] In sum, whether among Muslims, Jews, or Byzantine Christians, some prominent thinkers denied the resurrection of the flesh.

Let us return now to the ailing King Amaurry and his protégé William, conversing in Tyre's citadel. We have seen that William claimed to have been perturbed by the king's request for nonscriptural proofs for the future resurrection of the flesh. We have seen also that William's perturbation is understandable, as the king's request would have alarmed William's foremost teacher in theology, Petrus Lombardus, and indeed any conventionally trained Westerner of his age. On the other hand, our cursory excursion into the realms of Islamic, Jewish, and Byzantine thinking indicates that King Amaurry's request would not have surprised a learned Easterner familiar with some facet of the stormy discussions about the resurrection of the flesh.

Is it possible that Amaurry had become aware of some such facet?[36] We know that he first came to Egypt as the Fatimid caliph's ally; that he was known to have been on friendly terms with an Egyptian emir; that sometime between 1165 and 1168 he asked the Egyptians for a physician, whereupon they sent him an Eastern Christian famous for his knowledge of medicine and astrology, Abū Sulaymān Dāwūd, a native of Jerusalem.[37] Amaurry visited Constantinople in 1171, and the relationship between the courts of Byzantium and Jerusalem was close during his reign. About two years later Rashīd al-Dīn Sinān, Master of the Syrian Assassins, sent an envoy to Amaurry. William, who reports at some length on this mission, mentions that Sinān "abrogated *Mahumet*'s precepts, released his followers from fasts, and allowed them to consume wine and pork."[38] Hence, William—and most probably Amaurry, too—had at least an inkling of the religious revolution the Assassins had experienced a few years earlier, with the onset of their spiritual resurrection.

It is plausible, therefore, to assume that Amaurry got wind of some of the arguments against bodily resurrection then reverberating, primarily in the realm of Islam.[39] Indeed, when the greatly distressed William attempted to answer the king's question by insisting that the teachings of Christ and his apostles are unequivocal on the resurrection of the flesh, and went on to paraphrase a sentence from the Blessing of the Baptismal Water in the Easter Vigil and two verses from Matthew 25—all announcing the Last Judgment—the king reassured him that he did steadfastly believe in all these tenets, but that he was asking for a reasoning that would prove the future resurrection and the existence of another life after the present one to someone who does not recognize these tenets as true and does not accept Christ's doctrine. In other words, William was required to provide a rational, nonscriptural proof capable of convincing someone who was neither a

Christian nor a believer in bodily resurrection and yet was susceptible to rational argument. It stands to reason that Amaurry had in mind some Muslim who adhered to views such as those outlined above. Indeed, the Old French adapter of William's chronicle, who often displayed a keen understanding of William's intentions, designated those whom Amaurry sought to convince of bodily resurrection as *genz mescréanz* (disbelieving people)—the term the adapter habitually used to denote Muslims.[40]

Having failed to satisfy the king by restating the tenets of Christianity, William decided to resort to an argument capable of persuading all believers in divine justice, whether Christian or not, and to apply the skills in disputation he had acquired during his studies in the West. He proposed to Amaurry that the two of them engage in a debate, with the king assuming the role of the person who denies the resurrection. We may imagine Amaurry, his eyes glittering with fever and anticipation, embarking with relish upon this verbal tournament. It went—or so William relates—as follows:

WILLIAM: Do you admit that God is just?

AMAURRY: I admit nothing as more true.

WILLIAM: It is the quality of the just to repay good with good and bad with bad.

AMAURRY: That is so.

WILLIAM: Now, in the present life this does not happen, because some good people suffer in this world nothing but troubles and misfortunes, while some bad ones rejoice in continuous success, as we are taught by examples encountered every day.

AMAURRY: For sure.

WILLIAM: Therefore, it will come about in another life, for it cannot be that God is not a just rewarder. Therefore, there will be another life and the resurrection of this flesh: in that [flesh] in which anybody merited good or bad, he ought to receive his reward and be recompensed.

AMAURRY: I like this immensely; you have removed all doubt from my heart.[41]

Amaurry's last sentence marks William's triumph: he has won the case, resurrection has been proven; though one may wonder whether the king was really won over, or—as Susan Reynolds (d. 2021) cunningly remarked—whether his protégé saw fit to present himself as having discarded so improper a doubt.[42]

Yet William's own belief in bodily resurrection may have been less robust than his account of the conversation in Tyre's citadel suggests. Writing several years later about the crusader conquest of Jerusalem in July 1099, William asserted that Bishop Adhémar of Le Puy—Urban II's legate who died in Antioch a year previously—was seen by many crusaders as the first to ascend Jerusalem's wall; also, many of the men who fell during the march to Jerusalem appeared later to the victorious crusaders, joining them on the visit to the holy places.[43] Since William presents all these dead crusaders as resurrected in the spirit ("in spiritu"), and as extending momentous proof of the future resurrection ("magnum nobis future resurrectionis argumentum pretendentes"), one may infer that, in his view at that juncture, the future resurrection was not to be corporeal.

Let us return to the argument William set forth in his conversation with Amaurry. Did he devise it on the spot, as he insinuates? To what extent was it original?

William's reasoning amounts basically to a variant of what one may call the retribution argument in support of the resurrection of the flesh. This argument consists of two interrelated parts. According to Part One, God's just retribution for the deeds and misdeeds of mortals, unrewarded/unpunished during their earthly existence, necessitates their future resurrection. According to Part Two, since deeds and misdeeds were committed by the soul as well as by the flesh, both soul and flesh must be present at the Last Judgment. Earlier Latin writers do not appear to have favored, or even known of, this argument in its entirety, though they noted or espoused ideas congruent with it. Early in the third century, Tertullian mentions the view that the flesh must be resurrected before the Judgment because the soul alone is incapable of feeling torment or repose; he brands this opinion as vulgar. Tertullian regards the soul as capable of perception and suffering, yet asserts that since soul and flesh act together, both must be present at the Judgment—a variant of Part Two of the retribution argument.[44] Anselm of Canterbury (1033–1109) argues in his *Monologion* that justice requires eternal reward and punishment for the *soul*'s deeds; later, in *Cur Deus Homo* (Why God Became Man), he maintains that eternal remuneration will affect soul and body alike.[45] Hugo of St.-Victor (d. 1141) comes close to Part One of the retribution argument when he asserts that in this world the just appear to suffer the punishments of the wicked and the wicked to receive the rewards of the just, while in an occult way they receive their just recompense; at the Judgment, on the other hand, each will manifestly receive his due.[46] And Alain of Lille (ca. 1130–1203), polemicizing against the Cathar heretics, endeavors to prove the resurrection of the *flesh* by the necessity to punish eternally the very flesh through which the soul has sinned—a reasoning that resembles Part Two of the argument; his claim that the merits of the Bible's saints would be worthless if they did not entail rewards after their death recalls Part One. Alain's polemics have been dated to 1185–1200, which would preclude their use by William; but an earlier version might have existed.[47] None of the above reasonings is identical with the one presented by William; yet they attest to the existence of a broad nonscriptural discourse that linked retribution and resurrection, a discourse upon which he might have fallen back when Amaurry pressed him for an answer.

However, since long before William's time there had been in existence a body of Christian literature that contained almost exactly the same argument William was to employ. This was the literature of Eastern Christendom. Already at the end of the second century, Athenagoras, the early apologist from Athens, argued in his *Concerning the Resurrection of the Dead* that a just judgment requires that both soul and body be recompensed for deeds they committed together. Since such judgment occurs neither in earthly life, in which many wicked go unpunished and many virtuous suffer, nor after death, when the soul is separated from the body, it follows that soul and body must reunite at the resurrection and receive their just remuneration. For Athenagoras, however, this was merely a secondary argument in favor of bodily resurrection; he derived the primary one from the premise that each human being is permanent.[48]

It was Joannes the Damascene (ca. 650–ca. 750), the towering theologian of Eastern Christendom, who evolved the retribution argument in its full form, placing it at the very beginning of his discussion of the resurrection. Here the similarity to William of Tyre's argument, in both content and sequence, is striking. Very many of the just, wrote Joannes in his *On the Orthodox Faith*, suffer in this life, even as many sinners indulge in riches, and this cannot be their just judgment. There must therefore be a resurrection, for God is just and will repay his followers. And since the soul does neither good nor evil without the body, both must be rewarded or punished.[49] It is noteworthy that, about two centuries later, the Muslim Brethren of Purity ascribed a similar view to those whom they presented as more knowledgeable.[50]

As Joannes's *On the Orthodox Faith* was translated into Old Slavonic in about 900, into Arabic in the tenth century, and into Georgian first in the eleventh century and again in the early twelfth, one may assume that his retribution argument reached a considerable audience in the Christian East. Probably in the eleventh century, the monk Būlus (Paul) of Antioch, Greek Orthodox bishop of Sidon, restated it, in Arabic, at some length.[51] In the thirteenth century the argument would recur in the works of two Jacobite writers, Jacob of Bartella (d. 1241) and Bar-Hebraeus (1226–86).[52] But the argument was to have a considerable impact also on the West after Burgundio of Pisa translated Joannes's *On the Orthodox Faith* into Latin in 1153–54.[53] Commenting on Petrus Lombardus's discussion of the resurrection, Albertus Magnus (ca. 1200–1280) quotes verbatim the retribution argument as translated by Burgundio and explicitly ascribes it to "the Damascene." Thomas Aquinas in his *Summa against the Gentiles* briefly recapitulates the argument without mentioning his source; so does Ramón Llull, repeatedly.[54]

In Rome, presumably in the mid-1150s, Petrus Lombardus read at least a part of Burgundio's translation.[55] Could it be that his pupil, William of Tyre, read it too?[56] A comparison of Burgundio's translation with William's account of the disputation reveals no literal correspondence, but this is not conclusive.[57] Yet there is a weightier reason that militates against the possibility that William knew and used the Latin translation. For had he done so, it would follow that, while knowing perfectly well that an authoritative theologian had devised a cogent solution to the issue at hand, he nevertheless chose to present it as one he invented on the spot, vaunting a false resourcefulness. Moreover, if this were indeed the case, he had to take into consideration that some of the Western readers at whom he aimed did read Burgundio's translation and therefore would easily see through his deception. Hence it is likely that William devised the argument without relying on Burgundio's translation.

He may have invented—or unwittingly reinvented—it on his own. For it is noticeable that William's position in the discussion is consistent throughout. Initially, he attempts to answer Amaurry's question by paraphrasing a sentence from the Easter liturgy and two verses from the Gospels, all of which announce the punishments and rewards that will come to pass at the Last Judgment. The choice of these texts (and not, for instance, Paul's insistence on the centrality of the resurrection in Christian belief in 1 Corinthians 15) indicates that in William's mind resurrection primarily connoted just punishment and reward. When the paraphrase of these texts failed to satisfy the king, William continued to cling to the same idea, reformulating it, however, in nonscriptural terms. This internal consistency renders it conceivable that, even as the king was prodding him to proffer an answer he had not earlier contemplated, William hit upon the idea of presenting his original contention in a new, not specifically Christian garb.

Still, the similarity to Joannes the Damascene's argument is so close that one may assume a dependence of sorts. For instance, Joannes' retribution argument might have come up in a conversation William had with Eastern Christians in the Frankish Kingdom or in Constantinople, and when Amaurry insisted on a nonscriptural reasoning, it came back to his mind. He might not even have been aware who originally formulated it or on what occasion it came to his attention. In sum, we may assume that both the question of the Frankish king and the answer of the Frankish archdeacon, aired in a chamber of Tyre's citadel, ultimately originated in contacts with Easterners.[58]

A number of conclusions may be drawn from this body of evidence. First, dealing with an area of potential cultural interaction—such as the Frankish Kingdom of Jerusalem—we should more readily be willing to examine the possibility of an external influence. Second, considering some facet of one of the three religions nowadays relabeled as "Abrahamic," it may be worthwhile becoming acquainted with the form this facet assumes in the other two.[59] Doing so may require some effort on our part—and the boldness (or impudence) to rely, primarily or entirely, on secondary literature. But the investment is worthwhile, as it allows us to perceive basic similarities and differences, and to trace the facet in question on a broader canvas. In the present case we become aware that in the central Middle Ages, denial of bodily resurrection was considered a heterodoxy by all three monotheistic religions—but that there were significant differences between them. In Islam, some Shiʿis and a leading Sunni philosopher, Ibn Sīnā, espoused at one point this denial. In Judaism, no less a man than Maimonides offered a complex scenario that denied bodily resurrection in the world to come. In Western Christendom, on the other hand, a denial was definitely out of bounds. Additionally, our probe highlights that in medieval Islam and Judaism, but not in Western Christendom, denial of bodily resurrection was a major, hotly contested issue. It is also noteworthy that while studies on bodily resurrection in the various religious traditions abound, only a handful have employed a comparative approach.[60]

Some rudimentary guidelines then emerge for regarding an idea appearing in one tradition as being related to the same, or a similar, idea in another. Some relationships are clearly documented and can be taken for facts. Albertus Magnus, for example, quotes almost literally the Latin translation of Joannes the Damascene's retribution argument. Similarly,

Ibn Sīnā notes the Christian argument that the reason for bodily resurrection is the partnership of body and soul in actions both virtuous and wicked—in other words, he was aware of a Christian endorsement of Part Two of the retribution argument.[61] Again, a relationship may be assumed when, beyond a marked similarity in the content of views espoused by two thinkers, there are some unambiguous indications that one thinker was aware of the other's works. But what about a case where there is a similarity between the arguments of two thinkers yet no evidence for one knowing about the other? I propose that in such cases we should focus on (a) the extent of the similarity between the arguments and (b) the extent of intellectual interaction between the communities to which the two thinkers belonged.[62] In the present case, the similarity in structure of the quite complex retribution arguments employed by Joannes the Damascene and William of Tyre is striking, and there is considerable evidence, as we have seen, for Eastern Christian influence on the Frankish clergy of the Kingdom of Jerusalem. Both lines of reasoning, then, suggest that the two arguments were related.

In any case, Amaurry's query attests to an inquisitive, ingenious mind, open to unorthodox explanations. Yet there may have been also a more ordinary side to him; at least he was portrayed as possessing such. In 1167, during his third Egyptian campaign, when the Frankish army reached the Mountain of the Palm of the Hand (Jabal al-Kaff, about 125 miles south of Cairo), one of the places purportedly visited by the Holy Family during the Flight to Egypt, Amaurry allowed or encouraged his men to cut out and take to Jerusalem the piece of rock that was impressed with the mark of Christ's hand when he grasped the mountain that bowed to him in adoration and restored it to its original position.[63] And when near Daljā, about forty miles to the south of the now palmless mountain, Amaurry went to sleep on the eve of a battle against Shīrkūh—his rival for the mastery of Egypt—the long-dead Bernard of Clairvaux appeared in his dream, according to an account written at Clairvaux in about 1170. The account, based on information from Jerusalem—it calls Shīrkūh *Sarracon* and proffers many details about the battle—casts Amaurry in an entirely conventional role. Bernard rebukes the king for his sins and tells him he is unworthy of bearing, in the upcoming battle, the fragment of the True Cross that swings from his neck. When a terrified Amaurry confesses his sins, Bernard blesses the relic and announces that Amaurry will emerge unscathed from a danger the like of which he had never experienced. On the next day the king's life hangs indeed by a thread; remembering the dream that ended with the saint departing with the relic in hand, he vows to God and the saint that, should he survive the battle, he will send it to Clairvaux. Amaurry's men rescue him, the battle ends with a Christian victory, the king tells the story of the saint's apparition to Abbot Richer of Salvatio, who then makes it known in France.[64]

The account of the battle's outcome is out of true: in reality it ended inconclusively.[65] Amaurry's conventional behavior is possible: the same person can behave differently in various situations, and Amaurry would not have been the first or the last to emit zealous vows in a desperate situation on the battlefield. But he was by no means consistently subservient to ecclesiastical protocol. Returning from his last Egyptian expedition in December 1169, he hurried from Ascalon to celebrate Christmas in the lively harbor city of Acre, not in Jerusalem or Bethlehem.[66]

Amaurry as Patron

Amaurry's patronage of a French poet is referred to in a text that does not belong to the "canonical" writings about the crusades and therefore, like some other such writings, has remained unknown to historians of the Kingdom of Jerusalem. The text in question is the satirical *Bible* that the poet Guiot of Provins (ca. 1150 - after 1208) wrote late in life, in about 1206. In his youth Guiot spent some time in the south of France and was influenced by the poetry of its troubadours; by virtue of his own poems, written in the language of northern France, he became a welcome guest at dozens of courts. In his *Bible* he laments the passing away of the noble patrons of poetry who had been his benefactors and who have no counterparts in the younger, avaricious generation. In 170 verses he lists and briefly celebrates eighty-six patrons—all male—whom he met in person and from whom he received gifts. His long roll, which documents the spread of courtly literature in the second half of the twelfth century,[67] starts with Emperor Frederick I, Louis VII of France, Henry II of England and two of his sons, and ends with Geoffroy of Joinville, Count Henri of Bar-le-Duc, and Milles of Châlons-sur-Marne.[68] On Amaurry, who occupies the respectable eighteenth place, Guiot says:

Quel prince ot ou roi Amauri!	What a prince was there in King Amaurry!
Molt vi gloriouse sa vie	His glorious life much did I see
la riche terre de Syrie.[69]	[in] Syria's noble land.

The poet, who also mentions that he saw the Knights Hospitaller in Jerusalem and denounces their uncharitable behavior, must have visited the kingdom sometime before Amaurry's death in 1174. Possibly he went East again with the Third Crusade.[70] For the courtly culture of that age, it is significant that of the eighty-six patrons Guiot mentions, twenty-five took part in that crusade, and twelve of them found their death on it.[71]

Now, what does Amaurry's inclusion in Guiot's list mean? At the very least, that during a stay in Jerusalem Guiot recited some work of his in the king's presence, and that the gift he received was generous enough to remain etched in his memory three decades later. But possibly the inclusion implies that Amaurry patronized other French vernacular poets. The fact that their journeys are not documented does not prove that they did not occur; but for Guiot's decision to list his various patrons, his encounter with Amaurry would have remained unknown, too. As for a somewhat earlier period, it is likely that the anonymous author of the *Voyage of Charlemagne to Jerusalem and Constantinople* visited Jerusalem: his exact description of the city's market cannot be ascribed to imagination.[72] In the decade following Amaurry's death the troubadour Peire Vidal, exiled into pilgrimage beyond the sea by his "beloved with a dragon's heart," composed a poem in which he yearns to return to a small field between "Arle e Tolo" rather than possess "Lo Daro," "Lo Toro," or "Ibeli"—that is, Darum, Toron de los Caballeros, and Ibelin, three castles in the southwestern part of the Kingdom of Jerusalem. He appears to have enjoyed the patronage of Raymond III of Tripoli (d. 1187), Amaurry's cousin.[73]

Amaurry is also hailed in a Latin poem preserved in the *Carmina Burana*, the famous collection of medieval, often irreverent verse discovered in the monastery of Benediktbeuern (Bavaria) in 1803. The poem pleads for the success of a joint Byzantine-Frankish expedition against Egypt and may therefore be dated to the summer/early fall of 1169, when the allies were preparing to attack Egypt's new master, Ṣalāḥ al-Dīn. (About a year earlier, William of Tyre negotiated with Emperor Manuel the alliance that led to this attack.)[74] The poem's anonymous author stresses the Byzantine role in the expedition not only by praising the Byzantine emperor but also by modeling his Greek/Latin refrain on the Trisagion hymn. The poem runs as follows:

Imperator rex Grecorum,	The emperor, king of the Greeks,
minas spernens paganorum,	Spurning the threats of the pagans,
auro sumpto thesaurorum,	Took the gold out of his treasures,

parat sumptus armatorum.	To provide the warriors' expenses.
Ayos	Holy
o theos athanathos	God immortal,
ysma sather yskyros!	upon us, valiant Savior,
miserere Kyrios,	have mercy, O Lord,
salva tuos famulos!	save Your servants!
Almaricus miles fortis,	Amaurry, the mighty knight,
rex communis nostre sortis,	King of our common fortune,
in Egypto fractis portis	In Egypt, her gates shattered,
Turcos stravit dire mortis.	With fearful death laid flat the Turks.
Ayos . . .	Holy . . .
Omnis ergo Christianus	Let therefore every Christian
ad Egyptum tendat manus!	Stretch forth his hands toward Egypt!
semper ibi degat sanus,	Let him always be there wholesome;
destruatur rex paganus!	May the pagan king be ruined!
Ayos . . .[75]	Holy . . .

"Style simple. Sequence of ideas clear": this is the terse verdict of the poem's editors, Alfons Hilka and Otto Schumann, who also remark that the refrain's corrupt Greek may have originated with the author, not with some careless copyist.[76] They are right. The poem is a crude call to arms by a versifier at Amaurry's court who attempted to whip up enthusiasm for the king's fifth, and last, Egyptian expedition. But an ill-starred expedition it was. After several delays the Frankish-Byzantine attack took place in October 1169; two months later failure was unmistakable, and the allies retreated.

Amaurry does not figure only in French and Latin verse. It is a measure of his enemies' respect that he appears also in Arabic verses, those by the Yemenite poet Abū Ḥamza ʿUmāra that laud an unnamed Muslim leader:

You held off the Franks in every narrow pass,
  and ordered the feet of your horses: "Rush upon Murrī!"
And if the Franks were to throw a bridge over the sea,
  with a sea of iron you'd have traversed it.[77]

The battle cry, "Rush upon Murrī!"—in Arabic, *murrī ʿalā Murrī*—is a play of words on the name by which Amaurry was known in Arabic.

While Amaurry's patronage of French and Latin poetry may be deduced from a few surviving verses, his sponsorship of two historical works is explicitly attested. The first of these is the *History* of the First Crusade and of the Frankish Kingdom of Jerusalem, written by William of Tyre. William mentions on three different occasions that Amaurry urged him to compose this work.[78] It was to become the most comprehensive—and, in its thirteenth-century Old French adaptation, the most widely read—account of the kingdom's establishment and of its fortunes down to 1184, the year William laid down his pen.

One may wonder whether Amaurry would have been pleased by his depiction in this *History*—most probably written after his death—that highlights the discords in his physique as well as his deviations from proper Christian conduct. Also, William disapproves of some of the king's political decisions. He presents Amaurry's ill-fated descent to Egypt in 1168 as a breach of the advantageous treaty he had concluded with the Egyptians, and suggests that the king's avarice motivated his conduct during the campaign.[79] When he relates that immediately upon the death of Nūr al-Dīn in 1174, Amaurry went on the attack, an attentive reader cannot but remember that, in recounting the death of Amaurry's predecessor and brother Baldwin III in 1163, William approvingly reported that Nūr al-Dīn decided to refrain from attacking the Franks while they were mourning the death of their king.[80] The implied criticism of Amaurry's attack is unmistakable. In sum, the king's portrayal in the book he instigated is far from a panegyric. The way Amaurry himself wished to be remembered is more likely reflected by the Bethlehem inscription that eulogized him as "guardian of virtue, generous friend, companion of honesty and impiety's foe, fosterer of justice [and] piety, avenger of crime."[81]

The second historical work Amaurry sponsored is truly extraordinary. William relates that the king urged him to write a *History of the Oriental Rulers*, from the times of the "seductor Mahumet" (or "Mehemeth") onward, and provided Arabic books to allow him to do so.[82] This was an unprecedented assignment, attesting to Amaurry's curiosity about the history of the region into which the Frankish Kingdom had been implanted, the history of his Muslim neighbors, allies, and foes. No other twelfth-century Christian ruler envisaged a history of the Muslim realm, and the same is true of Western ecclesiastical writers. None of the works translated from the Arabic for Petrus Venerabilis in the 1140s amounts to a history of the Saracens. As Otto of Freising tersely put it, "hardly any deeds [of Jews and pagans] are worthy to be written down or to be commended to coming generations."[83] Only in the thirteenth century would there appear in the

West a counterpart to the book Amaurry commissioned: the *History of the Arabs* by Rodrigo Jiménez de Rada (ca. 1170–1247), archbishop of Toledo, which recounts the history of the Muslims of Iberia from their arrival in the eighth century down to the coming of the Almohads in the twelfth.[84] However, Rodrigo was a cleric, not a layman like Amaurry.

By placing Arabic works at William's disposal, Amaurry revealed his intention that the *History of the Oriental Rulers* should be based on Eastern accounts, not on bits of information gleanable from Western sources. Similar to his stance in the discussion about the resurrection of the flesh, he was unwilling to restrict himself to traditional Western lore and expected—not unlike Stephanus of Antioch—to find in the Arabic books new knowledge from which Latinity may profit.

But was William able to read these Arabic books? Möhring demonstrated that the content of the still existing Kufic foundation inscription in the Dome of the Rock is utterly different from what William pretends it to convey, and concluded that he was unable to read Arabic.[85] We may therefore hypothesize that some assistant orally translated or summarized the contents of the Arabic books into the Frankish dialect, and William used the information to write, in Latin, the *History of the Oriental Rulers* that—as he repeatedly attests—deals with the subject down to 1184.[86]

William mentions by name just one Arabic work, that of "Seith the son of Patricius, patriarch of Alexandria"—that is, Saʿīd ibn Baṭrīq/Eutychius (877–940)—and presents it as the main source of his *History of the Oriental Rulers*.[87] Yet Möhring has shown that, in his *History*, William used the continuation of Saʿīd ibn Baṭrīq by Yaḥyā ibn Saʿīd of Antioch (ca. 980–ca. 1066) and the chronicle of Sāwīris ibn al-Muqaffaʿ (d. 987) and his continuators, and plausibly concluded that he used them also in the *History of the Oriental Rulers*.[88] Now, all three works were written by Eastern Christians, which means that William's history of the Muslim realm was primarily (and perhaps exclusively) based on Christian, not Muslim, sources. The implication is obvious: truth about the Muslims' past ought to be obtained from Christian sources. This syndrome (not devoid of equivalents in our own times) was age-old by the twelfth century. For instance, Eulogius (d. 859), who could have easily obtained information about the Prophet from his many Muslim neighbors in Cordova, traveled all the way to northern, Christian Spain and brought thence back a Latin-written, pugnacious account about the heresiarch *Mahmeth*.[89] Was Amaurry or William responsible for the decision to rely, primarily or exclusively, on Christian sources? We do not know; but from what we have learned about the two men we may surmise that the decision was William's. In any case,

Amaurry's most original brainchild was a unique work of history. Unfortunately, it has not come down to us—yet we should not give up the hope that one day it will surface in some library or archive.

Another unprecedented patronage of Amaurry's is attested by a mosaic inscription. It consists of two parts, the first in Latin (just a few letters are visible, but the text was reconstructed on the basis of late medieval and early modern transcriptions), the second in Greek, and they celebrate the redecoration of the Church of the Nativity in Bethlehem under the joint sponsorship of Amaurry, Emperor Manuel, and Raoul, the local Frankish bishop. The date spelled out in the Greek part, 6677 (AD September 1168/August 1169), reveals that this unique Latin-Byzantine cooperation came to conclusion even as Amaurry and his Byzantine allies were preparing to attack Egypt.[90] The redecoration campaign brought into being one of the largest mosaic ensembles in Christendom: a fifteenth-century German pilgrim, Felix Fabri, was to liken Bethlehem's mosaic-covered walls to those of St. Mark's in Venice.[91]

What was Amaurry's role in this grand project? Was it another of his brainchildren? Did he comply with a wish of his Byzantine ally? Or did the joint patronage reflect a genuine convergence of two imperious wills? We do not know. We may suppose, though, that Amaurry had a hand in shaping the Latin part of the bilingual inscription that depicts him at length in glowing terms and then mentions the emperor briefly as generous donor and pious ruler of the Greeks—a presentation starkly contrasting with the Greek part, where the "great emperor" is mentioned before the "great king," and the conclusion of the artwork takes place "in the reign of" the first and merely "in the days of" the second. It is improbable that Amaurry was personally involved in the balancing of Eastern and Western components in the decorative program itself, which gave pride of place both to Byzantine mosaics and a Romanesque Tree of Jesse. But one cannot rule out that he gave some general guidelines to the monk, painter, and mosaicist Effrem/Efraìm, whom both the Latin and Greek parts present as having brought the artwork to completion.[92]

King Amaurry's Lots: Predicting a Crusader's Arrival

A divinatory tract referred to as "the lots of the most vigorous King Amaurry" is presented as the work that an unnamed physician of the king offered to him in the wake of the great victory he won in Egypt.[93] The tract's introduction, which dwells on this victory, attests to a considerable acquaintance with regional power struggles: Syraconus—that is Shīrkūh, Nūr al-Dīn's general, whom William of Tyre calls *Siracunus*—invades all of Egypt; the lord of Egypt and his men, confined to a stronghold called *Cassarum*, appeal to Amaurry for help; the king crosses the desert into Egypt, coerces Syraconus to flee to a well-fortified city, and after fighting against him there for a long time, drives him out of Egypt; the Egyptians become the king's tributaries forever.[94] As Charles Burnett has demonstrated, the account of this victory largely ties in with William of Tyre's description of Amaurry's second Egyptian campaign that took place in 1164; and *Cassarum* must be Cairo's citadel that William calls *Cascere*.[95] One may add that the tract's introduction rightly spells out that Kurds formed part of Shīrkūh's army—whereas William does not say so, nor does he mention anywhere that Shīrkūh and Ṣalāḥ al-Dīn were Kurds and that Kurdish contingents played an important role in their struggle against the Franks.[96] Also, the introduction presents King Amaurry as "the fifth lord of the Franks in Jerusalem," a formulation that has its analogues in Hospitaller charters issued during Amaurry's reign.[97] True, the introduction as it has come down to us does not appear to represent the original text, for neither the name of Amaurry's physician, the tract's purported author or compiler, nor the name of the Egyptian city to which Syraconus/Shīrkūh fled—namely, Bilbays—is spelled out.[98] It may well have received its present form in the West.

Haskins and Mirella Brini Savorelli believed that the tract, which presents the Arabic names of the twenty-eight "lunar mansions," was translated or adapted from the Arabic.[99] Burnett has pointed out, however, that *Almazene*, figuring in the tract as the name of the *first* mansion, is in reality a corrupt transliteration of the Arabic word *al-manzil*, that is, "mansion"; this blatant mistake leaves no doubt that the tract's compiler lacked an elementary knowledge of Arabic. Moreover, the same mistake appears already in a corpus of astrological works attested in the West from the end of the tenth century onward. Therefore, writes Burnett, there is nothing genuinely Arabic or Eastern in the tract and the "physician of King Amaurry" was possibly a fictitious creature, invented to add exotic flavor to the tract.[100]

And yet when we focus on the themes about which the tract purports to offer predictions, an unmistakable pointer to a Frankish origin turns up.

Those of us who dismiss astrological and other divinations as sheer humbug may be inclined to believe that all manuals that promise to forecast our future are alike, constantly delivering veiled assurances and vague admonitions about life, death, health, illness, love fulfilled or spurned, friends and enemies, success or failure. But a closer examination reveals that a manual very often expresses hopes, fears, and concerns typical of the people of the time in which it was written, providing thereby clues to the mentality of its author and prospective users. An analysis of Latin oracular sentences, preserved in a St. Gallen manuscript dating from the seventh century or later, has revealed that they reflect the reality of a small town of the later Roman Empire, the fear of its citizens lest they be appointed municipal councilors and become responsible for tax collection, their contemplation of flight, their dependence on a patron's protection, and their Christianity interspersed with remnants of paganism.[101] The oracular sentences often express disrespect for the clients who are appealing for a forecast, repeatedly branding them as fools.[102] The same approach appears in the much later *Lots of the Twelve Patriarchs*, dated to the eleventh century; here we read, for instance: "Your foolish soul muses over trifles."[103]

Like the oracular sentences preserved in the St. Gallen manuscript, the *Sortes regis Amalrici* disclose not a little about the preoccupations of the users the tract was to serve. All possible queries a user might have posed are subsumed under twenty-eight themes, each of which is supplied with twenty-eight different responses in verse form.[104] It is noteworthy that none of these convey disrespect for the user. Most themes are of universal appeal, like Life, Riches, Wife, Hope, Heir, Dream, Theft, Love, Female Friend (or: Concubine), Sickness, Fear. Four themes—Profit, Business, Loss, Debt—may have been of particular interest for merchants, while two others—War, Enemy—would have been especially pertinent for a ruler. "Your enemies flee and are afraid to prepare for war"; "[The two armies] will fight in like manner, but victory will go to your men"; "Your men will fight and suffer great losses"; "Sword and fire will lay waste your walls"—these are some of the responses to queries about War that show that the topic is approached from a ruler's perspective. Similarly, some responses about the Enemy pertain to a political entity: "Peace and concord with the enemies is given," "The band of enemies will inflict injury on you and yours."[105] This taking up of a ruler's viewpoint suggests an Eastern influence. Among the lots discussed by the eminent astrologer Abū Maʿshar (787–886)—known in the West as Albumasar—is "the lot of the king and the authority," and Muslim rulers used to consult astrologers with regard to military affairs.[106]

The one theme that points plainly to an origin in the Frankish East is that of the *Peregrinus*, the Latin term that meant in twelfth-century parlance "pilgrim" and "crusader." The *Peregrinus*'s slow or abortive progress is anxiously followed in several responses: "The *peregrinus* is fatigued, unable to come soon"; "The *peregrinus* halts; misfortunes cause the delay"; "The *peregrinus* is taken captive, therefore he is not coming soon"; "The *peregrinus* is very sick and dies."[107] Other responses announce his imminent arrival: "The one you are expecting will come soon"; "The *peregrinus* comes, already well-nigh at the entrance"; "The *peregrinus* comes, yet stays for a long time."[108] Still others celebrate his exploits: "The *peregrinus* comes with joy and a gain is made"; "He comes and brings gladness, extraordinary gains."[109] When we remember that embassies asking for help were sent to the West in at least ten out of the twelve years of Amaurry's reign, it is not surprising that the eager expectation of the *peregrinus*—a crusader with his retinue, or heading a contingent—occupies so prominent a place in the divinatory tract.[110] On the other hand, it is inconceivable that, elsewhere in the Latin world, *Peregrinus* would so figure.

Dungeon is another of the twenty-eight themes that must have been of major interest at Jerusalem's court. Renaud of Châtillon, the unruly prince of Antioch, was captured in 1160 by the governor of Aleppo and held in prison until 1176; Count Raymond III of Tripoli fell into Nūr al-Dīn's captivity in 1164 and remained in Aleppo's prison until 1173; and there were many others.[111] The Aleppo prisoners were alluded to in France in contemporary vernacular poetry; surely their prospects were discussed in the Frankish East time after time.[112] The responses in *King Amaurry's Lots* envisage a variety of outcomes: long or short captivity, successful escape or recapture, ransom for a large or small sum, liberation by a compassionate captor, or death in prison. Remarkably—and probably echoing the wishes of some users—one of the responses announces: "It is better that he remains in the dungeon than that he goes forth from it."[113]

In sum, the considerable acquaintance with Eastern politics observable in the introduction to *King Amaurry's Lots*, the inclusion of *Peregrinus* among the themes about which users pose queries, as well as several statements fitting a ruler's perspective, allow for the assumption that the divinatory tract was written originally at Amaurry's court. And, as we shall presently see, the unnamed physician who authored the tract would not have been the only physician in Amaurry's service to engage in astrology.

Amaurry's Western and Eastern Physicians

William of Tyre sternly rebukes the Frankish rulers who, swayed largely by their wives, scorn Latin medicine and imprudently put their trust in utterly ignorant Jewish, Samaritan, Syrian, and Saracen physicians.[114] At one point he divulges that Amaurry, too, had Eastern physicians in his service—and his account tacitly implies that their conduct on this occasion was sounder than that of their Western confrères.

It is the early summer of 1174 and Amaurry has just broken off the siege of the northern town of Paneas, which the Muslims conquered ten years earlier. While on his way south, he comes down with dysentery in Tiberias, the low-lying, hot Galilean town notorious for its fleas. Fearful of the sickness, Amaurry decides to ride to Jerusalem. He avoids the shorter route via the sweltering Jordan Valley, ascends to Nazareth, and thence takes the way that crosses the Jezreel Valley and twists south along the country's central ridge. In Jerusalem Amaurry's physicians manage to stop the dysentery, but he is seized by a crippling fever that persists for several days. No longer able to endure it, he summons physicians who are "Greek, Syrian, and men of those nations" and urges them to loosen his bowels with the help of some potion.[115] They refuse; William does not give their reasons, but from what soon happens we may assume that they considered the intervention dangerous, for the king and for themselves. Amaurry then calls the Latin physicians, asks them to administer the potion the Easterners were unwilling to employ, and promises them impunity should it have grave consequences. The Latins comply. The king discharges his bowels a number of times without difficulty and believes he is feeling better. But his body has been debilitated by the harsh remedy, and before he can reinvigorate it by consuming food, the fever recurs and he dies.[116] William, so generous with clinical details about the king's fatal illness, does not comment that the Eastern physicians may have been right.

Neither does William spell out the names of Amaurry's physicians, whether Latin or not. Nor is it possible to find information about them in Latin works devoted to a systematic presentation of physicians' biographies, because such works did not exist in the contemporaneous West, nor were they to exist there for many generations to come. But, fortunately for the present inquiry, the Frankish Kingdom of Jerusalem was surrounded by a civilization that did produce such works, and these contain some information about one of Amaurry's Eastern physicians.

The Egyptian author and official Ibn al-Qifṭī, whose *History of Learned Men* dates from the 1230s and survives in an abridgement of 1249, relates that, in the last days of the Fatimid dynasty, "the king of the Franks in Ascalon" asked the Egyptians for a physician and that they intended to send out to him Mūsā the son of Maymūn—that is, Maimonides—who however refused to go. The context indicates that this king was Amaurry, and that the episode took place between 1165, when Maimonides arrived in Egypt, and 1168, when Amaurry broke with his Egyptian allies. The notice appears in the section Ibn al-Qifṭī devotes to Maimonides's biography, and since he had known people close to him, it may be relied upon.[117] A probably related notice appears in Ibn Abī Uṣaybiʿa's encyclopedia of prominent physicians. Here we learn that Abū Sulaymān Dāwūd, a Jerusalem-born Eastern Christian, emigrated to Egypt and achieved fame there for his knowledge of medicine and astrology. "When King Mārī [Amaurry] arrived in Egypt, he was very impressed with Abū Sulaymān's medical skill and asked the caliph to allow Abū Sulaymān to remain with him. So, the caliph sent Abū Sulaymān and his five children to Jerusalem." There he treated Amaurry's leprous son, the future King Baldwin IV.[118] Since it was Abū Sulaymān's grandson who told the story to Ibn Abī Uṣaybiʿa, the gist of it may be relied upon. It should be dated to 1164 or 1167, as it is in these years that Amaurry descended to Egypt as the caliph's ally.

It is possible, though, that the two episodes occurred independently of one another. But, on the assumption that Abū Sulaymān's grandson embellished the story by letting his grandfather's fame reach Amaurry and by making the king ask specifically for his service, we may collapse the two episodes into one, and conjecture that Amaurry asked his Egyptian allies for a leading physician, without mentioning a specific name, and that they turned first to the Jewish physician-philosopher Maimonides, who declined to go, and then to the Eastern Christian physician-astrologer Abū Sulaymān. If so, the event must be dated to 1167, as in 1164 Maimonides had not yet arrived in Egypt.[119]

In any case, both Ibn al-Qifṭī and Ibn Abī Uṣaybiʿa leave no doubt that Amaurry endeavored, and succeeded, to bring to Jerusalem a prominent Eastern physician from Egypt. This physician, Abū Sulaymān Dāwūd, who was to forecast through astrological readings the day of Ṣalāḥ al-Dīn's conquest of Jerusalem, possibly doubled as Amaurry's court astrologer.[120] If so, the court of Jerusalem would have resembled in this respect the court of Ṣalāḥ al-Dīn and other Muslim rulers.[121] Also, according to a thirteenth-century Old French chronicle, Amaurry had recourse to physicians from Muslim Syria: when his son and heir, the future King Baldwin IV, was struck with leprosy, Amaurry brought physicians from Damascus to treat him, but their exertions were to no avail.[122] Evidently, he overvalued their capacities.

Indeed, while the vast Islamicate *medical literature* that existed in Amaurry's days undoubtedly eclipsed the one then accessible in Latin, several studies suggest that the *medical practice* of physicians in the Islamicate realm did not greatly differ from that of their Frankish counterparts: patients under either care were cured or harmed in about the same proportion. However, the Frankish licensing of medical practitioners, documented in the 1240s, was probably influenced by Eastern norms.[123]

Comparing Amaurry to His Contemporaries and Predecessors

Guiot of Provins mentioned Amaurry among the patrons of French vernacular poetry; an anonymous versifier composed in Latin a call to arms on the eve of his last Egyptian campaign; Amaurry urged William of Tyre to write a history of the Frankish Kingdom of Jerusalem as well as an unprecedented history of its Muslim neighbors and enemies; he sponsored, conjointly with the Byzantine emperor Manuel, the redecoration of the Church of the Nativity in Bethlehem; a divinatory tract, *King Amaurry's Lots*, was probably offered to him in 1164; he had in his employ both Western and Eastern physicians. Last but not least, he broached a remarkable query about the resurrection of the flesh.

What does all this add up to? Quantitatively not much, in comparison to Amaurry's leading counterparts in the West. William Stubbs (d. 1901) and Charles Homer Haskins hailed Henry II of England, Amaurry's half nephew and contemporary, as an outstanding patron of literature, and—as Ian Short has dryly observed—"from generation to generation [his] fabled literary patronage expands with repetition."[124] Of late, a more skeptical assessment is gaining ground, and a leading skeptic, John Gillingham, convincingly argues that Henry appears to have been uninterested in the history of his own times and in any historical work written in Latin—differing, we may add, from Amaurry in this regard.[125] Yet even Gillingham lists fourteen Latin-writing authors "who arguably were in some sense writing for Henry II," and states that the king probably commissioned two or three of their works, and certainly commissioned two compositions in vernacular verse.[126] He acknowledges also that several Latin authors appear to have composed their major works while being members of the royal court: Pierre of Blois; Richard FitzNigel, author of the *Dialogue on the Exchequer*; the historian Roger of Howden; the author of the treatise on English law known as "Glanvill"; Walter Map; and Gerald of Barri.[127] Besides, there were troubadours at Henry's court.[128] Obviously, this shrunken estimate of Henry II's literary patronage, too, far outstrips that of Amaurry, even when we take into consideration that Henry's reign lasted about three times longer than Amaurry's.

However, when originality of sponsorship and intercivilizational permeability rather than volume of literary output are considered, Amaurry emerges as the more complex figure. With much exaggeration, Walter Map hailed Henry II as having had knowledge of all languages spoken "from the French Sea to the Jordan"; yet as far as the Jordan was concerned, Henry knew only the language of the Frankish conquerors who lived along this river.[129] Henry's culture was exclusively Western.

Closer counterparts to Amaurry may be sought in the Mediterranean area. King Roger II of Sicily entrusted the theologian Neilos Doxapatres, a refugee from Constantinople, with writing—in Greek—a history of the five patriarchates that ascribed primacy to Constantinople, a work utilizable in a confrontation with the papacy. Also, interested in natural science, Roger commissioned the North African geographer Muḥammad al-Idrīsī to prepare a map of the then known world and to write—in Arabic—a description of it; if one may believe al-Idrīsī, Roger personally took part in gathering, for fifteen years, the required evidence. He was celebrated in Greek homilies and Arabic poems, and in his royal chapel in Palermo the sanctuary, representing the heavenly realm, was done in Byzantine style, whereas the nave, evoking the earthly realm, resembled an Islamic reception hall. A still existing trilingual inscription—Latin, Greek, and Arabic—commemorates Roger's construction of a water clock in 1142. But Latin culture appears to have been of secondary importance for him: the chronicle that Abbot Alexander of Telese wrote, in Latin, about the early years of Roger's rule was commissioned by the king's sister and aimed primarily at the Lombard nobility.[130]

Amaurry, who—similarly to his predecessors—styled himself "fifth king of the Latins in the holy city of Jerusalem,"[131] was far more attached to Latinity than Roger and never commissioned works from Greek or Muslim authors. Yet Amaurry's quest for a history of the rulers of the Orient was more exceptional than Roger's wish for a map and a description of the world: a history of the Other, and particularly of the enemy, is far less common than the intercivilizational flow of geographical knowledge.[132] Besides, Amaurry expected the *History of the Oriental Rulers* to be composed in Latin, while al-Idrīsī wrote his work in Arabic and the Latin translation of its abridged version was to appear only in 1619. On the other hand, Amaurry's query about the resurrection was surely surpassed by Emperor Manuel's order to delete the anathema of the "God of *Moámet*" from the ritual for the abjuration of Islam, maintaining that this God was identical with the God in whom he believed.[133]

How do Amaurry's cultural interests compare with those of previous kings of Frankish Jerusalem? King Baldwin I was originally a cleric and, according to William of Tyre, his deportment resembled that of a bishop more than that of a layman, but there is no direct evidence for his activity in the cultural sphere.[134] He may have instigated the insertion, on his royal seal, of the innovative inscription CIVITAS REGIS REGUM

OMNIUM (City of the King of all Kings).[135] Possibly he encouraged his chaplain Foucher of Chartres to write his chronicle, though Foucher does not say so. Neither is King Baldwin II known for cultural activities.

Things change with the reign of Fulk of Anjou (1131–43). The Psalter of Queen Melisende—his Jerusalemite wife—was commissioned sometime during his rule. It has been considered to be the work of four illuminators: two are Byzantinizing Westerners (or Franks born in the East), the third combines Italian, Anglo-Saxon, and Islamic ornamental motifs, while the fourth appears to emulate northern European models. The pair of ivory book covers appear to have been executed by an artist of Western, possibly English, origin who adopted Byzantine and Islamic patterns; for instance, the back panel shows a king, probably Fulk, performing the works of mercy while wearing a Byzantine-looking ceremonial costume.[136] The psalter reveals an eclectic yet definitely more Eastern than Western character that probably reflects the taste of Melisende, daughter of an Armenian noblewoman. Her Eastern temperament finds eloquent expression in the lament for her husband Fulk, fatally injured while hunting near Acre: "Wailing with her clothes and hair torn," so wrote William of Tyre a generation later, "and with sighs and moans attesting to the immensity of her anguish, she fell to the ground, embracing the lifeless body."[137] Anyone who has witnessed the traditional mourning of Middle Eastern women can easily visualize this scene.[138]

Baldwin III (1143–63), the firstborn son of Fulk and Melisende, and Amaurry's older brother, was according to William of Tyre "suitably lettered"—much more so than Amaurry—and enjoyed reading, listening to accounts about past events, and inquiring about the deeds of past rulers; also, he knew the kingdom's customary law exceptionally well.[139] William does not mention that, apparently in 1146, Baldwin III, then sixteen years old, "compiled and also caused to write down" a chronicle that bears his name.[140]

The compilation starts with the call for the First Crusade and concludes abruptly with the naval victories of the Venetian fleet in 1123, and not—as one would expect—with the Frankish-Venetian conquest of Tyre a year later. The work is skewed: sixty chapters for the four years of the First Crusade, twenty chapters for the first twenty-four years of the Frankish Kingdom. Like Foucher of Chartres before him and William of Tyre after him, the compiler tells a story in which the crusade seamlessly interweaves with the kingdom's establishment and growth. He relies mainly on Robert the Monk for the First Crusade, exclusively on Foucher for the kingdom's history—and utterly misunderstands the latter in one case.[141] His compilation does not offer any new factual information. Yet the way he abbreviates his sources is revealing. The emphasis is on military history—sieges, battles, numbers of combatants and casualties, sizes of fleets, distances. (At one point, the compiler sees fit to correct his source: where Foucher claims that the distance between Jerusalem's city wall and Mount Sion is "little less than a bow's arrow," he changes the wording to "a stone's throw.")[142] Clashes with the Muslim enemy conclude, with one exception, with Frankish victory. To King Baldwin I's expeditions in 1100 to the Dead Sea and in 1115 to Transjordan and the northern tip of the Red Sea are devoted two of the twenty chapters dealing with the kingdom's history, and the peculiarities of the two seas are highlighted.[143] On the other hand, ecclesiastical developments like the struggles between the claimants for the patriarchal see, problematic episodes like Baldwin I's marriage to Adelaide of Sicily, and internal conflicts in general are skipped. In sum, the compilation distinctly expresses—or is tailored to—the down-to-earth concerns of a young Frankish noble, who was crowned just three years earlier, in 1143, and came of age in 1145. Does the compilation also reveal a partiality to Eastern Christians? Perhaps. Where Foucher recounts that in 1099 the Frankish conquerors of Bethlehem gave the local Syrians the kiss of peace, the compiler replaces Syrians with "confrères" (*confratres*).[144] Surely the compilation is a child of its age: where Robert the Monk, in his rendition of the Clermont Address, has Pope Urban exalt Jerusalem as the city that the Redeemer of mankind consecrated by his passion and distinguished by his sepulture, the compiler adds, "and glorified with his resurrection."[145] Yes, we are in Jerusalem of the 1140s.

The compilation raises several questions. Why does it stop in 1123? Why is Baldwin III's father Fulk presented, in the rhymed prologue, not as king but as "Volco the Angevin count, who ruled for his father-in-law"?[146] Why does Baldwin III's mother Melisende, who in 1146 ruled the kingdom jointly with him, go unmentioned? What were the compilation's aims, in addition to glorifying the First Crusade and the first twenty-four years of the kingdom's existence as an era of God-willed conquest and triumphs?[147] In any case, it testifies to young Baldwin III's interest in history. Also, it provides a baseline for appreciating the chronicle Amaurry commissioned about two decades later, which contrasts with it so starkly. Besides, it reveals that not only Foucher's locally written chronicle but also the one Robert the Monk composed in France was available in Jerusalem of the mid-1140s.

Baldwin III was succeeded in 1163 by Amaurry, who was followed by his son Baldwin IV the Leper (1174–85). William of Tyre, Baldwin IV's tutor, relates that he made headway in the study of letters and, like Amaurry, was keen on listening to histories, but he is not known for cultural activities.[148] When he succumbed to his illness in 1185 at the age of twenty-four, he was succeeded by his nephew Baldwin V, an eight-year-old child, who died one year later; the child's tomb, reconstructed in 1987, displays Early Christian and Byzantine features.[149] The subsequent reign of Amaurry's daughter Sibylla and her husband Gui of Lusignan was cut short by Ṣalāḥ al-Dīn's triumph at Ḥaṭṭīn in July 1187 that put an end to the Frankish Kingdom of Jerusalem.

Thus, sponsorship of literary works is attested only for the two sons of Fulk and Melisende, Baldwin III and Amaurry. As we have seen, William describes the first as much more lettered (*litteratus*) than the second. The Latin term implies that both of them enjoyed, perhaps to a varying degree, some formal instruction. Although our sources are mute on the subject, there are reasons to believe that it was Fulk who provided for it.

Several of Fulk's ancestors, from Fulk II "the Good," count of Anjou in the mid-tenth century, onward, are said to have exhibited a precocious interest in learning.[150] Fulk's father, Count Fulk IV le Réchin (the Sullen One) (1043–1109), stands out for having written, possibly assisted by a scribe, a brief history of the achievements of his ancestors as well as of himself. The text, of which just a fragment survives, has been variously interpreted as one of the earliest Latin works conceived by a layman, an early example of secular autobiography, or a dynastic narrative aimed at instructing the next generation.[151] Original in any case, Fulk IV succeeded in transmitting—through a rudimentary, repetitious Latin—his pride in the deeds of the counts of Anjou.

Anjou and Maine, the counties Fulk—known there as Count Fulk V the Young—ruled until his departure for Jerusalem in 1129, were home to notable figures of the Twelfth-Century Renaissance. The most renowned of these was Hildebert of Lavardin, the great Latin poet and letter-writer who headed the cathedral school of Le Mans from 1085 onward and served as bishop of Le Mans between 1096 and 1125; Fulk certainly knew him.[152] Contemporaries did not portray Fulk himself as a man of letters, yet he did establish at the abbey of Notre-Dame-de-la-Charité in Angers a kind of proto-college, making provisions for the maintenance "in schools" of thirteen poor boys or scholar-clerics, natives of Anjou or Maine and offspring of legitimate marriages.[153] His son and heir Geoffroy Plantagenet enjoyed considerable schooling. An Angevin chronicle presents him as "most lettered and most eloquent among clerics and laymen."[154] In the biography that the monk Jean of Marmoutier wrote about three decades after Geoffroy's death, he is idealized as the compleat lettered knight, who delights in finding parallels between passages of scripture and classical literature and who, during a siege, consults Vegetius's *Epitome of Military Science* for a solution to a tactical problem.[155] (Historians tend to regard the latter incident as rooted in reality, and it has even been suggested that the incendiary weapon Geoffroy subsequently used may have been Greek fire, obtained from the Kingdom of Jerusalem.)[156] Moreover, the philosopher William of Conches dedicated in the 1140s to Geoffroy his *Dialogue on Natural Philosophy*, in which he praises him for imbuing his sons with the study of letters from early childhood and then presents the treatise in the form of a dialogue between Geoffroy and himself; yet, unlike his Jerusalemite half-brother, Geoffroy is not portrayed as having voiced queries with regard to William of Conches's carefully phrased confession of faith.[157] The education given to Fulk's sons in West and East may be regarded as complying with a tradition of Anjou's comital family. In the next generation it continued with Geoffroy entrusting William of Conches with the education of the future King Henry II of England, and with Amaurry choosing William of Tyre to tutor the future King Baldwin IV.

In Anjou, there was continued interest in the doings in the East of their former count, now king of Jerusalem. The "Chronicle of the Deeds of the Consuls of Anjou" proudly reports that he made the Damascenes and the Ascalonitans his tributaries and successfully defended Antioch against the Turks, then mentions the births of Baldwin and Amaurry and Baldwin III's accession to the throne; the Le Mans chronicle mentions King Fulk of Jerusalem before the kings of France and England.[158] The "Great Chronicle of Tours," on the other hand, relates with satisfaction that Fulk died "by miracle" while hunting a hare, and presents his death on the summer feast of St. Martin as a divine punishment for his erstwhile molestation of the Church of St. Martin of Tours.[159]

Conversely, Fulk's Angevin past was known in the East. William of Tyre writes that Fulk's father was denominated "Rechin" and presents a detailed if not wholly exact account of his descendants down to Henry II of England.[160] According to an imaginative hypothesis, Fulk may have brought his father's account about the achievements of the counts of Anjou to Jerusalem in 1129.[161] Perhaps; at any rate, we may assume that some of the stories from bygone times that Baldwin III and Amaurry liked to hear dealt with the deeds of their Angevin forefathers. And of their grandmother, Bertrada, who was a queen of France and in all likelihood an arresting figure.[162]

Thus, the sources allow for assuming an impact of Amaurry's Angevin heritage on his upbringing. But this heritage was just one conceivable inspiration. There was also Amaurry's mother Melisende, daughter of Morfia, an Armenian noblewoman from Melitene; Melisende's childhood passed in Edessa, a city with a predominantly Armenian population. There was Amaurry's first wife, Agnes of Courtenay, who likewise grew up in Edessa, a granddaughter of another Armenian noblewoman. We know nothing about Amaurry's awareness of his Armenian heritage, but this should not lead us into thinking that it was necessarily of no consequence. And there was Amaurry's second wife Maria Komnene, grand-niece of Emperor Manuel, whom he married in Tyre in August 1167. It is perhaps not accidental that only on seals postdating this marriage does Amaurry wear a long, narrow, embroidered band—the *loros*, the most important part of the Byzantine imperial costume.[163]

In any case, Amaurry's most original cultural enterprise—the history of Muslim rulers—has not survived. His most ambitious political venture met with a fate still worse: The repeated attempts to dominate Egypt led to Ṣalāḥ al-Dīn's rise to power and to the unification of Egypt and Syria that proved fatal for the Kingdom of Jerusalem. Ironically, these developments are chronicled with growing apprehension in the other historical work Amaurry urged William to write.

CHAPTER 8

The Inventiveness of the Kingdom's Knights and Military-Religious Orders

On 3 February 1138, at the instigation of his wife Melisende, King Fulk granted the *casale* of Thecua to the canons of the Church of the Holy Sepulcher, in return for the Church of St. Lazarus in Bethany, where the royal couple wished to establish a monastery.[1] This exchange of properties and the exceptionally long list of witnesses attesting to it have been studied in considerable detail.[2] But it has not yet been noted that among the sixty-nine witnesses—of whom twenty-five are clerics and twenty-seven nobles—were two brothers, *Rollandus Gunterius, Oliuarus frater eius* (Roland *Gunterius* and his brother Olivier).

No other pair of brothers in the Frankish East is known to bear these names. They are the names of the two heroes of the *Song of Roland*, the famous eleventh-century epic tale that exalts Christian warfare against the Saracens for the sake of God, Charlemagne, and glory, and extols a vassal's faithfulness to his lord. Harking back to the real-life Basque or Gascon ambush of Charlemagne's forces in 778 in the Roncevaux Pass high in the Pyrenean Mountains, the epic transforms the raiders into Saracens, thus turning the battle into a Christian-Muslim collision. Roland, Charlemagne's nephew who commands the rearguard, is depicted as the compleat warrior: valiant, battle-eager, proud, tenaciously upholding his honor. Olivier, Roland's comrade, is equally heroic, but displays prudence and levelheadedness. The two excel in the ensuing clash, the enemy suffer tremendous losses, but ultimately the Christians are overcome. Roland and Olivier lose their lives, but the epic renders them immortal.

Who were *Rollandus Gunterius* and his brother *Oliuarus*? Since this is their only appearance in the documentation, we must get the most out of their mention in the 1138 charter.[3] They are not pilgrims: these are recorded separately at the end of the roll of witnesses. They are listed among the nobles, but while five of these are designated as lords, two as viscounts, and one as marshal, the nineteen others—our Roland and Olivier among them—appear to be ordinary members of the knightly class, with only their names recorded.[4] Also, the brothers must have been born before 1123 in order to attain majority—the age of fifteen—by 1138 and thus become capable of attesting the charter.[5] A birth in the second decade of the twelfth century is more likely.

We do not know whether Roland and Olivier were born in the Kingdom of Jerusalem or whether they emigrated from the West. In the first case, the implication would be that a Frankish father—perhaps also a mother—who settled in the kingdom early in the twelfth century was aware of some variant of the *Song of Roland* and decided to name the two sons after the epic's two shining heroes.

The Jerusalem pair is one of the earliest in the documentation to have been so named. At the present stage of research, they are preceded only by Rollannus and Oliverius of Molesme (south of Troyes) in 1123, by Rollandus and Uliverius of Scafati (southeast of Naples) in 1131, and by Rothlandus and Oliverius of Saintes (southwest of Poitiers) in 1137.[6] Evidence for such pairs in England appears later: one pair was dead by 1165/66, another was living in 1185.[7]

Of course, the solitary appearance of Rollandus and Oliuarus in the 1138 charter does not necessarily mean that the *Song of Roland* was otherwise unknown in the Frankish East around that year. Similarly, the Sathanas episode of the *Chanson des Chétifs* (Song of the Captives), based on an Armenian folkloric motif and composed by a canon of St. Peter's in Antioch at the behest of Prince Raymond of Antioch (d. 1149)—the son of Duke William IX of Aquitaine, the Troubadour—must not be taken as evidence that no other vernacular piece of poetry was written there.[8]

There is, however, hard evidence that in later years the *Song of Roland* was known in the Frankish East. The chronicler Ernoul, who wrote about fifty years after the appearance of the brothers Rollandus and Oliuarus in Jerusalem, extolled the feats of the brothers Baldwin and Balian of Ibelin during the Battle of Montgisard in 1177, asserting—no less!—that they outdid those of *Rollanz* and *Oliviers* at *Rainscevaus* (Roncevaux)—that is, at the battle in which the two heroes fought gallantly until death.[9]

Experimenting with Writing in Old French

The Frankish East was also home to precocious vernacular works written in Old French. The Templar Rule was translated into Old French between 1135 and 1139, that is, within a decade after the Latin original had been drawn up in 1129; the translation constitutes one of the earliest French prose works anywhere.[10] The original, lost account that Ernoul, a youth in the service of the prominent Frankish nobleman Balian of Ibelin, wrote probably a short time after 1187 is one of the very earliest—possibly, the earliest—vernacular works of prose historiography written in Old French, with the lay author exhibiting a distinctly anticlerical stance.[11]

The early recourse to the vernacular was not necessarily just a switch to a different language; it could amount also to the adoption of a new way of expression that riveted a reader's mind not unlike a *chanson de geste*. For instance, this is how Ernoul describes a startling incident during a war council of 1183 that was attended by Patriarch Eraclius: "So it happened once in an army where the king was together with the patriarch and the barons of the land in order to take counsel about attacking Saracens who were nearby . . ., that a fool came upon them where they were in council, and [told] the patriarch: 'Lord Patriarch, give me a good reward, I bring you good news. Paske de Riveri, your wife, has [given birth to] a beautiful daughter.' The patriarch, ashamed, told him: 'Shut up, you fool.'"[12]

How to explain this early recourse to the vernacular? Is it possible that, in this faraway offshoot of Latin Europe that developed an impressive capacity to devise fresh solutions for problems of everyday life in a strange environment, the composition of prose works in the vernacular was still another experiment in sailing in uncharted waters? Possibly, although the new departure may also have been caused by more proximate reasons. As for the Knights Templar, their lay upbringing would not have allowed them to comprehend their order's Latin Rule; hence, its speedy translation into Old French became imperative.[13] As for the Frankish nobles, it is plausible to assume that their command of Latin was limited or less. In an age in which, in the West, the lettered knight was becoming increasingly common, he appears to have remained rare in the Frankish East. William of Tyre, who comments on the degree to which Frankish prelates and Kings Baldwin III and Amaurry were lettered, does likewise only with regard to just one Frankish noble: this is Count Raymond III of Tripoli, whom he presents as "slightly lettered" and as having attained this humble level with the utmost effort while imprisoned by the enemy (that is, during his captivity in Aleppo).[14] It may be that the remoteness of the Frankish nobility from Latin learning is related to the fact, pointed out by Rudolf Hiestand (d. 2023), that not a single male member of a leading Frankish noble family ever embarked on an ecclesiastical career.[15] Nor is there evidence for members of the lesser nobility having been destined for such a vocation. Did Frankish nobles receive in their early youth some instruction in letters, like that which their counterparts in the West were increasingly receiving alongside siblings who were to become clerics?[16] Or was their education restricted to military training? We do not know; but the routing of all noble male children toward a knightly career suggests that such a restriction may have taken place. In any case, Frankish nobles lacked firsthand, familial connections to clerics like the bond between, say, Count Henri the Liberal of Champagne (1126–81) and Archbishop William of the White Hands (1135–1202), his younger brother.

Whatever the explanation, some Frankish knights did exhibit ingenuity in harnessing the French vernacular to their needs. We shall see that they exhibited it even more forcefully in the military sphere.

Fighting against Muslims: A Silent Dialogue

ʿAbd al-Laṭīf al-Baghdādī went to see Ṣalāḥ al-Dīn in Jerusalem sometime after the conclusion of the truce with the Franks on 2 September 1192. In his autobiography, he relates that on the first night he found himself at a meeting at which men of learning discussed various sciences. The sultan "listened attentively and took an active part in the conversation, taking up the subject of building walls and digging moats. He had a good understanding of this matter and came up with all kinds of original ideas. He was concerned about the construction of the walls of Jerusalem and about the digging of its moats."[17] Thus, we get a rare glimpse of Ṣalāḥ al-Dīn discussing a military problem with men of his entourage. About the same time, Mardī al-Tarsūsī, honoring the sultan's exploits in the war against the infidels, presented him with a manual on weapons (the Frankish shield and mangonel included), the disposition of units in battle, and archery.[18]

There can be little doubt that Frankish knights and their leaders engaged likewise in discussions of military issues (even though the composition of Frankish manuals may be ruled out). The sources are silent about such discussions, but we can recognize them by their fruits.

Surely the Franks were aware of their small number, the tiny extent of their kingdom, the great distance from their Western homeland and the insecure communications with it, the danger posed by enemies who ruled vast, populated territories and who, if victorious, could expect the kingdom's subjected Muslims to join them in quashing the Frankish entity. Foucher of Chartres, the cleric who had seen battle, depicts the Franks as a tiny people persevering amazingly amidst many hostile kingdoms, with the Great Sea separating it from Christendom.[19] And the quite conventional speech that Foucher has King Baldwin I make just before the First Battle of Ramla (1101)—in which 260 knights and 900 foot soldiers faced a vastly superior Fatimid force—concludes with the wry observation: "If you want to run away—France is verily far off from you."[20]

How did the Frankish knights cope with this precarious situation? To neutralize the numerical superiority of their enemies, they evolved an aggressive style of warfare, perfecting the mass charge of heavily armored cavalrymen into a well-nigh irresistible tactic that gave them victory time and again. The success of this mounted shock combat, relatively rare in Europe, depended on the knights' willingness to give up the military individualism typical of their class in the Western homeland, and to learn to fight in a large, cohesive army that combined the retinues of various lords.[21] In this context it is instructive to examine the twenty-three instances in which William of Tyre uses the expression "military discipline." In twelve cases, he relates that "our" men were set in order, or drawn up in a line of battle, according to military discipline.[22] In two instances "our" men were defeated either because they broke ranks contrary to military discipline or because, surprised by the enemy, they were unable to draw up a battle array conforming to it.[23] Finally, in one case William expressly states that while "our" army was on the march and the enemy attacked its flanks, "our" men desisted from going on attack against them, because they knew that to break ranks contrary to military discipline would entail a punishment harsher than the one meted out to deserters.[24] Evidently William grasped that well-ordered disposition in battle and on march was a key feature of the Franks' art of war.

The massive shock-cavalry charge was a basic Western tactic the Franks perfected; the raising of a light cavalry was an improvement they introduced, probably under Byzantine influence, in the wake of their early battles against the Turks. The First Crusaders, whose host was composed of mounted knights wielding lances and foot soldiers with bows and spears, suffered many casualties from swift onslaughts by Turkish mounted archers of nomadic origin. In response, the Franks developed a light cavalry of their own, whose men were known as Turcopoles; similarly to the Byzantine name the Franks gave their imitation gold coins, they chose a Byzantine term for their cavalry's new component. Yuval Noah Harari discovered that the Turcopoles constituted about one half, and occasionally more, of the Frankish mounted arm. Of variegated ethnic descent—Muslim converts, Eastern Christians, and apparently, to a considerable extent, Frankish burgesses—their military roles were reconnaissance and message delivery, lightning strikes and raids, harassment, and skirmishes. When the Frankish army was on the march, the Turcopoles defended its van and rear against attacks by Muslim mounted archers; during a massive cavalry charge, the Turcopoles joined the heavily armored Frankish knights, thus augmenting, or doubling, the size of the shock cavalry. This creation, virtually from scratch, of the Turcopole light cavalry played a significant role in the Franks' ability to hold their own in a military theater that differed so strikingly from the one in which they originated.[25]

The Franks' adversaries were keen on neutralizing the Frankish massive cavalry charges that led to their defeat so often. The Fatimid vizier al-Afḍal (d. 1121) was credited by much later authors with establishing an elitist cavalry unit "on the model of the Frankish Templars."[26] Mardī al-Tarsūsī, in the manual presented to Ṣalāḥ al-Dīn, astutely points out that the arrangement of the Muslim army in a single mass, favors "the accursed Franks," who aim at storming and overwhelming it with all their forces. To confuse and stun them, it is imperative to array the army in several separate contingents: when the Franks strike at one, the others surround and break them.[27]

This dialectic between the doings of the Franks and their adversaries can also be discerned in Frankish castle construction. When the Muslims under Nūr al-Dīn, having learned from the Franks how to transport dismantled siege engines, employed heavier artillery alongside their time-honored sappers-tunnellers, and conquered several Frankish castles in the 1160s, the Franks countered by a radical advance in fortification. Their new, concentric castles—of which Belvoir, overlooking the upper Jordan Valley, is the striking example (see fig. 9)—stood out for an additional, outer line of walls that drastically impeded the

FIGURE 9. Belvoir Castle. *Above:* The Arab village Kawkab el-Hawā that existed within the castle's ruins until 1948. Source: Survey of Israel, Tel Aviv. The aerial photo was taken in 1956. *Below:* The castle, after its excavation in the 1960s. Photo: Duby Tal, Albatross Aerial Perspective, Herzlia

Muslim sappers and, even more importantly, allowed the Franks to fight simultaneously from the inner and outer walls, doubling effective firepower.[28]

Also, the concentric castles had larger and taller towers, thicker and higher walls, deeper and wider moats, massive vaults for the storage of food and water that also provided shelter from Muslim artillery during a siege, and postern gates that allowed for surprise sorties against the besiegers. As Ellenblum eloquently put it, these castles "should be regarded . . . as the most evident visual expression of the cultural dialogue between East and West. Not because one of the sides 'borrowed' an architectural expression from the other but because they were the outcome of a lengthy, ongoing dialogue between two schools of military tactics and approaches."[29] Fighting against Muslims and maintaining a silent dialogue with their art of war was the dominant facet of the Frankish knights' encounter with them. But it was not the only one.

Fighting alongside Muslims: Temporary Brethren in Arms

Albert of Aachen relates that when the crusader knights were riding to the Battle of Ascalon in August 1099, they were accompanied by a most noble Saracen, an erstwhile ruler of the city of Ramla who had become Godefrid of Bouillon's ally. As the crusaders were approaching Ascalon, they came upon a great multitude of camels, oxen, buffalos, and sheep scattered in the plain. The Saracen warned them that this dispersal of herds in front of them was an Egyptian trick, contrived to start the Christians' rush for booty that would encumber their army with plunder and render it an easy target. Godefrid and the other crusader leaders, put on guard by this warning, proclaimed that whosoever was to touch booty before the battle would have his ears and nose cut off. The Saracen converted to Christianity soon thereafter, either before or after fighting alongside the crusaders in the battle of 12 August 1099 that ended with their resounding victory.[30]

Some other Muslim warriors chose to serve the Franks; several of them apostatized and turned Christian.[31] In 1112, Countess Adelaide of Sicily brought to the Kingdom of Jerusalem "Saracen men who were very strong archers" as a gift to her husband, King Baldwin I.[32] And when in 1182–83 Renaud of Châtillon launched his daring raid into the Red Sea, apostate Bedouins aided his men.[33]

There were also alliances between Muslim rulers and the Franks that led to side-by-side fighting. In 1105, the Seljuk strongman Ertash conspired with the governors of Baalbek and Buṣrā against Toghtekin of Damascus, and the three conspirators entered into an alliance with King Baldwin I. Consequently, Ertash, with "one hundred Turkish archers," fought alongside the Franks in the Third Battle of Ramla—but Baldwin failed to support his designs on Damascus.[34] In 1140, Muʿīn al-Dīn Unur, the Seljuk governor of Damascus, wary of the intentions of Zengi, the powerful atabeg of Mosul, entered into an alliance with King Fulk of Jerusalem, and the Frankish and Damascene armies jointly besieged the Zengid-held town of Bāniyās (the Frankish Belinas). "It was not easy to discern," wrote William of Tyre, "which of the two forces fought more boldly, or pressed the attack more sharply, or persevered longer in the burden of warfare against the common enemy. Our knights and the Damascene cohorts were equal in will, in accord about aims; although greatly different in the experience and practice of arms, no army was inferior to the other in the wish to inflict injury."

After the Muslims brought huge beams from Damascus, Frankish artisans and wood-hewers constructed a tall wooden tower, its parts joined by iron nails: thus, the Muslims provided the raw material for a Frankish siege engine. The campaign ended with the surrender of Bāniyās, which became part of the Kingdom of Jerusalem.[35] In 1167, the Franks under King Amaurry allied with Egyptian troops under the Fatimid vizier Shāwar and fought along the banks of the Nile against the Turks of Shīrkūh. On two occasions Amaurry dispatched forces composed of Franks and Egyptians, yet in the main battle the Egyptian allies turned out to be, according to William, of little use.[36] Such feats of fighting alongside Muslims, as well as the many political alliances with them, attest to the Franks' partial integration into the regional power system. Yet this integration, however incomplete, estranged newly arrived crusaders from the West, for whom all Muslims were enemies, from the Franks. The estrangement became acute after the failure of the Second Crusade at Damascus in 1148, attributed to Frankish nobles who purportedly received bribes from the besieged Damascenes. Henceforward, states William of Tyre, Western rulers generally mistrusted the Frankish leaders, and eagerness to go on crusade dampened down.[37]

Curiosity about the other side existed even when the Frankish-Muslim encounter was adversarial. For instance, during the siege of Jerusalem in 1099, Baldwin of Bourcq—the future King Baldwin II—captured "a most noble knight, a bald-headed man, old and corpulent." Brought in fetters to Baldwin's tent, he promptly sat down on his purple-cloth-covered bed. "When the Christian princes saw that the Saracen was a wise, noble, and vigorous man, they frequently enquired about and discussed his life and customs."[38] When in 1124 the Franks and their Venetian allies succeeded in conquering Tyre, the inhabitants who emerged from inside the walls took delight in examining the Frankish war machines, siege towers, arms, and camps and even wished to know the names of the Frankish leaders, whereas the Franks entered the city and admired the sturdiness of its fortifications, buildings, towers, and walls, its harbor difficult of access, and the perseverance of its defenders.[39]

How much more intimate the mutual acquaintance between allies! In 1140, when the Franks and the Damascenes succeeded in demoralizing the defenders of Bāniyās, Muʿīn al-Dīn Unur, the ruler of Damascus, offered its commander an annual revenue from the income of the town's baths and orchards: "for it would seem scandalous and unsightly if a noble man and the lord of so famous a town, driven out of his inheritance, should be compelled to beg for alms." The Frankish leaders, with whom the notion that their foe deserved a settlement appropriate to his social standing must have struck a familiar chord, assented to this solution.[40] Later, Unur—whom William characterizes as "a man most prudent and a lover of our people"—made an unprecedented visit to the Frankish Kingdom.[41] While in Jerusalem, he was allowed to enter the

Christianized Dome of the Rock, accompanied by Usāma ibn Munqidh; a Frank insisted on showing him God when he was young, and led the two Muslims to an icon of Mary with the child Jesus in her lap. In Acre he visited King Fulk and asked him for a goshawk-hunter that a Genoese brought from the West.[42] And while riding from Acre to Tiberias, William of Buris, the kingdom's constable and lord of Tiberias, related to Muʿīn al-Dīn Unur and Usāma a story about Frankish medicine.[43] Usāma himself calls the Knights Templar of the Aqṣā Mosque/Temple of Solomon "my friends."[44] He became the constant companion of a Frankish knight who called him "my brother" and offered, before his return to the West, to take with him Usāma's fourteen-year-old son so that he might there "observe the knights and acquire reason and chivalry." Usāma, considering the proposal preposterous yet unwilling to offend his temporary friend, replied that although he fervently hoped to hear this offer, he must decline it because his mother, closely attached to his son, made him swear to return the boy to her. "Your mother," asked the Frank, "she is still alive?" "Yes," replied Usāma. "Then do not disobey her," the Frank said.[45] An arresting portrait of two warriors, each sure of his culture's intrinsic superiority, yet each steadfastly committed to polite discourse—a politeness that did not preclude combat. Usāma fought against the Franks both before and after these friendly encounters.

The Frankish-Fatimid alliance in 1167 led to an acquaintance with Fatimid grandeur and ceremonial. Hue, the young lord of Caesarea whom King Amaurry sent to Cairo together with a Templar knight in order to obtain Caliph al-ʿĀḍid's confirmation of the treaty between the two parties, described their reception at the caliphal palace to William of Tyre in great detail. Its sheer size and stupendous splendor dazzled him. Conducted through well-guarded passages, the Frankish envoys reached a spacious court open to the sky, its galleries resting on marble columns, its paneled ceilings gilded, its "floor consisting of small stones of variegated color" (that is, a mosaic pavement); marble pools overflowed with limpid water, and various kinds of birds, "which our world does not know," hovered above. Thence the chief eunuchs led them to still more graceful buildings, adorned with paintings of quadrupeds common in the East and South but never seen in the West. Finally, the envoys arrived at the royal residence, where the vizier Shāwar showed reverence to the caliph by throwing himself three times to the ground and laying down his sword. Then the richly decorated curtains were pulled aside and revealed the caliph sitting on a golden throne, with a few courtiers around him. The sultan kissed the caliph's feet and went on to explain the reason for the treaty with the Franks and its terms. The caliph approved it. The Frankish envoys demanded that he confirm it with his own hand as King Amaurry had done. The courtiers were aghast, but after a long deliberation and with Shāwar urging on, the caliph reluctantly extended a veiled hand. Hue of Caesarea insisted that the caliph, to demonstrate his sincerity, must bare his hand. The Egyptians were shocked, but ultimately the caliph, much indisposed, put his bare right hand into that of Hue.[46] A clash of customs and wills, in which the Frankish lord gained the upper hand.

Not all friendly interactions between Frankish knights and their Muslim counterparts were rooted in or reflected politico-military alliances; some appear to have been strictly personal. William of Tyre relates that during a clash between the armies of King Baldwin III and Nūr al-Dīn in 1150, a most powerful Turk, in steadfast fraternal pact with the kingdom's (future) constable, Onfroi II of Toron, passed on to him the critical information that Nūr al-Dīn's army, its provisions exhausted, was about to retreat.[47] More than a century later, the Templar knight Matheus Sauvage and the Mamlūk sultan Baybars maintained a close relationship, possibly propped up by a blood brotherhood.[48]

Crossing—and Recrossing—the Lines

In the morning of 4 July 1187—the day of the Battle of Ḥaṭṭīn—King Gui of Lusignan summoned a knight by the name of Johannes, "who oftentimes fought alongside the Turks and knew all their ways," and asked for his advice. Johannes recommended to the king and the assembled Frankish leaders to charge with all their forces, forming a compact wedge aimed at the spot where Ṣalāḥ al-Dīn's tall standard stood out; once the Turks around it were defeated, the other contingents would be easily overcome. His counsel was accepted by all; but Raymond of Tripoli argued that one cannot trust a man who first repudiated the Franks and then the Turks. The knight's helpful advice was rejected, and the proposal of the treacherous Raymond to occupy the high ground won the day—so reports Robert of Auxerre.[49] Yet during the final phase of the battle the Franks appear to have fallen back on the knight's advice, and the tactic he proposed almost gave them a last-minute victory.[50] In any case, Johannes's past fighting in the enemy's ranks did not disqualify him from serving in the Frankish army.

Another Frankish knight who crossed the lines was the Tyre-born Johan Gale. Having found his wife with his liege lord, Johan killed him and fled to Ṣalāḥ al-Dīn, where he was warmly received. The sultan appointed him to teach his nephew to fight according to the Frankish fashion and learn the ways of courtliness, but the knight broke his trust, sold the nephew to the Templars, used the money to reach a settlement with the relatives of his slain lord, and became able to return to the Kingdom of Jerusalem. The enraged Ṣalāḥ al-Dīn besieged the Templar castle of Roche Guillaume—the year must have been 1188—because he knew the hateful Johan Gale to be there; however, he raised the siege when induced to believe that Tyre was to fall into his hands. Later, Johan Gale advised the crusading King Philip II Augustus of France about the affairs of Outremer; this must have been in 1191.[51]

Raoul of Benibrac also crossed the lines after having been grossly ill-treated by his lord. When Baldwin of Ramla married Raoul's fiancée, the embittered knight went over to the Saracens and "caused great harm to Christendom," writes Ernoul. He promised to deal with his misdeeds later on, but unfortunately failed to do so.[52]

And Roger of Howden, the chronicler who participated in the Third Crusade, tells the story of Robert of St. Albans, an English Knight Templar who abjured Christianity, went over to Ṣalāḥ al-Dīn, and promised to deliver Jerusalem to him. Ṣalāḥ al-Dīn gave him his niece in marriage and appointed him commander of a huge army. Robert divided it into three contingents, two of which devastated the region between Montreal (in Transjordan) and Nablus, destroying Jericho and Sebaste. The third contingent attacked Jerusalem but was roundly defeated, and Robert himself escaped with difficulty.[53] The story was rightly rated by Röhricht as legendary; but the traversal of the Templar knight, whose name and origin are spelled out, is credible.[54]

The crossing of Frankish knights to the Saracen side was frequent enough to warrant its treatment in the *Book for the King*. This law collection lays down that if a knight crosses over to the land of the Saracens and returns within a year and a day, he is to recover his fief; if he does not return within this span of time, he may be disinherited, "if [his] lord so wishes." Yet the absolute precondition for regaining the fief is a steadfast adherence to Christianity while among the Saracens. The knight who crosses over "and renounces the law [that is, religion] of Jesus Christ for that of *Mahoumet*" loses his fief forever.[55] This law does not mention that the knight left the kingdom in order to fight alongside the Saracens; on the contrary, it refers to his detention at their hands and his endeavor to escape as soon as possible. Yet the phrase that he went to the land of the Saracens "for some affair of his" covers many possibilities, temporary service under Muslim leaders included.[56]

The Templar statutes adopt a harsher stance: a brother who escapes to the Saracens is cast out from the order; a brother who threatens to cross over to them may lose his habit.[57]

Some Knowledge of Arabic

We may assume that many Frankish knights acquired a bit of Arabic that allowed them to manage their serfs and slaves, just as the latter acquired a smattering of the Frankish dialect of French, and that the absorption of Arabic words into that dialect eased such limited communication. We may also assume that the longer a Frankish knight lived in the East, the more fluent did his pidgin Arabic become. Usāma ibn Munqidh famously remarked that Franks recently arrived from the West were "rougher in character than those who have become acclimatized and have frequented the company of Muslims."[58] It stands to reason that some Frankish old-timers, who met with Muslims of a social standing comparable to their own, gained a still better grasp of Arabic. And Frankish knights who spent time in Muslim captivity, in some cases for many years, also had an opportunity to do so.[59]

In one case we are expressly told that this happened. Renaud of Châtillon, the brutal prince of Antioch—he once forced the sickly Patriarch Aimery of Antioch to sit an entire day under a scorching summer sun, his bare head besmeared with honey attracting swarms of flies—fell into captivity in 1160 and remained imprisoned in Aleppo for about fifteen years.[60] In one of the most sensitive essays in contemporary crusade research, Carole Hillenbrand has reconstructed, almost ex nihilo, a plausible account of Renaud's long, probably harsh captivity. She assumes that he developed there an intense and relentless hatred for his captors and learned where Muslims were most vulnerable. Therefore, after his release in 1176, when he became the lord of Transjordan and its fortresses of Karak (Petra) and Montreal (Shawbak), he aimed implacably at attacking and annihilating Islam and set in motion, in 1182, the daring raid aimed at the holy cities of Mecca and Medina.[61]

This reconstruction can be buttressed by a statement by Pierre of Blois, who heard at the papal court reports about Ṣalāḥ al-Dīn's execution of Renaud immediately after the Battle of Ḥaṭṭīn; the reports were corroborated by Aimery of Lusignan—captured at Ḥaṭṭīn together with his brother King Gui of Lusignan and with Renaud—who described the event to Archbishop Baldwin of Canterbury and to Pierre of Blois after the two landed at Acre on 12 October 1190.[62] Consequently Pierre was able to state in his "Passion of Renaud, Prince of Antioch," that Renaud, when captured in his youth, kept hearing the Arabic language, which he did not know, but he "learned it after a long exercise, coached by necessity."[63] In other words, he acquired some knowledge of Arabic while in prison.[64] He may also have learned there from some Muslim inmate about Islam's holy cities; an exchange between a Muslim and a Christian during their sojourn in a Cairo jail allowed the Muslim to describe much later the countries of western Europe.[65]

Ibn Jubayr, who on 25 March 1183 saw in Alexandria Frankish prisoners who had participated in the raid into the Red Sea and Hejaz instigated by Renaud, learned that its aim was "to enter the City of the Prophet—may God bless and preserve him—and remove him from the sacred tomb."[66] Modern historians of the crusades, probably deeming Ibn Jubayr's statement fantastic, chose to disregard it, yet it is corroborated—and amplified—by other sources.[67] ʿAbd al-Laṭīf al-Baghdādī, whom we have already met visiting Ṣalāḥ al-Dīn in Jerusalem in 1192, and who knew the literati in his entourage, wrote that the Frankish raiders intended to dig up the Prophet's tomb, take his remains with them, and then charge Muslims money for permission to visit them. The work containing this statement has not survived, but it is cited by al-Dhahabī (d. 1348). Al-Maqrīzī (d. 1442), who does not indicate his source but who may have relied on ʿAbd al-Laṭīf, offers a slightly expanded statement: the raiders schemed to take the Prophet's body to their country, rebury it, and allow Muslims to visit it only upon the payment of a fee. Mujīr al-Dīn (1456–1522) offers the same information.[68] Recently a further account that partially concurs with Ibn Jubayr and ʿAbd al-Laṭīf has come to light. It appears in a marginal note to the chronicle of Prince al-Malik al-Manṣūr of Ḥamāh, the great-nephew of Ṣalāḥ al-Dīn who fought alongside his father Taqī al-Dīn at Ḥaṭṭīn and witnessed its aftermath. The marginal note, probably written by the prince-chronicler himself, offers some new details about the raid of 1182–83. It then relates that in 1186 Ṣalāḥ al-Dīn sent the envoy al-ʿĀdil to Renaud in Karak, and the latter told him that he had decided to launch a much larger expedition on land and sea and lead it in person to Medina, "the city of your Prophet," in order "to unearth his body and transport it here to my place; and no Muslim will be able to make a pilgrimage to his tomb without paying a fee."[69]

Is it conceivable that Renaud planned to snatch Muḥammad's remains, reinter them in his lordship—say, in Karak—and deflect Muslim pilgrims to the new tomb? About thirty-five years later the German pilgrim Thietmar, having visited Transjordan and Mount Sinai, related that a certain nobleman of Petra (Karak) or Scobach (Shawbak, Montreal) wished, at a monk's suggestion, to transfer the body of St. Catherine from the Sinai monastery "to another place." He made preparations to carry it off, assembled a multitude of men, and almost reached the church when God's miracles intervened and caused him to repent and bestow landed property on the monastery.[70] It stands to reason that this nobleman of Karak and Montreal was no other than Renaud of Châtillon.[71] If so, the Arabic accounts of ʿAbd al-Laṭīf al-Baghdādī and al-Malik al-Manṣūr and the Latin account of Thietmar allow for the hypothesis that the bold, ingenious lord of Transjordan aimed inter alia at creating a new holy site, attracting Muslim and Christian pilgrims.

In any case, the marginal note to al-Malik al-Manṣūr's chronicle reports that Renaud's intention concerning the Prophet's remains enraged Ṣalāḥ al-Dīn to the point that he vowed to kill him with his own hands. According to Pierre of Blois, Ṣalāḥ al-Dīn did so in the aftermath of the Battle of Ḥaṭṭīn after a sharp exchange between the two, in which each called on the other to convert to his religion. The exchange, emphasizes Pierre, took place in Arabic.[72]

A Frankish noble who learned Arabic under less exacting circumstances was Renaud, lord of Sidon, one of the four great barons of the kingdom. The *Lineages of Outremer*, dating from 1265–70, describes him as "extremely ugly and very wise."[73] Bahāʾ al-Dīn ibn Shaddād testifies that he knew Arabic and, moreover, "had some familiarity with histories and collections of *ḥadīth* [traditions of the sayings and deeds of Muḥammad]"—in other words, he attained direct knowledge of the history of Oriental rulers that King Amaurry was keen to obtain through William of Tyre's good services. Bahāʾ al-Dīn adds that he heard that Renaud kept a Muslim "who read to him and explained things."[74] In May 1189 Renaud negotiated with Ṣalāḥ al-Dīn about the surrender of his castle of Beaufort, and Bahāʾ al-Dīn, who was present, relates that he did "frequent the sultan's presence, disputing with us about his religion while we argued for its falsity. He was an excellent conversationalist and cultured in his talk."[75] The protracted negotiations, during which Renaud was seized and severely tortured, ended with the castle's surrender in April 1190.[76] Later, in November 1191, he negotiated with Ṣalāḥ al-Dīn on behalf of Conrad of Montferrat.[77] Another Arabic-speaking

Frankish knight, Onfroi IV of Toron, served as interpreter during King Richard the Lionheart's negotiations with Ṣalāḥ al-Dīn's brother al-ʿĀdil and during a meeting of Ṣalāḥ al-Dīn with "Franks from overseas."[78]

The Arabic of Renaud of Sidon and Onfroi IV of Toron is attested by chance remarks by Muslim chroniclers. Since it is not easy to generalize from them, historians have expressed diametrically opposed views on the Franks' knowledge of Arabic.[79] I believe that we are witness to an ongoing process rather than a static situation. In 1147 knowledge was still so rare that the Franks were constrained to send to Damascus an envoy who had been suspected of treachery during an earlier mission.[80] By the 1180s if not earlier, knowledge of Arabic had become considerably more widespread, and the trend intensified in the thirteenth century.[81] The last chronicler of the Frankish East, the so-called Templar of Tyre, translated from Arabic into French the beginning of the letter that the Mamluk sultan al-Malik al-Ashraf sent to the Templar Master William of Beaujeu a short time before besieging Acre in April 1291; the chronicler did so in order to demonstrate the stilted style of Mamluk diplomatic epistles.[82] The mirror image of this demonstration of pompousness is the view of al-Qalqashandī (d. 1418), the leading authority on the composition of Arabic chancery documents, about the Franks' Arabic. He believed that it was poor, and therefore the Mamluk-Frankish Arabic-written truce treaties of the years 1265–85 stand out for their vulgarity, lack of eloquence, and "stupid wording."[83]

The only Muslim known to have studied some Latin did so, like Renaud of Châtillon, while in captivity. This was Nāṣr al-Dīn (William of Tyre's *Noseradinus*), who in 1154 murdered the Fatimid caliph al-Ẓāfir and attempted to flee with his father ʿAbbās to Damascus but was captured by Frankish troops while underway in Transjordan. Having become part of the booty apportioned to the Knights Templar and held in chains for many days, he expressed the wish to convert to Christianity, "learned already the Roman letters and was instructed in the basics of Christian faith." However, the Templars chose to sell their captive for sixty thousand bezants to the Egyptians, who lynched him to death.[84]

The Knights Templar: A Religious Order of Warriors

The establishment of the Order of Knights Templar in Jerusalem amounted to a revolutionary innovation in the history of the Roman Catholic Church: a group of professed religious was permitted—and expected—to wage war against the infidel; contemplative and active life were conjoined, with licit killing conspicuous within the active one. The Founding Brothers of the new order resembled monks in some points, canons regular in other ones, lay brothers (*fratres conversi*) in some, and secular knights in many other respects.[85] Yet they were definitely distinct from all these, constituting a brand-new entity.[86] As the Templar Rule of 1129, addressing the order's members, put it, "this new sort of religion began from you at the Holy Places, so that you should mingle knighthood with religion [*religioni militiam admisceretis*] and thus religion, armed by knighthood, should advance and kill the enemy without sin."[87] A new sort of religion, but at the same time a new sort of knighthood; some time before the promulgation of the Templar Rule, Abbot Bernard of Clairvaux, the towering churchman of the age, titled his exhortation on the Templars *In Praise of the New Knighthood*, extolling them as *sancta militia* (holy knighthood).[88]

The preamble to a grant bestowed on the Templars at Noyon in 1130, in Bernard's presence, adds a further dimension to the order's originality. It refers to the three divinely instituted orders, namely, those who pray, those who work, and those who fight (here called *defensores*, those who defend), and claims that the latter order had almost entirely perished. However, God, in his mercy, deigned a short time ago to restore it in the Holy City, "so that where in time past the church took its origin, there the said order should begin its restoration."[89] In a formulation typical of traditional societies, the rise of the strikingly innovative Order of the Knights Templar is presented, or camouflaged, as the rejuvenation of an age-old Christian institution, restored to pristine purity.

In their internal stratification and governance, too, the Templars differed markedly from traditional religious orders. While these were increasingly led by ordained priests to whom the lay members were subordinated, the core of the Templar order consisted of lay brother-knights of whom one served as the order's Master, and the brother-priests were officially subordinated to them.[90] Hence, the Templar order was a religious entity governed, as it were, by lay brothers—a veritable inversion of the conventional monastic setup. Outwardly, the lay status of the Templar brother-knights was broadcast by their beards, which likened them to lay brothers. Inwardly, their lay origin entailed a limited or even nonexistent command of Latin that set them once again apart from traditional orders. A ruling issued by an Italian chapter of the new order some time before 1187 throws light on the astounding ignorance of some (perhaps many) early Templars: it stipulates that all brothers who do not know the Apostles' Creed and the Lord's Prayer must learn them according to their ability, either in Latin or in the Romance vernacular.[91] Surely the brothers' lay upbringing was the main reason for such scant knowledge. Nevertheless, the Templars themselves, and many contemporaries, were aware that, as members of a religious entity, they differed from ordinary laymen.[92]

Because of the Templars' revolutionary mingling of a warrior's way of life with that of a professed religious, and because of the lay status of the knight Hue of Payns, the order's founder and first Master, ecclesiastical approval of the new entity's Rule had to differ from the course habitual in conventional orders of monks or canons regular, where founders enjoyed spiritual authority and learning that allowed them to draw up Rules for their congregations and write treatises for their edification.[93] Hue evidently understood that he lacked the authority to promulgate a Rule, but in those early times of the Kingdom of Jerusalem, the Frankish prelates, too, did not consider themselves empowered to sanction so momentous a departure. The limit of their innovativeness at that stage was the decision taken in 1120 at the Council of Nablus, according to which a cleric who carries arms for the sake of defense must not be held culpable–a decision that, understandable against the background of extreme emergencies of the Frankish East in which clerics were pressed into military duties, ran squarely in the face of prevailing ecclesiastical rulings.[94] It is possible that in the margins of that council the Templars were recognized as a separate entity.[95] In any case, the approval of the Templar Rule required its endorsement by leading churchmen in the West. Abbot Bernard of Clairvaux instigated the convening of the Council of Troyes in January 1129, at which a papal legate, two archbishops, ten bishops, and eight abbots discussed and promulgated the Templar Rule. Hue of Payns's role in the proceedings was to present the usages that the Founding Brothers adopted in Jerusalem. The council either approved or forbade them.[96]

The mental setup of individual Founding Brothers remains unknown. It is a quirk of the documentation that, while Gerard of Nazareth offers rudimentary biographies of his "Men of God" who basically amounted to a Frankish offshoot of the eremitical and monastic stirrings in the West, no source sheds light on the personalities of the incomparably more original New Knights, whom the Rule of 1129 glorified as "Christ's companions in war." As a group, they appear to have started as a confraternity of warriors, attached to the Church of the Holy Sepulcher and lodged in the Jerusalem Hospital, who escorted pilgrims to the Holy Places; by 1120 they became autonomous, and King Baldwin II let them reside in the Temple of Solomon (see figs. 10a–b).[97] It is possible that before taking residence in that edifice they were known as "the devout" (*devotus* in Latin, *devot* in the vernacular).[98] This could explain their appellation in Arabic, *dāwiyya*.[99]

Yet there exists a document that sheds light on self-doubts that beset the early Templars: this is the letter that *Hugo peccator* (the Sinner) sent to the "Knights of Christ in the Jerusalem Temple." Previously it was assumed that Hue of Payns wrote it, but in 2013 Dominique Poirel has cogently established the authorship of Hugo of St.-Victor, the leading Parisian theologian; he may have sent it to Jerusalem in 1128–29, while Hue of Payns was in the West.[100] As Hugo puts it, the Devil made certain people perturb the Templars by denouncing their recourse to warfare as illegitimate and sinful, and by claiming that it obstructed their ascent to a higher, wholly spiritual order. Also, the Devil incited the order's lowly members against the brother-knights and advised them to join another group in which their work would be adequately appreciated. Hugo set out to rebuff one by one these diabolic attempts to undo, under the guise of piety, the fledgling order. Defending Templar warfare, he insisted—recalling thereby Abelard—on the centrality of intention. The Devil, he argued, tempts the brothers by injecting hatred and rage into their killing and cupidity into their despoiling. Yet—so Hugo—when they kill imbued by hatred of sin and not of man, when they despoil in punishment of his sins and not out of greed, their deeds as well as their intentions are pure. As for the longing for a higher order, Hugo retorts that the place one occupies is not important; ascent depends on true virtue; ergo, the Templars should stay in their place and fight, as Christ had done during his ministry. As for the order's subordinate members, Hugo assured them that all participants in the work will undoubtedly participate in the reward.

A glimpse of the ways in which the early Templars wished to lead their lives can be gauged by examining those of their usages that the prelates assembled at the Council of Troyes in 1129 decided to forbid. Fortunately, the prelates referred explicitly to these usages, thereby throwing some light on the pre-1129 situation. The first of the banned customs was to mark the death of a brother, as well as Easter and other feasts, by indiscriminate donations to the poor.[101] This custom implies that the early Templars were a tight-knit group intent on conspicuously commemorating the death of a member, in all probability in battle. The prelates looked askance at so unconstrained a commemoration and

FIGURE 10. Templar halls adjoining the Aqṣā Mosque (the Frankish Temple of Solomon). *Above:* On this rare aerial photo of the Dome of the Rock and the Aqṣā Mosque, taken from the north in the 1930s, the Templar halls are clearly visible to the left (east) of the mosque. Benjamin Z. and Nurith Kedar Archives. *Below:* The interior of one of the largest Templar halls, looking northeast. IAA, The Scientific Archive, 1919–1948. Jerusalem, photo 30.217. In 1943 the Waqf decided to demolish the halls: Kedar, "Vestiges," 17–19.

prescribed a much more limited one: celebration of the divine office and Mass by brother-chaplains, and giving a pauper, for forty days, the food and drink due to a living brother. Similarly, the prelates forbade the brothers to stay standing, "extravagantly and without measure," while hearing the divine office, and spelled out exactly when to sit and when to stand.[102] The custom of standing for too long a time reveals a bent toward self-mortification, faintly recalling one of Gerard of Nazareth's Men of God who recited daily the entire Psalter while on his feet.[103] Also, the prelates, having learned that exhausted knights were expected to rise for Matins, recommended that, by consent of the order's Master, they remain in bed and chant thirteen fixed prayers.[104]

In addition to prohibiting behavior the prelates regarded as too extreme, they also modified the order's internal organization. In Jerusalem, both brother-knights and brother-sergeants wore white clothes; the prelates condemned this egalitarian usage and ordered it eradicated: henceforth knights were to wear white, sergeants and squires black or brown, underscoring thereby the stratification Hugo of St.-Victor attempted to de-emphasize.[105] Also, the prelates ordered that not all brothers should always be called to council, but only those whom the Master considered suitable; when major issues were at stake, it would be proper to convoke the entire congregation "if it pleases the Master"; but once its advice was heard, the Master was to adopt the course he considered the best and most useful.[106] Finally, while the nascent order used to accept not only brothers but also sisters, the prelates decreed that henceforth no sisters were to be admitted, "because the ancient enemy removed very many men from the straight path to Paradise because of their association with women."[107] In sum, the Rule reveals that the pre-1129 Templars inclined toward a more ascetic way of life and a more egalitarian structure, and envisaged an order consisting of both brothers and sisters. Unfortunately, the prelates' prohibition does not spell out how the sisters' role had been construed, but the verb they use to describe their past admission, *coadunare* (to bring or join together), may hint at a closer setup than that of dual monasteries.

The limits of the early Templars' intellectual capacities can be gauged by the Old French translation or adaptation of the Rule, prepared for their sake by some cleric, within a decade of the promulgation of the Latin original. This Old French version was most likely intended to be heard rather than read; at the time, very few people were able to read in the vernacular.[108] The anonymous adapter frequently modifies the text in order to render it more easily comprehensible: for instance, the name of the *propheta* quoted in the original is spelled out as *David* in the adaptation, *Gehenna* reappears as *feu d'enfer* (hell's fire) and *superna retributio* (heavenly retribution) as *le regne de Paradis* (Kingdom of Paradise), while *interdictus* (interdict) is explicated as *entredis de oïr le servize Dieu* (prohibited to hear the divine service): evidently the adapter assumed that many Knights Templar would not be familiar with the ecclesiastical term *interdictus*.[109]

In other cases, the adapter painstakingly circumscribes a situation in order to avoid misunderstandings. For instance, where the Latin original states that the reader of the lessons at lunch and dinner should enjoin silence on the brothers, the Old French explains that the reader should do so "when he starts to read." And where the Latin text lays down that the brothers should go to Compline "upon hearing the signal," the adaptation enjoins them to go there "upon hearing the signal of the bell or of the clamor."[110] Evidently, the adapter aims at run-of-the-mill brothers of little learning, in need of clear-cut specifications. But at one point he profoundly alters the Latin text: a brother's willingness to *imitate*, through his death, the death of the Lord, becomes in Old French his willingness to *revenge*, through his death, the death of Christ.[111] A sublime endeavor envisaged by the prelates at Troyes gives way, in Jerusalem, to sanguinary retaliation.

The Knights Templar soon became the Kingdom of Jerusalem's first permanent military force—a novel, and critically needed, constituent buttressing a basically feudal army.[112] Their statutes regarding the various officeholders of the order add up to a very early military manual that stresses discipline (and not individual prowess, celebrated in chivalric culture), prescribes conduct on the march and in camp, instructs how to deliver the knights' charge, and much more.[113]

The Templars were the elite force of the kingdom's army. The Western Visitor who visited the kingdom between 1168 and 1187 wrote:

> The Templars are the very best knights. They wear white mantles with a red cross; a two-color standard, called *balcanum*, advances with them into battle. They join it in an orderly manner and without shouting. The first and sharpest clashes await them; they are the first to advance and the last to turn back, attending their Master's command. When they decide that the right moment to start a battle has come, and the sound of the trumpet resonates at the commander's order, they chant devoutly David's psalm: "Not to us, O Lord, not to us, but to thy name give glory" [Psalm 113:9 (Vulgate)] and,

> directing their lances, rush unto the enemy. Resolutely and of one mind, they seek out wedge- and horns-shaped battle dispositions; they never dare to retreat; and they either crush the enemy or die.[114]

The supreme tribute to the excellence of the Templars' fighting capacities came from the pen of the chronicler and logician Ibn Wāṣil (1208–98), who stood out for his less "jihādist" stance toward the Franks and for his acquaintance with Latin Europe.[115] Describing the rout of the Seventh Crusaders at the Battle of Fāriskūr (6 April 1250) and the capture of King Louis IX of France, Ibn Wāṣil dwells on the courage and fury exhibited in that battle by the Baḥrī Mamluks. The description is followed by the remarkable comment: "And they were the Templars of Islam [*dāwiyyat al-islām*]."[116] This comment appears, however, in only one branch of the manuscript tradition of Ibn Wāṣil's work and may even be the addition of a later redactor.[117] Similarly, the Western Visitor to the Kingdom of Jerusalem observes that the Assassins are as devout in their superstition as are the Templars in their religion. This observation was suppressed by some copyist: it appears in thirteenth-century manuscripts but does not recur in later ones.[118] Apparently, crediting the enemy with parity—no matter how limited—with one's own heroes struck some staunch believers, on both sides of the Christian-Muslim divide, as inappropriate.

Some Templars exhibited openness toward Eastern Christians. Two twelfth-century manuscripts from the Georgian Monastery of the Holy Cross in Jerusalem contain in their margins thirty-one donor commemorations, twenty-four of which refer to Westerners whose names are transcribed into the Georgian alphabet, for example Jirard, Per Gonsal, Ramond, Tsitsilia (see fig. 11). Three commemorations refer explicitly to Knights Templar: "Christ. True Cross, exalt and have mercy on Sir Per, Commander [*kumanduri*] of the Templars" (no. 7); "Christ. Have mercy on brother Peri of the Templars" (no. 8); "Christ. Holy Cross, have mercy and protect Sir Arberd [Robert?] *bche* [?] and brother of the Templars Juan" (no. 19).[119]

In addition, it has been suggested that *Jaufre Fausat* (no. 3) was the prominent Templar Gaufridus Fulcherii, and that *Gviliam Patera* (no. 10) was Guillelmus Petri, a Templar from Douzens.[120] *Philipe*, who appears together with *Elisabed*, *Elene*, and *Stephane* (no. 6), is undoubtedly the Frankish baron Phelippe of Nablus, the husband of Isabella (Elisabeth) and father of Helena and Stephania. The commemoration antedated Phelippe's entry into the Templar order in 1166 and his election to the order's mastership three years later.[121]

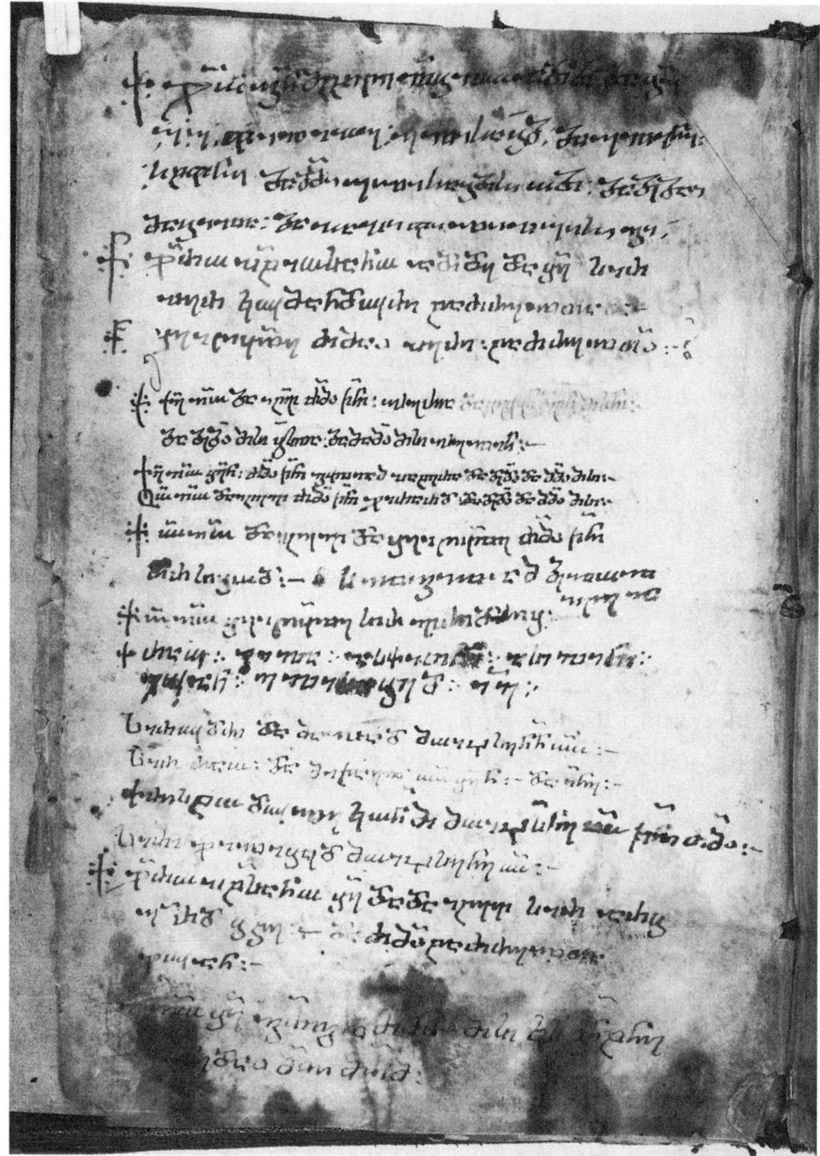

FIGURE 11. Templar donors listed in a Georgian manuscript. Giorgi the Athonite, "Great Synaxarion," copied in 1155 in the Monastery of the Holy Cross, Jerusalem. Tbilisi, National Centre of Manuscripts, shelfmark H-1661, fol. 1v.

Another Templar–Eastern Christian encounter took place at a distance of about 250 miles from Jerusalem, at Saydnāyā, in the mountains north of Damascus. The local Greek Orthodox convent was famous for an icon of the Virgin that exuded from the breasts an oil-like liquid that would heal the sick, Christian as well as Muslim. The story appears in Latin and Arabic from the late twelfth century onward. Templars played a central role in the diffusion, among Westerners, of the story of the miraculous icon and in the distribution of its thaumaturgic liquid to them. A Latin account mentions that the Templar Gautier of Marangiers, liberated from Muslim captivity sometime before 1186, passed through Saydnāyā and brought to Jerusalem some of the liquid emitted from the icon; it then made its way to the priory of Altavaux, southwest of Limoges.[122] Later accounts relate that during times of truce with the Muslims, Templars would go to Saydnāyā to pray, obtain the holy liquid, convey it to their houses, and then distribute it to pilgrims. They would also attest that they saw the icon and touched it with their hands.[123] The journey to a shrine deep in Muslim territory and the prospect of acquiring the rare, miraculous substance must have exerted a singular fascination on these knights.

And what happened to the initial doubts of the Founding Brothers that Hugo of St.-Victor attempted to dispel? Some Templars continued to feel the urge for a more spiritual way of life. Bartolomeus, one of Gerard's Men of God, went on pilgrimage to Jerusalem, where he joined the Templars, and later decided to serve the city's lepers. Fasts and vigils almost brought death upon him, and finally he joined a monastery on the Black Mountain.[124]

A far more prominent Templar who opted to leave the order and become a monk was Everard of Barres, the Templars' third Master. By 1143 he was in charge of the order in France; in 1147 he went on the Second Crusade with King Louis VII of France; early in 1149 he was elected in Jerusalem Master of the Templar order, but chose to return to France with the king. Later that year, after Nūr al-Dīn's annihilation of Raymond of Antioch's army, the Templar seneschal André of Montbard dispatched a panicky letter to Everard, urging him to come back: "For assuredly we believe that, even if you were to hasten very much, you would find us barely alive. Therefore, come and don't be tardy," adding rather incoherently a few lines later, "And though we understand that you will be tardy, come nevertheless."[125] Everard did take his time to return to Jerusalem. In 1152 he went West again, quit the order, and became a Cistercian monk at Clairvaux where he lived for many years.[126]

On the other hand, later Templars were no longer troubled by apprehensions that their shedding of blood might be illegitimate and sinful. Bernard of Clairvaux's emphatic assurance that the death they inflict, for Christ, on the enemy, is not a crime at all and rather merits the greater glory, the enthusiastic endorsement of their way of life by the prelates assembled at Troyes, the privileges bestowed on them by the papacy, and the intense backing by believers throughout the West eased such initial doubts out of existence.[127]

But outside the order such doubts hardened into outright condemnation. Isaac, the Cistercian philosopher and theologian who in about 1147 became abbot of the monastery of L'Étoile, probably had in mind the Templars when, in one of his sermons, he presented a new military order as a new monstrosity (*monstrum novum*) set out to kill unbelievers. He called it also "a new knighthood" (*nova militia*), a term that evokes the title of Bernard of Clairvaux's exhortation in support of the Templars, and observed acidly that the new order "despoils licitly and murders religiously," a formulation that sounds like a parody of the assertion of Hugo of St.-Victor that the Templars "do not wrongfully hate when they kill and do not unjustly covet when they despoil."[128] And in about 1190 Walter Map, a courtier of Henry II of England, unequivocally condemned Templar warfare as irreconcilable with Christ's teaching:

> [In Jerusalem the Templars] take up in protection of Christianity the sword that Peter was prohibited to take up in the defense of Christ. Peter learned there to seek peace by patience; I do not know who taught them to overcome force by violence. They take up the sword and they perish by the sword.[129] They assert however: "All laws and all legal systems permit to repulse force by force."[130] Yet He rejected this law when, with Peter striking, He did not command His legions of angels.[131]

Presumably Map was not persuaded by Bernard of Clairvaux's enthusiastic embrace of Templar warfare. He was no admirer of Bernard and included in his book some mocking anecdotes about his purportedly failed miracles. One of those, which dealt with Bernard laying down, praying, on a dead boy in a futile attempt to revive him, triggered Map's comment, loaded with double entendre: "Then he was the most unlucky of monks. Never have I heard of a monk laying down on a boy, without the boy instantly arising after him."[132]

That this anecdote—which, according to Map, was related in the presence of Gilbert Foliot, bishop of London—could have been put down in writing, speaks volumes for the openness of the Twelfth-Century Renaissance.[133]

The Novelties of the Jerusalem Hospital

Both the Knights Templar and the Knights Hospitaller originated in confraternities that took care of pilgrims from the West: the early Templars, by protecting and defending them, sword in hand, on their way to and from the Holy Places; the early Hospitallers, by nursing poor, frail, and sick pilgrims in their charitable institution in Jerusalem, the Hospital. Thus, while the Templars—professed religious engaging in warfare—amounted to a startling innovation, the Hospitallers began their existence as a conventional religious group engaged in works of mercy. These were, as Riley-Smith rightly put it, "two very different orders."[134] The subsequent militarization of the Hospital, that is, the transformation of the Hospitallers into an order that added warfare to its charitable work, is an ill-documented process: the sources are few and vague, and the first unambiguous evidence dates from 1136, when King Fulk entrusted "to the brothers of the House of the Hospital, which is in Jerusalem," the castle of Bethgibelin, constructed to restrain Fatimid raids from Ascalon and facilitate attacks against it.[135]

By the 1160s the order's militarization had become so obvious that Gilbert of Assailly, Master of the Hospital, could write to the archbishop of Trani that he and his brothers, "mingling together knighthood with religion [*religioni miliciam commiscentes*], sweat unceasingly in the defense of the Holy Land, resisting the enemies of Christ's cross, not unwilling to shed our blood."[136] The similarity of Gilbert's *religioni miliciam commiscentes* to the *religioni militiam admisceretis* (you should mingle knighthood with religion) of the Templar Rule of 1129 is hardly accidental. And for the Western Visitor the Hospitallers are, first and foremost, warriors who go into battle together with the Templars, and "alongside their warfare they take care of the poor and the sick."[137]

It was probably in the mid-twelfth century that an unknown Hospitaller devised an intricate legend about his order's foundation, locating it squarely within biblical times. Many years before the Incarnation, claims the legend, Christ ordered two men to build for him, next to Calvary, a lofty house in which he was to receive many poor saints. Later, Judas Maccabeus dispatched twelve thousand silver drachmas to the Hospital for distribution among the poor. Then the Son of God sent Zacharias and, later, a Roman legate to serve the poor there. After Incarnation, Christ lived and taught in the Hospital, nurturing and curing the poor; during the Crucifixion the apostles hid there, and it was thence that Mary and John the Evangelist left for Calvary. Finally, eight days after the Resurrection, the risen Christ appeared before his disciples in the Hospital.[138] A daring attempt to invent a grandiose biblical origin, possibly rooted in competition with the Knights Templar whose very name evoked the Bible, or in a desire to conceal the order's recent, mundane beginnings.[139]

Yet the most innovative, unprecedented facet of the Order of the Knights Hospitaller was the Jerusalem Hospital. It was not only a traditional hospital—habitual in the West—that offered accommodation and care to the poor and feeble and resembled a hospice, but also a medicalized hospital, that is, an institution in which salaried physicians treated the sick by medications and diets tailored to their individual afflictions.[140] In fact, it was the first medicalized hospital of the Latin world, subsequently emulated to some extent in the West.[141]

The Hospitaller statutes of 1182 contain the earliest dated evidence for the activity of physicians in the Jerusalem Hospital. They lay down that four wise physicians, "knowledgeable of the properties of urines and the diversities of illnesses," should be hired to serve the Hospital's poor and determine their medications.[142] This must not necessarily mean that in 1182 the number of physicians jumped from zero to four; it is plausible to assume that fewer physicians served there in earlier years, perhaps even from the institution's very beginnings.

According to the sparse documentation about these beginnings, about thirty years before the First Crusade a group of Amalfitan merchants established in Jerusalem two hospices for pilgrims from the West, one for men, the other for women. A brief, anonymous notice about Archbishop Johannes of Amalfi (ca. 1070–ca. 1082) relates that he made a pilgrimage to Jerusalem, where he was received by the Amalfitan founders of these hospices, in which men and women "were sustained and the sick healed" by persons who followed a quasi-religious way of life.[143] Evidently, the cure of the ill was practiced in the institution right from the beginning.

Unlike in the contemporary West, a number of medicalized hospitals flourished in the Islamicate and Byzantine East. It is symptomatic of this important East/West disparity that when, in the late eleventh century, Constantine the African translated into Latin *The Complete Book of the Medical Art* by ʿAlī ibn al-ʿAbbās al-Majūsī, he omitted the advice to visit hospitals in order to gain medical knowledge, for hospitals in which such knowledge could have been acquired did not yet exist in the Latin West.[144] In the Islamicate realm, however, professional medical treatment was quite commonly available also outside of hospitals, as the Cairo Geniza amply documents.[145]

The Amalfitan merchants who established the Jerusalem hospices were no newcomers to the East. The Amalfitan Lupino de Rini traveled to Cairo in 976; twenty years later a mob massacred there 107 (or 160) Amalfitans while others were able to escape; Geniza letters attest to Amalfitan commercial activity in Egypt and in the eastern Mediterranean in the eleventh century.[146] Therefore we may assume that the Amalfitans who decided to establish hospices in Jerusalem were aware of the availability of professional medical services in the Islamicate world. Moreover, there is evidence for the existence of a medicalized hospital in Jerusalem about two decades before they established those hospices. Nāser-e Khosraw, who arrived in Jerusalem on 5 March 1047, relates that the city "has a fine, well-endowed *bīmāristān* [hospital]. Many people are given drugs and elixirs. The physicians who are there receive salaries from the endowment for this *bīmāristān*."[147] The existence of this hospital could hardly have escaped the Amalfitan founders. Given that the Jerusalemite al-Muqaddasī, writing in the 980s, reported that in al-Shām (that is, Syria/Palestine) the physicians were generally Christians, one may hypothesize that the Amalfitans hired some Eastern Christian physician(s) to heal the sick of their hospices.[148]

Little is known about the functioning of the Jerusalem Hospital, which originated in the Amalfitan foundation in the first half of the twelfth century. Later pilgrim accounts indicate that the Hospital had become a vast enterprise: Nikulás, in about 1150, stated that it was the richest *spitali* in the world; Johann of Würzburg reported in the mid-1160s that a "huge multitude" of sick women and men were taken care of and fed in its different lodging places; he was told that the number of the feeble reached at the time two thousand, of whom sometimes more than fifty died in a single day. Benjamin of Tudela noted in about 1170 that in the house of the *Ospitāl* "rest all the sick who come there, and they are given all their needs in life and death." Theoderich, perhaps two years later, was unable to estimate the number of poor, sick, and feeble who lay in the hospital, but he noted that the number of beds exceeded one thousand. Of our witnesses, he was the first to call the building in which the sick were housed a *palatium* (palace).[149] Theoderich does not explain why the sick were put up in a "palace," but the term becomes comprehensible once we recall that the first statutes of the order, confirmed by 1153, refer to the poor as "lords" and to the Hospitallers as their "servants."[150] Evidently, the ailing lords were perceived as residing in a palace.[151]

An excavation conducted in 2013 by the Israel Antiquities Authority in the southeastern part of the complex that the Knights Hospitaller erected in Jerusalem has apparently revealed several wards of the Palace of the Sick, the order's hospital. Interpreting the results of this excavation, Ilya Berkovich and Amit Re'em argue that the Palace was an imposing vaulted structure, at least seven meters high, covering between 3,500 and 4,000 square meters, and capable of accommodating more than 1,000 beds.[152]

Two texts discovered in the late twentieth century throw much light on the institution's functioning. The first, preserved in Old French in a Vatican manuscript that appears to have been copied in Acre in about 1280, contains administrative regulations for the Palace of the Sick, datable to the years 1181/83. The regulations deal with admission to the institution: first, confession and communion; second, a meal near the palace's altar; third, the meting out of bed utensils and cutlery; finally, the escort to a bed. Ample space is then devoted to daily routine and, especially, to the foodstuffs provided to patients on various days of the week and on Christian feast days.[153] Much of the same ground is covered in greater detail by the second text, a Latin account carelessly copied in a fourteenth-century manuscript now in Munich. The anonymous author relates that he spent some time in the Jerusalem Hospital; his frequent biblical citations, quotations from Ovid and Horace, as well as his remarkably rich vocabulary suggest that he was a cleric, while his mention of *talenta* (units of account) may point to a German origin.[154] Because of the similarities between this account and the Hospitaller statutes of 1182 one is tempted to date it between 1182 and 1187; but—as I cautioned when introducing my edition of this text—"it is of course possible that the statutes merely codified prevailing practices," in which case the anonymous visitor might have stayed in the Hospital at an earlier date.[155]

The visitor's account reveals that the Palace of the Sick was divided into eleven wards, each served by a brother assisted by twelve attendants. Sick women had a Palace of their own, also divided into wards and served by the order's sisters. The visitor presents the care extended to the sick as a supreme expression of Christian charity, and highlights the divine remedy offered to the sick upon admission, the attendants' procession after Compline through all wards of the palace, and the proclamations to the sick at night: "O Lords, wine on the part of God!" or "Warm water, in the name of God."[156]

The salaried staff consisted of four doctors as well as of surgeons and bloodletters.[157] The administrative regulations that lay down that a physician must "swear by the saints *or vow*" to do all he can for the sick, in all probability aimed at enabling the employment of non-Christian doctors.[158] Eastern Christian physicians, who could of course swear by the saints, posed no problem. Yaʿqūb ibn Siqlāb, the Eastern Christian who studied and practiced medicine in Frankish Jerusalem and then rashly wore in Damascus "the usual dress of Frankish physicians," might have worked previously in the Palace of the Sick.

The anonymous visitor relates that, with the exception of lepers, the hospital admits all sick, of whichever origin, status, or gender. Moreover, non-Christians, too, were welcome: "In this holy house—which knows that the Lord invites all to salvation and does not want anyone to perish—men of the Pagan faith [Muslims] find mercy, and even Jews, if they hasten to it."[159] This willingness to admit Muslims and Jews was unheard-of in the contemporary West; the closest counterpart was the hospital of Mérida in Visigothic Spain, where, in about the year 600, medical care was provided to slaves and free men, Christians and Jews. Of course, from the tenth century onward, the *bīmāristān*s of the Muslim realm were open to patients of all three monotheistic religions, and Muslim, Christian, and Jewish physicians treated them. But these Islamic hospitals lacked mosques or specific locations for religious ritual, and the medicine practiced there was secular, whereas the Jerusalem Palace of the Sick was pervaded, as we have seen, by Christian rites.[160] The Geniza evidence indicates that Jews did not make use of the ritually neutral *bīmāristān*s, probably reluctant to transgress their dietary laws.[161] Hence it is hardly likely that they availed themselves of the services of the distinctly Christian Palace of the Sick; and the wording used by the anonymous visitor with regard to Jewish admission, "if they hasten to it," appears to hint that the Hospitallers' willingness to accept them was rarely tested.

Despite this fundamental difference between the *bīmāristān*s and the Palace of the Sick, their daily medical routines disclose striking similarities. In Jerusalem, the brother in charge of a ward ties up the belongings of every patient upon admission, holds them in custody in a room called *karavane*, and returns them upon convalescence—the same procedure as in the hospital at Fusṭāṭ established by Aḥmad b. Ṭūlūn in 872.[162] In Jerusalem, the four resident physicians make their rounds twice a day and examine the patients' urine and pulse; in the ʿAḍudī Hospital in Baghdad, originally established in 982, doctors visit the sick every Monday and Thursday to prescribe treatment, whereas those of the hospital that Nūr al-Dīn founded in Damascus examine the ill early each morning: so reports Ibn Jubayr, who visited the two cities in 1184. In Jerusalem, each doctor is accompanied by two attendants: one carries syrup, oxymel, electuaries, and other medicines, the other checks the urine, cleans the urine-flasks, and notices the diet the doctor prescribes for each patient; in Damascus, according to Ibn Jubayr, the overseer maintains registers in which the names of the patients are recorded, and the doctors order the preparation of drugs and foods as suitable for each patient.[163] Ibn Abī Uṣaybiʿa devotes an entry of his *Best Accounts of the Classes of Physicians* to Abū al-Majd ibn Abī al-Ḥakam, whom Nūr al-Dīn, upon the foundation of his hospital in Damascus in 1154, put in charge of the medical college. The entry amounts to a revealing portrait of this prominent physician of variegated interests.

> Outstanding in medicine, geometry, and astronomy, he also played the lute, the flute, percussion instruments and excelled as a singer. He visited the hospital frequently, making his rounds, seeing the patients, examining their conditions and determining the importance of their cases. He would be accompanied by the overseers [of the wards] and the superintendents, who would immediately, without hesitation, execute his orders concerning the treatment of each patient and the management of the cases. After finishing with all this, Abū al-Majd would go to the castle and visit any state dignitaries who might happen to be indisposed. Finally, he would go and sit in the great hall of the hospital, which was abundantly furnished and carpeted, and engage in study; for Nūr al-Dīn—may God have mercy upon him—had donated a large number of medical works to the hospital. . . . Physicians and students [of medicine] would come there to Abū al-Majd and sit before him to discuss medical matters. He taught his students [there] and would engage in discussion and study with them. After three hours with his books, he would make his way home.[164]

Had Abū al-Majd some counterparts in the Palace of the Sick? Possibly. The anonymous visitor's silence on the issue of medical instruction is not conclusive; he was hardly privy to the doctors' internal interactions.[165] Likewise, the author of the regulations of 1181/83, clued-up with regard to the attendants' routine and the fare doled out on Christian feast days, is silent about the rationale behind the advice and instructions of the physicians, whose professional world he evidently did not share.

Ibn Jubayr—who dwells on the hospitals of the major cities through which he passed, from Alexandria to Baghdad to Mosul to Aleppo to Damascus—halted in the Frankish kingdom for less than a month and did not visit Jerusalem. From a historian's point of view, this is unfortunate: as "Otto" Smail put it, "Ibn Jubayr was so observant a traveller that we wish he could have stayed in the kingdom for a little longer. Every few lines he brings momentarily to life some fresh aspect of [Frankish] society."[166] Had he visited Jerusalem, he would have surely mentioned the Palace of the Sick and possibly compared it with Islamic hospitals. Nevertheless, he made a highly pertinent remark, overlooked by crusade historians probably because it appears in the part of his account that deals with Sicily. Near Palermo, he writes, "we observed along the way that the Christians had churches fitted out for Christians who are ill, and that in their cities they have some such, along the lines of the Muslim *māristān*s, and we have seen some such [belonging] to them in Acre and Tyre. We marvelled at such solicitude."[167]

Evidently, Ibn Jubayr realized that the Christian hospitals he saw in Sicily and in the Frankish Kingdom were religious institutions, yet he considered them to be similar to the Muslim ones. It stands to reason that the Jerusalem hospital, the kingdom's earliest and largest, served as model for the hospitals of Acre and Tyre.

An examination of the foods offered in the Palace of the Sick, too, suggests an influence of Eastern (that is, Islamic—or rather Islamicate—and Byzantine) medicine. The emphasis on white bread may be taken as one example. In 1176 the Hospitaller Master Josbert laid down that the sick should always receive white bread; the regulations of 1181/83 stipulated that "every day there should be bought the whitest bread . . . and each of the sick should have of it," and the anonymous visitor observed that only the sick receive bread of the finest wheat flour.[168] This recalls the 1136 regulations of the Pantokrator Monastery in Constantinople that oblige the superior to often visit sick monks and provide them with white bread and the best wine.[169]

In the Islamic realm, white bread was repeatedly recommended by physicians. Ibn Riḍwān (d. 1068) counseled consuming high-quality wheat bread; Ibn Zuhr, who came to be known in the Latin West as Avenzoar, wrote in about 1150 that the best bread is made of wheat;

Ṣalāḥ al-Dīn's physician, Ibn Jumayʿ, advised him to eat white bread only; and Maimonides placed "well prepared wheat bread" at the head of his list of "excellent foods on which everyone who desires to stay healthy should rely."[170] Another example is the bias against the meat of female animals. The anonymous visitor relates that all physicians agree that such meat is "harder, thicker, stickier, and less digestible" than that of males, and therefore is never served to the sick.[171] In very similar terms, Maimonides advises against serving the meat of female sheep to asthmatics, "because it is sticky and hard to digest and contains many superfluities."[172] A third example is the serving of lighter meat to the sick. The visitor describes two kitchens. In the first, heavier food like the flesh of pigs and rams was prepared on Sundays, Tuesdays, and Thursdays, grain cakes and chickpeas on the other days. The brothers in charge of the wards and their attendants were to check who of the sick did not eat these at all or partook of them just a little. For such patients they hastened to fetch, from the second kitchen, the meat of hens, chickens, doves, partridges, lambs, young goats, eggs, and fish. The brothers received money to buy such delicate food outside the house—most probably at the poultry market nearby.[173] Similarly, Ibn Zuhr asserts that the meat of the hen is beneficial for the exhausted and convalescent and that all physicians agree that it is the best of meats.[174] For Maimonides, the best meat of birds is that of chicken, francolin, partridge, and turtledove, and he counsels to consume it because "the meat of birds is lighter than that of land animals and is digested quicker."[175]

Riley-Smith, revealing a touching pro-Hospitaller bias, wrote that "a [Hospitaller] respect for the dietary requirements of its Muslim and Jewish patients, who must have been pilgrims to their own shrines, may have been reflected in a statute which laid down that the sick were to have chicken if they could not stomach pork."[176] He even went so far as to suppose that the second kitchen that the anonymous visitor mentioned and in which chicken was cooked took into account Muslim and Jewish dietary constraints. Yet the statute on which he bases this daring hypothesis does not deal with the sick who could not consume pork and were given chicken, but with those who could not eat pork *or mutton* and received that substitute.[177] Now, Muslims and Jews are allowed of course to eat mutton, and therefore the statute cannot be interpreted as reflecting respect for their dietary laws: it undoubtedly refers, as the anonymous visitor clearly spells out, to patients who were unable to consume heavy meat and were therefore given lighter fare, quite in accordance with Islamicate medicine.[178]

Does the great emphasis, in the Latin and Old French texts, on foodstuffs, coupled with an absence of details about medical treatment, indicate that *caring* rather than *curing* was the fundamental objective of the Palace of the Sick and that its "modern analogy is not the hospital, but the convalescent home"?[179] The situation, I believe, was more complex. Islamicate medicine, as well as its classical antecedents, regarded dietary regulation as the primary *cure* of disease and recommended a very cautious recourse to medicinal treatment and drugs. Thus, Maimonides explains:

> The physicians have instructed every physician not to treat a patient with medication, if he can be treated only by a dietetic regimen. If one cannot manage without treating [him] with medication, one should treat him with things that are customary, such as medicines with nutritional properties and nutrients with medicinal properties. But if one cannot manage without a purely medicinal treatment, one should start with the mildest remedies, and if this is sufficient, it is good. But if it is not sufficient for the disease, one should resort to stronger [remedies] and then to [even] stronger ones. . . . One should not resort to very complex remedies, except when absolutely necessary.[180]

Evidently, foodstuffs served for *cure*.[181] Indeed, the opening paragraph of the 1181/83 regulations spells out no less than four times that, in the Palace of the Sick, foodstuffs were to be dealt out to the sick according to the physician's instruction or advice.[182]

And yet the Jerusalem institution was not only an early medicalized hospital that offered professional treatment to the sick. It was also a traditional Western-type hospice that took care of poor pilgrims enfeebled by the long voyage from Europe. It is impossible to estimate the ratio between the sick and the feeble, yet the wish to accommodate the latter must have been a main reason why the estimated 3,500 to 4,000 square meters of the Palace of the Sick dwarfed the 138 square meters of the wardrooms of Nūr al-Dīn's *bīmāristān* in Damascus.[183] Like in the Western hospices, both sick and feeble "lords" were offered—to use Peregrine Horden's happy formulation—the "therapy of the sacraments."[184]

The Jerusalem institution also took up other charitable work. Pregnant women who give birth there, writes the anonymous visitor, are watched over and bathed with their newborns down to recovery in the Palace earmarked for females.[185] The statutes of 1182 lay down that small cradles be prepared for infants of the female pilgrims who give birth in the house of the Hospital; the sucklings should sleep separately, so as not to disturb their mothers.[186] *The Miracles of Our Lady of Rocamadour* provide independent testimony: A pregnant woman from Burgundy enters the Hospital of St. John the Baptist in Jerusalem and, while in labor, loses her eyesight. After purification her husband leads her to the Church of the Holy Sepulcher and their prayers remain unanswered, but once they vow to pilgrimage to Rocamadour, her eyes immediately open.[187]

A further kind of charitable work undertaken in the Jerusalem Hospital was the care of foundlings. The 1182 statutes lay down that infants abandoned by their *fathers and mothers* should be accepted and nurtured.[188] The anonymous visitor speaks more specifically—and probably more realistically—of little children cast away by starving or unwilling *mothers*, who were brought to the Hospital by the first person who found them; of mothers who secretly, with forehead covered, deposited their infants there; and of mothers who, having given birth to twins, retained one child and abandoned the other. The foundlings were entrusted to nurses who were remunerated by money and food. Constantly supervised, they had to bring the children to the hospital for inspection by the sisters of the house; if these found that a child had been badly attended, they committed it to the custody of another nurse. The children were known as *filii beati Johannis* (Sons of St. John) and, on reaching adulthood, were given the choice to serve the one who had raised them—St. John—or "to embrace the seductive allurement of the frivolous world."[189] The account implies that in Frankish Jerusalem the abandonment of infants by poor mothers was quite common. If so, Jerusalem was unusual in this respect, for John Boswell (d. 1994), in his general study of the subject, found that, except for Scandinavia, there is little evidence for the abandonment of children in twelfth-century Europe.[190]

In addition to all this, the anonymous visitor reveals that the Hospitallers organized what in modern parlance might be called emergency medical treatment on the battlefield. Whenever the Franks moved out on an expedition against the "pagans," the wounded in battle sought help in tent hospitals, where the institute's surgeons would attend to them. Those who needed further care were transported—on camels, horses, mules, and donkeys—to the Palace of the Sick, or to closer retreats. And when the order's beasts of burden did not suffice for the transportation, the Hospitallers hired beasts from others; and when these, too, did not suffice, the wounded were hoisted on the Hospitallers' mounts, with these—even the noblemen among them—returning on foot.[191] The visitor, the only one to mention this innovation, unmatched in the West, does not spell out at what stage in the order's history it was introduced.[192] If in the early days, it may have triggered the order's militarization, with care for the sick in the Hospital leading to the care of the wounded on the battlefield, and with the surgeons providing this care requiring and receiving protection by knights.

In sum, I believe that the question whether the modern analogy to the Jerusalem institution is the hospital *or* the convalescent home is inapposite. In modern terms, it was *both* a hospital and a convalescent home; in addition, it was a maternity clinic, a home for foundlings, and the base of a combat medical unit. In twelfth-century terms, it combined traditional Christian cure of the soul with a novel, medicalized cure of the body; it also stood out for catapulting the sufferers into the role of lords residing in a palace, attended by devout servants acting in the spirit of Christian charity.

As for the medical component, the daily routine in the Palace of the Sick as observed by the anonymous visitor and Ibn Jubayr's explicit remark render most likely an inspiration by Islamic prototypes, perhaps already in the Amalfitan stage. But some Byzantine influence must not be ruled out. Like the Jerusalem institution, Byzantine hospitals were administered by religious communities, not by government officials like the Islamic ones. The 1136 regulations of the Constantinopolitan hospital of the Pantokrator Monastery and those of the provincial hospital of Kosmosoteira, attached to a monastery founded in 1152, contain instructions with regard to bedding that resemble the practice in the Palace of the Sick.[193] The allotment of one hundred *litrai* of sugar per year to the Pantokrator's infirmarian recalls the four quintals of sugar that the statutes of 1182 ordered the prior of Mont Pèlerin and the bailiff of Tiberias to send to Jerusalem for the preparation of syrups and medicines.[194] The two brothers who performed night duty in the Palace had five counterparts in the Pantokrator hospital; in both institutions, lamps illuminated each ward at night; and the chief physician at the Pantokrator, enjoined to pass every day from one bed to another, to ask every sick person how he was looked after, and to supervise that he was given all that was due to him, would have found familiar the doctors' routines in Baghdad, Damascus, or Jerusalem.[195]

From the standpoint of medicalization history, the Palace of the Sick lagged behind the leading Islamic and Byzantine hospitals, which were divided into wards reserved for patients suffering from different diseases.[196] They were serviced by many more than Jerusalem's four resident doctors: the ʿAḍudī Hospital in Baghdad had twenty-five doctors when founded in 982 and the number rose to twenty-eight in 1068; the Pantokrator is said to have had eleven.[197] Yet the four doctors of the Jerusalem Hospital, so pathetically few when regarded from Baghdad or Constantinople, amount to a dramatic innovation when viewed from contemporary Rome, Paris, or London.[198] And the institution's original engagement in traditional as well as novel therapy, battlefield surgery, and tutelage of foundlings attests to the remarkable capacity of the Knights Hospitaller to deal imaginatively with a varied gamut of problems and proffer unprecedented solutions.

Karl Borchardt has pointed out that the Hospitallers and Templars stood out for their innovativeness in administration. Theirs were Europe's first truly centralized religious orders, governed from a single Eastern headquarters; they established territorial districts, and they limited the appointment of officers to a relatively short time.[199] The eclectic terms chosen to designate them amount to a further testimony to the novelty of the orders' internal government.[200] The inventiveness of the two orders flourished on several planes.

Two Modes of Interaction with Non-Franks?

A comparison between the kingdom's clergy and knighthood suggests that each of these social groups maintained contacts with, or was typically oriented toward, a different category of non-Franks. Clerics learned many a local tradition and obtained some of their relics from Eastern Christians, appropriated from them the stirring miracle of the Holy Fire and the perception of Jerusalem's main sanctuary as the Church of the Holy Resurrection, devised its sharing with Eastern clerics, engaged in some religious polemics with them, and introduced a modified version of Byzantine laws into the canons of the Council of Nablus. The knights, on the other hand, were habitually preoccupied with Muslims. They were the enemy whose tactics had to be blunted, whose advances in siege warfare had to be counteracted, and in whose captivity many a knight fell, sometimes for a long time. It was the Muslim menace that brought into being two of the kingdom's main innovations—the Orders of the Knights Templar and Hospitaller, that is, of professed religious committed to warfare. But Muslims were also potential allies, their internal conflicts an opportunity for territorial expansion or the imposition of tributes. And, for the individual knight, the realm of Islam offered prospects of professional service or asylum. It is symptomatic, from this point of view, that we hear about one Frankish cleric who knows Greek and about some Frankish knights who know Arabic, but not about Arabic-speaking clerics or Greek-speaking knights. The Templars, who exhibited an openness toward Eastern Christians, appear to have occupied a middle ground.

A twelfth-century Frank may have believed that those who pray contribute to the safety of the kingdom as much, or more, than those who fight. Some present-day observers may subscribe to this view, but even they will admit that a knight's exposure to mortal danger loomed much larger than that of a cleric. At any rate, knights were constrained to develop an inventiveness that surely surpassed that of the clerics—no liturgical innovation is a match for the decision of Hue of Payns and his fellow knights to embark on an unprecedented mingling of knighthood with religion, or of Renaud of Châtillon to launch a naval expedition deep into the Red Sea.

CHAPTER 9

Burgesses, Urban and Rural

Clerics and knights constituted the Frankish elites. The bulk of the Frankish population consisted of burgesses (*burgenses*) who—unlike in the West—enjoyed this status whether they lived in towns or in the countryside.[1] All of them were legally free: as a later Frankish law was to solemnly declare, "The land of the Christians is called *la terre des Frans* [that is, "the land of the Franks," as well as "the land of the free"], and for this reason they should enjoy all freedoms there."[2]

Yet while from the legal viewpoint all burgesses were equal, not all of them enjoyed the same socioeconomic status. Ernoul, a keen and sympathetic observer of this class, repeatedly juxtaposes the burgesses proper with the "little people" (*menu peuple*), to whom he also refers as "poor folk" (*povres gens*).[3] These little people, while legally burgesses, were of a definitely lower status than their more affluent confrères.

A burgess living in a town could engage in viticulture or agriculture; in 1124 we hear about citizens of Jerusalem who were working in vineyards and fields outside the city walls when Ascalonite raiders fell upon them.[4] An urban burgess could also seek advancement by moving to the countryside: when King Amaurry erected the castle of Darum south of Gaza in the late 1160s, peasants and traders from neighboring places flocked there and established a suburb, because—as William of Tyre observes in a rare reference to humble contemporaries—"it was a favorable place where poorer people could make progress more easily than in towns."[5]

In 1998, Ellenblum revolutionized our understanding of the extent of Frankish settlement in the countryside. While earlier scholars had assumed that almost all Franks lived in towns and castles, Ellenblum conducted an archaeological survey of hundreds of rural sites and identified many buildings presumably erected by Frankish builders. This survey, together with a rereading of the written evidence, led him to conclude that (a) Frankish rural settlement was far more widespread than previously assumed, and (b) it took place in the parts of the kingdom largely inhabited by Eastern Christians.[6] In 2003, Denys Pringle argued that the distribution of twelfth-century churches permits assessing the extent of Frankish rural settlement more reliably, yet this distribution agrees with Ellenblum's main conclusions.[7]

What impelled people to go East and settle in the kingdom's countryside? Here, too, we may assume an amalgam of the spiritual and the material, a wish to live in Christ's country and a hope to better one's position. Some may have been serfs who hoped to gain free, burgess status; others may have got wind about the lucrative cultivation of sugar and other exotic foodstuffs. Also, William of Tyre claims that after the conquest of Ascalon in 1153, the land, which had not been tilled for half a century because of ongoing Frankish-Ascalonite hostilities, rendered a sixtyfold yield.[8] This stunning seed-to-yield ratio goes, of course, back to Jesus's parable in Matthew 13, yet it is conceivable that fields uncultivated for several decades did yield an unusually high product. The second wave of settlement at Bethgibelin, which occurred after the conquest of Ascalon, and the growth of the suburb underneath the castle of Ibelin may be understood against this background.[9] There is, however, no reason to assume that a majority of the Franks engaged in agriculture.

Burgess life in towns differed from that in the countryside on several counts. An urban burgess would typically reside in an old Eastern-type house or in a new one of similar layout, whereas his rural counterpart would normally live in a humbler but new house, standing on the single street of a recently planned Frankish village. While the urban burgess lived in a city that could encompass several thousands of people of various origins, the rural one belonged to a homogeneous community, totaling a few hundred in the largest villages, and much less in the far more common small ones: speaking of the region north of Jerusalem, an anonymous chronicler mentions the *villulas Francorum* (the Franks' hamlets) laid waste there by Ṣalāḥ al-Dīn's men in 1187.[10]

The Evidence of Pottery

There were also disparities in affluence between town and village. A pioneering study by Edna J. Stern allows for a glimpse of differences in the use of pottery between town and village, and between a Frankish and an indigenous village. Stern examined 10,500 whole vessels and rims unearthed in two large excavations in Frankish Acre, 749 rims excavated in the Frankish village La Hadia (Arabic: Khirbat al-ʿAyadiya, modern Hebrew: Ḥorvat ʿUza) five miles east of Acre, and 455 rims yielded in the indigenous village that appears in Latin as Zoenite or Iunite (Arabic: Khirbat Zuweinita, modern Hebrew: Ḥorvat Beyt Zeneta), eleven miles northeast of Acre.[11] She classified these finds into five categories: cooking ware, imported glazed tableware, local glazed tableware (produced in Beirut and Acre), undecorated wheel-made coarse vessels, and handmade vessels.[12] When we tabulate the data appearing in her text and add to them data extrapolatable from one of her figures, we arrive at table 9.1.

The percentage of cooking vessels is roughly similar in all three locations, but there is a vast, almost three-to-one discrepancy between the Frankish city and the Frankish village in the use of glazed tableware imported from afar, highly taxed and expensive; and this category is barely present in the indigenous village.[13] On the other hand, glazed vessels produced locally, and much cheaper, are almost four times more

Table 9.1 Percentage of various categories of pottery wares in a Frankish city, a Frankish village, and an indigenous village

	ACRE	LA HADIA FRANKISH VILLAGE	ZOENITE INDIGENOUS VILLAGE
Cooking ware	20.0	18.7	16.7
Imported glazed tableware	44.0	15.6	0.4
Local glazed tableware	11.9	46.6	23.3
Undecorated wheel-made vessels	23.5	8.2	16.3
Handmade vessels	0.6	10.9	43.3
Total	*100*	*100*	*100*

Figures 12a–d. Types of pottery excavated at Frankish sites. *Top left*: Imported glazed tableware. Photo: Vladimir Zeev Nayhin IAA B-384511-300118104161. *Top right*: Local glazed tableware. Photo: Mariana Saltzberger IAA B-170731-29071329213. *Bottom left*: Undecorated wheel-made vessel. Photo: Vladimir Zeev Nayhin IAA B-384102-300118020331. *Bottom right*: Handmade vessel. Photo: Edna Stern IAA B-991892-100181531344401.

frequent in the Frankish village than in the Frankish city, and constitute almost one-quarter of the pottery unearthed in the indigenous village. Finally, the distribution of cheap handmade vessels presents a mirror image of that of the expensive, imported glazed tableware: barely existent in Acre, in the indigenous village these plain vessels are as predominant as the glazed imports in Acre (see figs. 12a–d).

One should beware of generalizing from these data. Possibly future excavations in other parts of Acre may hint at a less affluent reality, while future work at other rural sites may show that the difference between La Hadia and Zoenite reflected their relative prosperity, or distance from Acre, rather than the ethnic identity of their inhabitants. Nevertheless, the method proposed in Stern's study holds the promise of throwing light on the affluence and preferences of various groups.

The Evidence of Personal Names

Another pioneering quantitative study, published by Iris Shagrir in 2003, throws light on the naming preferences of Frankish burgesses and knights. As students of anthroponymy know, the names parents give to their children afford some hint about their mentality and culture. Shagrir's data allow for a comparison of the names prevalent in the two social classes.

As tables 9.2 and 9.3 show, Petrus was the most frequent name borne by burgesses throughout the duration of the Frankish Kingdom of Jerusalem, while among knights the name was much less common. The trend toward saints' names, known from studies of Western anthroponymy, is discernible among Frankish burgesses earlier than among the knights, while names with an aristocratic flavor like Hugo and Balduinus, frequent among the latter, are scarce among burgesses. The name-stock of twelfth-century Frankish burgesses may have resulted from several

Table 9.2 Top ten names of Frankish burgesses, 1100–1187

1100–29 (N=40)		1130–59 (N=199)		1160–87 (N=142)	
NAME	%	NAME	%	NAME	%
Petrus	*12.5*	**Petrus**	*9.5*	**Petrus**	*12.0*
Berengarius	*5.0*	Guillelmus	*8.0*	**Johannes**	*7.0*
Gaufridus	*5.0*	Bernardus	*7.0*	Bernardus	*6.3*
Radulfus	*5.0*	Gerardus	*4.0*	Guillelmus	*5.6*
Robertus	*5.0*	**Johannes**	*4.0*	Guido	*4.2*
Achardus	*2.5*	Robertus	*4.0*	**Stephanus**	*3.5*
Albertus	*2.5*	Pontius	*3.5*	Gaufridus	*2.8*
Andreas	*2.5*	**Stephanus**	*3.5*	Hugo	*2.8*
Anschetinus	*2.5*	Galterius	*3.0*	Robertus	*2.8*
Bernardus	*2.5*	Rainaldus	*3.0*	**Andreas**	*2.1*

Source: After Shagrir, *Naming Patterns*, figures 16 and 17 and appendix 1. Saints' names are in bold.

Table 9.3 Top ten names of Frankish knights, 1100–1187

1100–29 (N=74)		1130–59 (N=158)		1160–87 (N=305)	
NAME	%	NAME	%	NAME	%
Hugo	6.8	Guillelmus	8.2	Hugo	6.8
Balduinus	5.4	Robertus	4.4	Guillelmus	4.9
Gerardus	5.4	Galterius	3.8	Rainaldus	4.9
Guido	5.4	Gaufridus	3.8	Raimundus	3.9
Guillelmus	5.4	**Petrus**	3.8	Balduinus	3.6
Bertrandus	4.1	Balduinus	3.2	**Petrus**	3.3
Eustachius	4.1	**Johannes**	3.2	Balianus	2.6
Simon	4.1	Adam	2.5	**Johannes**	2.6
Balianus	2.7	Gerardus	2.5	Galterius	2.3
Boemundus	2.7	Joscellinus	2.5	Bernardus	2.0

Source: After Shagrir, *Naming Patterns*, figures 16 and 17 and appendix 1. Saints' names are in bold.

causes: the impact of traditional names among peasants in rural regions of southern France from which numerous burgesses may have come; intermarriage with Eastern Christians, among whom saints' names had been common for centuries; the more intense religiosity of the Westerners who chose to settle in the Frankish Kingdom. Be that as it may, the naming pattern of the twelfth-century Frankish burgesses was markedly distinct from the knightly one. Burgesses also stood out for an early adoption of bynames.[14]

A comparison of the most frequent names among the 142 burgesses of Mahumeria (the "new town" established by the 1120s) who in 1156 swore fealty to the convent of the Church of the Holy Sepulcher, and the 144 burgesses of Jerusalem who appear in the documentation between the years 1148 and 1164, reveals that the two groups shared the same name-stock.[15] The percentage of saints' names in the two groups was similar: 26.76 percent and 26.38 percent, respectively. Evidently, the burgesses, whether living in cities or in the newly founded settlements in the countryside, constituted a roughly homogeneous group.

The "Little People"

The "little people" or "poor folk" constituted the lowest stratum of the burgess class. When such people fell into Muslim captivity, their chance of being ransomed by the rulers of Jerusalem was slight or less, and they had to face many years of slavery, often until death. A work ascribed to a twelfth-century Coptic priest, Abū al-Makārim, sheds some light on the fate of such captives. They dwelt in a quarter of Cairo where they worked under their captors' supervision, spinning cotton, making leather slippers, raising chickens. Some were married, others were celibate; they prayed in two churches, one dedicated to the Virgin, the other named after St. George. Under the Fatimid caliph al-Ḥāfiẓ—that is, in the years 1132–49—Abū al-Karam al-Tinnīsī, the official in charge of the treasury, notified the Frankish headman that if the captives were to pay a sizable sum, the caliph would let them go home; were they not to do so, they had to convert to Islam. The captives refused to pay and purportedly declared: "We would sooner have our own blood spilled by the sword than renounce the religion of Christ." Abū al-Karam nevertheless succeeded in extorting whatever they had, conveying the money to the caliph—but none of the Frankish captives was set free. It was only in 1164, when King Amaurry arrived in Egypt as the ally of Shāwar, that the captives regained freedom and returned to the Kingdom of Jerusalem.[16] William of Tyre, who devotes much space to describing Amaurry's Egyptian campaigns, sees no need to mention the liberation of these humble captives. However, Patriarch Aimery of Antioch, in a letter to Louis VII of France, does spell out that the Franko-Egyptian agreement stipulated that all Christian captives were to be freed.[17]

Robert Kool, the doyen of Frankish numismatists, suggested that the motifs appearing on low-value token money in lead—excavated in large numbers in some thirty urban and rural localities—allow a glimpse at the symbolic ambit such humble Franks encountered in everyday life. Some motifs are Christian: many simple crosses, others patriarchal, still others double- or triple-lined, or with pellets in each quarter; on one token the infant Jesus in his crib appears, flanked by the ox and the donkey, with the Star of Bethlehem above, while another presents a simplified version of the Lamb of God. Other motifs represent the realm of warfare: triangular and kite-shaped shields, a quiver with arrowheads, a wall with crenellations, a bust of a helmeted warrior, a mounted knight with shield and lance. There are many animals (birds, eagles, dolphins, fish, bull's heads, lions, or leopards), flowers (mainly fleur-de-lis), numerous waterwheels, some rosettes, and a few working utensils (axe, hammer, sickle, masons' planes). A handful of tokens imitate Fatimid coins of the bull's-eye type. With few exceptions, the tokens are devoid of inscriptions; apparently this substitute cash, cast in crudely made molds, was destined for illiterate people.[18]

Another glimpse of the mentality of such people may be gained from observations by Otto of Freising and the pilgrim Theoderich. Otto, who reached Jerusalem in 1148 with the Second Crusade, wrote that simple people who come to pray at the Lord's Sepulcher set up piles of pebbles or some other signs in the Valley of Josaphat so as to reserve their places there on the Day of Judgment; the learned bishop presents the custom as "a pious error, resulting from devotion and simplicity of faith" that he neither condemns nor approves. A generation later, Theoderich saw "many heaps of stones" in a field on the road from Jerusalem to Bethlehem and explained that simple pilgrims placed them there, believing that they were to sit on them on the Day of Judgment.[19] Both Otto and Theoderich ascribed the custom to humble pilgrims, but it stands to reason that ordinary Franks, too, took it up.

Rank and File Burgesses

Let us move upward the social ladder to the core, more affluent, stratum of burgesses. Usāma ibn Munqidh uses the Frankish term *burjāsī* (burgess) in one of his stories and explains that it means "merchant" (*tājir*).[20] This is the impression of an outside observer. Surely merchants formed part of the burgess class, but it comprised also members of many other professions. Of the 412 Jerusalemite burgesses figuring in the extant twelfth-century documentation, forty-seven bear bynames that may be taken to designate their occupations.[21] Of these, just three appear to have engaged in commerce.[22] Three were moneychangers, two dragomans, and one a toll-gatherer, whereas one burgess appears as Nicolas the Scribe and another as Robert the Physician. All the rest are artisans: six goldsmiths, five butchers, three shoemakers, three cooks, three tailors, two blacksmiths, two masons, two saddlers, one baker, one carpenter, one glassworker, one miller, one potter, one weaver, and four others whose occupations are not easily identifiable. Crafts workers were active also in Frankish settlements of the countryside. Among the 142 burgesses of Mahumeria listed in 1156, there were five masons, three blacksmiths, three carpenters, one baker, one shoemaker, and one weaver.[23]

Some masons chose to leave behind a pithy record of their existence. They carved their names on stones they cut, revealing thereby a certain familiarity with the letters of which they consisted; but as some of these letters are positioned upside down, one may wonder whether the names attest even to a partial literacy. One of the masons whose letters are positioned correctly was VILLELM(US) (William), whose name has been discovered at Belvoir; perhaps he was involved in the construction of the castle's chapel.[24] Other Latin names are carved on the walls of the Frankish Church of the Annunciation in Nazareth. The name OGER or OGIER appears eight times, ELIA six times, IOH(ANNE)S three times, and PE(T)R(US) just once.[25] The name OGER/OGIER, appearing as it does in the vernacular, raises the question whether Oger's parents named him after Oger/Ogier the Dane of the *Song of Roland*, Charlemagne's count (or duke) who never knew cowardice.[26]

A Frankish mason could be a quite wealthy person. In 1158, the mason Theobald of Tyre lent 500 bezants to the knight Jacques of Sidon, who was to repay him the sum over twelve years, by produce from one of his villages, to the value of 150 bezants.[27] Hence, the mason wrung from the knight an annual interest of ca. 22 percent, or more![28]

Frankish Craftsmen in Western Sources

An anonymous Frankish artisan made his way into a major European chronicle. Describing Frederick I's siege of Crema in 1159, Vincent of Prague (ca. 1130–67) relates that "a man from Jerusalem, who alongside the Jerusalemites had destroyed many Saracen castles with his instruments, approached the emperor and promised to construct a wooden tower [peopled] with warriors and position it right at the [enemy] fortress." Vincent, an eyewitness of the siege, goes on to describe the tower's construction and movement:

> First, two quadrate oak beams are laid out like in a four-wheeled wagon. The breadth and length of the tower are delineated on the ground; then, with a singular contrivance, it is raised to the position in which it was to move toward the fortress. There are six domiciles for the warriors who are about to fight. The first domicile is as high as the fortress. The master of the tower placed there a big bridge, to be positioned at the fortress in order to allow the warriors to break into it. At the ground level the tower is broad, in keeping with the beams' disposition; higher up it is narrower, constructed of beams suitably set up, secured by thin iron pieces and steadfast nails. Up to ten warriors can occupy this domicile; the [five] inferior ones, up to one thousand. This contraption, enclosed from the front, the right, and the left by scarlet oak coverings, was transported up to the great water-filled moat surrounding the

> fortress. . . . Around five hundred men stationed in the domicile on the ground, fastening sticks to the beams, moved the tower forward and backward as they wished [and] placed it on the moat's bank. The two beams that, as we have said before, were laid out like in a four-wheeled wagon, were the foundation of the entire tower. Other beams [extending] in the breadth were most powerfully affixed by many tools and iron, and by them [the men] moved the tower forward and backward as they wished—by equal, little beams, frequently oiled to ensure mobility.[29]

The account by Vincent, canon of Prague's cathedral, arguably offers a description of the procedure the Franks followed in constructing their siege towers in the mid-twelfth century. It stands to reason that the anonymous Frank, who was at work in Crema in 1159, had taken part in the construction of the huge "wooden castle" that, according to William of Tyre, artisans erected during the siege of Ascalon in 1153.[30] Evidently, the Franks made notable progress in siegecraft: in 1099, the First Crusaders forced their way into Jerusalem from the top of a three-storied siege tower that lacked a drawbridge; in 1124, during the siege of Tyre, the Franks had to rely on an Armenian expert from Antioch, Havendic, to toss stones accurately at targets inside the city; but a generation later, a Frankish artisan constructed for the Holy Roman Emperor a six-storied tower that—as the contemporary chronicler Otto Morena put it—"was of a size so extraordinary that none equal or similar to it had ever been seen on this side of the sea."[31]

Another Frankish artisan comes into view in *Girbert of Metz*, a contemporary *chanson de geste*. His name is Maurin; he hails from beyond the sea, was taken prisoner by the Saracens in Alexandria, and somehow made his way to the West. He is an *engigneor*—one who conducts works for the attack, defense, or fortification of places—and, as the anonymous poet declaims,

> He knew more about wood than any cleric did of Latin;
> There is no tower under the sky, nor any castle fortified enough,
> No refuge, no vault, no wall, no palisade,
> That, should he sojourn there fifteen days,
> He could not burn, demolish, or capture.[32]

Clearly, Frankish siegecraft aroused the admiration of some Westerners.

A far less successful Frankish craftsman was the anonymous shipbuilder of Jaffa, alluded to in a story told by Eudes of Champagne in his treatise on the efficacy of astrology. Eudes, who passed through Jaffa in the late twelfth century, relates that he was asked to forecast the fate of a brand-new ship. He turned immediately to the poop's chamber, carried out astrological observations, and these rendered his members stiff with fear: it was crystal-clear that shipwreck was imminent. This indeed took place three days later, during the ship's maiden voyage. Eudes persuaded his companions, who were to sail on it, to remain in Jaffa; his know-how saved their lives.[33] The story indicates, inter alia, that interest in astrology was not restricted to King Amaurry's court.

A Lettered Burgess: Raimon Anciaume

The highest stratum of the burgess class consisted of jurors of the Burgess Courts. These existed in some three dozen localities, presided over by a viscount who represented the local lord.[34] Some burgesses who sat on them became experts in law. Raimon Anciaume, who attested a charter drawn up in Acre in 1193, and whom his son Nicole characterized as a "wise burgess," was presumably a Burgess Court juror, even though he is not mentioned as such.[35] When in 1197 King Aimery invited Raoul of Tiberias, titular prince of Galilee and seneschal of the kingdom, to join him in writing down the laws of the kingdom together with Raimon Anciaume and another subvassal, Raoul haughtily replied that "he would never accept Raimon nor any other cunning burgess or low-born lettered man as his equal."[36] The exchange reveals that the king valued Raimon's legal knowledge and that some burgesses were known to be lettered—and that Raoul drew a rigid line between his class and the burgesses, belittling their learning on account of their social inferiority. He would have been chagrined to learn that Raimon's son Nicole became a respected legal expert, guardian of Acre's citadel, and possibly a knight, and that his grandson Balian, certainly a knight, married into the high nobility of the Kingdom of Acre.[37]

Some burgess upward mobility took place already in the days of the Kingdom of Jerusalem. During an emergency in 1101, when few knights were at hand, King Baldwin I ordered that whosoever could make his squire a knight should do so.[38] But there was also upward mobility in less dramatic circumstances. Johannes Vaccarius, who in 1143 attested to a deed as one of the burgesses of Jerusalem, had a son, Isaac de Naalein, who in 1167 attested as a knight.[39] The viscount Anschetinus, whose status is uncertain, had one son, Gybelinus, who appears to have been a knight, and another one, Albertus, probably a burgess.[40] The cases of Fulco Niger, who in 1163 was listed under the knights and in 1167 under the burgesses, and of Thomas Patricius, who in 1163 appeared as a knight and in 1174 was listed among Jerusalem's burgesses, suggest that it was possible also to move down the social ladder, perhaps by acquiring a burgage tenure.[41]

Furthermore, there were cases of intermarriage between knightly and burgess families, and between burgess and Eastern Christian ones. The boundary between the burgess class and the adjoining strata was not a rigid one. Christiane Tischler has calculated that of the twenty-four Jerusalemite burgess couples appearing in the documentation, four or five consisted of a Frankish man and an Eastern Christian woman, while in one case a Frankish woman, Stephania, married Nicolaus Manzur (Manṣūr?), possibly an Eastern Christian. If five of these couples were indeed Franko/Eastern Christian, "mixed marriages" would have amounted to slightly more than 20 percent of the total.[42]

Ernoul: A Frankish Chronicler Attentive to Jerusalemite Burgesses

As we have seen, William of Tyre, the son of Frankish burgesses who attained high status by embarking on an ecclesiastical career, mentioned *burgenses* only when the term appeared in a document he was transcribing and preferred to refer to them as members of the "second class."[43] The heroes of his chronicle were kings and prelates, clerics and knights; no person of a lower status did he ever mention by name. However, in two instances William recorded the presence of more lowly people and, significantly, both times the imposition of an emergency tax was at stake. In the first case he relates that in 1166, King Amaurry convened a general assembly in Nablus and explained to the prelates, the princes, and the people the dangers the kingdom was facing in Egypt, and that it was then resolved that everybody must pay one-tenth of his movable property. In the second case, he quotes the decree issued in Jerusalem in February 1183 by which a general tax was imposed by all great men of the realm, whether ecclesiastic or secular, "and by the assent of all the common people of the kingdom of the Jerusalemites."[44] Unfortunately for modern constitutional historians, he did not see fit to dwell on their role in the assemblies of 1166 and 1183.

How different the prominence of the burgesses in the romance-like chronicle written by Ernoul, the youth in service of Balian of Ibelin. Ernoul's original account has not survived, and only a version dating from the 1230s has come down to us, but his voice is discernible in the partisan, flattering references to Balian—and (a feature hitherto unnoticed) in his repeated mentions of the burgesses of Jerusalem. While William, in his immense chronicle, obliquely refers to them in just a handful of cases, the burgesses figure more than twenty times in the part of Ernoul's narrative that focuses on the decade 1177–87.[45]

They appear for the first time in the account of Ṣalāḥ al-Dīn's incursion into the kingdom in November 1177. Ernoul writes that when King Baldwin IV realized how large Ṣalāḥ al-Dīn's army was, he ordered all men of arms to join him at Ascalon. When the burgesses of Jerusalem approached the city, Ṣalāḥ al-Dīn captured them, and they were bound to camels in his baggage train. Then the sultan decided to attack Jerusalem, defenseless after all burgesses had been seized. But the Franks unexpectedly gained the great victory at Montgisard, in which—according to Ernoul, as we have seen—the brothers Baldwin and Balian of Ibelin outdid the feats of Roland and Olivier at Roncevaux. Ernoul returns to dwell on the fate of the captive burgesses: When they learned of the Saracen rout, they untied one another, killed the guards, and took possession of the stored equipment.[46]

Describing the coronation of the child Baldwin V during which Balian of Ibelin held the child in his arms, Ernoul mentions that the ceremony was customarily followed by a banquet in some part of the Temple of Solomon, at which the burgesses of Jerusalem served the king and his barons.[47]

When after the leper king's death in 1185 a severe drought struck the country—so relates Ernoul—a Jerusalemite burgess by the name of Germain, eager to do good for God, saw to it that bowls chained to three marble basins were constantly full of water, so that men and women could sate their thirst. But as rains were not forthcoming, the basins were about to go dry, and Germain, afraid that he would no longer be able to provide water to the poor, prayed to God to let him discover an ancient well, said to exist in the Valley of Josaphat near the Spring of Syloé (the Shiloaḥ of the Bible). His workmen found the well, built it up, and with the help of a wheel turned by a horse, pots full of water would come up and empty ones go down. The water was collected in stone basins, townsmen carried it into the city, Germain's horses worked day and night, and all who needed water obtained it at his expense. When the rains resumed, the city's cisterns were refilled, and henceforth Germain bade three sergeants with three pack animals to carry water to his marble basins. Later, as Ṣalāḥ al-Dīn was approaching to lay siege to

Jerusalem, the Franks filled in the well.[48] Evidently Ernoul relishes recording, in considerable detail, the good deeds of this generous burgess.[49]

Somewhat later, Ernoul writes:

> I have forgotten to tell you, when I was speaking of the Spring of Syloé, of an act of charity that the burgesses of Jerusalem used to perform, but I shall tell you now. And they did it during Lent, on the day on which one reads the Gospel of the poor man for whom Jesus Christ made eyes out of mud. And He asked him to go and wash in the Spring of Syloé, and he did so, and received eyes and saw.[50] In remembrance of that they performed this act of charity of which I shall tell you. They had basins brought and placed over the spring, and they had them all filled with wine and they had the pack animals brought loaded with bread and wine in such abundance that all the poor people who went there had bread and wine in great abundance, and they also received money with it. And the men and women went in procession on that day to make this act of charity.[51]

Still another testimony to Ernoul's interest in, and admiration for, the burgesses of Jerusalem. After the Battle of Ḥaṭṭīn that left the Frankish Kingdom denuded of almost all knights, the burgesses come to the fore of Ernoul's account. When Ṣalāḥ al-Dīn appeared before Ascalon late in August 1187 and offered to free King Gui in return for the city's capitulation, Gui conferred with the local burgesses, "as there was no knight there." Gui advised them not to surrender Ascalon just in order to free him, adding, however, that, should they arrive at the conclusion that the city cannot be held, they should attempt to obtain his liberation. The burgesses returned to Ascalon, deliberated with the town's commonalty, and, arguing that no Frankish force would come to their rescue, decided to surrender.[52]

The burgesses of Jerusalem came to Ṣalāḥ al-Dīn, on his invitation, on the day he occupied Ascalon. According to Ernoul, the sultan proposed to give them thirty thousand bezants so that they might fortify Jerusalem; an area around the city in which they may work freely; and plenty of meat—and offered a truce until Pentecost. If by that time aid were forthcoming, they would hold on; if not, they would surrender the city and be safely conducted, with their possessions, to Christian territory. The burgesses rejected the offer, declaring that they would never surrender the city where God had shed his blood for them, ready as they are to shed theirs for him. Consequently, Ṣalāḥ al-Dīn realized that he must take the city by force.[53] Ernoul's—evidently fictional—account presents the Jerusalemite burgesses as more zealous than their Ascalonite confrères.

About that time Balian of Ibelin, who had not been captured at Ḥaṭṭīn and had escaped to Tyre, obtained Ṣalāḥ al-Dīn's permission to conduct his wife and children, under Muslim protection, from Jerusalem to Tripoli. (Ernoul repeatedly refers to Balian's wife as "the Queen"—that is, the Byzantine princess Maria Komnene, widow of King Amaurry.)[54] Balian swore to the sultan that he would stay in Jerusalem for just one night. But his arrival aroused the spirits of the city's inhabitants, who asked him to rule it, and Patriarch Eraclius absolved him from the oath to Ṣalāḥ al-Dīn. Balian started to prepare Jerusalem for the imminent siege and, since only two knights—escapees from the battlefield of Ḥaṭṭīn—were in the city, he proceeded to knight about fifty sons of burgesses, perhaps unwittingly following the example of King Baldwin in 1101.[55]

In Ernoul's description of the final days of Frankish Jerusalem, the burgesses appear time and again. With Ṣalāḥ al-Dīn's final assault imminent, the burgesses, alongside the knights and sergeants, decided on a suicidal night sortie, but Eraclius dissuaded them from doing so, and Balian was dispatched to make terms with the sultan.[56] When he returned with Ṣalāḥ al-Dīn's terms, he announced them to all the burgesses, who were dismayed to learn that the ransom demanded by the sultan was much too high for the "little people" to pay. Therefore Eraclius, Balian, and the burgesses approached the commander of the Order of the Hospital and insisted that he earmark for the ransom of the city's poor the thirty thousand bezants that King Henry II of England had deposited with the Hospitallers. Having consulted with his brothers, the commander announced to Eraclius, Balian, and the burgesses that the sum would be allocated for this purpose.[57] After a further round of talks with Ṣalāḥ al-Dīn, Balian and Eraclius announced the final terms to the Templars, Hospitallers, and "the burgesses of the city."[58] Once Eraclius and Balian paid the thirty thousand bezants for the ransom of seven thousand of the poor, they convened the burgesses, and two of the worthiest men of each street were entrusted to establish who these seven thousand poor should be. Eraclius and Balian then beseeched the Templars, Hospitallers, and burgesses to provide for the ransom of the remaining poor, but they did so only sparingly; it is only here that Ernoul disapproves of the behavior of the Jerusalem burgesses.[59] Punishment soon followed. When Jerusalem's refugees arrived outside Tripoli, Count Raymond III ordered the city gates closed and sent his knights into the fields to despoil the "rich burgesses" of Jerusalem of the possessions with which Ṣalāḥ al-Dīn had permitted them to depart.[60]

Ernoul's chronicle is blatantly tendentious in its pro-Balian and anti-Raymond stance. But how should we understand the prominence it accords to the burgesses? Balian, as de facto ruler of besieged Jerusalem, must have given them a say because of the virtual absence of knights in the city. But what about the references to Jerusalem's burgesses in the account of the Battle of Montgisard, the lengthy description of the pious deeds of Germain the Burgess, the annual act of charity the Jerusalem burgesses performed at the Spring of Syloé, and much more? Is it possible that Ernoul was a son of Jerusalemite burgesses who made a career in Balian's service?

At any rate, Ernoul's work is not only one of the earliest prose chronicles in Old French; it is also one of the first chronicles that accords a major role to burgesses and treats them with obvious sympathy.

Chapter 10

The Non-Franks

The demography of the Frankish Kingdom of Jerusalem is a difficult, rarely taken up subject, and the few estimates in the research literature are open to serious doubts.[1] Yet, it is clear that the Franks were a minority within their kingdom, amounting perhaps to just one quarter of the total population. Nevertheless, with a few exceptions, modern histories of the kingdom deal almost exclusively with the Franks. Conversely, in this chapter the cultural activities of the subjected non-Frankish communities will be delineated and compared both one to another as well as to the Franks. The communities will be dealt with in an order that roughly reflects the differing extent of their cultural creativity under Frankish rule.

Samaritans

The Samaritans believe that they descend from the biblical Israelites, but, unlike the Jews, they accept as holy scripture only the five Books of Moses, and consider Mount Gerizim overlooking Nablus, not Mount Zion in Jerusalem, as God's chosen place. In Roman times, the Samaritans spread out throughout much of Palestine as well as in a diaspora, but their revolts against Byzantium were harshly suppressed and their numbers dwindled. By the time of the crusader conquest, they were one of the smallest groups within the indigenous population. The Western Visitor claimed that in the entire world there were less than a thousand Samaritans, "nay, hardly three hundred can be found."[2] This was an exaggeration: Benjamin of Tudela, in about 1170, mentioned one thousand Samaritans in Nablus, two hundred in Caesarea, and three hundred in Ascalon and, outside the kingdom, four hundred in Damascus.[3] Other sources mention Samaritans in Gaza and Acre, as well as in Egypt.[4] Still, it was a small community. The crusader conquest did not affect it adversely, because Nablus passed peacefully into the hands of Tancred and Eustache of Boulogne a few days after the fall of Jerusalem.[5] However, at some point the Franks destroyed the Samaritan ritual bath and the fourth-century synagogue adjoining Mount Gerizim. So relates Abū al-Fatḥ, a Samaritan who in 1355 compiled a chronicle in Arabic.[6]

The Samaritans suffered twice from Muslim incursions. In 1137, when the Damascene emir Bazwāj raided Nablus, many Samaritans were abducted to Damascus, and when Ṣalāḥ al-Dīn raided the city in 1184, "the hands of the Muslims were filled with prisoners beyond numbers from the Franks and from a sect of Jews called Samaritans."[7] It is not clear why this treatment befell the Samaritans. Perhaps the Franks, remembering the favorable references to the Samaritans in the New Testament, treated them kindly, and therefore the Muslim raiders took them captive alongside the Franks.[8]

The information about Samaritan cultural activities is considerable. The high priests continued to dwell in Nablus and preside over the Passover sacrifice ceremony on Mount Gerizim. In 1139/40, the Samaritan punctuation system was established in Fatimid Ascalon.[9] In 1149/50, El'azar b. 'Amram—brother of Aharon b. 'Amram, high priest in the years 1115–37—wrote the earliest Samaritan chronicle, the *Tulida* (Genealogy). El'azar notes the Seljuk conquest of Ramla in 1070/71, but ignores the crusader conquest and Frankish rule.[10] Focusing on Samaritan affairs, he dwells on the 1137 raid on Nablus during which Bayzūga Zaydna (Bazwāj) "abducted five hundred men, women and children to Damascus," and goes on to relate that a wealthy Samaritan of Acre, Ab Gillūga, "saved" (ransomed) them.[11] A descendant of a family from Gaza, Ab Gillūga donated food, clothing, gold, and silver to his Samaritan brethren, repaired synagogues, built a new one in Nablus, and had the waters of the spring of 'Awartā (southeast of Nablus) conveyed to the city. He also "revealed the right faith in God through joyful trumpets"—an obscure statement, which a post-1355 Hebrew chronicle renders as "he introduced the blowing of trumpets on Sabbaths and feast days."[12] In the last quarter of the twelfth century, Abū Isḥāq Ibrāhīm b. Faraj b. Mārūth wrote the first true Samaritan grammar and *The Book of Inheritance*, in which he refuted Karaite and Islamic teachings.[13] Somewhat later, Munajjā b. Ṣadaqa composed *The Book of Differences* that examines halakhic disparities between Samaritans and Jews.[14]

On a more pedestrian level of cultural activity, many Samaritan Torah scrolls were written. A fragment containing twenty chapters of Deuteronomy dates from 1149/50. In the same year, a Samaritan sold a Torah scroll to his brother for twenty-five *sheqels*.[15] Another scroll (see fig. 13) was written, according to a cryptogram concealed within the text, "in the year 562 of the Kingdom of Ishmael" (AD 1166/67) for the synagogue of ʿAṣāfa (now Khirbet ʿAṣāfa, west of Nablus).[16] This locality appears in a Latin charter of 1123 as *Saphe*, designated as "a certain village of Samaritans," which indicates that it was inhabited solely or mainly by Samaritans.[17]

A part of a codex containing Deuteronomy bears the date 1181/82.[18] But the extant scrolls form only a small part of the very many written

Figure 13. A column of the Samaritan Torah scroll, written in AH 562/AD 1166–67 for the synagogue of ʿAṣāfa (the column contains Deuteronomy 5:18 to 6:25). John Rylands Library, Manchester. Gaster Manuscripts, no. 88 (1868).

in that period. The scribe Abraham b. Israel b. Ephraim b. Joseph ha-Nasī' relates in a scroll he concluded in AH 629/AD 1231–32 that he is sixty years old and that the scroll in question is the seventy-fourth he had written.[19] Evidently, not only Samaritan communities but also many individuals were in possession of a scroll. For scribes, the writing of scrolls was apparently also an act of piety, like it was for Usāma ibn Munqidh's father, who prepared forty-three copies of the Qur'an.[20]

William of Tyre complained, as we have seen, that Frankish nobles preferred Jewish, Samaritan, Syrian, and Saracen physicians to Western ones.[21] Three Samaritan doctors who may also have worked for Frankish nobles appear in Ibn Abī Uṣaybiʿa's encyclopedia of prominent physicians. The first is Ibrāhīm al-Sāmirī (that is, the Samaritan), known as "the Sun of the Physicians," who ended up serving as Ṣalāḥ al-Dīn's doctor; he has been identified with the aforementioned Samaritan author Abū Isḥāq Ibrāhīm.[22] The second is Ibrāhīm's student Muhadhdhab al-Dīn Yūsuf, who stood out also for his knowledge of philosophy and literature, and composed poetry and a commentary on the Torah.[23] The third is Ṣadaqa al-Sāmirī, the son of Munajjā b. Ṣadaqa who wrote *The Book of Differences*. Ibn Abī Uṣaybiʿa acclaims Ṣadaqa as a leading physician who also taught medicine and adds that he was well-versed in philosophy and "composed mediocre poetry, in which he often included philosophical witticisms." Nevertheless, Ibn Abī Uṣaybiʿa quotes at length from this poetry and goes on to list Ṣadaqa's eight works. Four deal with medicine, four with religious subjects: a commentary on the Torah, and treatises on the soul, the unity of God, and the principles of faith.[24] We may assume that some of William of Tyre's Samaritan physicians were knowledgeable in Samaritan and Islamicate lore.

Samaritans were aware of the opportunities provided by the region's partition between Muslims and Franks. When Amīn al-Dawla, still another prominent Samaritan physician, converted to Islam, his uncle Muhadhdhab al-Dīn Yūsuf told him: "My son, if you regret your conversion to Islam, I will transport you to a Frankish land, where you may live and return to your [original] faith." The nephew answered that his conversion was sincere; but the uncle's offer reveals that he knew that one could persevere in apostasy—punishable by death in the realm of Islam—by crossing over into Frankish territory.[25] Decades earlier, on 16 May 1165, Maimonides—coerced to accept Islam in the Maghreb—landed in Frankish Acre, where, as he put it, he was "saved from apostasy" and could revert to Judaism. Frankish converts to Islam, who settled in Muslim territory and then decided to return to the Frankish Kingdom and their Christian faith, availed themselves of the same opportunity.[26]

Samaritan writings of the twelfth century hint at some intellectual openness toward Rabbanite and Karaite Jews as well as Muslims—but not toward Christians, whether Frankish or Eastern. Still, there was some interaction with Franks, as attested by the knowledge of the Western Visitor and Ernoul about Samaritans. Also, Rorgo Fretellus relates that the Samaritans assert that the mountains Ebal and Gerizim are located above Nablus. He goes on to reject their testimony and repeats the authoritative if erroneous opinion of Jerome (ca. 342–420) that they are located above Jericho.[27]

Jews

The mode in which the crusaders took over a locality determined the fate of its non-Christian inhabitants.[28] Luckily for the Samaritans, their chief community was in Nablus, which surrendered right after the crusader conquest of Jerusalem. Therefore, the community remained intact, the chain of high priests was not broken, and the cultic center on Mount Gerizim continued to serve believers.

The fate of the Jews was different, because many of them lived in towns taken by assault, like Jerusalem, Haifa, Caesarea, and Beirut; in Haifa, where Muslims and Jews fought together against the crusaders and rejected an offer to surrender, a massacre took place upon the town's fall.[29] The inhabitants of Ramla, the capital of the Muslim district of Filasṭīn that had a sizable Jewish population in the eleventh century, fled upon the advent of the crusaders in June 1099, and most of them did not return.[30] In Tyre, which surrendered in 1124 after a long siege, and in Ascalon, which did likewise in 1153, many—perhaps all—Jews decided to stay put under Frankish rule.

Some Jewish communities decimated during the conquest were recreated fairly soon. In Acre, a few years after the conquest, there existed an organized community, a cantor who doubled as a ritual slaughterer, and a slaughterhouse; Jewish oyster fishers from Alexandria purportedly misbehaved in local taverns.[31] In later years a rabbinical court is attested there.[32] In Jerusalem, however, Jews and Muslims were not allowed to reside, because—as William of Tyre put it—"to permit people not belonging to the Christian faith to live in so venerable a place, seemed like sacrilege to the leaders [of the First Crusade]."[33] Yet with the passage of time, a few Jews managed to settle in the city. About seventy years after the conquest, Benjamin of Tudela mentions 1,287 Jews in sixteen localities of the Frankish Kingdom; four of them lived in Jerusalem. The largest communities were Tyre (five hundred Jews), Acre, Caesarea, and Ascalon (two hundred each); the middle-sized ones were Beirut, Tiberias, the Galilean village of ʿAlma (fifty each), and Sidon (twenty); whereas eight localities had just between one to four Jewish inhabitants.[34] If Benjamin's figures are given credence, the 1,500 Samaritans living in the kingdom outnumbered the Jews.

Only with regard to Tyre did Benjamin mention the presence of Talmudic scholars.[35] In Jerusalem he met Rabbi Avraham al-Qonstantini (from Constantine, present-day Algeria, or Constantinople), a pious ascetic who belonged to "the Mourners of Jerusalem," that is, recluses intent on hastening the coming of the Messiah.[36] Benjamin provides no further allusions to cultural activity. In five of the eight localities that had one to four Jewish residents he noted that they were dyers. The four Jews who lived in Jerusalem near the Tower of David paid the king an annual sum for the local dyeing house, to ensure that only they should dye in the city.[37]

The Jews of the Frankish Kingdom lacked a central leadership. The Palestinian Academy left Jerusalem in the 1070s, moving first to Tyre, then to Damascus, and after 1120 to Fusṭāṭ.[38] Therefore the kingdom's Jews had to address their queries about legal issues to rabbinic authorities in surrounding Muslim countries.

A batch of thirty-two queries that Rabbi Efrayim of Tyre and his disciples sent in the late 1170s to Maimonides in Egypt, as well as his answers, has survived. So did a responsum Maimonides sent to Acre, a letter he dispatched in 1185 to Judge Yefet of Acre, and another he addressed to a Muslim convert to Judaism "in the Land of Israel."[39] Three of the thirty-two queries deal with religio-legal issues specific to the community of Tyre, and one asks about the geographical extent of the Land of Israel.[40] Two queries focus on Jewish interaction with non-Jews. The first asks whether a Jew may circumcise a Muslim and a Christian, and Maimonides answers in the affirmative.[41] Since this answer tallies with an enactment attributed to King Baldwin II that mentions Frankish conversion to Judaism, we may assume that some such conversions took place.[42] The second query asks whether a Jew may teach the Torah to a non-Jew, and Maimonides rules that he may teach it to a Christian "and draw him to our religion," because the Christians acknowledge the Hebrew scripture as authentic, and even though they grievously misinterpret it, one may persuade them to accept the correct—that is, Jewish—interpretation. The Muslims, on the other hand, do not believe that the

Torah is God's word, and when they find in it a passage that conflicts with their confused stories, they do not concede to be in the wrong, but interpret it according to their false suppositions, and may even use it to confound Jews. Therefore, a Jew should not teach the Torah to a Muslim.[43] Evidently, the query attests to an interest among some Christians and Muslims of Tyre in the Hebrew Bible and in Judaism's precepts.

In his letter to the Muslim convert to Judaism—who assumed the Hebrew name ʿOvadyā (God's servant)—Maimonides defends Islam against the charge of idolatry. ʿOvadyā's rabbi rebuked his pupil for maintaining that the Muslims are not idolaters and called him a fool; in other words, the rabbi was in agreement with the Franks who called the Muslims pagans. In his response, Maimonides emphatically asserted that "the Ishmaelites are by no means idolaters . . . and properly insist on God's flawless unity." The idolatry of their forefathers is a matter of the past. "Their error and foolishness lie elsewhere, and this cannot be put in writing because of the wicked in Israel." He sternly chastises ʿOvadyā's rabbi for having called his pupil a fool and bids him to ask for forgiveness.[44]

Maimonides speaks with great respect of Rabbi Efrayim of Tyre and his disciples.[45] Yet, elsewhere he speaks gloomily about the level of learning among the country's Jews. In the commentary on the Mishnah he writes: "I saw in the Land of Israel people titled Fellows of the Academy and in other places called Head of the Academy—and even a student who learned just one day is not there."[46] And in a letter to the scholars of Lunel (northeast of Montpellier) he asserts that "in the Land of Israel and in all Syria there is just one city, Aleppo, in which scholars study the Torah, but not in a truly steadfast manner."[47]

By these extreme, exaggerated statements, Maimonides—hailed in 2008 as "one of civilization's greatest minds"—disclosed some underlying resentment, perhaps rooted in experiences at Acre or Tyre in 1165.[48] Yet basically he was right. While Samaritans produced the *Tulida* and several treatises, their Jewish neighbors did not author a single work. A Hebrew dirge on the crusader conquest and Christianization of the Holy Land was discovered in 2012—yet it was written in Germany.[49]

Muslims

Evidence about the cultural life of the Muslims, who may have amounted to one-half or more of the Franks' indigenous subjects, is hardly more abundant than that regarding the small Jewish minority.

The mode of Frankish takeover impacted the structure of the Muslim communities. Where the terms of surrender allowed for a choice between staying or going into exile, members of the leading Muslim strata chose to leave. Ibn al-Athīr writes that "a large group of the important people" of Sidon left in 1110, and Foucher of Chartres refers to the Muslims who remained there as peasants. Ibn Qalānisī writes that in Tyre, in 1124, the only Muslims who stayed were those too weak to embark upon a journey, and that at the surrender of Ascalon in 1153 all Muslims able to depart did so.[50] Possibly, these statements are exaggerations aimed at playing down the size and importance of the Muslim population that chose to remain under Frankish rule. However, evidence in the guide to pilgrimage sites by ʿAlī al-Harawī (d. 1215) and in the *History of Jerusalem and Hebron* by Mujīr al-Dīn (d. 1522), indicates that the remaining Muslims were too weak to preserve the tombs of famous local personages, or too uninformed to uphold the traditions about their exact location.[51] Like the Jews, the Muslim inhabitants of the kingdom were largely bereft of their elites.

Some local spiritual leadership, albeit of modest intellectual stature, persisted. As we have seen, Ḍiyāʾ al-Dīn reveals that in some villages of the Nablus region lived shaykhs, that is, holy persons believed to be endowed with supernatural powers. Some of these quoted the Qur'an or *ḥadīth* and dealt with religious issues. For instance, Shaykh Saʿd ibn ʿAbd Allāh of the village of Qīra (southwest of Nablus) appeared to his nephew in a dream and answered several of his questions. Thus, he reassured him that Munkar and Nakīr—the angels who question the dead about their faith—are real, and when asked, "If a man is buried next to a righteous man, is it of benefit to him?" he answered, "Only his deeds can be of benefit."[52] Yet no work is known to have been written by a Muslim subject of the Franks.

In this respect, too, the Principality of Antioch differed from the Kingdom of Jerusalem. The man of letters and physician Ḥamdān al-Athāribī (ca. 1067–1147) moved repeatedly between the Frankish and Muslim areas in northwestern Syria. He first administered lands for the Franks until they confiscated his wealth; he then worked as an envoy and possibly as a civilian administrator for the Muslim lords of Aleppo; in 1127, having healed the Frankish lord of al-Athārib, he was recompensed with a deserted village, which he developed and made his home, drawing criticism for having chosen to dwell among the Franks. Later, after Zengi conquered Aleppo, Ḥamdān administered the lands on his behalf. This colorful individual, famous for his drinking parties and poetry, is known to have written also about the Frankish incursion into the East. He appears to have dealt with it in two works, both unfortunately lost: a history of Aleppo, and a *History of the Franks Who Went Out to the Lands of Islam in These Years*—the latter being the Arabic counterpart of William of Tyre's Latin *History of the Oriental Rulers*, equally lost.[53] Apparently, contemporaries did not exhibit much interest in works focusing on the adversary's history.

While little is known about the cultural life of the Franks' Muslim subjects, evidence about the cultural attainments of several Muslim refugees and emigrants from the Frankish Kingdom, and the espousal of the anti-Frankish *jihād* by some of them, is considerable. Ibn Munīr al-Ṭarābulusī (1080–1153) was born in Tripoli and fled the city when the Franks conquered it in 1109. Ibn al-Qaysarānī (1085–1153) was born in Acre and grew up in Caesarea (hence his name) until his family fled the city, taken by the Franks in 1101. The two refugees became Muslim Syria's most prominent poets, celebrating Zengi's victories over the Franks, and positing the reconquest of all Frankish-held lands as the supreme goal of the *jihād*.[54] Ibn al-Qaysarānī stands out also for poems, written upon his visit to Antioch in 1146, that divulge his intense agitation at the sight of Frankish women, their uncovered faces, white skin, blue eyes, long necks, slender waists, broad hips, and hefty buttocks.[55] The erotic pleasure he derived from observing them, and his readiness to publicize it, may be contrasted with the description, about fifteen years later, of the Frankish princess Melisende of Tripoli by the Byzantine envoy Konstantinos Manasses. He lauds Melisende's exceptional beauty in some fifty verses, but he focuses almost exclusively on her face, briefly referring to her steady gait and tall stature.[56] Neither are the enchanting Saracen maidens of the *chansons de geste* described so uninhibitedly as the womenfolk of Antioch in Ibn al-Qaysarānī's poetry. Yet his attraction is mixed with condescension.

Aḥmad ibn Qudāma, the Ḥanbalī preacher who fled in 1156 to Damascus, and his relatives and followers who did likewise somewhat later, founded there the quarter of Ṣāliḥiyā, which soon became a hub of Islamic scholarship coupled with severe piety, and famous for public readings of traditional texts.[57] Aḥmad's eldest son Abū ʿUmar (1134, Jammāʿīl, - 1210, Damascus) stood out for rigorous asceticism and strict conservatism. His younger brother Muwaffaq al-Dīn (1146, Jammāʿīl - 1223, Damascus) studied in Damascus and Baghdad and became a leading jurisconsult and theologian who wrote about twenty works, the main one of which—the treatise of Ḥanbalī law, *al-Mughnī*—remained influential for centuries.[58] Muwaffaq al-Dīn's cousin ʿAbd al-Ghanī (1146, Jammāʿīl – 1203, Cairo) studied with him in Baghdad and came to be known for works on the transmission of *ḥadīth*. ʿAbd al-Ghanī's younger brother ʿImād al-Dīn Abū Isḥāq Ibrāhīm (1148, Jammāʿīl – 1217, Damascus), also educated in Iraq, became a jurisconsult of some stature.

Muwaffaq al-Dīn and ʿAbd al-Ghanī engaged in *jihād* propaganda and, together with Abū ʿUmar, volunteered in the 1180s to join Ṣalāḥ al-Dīn's anti-Frankish campaigns.[59] Muwaffaq al-Dīn, who participated in the Battle of Ḥaṭṭīn, dispatched an eyewitness account to Baghdad.[60] In 1202, Abū ʿUmar founded the Grand Mosque of the Ḥanbalīs and, somewhat later, the ʿUmarīyya Madrasa next to it, both in the Ṣāliḥiyya Quarter.[61] The niche (*miḥrāb*) in the wall of each building that indicated the direction of Mecca was adorned with Frankish capitals, trophies from the vanquished Kingdom of Jerusalem.[62] In the mosque's court, a large capital with a rectangular configuration on top serves, in secondary use, as a well-head; on one of its frontal faces a mounted warrior is clearly discernible.[63] May we imagine that Abū ʿUmar, who during his childhood and youth in Jammāʿīl beheld a Frankish knight on horseback with apprehension or worse, was exhilarated to see a knight's likeness locked up in his mosque?[64]

Eastern Christians

For the First Crusaders of 1096–99, Muslims and Jews were the enemy; the Eastern Christians—the purported victims of Muslim oppression—were whom they were determined to liberate. Hence, while the crusader conquest entailed the massacre and dislocation of numerous Muslims and Jews, the Eastern Christian communities remained intact and many of its members were to collaborate with the Franks.

Greek Orthodox (or Melkites)

The only Eastern Christians whom the crusader conquest affected negatively were the Greek Orthodox patriarch and his bishops, who had to cede their posts and major sanctuaries to Latin prelates; several of them chose to emigrate. The Franks, who considered the Greek Orthodox to basically adhere to the one true church to which they themselves belonged, did not grant them the autonomy they did concede to the Miaphysite churches branded by Rome as heretics.[65]

The emigration of the leading Greek prelates was not immediate. Joannes VIII appears to have been elected Greek patriarch of Jerusalem in 1106 and to have resided in the city for about a year.[66] During that time, he composed two anti-Frankish tracts about the *azymes*, the unleavened eucharistic bread that the Latins used in disagreement with the Greeks, who used leavened bread. In the first tract, Joannes marshals traditional and original arguments against the *azymes* but is well aware that the obduracy of his—probably fictitious—Latin interlocutor will prevent him from conceding that the Greeks were right; also, even if persuaded to so concede, the fear of the rabble under his charge would make him stick to the Latin rite. This Latin interlocutor is a man of authority, possibly the Frankish patriarch of Jerusalem: Joannes claims that he ridicules the Greeks, calls them bad Christians, and treats them tyrannically. Consequently, the tract brings into sight a strained relationship between Greek and Frankish clerics in the early years of the Kingdom of Jerusalem.[67]

The second tract purports to render a conversation between Joannes, "the patriarch of Jerusalem," with an unnamed "Latin philosopher." At first, the philosopher, accompanied by several armed men, asks the patriarch to cure his aching hip. The patriarch complies, revealing a knowledge of medicine. Restored to health, the philosopher returns to pay his thanks and goes on to ask for guidance with regard to the *azymes*. Joannes employs once again both traditional and original arguments. When his interlocutor points out that the Church of Rome enjoins the use of unleavened bread, Joannes explains that Rome is the only patriarchal church to uphold this erroneous view, whereas "I have the three churches testifying together with me, namely those of Constantinople, Alexandria, and Antioch. In addition, I have also in my support that, at my place, this holy rite was for the first time performed by Christ himself in front of all his disciples." A powerful rejection of the primacy of Rome (or Constantinople), and an insistence on Jerusalem's special authority. Like in the first tract, the Latin interlocutor remains unconvinced.[68]

Symeon II, the last Greek Orthodox patriarch to reside in Jerusalem before the crusader conquest, wrote in the 1090s a tract against the *azymes*. It is addressed to the Latins and displays a much friendlier tone than that of Joannes VIII.[69] And the titular patriarch of Jerusalem in the years 1176–85, Leontios II, was the author of a short treatise on the Holy Trinity, and perhaps also of a tract on earthly and heavenly love; his biographer, Theodosios Goudeles, stressed his ability to provide "easy solutions for scriptural difficulties."[70] Evidently, some

Greek patriarchs of Jerusalem—unlike their Frankish rivals—composed works on ritual and theological topics.

Yet none of the lower Greek clergy in the Frankish Kingdom, who had to function under the authority of the Frankish prelates, is known to have written works on these or other subjects. It is symptomatic that, when, apparently some time before 1169, disputes arose between the Greek Orthodox and the Franks of the village of ʿAyn Kārim about various customs, a local Greek did not turn for guidance to a member of the kingdom's Greek Orthodox community, but to Theorianos the Philosopher, who served Emperor Manuel as envoy to the Armenian and Jacobite patriarchs, and was acquainted with Enrico Dandolo, patriarch of Grado. Theorianos sent a conciliatory letter to the Greek priests of the village, advising them to maintain fraternal relations with the Franks, and warning against a breakup on account of mere differences of custom. He then went on to explain at length that both unleavened and leavened bread are valid, equally becoming the Body of the Lord after consecration.[71] It is not known whether his advice was heeded.

The production of codices, on the other hand, took place quite often. Johannes Pahlitzsch has established that eight dated Greek manuscripts were prepared in the Kingdom of Jerusalem between the years 1122 and 1174/75: of these, two were copied in Jerusalem, two in Bethlehem, two in the Monastery of St. Sabas, one in Tiberias, and one in the Prodromos Monastery on the River Jordan; two further codices, dating from 1163 and 1186, may have been copied in the kingdom; and thirty-eight undated codices produced there are attributable to the twelfth century.[72] There are also indications for the continuous functioning of libraries.[73]

Three of the dated manuscripts throw some light on religio-cultural realities and attitudes. The *Typikon* of 1122 that presents the tenth-century liturgy of Easter Week in the Church of the Resurrection contains some contemporary additions. The colophon states that it was commissioned by Georgios, who held simultaneously three different posts, and was copied by Basileios, scribe and lector; the accumulation of offices suggests that the number of Greek clerics at the sanctuary was limited. An openness of the Greek clergy toward lay members of their community whose language was Arabic—that is, the Syrians—is revealed by a rubric that lays down that a sermon should be delivered first in Greek and then in Arabic translation; the Arabic text was indeed inserted into the codex. And in the intercessory prayer the name of the titular, exiled Greek patriarch, Nikolaos, is spelled out, eloquently declaring thereby that Nikolaos—not Warmund of Picquigny, the Frank—is the legitimate patriarch of Jerusalem.[74]

In the same vein, the colophon of a manuscript containing the Gospels, copied at St. Sabas in 1135/36, announces that this took place at the time of Emperor Joannes II Komnenos and of Konstantinos Kamytzes, the governor of Cyprus under Byzantine rule.[75] Fulk, the Frankish king of Jerusalem, is ignored.

The colophon of the Gospel lectionary made by the priest Georgios in 1152/53 for the Church of the Theotokos in Tiberias designates the city as the seat of an archbishopric.[76] Possibly some Greek clerics moved the archiepiscopal seat from Scythopolis—the capital of Palaestina Secunda in antiquity, which by the twelfth century became the insignificant township of Bethsan/Baysān—to Tiberias, just as the Franks moved it to Nazareth.[77] The lectionary also contains a full-page miniature of an enthroned Virgin holding Christ: an inscription identifies her as the Mother of God of Tiberias. Panayotis Vocotopoulos, the leading expert on Byzantine painting, upholds that the miniature is a copy of an icon renowned in Tiberias.[78] If so, it allows to observe at one remove a hub of local Greek Orthodox devotion in the capital of the Frankish Principality of Galilee.

Jotischky has summarized the contents of three undated manuscripts attributable to the twelfth century.[79] All three attest to a conservative outlook and an endeavor to ensure the continued knowledge of hagiographical and liturgical traditions.[80] Outlook and endeavor were basically common to Georgian, Armenian, and Jacobite monks and to local Muslim and Jewish leaders living under Frankish rule. The Samaritan literati were the only exception.

While the number of manuscripts copied in the Greek Orthodox scriptoria of the Kingdom of Jerusalem was substantial, only one author has been considered by some present-day historians as having produced original work. This is the monk Būlus (Paul) of Antioch, Greek Orthodox bishop of Sidon, who wrote at least five theological treatises in Arabic. The "Brief Letter on Reason" expounds Christianity's basic tenets.[81] In "On the Christian Sects" Būlus states that at this time there are four such factions: Melkites (to whom he belongs), Nestorians, Jacobites, and Maronites. He expounds the Melkite beliefs and polemicizes against those of the other groups.[82] The best known of his works is the "Letter to One of His Muslim Friends in Sidon," in which he presents the views about "Muḥammad, peace be upon him" that he heard from Christian sages during his journey, as bishop, to Constantinople, Amalfi, some Frankish districts, and Rome.[83] On the surface, the treatise stands out for its irenic attitude toward Islam, but, as David Thomas has shown, underneath the polite friendliness is a subtle, Christianizing, reading of the Qur'an that subverts traditional Muslim teachings and must have outraged Muslim readers.[84] The Egyptian jurist Shihāb al-Dīn al-Qarāfī wrote a wide-ranging rejoinder.[85] When in 1316 and 1321 Cypriot Christians sent an extended, less aggressive version of Būlus's "Letter" to two Damascene theologians, Ibn Taymiyya and Ibn Abī Ṭālib, they composed harsh replies.

But in which period was Būlus active? Since he used works by Elias of Nisibis (975–1046) and since 1232 is the date of the first known copy of the "Letter to One of His Muslim Friends," historians place him between the late eleventh and early thirteenth century.[86] Paul Khoury (d. 2021), the editor of his tractates, opts for the period 1140–80, and Jotischky appears to concur, presenting Būlus as a Greek Orthodox coadjutor-bishop of Sidon under the Franks.[87] On the other hand, Cahen and Pahlitzsch argue that the absence of any allusion to the Latin church in Būlus's writings militates against the possibility that he lived under Frankish rule; Cahen, who highlights Būlus's visit to Amalfi, assumes that he lived in the eleventh century.[88] One may add that Būlus's ascription of the subversive anti-Muslim statements—which are undoubtedly his own—to Christian sages in Constantinople and in the West would have amounted to a sensible defensive stratagem by an Eastern Christian living under Muslim rule; a subject of the Frankish Kingdom would have no need for such a subterfuge. Also, the notion that a twelfth-century Būlus believed that the Latins may be subsumed under the Melkites is hardly tenable. In "On the Christian Sects," Būlus claims that the Niceno-Constantinopolitan Creed is accepted by all Christians and goes on to quote it verbatim, including the statement that the Holy Spirit proceeds from the Father—and not from the Father and the Son, as taught in the West. A Melkite theologian, coadjutor in a Latin see, would surely have known that the Church of Rome does not believe in the procession of the Holy Spirit solely from the Father. Consequently, it is more plausible that Būlus lived in the eleventh century.[89]

Greek Orthodox monasteries, from Mount Tabor to the Judaean Desert, experienced a revival under Frankish rule, with Emperor Manuel paying for repair and redecoration and donating books.[90] In the cave monastery of St. Theoktistos in the Judaean Desert, vestiges of paintings dated to the years immediately preceding 1187 attest to a provincial version of the Komnenian style.[91] In the monastery of Choziba above Jericho, floor mosaics possibly dating from the twelfth century survive; in 1873, apparently coeval fresco paintings of saints and biblical scenes, with explanatory inscriptions, could still be seen. Over the outer gate, a Greek inscription gives a date equivalent to AD 1179, while an Arabic one announces: "This work Ibrāhīm and his brothers, the sons of Mūsā al-Jifnāwī [of Jifnā, Frankish Jafenia, north of Jerusalem] have done."[92] Still another testimony to the coexistence of the Greek of clerics and monks and the Arabic of the Syrians.

The schooling of one Syrian of the Frankish Kingdom is described in some detail. This is Yaʿqūb ibn Ṣiqlāb, the doctor who came to Damascus wearing the dress of Frankish physicians. He was born, probably in the 1160s, in Jerusalem's Quarter of the Easterners to one of the peasant families whom King Baldwin I induced to move from Transjordan to Jerusalem in order to enlarge the city's sparse population. According to Ibn Abī Uṣaybiʿa, young Yaʿqūb attached himself to an ascetic philosopher of the St. Sabas Monastery who was an expert in the natural sciences, geometry, arithmetic, and astrology. Ibn al-Qifṭī, in his turn, writes that Yaʿqūb studied philosophy and medicine in Jerusalem with a man from Antioch who excelled in some of the Greek branches of learning; this "philosopher from Antioch" turned his Jerusalemite home into a church of sorts, worshipping and teaching there until his death in about 1184/85. Possibly Yaʿqūb first studied with the St. Sabas ascetic and then, focusing on medicine, with the Antiochene scholar. At any rate, his wide-ranging studies and quotations of poetry recall those of his Samaritan contemporaries though—unlike them—he did not deal with religious issues. He stood out for an unequaled familiarity with the works of Galen, which he read and studied in the original Greek, yet—as Ibn Abī Uṣaybiʿa, who knew him, attests—"he would act independently and also used contemporary insights."[93] One is left to wonder how many of the Jerusalemite laymen of the Greek Orthodox rite were proficient in Greek and capable, like Yaʿqūb, of translating from it into Arabic.

Georgians

Georgian ties to Jerusalem and other hallowed places in the country go back to the fourth century.[94] Since the mid-eleventh century, the Georgians' principal center was the Monastery of the Holy Cross just west of Jerusalem, but monks and nuns from Georgia also lived in other communities, and some joined Greek Orthodox monasteries.[95] The Franks regarded the Georgians, like the Greek Orthodox, as belonging to the one true church that upholds the Chalcedonian Confession of 451, and appreciated their skill in combat.[96] The widow of Georgia's king came to Jerusalem and, on the authority of Patriarch Gibelin of Arles (1108–12) entered the city's Georgian nunnery and later became its abbess.[97] And, as we have seen, Knights Templar and Frankish nobles are commemorated as donors in the margins of two manuscripts of the Monastery of the Holy Cross.[98]

The first of these contains the translation of the *Great Synaxarion* by Giorgi the Athonite (1009–65), copied in 1155 by the hieromonk Giorgi Dodis "in the holy city of Jerusalem, in the Monastery of the Cross."[99] The second, containing the four Gospels, was copied in Georgia and donated to the monastery.[100] Another manuscript that belonged to the monastery was copied in 1167, but it does not disclose where the copying had taken place.[101] On the other hand, six manuscripts were copied in the Monastery of the Cross or in Jerusalem, but the date of copying is not given; scholars attribute one to the eleventh–twelfth, another to the twelfth, two to the twelfth–thirteenth, and two to the twelfth–fourteenth centuries.[102] A further manuscript, containing the *Life of the Mother of God* by Maximos the Confessor and copied by the Georgian scribe Iovane Q'ia in the Greek Orthodox monastery of St. Sabas "at the old people's home," is attributed to the twelfth century.[103] We may assume that several of the many manuscripts that do not contain information about the date and place of copying, but are attributable on paleographical grounds to the twelfth century and formed part of the library of the Monastery of the Cross, were copied there at the time of the Kingdom of Jerusalem. In any case, considering the small number of Georgian monks, their copying activity was substantial.

An Arabic-written contract by which Abbot Makharebeli of the Monastery of the Cross and his monks purchased in 1169 a vineyard from a family of Syrians sheds light on the influences affecting these Eastern Christians. The contract adheres essentially to the conventions of Islamicate juridical practice; the year is Islamic, 564; the month is Naysān, the Arabic name of April.[104] But the price of the vineyard is given in royal gold coins of full weight—a formulation that refers to the Frankish imitation dīnārs.[105]

The presence of the Georgian Iovane Q'ia in the Greek Orthodox monastery of St. Sabas is not surprising. A version of the *Rule of St. Sabas*, probably dating from the twelfth century, lays down that "the Iberians

[Georgians] or the Syrians or the Franks" may gather in their churches within the monastery and chant and read there in their own languages, but the complete prayer service must be conducted in the great church, together with the entire brotherhood.[106]

There were in the kingdom Georgian hermits, too. Joannes Phocas (or Doukas), who visited the country in 1177, mentions an Iberian monk who shut himself within a rock monument resembling a sharp-topped pyramid, near Gethsemane in Jerusalem—probably the structure known as Zechariah's Tomb. Near the Jordan, Joannes met an old, miracle-working Georgian hermit who dwelled on the top of his column and habitually fed a pair of lions; these played a key role in the miracle he recounts at some length. Not far from there he was impressed by another Georgian at his hermit's column.[107]

The mental turmoil that befell the Georgian hermit Gabriel is disapprovingly described by Neophytos the Recluse (1134–after 1214), the self-proclaimed Cypriot saint. Neophytos went on pilgrimage to the Holy Land in 1158, hoping to become some hermit's disciple, but after a six-months-long futile quest he returned to Cyprus.[108] His account about the Georgian hermit, whom he never met, was based on what he heard from a monk who knew him well. Neophytus relates that Gabriel was an esteemed monk deemed worthy of the sacerdotal order who, having arrived in Jerusalem, spent many years at different sites in the desert and, finally, in the monastery of St. Sabas. He persuaded the superior to allow him to ascend a column not far from the monastery, where he exerted himself for three years as a stylite in quest of God. He underwent many deprivations, but the quest was beyond his spiritual powers and turned out to have been—so Neophytus claims—inspired by the Devil. One night in 1164/65 the Devil appeared to Gabriel in the guise of St. Sabas, divulging that Christ assigned him an illustrious role. The following evening the bogus Sabas materialized again, together with demons pretending to be St. Symeon the Stylite and St. Stefanos the Sabaite, and the trio persuaded Gabriel to stop venerating the Virgin as the Mother of God. Subsequently they let him behold angels, apostles, prophets, martyrs, holy men, and, enthroned in their midst, Christ—in reality, Antichrist surrounded by demons. Gabriel, having made obeisance to him, was promised three great gifts, which he was to obtain the next evening upon calling out northward to Sabas, Symeon, and Stefanos. Neophytos sternly rebukes Gabriel for this reckless gullibility. (He might have likewise chided Ranieri of Pisa for trusting his visions.)

In due time, Gabriel, on his pillar, turned northward—the region symbolizing disaster—and shouted the three names so loudly that the monks of the St. Sabas Monastery were alarmed. Soon the demonic trio appeared, made the hermit vacate all traces of the Eucharist from his body, then invaded it through mouth and ears and gained almost complete control over him. Thereafter a demon in the form of a woman urged him to fornicate—and a flabbergasted Neophytos recoils from spelling out what then happened. However, Gabriel now comprehended that he had fallen into the trap of the Devil and his demons. Yet these did not give up. One of them assumed the form of the esteemed monk David, who dwelled nearby, and attempted to reassure Gabriel that he had been approached by angels. Furious, Gabriel was about to kill this tormentor, but soon the real David exposed the deceit and led the shaken stylite to the St. Sabas Monastery. The superior sent him to the Monastery of St. Euthymios, also in the Judean Desert, where he was ordered to carry wood for the bakery and kitchen. Evidently, hard manual work was supposed to rid him of the demons. Yet these continued to torment him. Eventually the superior succeeded in expelling the two who had entered his ears, but the third continued to lurk in his entrails. When *Salakhantes* (Ṣalāḥ al-Dīn) conquered the kingdom in 1187, Gabriel was carried off as a prisoner to Damascus.[109] Eighteen years later, Neophytos learned that he managed to make his way to the environs of Antioch, get rid of his travail, and find peace.[110]

Armenians

While the Latins regarded the Greek Orthodox and the Georgians as part of the one true church to which they themselves belonged, the Armenians were not so considered. The Western Visitor learned from the Franks he encountered that the Armenians "disagree on many issues with both Latins and Greeks" and act in many ways "contrary to ecclesiastical regulations."[111] He did not go so far as to brand them as heretics (as he did the Jacobites and Nestorians), but clearly considered them as being outside the fold. Frankish prelates must have thought likewise, because they left the local Armenian hierarchy in place and did not attempt to incorporate the Armenian believers into their church. Only once—at the Council of Jerusalem in 1141—was an attempt made to bridge over the doctrinal differences but, as Christopher MacEvitt has convincingly shown, this attempt was initiated by the papal legate, Alberic of Ostia.[112] On the practical level, the relations between Frankish and Armenian clerics were good. No less a Westerner than Joachim of Fiore, the towering apocalyptic thinker, was impressed by the fasts and prayers of the Armenians whom he encountered during his pilgrimage to Jerusalem, and gave the opinion that they are closer to the Roman faith than other non-Latin churches of those parts.[113] And because of King Baldwin II's marriage to Morfia of Melitene, an Armenian noblewoman, three generations of rulers of Jerusalem could look back to an Armenian ancestry, and may have felt some closeness to the kingdom's Armenian community.[114]

There is some evidence for an Armenian scriptorium in Jerusalem as early as the fifth century and for translations carried out there in 879, but the earliest extant manuscript copied in Jerusalem dates from 1215.[115] However, the arrival of Armenian books in Jerusalem is mentioned in the work ascribed to Abū al-Makārim. When the Ghuzz (Turks) and the Kurds took over Egypt in 1169, the Armenian patriarch and monks were driven from their monastery, and in 1172 the patriarch departed for Jerusalem. "He took with him 75 sacred books, among which was a copy of the Four Gospels with illuminations in colors and gold, representing the miracles of Christ." On arrival in Jerusalem, he was joyfully welcomed by "all the Christians." Outside the city, the patriarch later founded a monastery named after St. Sarkis, in which twenty monks were said to dwell. The Armenian bishop of Jerusalem, full of envy, poisoned him.[116] It is possible that the seventy-five books formed the basis of the renowned library of the Armenian patriarchate of Jerusalem.[117]

The Armenian imprint on the Frankish Kingdom is principally visible in the sphere of art. The goudron frieze (known also as "pillow arch") is apparently an Armenian form, with predecessors figuring in many variations on church portals of Greater Armenia at least since the sixth century. In Jerusalem, the goudron frieze is one of the most prominent components of the main entrance to the Frankish Church of the Holy Resurrection. The two gates on the first floor and the two windows on the second are framed by this frieze, and so is the upper, single window of the façade of St. Anne's Church in the eastern part of the city. A goudron frieze could be seen, until 1950, above the western entrance to the church of Frankish Ibelin (see fig. 14).[118]

In Jerusalem, the frieze recurs in two twelfth-century Armenian churches: it frames the portal leading from the narthex into the Cathedral of St. Hagop (Jacob), as well as the portal from the narthex into the Church of the Holy Archangels. The four Jerusalemite goudron friezes may be ascribed to the patronage of Queen Melisende, daughter of Morfia of Melitene.

Figure 14. Church of Ibelin, western entrance. Photo: Salem 'Abd es-Salam Husseini. IAA, The Scientific Archive, 1919–1948. Yibna, 2-7.654. Some time after 1187, the church became a mosque. It was blown up on 9 July 1950 on the orders of Moshe Dayan, OC Southern Command, IDF: Kedar, "In Search of Ibelin Castle," 14–15.

Armenian heritage is also conspicuous in Melisende's sepulchral chamber in the Church of St. Mary in the Valley of Josaphat. Its most outstanding element is the domed lantern above the chamber's center. Built on a square ground plan followed by an octagonal base on squinches and topped by a round form, it has no local parallels yet resembles antecedents in the churches of Haghpat Monastery (present-day northern Armenia).[119]

There is, however, no evidence that Armenian residents of the kingdom composed original works or translated works from the Latin. The *Poem of Lamentation over the Capture of Jerusalem* by Ṣalāḥ al-Dīn was written hundreds of miles north of the city, by Grigor IV Tłay, Catholicos of all Armenians.[120]

Here, too, the Frankish north differed from Jerusalem. Nersēs of Lambron (1153–98), the Armenian archbishop of Tarsus (northwest of Antioch), was fascinated by Frankish devotion, writing in 1177 to Levon of Cilicia: "In just a few years the Franks filled the entire country with their piety." Elsewhere he mentioned that during a visit to the Black Mountain he "admired, full of astonishment, the life of solitude, virtue, and mortification of the Roman monks called today Franks." When he asked a Greek monk, Basil, why these Franks were outdoing their Greek and Armenian counterparts, Basil directed him to Gregory the Great's *Life of St. Benedict*, and Nersēs decided to have both the *Life* and the *Rule of Benedict* translated into Armenian. Introducing his translation of the Rule, Nersēs stated that he did so in the Frankish monastery of St. Paul in Antioch (whose treasurer Stephanus Philosophus probably had once been) with the help of the monk William. Later he translated other Latin works. Nersēs was also impressed with the Franks' charitable works and set out to follow their example.[121]

Jacobites

Three twelfth-century colophons, written in Syriac in Jerusalem, amount to important sources for the history of the Jacobites—or Syrian Orthodox—in the Kingdom of Jerusalem and their relations with the Franks.

On 10 February 1138 the monk Michael of Marʿash (northwest of Edessa) placed the first colophon at the end of a book of liturgical chants that Ignatius III, Jacobite archbishop of Jerusalem, had copied. Michael's attitude toward the Franks is decidedly positive: They conquered Jerusalem "by the will of God," King Fulk is referred to as "victorious," his subjects as "the believing people of the Franks." Queen Melisende is especially extolled: she "had learned the fear of God from her mother the queen" (the Armenian Morfia); favorably inclined toward the Jacobites, she intervened on behalf of Archbishop Ignatius III in the protracted dispute that the colophon describes in detail and whose highlights are as follows. At the time of the 1099 conquest the Jacobite community was weak, as the archbishop and his monks had fled to Egypt, and a First Crusader, whose name is given as Gonfré, took possession of the two Jacobite villages of Beth ʿArīf (east of Lydda) and ʿAdse (north of Jerusalem).[122] Soon thereafter he fell into Fatimid captivity, and Jacobite prelates persuaded King Baldwin I to return the villages to them. In ʿAdse the Jacobites erected two churches, and a sizable monastic community came into being. But in the 1130s, Armenian influence in Egypt paved the way for Gonfré's release, and upon his arrival in Jerusalem King Fulk ordered to give him back the villages. The ailing Ignatius III, accompanied by the monk Michael and others, set out for Beth Gavrin (*sic*; meaning Bethgibelin), where Fulk was then staying, and presented his case. The king—whose entourage was instructed by Melisende to help the Jacobite prelate—eventually convinced Gonfré to give up the villages. Michael relates that Ignatius promised to give him two hundred dīnārs in charity.

The second colophon was written six months later, on 25 August 1138, by the monk Romanos, who after Ignatius's death was to succeed him as Ignatius IV. Romanos basically repeats Michael's account but adds many details. He relates that Archbishop Ignatius II Hesnūn (d. 1124/25) rebuilt the Monastery of St. Mary Magdalene and Simon the Pharisee close to Jerusalem's northern wall and ordered all of the city's Jacobite monks to dwell in it. Ignatius III, who succeeded him, enlarged the monastery, constructed at its gate three cisterns, and built a hostel for pilgrims. In ʿAdse he completed the tower, which had four stories, with a church on the upper one (this explains why Gonfré, according to Michael, referred to the place as "the fortress"), and at the tower's foot he constructed large cisterns. The rooms above them served as a monastery or convent, in whose corner stood a large church. The Gospel lectionary that Romanos copied, and into which he placed his colophon, was destined for this Monastery of the Tower. Romanos also spells out that the two hundred dīnārs that, according to Michael, Ignatius promised to give Gonfré in charity, were in reality part of the settlement Fulk imposed; Romanos reveals that the king received the same amount and so did his "chieftains."[123]

The third colophon appears in a Gospel lectionary, which the monk Sōhdō from Edessa finished copying in Jerusalem on 15 September 1149, and which was destined for use in the Church of St. Mary Magdalene in Tyre. In the colophon, Sōhdō (who was to become in 1193 Archbishop Ignatius VI) describes Zengi's conquest of Edessa in 1144 and the Second Crusade. He then focuses on Jerusalem and relates that in 1148 the city was flooded with paupers, among them refugees from Edessa, who pressed at the monasteries' gates. Ignatius III did all he could to help them, whether they were Jacobites or Franks, but ran out of supplies. At this juncture he obtained an audience with the young King Baldwin III and his mother, Queen Melisende, and asked for the restitution of the village of Dayr Dakariyya that had belonged to the Jacobite monastery under Muslim rule and was appropriated by an unnamed First Crusader.[124] The story of ʿAdse repeated itself. Baldwin and Melisende persuaded the Frankish owner to return the village, and Ignatius to pay him about one thousand dīnārs. Once the village was in the archbishop's possession, "he began to build a defensive tower in it with a church and houses surrounding the tower."[125] The Jacobites' decision to erect defensive towers in villages situated in the kingdom's center points to a widespread sense of insecurity.

An autograph notice by Michael the Syrian, Jacobite patriarch of Antioch in the years 1166–99 and author of a renowned chronicle, records the presence in the Monastery of St. Mary Magdalene in Jerusalem of a book that prescribed the correct pronunciation of foreign and rare words occurring in Syriac translations of the Bible and the Greek Fathers. In this notice, bearing a date equivalent to 1179, Michael forbids removing this book "from our monastery in Jerusalem that bears the name of St. Mary Magdalene."[126] The central and northern apses of the monastery's church could still be seen in Jerusalem in the 1860s, but in 1915, during World War I, the ruins were totally demolished. In 1978, however, the rectangular cloister with some of its arcades was unearthed. The elongated ground plan, the relatively slight walls, and the external buttresses may disclose Western influence.[127]

But even as Jacobites of the Kingdom of Jerusalem copied and possessed books, none of them is known to have composed one. For written guidance they—like the Jews of Tyre and Acre, and the Greek Orthodox of ʿAyn Kārim—turned to leading thinkers abroad. When sometime between 1166 and 1171 Ignatius IV wished to obtain an exposition of Jacobite liturgy that would be helpful in encounters with the Franks, he turned to Dionysius Bar Salībī who in those years was archbishop of Amida in Upper Mesopotamia. Dionysius—whom Michael the Syrian hailed as the "star of his generation"—complied, and decided to send the archbishop of Jerusalem also a discussion of the Incarnation and the Eucharist.[128]

Here, again, the Frankish north differed. Michael the Syrian wrote with admiration about the Knights Templar and Hospitaller, and his relations with his Latin counterpart, Patriarch Aimery of Antioch, were so close that the latter formally invited him to attend the Third Lateran Council of 1179, informing him that the Cathar heresy was to be discussed there. Michael responded by writing a treatise against the Manichaeans earmarked for use at the council.[129]

A bird's-eye view of the cultural activities of the non-Frankish communities in the Kingdom of Jerusalem reveals a spectrum of conducts. The Samaritans, who constituted the only autochthonous community that retained its cultic center and traditional leadership, stand out for considerable creativity. Jews and Muslims, who lost their leadership in the wake of the crusader conquest, engaged in low-level activity that endeavored to conserve traditional rites and customs. The Greek Orthodox, too, lost their leadership, with their patriarchs and some bishops residing in Constantinopolitan exile; but, as the Greek Orthodox preserved their monasteries and many churches, they were capable of undertaking ample low-level activities, especially the copying of manuscripts. The Georgians, Armenians, and Jacobites, few in number and with their cultural centers far away, did likewise, albeit on a smaller scale. On the other hand, some Muslim refugees were creative, stimulated by dislocation and exile.

A juxtaposition of the non-Franks with the Franks underscores the marked originality of the latter, whether in fashioning new foci of religiosity, an unprecedented amalgam of knighthood and monastic life, of medical and sacramental therapy, a new dialect of French, or experimenting with writing in the vernacular. Evidently, challenges of life in a radically new frontier environment generated the vibrant, innovative cultures of Frankish knights, clerics, and burgesses, contrasting with the largely stagnant ones of the indigenous.

Chapter 11

Cultural Activities in the Kingdom of Acre (1191–1291)

The thirteenth-century Kingdom of Acre was much smaller than the twelfth-century Kingdom of Jerusalem. Most of the time it was reduced to a strip along the Mediterranean coast: only between 1229 and 1244 did Jerusalem and Bethlehem—linked to the coast by a narrow corridor—belong to the kingdom, and Galilee was in Frankish hands only between 1241 and the mid-1260s. The Kingdom of Acre was also much more dependent on outside help. While local Frankish forces fighting under their kings played the leading role in the expansion of the Kingdom of Jerusalem, the more modest territorial gains of the Kingdom of Acre resulted mostly from military or diplomatic moves by crusaders from Europe. Crusaders also fortified the kingdom's coastal towns and castles, and between 1254 and 1291 the kings of France stationed a French contingent in its capital, Acre.[1]

Internally, the Kingdom of Acre was less stable than that of Jerusalem. During most of its existence, it lacked a resident king, and the local dominant powers—the Frankish nobility, the military orders, and the Italian communes—pursued their particular and often conflicting interests. The kingdom was also weakened by Cyprus becoming, in 1192, a nearby but separate Frankish-ruled entity. Numerous knights and burgesses were enticed to leave the kingdom and settle there, and leading nobles chose to add lands on the island to their possessions on the Levantine mainland. From the 1260s onward, as the Mamluk sultans Baybars and Qalāwūn conquered the kingdom step by step, Cyprus turned into a refuge for many Franks and some Eastern Christians.[2] The kingdom's fragility was so evident that even before the rise of Baybars some inhabitants took into consideration the likelihood of another Ḥaṭṭīn-like calamity. A charter drawn up at Acre in 1248 deals with these gloomy scenarios: the loss of the entire kingdom with the exception of Acre or Tyre; the loss of the kingdom and of one of these cities; and the loss of the kingdom as well as of both cities.[3]

The Clergy's Growing Integration into the West's Intellectual Scene

From a cultural point of view, a main difference between the Kingdoms of Acre and Jerusalem was the demise of the three foci of Frankish religiosity. The True Cross, captured by Ṣalāḥ al-Dīn's men at the Battle of Ḥaṭṭīn, was never, despite many efforts, recovered. Frankish clerics were able to contrive the Miraculous Fire once again when most of Jerusalem was temporarily restored to Christian rule according to the 1229 agreement between Emperor Frederick II and the Ayyubid sultan al-Kāmil. But on 9 March 1238, Pope Gregory IX instructed Patriarch Gérold of Jerusalem to forbid the canons of the Church of the Holy Sepulcher to presume that, on the Vigil of Easter, fire descends on the Sepulcher from Heaven.[4] The miracle was declared a fraud; thereafter, only Eastern Christians continued to regard it as genuine. And the presentation of Jerusalem's main sanctuary as the Church of the Holy Resurrection gradually fell into abeyance; Gérold's successors no longer mentioned "the Church of the Holy Resurrection" on their seals and referred instead to "Christ's Sepulcher."[5] Neither did they call into question the papacy's absolute supremacy over the four Eastern patriarchs, formally proclaimed at the Fourth Lateran Council of 1215.[6]

Acre, the capital of the kingdom in which the patriarchs of Jerusalem resided from 1191 onward, was devoid of significant biblical reminiscences. It is mentioned just once in the Old Testament—as a town the Israelites did not conquer (Judges 1:31)—and just once in the New Testament: according to Acts 21:7, Paul spent one day in Ptolemais (as the city was then known) while on his way to Jerusalem. The city's occasional confusion with Accaron, that is, ʿEqron of the Philistines, was hardly fit to boost its status in sacred history.[7]

The *Pardons of Acre*, probably written between 1258 and 1263, endeavored to attract pilgrims to the unhallowed city by promising extravagant indulgences (expressed in years and days of remission from purgatory) in return for visits to forty of its sites. For instance, visitors to the Church of St. Thomas on any day of the year were to obtain fifteen years of remission—which is truly astounding, seeing that Pope Alexander IV granted in 1260 to all those who visited St. Peter's Basilica in Rome on 25 April (the feast of St. Mark) just two years and eighty days.[8] Similarly, while Pope Nicholas IV was to grant in 1288 one year and forty days for visiting the Hospitaller church in Acre on the feasts of St. John the Baptist, St. Mary, and St. Michael, the *Pardons* promised no less than eight years for visiting this church on any date, with an extra forty days for each time one went around the Palace of the Sick and 240 days for partaking in the Sunday procession.[9] Moreover, the pilgrims were promised that their very arrival at the edge of the city would earn them four years and forty days![10] Evidently, the anonymous author or authors of the *Pardons* aimed at transforming Acre into a major, substitute expiatory pilgrimage center whose visitors were to reap stupendous spiritual benefits. Also, Acre's forty indulgence-yielding sites are listed in the *Pardons* in an order—as David Jacoby (d. 2018) was the first to realize—that allowed a pilgrim to make his way through the city according to a preset itinerary.[11] The route prescribed is, however, occasionally erratic.[12]

In any case, there is no evidence that the far-fetched promises of the *Pardons* converted Acre into a sacred space. When one remembers the ringing successes of the clerics of the Kingdom of Jerusalem—the appropriation of the Miraculous Fire, the Christianization of the Dome of the Rock, and so much more—the plan to sacralize Acre, if it was ever embarked on in earnest, looks pathetic. Indeed, an Old French itinerary datable to before 1265 proclaimed, "And know that Acre is not of the Promised Land," and the German Dominican Burchard of Mount Sion, who journeyed in the country in 1283–85, likewise observed that Acre has never been part of the Holy Land.[13] The city's reputation was unsavory. Jacques of Vitry, in 1216, famously denounced Acre as a "monstrous city replete with countless shameful deeds and crimes."[14] In 1254 Eudes of Châteauroux, the papal legate, told Joinville: "No one knows as well as I do about the dreadful sins that are committed in Acre; that is why God will avenge them by washing the city with the blood of its inhabitants."[15] And Manuello Romano (ca. 1260–ca. 1330), the poet who wrote both in Hebrew and in Italian, commented: "And what caused Acre's crash? Its corruption of all flesh."[16] The assumption that

Acre became "a kind of sacred place" and that its new religious role, the pilgrimage flow allegedly attested by the *Pardons*, and the prominence of the Knights Hospitaller in it caused the city to be known as Saint-Jean d'Acre toward the end of the thirteenth century is unwarranted.[17] That appellation appears in early modern times, when pilgrims and travelers were impressed by the ruins of the Hospital of St. John.[18]

The number of ecclesiastical buildings in twelfth-century Jerusalem and in thirteenth-century Acre appears to have been quite similar: the figures—based on a count of the edifices dealt with by Pringle in his masterly *Churches of the Crusader Kingdom of Jerusalem*—are eighty-nine and eighty-three, respectively. But the ratio of Roman Catholic to Eastern ecclesiastical buildings radically differed: forty-nine to forty in Jerusalem, seventy-three to ten in Acre.[19] As a result, the capital of the Kingdom of Acre displayed a decidedly more Occidental character than twelfth-century Jerusalem. Yet Occidental conspicuousness extended much beyond the number of Acre's Roman Catholic churches.

From the time of Pope Innocent III (1198–1216) onward, the popes considered the "translation" (transfer) of bishops from one see to another as their prerogative, exercising it frequently. A bishop would be transferred to a diocese remote from the one in which he was born and might expect translations to still other sees; consequently, the Roman Catholic Church, as Kenneth Pennington put it, "was becoming more national, or even international." Also, from the thirteenth century onward, papal provisions of benefices entailed the circulation of clerics all over Western Christendom.[20] These general processes also affected the clergy of the Kingdom of Acre, rendering it markedly different from that of the Kingdom of Jerusalem. The autonomous episcopal elections of the twelfth century gave way to papal provisions for Western clerics that rendered them bishops or lesser officials of the Frankish church. Especially in the second half of the thirteenth century, clerics so provisioned often returned to Europe after a stint in the Frankish East, with the popes promoting such traffic to and fro.

Since the popes were Italians, they provisioned numerous Italian clerics; this must have been one of the reasons why, in the Frankish East, the ratio of French-born to Italian-born bishops changed from 29:6 in the pre-1187 period to 22:17 in subsequent years.[21] The papacy also virtually chose the patriarchs of Jerusalem, usually opting for Western bishops with no previous contact with the Frankish church. These patriarchs served at the same time as papal legates, and their legatine status was the mainstay of their authority—a far cry from Patriarch Amaurry's acting "by the authority of the Lord's Passion and Resurrection."[22] The popes watched closely over the doings of the patriarchs and other prelates: the nine letters concerning the Frankish church that Pope Gregory IX issued on a single day, 9 March 1238, demonstrate this supervision.[23] Two popes had firsthand acquaintance with the Frankish East and its clergy. Pope Urban IV (1261–64), born in Troyes as Jacques Pantaléon, served as bishop of Verdun in 1252–55 and as patriarch of Jerusalem in 1255–61.[24] Tedaldo Visconti, the archdeacon of Liège who in 1271 arrived in Acre, joined Lord Edward and his crusaders, and learned there that he had been elected pope, returned West a few months later and upon his consecration took the name Gregory X. In subsequent calls for a crusade he repeatedly emphasized his familiarity with conditions in the Frankish East, "which we saw with our eyes and touched with our hands."[25]

Thus, the fragment of Western clergy that, in the Kingdom of Jerusalem, stood out for its preoccupation with places pervaded by sanctity, was increasingly replaced by a cross-section of Western clerics persistently overseen by the papacy: most of them had no previous acquaintance with the Frankish East, and some returned to Europe after a while. Hamilton found that of the forty bishops of the years 1192 to 1291 in the patriarchate of Jerusalem whose background is known, twenty-five came directly from the West to assume episcopal office, while fifteen were trained in the East. "As a result of greater western influence," he concluded, "a wider range of talent was found on the Jerusalem bench in the thirteenth century than had been present in the twelfth. . . . As a result, the church of Jerusalem was no longer a backwater in relation to the universal church as it had in some measure been earlier. Latin Syria through its bishops felt the impact of the complex revival of scholarship, jurisprudence and literature commonly called the twelfth-century renaissance."[26] After a century-long lag, some mainstream trends of that renaissance reached the Frankish East.

Literary creativity on the patriarchal level grew significantly. While no Latin patriarch of the Kingdom of Jerusalem is known to have authored a work, three patriarchs of the Kingdom of Acre did so, whether before or during their tenure of office.[27] Albert, bishop of Vercelli (Piedmont) in the years 1185–1205 and patriarch of Jerusalem from 1205 to 1214, drew up the Rule for the hermits of Mount Carmel.[28] Tommaso a Lentini (Sicily), patriarch in the years 1272–77, wrote the biography of the inquisitor Peter Martyr of Verona, killed by heretics in 1252.[29] Nicholas of Hannappes (northern France), the apostolic penitentiary whom Pope

Nicholas IV nominated as patriarch in 1288, was the author of a widely circulating collection of biblical examples; he also left behind a series of Lenten sermons. He drowned during the chaotic flight from Acre at the Mamluk conquest on 18 May 1291.[30]

The growing integration into the Western intellectual scene may be illustrated by the composition and diffusion of Benoît of Alignan's *Treatise on the Errors* both in the West and in the East.[31] Benoît, bishop of Marseille in the years 1229–68, first landed in Acre in 1239 with Count Thibaud IV of Champagne's crusade.[32] In the wake of the alliance with Sultan al-Ṣāliḥ Ismāʿīl of Damascus, Benoît was able to pilgrimage to the Greek Orthodox shrine at Saydnāyā and on his return to Acre persuaded Armand of Périgord, the Master of the Knights Templar, to refortify the important castle of Safed.[33] He also gathered information about the beliefs and practices of Greeks, Armenians, Jacobites, Nestorians, Maronites, and Nubians, gaining knowledge of at least one detail through direct contact.[34] He later used this information in his *Treatise*, which challenges "the errors deviating from the Catholic faith that we found on this as well as on the far side of the sea."[35] In two letters he points out that he started work on the treatise "in time past, when we first came thither [to Acre] for the relief of the Holy Land."[36] On 4 October 1260 Benoît was again in the Frankish East, this time to drum up help against the Mongol threat (which, however, vanished a month earlier as a result of the Mamluk victory at ʿAyn Jālūt). At an undisclosed date he sent the completed *Treatise* to Pope Alexander IV, who died on 25 May 1261. On 21 September 1261, still in Acre, he presented a copy to Tommaso Agni da Lentini, then titular bishop of Bethlehem and papal legate.[37] Tommaso, who in 1243 received Thomas Aquinas into the Dominican order and was to become archbishop of Cosenza in 1267 and patriarch of Jerusalem in 1272, shared with Benoît the desire to gain knowledge about Eastern Christian "errors" and refute them.[38] In the letter to Tommaso that introduces the *Treatise*, Benoît mentions its previous dispatch to the late pope, the Dominicans, Franciscans, Cistercians, Friars of the Sack, and many others, as well as to the prelates of the Frankish East.[39] On 9 August 1263, back in Marseille, Benoît sent a further copy of the *Treatise* to Bishop William of Agen (Aquitaine), whom Pope Urban IV appointed papal legate and patriarch of Jerusalem, as well as bishop of Acre, and who was to arrive there in September 1263.[40] Thus, a Western prelate who visited the Frankish East twice and started there a work on theological issues concerning both West and East, relayed it to leading ecclesiastics in the West as well as in the East.

The intensified links with the Western intellectual scene may also be observed in the sphere of law. Patriarch William of Agen requested a professor of civil law from Italy, Giovanni of Ancona, to write a compendium of canon law. Giovanni was a student of the versatile and prolific jurist Martino of Fano (ca. 1190–ca. 1272).[41] He composed his compendium in Acre in the years 1265–68, aiming to provide solutions to problems unsatisfactorily dealt with in the authoritative *Summa* by Goffredo of Trani (d. 1245) that was habitually consulted by Outremer's judges and lawyers. Yet, even as Giovanni wrote his bulky compendium in Acre, he underscored his Westernness by dedicating the work not only to the patriarch of Jerusalem but also to the bishop of Ancona. Giovanni—who takes pride for having handled legal issues concerning the Knights Templar and "nearly all prelates and nobles of this kingdom"—also wrote a treatise on feudal law. Standing squarely in the learned juridical tradition of the West, the treatise refers also to local practices and reveals a complex relationship to the Frankish East's customary law.[42]

No catalog of books owned by a church of the Kingdom of Acre has come down to us, but thirteen codices preserved in Rome, Paris, and Florence bear the mark *ecclesie Sydonensis* (of the church of Sidon); evidently, they formed part of the library of Sidon Cathedral before the Mamluk conquest of that city in July 1291.[43] Of the thirteen codices, eight date from the twelfth century and contain works by Fathers of the Church, Haimo of Halberstadt (d. 853), homilies, a pre-Gratian canon law collection, the decisions of the Council of Nablus in 1120, the commentary on the Apocalypse by Bruno of Segni (d. 1123), and the like.[44] The eight codices resemble the ones that the twelfth-century catalog of Nazareth Cathedral lists as dealing *de divinitate*, that is, with theological and ecclesiastical subjects. A codex copied in the twelfth/thirteenth century contains works by Seneca the Elder and the Younger, and constitutes the one Sidonese counterpart of the many Nazareth books listed as dealing *de grammatica*, that is, with language and literature.[45] The remaining four Sidonese codices, dating from the thirteenth century, are of a more variegated content and include recent works. BnF, lat. 1794 contains—in addition to works by Jerome, Nicetas of Remesiana (d. after 414), and Pope Gregory the Great—the liturgical book for ordinary services of the canons regular of St.-Jean-en-Vallée near Chartres, whose liturgy exerted great influence on that of Frankish Jerusalem.[46] Most of BAV, Vat. Borgh. 287 is taken up by the authoritative *Summa* on Gratian's *Decretum*, written by Étienne of Tournai.[47] BAV, Vat. Borgh. 6 contains sermons by Jean of Abbeville, the university professor and cardinal (d. 1238), and by the English preacher Odo of Cheriton (d. 1247).[48] But the great surprise comes into view in BAV, Vat. Borgh. 141, most of which is taken up by sermons. Between their inventory and the text of the sermons are inserted two folios containing four dense pages written in a different hand: they present a Latin translation of a part of *Philosophers' Intentions* by al-Ghazālī.[49] However, the text was not rendered into Latin in the Frankish East: Dominicus Gundissalinus of Segovia and a *magister Iohannes* translated it in Toledo in the twelfth century.[50] In the thirteenth, it was read by at least forty members of the university-trained elite of the West—and by at least one cleric of Sidon.[51] Accordingly, the thirteenth-century Sidonese codices, too, point to a greater familiarity with ongoing intellectual developments in the West.

The Dominican and Franciscan friars who arrived from Europe from the 1220s onward also helped bring the Frankish East in line with developments in the West. In 1236, the Dominican General Chapter held in Paris decreed that friars of all provinces and convents should learn the languages of the people near them, and in 1237 Philip, prior of the Dominican Province of the Holy Land, reported to Pope Gregory IX that he had introduced the study of languages into every convent and that the friars already speak and preach in the new languages, especially in Arabic, the more common one among the people.[52] In 1238, Gregory IX granted the crusading indulgence to the Franciscans and Dominicans in the Frankish East who were endeavoring to convert "pagans and others" by word and deed.[53] Theirs was the first institutionalized attempt at missionizing among Muslims who lived under Frankish rule—an attempt rooted in the evangelization programs espoused by their orders in the West. Thus, while in the twelfth century the innovative Military Orders of the Temple and the Hospital that arose in the Kingdom of Jerusalem spread in the West, in the following century the new, innovative mendicant orders of the West came to play a substantial role in the East.[54]

Were all Mendicants who went East motivated solely by the ideology of their orders, or were some of them—comparably to the twelfth-century clerics whose pilgrimage solved a knotty situation—more or less banished there? A decision of the Franciscan General Chapter that convened in Montpellier in 1287 implies that there were officials in the order who deliberately dispatched problematic friars to the Franciscan Province of the Holy Land.[55]

The number of mendicant friars was not large: at the election of Acre's Dominican prior in 1279, only thirteen friars were qualified to vote.[56] But the mendicant convents offered their friars access to institutionalized, if modest, higher studies—at any rate, studies that had no precedent in the Frankish East.[57] In 1255, the Franciscan William of Rubrouck (Flanders), back from his mission to the Mongol capital at Qara-Qorum, was appointed by the Minister of the Franciscan Province of the Holy Land to teach in the order's convent in Acre, where he then wrote the famous account, addressed to King Louis IX of France, of his journey to Mongolia. He does not spell out the subjects he taught in Acre; what with his background in theology and polemical experience gained in Qara-Qorum, he may have instructed the friars how to engage in disputations with infidels.[58] And Arabic and other Eastern languages were taught in Acre's Dominican convent, as we have seen.

The hope that preaching in Arabic would lead to large-scale Muslim conversion did not materialize. Yet the Dominicans' study of Eastern languages allowed them to instruct Muslim converts, discuss theological issues with Jacobites, Nestorians, and Armenians, "correct" Maronite books (that is, bring them in conformity with Roman Catholic teachings), and serve as translators and envoys.[59] One of these was the Dominican friar Yves the Breton, "who knew the Saracen language," as Joinville attests. In 1250, King Louis IX, then in Acre, sent him on a mission to the sultan of Damascus. Upon his return, Yves related that he saw there an old woman who passed through a street carrying a ladle full of fire in her right hand and a vial full of water in her left. When he asked what she intended to do with these, she explained that she wanted to burn paradise with the fire and quench hell with the water, so that thereafter no one would ever do good because of the hope of paradise or out of fear of hell, but simply for the love of God. Now, as Marie-Thérèse d'Alverny and Annemarie Schimmel have noted, this story is based on a tale about the female mystic Rābiʿa al-ʿAdawiyya, who died in Baṣra in 801. The good friar apparently disguised its origins by presenting the event as if he had taken part in it, and by avoiding typically Islamic terms, and paved the way for its inclusion in a major Western work.[60] Such percolation of an Arabic tale, with no precedents in the twelfth-century Kingdom of Jerusalem, had occurred in Acre already in about 1220. Jacques of Vitry, well known for his acerbic denunciation of the Prophet, mentions in one of his moralizing stories that people who proffer various excuses in order to evade work are likened by the Saracens to an ostrich, the animal that has a camel's feet and a bird's wings. When told to fly, the ostrich points to its feet, claiming, "I cannot fly, being a camel," and when told to carry a load, it points to the wings, saying, "I am a bird, and cannot carry loads."[61] The fable, which goes back to Aesop, was not known in medieval Europe, yet figured in the collection of parables by Abū al-Faḍl al-Maydānī (d. 1124).[62]

The linguistic and scriptural competences of just one friar of Acre's Dominican convent have been closely examined. This is William of Tripoli, who appeared before Pope Urban IV in 1264, entreating him to send immediate help to the Frankish East; he probably continued to France to alert King Louis IX. Later he was to accompany Niccolò and Maffeo Polo—and young Marco—to China, but got cold feet underway and returned to Acre.[63] In 1271, while in Acre, William presented his report on Islam and the Muslims, entitled *Account about Machomet*, to Tedaldo Visconti, the archdeacon of Liège soon to become Pope Gregory X.[64] An examination of the *Account* has revealed that William's knowledge of the Qur'an was limited, that he probably had no command of written Arabic, and that many of his Arabic-to-Latin translations were clumsy or erroneous, while his Latin was "wooden, the style awkward and inelegant."[65] Still, the report presents an account of Muḥammad's life (with an extraordinarily positive depiction of his teacher Baḥīrā) and of the contents of the Qur'an, reviews the early Muslim conquests and the main contemporary Muslim states, and dwells at some length on the Friday prayer.[66] Having condemned many teachings of the Qur'an, William goes on to announce rather surprisingly that it mentions Jesus with so much devotion and piety "that a simple person might believe that these words are truer than the text of the holy Gospel."[67] He then reproduces thirty-eight testimonies about Christ and the Virgin Mary appearing in the Qur'an, and polemicizes against Muslims who, despite being confronted with these texts, decline to convert to Christianity. The report, which also attests to some familiarity with Jewish lore, concludes with an emphatic call on all knowledgeable Christians to rescue Muslim souls from the Devil's snares. The subsequent assertion that the Muslims are well aware that the end of Islam and Christianity's victory are near probably aimed at persuading the future pope that Christian missionizing stood a fair chance of success.[68] William's *Account* was read by Cardinal Nicolaus Cusanus (1401–64) and quoted by the Dominican theologian and pilgrim Felix Fabri (1441–1502).[69]

The Frankish East's growing cultural enmeshment with the West can be discerned also on the level of popular religiosity. The Flagellants of 1260, who passed through the cities of northern Italy and ventured north of the Alps as far as Thuringia, Bohemia, and Poland, made their way also to Acre, possibly in response to the Mongol menace of that year.[70] The Coptic chronicler Jirjis Makīn ibn al-ʿAmīd (1205–73), the only author to record the arrival of these self-punitive penitents in Acre, dismisses them as charlatans, relating that, naked and holding whips in their hands, they flogged themselves, claiming that a rain of red sand descended on them.[71] Unfortunately, the Coptic chronicler does not spell out how the inhabitants of Acre—a city considered exceedingly sinful—received the Flagellants. Were they met with reserve or derided, as they were at first in Genoa? Or did they, as later on in Genoa, trigger a frenzied public repentance?[72] At any rate, thanks to Jirjis Makīn, we know that an offshoot of this lay movement reached the East. This may have been true of other Western factions, triggering the papal decision of 1290 to appoint inquisitors in Acre.

Were there also, at the same time, westward passages by would-be Frankish scholars? In 1249, Eudes of Châteauroux remarked in Nicosia that few or no men "of these parts" dare or are able to go to places where there exists a *studium* (institution of higher learning), "either because they are constrained by poverty, or frightened by the distance, the difficulty of the roads, or the danger of the sea."[73] This would have been a fortiori true for the Kingdom of Acre and the other Frankish possessions on the mainland. Yet, some Franks did decide to study in the West. In 1244, Pope Innocent IV acceded to the request of a treasurer of the church of Tripoli to use the income of his Tripolitan prebends while studying the "scholastic disciplines" beyond the sea; the permission to do so was limited to five years.[74] Ten years later, in 1254, the pope allowed Petrus, canon of Acre, to enjoy during his time "in the schools" the income of his prebend in the church of Acre.[75] In March 1269, Petrus, dean of Acre, appears in the documentation relating to the University of Bologna; he is hardly the same as the canon of 1254, but he may be identical with Petrus de Charta, of Acre, who appears as scholar at Bologna in August 1269.[76] Tripolitan Franks appear in the Bolognese documentation somewhat more frequently. On 19 July 1268 the scholar Guarinus of Antiozia sold two books of Decretals; the transaction was witnessed by the scholar Simon of Tripoli.[77] On 12 November 1268, Rambertus of Lambesco, scholar of Tripoli, bought a copy of Gratian's *Decretum* with the commentary of Johannes Teutonicus; master Paulus of Tripoli headed the list of witnesses.[78] A month earlier, master Henricus from Outremer was witness to a loan.[79] The published Bolognese documentation throws light only on a few years in the 1260s, and it is therefore plausible to assume that in reality more Franks studied there. In later years, such Easterners constituted one of the "nations" that made up the universities' student bodies. The statutes of Padua

University promulgated in 1331 list ten non-Italian nations, the last of which was that of the *Ultramarini*, students from Outremer.[80] As the Kingdom of Acre ceased to exist forty years earlier, these *Ultramarini* must have come from Frankish Cyprus and the Frankish-ruled parts of what had been the Byzantine Empire.[81]

Did such Ultramarine students tend to return to the Frankish East upon concluding their studies in the West? There is one indirect pointer to a negative answer. At the Dominican Chapter General that took place in Lucca in 1288, some provincial delegates requested the Master of the order that students from Greece and the Holy Land, sent to undertake higher studies in the West, should not be assigned to other provinces before they had served time as lecturers in their provinces of origin.[82]

The one churchman of the Frankish East whose work—the Latin translation of the pseudo-Aristotelian *Sirr al-asrār* (Secret of Secrets)—enjoyed phenomenal success in the West, presents himself in its prologue as Philippus, the least of the clerics of Bishop Guy of Tripoli.[83] As he was born in Umbria, spent many years in Italy and appears repeatedly in the documentation as Philippus Tripolitanus, it may be appropriate to refer to him as Filippo of Tripoli.

His career, like those of so many thirteenth-century clerics of Outremer, spanned East and West. He enjoyed an education that gained him the title *magister* and went East, where he benefited from the patronage of his uncle, Patriarch Rainiero of Antioch (1219–25), and exhibited medical skills that came to the attention of Pope Honorius III. In 1225 the pope addressed him as "our [papal] subdeacon and canon of Antioch." Presumably it was in Antioch that he learned Arabic. In 1227 he received a canonry in Tripoli, in the 1240s he held prebends in Gibeleth, Tyre, and Sidon, and in 1244 he was elected archbishop of Tyre, but because of unspecified objections he resigned. In 1257, as cantor of Tripoli, he received a loan from the Knights Hospitaller for an overseas trip of Tripoli's bishop, Opizo. During the same period, he was active in the West. In 1230 Pope Gregory IX addressed him as "prior of Todi [Umbria] and canon of Antioch." In 1238, functioning as "the pope's cleric," he collected dues from the prelates of Morea (the Frankish Peloponnese). In 1243, as canon of Gibeleth and master, he appeared before Pope Innocent IV and accused Gibeleth's bishop of insufficient learning. Two years later, when the papal court sojourned in Genoa, Filippo was there as envoy of Archbishop Henri of Nazareth and Patriarch Robert of Jerusalem. In the years 1248–50 he served as chaplain of Cardinal Hugues of St.-Cher. In 1267, as archdeacon of Tripoli and chaplain of the Apostolic see, he accompanied the pontifical legate for the Kingdom of Sicily, and two years later, the cardinals instructed him to see to the hosting of a troop of soldiers from Velletri. It is not known where Filippo ended his days.[84]

In the prologue to his translation, dedicated to Bishop Guy of Tripoli—whom he presents as originating in Valencia (probably Valence on the Rhône River), but who does not appear elsewhere—Filippo relates that he was with the bishop in Antioch when the "most precious pearl of philosophy" was discovered, and the bishop asked him to translate it from Arabic into Latin. The work so emphatically extolled is the *Sirr al-asrār*, which Filippo translated, probably in about 1232, under the title *Secretum Secretorum*. Perhaps originally written in Syriac, the work pretends to constitute a lengthy epistle in which Aristotle—unable to join Alexander on his campaigns of conquest—reveals to him the most profound secrets in an allegedly enigmatic language.[85] In reality, it is an encyclopedic work written in quite plain prose. Its core is a "mirror for princes" that instructs Alexander how to govern his realm and how to sustain his health, to which sections on astrology, alchemy, the power of stones and plants, physiognomy, and much more are added. A short section dealing with diet and health had been translated in Iberia by Johannes Hispalensis in about 1120.[86] Filippo had this Latin translation before him, but put it to use rather clumsily: he first quoted a passage from it, and later unwittingly translated the self-same passage from the Arabic.[87] In any case, the Latin rendering of al-Ghazālī's *Philosophers' Intentions* was not the only twelfth-century Iberian translation to reach the Frankish East.

A careful study of Filippo's translation has highlighted the limits of his knowledge of Arabic. Some words and expressions he misunderstood; faced with a word with a spectrum of meanings, he revealed his unawareness of the one required by the context; not sure of the Latin equivalent of some technical terms, he merely transliterated them; philosophical and metaphysical issues, as well as Islamic political theory, he misunderstood or misrepresented. Nevertheless, his translation is much of the time accurate.[88] Often it is attuned to the knowledge of his readers: for instance, instead of using the unfamiliar term "bedouin" he refers to "Arabs and those who often traverse deserts and [undertake] long journeys."[89] Sometimes he also adapts the content to his readers' sense of decorum, like in his presentation of the *ḥammām*.[90] But his Latin is definitely less graceful than that of Johannes Hispalensis.[91]

Roger Bacon, the Franciscan "wonderful teacher," was so much impressed by Filippo's text that he decided, in about 1275, to edit and gloss it.[92] The text was also used in some university courses. Yet there were scholars who doubted that Aristotle was the author of the treatise: Bacon himself refers to such skeptics in one of his glosses, and in the fourteenth century Nicole Oresme (d. 1382) squarely denounced the treatise as inauthentic. According to Ibn Khaldūn (d. 1406), Muslim scholars of his time also doubted its attribution to Aristotle.[93] But even as the treatise's reception among scholars was restricted, it became—to quote the apposite characterization by Mahmoud Manzalaoui (d. 2015)—"the great middle-brow classic for the layman."[94] It was one of the most widely read books of the later Middle Ages: fifty-seven manuscripts containing the full Latin text, and twenty-two manuscripts holding fragments or excerpts, were copied before 1325, and the treatise was also translated into several vernacular languages.[95] Its impact on the popular culture of the age deserves a special study.[96]

This spectacular success should not surprise. In the thirteenth century as in the twenty-first, a book that purports to offer a shortcut to the allegedly most profound secrets of an illustrious sage captures the imagination of countless middle-brow semisavants, and when it is also endowed by a touch of the occult, the fascination becomes still more sweeping.[97] The members of the Institut de France, who, as we have seen, wished in 1806 to learn about the influence of the crusades on the civilization of the peoples of Europe, would have been surprised to hear that the only Arabic work to come from the Frankish East and to widely circulate among Europe's peoples was a pseudo-Aristotelian text of little scholarly value.

Knightly Creativity in Old French

The precocious recourse to writing in the vernacular, attested in the Kingdom of Jerusalem by the translation of the Templar Rule into Old French and by Ernoul's Old French chronicle, became widespread in the Kingdom of Acre. The first legal treatise of the Frankish East that has come down, the *Book for the King*, instigated by King Aimery of Lusignan and written in Acre between 1197 and 1205, is one of the earliest collections of customary feudal law written in Old French.[98] Later, from 1228 on, Frankish charters began to be written in Old French: first in the princely chancery of Antioch, then in the royal chancery of Cyprus, and from 1249–50 onward the feudal lords of the Kingdom of Acre followed suit. Hiestand, who dedicated a painstaking study to these charters, pointed out that throughout Western culture, Frankish laymen were the first to abandon Latin and use the vernacular as the official language of chancery acts.[99]

The shift from Latin to Old French is striking in the realm of historiography. While the chronicles of the Kingdom of Jerusalem were written in Latin and only that by Ernoul, written during the kingdom's collapse, was in Old French, the chronicles of the Kingdom of Acre were written in Old French, with the exception of the *Oriental History* by Jacques of Vitry, who lived, however, in Outremer for just nine years.[100]

Almost all thirteenth-century Frankish chronicles written in Old French were composed either by knights or by members of their retinue who espoused knightly values.[101] Ernoul eulogized his master Balian of Ibelin; Phelippe of Novara—a noble of Italian origin—who wrote an account of the struggle from the mid-1220s to 1242 between Emperor Frederick II and a part of the Frankish nobility, described it from the standpoint of Balian's son Johan, "the Old Lord of Beirut," and his brother Phelippe, a prominent Cypriot noble.[102] The so-called Templar of Tyre, apparently a member of the lower Frankish nobility, expressed his admiration for William of Beaujeu, Master of the Knights Templar in the years 1273–91, to whose entourage he belonged.[103] Knightly attitudes also pervade the anonymous continuations of William of Tyre's chronicle written in the Frankish East. The account covering the years 1184 to 1247, labeled in the research literature as the "Colbert-Fontainebleau Continuation," was written by an author who expressed the viewpoint of the nobles who served King Johan of Brienne (1210–22), last resident ruler of the Kingdom of Acre.[104] The continuation labeled as "the Lyon *Eracles*" may have been written by a cleric, but it strikingly expresses knightly disdain for burgesses.[105] The bulk of the texts known as the *Annals of the Holy Land*, originally compiled in Acre in the mid-1250s, points to a clerical authorship, yet the early entries, which greatly expand those recorded in Latin by the twelfth-century canons of the Church of the Holy Sepulcher, betray a knightly outlook.[106]

Two chronicles attest to familiarity with literary works typical of Western chivalric culture. Phelippe of Novara repeatedly pours scorn on his—and the Ibelins'—main adversaries by bestowing on them the names and characteristics of animals that figure in the *Tale of Renart the Fox*; since he reports that the knights of Acre to whom he addressed his satire received it with great joy, they must have been acquainted with the story of the trickster fox.[107] Phelippe also relates that when in 1223, in Cyprus, Johan of Ibelin conferred knighthood on his two oldest sons, he threw a magnificent feast unprecedented in the Frankish East, with reenactments of "the adventures of Brittany and the Round Table," and with sundry spectacles taking place.[108] The Templar of Tyre, in his turn, recounts that in 1286, after King Henry II of Cyprus was crowned king of Jerusalem, he came to Acre and held for fifteen days grand festivities in the residence of the Knights Hospitaller—meaning the great hall of this complex, situated in the suburb of Montmusard. Tournaments took place there, the Round Table and the Queen of Amazons were enacted, "that is, knights dressed up as ladies fought together, and then impersonated nuns who stayed with monks and blindfolded one another. And they enacted Lancelot and Tristan and Pilamedes [*sic*] and many other beautiful, delightful and enjoyable spectacles."[109]

More than just chronicles testify to Frankish familiarity with Western chivalric literature. In his treatise on the procedures and law of the High Courts of the kingdoms of Cyprus, Jerusalem, and Acre, Phelippe of Novara relates that during the first siege of Damietta—that is, when the Fifth Crusaders were besieging the city in 1218–19—he was asked by his lord Piere Chape, a Cypriot noble, to read to him and to Raoul of Tiberias from a romance. Raoul liked what he heard, and when he later fell ill, requested Piere Chape to tell Phelippe to read to him. As Phelippe did so for more than three months, it is obvious—as Jacoby remarked—that he read to him not just from one but from several romances, which Piere or some other knight took along to Egypt.[110]

Some Knights Hospitaller shared Piere's and Raoul's predilection for such works: the Hospitaller statutes promulgated in Acre in 1262 stipulated that all books belonging to a deceased brother—with the exception of breviaries, romances, and psalters—will be returned to the treasury; later, the statutes call for the punishment of sick brothers who play chess or read romances while in the infirmary.[111] Two fragments of the *chanson de geste* about the Saracen knight Fierabras that forms part of the Charlemagne Cycle, two passages of *Enfances Godefroi* that deal with the exploits of young Godefrid of Bouillon, a short portion of the Old French *Life* of St. Mary of Egypt, and a fragment of an otherwise unknown Old French apologetic treatise that rebuts the Jewish denial of the Incarnation and the Virgin Birth, all of which made their way to the treasure trove of the Umayyad Mosque of Damascus, may have formed part of the booty the Mamluks took upon the conquest of Acre in 1291, or elsewhere in the Frankish East.[112] The two folios of Tristan, copied in a mid-thirteenth Parisian Gothic minuscule and now deposited in the National Library of Israel in Jerusalem, may have met a similar fate.[113]

But how did such pieces of chivalric literature reach the Frankish East in the first place? The inventory of Count Eudes of Nevers, who died in Acre in 1266 while leading a small crusade, may provide one answer. It lists among his possessions three books: the *romanz des Loheranz*, that is, a *chanson de geste* of the Lorrain Cycle; the *romanz de la terre d'outre mer*, that is, an Old French adaptation of William of Tyre, probably with some continuation appended; and a *Chançoners*, that is, a manuscript containing lyrical works by trovères or troubadours.[114] Such books brought to the East by crusaders may have remained, or been copied, there. To judge from the count's inventory, they were not considered of great worth; all three books were sold for 31 bezants, as were 155 hens.[115]

Some vernacular texts were composed in the Frankish East. The regulations of the Knights Templar, some mentioning events datable to the years 1257–65, were recorded in Old French, and the Templar Ricaut Bonomel lamented, in a poem written in Provençal, the Mamluk conquest of Caesarea and Arsur in 1265, famously complaining that God is asleep while *Bafometz* (Muḥammad) brims with activity.[116] As for the Knights Hospitaller, a prayer recited every night in Old French to the "Sick Lords," bedridden in the order's hospital in Acre, has come down to us; it appears to be an adaptation of a vernacular text that formed part of Sunday services in France.[117] In 1282, in Acre, the Hospitaller William of St. Estiene requested master Johan of Antioch to translate Cicero's treatise on rhetoric into Old French.[118] While the translation is marred by numerous mistakes that attest to a scant linguistic competence and to an ignorance of Roman history and law, the original epilogue appended to it stands out for the remarkable insinuation that Old French is not inferior to Latin and for application of rules of grammar to Old French.[119] About the same time, William of St. Estiene instigated the translation into Old French of an assemblage of Hospitaller records. The translator was, most likely, Johan of Antioch.[120] William himself authored a brief, realistic account of the Jerusalem Hospital's foundation, dismissing the legend about its biblical origins.[121]

It was not only Knights Templar and Hospitaller who wrote in or translated into the vernacular. In about 1271 in Acre, a master Richard translated into Old French the *Epitome of Military Science* by Vegetius, a work of considerable interest for the knightly class, which—as we have seen—already Geoffroy Plantagenet is said to have consulted in the Latin original; apparently, the translation was made for Eleanor of Castile, who was to present it to her husband, the Lord Edward.[122] A knight and a convert from Islam joined forces to produce at an unknown date an Arabic-French glossary of remedial stuffs used in medicine.[123] And a no longer extant Old French translation of the books of Genesis and Exodus, made in the West, served as the basis for an adaptation prepared in the Frankish East, possibly in Acre. The adaptation, whose lost archetype must have existed before 1250, formed part of a compilation that presented vernacular versions of several biblical books—an early attempt to render much of the Old Testament in Old French.

Probably but not necessarily aiming at a knightly audience, the adaptation offers a brief summary of Genesis and Exodus, omits lists of generations and events that have no bearing on the core narrative, and is often unfaithful to the original. The adaptation's Frankish authorship is attested by a recourse to Arabic words like the already mentioned *dāye* (midwife) and by marginal glosses that offer Frankish equivalents of biblical toponyms, with some of the localizations erroneous.[124] Remarkably, the glossator time and again chooses *Naples* (Nablus) as his point of reference.[125] Also noteworthy is the gloss on the name *Ysmael*: "Of him descend the pagans of nowadays, whom one calls *Sarrazins*. This name is given to them mistakenly because they are [descended] from the slave [Hagar]. However, we are the sons of Sarah [and therefore] we Christians are justly called *Sarrazins*."[126] The view that the Saracens wrongfully pretend to descend from Sarah, first voiced by Isidore of Seville (ca. 560–636), was widespread; the subsequent assertion possibly reflects a local joke according to which the Franks—and not their enemies—were the true Saracens.[127]

Creativity in the vernacular was especially pronounced in the legal sphere. Riley-Smith drew attention to several jurists who formed a veritable school of feudal law, "confined, it is true, to a small circle of relatives and dependents, in which ideas and details of the techniques of court practice were passed from generation to generation."[128] The most prominent of these jurists was Johan of Ibelin (1215–66), namesake of his uncle the "Old Lord of Beirut" and, in his later years, count of Jaffa and Ascalon. The bulky *Book of Assizes* he composed in the 1260s offers the most comprehensive account of the customary law of the Frankish East that regulated court procedures, vassalage, fief-holding, and much more. He also wrote a short tract on the regency of the Kingdom of Acre.[129] In his *Book of Assizes*, Johan made use of the *Book about the Method of Pleading* by Phelippe of Novara, a shorter treatise, probably written in the early 1250s, that deals with the customary law and procedures in the High Court. Phelippe and Johan decidedly favored the kingdom's nobility and went so far as to deny the very existence of the earlier, pro-royal *Book for the King.*[130] After 1265, Jofrei Le Tor—member of a middle-ranking noble family mentioned already in the 1120s[131]—wrote a *Livre* on homage and other feudal customs, deriving a substantial part of his text from Phelippe's treatise.[132] And Jacques of Ibelin, son of Count Johan of Jaffa and Ascalon, wrote after 1271 a lawbook summarizing, but occasionally correcting, his father's *Book of Assizes.*[133]

No other cultural sphere in the Frankish East witnessed the activity of so numerous and interrelated authors, all dealing with local customary law and discussing issues of major political importance, like the constitutional position of the monarchy. Yet Western lore, too, had some impact on Frankish legal procedure and decisions, while Roman legal terms began to turn up in charters drawn up in Acre. The legal experts who arrived from the West spread the knowledge of Roman law, and the local knight-jurists had to take it into account.[134]

On the other hand, Frankish law was known in the West to some extent and on one occasion served to buttress an argument in the interminable clash between the empire and the papacy. When in 1238 the envoys of Pope Gregory IX charged that Emperor Frederick II did not fully restore to the Knights Templar and Hospitaller their properties in Sicily, Frederick retorted, inter alia, that Sicilian law forbids to grant them property held in burgage tenure (*burgasatica*), because otherwise they would take possession of the entire Kingdom of Sicily in a short time; and he added: "and this same statute is in force beyond the sea."[135] Evidently, the emperor—who went on crusade in 1228–29—learned of the stipulation of the *Book for the King* that forbade the grant of burgage tenures to a church or an order.[136]

Phelippe of Novara, whom we encountered as having authored both a chronicle and a lawbook, was a versatile writer. Having passed his seventieth year, he composed a moral treatise, *On the Four Ages of Man*, in which he advised male and female members of the knightly class how to behave in the different phases of their lives. The treatise's concluding section reveals that Phelippe's above-mentioned chronicle, describing the struggle between Emperor Frederick II and the Ibelins, formed part of a larger work that has not come down to us. The lost sections were partly autobiographical: "For there it is told where he [Phelippe] was from and how and why he came to this side of the sea and how, by the grace of Our Lord, he got on and supported himself for so long. Then there are plenty of rhymes and songs he himself had made, some of them about the great follies of the world that one calls love lyrics." These sections were followed by the extant account of the struggle between the emperor and the Ibelins and then by another section that has not survived: "After that there are songs and rhymes, of which he [Phelippe] made many in his old age, about Our Lord and Our Lady and about male and female saints."[137] The composer of love songs, a chronicle, a lawbook, a moral treatise, and devotional poems, Phelippe was surely the outstanding literary personage of the Frankish East in the thirteenth century.[138] Significantly, the most prominent man of letters in the Frankish East in the twelfth century, William of Tyre, was a churchman who wrote in Latin, whereas his thirteenth-century counterpart was a knight writing in Old French.

An unnoticed similarity between William and Phelippe concerns their conviction that life in the present world must be followed by life in a different one. William, as we have seen, answered King Amaurry's query about the resurrection of the flesh by arguing that it must take place because God, being just, recompenses befittingly the good and the bad, and as this compensation does not happen in the present life, it will occur in the future one. Phelippe, in his *On the Four Ages of Man*, relates that those who lost all hope and the unbelievers claim that there is no world beyond the present one. He then goes on to assert at considerable length that it is easy to prove that they err, because one sees frequently in this world how the good suffer and the bad prosper, and if there were not another world, God's promise that no good deed remains without reward nor a bad one without punishment would turn out to be untrue. Evidently, Phelippe reiterates Part One of the retribution argument.[139] But he then adds on his own that in the absence of another world, "all religions would cease to be true, because the Jews and even the Saracens say and believe that God is great and just and all-powerful, and if this is true, then there exists another world in which he gives justice to good and bad, which does not happen in this world."[140] Thus, Phelippe mobilizes the Jews and the Muslims in support of his argument, divulging in passing that he regards the latter to be monotheists.

Was Phelippe aware of William's argument? Probably not, because William also deals conspicuously with the resurrection of the flesh, while Phelippe does not mention resurrection at all. Yet it is possible that he knew of William's argument as paraphrased in the Old French adaptation of his chronicle. There, too, the resurrection goes unmentioned, while the phraseology resembles Phelippe's on occasion.[141]

Phelippe's reference to the beliefs of Jews and Saracens amounts to a rare instance of knightly openness toward external cultures. The manifold cultural activities in their milieu—whether the writing of chronicles, legal treatises, or poems in Old French, or the translation of Latin works, classical and recent, into Old French—were essentially inward-oriented. However, the two Western rulers who came to the kingdom during the thirteenth century displayed, in varying degrees, a contrary orientation. Emperor Frederick II, who sent questions about medicine, optics, mathematics, and metaphysics to Muslim rulers, used the negotiations with the Egyptian sultan al-Kāmil—which led in 1229 to the Christian reacquisition of most of Jerusalem—to make enquiries about philosophical and mathematical issues.[142] When he refortified Jaffa in the same year, he set, probably above the citadel's gate, a Latin and an Arabic inscription, fragments of which have come down to us (see figs. 15a–b). The Latin fragment, published in 1899, reads:

> [Fridericus Romanorum imperator semp]**er Augustus, Ie**[rusalem rex. Anno Domi]**nice Incarnatio**[nis]
>
> [Frederick, Emperor of the Romans, alw]**ays august, Je**[rusalem's king in the year of the Lo]**rd's Incarnation**].[143]

The Arabic fragment, discovered in 2012, reads:

1. قيصر المـ(عظم إمبراطور رومية فر)دريك المنصور بالله مالك ألما
2. نيـ(ة ولمبردية وتسقانة وإيطالية وأ)نكبردة وقلورية وصقلية ومملكة
3. الشا(م القدسية معز إمام رومية الناصر للملة)المسيحية بشهر فورارو سنة ألف
4. ومـ(تين وتسع وعشرين لتجّسد سيدنا يسوع المسيح . . .

1. [The august Caesar], **Emperor** (*Imbrāṭūr*) **of Rome, Fre**[derick, the victorious by God, ruler of Germa]
2. **ny and Lombardy and Tuscany and Italy and** [Longobardia and Calabria and Sicily and the Syrian kingdom]
3. **of Jerusalem; the fortifier of the** *imām* **of Rome, the protector of the Christian community**, [in the month of February (?) of the year one thousand]
4. **two hundred and twenty-nine of the Incarnation of our Lord Jesus Christ** . . .[144]

Figures 15a and 15b. Fragments of Emperor Frederick II's Latin and Arabic Inscriptions in Jaffa, 1229. *Left*: The Latin fragment (size: 77 x 27 cm). Drawing: Charles Clermont-Ganneau, *Archaeological Researches in Palestine during the Years 1873–1874*, 2 vols. (London, 1896–99), 2:155. *Right*: The Arabic fragment (size: 58 x 35 cm). Photo: B. Z. Kedar.

This Arabic inscription, with parallels in Sicily and Iberia, is unique in the Frankish East.

King Louis IX of France, who spent the years 1250–54 fortifying Acre, Caesarea, Jaffa, and Sidon, exhibited a similar orientation. Having heard about "a great sultan of the Saracens" who had copied and stored all books that Saracen philosophers may need, he decided that, upon his return to France, he would do likewise with regard to all books of holy scripture, and indeed he did store them thereafter in his chapel's treasury. Geoffroy of Beaulieu, the king's confessor and biographer who relates this, has him reflect, with regard to the sultan's deed, that "the sons of darkness appear to be more prudent than the sons of light, and more zealous in their error than the sons of the true Church in the Christian faith"– inadvertently using Luke 16:8 exactly as Arnold of Lübeck had done while pondering over Muslim advantages over Christians.[145]

Acre's Burgesses: Western Influences in Law, Art, and Medicine

Raimon Anciaume, the "wise burgess" who grew up in the Kingdom of Jerusalem, was snubbed by the prominent knight-jurist Raoul of Tiberias as unfit—because of his burgess status—to take part in the codification of the laws of the realm. This, as we have seen, occurred in the early years of the Kingdom of Acre.[146] Later, burgesses became a powerful component of Outremer's society, especially when between 1231 and 1243 they formed part of the revolutionary Commonalty of Acre.[147] In his chronicle, Phelippe of Novara mentions two "eminent burgesses" of Acre, Johan Vaalin and William of Conches, "who had very great power over the city's people."[148] He presents a member of William's family, Raymond of Conches, as a "very wise burgess," "who came and pleaded very often in the High Court."[149] Phelippe also claims that he himself, together with a wise burgess, Phelippe of Baoduyn, drew up the agreement of 1242 that aimed at transferring the rule of the kingdom to Alice of Cyprus, granddaughter of King Amaurry, and not to Emperor Frederick II's son Conrad.[150]

Elsewhere, Phelippe presents this burgess as "sire Phelippe de Baudoin," who together with Nicole Anteaume (son of the disparaged "wise burgess" Raimon), were "great pleaders in and outside the court."[151] So the names of four burgesses who stood out for their expertise in the customary law of the kingdom have come down to us; a considerable number, seeing that the number of knightly experts whose names are spelled out is twelve.[152] But while four of the knight-jurists left behind writings on the subject, none of the burgesses did so.

There was, however, a Frankish burgess who did compile a legal treatise, known as the *Book of the Assizes of the Court of Burgesses*.[153] It is a remarkable work because—as Prawer put it—"in the thirteenth century and for many centuries to come, it is the only treatise that specifically dealt with one strata [*sic*] of society, the burgesses."[154] It has been variously dated to 1229–44, 1240–44, the 1250s, and the 1260s; in 2006 Marwan Nader suggested that this book is a compilation, with some parts written in the late twelfth century, a main author composing the bulk of the treatise between 1229 and 1244, and a later author inserting additions after 1251.[155]

The *Book of the Assizes of the Court of Burgesses* presents the local law relating to the burgesses, yet it is permeated with Roman law as studied in the West from the Twelfth-Century Renaissance onward, and attests also to an impact of canon law and Germanic customary law.[156] Back in 1843, Charles Giraud noted the similarity between the chapter on ex-hereditation in this work and the corresponding chapter in *Lo Codi*, a compendium of Roman law written in Provençal.[157] In 1954, Prawer argued that the mid-twelfth-century *Lo Codi* served to a considerable extent as the template for the presentation of Frankish usages in the *Book of the Assizes of the Court of Burgesses*.[158] In 2019, Adam Bishop contended that this work contains sections apparently taken directly from Roman law as codified under Emperor Justinian, and adapted to the circumstances of the Frankish East.[159] Thus, even if the work were merely a private law treatise, compiled by some jurist in Acre intent on describing the judicial reality of the kingdom, and all the more so if it were the public law book of Acre's Court of Burgesses, consulted by its jurors, it attests to an impact of Western legal learning on local burgess culture that far exceeds that learning's effect on local customary feudal law.[160] A close reading of the *Book of the Assizes of the Court of Burgesses* reveals, however, that it aims at readers with very limited knowledge of the Latin language and of Roman law.[161]

Another work related to Acre's burgess milieu is a manual of commercial practice, that is, a work of a distinctly Western character. If we accept Jacoby's dating of the work to around 1270 at the latest, it would be the earliest specimen of the merchant handbook (*pratica di mercatura*) genre known in the West. Acre, mentioned in fifty-one entries, is surpassed only by Venice with fifty-two entries, yet the information on trade to and from Acre is far more plentiful than that on trade between Venice and other places. Also, the manual is followed by a fragment of a portolan that describes the maritime routes from Acre to Venice and from Acre to Alexandria. The manual's link to Acre is obvious; Jacoby surmised that it was compiled by a Venetian resident in the city.[162]

The arrival of Western legally trained masters in the Frankish East is documented in written sources; many of them appear to have stayed for just a year or two, recalling the brief terms of service of many Western clerics.[163] The arrival of French architects, sculptors, and illuminators may be inferred from works in stone and on parchment, and such inference depends on an art historian's interpretation. As for architecture, alongside the local Frankish variant of the Romanesque style there appeared, already during the Kingdom of Jerusalem, some Gothic elements: in the Church of the Holy Sepulcher, in the Cenacle on Mount Sion, and in the cathedral of Sebaste, whose connection to the Gothic cathedral of Sens has been convincingly established.[164] Later, in the first half of the thirteenth century, distinct manifestations of the Gothic style can be observed at Tortosa, Montfort, and elsewhere.[165] But was this Gothic influence imported by a flow of French architects and sculptors, or did local artisans learn it from imported models? It is tempting to think that the two decorated capitals within the northern gate of Caesarea, characterized by Jean Mesqui as "refined sculpture in the best [Gothic] style of the 1250s," were executed, alongside the consoles within the eastern gate, by French sculptors whom King Louis IX brought to the

East and who worked for him at Caesarea while he fortified the city in 1251–52.[166] Possibly such artisans came East with the French contingent, stationed in Acre and periodically reinforced after Louis IX's return to France. At any rate, a glance at the seventeenth-century drawings of the no longer existing Church of St.-André in Acre, or at the doorway of a church of Acre that the Mamluks installed after 1291 as a trophy in the mausoleum-*madrasa* of Sultan al-Nāṣir Muḥammad in Cairo—which al-Maqrīzī hailed, with startling exaggeration, as "one of the most marvelous things made by man"—suggest that the French Gothic norms that had become canonical in large parts of the West came to be paramount in the Frankish East as well.[167]

And what about the illuminators? Jacoby offered a convincing reconstruction of the production of illuminated manuscripts in Acre, emphasizing the economic aspects. A manuscript-and-illuminator workshop would not have been sustainable over time had it depended only on occasional orders for luxury manuscripts of the kind that have come down to us. To survive economically, it also had to produce sparsely decorated, or even totally unadorned, manuscripts for buyers of limited means. Therefore, we should envisage workshops producing manuscripts of varying quality for a broad clientele, ranging from wealthy nobles who may have commissioned specific illuminations to humble customers constrained to buy cheap specimens off the shelf.[168] The artistically most creative members of these workshops were the illuminators, who conceived and executed the miniature panels that adorned the texts. In thirteenth-century Paris, they—and other workers in the book trade—married, begot legitimate children, and even though technically clerics in minor orders, belonged in effect to the burgess class.[169] It stands to reason that the same was true of the contemporary Acre illuminators, especially those who came from Paris.

Jaroslav Folda studied the works of leading French illuminators active in Acre in the second half of the thirteenth century. The first of these illustrated the "Arsenal Bible" that contains Old French paraphrases of numerous books of the Old Testament. The codex was probably commissioned by Louis IX while in Acre and executed during his sojourn in the kingdom in 1250–54. Folda's examination of its illuminations led him to conclude that the artist was a French-trained painter who studied Byzantine manuscripts in Constantinople and then came to Acre; there he decorated the "Arsenal Bible" in an original style that amounts to "a marriage of Gothic naturalism with Byzantine figure design," with

Eastern touches like camels in the creation scene or King David wearing a turban. This is "the Acre Franco-Byzantine Crusader style," discernible in other illuminated manuscripts, as well as icons, down to the 1280s.[170] It amounts to the rebirth, in about 1250, of the multisource Frankish style that evolved in the twelfth-century Kingdom of Jerusalem.[171]

A second French illuminator—whom Folda calls "the Paris-Acre Master" because three works done in Paris in the 1270s and eight in Acre in the 1280s can be attributed to him—employed a clearly different, purely Parisian Gothic style. In Acre, the Master first illuminated the codex that contains inter alia the Frankish paraphrases of Genesis and Exodus. He then worked on the codex containing the Old French translation of Cicero's treatise on rhetoric that William of St. Estiene commissioned in Acre in 1282. He adhered to the Parisian Gothic style also in later works, and was influenced just marginally by local confrères, for instance in adopting a richer colorism. To judge by the extant manuscripts, the new style became dominant, denoting a growing demand for works decorated in the manner fashionable in the West.[172] And the ratio—highlighted by Folda—of one religious versus twelve secular, vernacular books among the extant illustrated codices of the years ca. 1270–ca. 1288, points to a sizable Old-French-reading clientele.[173]

Finally, let us turn to a physician who left behind a Latin treatise, *The Well-Proven Art of the Eyes*, that survives in twenty-five manuscripts and was translated in medieval times into Provençal, Italian, French, and English. Printed four times between 1474 and 1549, it remained influential in ophthalmology well into early modern times. Calling himself Benvenutus Grapheus Hierosolymitanus, this itinerant physician may have originated in Sicily, probably studied in Salerno and practiced in various parts of Italy as well as in northern Africa, and employed medications from Jerusalem or Alexandria. In his treatise, Benvenutus employs some Arabic terms, yet quotes "Johannicius" (the Nestorian physician and scholar Ḥunayn ibn Isḥāq, 809–73) from a Latin adaptation of his Arabic-written introduction to medicine.

Benvenutus exhibits no modesty whatsoever, no trace of scholastic subservience to authorities, boasts of his vast experience and the innumerable patients he cured, and does not forget to mention that he made a lot of money thereby. Apparently, he did spend some time in the Frankish East. Introducing his most recommended medicine, he explains that it is made "of *nabet* sugar according to the Arabic language"—and *sukkar al-nabāt* appears for the first time in Western garb in the customs tariffs of Acre that form part of the *Book of the Assizes of the Court of Burgesses*; it is called there *sucre nabet.* Also, speaking of a grave affliction caused by the melancholic humor, Benvenutus observes that the *Ultramarini* (inhabitants of Frankish Outremer) and the Frenchmen call it most appropriately *maledicta* (the accursed one), revealing thereby not only knowledge of a Frankish term, but also of the closeness of Frankish and French idioms.[174]

Recently, Jonathan Rubin and Cornelia Linde discovered another general medical treatise by Benvenutus, extant only in German translation. Here *Wenefemitus Grapheus Jerosolimitanus* presents himself as the "sultan's physician," relates that the masters of Damascus asked him to pick out the best of his experiences, and goes on to discuss various medicines and surgical procedures. Since Benvenutus quotes three Western medical sources whose dates are known, his activity must have taken place after 1200, whereas the mention of his service as the sultan's physician alongside the request of the Damascene masters implies that he served a sultan of Damascus—and since no sultan resided in this city after the Mamluk conquest in 1260, Benvenutus probably wrote his treatise before that date.[175]

Benvenutus's service as a sultan's physician and the wish of the Damascene masters to benefit from his knowledge indicates that, by the thirteenth century, Western medical lore was not considered inferior in the Islamicate world. Western and Eastern physicians may have been competing, but success could be achieved by either side. Gilbertus Anglicus (ca. 1180–ca. 1250), the "most sought-after doctor" who taught medicine in Montpellier, relates proudly that he cured Bertranninus, the son of Hugo of Gibeleth, who almost lost his sight and of whom "famous Saracens and Christian Syrians had despaired."[176] On the other hand, Benvenutus recounts that a Saracen physician succeeded in curing the everted eyelid of a brother of a bishop of Verona whom neither he nor any of the countless physicians who had been consulted could help.[177]

Non-Franks in Acre

Contrary to the relative abundance of information about the cultural activities of the Samaritans in the Kingdom of Jerusalem, almost nothing is known about their doings in the Kingdom of Acre. Nablus, the Samaritans' major center, was never part of the kingdom, yet their mention in the *Book of the Assizes of the Court of Burgesses* suggests that some of them lived in Acre.[178]

Inversely, information about the cultural activities of Jews in the Kingdom of Acre, and specifically in its capital, is considerably richer than about their doings in the Kingdom of Jerusalem. Numerous Jews from western Europe, partially roused by apocalyptic expectations, reached Jerusalem and Acre—but also Alexandria—from 1209 onward.[179] Several prominent scholars settled in Acre, above all Rabbi Shimshon of Sens (d. 1214, Acre), who—first in France, then "in Galilee"—defended the traditional position on the resurrection against Maimonides's two-stage scenario, and Naḥmanides (1194, Girona - 1270, Acre), who defended Judaism at the Disputation of Barcelona in 1263 and established himself in 1268 in Acre.[180] There he completed his *Commentary on the Torah* and delivered an extant New Year sermon.

With Jewish scholars from different regions living side by side in Acre, unprecedented contacts, acquaintance with previously unknown written works, and the acquisition of knowledge from local informants became possible. Consequently, Naḥmanides was able to solve issues in his *Commentary* because some Samaritans read for him the legend—in ancient Hebrew script—on a coin of the Second Temple period, and some students from Mesopotamia enlightened him about the geography of their country. There were Jewish schools in the city, and Rabbi Yitzḥaq of Acre, who studied in one of them under Rabbi Shelomo Tzarfatī (the Frenchman) Petit, describes two classroom scenes: in the first, the tale of Aristotle and Alexander's wife came up, while in the second a student knowledgeable in Arabic silenced the teacher, whose grasp of the language was slight. But not only Jewish subjects were pursued in Acre: one—unnamed—scholar also studied geometry.[181] Acre's Jewish scholars enjoyed authority in the Frankish East, as attested by a request for instruction concerning a levirate marriage that the scholars of Gibeleth sent to those of Acre. Yet, when no scholar of Naḥmanides's stature resided in the city, and the local rabbis were unable to solve legal or exegetical issues, they asked for instruction from leading scholars in the West, Rabbi Meir ben Barukh of Rothenburg ob der Tauber and Rabbi Shelomo ben Avraham ibn Adreth of Barcelona.[182]

Prawer, who dealt in detail with the history of the Jews in the kingdom, concluded that "in the second quarter of the thirteenth century the Jewish community of Acre settled down; one has the impression that it became 'westernized,' in that the leading men of the community were now of European origin."[183] Thus, the Jews of Acre shared with the Frankish Kingdom's clergy a process of westernization, with leading churchmen and rabbis hailing from western Europe. But there were differences. The churchmen came East, as we have seen, for short spans of time, whereas the rabbis usually settled down for good. They continued to use Hebrew as their written language, while Eastern Jews typically wrote in Judeo-Arabic.

There is evidence of friction between Jewish newcomers from the West and native, local Jews. A main bone of contention were Maimonides's philosophical writings, especially his *Guide for the Perplexed*. In the 1280s a bitter confrontation erupted in Acre between the two groups, the one led by David, Maimonides's grandson and leader of Egypt's Jewry then temporarily residing in the city, and the other by the aforementioned Rabbi Shelomo Petit. The latter condemned the writings of Maimonides, went on a tour of the West, returned with a prohibition—signed by several rabbis—to read the *Guide*, and proclaimed it in Acre. The exilarch of Damascus countered by excommunicating those who disparaged the study of Maimonides's works as well as those who owned the text of the prohibition and did not hand it over to David to be burned. "Some of the scholars of Acre"—evidently, the Eastern ones—joined the rabbinical court of Safed in issuing a solemn excommunication along these lines. The exilarch of Mosul and the head of the Baghdad Academy followed suit, with the first ordering to evict Shelomo Petit and his followers from the Jewish community, and the second anathematizing those who kept letters against Maimonides. It is unknown how this clash, in which much of contemporary Jewry became involved, ended. Possibly it went on down to the Mamluk conquest of Acre on 18 May 1291, when many of the inhabitants, the Jewish ones included, were killed or enslaved.[184]

Little is known about relations between Jews and Franks in the Kingdom of Acre. William of Tripoli, of the Dominican convent in Acre, mentions in his *Account about Machomet* that the Law of Moses contains 613 precepts, of which 248 are positive and the rest (that is, 365) negative—and it is possible that William acquired this bit of lore from some Jewish scholar of Acre.[185] An Acre Jew dwells, in a letter preserved in the Cairo Geniza, on the sorrow that engulfed the city when the Sons of Esau (Christians) died of hunger and drowned in the Nile—a surprising record, in Hebrew, of the Frankish reaction to the crusader defeat in Egypt in 1221 or 1250, a reaction with which the anonymous author appears to empathize.[186] Yet in later popular memory, Jews are portrayed as siding with the Muslims against the Franks, or as living with them in harmony under stern Frankish rule.

In one Galilean tale, preserved in a Hebrew manuscript copied in the sixteenth century, Jonathan b. ʿUziel, a first-century AD sage regarded as a *tsaddīq* (a Righteous One), appears in the dream of an Ishmaelite king of Egypt, who is about to give up the attempt to conquer "the high and strong castle called Safed" from the Christians. The Righteous One encourages him to launch an attack and, heartened by the dream, the king captures the castle on the following day. The tale undoubtedly relates to the 1266 conquest of Templar Safed by Baybars.[187] Another tale in the same manuscript takes place in the village of ʿAlma in eastern Upper Galilee, which was under Frankish rule throughout the duration of the Kingdom of Jerusalem and then between 1240 and 1266. According to the tale, ʿAlma is inhabited by Jews and Ishmaelites and ruled firmly by a lord, evidently a Frank. The village is famous for the tomb of Rabbi Elʿazar b. ʿArakh, another first-century AD Righteous One, with branches of a beautiful tree bending over it on all sides. On every Sabbath Eve—that is, on Friday before nightfall—Jews and Ishmaelites light candles at the tomb, the Jews to honor the Sabbath as well as the Righteous One, the Ishmaelites to honor the Righteous One as well as Friday, "which is their feast day like Sunday is that of the Christians." And it came to pass that on one Friday, shortly before nightfall, a great flame sprang up from the many candles and set the tree on fire. The village was abuzz over the conflagration that threatened to reduce the tree to ashes. The Jews, forbidden to extinguish the fire on the Sabbath, beseeched the Ishmaelites to do so, and these, afraid to act without the lord's permission, asked him whether they might go ahead and save the rabbi's tree. He asked, "Why do not the Israelites, his people, do so?" The Ishmaelites explained: "They cannot, because today is the Sabbath." Forthwith the lord determined: "Since God wished the Righteous One's tree to burn during the night in which the Israelites cannot put out the fire, you must not extinguish it. . . . Beware not to touch it—and do not disobey my order, lest you lose your heads." All went home and left the tree burning. When they returned in the morning to see whether some branch remained unscorched, they found the tree in its pristine beauty, just as it had been before the fire. God let the Righteous One's tomb manifest its glory, concludes the tale's narrator.[188]

An erstwhile Muslim subject of the Franks who rose to fame in the thirteenth century was Rashīd al-Dīn Ibn al-Ṣūrī. As his name indicates, he was born in Tyre, in 1177, two years after William of Tyre had been consecrated as the city's archbishop. He grew up there, but at some point moved to Ayyubid territory, where he studied medicine; one of his teachers was ʿAbd al-Laṭīf al-Baghdādī. For two years he worked as physician in a Jerusalem hospital, probably the one established by Ṣalāḥ al-Dīn. From 1215 onward, he was the personal physician of three Ayyubid sultans, first of al-ʿĀdil, Ṣalāḥ al-Dīn's brother, then of al-ʿĀdil's son al-Muʿaẓẓam ʿĪsā, "with whom he witnessed a number of battles with the Franks, when they fell upon the port of Dimyāṭ [Damietta, during the Fifth Crusade]." Finally—down to 1229—he served al-Muʿaẓẓam ʿĪsā's son al-Nāṣir Dāwūd, who appointed him chief physician. In Damascus he established a scholarly salon that discussed medicine. A successful, influential physician, Ibn al- Ṣūrī was also an expert on medicinal herbs; back in 1876, Lucien Leclerc lauded him as "the most original of all Arab botanists."[189] To study these herbs, he undertook travels to various regions—including the Frankish-ruled ones of Tyre, Tripoli, and Antioch—and instructed the painter who accompanied him to draw the plants realistically in three stages: at sprouting, in full bloom, and dried up. His empirical work also made use of knowledge gathered from fellaheen and farmers. Unfortunately, only excerpts from the resultant *Book of Simple Drugs*—which he dedicated to al-Muʿaẓẓam ʿĪsā—survive, and the illustrations were lost. He also wrote a refutation of another author's book of drugs, and a very personal book whose title is a further testimony to his originality: "Explanatory remarks, useful lessons and instructions regarding medicine, dedicated to myself." Ibn al-Ṣūrī died in Damascus in 1242.[190]

Jacques of Vitry wrote that the *Suriani* had their own Greek bishops and mentioned that he met in Acre a Syrian bishop and in Sidon a Syrian archbishop.[191] A richly illuminated Greek liturgical calendar—or at least one of its parts—was looted by the Mamluks at the conquest of Acre in 1291 and redeemed by the monk Bessarion; the manuscript had been prepared in 1055/56, most likely in Constantinople, became the property of the Chariton Monastery in the Judaean Desert until its dispersal in the mid-thirteenth century, and was then brought to some Greek Orthodox institution in Acre.[192] Similarly, the nun Matrona redeemed from the booty of Acre a Greek evangeliary prepared in 1019, probably in the Monastery of St. Sabas.[193] But no original works are known to have been written by Greek Orthodox or other Eastern Christian subjects of the Kingdom of Acre. Also, while the influence of Byzantine legislation on the decisions promulgated in Frankish Nablus in 1120 is unmistakable, no such influence on the thirteenth-century *Book of the Assizes of the Court of Burgesses* is discernible. Still, Easterners continued to serve as informants for curious visitors from the West; Burchard of Mount Sion relates that, crisscrossing the Holy Land, he noted down what he learned by questioning Syrians, Saracens, or other inhabitants of the land; significantly, unlike his twelfth-century predecessors, Burchard mentions Muslims among his informants.[194]

In the Kingdom of Acre, Dominican friars attempted to reconcile Jacobites, Copts, and Nestorians with the Church of Rome and gained some short-lived successes.[195] Tommaso Agni, the Dominican who then served as papal legate as well as bishop of Bethlehem, convened in 1262 an assembly in Acre aimed at bolstering the 1198 union with the Armenian church, while insisting on Rome's primacy. The learned Mxit'ar, who represented the Armenian Catholicos of Cilicia, countered—if we may believe his report—by bluntly pointing out that the apostles, scandalized to learn that Peter had baptized the Gentile Cornelius, served as Peter's judges and Peter did not regard himself as their superior (Acts 11:1–18); hence, Rome's pretension to judge the other apostolic sees, without herself being submitted to their judgement, is unfounded.[196] Fourteen years later, in 1276, Tommaso Agni—by now papal legate, patriarch of Jerusalem, and bishop of Acre—attempted to convince Nikephoros and Klimentos, two monks from Mount Athos, to assent to the union of the churches of Rome and Constantinople, promulgated at the Second Council of Lyon in 1274. When the two refused, Tommaso—the biographer, we remember, of the inquisitor-saint Peter Martyr—let them undergo some physical torture, then a lengthy interrogation, which Nikephoros purports to document in his account. Thereafter they were dispatched as prisoners to Cyprus, whence they returned to Byzantium. Nikephoros claims to have written his account for the benefit of other faithful brethren who may be interrogated by Italians "or others who resemble them."[197] It is noteworthy that both Mxit'ar and Nikephoros refer to Tomasso just as "the legate," portray him as irascible, and present the members of his entourage as rude, with Mxit'ar remarking that he spoke a lot and listened a little.[198]

The one Eastern Christian of the Frankish East who came to play a meaningful role in the West was Theodore (*Thādhūrī*) of Antioch, a Jacobite.[199] Born in Antioch probably in the 1190s, he mastered there the Syriac and Latin languages, then moved to Mosul to study philosophy and mathematics under Kamāl al-Dīn ibn Yunūs (1156–1242), the leading teacher in the Islamic realm of those days. He returned to Antioch but, feeling unable to study there by himself, traveled once again to Kamāl al-Dīn. Later he studied medicine in Baghdad. Probably in the 1220s, Theodore entered into the service of a Seljuk sultan, then of an Armenian regent, and finally decided to join an envoy of Emperor Frederick II on his return trip to Sicily. There Theodore became the emperor's philosopher, and wrote, in Latin, a short treatise in which he set down for his patron the basic rules for preserving one's health.[200] In February 1240 Frederick asked him to write, in Arabic, a letter to the king of Tunis, and to prepare syrups and violet-sugar for him and his household. On Frederick's order, Theodore translated from Arabic the *Book of Moamyn the Falconer*, and Frederick corrected the translation in 1240–41; Theodore's Long Prologue to his translation reveals an occasionally awry syntax and some impact of Arabic phraseology, discernible for instance in the use of comparative instead of superlative forms.[201]

The emperor bestowed on Theodore—according to the Jacobite author Bar-Hebraeus—a town called Kamāhā; a Latin document from Messina, drawn up in 1243, mentions the vineyard of "Theodore, the imperial philosopher," near Camaro; conceivably, the name was distorted into Kamāhā.[202] Petrus Hispanus (d. 1277), the scholar who wrote on logic and ophthalmology and was to end his days as Pope John XXI, mentioned Theodore, "the emperor's physician," as his master.[203] Leonardo Fibonacci, the West's leading mathematician, corresponded with Theodore, expressing esteem; scholars at Padua asked him to translate Ibn Rushd's introduction to his commentary on Aristotle's *Physics*; he also translated Aristotle's *On Animals*, presumably from the Arabic. However, when Roland of Cremona, the Dominican theologian and philosopher, challenged Theodore in 1238 in a philosophical dispute, he utterly defeated him—so relates a Dominican author. Theodore's sojourn in the West came to a fatal end when, feeling homesick but forbidden by Frederick to leave, he used his absence in order to board a ship headed for Acre. A storm thrust it ashore at a town at which Frederick had anchored, and Theodore, "from shame rather than fear," took poison and died. In 1250 Frederick mentions him as no longer alive.

On 11 September 1098, the leaders of the First Crusade, perplexed by their encounter with Jacobites and other heretical Eastern Christians, wrote from Antioch to Pope Urban II, beseeching him to come there and "eradicate and destroy all the heresies, of whatever kind they might be, by your authority and our valor."[204] About 140 years later, an Antiochene

Jacobite became a Western emperor's philosopher and master of a future pope. Yet he was also the only non-Frank easterner of the entire 1099–1291 period to gain ingress into the Western intellectual scene and play there a substantial role. It is hardly accidental that he learned his Latin in Antioch, not in the land called holy.

Conclusion
Footprints in the Sand

From a world-historical perspective, Frankish Jerusalem was an anomaly. It was the only major sacred center to be managed by people for whom it was situated far beyond the periphery of their ancestral lands. This unique center-beyond-the-periphery phenomenon had various repercussions. It bestowed epic dimensions on the march to Jerusalem and the conquest of the city in 1099. It led to a constant stream of fighting men for the defense of the distant, often embattled entity. It required the eastward flow of vast funds for the construction of ecclesiastical edifices and the fortification of towns and castles. It triggered a maritime pilgrim traffic from the West to the newly accessible center; the Western, mainly Italian, ships that transported the many pilgrims also boosted the trade of Acre and Tyre, deflecting in part the import of Oriental goods from Alexandria to the Frankish harbors. And its remoteness from the Western motherland played a decisive role in Frankish Jerusalem's downfall: in the long run, the hard fact of geographical peripherality, not the fervent devotion to the sacred center, had the upper hand.

This remoteness also goes some way to explain the inventiveness of the Franks, who, facing manifold challenges in their new, holy yet unfamiliar abode, responded by contriving unprecedented solutions whose adoption was facilitated by the great distance from the motherland and its conventions. The churchmen of the Kingdom of Jerusalem invested much energy and exhibited remarkable creativity in fashioning this holy center by a variety of means, especially by drawing on local Greek Orthodox traditions to construct the main foci of Jerusalemite religiosity. The kingdom's knights displayed much inventiveness in defending it, first and foremost by engendering an entity that mingled knighthood with religion, setting thereby a new standard of Christian fighting and leading also to early experimentation with writing in the vernacular. Other knights combined the West's traditional hospice with the East's medicalized hospital. The kingdom's rulers made Jerusalem—for the first time since Herodian days—their capital city, presenting it on their seals as the "City of the King of all Kings," an innovative formulation that conjured sundry biblical reminiscences. Amaurry, "fifth king of the Latins in the holy city of Jerusalem," stood out for his unconventional thinking and for the unprecedented sponsorship of a history of Muslim rulers. The kingdom's burgesses, who found an early spokesman in the chronicler Ernoul, participated in the processes by which local practices were adopted, novel habits arose out of the amalgam of disparate components, the Frankish dialect of Old French evolved, and thus a new, distinct, often vilified identity came into being.

An examination of the cultural activities of the kingdom's autochthonous communities reveals that even as the Franks exhibited creativity and inventiveness in many areas, their indigenous subjects, largely bereft of leaders, were stagnating and merely endeavored to conserve traditional rites and customs. Only the minuscule Samaritan community, which retained its leadership and cultic center, displayed some creativity.

The cultural activities that the Franks developed in the days of the Kingdom of Jerusalem came to an abrupt end with its collapse in 1187. The Kingdom of Acre, which differed from it in many respects, stood out also for a quite altered cultural scene. The sancterranean churchmen of the Kingdom of Jerusalem, devoted to the celebration and husbanding of the country's sacred treasures, were largely replaced with appointees from the West, many of whom came to stay for just a short time and remained part and parcel of Europe's clergy. Besides, as Jerusalem and many other Holy Places were under Muslim rule most of the time, the salience and proximity of sanctity receded. The clerics from the West brought with them some impulses of the new age, patriarchs sent to serve in Acre authored—unlike their Jerusalemite predecessors—some works, and one of them, a former bishop of Agen in Aquitaine, asked an Italian professor of civil law to write a compendium of canon law. A cleric from Umbria translated a pseudo-Aristotelian treatise from Arabic into Latin. The Dominicans and Franciscans—imports from the West—established schools of higher learning, and a Dominican friar in Acre wrote a report on Islam and the Muslims. Consequently, the Frankish East's clergy became enmeshed with that of the West and shared its intellectual interests, exhibiting no longer the peculiarities of a new center situated in a faraway periphery, but rather the ordinary traits of a periphery attuned to its center.

The cultural activities of the Kingdom of Acre's knights were of a different character. Although the most outstanding man of letters among them originated in Lombardy, most were born and raised in the East. Several prominent members engaged in an original, locally important endeavor: the composition of treatises dealing with the kingdom's customary law. These were written in Old French, and it was in this language that chronicles written by or for knights were authored, and so were some poems and prayers: the recourse to Old French, first attested by the vernacular version of the Templar Rule, was in full swing. In addition, several Latin texts were translated into Old French, and the epilogue to one of them negates the hierarchical ordering of source and target languages. Yet all these activities were inward looking. One looks in vain, among the kingdom's knights, for counterparts to Renaud of Sidon or King Amaurry, and their openness toward the surrounding civilization. The golden age of Frankish inventiveness unfolded in twelfth-century Jerusalem.

What footprints were left by Frankish society and culture? Frankish society ceased to exist in Palestine after the Mamluk conquest of Acre in 1291, although some individual Franks probably remained there as converts or slaves. The Franks who fled to the West did not establish cohesive, permanent communities but assimilated bit by bit into their new environs.[1] Thus, the tax lists of Paris record in 1292 sixteen individuals whose toponymic surnames link them to Outremer, Acre, and Tiberias, or are designated as Poulains; by 1313 their number dwindles to eight.[2] A fourteenth-century Venetian chronicle relates that many refugee families from Acre settled in Venice and were admitted into the republic's Major Council, becoming thereby part of the Venetian nobility.[3] A far larger number of Frankish refugees settled in Cyprus. In Nicosia, the capital of Cyprus, the Church of Saint

George of the Poulains existed by 1306.[4] In Famagusta, the island's main harbor, the population increased after the fall of Acre so much that in 1313 and 1318 the popes called for contributions to construct a new, larger cathedral.[5] Yet these numerous refugees appear to have merged before long with the Western inhabitants of Cyprus, who shared their religion, language, and customs. Indeed, the ancestors of many Cypriot Westerners originated in the Frankish East and were lured in 1192 to move to the island by its ruler, Gui of Lusignan, who promised them lands and benefits. Moreover, leading nobles of the Kingdom of Acre owned lands in Cyprus.[6] Similarly, Eastern Christian refugees—Melkites, Jacobites, Nestorians—could blend into the Cypriot congregations that followed their rite.[7] The only Franks known to have maintained a distinctive identity for several generations were the captives whom the Mamluks held, with their wives and children, in Cairo. Originally, they had to perform the toughest tasks on building sites; later they became wine producers and sellers, and apparently also engaged in other activities that Muslims considered unclean. In 1342, the captives and their women suffered during a riot, and thereafter were scattered throughout the city, mainly near its rubbish hills. They appear for the last time in the documentation—inasmuch as it has been studied—in 1389. Presumably they converted to Islam or were submerged in the local Christian (that is, Coptic) population.[8]

On the other hand, the physical footprint on the ground is instantly recognizable. From Sidon to Ascalon, from Beaufort (Shaqīf Arnūn) to Montreal (Shawbak), the area of the erstwhile Kingdom of Jerusalem is dotted with the remains of Frankish fortifications and churches, far more salient than those of other periods, and archaeological excavations from the 1920s onward bring ever more of them into sight. Within the walls of ruined inland castles came into being, at unknown dates, Muslim villages: for instance, the village of Kawkab al-Hawā within the ruins of Belvoir (see fig. 9), Qāqūn in those of Caco southeast of Caesarea, and Ṣūbā in those of Belmont, west of Jerusalem. Rebellious Muslim peasants from Qāqūn and Ṣūbā in 1834 sought refuge within what remained of the Frankish walls, but Egyptian artillery smashed them.[9] In the coastal plain, the Mamluk scorched-earth policy, aimed at denying a foothold for future crusading invaders from the West, rendered much of the region uninhabited, with sand dunes expanding from the seashore inward and swamps, caused by clogged drainage channels, covering large tracts of land. An inadvertent result of this Mamluk policy was, more than six centuries later, the concentration of early Zionist settlement activities in these by and large untilled coastal areas.

One may also discern a continuation of trends that had solidified during the Frankish period. After a disruption that lasted several decades, the maritime pilgrim traffic from the West resumed in force after 1345, with most pilgrims making the passage on Venetian vessels sailing regularly to Jaffa. Western pilgrims' accounts (or itineraries), sparse in precrusade times and ever more frequent in the days of the Kingdoms of Jerusalem and Acre, became abundant in the subsequent period, many of them dwelling on Frankish vestiges.[10] Western trade with the ports of Palestine, barely existent before the establishment of the Kingdom of Jerusalem and robust in the following two centuries, continued to some extent in the Mamluk period and beyond, with cotton being one of the main products exported to the West. Already in the early fourteenth century, Acre played a prominent role in this export; in 1353 Western merchants held a religious celebration among Acre's ruins; by 1471, a small group of Venetian merchants, under a vice-consul, were buying cotton at Acre, and at least sixteen Venetian ships anchored or were expected to do so there between the spring of 1471 and the autumn of 1472.[11]

And what about the footprints of Frankish culture? The dictum of Jacob Burckhardt (d. 1897) about the First Crusade, that its "true, world-historical, enduring consequences revealed themselves in a completely different sphere than in longed-for Palestine," is applicable to these traces as well.[12] The mingling of knighthood with religion, first successfully institutionalized in Jerusalem, inspired the military-religious orders that fought the pagans in the Baltic region and the Muslims in Iberia and, later, defended the western Mediterranean against Ottoman expansion. The medicalization of the Jerusalem Hospital influenced the routine in Hospitaller establishments in Europe. The Carmelite order, founded on Mount Carmel by hermits akin to those described by Gerard of Nazareth, rapidly spread throughout Catholic Europe as one of its four mendicant orders and, in modern times, expanded throughout the world. The liturgy evolved at the Church of the Holy Sepulcher influenced the Carmelite rite and was partially adopted by various churches across Catholic Europe. And many of the relics dispatched from twelfth-century Jerusalem are venerated in European monasteries and cathedrals to this day.

Of the works written in Frankish Outremer, Filippo of Tripoli's Latin translation of the pseudo-Aristotelian *Secret of Secrets* enjoyed exceptional success in the West. The Latin-written *Well-Proven Art of the Eyes* by Benvenutus Grapheus Hierosolymitanus, possibly composed in the Frankish East, served as a leading ophthalmological text well into early modern times. But the influence of William of Tyre's *History* was the most significant and wide-ranging. Not through its Latin original: only nine manuscripts containing it, and a small fragment of a tenth, have come down to us. Indeed, it was so little known that Vespasiano da Bisticci (d. 1498), the major bibliophile of his times, could maintain that Godefrid of Bouillon's expedition had hitherto "never been described except in French."[13] However, the Old French adaptation of William of Tyre's *History* reached a far larger audience, attested by sixty-four surviving manuscripts. Furthermore, this adaptation was translated in late medieval times into Castilian, Italian, and Middle English, and even repeatedly retranslated into Latin, thus doubling and redoubling its original audience. The author of this Old French adaptation, a Western cleric writing in the early thirteenth century somewhere in France for noble readers or listeners, transformed William's solemn text into "a prose version of a *chanson de geste*," as John Pryor appositely characterized it.[14] Simplifying and diluting William's chronicle, the adaptation tells the story of pious knights and devout commoners setting out to liberate the Sepulcher and the oppressed Christians of the East, struggling against all odds while underway, conquering Jerusalem, establishing a new Christian kingdom, and valiantly defending it. The story, told also in other works, perpetuated the image of the crusade as a glorious, unselfish striving for a just, exalted goal and of the kingdom as the scene of the good fight for the true faith.

This decidedly positive perception also colors the secularized usage of the term "crusade" in much of present-day Western civilization: a crusade against alcoholism, a crusade against vice, a crusade against animal cruelty, a crusade against prostitution, are all meritorious enterprises fired by virtuous fervor. Let us remember that Dwight Eisenhower, in 1948, gave his World War II memoir the title *Crusade in Europe*.

Yet this highly positive view is by no means the only one. Protestant writers forcefully rejected the crusade idea, Enlightenment authors emphatically condemned it, among Jews the crusade chiefly connotes the massacres of the Rhineland communities in 1096 and of the Jerusalem community in 1099, and in the contemporary Middle East the crusades are largely perceived as aggressive imperialist undertakings, and the Kingdom of Jerusalem as an early instance of European colonialism. Tellingly, the Hebrew and Persian translations of Eisenhower's memoir avoid the term "crusade" because of its negative connotation for their prospective readers. The Hebrew translation, published in Tel Aviv in 1951, is titled *Campaign for Europe's Liberation*. The title of the Persian translation, published in Tehran in 1956, startles at first sight but turns out to be, on reflection, culturally sensible. It reads: *Jihād in Europe*.[15]

APPENDIX 1

Amalric, Amalrich, Amalrico, Amaury—or Amaurry? How Should We Render Frankish Names?

Most medievalists render Frankish names according to their present-day forms in the language in which they are writing. For instance, the man who introduces himself as Willelmus (or Guillelmus) of Tyre at the outset of his chronicle appears in English-language studies as William, in French as Guillaume, in Italian as Guglielmo, in Spanish as Guillermo, in German as Wilhelm, in Czech as Vilém, and so forth. Thus, Frankish men and women (and other medieval Europeans) are given names that indisputably differ from those by which they were known in their lifetime.[1] Such adjustment—or, if you wish, imposition—of identity is not applied to moderns: for instance, while English-writing medievalists routinely refer to Jacques of Vitry (d. 1240) as "James," even the most ardent devotee of the English language would not dream of referring to Jean-Jacques Rousseau (d. 1778) as "John James." Asked to explain their ahistorical, "nationalizing" appellations, medievalists either claim that it is impossible to know how Frankish names were pronounced in the twelfth–thirteenth centuries, or that they are following long-established custom. Yet, in most

1. There are a few exceptions among medievalists. For instance, in an English-written article Luttrell speaks of Hugues de Payns, Geoffroi of Saint Omer, etc.: Luttrell, "The Earliest Templars," 199–200.

cases it is possible to establish with reasonable certitude how a Frankish name was pronounced at the time, and invoking custom is the last refuge of the standpatter.

There are two clues to the contemporary pronunciation of Frankish names. The first is to check how a name known from a Latin source is rendered in an Old French version of it. For instance, Gaufridus de Novo Vico, the intrepid canon of the Church of the Holy Sepulcher who earned William of Tyre's censure for having taken the sword in 1182 during the Battle of Forbelet, appears about forty years later in the Old French adaptation of William's chronicle as Jefroiz de Nuefvi.[2] I believe that it is more appropriate to slightly alter the name's spelling to Jefroi (as Paulin Paris, the editor, did) than to anglicize it into Geoffrey. In short, for Franks originating in French-speaking regions, it is reasonable to employ the form appearing in the Old French adaptation of William's chronicle.

This approach is not devoid of problems. The Old French adaptation may be a dependable guide for names appearing in the later part of William's chronicle, fairly close to the date at which the adapter was writing; but how reliable is it for the earlier parts that mention individuals who lived more than a century before the adapter started working? Also, the Old French form used by the adapter does not always provide a sure guidance as to a name's pronunciation: see, for instance, the archbishop of Caesarea whom William presents in Latin as Hernesius and who appears in the adaptation as Erneys, Ernays, Herneis, and Hernaïs.[3] Furthermore, we do not always know which vernacular a person who lived in a linguistic borderline area used. In such cases we may follow the example of Amnon Linder, who refers to Jerusalem's first Latin ruler as Godefrid.[4]

The second clue to the contemporary pronunciation of a Frankish name is its form in a text written in a different alphabet. Such cross-utilization of alphabets is helpful even for Europe: for instance, the reference in medieval Hebrew texts to the city of Troyes as טרווייש [Trwyys] proves that the three final letters of the city's name were still being pronounced, in the central Middle Ages, in a way resembling the English "yes." Similarly, the Hebrew-written autobiography of the priest Johannes of Oppido (west of Bari) reveals that the vernacular form of his name was

2. WT 22.18 (1032). WT OF 22.15 (2:438; also index, 520).

3. WT 18.20 (841), 20.1 (913), 20.12 (926), 21.9 (974). WT OF 18.20 (2:226), 20.1 (2:311), 20.11 (2:326), 21.8 (2:377).

4. See, for instance, Linder, "The Liturgy," 111.

גְּוָאן [Juwān], that is, Giuàn, the dialectal form of "Giovanni" current in the region to this day.[5]

A Hebrew text helps to ascertain the contemporary pronunciation of a leading figure of the First Crusade, *Petrus heremita*—called in present-day works Pierre, Peter, Pietro, Pedro, Petr, and so forth. The Old French adapter of William of Tyre's chronicle added on his own that "Pierres, qui avoit esté ermites en bois, por ce l'apeloit l'en Perron l'ermite."[6] But is it likely that the adapter, writing some 120 years after the event, knew that the Hermit was called Perron? The Hebrew chronicle relating the persecutions of 1096, which Shelomo bar Shimshon compiled in about 1140, allows for a positive answer, because the compiler refers to the Hermit repeatedly as פידרון [Pedron].[7] The Hebrew form apparently represents "Peðron," which was about to turn a little later into "Perron." Therefore, Pedron may be a fair approximation of the way the name was pronounced at the time.

The cross-utilization of alphabets is still more useful in the Frankish East, where names may appear in several alphabets. The name of Bethlehem's bishop in the years 1156–74 is a telling example. William of Tyre gives it as Radulfus.[8] Since he characterizes him as "English by birth" and compatriot of Pope Hadrian IV, medievalists writing in English understandably call him Ralph. But the bilingual mosaic inscription in the *bema* of the Church of the Nativity in Bethlehem, which celebrates him as patron alongside the Byzantine emperor and the king of Jerusalem, called him Radulphus in the Latin part and Ραοὺλ [Raoul] in the Greek one.[9] Consequently, the Greek inscription vindicates the Old French adapter, who refers to the bishop as Raoul or Raous.[10] Apparently, he was Anglo-Norman.[11]

5. B. Z. Kedar, "The Voyages of Giuàn-Ovadiah in Syria and Iraq and the Enigma of his Conversion," in *Giovanni-Ovadia da Oppido, proselito, viaggiatore e musicista dell'età normanna*, ed. Antonio De Rosa and Mauro Perani (Florence, 2005), 133 n. 1.

6. WT OF 1:21.

7. *Hebräische Berichte über die Judenverfolgungen während des Ersten Kreuzzugs*, ed. and trans. Eva Haverkamp, MGH Hebräische Texte aus dem mittelalterlichen Deutschland, 1 (Hanover, 2005), 470–71, 484–87; on the author and the chronicle's date, 49–63.

8. WT 16.17 (738–39); see also 18.1 (809), 18.20 (841), 19.25 (899), 20.19 (950), 20.26 (950), 20.30 (955), 21.5 (967).

9. Lamberz, "The Bilingual Inscription," 148–50.

10. WT OF 16.17 (2:116), 18.1 (2:191), 18.20 (2:226), 19.26 (2:294), 20.18 (2:338), 20.25 (2:354), 20.29 (2:360), 21.4 (2:369).

11. For the hypothesis that he was a Fleming, see Mayer, "Einwanderer in der Kanzlei," 30–37.

The king of Jerusalem appeared in the Greek inscription as Ἀμμορὶ [Ammorí]. Ibn al-Athīr calls him مُرّي [Murrī, probably pronounced Morrī].[12] The geminate "rr" appears also in the chronicle of Niketas Choniates (d. 1217) as Ἀμερρίγος [Amerrígos].[13] The gemination probably reflects the way the Franks pronounced the name, because on sixteen occasions the chronicle of Ernoul has Amaurri or Amaurris and only three times Amauri, while the *Book for the King* has Amaurry.[14] The Old French adapter of William of Tyre, on the other hand, calls the king Amauris or Amauri, while Johan of Ibelin constantly opts for the second of these forms.[15] We may therefore securely discard the forms Amalric and Amalrich, now dominant in English and German research literature, and opt for Amaurri, Amauri, or—as I have decided to do—Amaurry, akin to Amaury, the form nowadays used mainly by historians writing in French.

The Latin name Balduinus, spelled in different ways, is rendered in English as Baldwin (with the "a" usually pronounced as "o"), in French as Baudouin, in German as Balduin, and so forth.[16] In Anna Komnene's chronicle, Godefrid's brother appears as Βαλδουΐνος.[17] On the copper coins of his homonymous successor as count of Edessa the name appears, in Greek letters, as ΒΑΛΔΟΥΙΝΟC [Baldouinos], with some slightly diverging spellings, but the second letter is consistently an "a," and the "d" is followed by three vowels.[18] Two twelfth-century Armenian texts from Edessa present the name as Պաղտոււնին [Bałdounin], with the letter Պ [P] pronounced in western Armenian as B, and տ [T] as D.[19] An unpublished Geniza document, dated 1104, presents the first Frankish king of Jerusalem as ברדויל [Bardwīl; or perhaps Bardawīl, a spelling

---

12. Ibn al-Athīr in *RHC Or*, 4:553, 619. Michael the Syrian calls the king *ʾmry*, which can stand for Amari or Amori: *Chronique de Michel le Syrien*, 4:699, 707, 747.

13. Nicetas Choniates, *Historia*, ed. Ioannes Aloysius van Dieten (Berlin, 1975), 160, 161.

14. *Ernoul*—Amaurri or Amaurris: 71–73, 75, 77, 88, 91–92, 116, 143, 177, 196. *Ernoul*—Amauri: 74–75, 100 (the variant Amalri also appears three times: 115, 164, 482). *Le Livre au Roi*, 198, c. 21. See also "regnante venerabili domino Almarrico Latinorum rege quinto": *Cart Hosp*, 1:225, no. 312 (a. 1163).

15. WT OF 2:88, 90, 160, 189, 234, and passim. John of Ibelin, *Le Livre des Assises*, 307, 571, 591; also 650, 684.

16. For Latin spellings, see the index in *UKJ*, 4:1615–17.

17. Anna Comnena, *Alexias*, ed. Diether R. Reinsch and Athanasios Kambylis (Berlin, 2001), 316, 343, 346, 436 (X.10.6, XI.7.2, XI.8.1, XIV.3.4).

18. Porteous, "Crusader Coinage," 365, 389–90; Metcalf, *Coinage of the Crusades*, 31–38; Murray, *Baldwin of Bourcq*, 44–45.

19. See Cyril Aslanov, "Old French and Armenian in Contact in Cilicia: A Short-Lived Episode?," in *Transferts*, 175–76; further clarification in Aslanov, "*Babiloine* vs. *Baldach* en ancien français d'outremer et d'en déça la mer," *Francigena* 7 (2021): 288–89.

that would prefigure the name of the lagoon on the Sinai coast near which the king died in 1118, and which is called after him Buḥayrat al-Bardawīl to this day].[20] When we take into consideration the common substitutions in Arabic of "l" with "r," and of "n" with "l," we may postulate the form *Baldwīn (or *Baldawīn). In sum, the Greek of Anna Komnene and the Edessene coins, the Armenian of the Edessene texts, and the Judeo-Arabic of the Geniza document all suggest that the name was pronounced, in the early twelfth century, with an "a" after the initial "B" and with a diphthong in the second syllable. Hence the form "Baldwin" (with the first vowel an "a," not an "o") may offer an approximation of the way the name was pronounced at the time.

The name of King Amaurry's father appears in modern French studies as Foulques, in German ones as Fulko, while English historians opt for the form Fulk. Since Usāma ibn Munqidh, who met the king, calls him فلك بن فلك [Fulk bin Fulk], we may safely adopt the variant used in English works.[21]

The name William poses a more difficult problem. Usāma transliterates this name, twice, as كليام [Kilyām].[22] As the Arabic alphabet has no "g," the "k" at the name's beginning evidently attempts to reproduce it; the "l" of the Arabic transcription indicates that the "ll" of the Frankish name was still pronounced, and had not yet been converted into a "yy" as in the modern French "Guillaume"; the "ām" denotes how the second syllable sounded to Usāma's ears. Introducing his translation of the Benedictine Rule into Armenian, Nersēs of Lambron states that he did so in the Frankish monastery of St. Paul in Antioch with the help of the monk whose name is transliterated as Գիլամ [Kilam].[23] The letter Գ [historical G] is pronounced in western Armenian as K; as for the second syllable, we see that not only Usāma heard it as "-am." The twelfth-century Georgian transliterations გვლიამ [Gviliam], გილამ [Gilam], and გლიამ [Gliam] point in the same direction.[24] So does the name of "Me sire Willame li Pulains [*Poulain*] ch[evalie]r," responsible for the Arabic-French glossary of *materia medica*.[25] All this leads to the counterintuitive conclusion that "William" approximates the Frankish pronunciation better than "Guillaume."

20. Oded Zinger brought this document to my attention.
21. *Usāmah's Memoirs*, 65, 132. Usāma calls Baldwin بغدوين [Baghdwīn]: 81, 103.
22. *Usāmah's Memoirs*, 81, 137.
23. See Weitenberg, "Literary Contacts in Cilician Armenia," 68–69.
24. See Tsurtsumia, "Commemoration of Crusaders," 325, 326, 329 (nos. 10, 12, 22).
25. "Il glossario arabo-francese," 363 and tavola I.

Finally, the last Frankish patriarch to reside in Jerusalem spelled his name consistently as Eraclius. A master who studied law at the nascent university of Bologna, he surely knew what he was doing. I see no reason why he should be referred to as Heraclius. Likewise, since the most prominent man of letters in the thirteenth-century Frankish East spelled his name Phelippe (or Phelipes, or Felippe), there is no compelling justification for anglicizing it to Philip.

This is the rationale behind the Frankish names appearing in the present book. Further studies will hopefully lead to closer approximations.

I decided to conform to current Anglo-American convention with regard to the names of biblical persons, church fathers, popes, Western emperors, and some others, and render them in their English form. Names of some authors and scholars—for example, Petrus Lombardus, Petrus Venerabilis, Gaufridus, Bulgarus, Stephanus Philosophus—appear in their Latin form. As for place-names in the Frankish Kingdom of Jerusalem, some historians prefer to use the Arabic forms, others the Hebrew ones—often because of a political agenda. I stick to the Latin or Old French forms that appear in the contemporary documentation.[26]

---

26. My thanks to Cyril Aslanov, Shraga Assif, Michael Stone, and Mamuka Tsurtsumia for their help with the Armenian, Georgian, and Syriac texts; and to Richard Kelleher for information on the Edessene coins.

Appendix 2

Was There a Large-Scale Massacre in Jerusalem in July 1099?

Some historians of the crusades, especially of the sanctimonial persuasion, exhibit an uneasiness when dealing with the massacre of Jerusalem's Muslims and Jews upon the crusader conquest of the city on 15 July 1099. Thus, Richard, who in 1996 dedicated to the massacre a single paragraph in which, at three points, he attempted to downgrade its exceptionality, went on to comment: "Ce massacre, dont la description a été répétée à satiété, n'a cependant pas été systématique."[1] Riley-Smith, in his history of the crusades published in 1987, did not mention the massacre at all and just wrote: "Jerusalem was given over to sack."[2] After I drew attention to this omission in the opening lecture of the conference of the Society for the Study of the Crusades and the Latin East that, in July 1999 in Jerusalem, commemorated the crusader conquest of 1099, he added in his book's second edition, after the mention of the city's sack, the telling sentence: "Although the only contemporary Muslim evidence suggests that the number of deaths may not have been as high as has been supposed, the eyewitness Christian writers wallowed in their descriptions of a massacre."[3]

---

1. Richard, *Histoire des croisades*, 79.
2. Riley-Smith, *The Crusades: A Short History*, 34.
3. Riley-Smith, *The Crusades: A History*, 43. For an enlarged version of my 1999 lecture, see Kedar, "The Jerusalem Massacre."

The downgrading of the massacre was significantly boosted in 2014 by the prominent orientalist Konrad Hirschler. In an analysis of the references to the conquest of 1099 in Arabic sources, he contends that a large-scale massacre is mentioned for the first time in the chronicle of the Baghdadi scholar and preacher Ibn al-Jawzī (1117–1200). Consequently, he concludes that "it is beyond doubt that there was a massacre," which presumably "targeted the Jewish population in particular but also parts of the Muslim population." However, "that Jerusalem witnessed a large-scale massacre as brutal as the one described in the Latin sources, without contemporary and near-contemporary Arabic sources recording it, simply beggars belief. The question why Latin chroniclers chose to insert the full-scale massacre into their narratives is beyond the scope of this article. Yet the Arabic sources make it impossible to claim that it took place."[4]

However, there is a contemporary Arabic-written source, albeit not a historiographical one, that does mention a large-scale massacre in Jerusalem, with the few inhabitants who escaped death falling into captivity. This is the letter, preserved in the Cairo Geniza, by a Jew who left northern Africa or Iberia in about 1094, wishing to pilgrimage to Jerusalem. Because of the unstable conditions in Palestine in the 1090s, and the subsequent crusader conquest, he was not able to proceed beyond Egypt. Writing in Judeo-Arabic in Hebrew letters, probably early in 1100, to a relative in the Muslim West, he expresses the hope that the Fatimids will soon expel the Franks from Jerusalem and enable him to make the pilgrimage. About the conquest of 1099 he writes: "The *Ifranj* [Franks] arrived and killed everybody in the city, whether of Ishmael [Muslims] or of Israel [Jews]; and the few who survived the slaughter were made prisoners. Some of these have been ransomed since, while others are still in captivity in all parts of the world."[5] An unequivocal, contemporary statement, albeit by a person leaning toward strong-worded formulations.[6]

---

4. Konrad Hirschler, "The Jerusalem Conquest of 492/1099 in the Medieval Arabic Historiography of the Crusades: From Regional Plurality to Islamic Narrative," *Crusades* 13 (2014): 37–76, quotation on 74.

5. Shelomo Dov Goitein edited this letter in "New Sources on the Fate of the Jews during the Crusaders' Conquest of Jerusalem," *Zion* 17 (1951–52): 144–47 [in Hebrew]; its English translation, from which I quote, appears in Goitein, "Contemporary Letters," 175–77. Gil assumes that the letter was probably written early in 1100: Moshe Gil, *Palestine during the First Muslim Period (634–1099)*, 3 vols. (Tel Aviv, 1983), 3:442, n. 31 [in Hebrew].

6. Describing the situation of Alexandria after several sieges, he writes that the city was "ruined"; when the sultan conquered it, he "caused justice to abound in it in a manner unprecedented in the history of any king in the world": Goitein, "Contemporary Letters," 176.

Surely his terse account of the massacre parallels the reports of the Western chroniclers, while his reference to captive and ransomed survivors ties in with details in a letter of the Karaite elders of Ascalon, written possibly still closer to the 1099 conquest.[7]

And there is also a strictly contemporary Armenian source. In Alexandria, the monk Ahaṙovn [Aaron] wrote approvingly in 1099, in the colophon of a Gospel he copied, that "the valiant people of the Romans, that is, the Franks . . . entered the great and famous city of Jerusalem and, by the might of Christ, put the infidels to the sword."[8]

A statement by Ṣalāḥ al-Dīn's secretary and companion ʿImād al-Dīn also militates against Hirschler's argument. Describing an early stage of the negotiations between Jerusalem's Frankish leaders and the sultan, which were ultimately to result in the city's capitulation on 2 October 1187, he relates that Ṣalāḥ al-Dīn rejected the initial Frankish offer, stating: "I will take Jerusalem the way they took it from the Muslims ninety-one years ago. They inundated it with blood, leaving it not a moment's peace. I will annihilate their men and take their women prisoner."[9] Hirschler underlines the brevity of this reference to the crusader conquest of 1099 and points out, in a footnote, that this conquest "is not employed as a central element" in other surviving parts of ʿImād al-Dīn's oeuvre.[10] Yet the critical question is a factual one: Was Ṣalāḥ al-Dīn, in the fall of 1187, indeed aware that the Christian conquest of 1099 had been followed by a mass killing, and that he intended to avenge it by

---

7. This letter is translated in Goitein, "Contemporary Letters," 171–75. I dealt with these letters in "The Jerusalem Massacre," 59–64. I am grateful to Konrad Hirschler for having pointed out my mistaken assumption, in that article, that Ibn al-ʿArabī's figure of three thousand killed refers to the Aqṣā Mosque and not to Jerusalem in its entirety: Hirschler, "The Jerusalem Conquest of 492/1099," 49 n. 31; I corrected the mistake in my *Crusaders*, Study VIII, Addenda and Corrigenda, 1. Hirschler does not deal in his article with the Geniza evidence.

8. Gérard Dédéyan, "Les colophons de manuscrits arméniens comme sources pour l'histoire des Croisades," in *Crusade Sources*, 95–96. Ahaṙovn has the conquests of Antioch and Jerusalem occurring in the same year, 1099. Gérard Dédéyan kindly checked for me the date and the translation.

9. Hirschler, "The Jerusalem Conquest of 492/1099," 64. For the text of ʿImād al-Dīn in Abū Shāma and its French translation, see *RHC Or*, 4:327–28. On "They inundated it with blood," Elon Harvey observes: "Literally, *fa-inna-hum istabāḥū al-qaṭl* means 'They made murder legal,' 'They legitimized killing.' As for 'They inundated it with blood,' this clearly translates the French 'Ils l'ont inondée de sang,' appearing in RHC Or 4:328" (pers. comm.)

10. Hirschler, "The Jerusalem Conquest of 492/1099," 64 and n. 80. There exists, however, a version of this passage in al-Bundarī, *Sanā al-barq al-Shāmi*, 311. Here Ṣalāḥ al-Dīn says: "I will take Jerusalem the way they took it from the Muslims ninety-one years ago. They made murder lawful, letting no eye incline toward [a moment of rest]. They thoroughly killed the men and took the women as prisoners." Elon Harvey brought this passage to my attention and translated it.

killing all male Franks? Fortunately, it is possible to answer this question unequivocally. A continuator of William of Tyre has Ṣalāḥ al-Dīn, at precisely the same point in the negotiations, reject the Frankish offer, asserting: "Por quei me requerés vos la cité rendre et faire pais? . . . Bien veés vos que la cité est moie. Et ensurquetot les faquirs [*fuqahā'*] et les hages [pl. of *ḥājjī*] et li autres religious de la lei de Mahomet m'angoissent et hastent mout que je ne vos doigne nule fiance, ains revenge par ceaus qui sont en Jerusalem de lor sanc espandant par mi les rues de Jerusalem et au Temple autretant come Godefrei espandi de celui des Sarazins."[11]

It follows that, by 1187, Ṣalāḥ al-Dīn and Muslim scholars in his entourage were well aware of the large-scale massacre of 1099. Hirschler maintains, however, that such massacre is mentioned in Arabic historiography for the first time, "out of a historiographical void," in the work of Ibn al-Jawzī, who was apparently writing in about 1180, or even later.[12] As I see it, the notion that an assertion purportedly appearing for the first time in about 1180 in the writings of a Baghdadi scholar became well-known in Ṣalāḥ al-Dīn's entourage a few years later is quite implausible.

The same goes for the notion that Western chroniclers chose, without factual basis, to describe a full-scale massacre in their narratives. Even if we posit, for the sake of argument, that these chroniclers joined up to invent an all-out massacre, there is an important if largely overlooked statement that militates against such invention. Foucher of Chartres, who was in far-away Edessa at the time of the conquest of Jerusalem, relates—in the first version of his chronicle—that when he

---

11. WT Cont. Lyon, §53, 66. "Why do you seek to surrender the city and make peace? . . . As you see, the city is mine. And in any case, the faquirs and the hages and the other religious of the law of Mahomet are pressing and urging me not to give you any trust, but to take revenge through those who are in Jerusalem, shedding their blood in the streets and in the Temple, exactly as much as Godefrei had shed that of the Saracens." Cyril Aslanov helped with this translation. See also the introduction of Keagan Brewer and James H. Kane to the *Libellus*, 39–40.

12. "Out of a historiographical void": Hirschler, "The Jerusalem Conquest of 492/1099," 56, 73. Hirschler does not explicitly date Ibn al-Jawzī's chronicle (which ends with the year AH 574/AD 1178–79), but he observes that he wrote it "several decades after Ibn al-Qulzumī, Ibn al-ʿArabī, al-Azīmī, and Ibn al-Qalānisī [d. 1160] put their reports down on paper," and mentions that Ibn ʿImrānī's chronicle was "finished between 555/1160 and 560/1165 and thus some two decades earlier than Ibn al-Jawzī's chronicle": Hirschler, "The Jerusalem Conquest of 492/1099," 54, 64. Drory, to whom Hirschler (54 n. 43) refers for Ibn al-Jawzī's views on the early crusades, writes that Ibn al-Jawzī "wrote at the end of the 12th century," "several years after the Franks had already been defeated on the battlefield": Joseph Drory, "Early Muslim Reflections on the Crusaders," *Jerusalem Studies in Arabic and Islam* 25 (2001): 93, 94.

arrived in December 1099 to celebrate Christmas, the rotting cadavers of the Saracens whom the crusaders had killed at the conquest set off such a stench around Jerusalem's walls, both inside and outside, that he and his companions were constrained to cover their noses and mouths.[13] Foucher speaks here matter-of-factly about a personal experience; even a conspiracy-prone historian will find it difficult to detect an ulterior motive behind his remark, which does not form part of his description of the 15 July 1099 massacre.[14] The overwhelming stench of cadavers more than five months after the event, despite attempts to set the corpses outside the walls on fire,[15] leaves little doubt that the massacre was indeed a large-scale one.

In numerous modern histories of the crusades, one reads that Muslim survivors of the 1099 massacre settled in the al-Ṣāliḥiyya suburb of Damascus. René Dussaud, in 1927, was the first to make this claim, ultimately based on a misinterpretation of a statement by ʿAbd al-Muʾmin (d. 1339). In reality, the al-Ṣāliḥiyya suburb was founded in the late 1150s by the Banū Qudāma émigrés from the Nablus region.[16]

A massacre is rarely total. In most cases some potential victims manage to escape or (as my own biography shows) hide, or—in medieval situations—to be ransomed. This was also what happened in Jerusalem in 1099—a large-scale but not a total massacre.[17]

---

13. "unde nares nostras et ora oppilare nos oportebat." FC 1.33 (333, n. b). Guibert of Nogent, who read Foucher's first version, describes the same event as follows: "ea adeo fetida recens cesorum cadaverum numerositate repperitur, ut nusquam aura nisi corruptissima narium orisve spiraculo hauriretur." GN 7.37 (336).

14. For this description, see FC 1.27–28 (299–303).

15. See, for instance, Petrus Tudebodus, *Historia de hierosolymitano itinere*, 142.

16. Talmon-Heller and Kedar, "Did Muslim Survivors."

17. Goitein emphasized in his writings that, in Jerusalem, the crusaders brought an end to a Jewish community that had been dwindling years before their arrival. See, for instance, Goitein, "Geniza Sources for the Crusader Period," 308. Having realized that his statement was used to make little of the 15 July massacre, he wrote, in his final reference to the issue: "There was a gruesome massacre, no doubt, but it was not as all-embracing as the summary reports of the chroniclers led us to believe." S. D. Goitein, "al-Ḳuds," in *Encyclopaedia of Islam*, 2nd ed., 5:330.

APPENDIX 3

The Nazareth Catalog

Erfurt, Bibliotheca Amploniana, Q 102, fol. 167v.[1]

Editions: Wilhelm Schum, *Beschreibendes Verzeichniss der amplonianischen Handschriften-Sammlung zu Erfurt* (Berlin, 1887), 361–62, no. 10; James S. Beddie, "Some Notices of Books in the East in the Period of the Crusades," *Speculum* 8 (1933): 241.

For two corrections, see Paul Lehmann, "Von Nazareth nach Erfurt," *Zentralblatt für Bibliothekswesen* 50 (1933): 483–84. A photocopy of the catalog, its diplomatic transcription, and translation appear in Yolles, *Making the East Latin*, 28, 239–41.

Date: Schum dated MS Q 102 to the late twelfth century; Beddie, to the late twelfth/early thirteenth century; Lehmann, to "about 1200." Malcolm Parkes, who painstakingly examined the catalog for me, dated it to the late twelfth century.

1. In 2001 the Bibliotheca Amploniana was deposited in the library of the reestablished University of Erfurt. My thanks to Christa Becker, librarian at the MGH, Munich, who in 1983 obtained for me a photocopy of the catalog from the municipal library of Erfurt, then in the (for me inaccessible) German Democratic Republic.

I added two sets of numbers: those in square brackets designate titles; those in round brackets, the number of volumes.

Hii sunt libri conventus Nazarene ecclesie.

[1] Ieronimus super Psalterium (1)
[2] Anbrosius [*sic*] super Lucam (2)
[3] Matheus (3)
[4] Iohannes (4)
[5] Apocalysis [*sic*] Iohannis[2] (5)
[6] Gregorius super II libros Ezechielis (6)
[7] Textus Marci evangeliste[3] (7)
[8] Gesta pontificum (8)
[9] Isidorus ethimologiarum (9)
[10] Isidorus de summo bono (10)
[11–12] Dialogus Ieronimi presbyteri et Vita patrum in eodem volumine (11)
[13] Liber quidam qui dicitur Paradisus (12)
[14] Cur Deus homo (13)
[15] Textus IIII evangeliorum (14)
[16–17] Epistole Ieronimi et Augustini in uno volumine (15)
[18] Duo libri canonum (16–17)
[19–20] XV^{cim} libri beati Augustini,[4] etiam Gregorius super Cantica canticorum in eodem volumine (18)
[21] Augustinus de Trinitate (19)
[22–23] Augustinus super Iohannem et glosule super[5] Iohannem (20)
[24] Epistole magistri Ivonis (21)
[25] Elucidarium (22)
[26] Gregorius super moralia Iob (23)
[27] Epistole Pauli glosate (24)
[28] Augustinus de agone christiano (25)
[29–30] Episcopus Sidoniensis Augustinum de retractatione, Augustinum [*sic*] encheridion habet (26–27)
[31] Ieronimus de interpretacionibus nominum (28)
[32–38] Liber Ieronimi questionum hebraicarum et de X^{cem} tempt[at]ionibus et de paralipomenon et canticum Debore[6]

2. Schum: *sancti Iohannis.*
3. *g* corrected from *d*; also in nos. [15] and [56].
4. Possibly another copy of Augustine's *De Trinitate*, a work consisting of fifteen books.
5. *super*—added above the line.
6. MS: *debofre*. Schum and Beddie read: *de Befre [Efrem]*; Lehmann corrects to *Debore*.

et lamentaciones Iheremie et epistola ad Dardanum [;] de distanciis locorum (29)

[39] Epistola de vesti sacerdotali (30)
[40] Registrum Leonis pape (31)
[–] alius Isidorus de sumo [*sic*] bono (32)[7]
[41] de Egisippo[8] IIII quaterniones et dimidius (33)
[42] VII libri de sententiis (34–40)
[43] X[9] libri de phisica (41–50)
[44–45] Scintilarius[10] [;] Pastoralis Gregorii[11] (51)
[46] et duo libri dialogorum Gregorii (52–53)
[47] II libri de luna (54–55)
[48] Arimethica[12] (56)
[49] Magnus Pri[s]cianus (57)
[50] Alius de construcione (58)
[51] IIIes Boetii cum glosulis[13] (59–61)
[52] II° Oratii cum glosulis (62–63)
[53] II° Stacii cum glosulis (64–65)
[54] Persius (66)
[55] II° Salustii (67–68)
[56] Eneis Virgilii (69)
[57] Lucanus cum glosulis (70)
[58] Iuvenalis duplex (71–72)
[59] duo Stacii Achilleidos (73–74)
[60] Tullius[14] de amicicia (75)
[61] IIIes Prudencii (76–78)
[62] Commenta Boetii (79)
[63] II Sedullii (80–81)

---

7. See no. [10] of the catalog, above.

8. Schum: Egesippo.

9. MS: *IX*, corrected above the line to *X*.

10. Before *Scintilarius*, in the margin: *Hi supradicti de divinitate*.

11. Defensor's *Liber Scintillarum* and Gregory I's *Liber regulae pastoralis* take up most of MS Q 102, the volume of the Nazareth library on whose last folio our catalog is inscribed; evidently, *Scintilarius, Pastoralis Gregorii* designate the volume in question. It contains, in addition, seven short texts, six of which are very short: Libellus b. Augustini de dominica oracione; Eiusdem libellus de symbolo; Interpretatio nominum apostolorum; Notae de confessione, de remissione peccatorum, de poenitentia; Alter libellus de symbolo; Diverse omelie a doctoribus [=Augustino et Hieronymo] conscripta; De misterio sancte crucis. See Schum, *Beschreibendes Verzeichniss*, 360–61.

12. Before *Arimethica*, in the margin: *Hi aū de de* [*sic*] *gramatica* [*sic*].

13. *cum glosulis*—added above the line. Also in nos. [52], [53], and [57].

14. Beddie: Tullis.

[64] duo Ovidii epistolarum (82–83)
[65] Ovidius de Ponto (84)
[66] Ovidius de amatoria arte (85)
[67] II Ovidii stristium [*sic*] (86–87)
[68] II O[vidii]. de remedio amoris (88–89)
[69] duo Catones (90–91)
[70] V Spropiri[15] (92–96)
[71] duo Maximiani (97–98)
[72] duo Donatuli[16] (99–100)

---

15. Schum explains: *Prosperi*; Beddie reads: *Sprosperi*.
16. Lehmann's accurate deciphering. Schum: *Don*.

Appendix 4

Shaykh Rabīʿ Visits the Christianized Dome of the Rock

Ibn al-ʿAdīm, *Bughyat al-ṭalab fī tārīkh Ḥalab*, ed. Suhayl Zakkār, 11 vols. (Damascus, 1988–89), 8:3593. Translation: Daniella Talmon-Heller and Elon Harvey.

The Shaykh Abū ʿAbdallāh Muḥammad b. Abī Saʿd al-Ḥalabī reported to me [the author, Ibn al-ʿAdīm], saying: The Shaykh Rabīʿ [b. Maḥmūd b. Ḥibat Allāh (d. AH 602/AD 1205)] was of the people of Mārdīn, and I was told that he went to Jerusalem to perform a *ziyāra* (ritual visit) of it, when it was in the hands of the Franks. He [Rabīʿ] said: [At that time,] I was making a living as a laborer. I knew a group of Christians in Mārdīn, and I stayed with them in Jerusalem. I used to work for the monks, as they did not prevent me from praying. I used to sustain myself with my wages, using the surplus to perform the *ziyāra* at the Dome of the Rock. I would pay the man at the entrance to the Dome, [who was responsible] for collecting the fee from the Muslims, a coin of little value[1] each time. Whenever I had some extra money, I used to spend it this way and enter the Dome of the Rock, perform the *ziyāra*, and pray. Sometimes, I had nothing. One day, I went to him

1. *Qirṭāsiyyan*. Probably a Frankish billon *denarius* or a Damascene copper coin: see Heidemann, *Die Renaissance der Städte in Nordsyrien und Nordmesopotamien*, 404–9.

empty-handed. He said: Pay up! I said: I don't have anything. He said: Enter! The Christians reproached him, saying: How do you allow this man to enter without taking anything from him?! He replied: That is because he pays whatever he pays from the bottom of his heart. If he had anything, he would use it to pay. That is why I allowed him in.

APPENDIX 5

Frankish Captives in Cairo in the Twelfth Century

Abū al-Makārim, *History of the Churches and Monasteries of Egypt and Some Neighboring Countries* (Munich, Staatsbibliothek, Codex arabicus 2570, fols. 20r–21r). Translation by Elon Harvey, based on that by Bishop Samuel [al-Suryānī], Abu al Makarem, *History of the Churches and Monasteries in Lower Egypt in the 13th Cent.* (Cairo, 1992), 22–24.

Al-ʿUṭūfiyya Quarter

The quarter known as al-ʿUṭūfiyya, was named after ʿUṭūf who was the servant master in charge of manufacturing provisions, weapons, the hanging millstones for the grinding of special flour and so forth, and of the storage of wood, materials used for whitewashing, and other equipment. In that quarter, there was a group of captive Frankish workmen—some married, some celibate. They had two churches in that quarter. One of them, the large one, was dedicated to the Lady, the pure Virgin. The second church was above the houses, named after St. George. For prayers and masses, a large group of various types of Christians [and Franks] who work in the industry of Egypt, congregated there. They would light up many candles on every [. . . . . .] with a torch in his hand accompanied by the candles and flashes. And [there was] happiness and rejoicing. Those two churches were destroyed on [one][1] occasion. There was a man named Abū al-Karam al-Tinnīsī. The Devil possessed his heart so that he sought to harm everybody. He oversaw the *dīwān al-naẓar*,[2] in the caliphate of al-Ḥāfiẓ.[3] His harm was eventually directed to those captive Franks. These miserable souls used to beg the people for assistance, and they would spin cotton, and some of them would make leather slippers. Others raised chickens, profiting from the eggs they were able to collect from them and from the wages of their work. This aforementioned oppressor Abū al-Karam came to the *manākhāt*[4] and sent for the chief man of the Franks and said: "Our Lord is sending you back to your country. Therefore, buy the freedom of your souls from him! And if you do not, you must convert to Islam." They refused to pay and said: "We would sooner have our own blood spilled by the sword than renounce the religion of Christ." They each began searching for the sum that would save each person's religion and soul. And they complained to him of their bad condition, and that they had become very poor, lacking in means, and in a wretched state. But he did not show them mercy, nor did he feel compassion for them. He did not let them go until every one of them gave him whatever they had in their possession or could obtain. He collected much money from them and carried it to al-Ḥāfiẓ who took it without setting a single one of them free. It was a deceitful act on his part. They remained in bondage [. . .], until the time of Shāwar al-Saʿdī[5] and the arrival[6] of Amurrī king of the Franks and his army in Cairo; and God released them from captivity [. . .] and took them back to their country, and the prophecy was fulfilled in them: "Blessed is the Lord who brings back his people from captivity[7] and saves them from the hands of the enemy, and does not make them [stay] in error forever." And it is written in the Catholic Epistle that "the Lord will rescue the righteous from trials and tribulations, and that he will subject the oppressors to torment on the Day of Judgment."[8]

---

1. I supply here the word *ba'ḍ*, based on other occurrences of the expression *fī ba'ḍ al-nuwab al-ḥāditha* in Abū al-Makārim's work (e.g., in Paris, BnF, arabe 307, fols. 39a and 50a). E.H.

2. The treasury: See Anne-Marie Eddé, "Ayyubids, 2: Power and Institutions," in *Encyclopaedia of Islam* THREE.

3. Ruled in the years 1132–49.

4. The royal camel pens.

5. The vizier Shāwar al-Saʿdī, de facto ruler of Fatimid Egypt, 1162–69.

6. I am unsure about the exact wording here, but this is approximately the meaning. E.H.

7. Cf. Jer. 31:23, Ps. 106:10, Luke 1:68–71.

8. 2 Pet. 2:9.

Appendix 6

Kings and Patriarchs of Jerusalem

Kings

resident in Jerusalem

Godefrid of Bouillon (duke)	1099–1100
Baldwin I	1100–1118
Baldwin II	1118–1131
Fulk	1131–1143
Baldwin III	1143–1163
Amaurry	1163–1174
Baldwin IV	1174–1185
Baldwin V	1185–1186
Gui of Lusignan	1186–1187

resident in Acre

Conrad of Montferrat	1191–1192
Henri of Champagne ("Lord of the Kingdom")	1192 -1197
Aimery of Lusignan	1198–1205
Johan of Brienne	1210–1222

Patriarchs

resident in Jerusalem

Arnoul of Chocques	1099
Daibert of Pisa	1099–1101
Evremar of Chocques	1102–1108
Gibelin of Arles	1108–1112
Arnoul of Chocques	1112–1118
Warmund of Picquigny	1118–1128
Etienne of Chartres	1128–1130
William of Messines	1130–1145
Foucher of Angoulême	1145–1157
Amaury of Nesle	1157–1180
Eraclius of Auvergne	1180–1187

resident in Acre

Haymarus Monachus	1197–1202
Soffredo (cardinal)	1203
Albert of Vercelli	1205–1214
Raoul of Mérencourt	1215–1224
Gérold of Lausanne	1225–1239
Robert of Nantes	1240–1254
Jacques Pantaléon	1255–1261
William of Agen	1262–1270
Tommaso Agni of Lentini	1272–1277
Elias Peleti of Périgueux	1279–1288
Nicholas of Hannappes	1288–1291

Sources: For kings, *UKJ*, ed. Mayer; for patriarchs, Hamilton, *The Latin Church*, 373–74.

Acknowledgments

My thanks to the following presses for the permission to reproduce texts for which they hold the copyright: Presses Universitaires de Provence, a stanza by Bertran de Born; Universitätsverlag Winter GmbH, a poem of the *Carmina Burana*; Brill Academic Publishers, passages from the translations of Maimonides's *On the Regimen of Health* and Ibn Abī Uṣaybiʿa's *Literary History of Medicine*; and to Prof. Daniella Talmon-Heller and the Taylor and Francis Group for the permission to reproduce a passage from her translation of Diyāʾ al-Dīn al-Maqdisī's *Cited Tales of the Wondrous Doings of the Shaykhs of the Holy Land*. I am grateful to Professor Adrian Boas and to Brill Academic Publishers for allowing me to reproduce his plan of an Acre courtyard house; to the Israel Antiquities Authority for granting permission to publish photos of gold coins, a no longer existing Templar hall in Jerusalem, types of pottery, and the church of Ibelin; to Dr. Nazmi al-Juʿbeh for allowing me to publish his photo of a Frankish letter of 1179/84; to the Winchester Excavation Committee for permission to reproduce photos of the seal of Patriarch Sophronios of Jerusalem; to the Bayerisches Hauptstaatsarchiv, Munich, for granting permission to reproduce photos of the seal of Patriarch Eraclius of Jerusalem; to the Syndics of Cambridge University Library for permitting me to publish a page from the Cairo Geniza; to the Bibliothèque nationale de France, for graciously allowing users to reproduce the daguerreotype of the apse of Sebaste Cathedral, taken by Joseph-Philibert Girault de Prangey in 1844; to Duby Tal, of Albatross Aerial Perspective, Herzlia, for allowing me to publish his photo of Belvoir Castle; to the Korneli Kekelidze Georgian National Centre of Manuscripts, Tbilisi, for granting permission to publish the photo of a page of a Georgian manuscript copied in 1155 in Jerusalem; and to the John Rylands Research Institute and Library at the University of Manchester for permitting me to publish the photo of a column of a Samaritan Torah scroll copied in 1166–67. My thanks to the following publishers and institutions for having granted permission to reuse segments of my articles (their full details are spelled out in the bibliography): to the Dumbarton Oaks Research Library and Collection for a part of "Gerard of Nazareth" (published in 1983); to Leuven University Press for a part of "Raising Funds for a Frankish Cathedral" (1994); to the Taylor and Francis Group for parts of "A Twelfth-Century Description of the Jerusalem Hospital" (1998), "Frankish Bathhouses" (2018), and "The Use of Paper in the Frankish Levant" (2019); to Professor Denys Pringle and Yad Izhak Ben-Zvi for a part of "1099–1187: The Lord's Temple and the Temple of Salomon" (2009), an article I coauthored with him; and to Professor Mahmoud Yazbak for a part of "On Books and Hermits in Nazareth's Short Twelfth Century" (2012). Finally, I would like to thank Royal Holloway University of London for allowing me to reproduce a part of "Holy Men in a Holy Land," the Hayes Robinson Lecture I delivered there in 2005. With the exception of the Taylor and Francis Group, who charged US$90 for the reproduction of 270 words of the translation of Diyā' al-Dīn's *Cited Tales*, the permissions were granted gratis.

Very many friends and colleagues extended help by discussing specific issues, answering queries, or supplying bibliographical items, particularly during the COVID-19 pandemic. I would like to mention first and foremost Eliyahu Ashtor (Jerusalem), Claude Cahen (Paris), Peter Landau (Munich), Hans Eberhard Mayer (Kiel), Shelomo Pines (Jerusalem), Joshua Prawer (Jerusalem), Jean Richard (Dijon), and Jonathan Riley-Smith (Cambridge), who are no longer with us; and to thank Mustafa Abbasi (Tel Hai), Cyril Aslanov (Aix-Marseille), Shraga Assif (Jerusalem), Martin Aurell (Poitiers), Laura Balletto (Genoa), Katherine Ann Barclay (Kidlington), Martin Biddle (Oxford), Karl Borchardt (Munich), Charles Burnett (London), Manuel Castiñeiras (Barcelona), Gérard Dédéyan (Montpellier), Luc Deitz (Luxembourg), Paul Doty (Canton, NY), Gisela Drossbach (Augsburg), Peter Edbury (Cardiff), Oren Falk (Ithaca, NY), Gil Fishhof (Haifa), Moshe Florentin (Tel Aviv), Deborah Gerish (Santa Barbara), Brendan Goldman (Seattle), Yuval Noah Harari (Jerusalem), Elon Harvey (Chicago), Martin Henig (Oxford), Peter Herde (Würzburg), Kevork Hinklian (Jerusalem), Ivan Hlaváček (Prague), Hubert Houben (Lecce), Estelle Ingrand-Varenne (Poitiers), Andreas Kaplony (Munich), Isidoros Katsos (Oxford), Richard Kelleher (Cambridge), Rabei Khamisy (Haifa), Etan Kohlberg (Jerusalem), Richard A. Landes (Boston), Ryan Lavelle (Winchester), Laura Minervini (Naples), Frankwalt Möhren (Heidelberg), Kenneth Pennington (Washington), Edward Peters (Philadelphia), Jonathan Phillips (London), Denys Pringle (Cardiff), John Pryor (Sydney), Marina Rustow (Princeton, NJ), Shulamit Schneidermann-

Wilkansky (Jerusalem), Ian Short (London), Philip Slavin (Stirling), Damian J. Smith (St. Louis), Anna Soffici (Florence), Edna Stern (Acre), Michael Stone (Jerusalem), Guy Stroumsa (Jerusalem), Sarah Stroumsa (Jerusalem), Daniella Talmon-Heller (Beersheba), Paolo Trovato (Ferrara), Mamuka Tsurtsumia (Tbilisi), Julian Yolles (Turnhout), Oded Zinger (Jerusalem) and—last but not least—my erstwhile PhD students, the late Ronnie Ellenblum and Emanuel Wardi, as well as Daniel Baraz, Hervé Barbé, Nirit Ben-Aryeh Debby, Adrian Boas, Diego Holstein, Robert Kool, Ora Limor, Jonathan Rubin, Iris Shagrir and Vardit Shotten-Hallel.

My thanks to the following colleagues for having provided or checked translations from various languages: the late Professor Eliyahu Ashtor, Professors Reuven Amitai, Cyril Aslanov, Gérard Dédéyan, Shay Eshel, Isidoros Katsos, Etan Kohlberg, Michael Stone, Guy Stroumsa, Daniella Talmon-Heller, Mamuka Tsurtsumia, and especially Dr. Elon Harvey. I am indebted also to Nomi Morag for having enhanced several of the illustrations; to Reuven and Tammy Soffer who prepared the map and the plan of the Hebron sanctuary and cave; to Dr Leigh Chipman, who read the entire text, rescued me from sundry pitfalls, and attempted to improve my English; to Mahinder S. Kingra, editor in chief at Cornell University Press, whose incisive comments helped me to restructure chapters and render the book more reader-friendly; to India Miraglia, for having meticulously prepared the manuscript and the illustrations for editing and production; to Karen Hwa, senior production editor; to Shannon Li, who prepared the index; and to Deborah A. Oosterhouse, princess of copy editors.

Finally, I would like to thank M. Cecilia Gaposchkin and Anne Lester for including this book in their series and the two anonymous readers on behalf of Cornell University Press for their helpful comments. My indebtedness to Cecilia goes far beyond the one an author owes his editor. She steadfastly raised my spirits while I worked on the final version of the manuscript, with Ḥamās rockets exploding time and again some miles away. When, apprehensive of power outages or worse, I decided to dispatch abroad each revised chapter upon completion, she turned her e-mail account into their temporary shelter. *Gratias tibi ago, editrix unica*!

Modiʿin, December 2024

Abbreviations

AA	Albert of Aachen, *Historia Ierosolimitana*, ed. and trans. Susan B. Edgington (Oxford, 2007)
AMS	Shelomo Dov Goitein, *A Mediterranean Society: The Jewish Communities of the Arab World as Portrayed in the Documents of the Cairo Geniza*, 6 vols. (Berkeley, 1967–93)
AOL	*Archives de l'Orient latin*
"Assises des Bourgeois"	"Livre des Assises de la Cour des Bourgeois," ed. Auguste-Arthur Beugnot. In *RHC Lois*, vol. 2 (Paris, 1843), 1–226.
Autour	*Autour de la Première Croisade: Actes du colloque de la Society for the Study of the Crusades and the Latin East, Clermont-Ferrand, 22–25 juin 1995*, ed. Michel Balard (Paris, 1996)
BAV	Biblioteca Apostolica Vaticana
BnF	Bibliothèque nationale de France
Bourgogne/Orient	*De la Bourgogne à l'Orient: Mélanges offerts à Monsieur le Doyen Jean Richard*, ed. Jacques Meissonnier (Dijon, 2020)
Cart Hosp	*Cartulaire général de l'ordre des Hospitaliers de Saint-Jean de Jérusalem, 1100–1310*, ed. Joseph Delaville Le Roulx, 4 vols. (Paris, 1884–1906)
Cart St Sép	*Le cartulaire du chapitre du Saint-Sépulchre de Jérusalem*, ed. Geneviève Bresc-Bautier, DRHC 15 (Paris, 1984)
Cart Tem	*Cartulaire général de l'ordre du Temple 1119?–1150: Recueil des chartes et des bulles relatives à l'ordre du Temple*, ed. Guigue A. M. J. A. Marquis d'Albon (Paris, 1913)

CCCM	Corpus Christianorum, Continuatio Mediaevalis
Chartes Josaphat	*Chartes de la Terre Sainte provenant de l'abbaye de Notre-Dame de Josaphat*, ed. Henri-François Delaborde, Bibliothèque des Écoles françaises d'Athènes et de Rome 19 (Paris, 1880)
I comuni italiani	*I comuni italiani nel Regno Crociato di Gerusalemme*, ed. Gabriella Airaldi and B. Z. Kedar (Genoa, 1986)
Crusade Sources	*The Crusades and Their Sources: Essays Presented to Bernard Hamilton*, ed. John France and William G. Zajac (Aldershot, 1998)
Crusades, ed. Setton	*A History of the Crusades*, general editor Kenneth M. Setton, 2nd ed., 6 vols. (Madison, 1969–89)
CS	*Crusade and Settlement: Papers Read at the First Conference of the Society for the Study of the Crusades and the Latin East and Presented to R. C. Smail*, ed. Peter W. Edbury (Cardiff, 1985)
Deeds Done beyond the Sea	*Deeds Done beyond the Sea: Essays on William of Tyre, Cyprus and the Military Orders Presented to Peter Edbury*, ed. Susan B. Edgington and Helen J. Nicholson (Farnham, 2014)
D'Orient en Occident	*D'Orient en Occident: Les Templiers des origines à la fin du XII*[e] *siècle. Actes du colloque international Troyes-Abbaye de Clairvaux, 3–5 novembre 2021*, ed. Arnaud Baudin and Philippe Josserand (Ghent, 2023)
DRHC	Documents relatifs à l'histoire des croisades
EC	*The Experience of Crusading* [Festschrift Jonathan Riley-Smith], vol. 2: *Defining the Crusader Kingdom*, ed. Peter Edbury and Jonathan Phillips (Cambridge, 2003)
EO, 1	*Exploring Outremer*, vol. 1: *Studies in Medieval History in Honour of Adrian J. Boas*, ed. Rabei G. Khamisy, Rafael Y. Lewis, and Vardit R. Shotten-Hallel (Abingdon, 2023)
EO, 2	*Exploring Outremer*, vol. 2: *Studies in Crusader Archaeology in Honour of Adrian J. Boas*,

	ed. Rabei G. Khamisy, Rafael Y. Lewis, and Vardit R. Shotten-Hallel (Abingdon, 2023)
Ernoul	*The Chronique d'Ernoul and the Colbert-Fontainebleau Continuation of William of Tyre*, ed. Peter Edbury and Massimiliano Gaggero, 2 vols. (Leiden, 2023), 1:64–548.
EWCS, 1	*East and West in the Crusader States: Context—Contacts—Confrontations*, vol. 1: *Acta of the Congress Held at Hernen Castle in May 1993*, ed. Krijnie Ciggaar, Adelbert Davids, and Herman Teule (Leuven, 1996)
EWCS, 2	*East and West in the Crusader States: Context—Contacts—Confrontations*, vol. 2: *Acta of the Congress Held at Hernen Castle in May 1997*, ed. Krijnie Ciggaar and Herman Teule (Leuven, 1999)
EWCS, 3	*East and West in the Crusader States: Context—Contacts—Confrontations*, vol. 3: *Acta of the Congress Held at Hernen Castle in September 2000*, ed. Krijnie Ciggaar and Herman Teule (Leuven, 2003)
EWMEM	*East and West in the Medieval Eastern Mediterranean: Antioch from the Byzantine Reconquest until the End of the Crusader Principality*, vol. 1: *Acta of the Congress held at Hernen Castle in May 2003*, ed. Krijnie Ciggaar and Michael Metcalf (Leuven, 2006)
FC	Foucher of Chartres, *Fulcheri Carnotensis Historia Hierosolymitana (1095–1127)*, ed. Heinrich Hagenmeyer (Heidelberg, 1913)
France and the Holy Land	*France and the Holy Land: Frankish Culture at the End of the Crusades*, ed. Daniel H. Weiss and Lisa Mahoney (Baltimore, 2004)
The French of Outremer	*The French of Outremer: Communities and Communications in the Crusading Mediterranean*, ed. Laura K. Morreale and Nicholas L. Paul (New York, 2018)
Fretellus	*Rorgo Fretellus de Nazareth et sa description de la Terre Sainte: Histoire et édition du texte*, ed. P. C.

	Boeren, Koninklijke Nederlandse Akademie van Wetenschappen, Afdeling Letterkunde, Verhandelingen, n.s., 105 (Amsterdam, 1980)
GN	Guibert of Nogent, *Dei gesta per Francos*, ed. Robert B. C. Huygens, CCCM 127A (Turnhout, 1996)
Horns	*The Horns of Ḥaṭṭīn*, ed. B. Z. Kedar (Jerusalem, 1992)
IAA	Israel Antiquities Authority
JdV	Jacques de Vitry, *Historia orientalis*, ed. and trans. Jean Donnadieu (Turnhout, 2008)
Kedar, *Crusaders*	B. Z. Kedar, *Crusaders and Franks: Studies in the History of the Crusades and the Frankish Levant* (Abingdon, 2016)
Kedar, *The Franks*	B. Z. Kedar, *The Franks in the Levant, 11th to 14th Centuries* (Aldershot, 1993)
Kedar, *Franks, Muslims*	B. Z. Kedar, *Franks, Muslims and Oriental Christians in the Latin Levant: Studies in Frontier Acculturation* (Aldershot, 2006)
Kreuzfahrerstaaten	*Die Kreuzfahrerstaaten als multikulturelle Gesellschaft: Einwanderer und Minderheiten im 12. und 13. Jahrhundert*, ed. Hans Eberhard Mayer with Elisabeth Müller-Luckner (Munich, 1997)
Libellus	*The Conquest of the Holy Land by Salāh al-Dīn: A Critical Edition and Translation of the Anonymous Libellus de expugnatione Terrae Sanctae per Saladinum*, ed. and trans. Keagan Brewer and James H. Kane (Abingdon, 2019)
Mansi, *Concilia*	Giovanni Domenico Mansi, *Sacrorum conciliorum nova et amplissima collectio*
MGH	Monumenta Germaniae Historica
SS	Scriptores
Montjoie	*Montjoie: Studies in Crusade History in Honour of Hans Eberhard Mayer*, ed. B. Z. Kedar, Jonathan Riley-Smith, and Rudolf Hiestand (Aldershot, 1997)
Occident et Proche-Orient	*Occident et Proche-Orient: Contacts scientifiques au temps des Croisades*, ed. Isabelle Draelants,

	Anne Tihon, and Baudouin van den Abeele (Turnhout, 2000)
Outremer	*Outremer: Studies in the History of the Crusading Kingdom of Jerusalem Presented to Joshua Prawer*, ed. B. Z. Kedar, Hans E. Mayer, and R. C. Smail (Jerusalem, 1982)
OV	*The Ecclesiastical History of Orderic Vitalis*, ed. and trans. Marjorie Chibnall, 6 vols. (Oxford, 1969–80)
PG	Patrologia Graeca
PL	Patrologia Latina
Pringle, *Churches*	Denys Pringle, *The Churches of the Crusader Kingdom of Jerusalem: A Corpus*, 4 vols. (Cambridge, 1993–2009)
RHC	*Recueil des Historiens des Croisades*
Oc	*Historiens occidentaux*
Or	*Historiens orientaux*
RHGF	*Recueil des Historiens des Gaules et de la France*
ROL	*Revue de l'Orient latin*
RRH	Reinhold Röhricht, comp., *Regesta Regni Hierosolymitani* and *Additamentum* (Innsbruck, 1894–1904)
RRR	*Revised Regesta Regni Hierosolymitani Database*, ed. Jonathan Riley-Smith et al. http://crusades-regesta.com
RS	Rolls Series
Tractatus	"The *Tractatus de locis et statu sancte terre ierosolimitane*," ed. B. Z. Kedar, in *Crusade Sources*, 123–31; repr. in. Kedar, *Franks, Muslims*, Study II.
Transferts	*Transferts culturels entre France et Orient latin (XIIe–XIIIe siècles)*, ed. Martin Aurell, Marisa Galvez, and Estelle Ingrand-Varenne (Paris, 2021)
UKJ	*Die Urkunden der lateinischen Könige von Jerusalem*, ed. Hans Eberhard Mayer, MGH Diplomata regum latinorum hierosolymitanorum, 4 vols. (Hanover, 2010)
WT	William of Tyre, *Chronicon*, ed. Robert B. C. Huygens, CCCM 63–63A (Turnhout, 1986)

WT OF	*Guillaume de Tyr et ses continuateurs: Texte français du XIIIe siècle*, ed. Paulin Paris, 2 vols. (Paris, 1879–80)
WT *C-F Cont*	*The Chronique d'Ernoul and the Colbert-Fontainebleau Continuation of William of Tyre*, ed. Peter Edbury and Massimiliano Gaggero, 2 vols. (Leiden, 2023), 2:77–380.
WT Cont. Lyon	*La continuation de Guillaume de Tyr (1184–1197)*, ed. M. Ruth Morgan. DRHC 14 (Paris, 1982)

Notes

Introduction

1. Hans Prutz, *Kulturgeschichte der Kreuzzüge* (Berlin, 1883; repr. Hildesheim, 1994).

2. Arnold Hermann Ludwig Heeren, *Versuch einer Entwickelung der Folgen der Kreuzzüge für Europa: Eine vom Nationalinstitut von Frankreich gekrönte Preisschrift* (Göttingen, 1808), iii. For the answers given by two winners, Arnold Hermann Ludwig Heeren (1760–1842) and André-Maxime-Urbain de Choiseul-Daillecourt (1782–1854), see B. Z. Kedar, "La *Via sancti sepulchri* come tramite di cultura araba in Occidente," in *Itinerari medievali e identità europea*, ed. Roberto Greci (Bologna, 1999), 181–84. For information on the reprinting of this and other articles, see the bibliography.

3. The term "First Crusaders"—meaning the participants of the First Crusade—was coined by Jonathan Riley-Smith, *The First Crusaders, 1095–1131* (Cambridge, 1997).

4. Prutz, *Kulturgeschichte*, esp. 6–9, 451, 475. For a more detailed discussion that highlights the impact on Prutz's thinking of the nexus between spatial and spiritual expansion proposed by Oscar Peschel, see Kedar, "La *Via sancti sepulchri*," 185–87.

5. Ernest J. Passant, "The Effects of the Crusades upon Western Europe," in *Cambridge Medieval History*, vol. 5 (Cambridge, 1926), 320–33, quotation on 331.

6. Charles H. Haskins, *Studies in the History of Mediaeval Science* (Cambridge, MA, 1924), 130.

7. Steven Runciman, *A History of the Crusades*, 3 vols. (Cambridge, 1951–54), 3:489–92.

8. Joshua Prawer, *The Latin Kingdom of Jerusalem: European Colonialism in the Middle Ages* (London, 1972), 524.

9. See most recently Julian Yolles, *Making the East Latin: The Latin Literature of the Levant in the Era of the Crusades* (Washington, DC, 2022), 12–13.

10. For underlying conceptions, see for instance Peter Burke, *What Is Cultural History?* (Cambridge, 2004).

11. The term "crusader art" was introduced in 1963 by an eminent art historian whose knowledge of the history of the crusades was limited: see Kurt Weitzmann, "Thirteenth Century Crusader Icons on Mount Sinai," *Art Bulletin* 45 (1963): 182 (a page earlier he asserts: "After the fall of Jerusalem in 1244 Acre had become the new capital of the shrinking Crusader kingdom"). On the use of the term "crusader states," see the diametrically opposed views of Christopher MacEvitt, "What Was Crusader about the Crusader States?," *Al-Masāq* 30 (2018):

317–30, and Andrew D. Buck, "Settlement, Identity and Memory in the Latin East: An Examination of the Term 'Crusader States,'" *English Historical Review* 135 (2020): 271–302. For the advocacy of the term "Levantine Latinity" rather than "Crusader Latinity," see Yolles, *Making the East Latin*, 3–4.

12. "Lettres de Jacques de Vitry," Ep. 2, in *Serta Mediaevalia: Textus varii saeculorum X–XIII in unum collecti. Tractatus et epistulae*, ed. Robert B. C. Huygens, CCCM 171 (Turnhout, 2000), 568–69; see also 571, 573.

13. For discussion, see Timo Kirschberger, *Erster Kreuzzug und Ethnogenese: In novam formam commutatus—Ethnogenetische Prozesse im Fürstentum Antiochia und im Königreich Jerusalem* (Göttingen, 2015), 75–102; Alan V. Murray, "Ethnic Identity in the Crusader States: The Frankish Race and the Settlement of Outremer," in *Concepts of National Identity in the Middle Ages*, ed. Simon Forde, Lesley Johnson, and Alan V. Murray (Leeds, 1995), 59–73. A Western Visitor to the Kingdom of Jerusalem in the years 1168–87 writes: "Franci, qui Latini verius appellantur": *Tractatus*, 124. That is, the usual appellation is "Franks," but the visitor believes that "Latins" is more appropriate.

14. Thus, Jaroslav Folda in his *The Art of the Crusaders in the Holy Land, 1098–1187* (Cambridge, 1995), speaks of Crusader masons (225), a Crusader artist (238), states that "the Crusaders . . . arrived at a specific 'core' plan to enclose all of the holy sites . . . in one unified and unique architectural complex" (202), and passim. Yet the terminology is not consistent; see for instance, "our proposition here is that the major art produced in the mainland Crusader States between 1098 and 1291 was produced . . . by local Crusader or even Frankish and sometimes indigenous Christian artists": Folda, *Crusader Art in the Holy Land from the Third Crusade to the Fall of Acre, 1187–1291* (Cambridge, 2005), 524.

15. For quotation, see WT 14.22 (660).

16. I obtained a microfilm of the manuscript containing Ḍiyā' al-Dīn al-Maqdisī's descriptions, but because of my rudimentary grasp of Arabic I gave the text to Daniella Talmon-Heller, who published it as "*The Cited Tales of the Wondrous Doings of the Shaykhs of the Holy Land* by Diyā' al-Dīn Abū ʿAbd Allāh Muhammad b. ʿAbd al-Wāhid al-Maqdisī (569/1173–643/1245): Text, Translation and Commentary," *Crusades* 1 (2002): 111–54.

17. Realizing my inability to deal with the Kingdom of Acre in the present book, I placed my files at the disposal of Jonathan Rubin, who used them, alongside a vast number of sources he gathered, in his PhD dissertation of 2012. See Rubin, *Learning in a Crusader City: Intellectual Activity and Intercultural Exchange in Acre, 1191–1291* (Cambridge, 2018).

18. On the author's visit in about 1135, see Jean Richard, "Sur un passage du 'Pèlerinage de Charlemagne': Le marché de Jérusalem," *Revue belge de philologie et d'histoire* 43 (1965): 552–55. For the boast, see *Voyage de Charlemagne*, ed. Massimo Bonafin (Parma, 1987), 60, 76–78, vv. 484–92, 705–33. For an attempt to bring Olivier's boast into conformity with conventional morals, see Paul Aebischer, "Le gab d'Olivier," *Revue belge de philologie et d'histoire* 34 (1956): 659–79. The attempt came under scathing attack by Alain Corbellari, "Paul Aebischer," in *Portraits de médiévistes suisses (1850–2000): Une profession au fil du temps*, ed. Ursula Bähler and Richard Trachsler (Geneva, 2009), 254–57.

19. "Farei un vers, pos mi somelh," xiii–xiv, vv. 77–86, in *Les Chansons de Guillaume IX, duc d'Aquitaine (1071–1127)*, ed. Alfred Jeanroy (Paris, 1913), 12–13. Jeanroy opted to dispense with translating the verses starting with "Tant las fotei," following thereby in the footsteps of an earlier scholar who exclaimed that "Die folgenden Strophen sind unübersetzlich": Friedrich Diez, *Leben und Werke der Troubadours*, 2nd ed. (Leipzig, 1882), 11. William, the monk of Malmesbury Abbey, condemned the duke as foolish and lewd, wallowing in vice and seasoning his trifles with witty elegance: William of Malmesbury, *Gesta regum Anglorum* 5.439, ed. and trans. Roger A. B. Mynors, Rodney M. Thomson, and Michael Winterbottom (Oxford, 1998), 782–85.

20. See for instance JdV 5 (116). For overviews, see Norman Daniel, *Islam and the West: The Making of an Image* (Edinburgh, 1960), 96–102; Ruth Roded, "Alternate Images of the Prophet Muḥammad's Virility," in *Studies in Islamic Masculinities*, ed. Lahoucine Ouzgane (London, 2006), 57–71. To this may be added William of Tripoli's assertion that at the conquest of a city ninety-nine virgins were Muḥammad's part of the booty, "quas omnes cognovit sequenti nocte"; see his *Notitia de Machometo: De statu Sarracenorum*, ed. and trans. Peter Engels (Würzburg, 1992), 220.

21. *Mahomet et Charlemagne* is the title of the influential book by Henri Pirenne (1862–1935), published posthumously in 1937, that linked the rise of Islam with Carolingian ascendance.

22. "Islamicate," the term referring to the culture shared by Muslims and the Christians and Jews who lived in their midst, was coined by Marshall G. S. Hodgson, *The Venture of Islam: Conscience and History in a World Civilization*, vol. 1: *The Classical Age of Islam* (Chicago, 1974), 57–60.

23. See Claude Cahen, *Orient et Occident au temps des Croisades* (Paris, 1983), 5.

24. Jürgen Kocka, "Asymmetrical Historical Comparison," *History and Theory* 38 (1999): 40–50; Kocka, "Comparative History: Methodology and Ethos," in *Explorations in Comparative History*, ed. B. Z. Kedar (Jerusalem, 2009), 29–35.

25. *Autour*, 173 (emphasis added).

26. Jean Richard, *L'esprit de la croisade* (Paris, 1969), 53.

27. Jonathan Riley-Smith, *The Crusades: A Short History* (New Haven, CT, 1987), 271; Riley-Smith, *The Crusades: A History*, 2nd ed. (London, 2005), 327 (emphasis added). The decision to refer to crusading as an act of love is no less revealing: see Riley-Smith, "Crusading as an Act of Love," *History* 65 (1980): 177–92.

28. "Address by Father Bernhard Demel, OT," in *The Military Orders*, vol. 2: *Welfare and Warfare*, ed. Helen Nicholson (Aldershot, 1998), xxi–xxiii.

29. Jonathan Riley-Smith, "The First Crusade and the Persecution of the Jews," in *Persecution and Toleration*, ed. William J. Sheils (Cambridge, 1984), 56 (emphasis added); Riley-Smith, *The First Crusade and the Idea of Crusading* (Philadelphia, 1986), 52.

30. Joshua Prawer, *The History of the Crusaders' Kingdom in the Land of Israel*, 2 vols. (Jerusalem, 1963), 2:359, 370. The first statement is toned down, the second deleted in the French version, *Histoire du Royaume latin de Jérusalem*, trans. Gérard Nahon, 2 vols. (Paris, 1969–71). For an appraisal, see B. Z. Kedar, "Joshua Prawer

(1917–1990), Historian of the Crusading Kingdom of Jerusalem," *Mediterranean Historical Review* 5 (1990): 107–16.

31. Joshua Prawer, *The History of the Jews in the Latin Kingdom of Jerusalem* (Oxford, 1988), 93, 115, 254, 259.

32. Ronnie Ellenblum, *Crusader Castles and Modern Histories* (Cambridge, 2007), 61.

33. See Zvi Gal, "Saladin's Dome of Victory at the Horns of Ḥaṭṭīn," in *Horns*, 213–15.

34. For instance, William Stubbs wrote in 1864: "The original settlers [in the Kingdom of Jerusalem] did not live long in their new possessions, and their children born in the land were a degenerate race. There were eleven kings of Jerusalem in the twelfth century: under the first four, who were all of European birth, the state was acquired and strengthened; under the second four, who were born in Palestine, the effects of the climate and the infection of Oriental habits were sadly apparent." *Itinerarium Peregrinorum et gesta regis Ricardi*, ed. William Stubbs, RS 38.1 (London, 1864), introduction, xcv–xcvi. And Adolf Waas maintained in 1956: "Es ist sicher damals eine gewisse Degeneration durch die häufigen Ehen mit volksmäßig weit abstehenden fremden Völkern eingetreten." Adolf Waas, *Geschichte der Kreuzzüge*, 2 vols. (Freiburg im Breisgau, 1956), 1:218.

35. "Le secret d'ennuyer est celui de tout dire." Voltaire, "Discours en vers sur l'homme, 6: De la nature de l'homme," in *Poèmes et discours en vers de Voltaire* (Paris, 1813), 35.

36. Eileen Power, *Medieval People* (London, 1924).

37. "(par hasard, direz-vous peut-être, mais souvenez-vous que dans les champs d'observation le hasard ne favorise que les esprit préparés)." *Oeuvres de Pasteur*, ed. Louis Pasteur Vallery-Radot, 7 vols. (Paris, 1922–39), 7:131.

1. A Tiny Kingdom of Diverse Peoples

1. This is the adapter of William of Tyre's chronicle, who writes: "Je ai apelé le roiaume baronie, porce qu'il estoit si petiz." WT OF 2:136; this interpolation into WT 16.29 was copied by Primat: *Les grandes chroniques de France*, ed. Jules Viard, 10 vols. (Paris, 1920–53), 6:42. See also Cahen, *Orient et Occident*, 156.

2. For the numbers in 1100, see FC 2.6 (389); William gives the number of foot soldiers as two thousand: WT 9.19 (445). For chroniclers' data on the size of King Baldwin I's army in the years 1100–1108, see Prutz, *Kulturgeschichte*, 94–95, 518–19. The apposite designation "Founding Fathers" was coined by Amnon Linder, "A New Day, New Joy: The Liberation of Jerusalem on 15 July 1099," in *L'idea di Gerusalemme nella spiritualità cristiana del Medioevo*, ed. Walter Brandmüller (Vatican City, 2003), 52.

3. See esp. Riley-Smith, *The First Crusade*, 17–49; Riley-Smith, *The Crusades: A History*, 2–23; Riley-Smith, *Templars and Hospitallers as Professed Religious in the Holy Land* (Notre Dame, IN, 2010), 12–13.

4. "en leur imposant pour pénitence de suivre la plus grande de leurs passions, d'aller faire la guerre." Voltaire, *Histoire des croisades* (Berlin, 1751), 17. Similarly, Carl Erdmann highlighted the "unvergleichliche Geschicklichkeit" with

which Urban accommodated himself to the temper of his contemporaries: Carl Erdmann, *Die Entstehung des Kreuzzugsgedankens* (Stuttgart, 1935), 325.

5. See the review by Hans Eberhard Mayer of Riley-Smith, *The First Crusade*, in *Deutsches Archiv* 43 (1987): 277.

6. *Le "Liber" de Raymond d'Aguilers*, ed. John H. Hill and Laurita L. Hill, DRHC 9 (Paris, 1969), 137.

7. William mentions that some people went East for reasons he considered ignoble: WT 1.16 (136). Cf. Conor Kostick, *The Social Structure of the First Crusade* (Leiden, 2008), esp. 291–300. For a portrayal of Godefrid of Bouillon's motivation as resulting from an interplay of "spiritual, dynastic and political impulses," see Simon John, *Godfrey of Bouillon, Duke of Lower Lotharingia, Ruler of Latin Jerusalem, c.1060–1100* (Abingdon, 2018), 99–103, 220.

8. GN 5.25 (228). A few lines earlier he writes: "Attendamus illos, qui de Iherosolimitana, quia ibi interfuerint, captivitate superbiunt, et videbimus quia in flagitiis, proditionibus, periuriis nemo eorum alicui se patitur esse secundum"; see also 7.7 (278), where he obliquely refers to Raimbold Croton, who was the first to mount Jerusalem's wall and, upon his return to the West, had a monk castrated for a trivial reason. Cf. Christopher Tyerman, *God's War: A New History of the Crusades* (London, 2006), 87, 156, 249; Riley-Smith, *The Crusades: A History*, 113–14.

9. Honorius Augustodunensis, *Elucidarium* 2.77, in Yves Lefèvre, *L'Elucidarium et les lucidaires: Contribution, par l'histoire d'un texte, à l'histoire des croyances religieuses en France au moyen âge* (Paris, 1954), 434–35; see also 158; Diana Webb, *Pilgrims and Pilgrimage in the Medieval West* (London, 1999), 246.

10. B. Z. Kedar, "Gerard of Nazareth: A Neglected Twelfth-Century Writer in the Latin East. A Contribution to the Intellectual and Monastic History of the Crusader States," *Dumbarton Oaks Papers* 37 (1983): 55–77.

11. Andrew Jotischky, *The Perfection of Solitude: Hermits and Monks in the Crusader States* (University Park, PA, 1995); Jotischky, "Gerard of Nazareth, John Bale and the Origins of the Carmelite Order," *Journal of Ecclesiastical History* 46 (1995): 214–36; B. Z. Kedar, "The Latin Hermits of the Frankish Levant Revisited," in *"Come l'orco della fiaba": Studi per Franco Cardini*, ed. Marina Montesano (Florence, 2010), 185–202.

12. *Acta Sanctorum, Septembris VII* (Antwerp, 1760), 523; Stefano Pedica, "Bonfiglio," in *Bibliotheca Sanctorum*, vol. 3 (Rome, 1963), 305–6.

13. Henrietta Leyser, *Hermits and the New Monasticism* (London, 1984), esp. c. 3; Clifford H. Lawrence, *Medieval Monasticism*, 3rd ed. (Harlow, Essex, 2001), 146–56.

14. Gerard of Nazareth, *De conversacione virorum Dei in Terra Sancta morantium*, ed. in Kedar, "Gerard of Nazareth," c. 20 (73).

15. Gerard of Nazareth, *De conversacione*, c. 19 (73). Galbert of Bruges reports that Jerusalemite knights hated Baldwin for being stubborn and stingy, "not ruling the people of God well": Galbert of Bruges, *De multro, traditione, et occisione gloriosi Karoli comitis Flandriarum*, ed. Jeff Rider, CCCM 131 (Turnhout, 1994), 15; see Alan W. Murray, *Baldwin of Bourcq, Count of Edessa and King of Jerusalem (1100–1131)* (Abingdon, 2022), 152.

16. Jotischky, *The Perfection of Solitude*, xiii, 133.

17. Benincasa, *Vita sancti Rainerii confessoris de civitate pisana*, ed. Réginald Grégoire, in *San Ranieri di Pisa (1117–1160) in un ritratto agiografico inedito del secolo XIII* (Ospedaletto, 1990), 99–254; B. Z. Kedar, "A Second Incarnation in Frankish Jerusalem," in *EC*, 79–92; Kedar, "Un Santo venuto da Gerusalemme: Ranieri Scacceri," in *I Santi venuti dal mare*, ed. Maria-Stella Calò Mariani (Bari, 2009), 173–80.

18. For an early survey, see Prutz, *Kulturgeschichte*, 117, 525.

19. Mansi, *Concilia*, 21:237; for discussion, see Hartmut Hoffmann, *Gottesfriede und Treuga Dei*, MGH Schriften 20 (Stuttgart, 1964), 226–27. Riley-Smith asserted that Urban II presided over a council in Rome in 1099 that decreed that an arsonist's penance should be "to remain in the service of God in Jerusalem or in Spain for one year": Riley-Smith, *The First Crusaders*, 108. The assertion is based on *Acta pontificum Romanorum inedita*, ed. Julius von Pflugk-Harttung, 3 vols. (Stuttgart, 1881–86), 2:167–68, no. 203. But Pflugk-Harttung proposed only tentatively that the unidentified council whose decrees he edited had taken place in Rome in 1097 or 1099; the arguments proffered are not cogent.

20. Mansi, *Concilia*, 21:440 (Clermont, 1130), 462 (Reims, 1131), 531 (Lateran II, 1139), 717 (Reims, 1148). See also Gratian, C. 23 q. 8 c. 32, in *Corpus iuris canonici*, ed. Emil Friedberg, 2 vols. (Leipzig, 1879–81), 1:964–65; c. 8 of Frederick I's *Constitutio contra incendiarios* of 1186, in *Constitutiones et acta publica imperatorum et regum*, vol. 1, ed. Ludwig Weiland, MGH Legum sectio 4 (Hanover, 1893), no. 318 (450); Alain of Lille, *Liber poenitentialis*, c. 31, ed. Jean Longère, 2 vols. (Louvain, 1965), 2:64; Robert of Flamborough, *Liber penitentialis* 5.315, ed. J. J. Francis Firth (Toronto, 1971), 255.

21. "Qar tuit ceste custome tenent: / Qui bon i vont, mal en revenent." Branche I, vv. 1351–1414, in *Le Roman de Renart*, ed. Ernest Martin, 3 vols. (Strasbourg, 1882–87), 1:38–40, quotation on 40. For the date, see Lucien Foulet, *Le Roman de Renard* (Paris, 1968), 106–8. Following Martin, the manuscripts of the Renart cycle are classified into three groups, α, β, γ. Martin's edition is based on an α manuscript. The passage quoted above recurs in manuscripts of the γ group: see *Le Roman de Renart, Branches 1 et 1a*, ed. Naoyuki Fukumoto (Tokyo, 1974), 139. It is missing in the β group. My attention to this passage, important for the history of the criticism of crusading, was alerted by its partial use by Urban Tignor Holmes, "Life among the Europeans in Palestine and Syria in the Twelfth and Thirteenth Centuries," in *Crusades*, ed. Setton, 4:5.

22. "fugiunt multi ad heremum ut egyptiaca vel ad monasteria vel ad partes ultramarinas, ut habeant minorem occasionem peccandi. Sed proh dolor aliqui plures inveniunt ibi occasiones peccandi quam in patria sua et ubi debent sanctificari a peccatis ibi amplius inquinantur." BnF, lat. 15959, fol. 208rb.

23. "Landsdowne Anonymous," ed. James C. Robertson, in *Materials for the History of Thomas Becket*, RS 67, 7 vols. (London, 1875–85), 4:163–64.

24. Roger of Howden, *Chronica*, ed. William Stubbs, RS 51, 4 vols. (London, 1868–71), 2:17; Romuald of Salerno, *Chronicon*, ed. Carlo A. Garufi, Rerum Italicarum Scriptores, n.s., 7.1 (Rome, 1935), 261; Pringle, *Churches*, 3:105. On the possibility that the four barons did not die in the Kingdom of Jerusalem, see Frank Barlow, *Thomas Becket* (Berkeley, 1986), 258–59.

25. Mansi, *Concilia*, 22:430–31; partially included in Gregory IX's *Decretals*: see X 5.10.1, in *Corpus iuris canonici*, ed. Friedberg, 2:792. Alexander III's letter, partly summarized by Alphonse Wauters, *Table chronologique des chartes et de diplômes imprimés concernant l'histoire de la Belgique*, 11 vols. (Brussels, 1866–1946), 2:590, led Reinhold Röhricht to present the case as: "Kindesmörderin, eine, 1179 zur Strafe auf 7 Jahre nach dem heiligen Lande geschickt." Reinhold Röhricht, *Beiträge zur Geschichte der Kreuzzüge*, 2 vols. (Berlin, 1874–78), 2:323; Röhricht, *Die Deutschen im Heiligen Lande, 560–1291* (Innsbruck, 1894), 48. Röhricht's error was repeated by Sabine Geldsetzer, *Frauen auf Kreuzzügen, 1096–1291* (Darmstadt, 2003), 212.

26. The Englishman's story appears in a 1243 letter by Ivo of Narbonne, a former Patarine, to the archbishop of Bordeaux: Matthew Paris, *Chronica majora*, ed. Henry R. Luard, RS 57, 7 vols. (London, 1872–80), 4:274–77; partially utilized by Jean Richard, *The Latin Kingdom of Jerusalem*, trans. Janet Shirley, 2 vols. (Amsterdam, 1979), 1:260.

27. Ralph Niger, *De re militari et triplici via peregrinationis ierosolimitanae (1187/88)* 3.84, ed. Ludwig Schmugge (Berlin, 1977), 194. For a study of this topos, see Martin Aurell, *Des chrétiens contre les croisades, XIIe–XIIIe siècle* (Paris, 2013), 85–86, 152–54, 264, 304, 338–40.

28. William of Newburgh, *Historia rerum Anglicarum* 3.15, ed. Richard Howlett, RS 82.1 (London, 1884), 254.

29. *Cart Hosp*, 2:523, no. 2185.

30. Burchard of Mount Sion, *Descriptio Terrae Sanctae*, ed. and trans. John R. Bartlett (Oxford, 2019), 190, c. 111. On the date of his travels, see Jonathan Rubin, "Burchard of Mount Sion's *Descriptio Terrae Sanctae*: A Newly Discovered Extended Version," *Crusades* 13 (2014): 180–81. On Western denigration of the Franks of the Latin East, see Martin Aurell, "De l'acculturation à l'ethnotype: L'alterité du Latin d'Orient," in *Transferts*, 337–53.

31. See the diverging remarks by Hans Eberhard Mayer, *Geschichte der Kreuzzüge*, 10th ed. (Stuttgart, 2005), 190, and Aurell, *Des chrétiens contre les croisades*, 137, 349.

32. FC 3.37 (748).

33. Bernard of Clairvaux, *Éloge de la Nouvelle Chevalerie*, ed. and trans. Pierre-Yves Emery (Paris, 1990), 76–77. The editor observes (on 22) that the Templar order "prend ici un petit air de Légion étrangère!" But Bulst-Thiele rightly observed that Bernard speaks here of crusaders, not of Templars: Marie-Luise Bulst-Thiele, *Sacrae Domus Militiae Templi Hierosolymitani Magistri: Untersuchungen zur Geschichte des Templerordens 1118/19–1314* (Göttingen, 1974), 45–46.

34. *Les registres de Grégoire IX*, ed. Lucien Auvray, 4 vols. (Paris, 1896–1955), 2:915, no. 4145. For some cases in the years 1178–1236, see John H. Mundy, *The Repression of Catharism at Toulouse* (Toronto, 1985), 12–18, 46–47, 83, 94, 226, 229–31, 257.

35. *Concilium Bitterense*, cc. 26, 29, in Mansi, *Concilia*, 23:720–22.

36. *Layettes du Trésor des Chartes*, ed. Alexandre Teulet et al., 5 vols. (Paris, 1863–1909), 3:19, no. 3625.

37. B. Z. Kedar, "The Passenger List of a Crusader Ship, 1250: Toward the History of the Popular Element on the Seventh Crusade," *Studi Medievali* 13,

no. 1 (1972): 267–79; Gauthier Langlois, *Olivier de Termes: Le cathare et le croisé* (Toulouse, 2001); Tyerman, *God's War*, 604, 722, 774.

38. *Bullarium Franciscanum*, ed. Giovanni Giacinto Sbaraglia, 4 vols. (Rome, 1759–68), 4:136–37. Characteristically, Henry Charles Lea quipped: "Even the decaying fragments of the Kingdom of Jerusalem could not be allowed burial without an inquisition to attend the obsequies." *A History of the Inquisition of the Middle Ages*, 2 vols. (London, 1887–88), 1:355–56.

39. *Die Chroniken Bertholds von Reichenau und Bernolds von Konstanz, 1054–1100*, ed. Ian S. Robinson, MGH SS. rer. Germ. n.s. 14, 530, 533–34, 537, 540; Berthold of Zwiefalten, *Liber de constructione monasterii Zwivildensis*, ed. Otto Abel, in MGH SS 10:108; Riley-Smith, *The First Crusaders*, 207.

40. Petrus Venerabilis, *De miraculis libri duo*, ed. Denise Bouthiller, CCCM 83 (Turnhout, 1988), 118.

41. OV 12.30 (6:310–12); *Anselmi Gemblacensis Continuatio*, ed. Ludwig Conrad Bethmann, in MGH SS 6:79.

42. Gerd Tellenbach, "Der Sturz des Abtes Pontius von Cluny und seine geschichtliche Bedeutung," *Quellen und Forschungen aus italienischen Archiven und Bibliotheken* 42–43 (1963): 13–55; H. E. J. Cowdrey, "Abbot Pontius of Cluny (1109–22/6)," *Studi Gregoriani per la storia della "Libertas Ecclesiae"* 11 (1978): 177–277.

43. "Chronicon monasterii S. Petri Aniciensis," in *Cartulaire de l'abbaye de St. Chaffre du Monastier*, ed. Ulysse Chevalier (Paris, 1884), 165–66.

44. WT 14.11, 16.17 (643–44, 738). Bernard Hamilton, *The Latin Church in the Crusader States: The Secular Church* (London, 1980), 70–75; Hans Eberhard Mayer, "Guillaume de Tyr à l'école," in *Mémoires de l'Académie des sciences, arts et belles-lettres de Dijon* 127 (1988): 258.

45. Saxo Grammaticus, *Gesta Danorum*, 14.26, 45, ed. Karsten Friis-Jensen, trans. Peter Fisher (Oxford, 2015), 1180–90, 1366.

46. WT 20.3 (914–15).

47. "Appendix ad Concilium Lateranense III," c. 26, in Mansi, *Concilia*, 22:372–73.

48. *Chronica Adefonsi Imperatoris* 1.74, 77, 87, in *Chronica Hispana saeculi XII*, ed. Emma Falque et al., CCCM 71 (Turnhout, 1990), 185–86, 189–90; *Cart St Sép*, 170–71, no. 72; B. Z. Kedar, "Iberia y el reino franco de Jerusalén," *Ad Limina* 8 (2017): 49–50.

49. *Chronica Adefonsi Imperatoris* 1.47–48, 2.30 (172, 209); Kedar, "Iberia y el reino franco," 50–56.

50. Roger of Howden, *Chronica*, 1:273–74; Clément de Vasselot de Régné, "A Crusader Lineage from Spain to the Throne of Jerusalem: The Lusignans," *Crusades* 16 (2017): 102.

51. Geldsetzer, *Frauen*, 49–53.

52. Geoffrey of Vendôme, *Oeuvres*, ed. and trans. Geneviève Giordanengo (Turnhout, 1996), 62–63, 94–95, 174–77, 312–15, epp. 33, 53, 92–93, 145–46.

53. *Cartulaire de l'abbaye de Saint-Aubin d'Angers*, ed. Arthur Bertrand de Broussillon and Eugène Lelong, 3 vols. (Paris, 1903), 2:345–46.

54. Anatole de Barthélemy, "Libre exercice de commerce octroyé à un pèlerin champenois (1153)," *AOL* 1 (1881): 535–36.

55. "Appendix ad Concilium Lateranense III," c. 50, in Mansi, *Concilia*, 22:451; *Papsturkunden für Kirchen im Heiligen Lande*, ed. Rudolf Hiestand (Göttingen, 1985), 343, 371, nos. 164, 186; Hans Eberhard Mayer, *Die Kanzlei der lateinischen Könige von Jerusalem*, MGH Schriften 40, 2 vols. (Hanover, 1996), 1:297–98, 2:455.

56. JdV 68, 73 (276–77, 292–93).

57. "magna societas solummodo pauperum et egenorum tunc insimul congregata, qui derisorie filii Arnaldi appellabantur." Otto Morena, "Historia," in *Das Geschichtswerk des Otto Morena*, ed. Ferdinand Güterbock, MGH SS rer. Germ. n.s., 7:73. Ducange considered *filli Arnaldi* a variant of *filli Hernaudi*: *Glossarium mediae et infimae Latinitatis*, vol. 3 (Paris, 1844), 296. Is it possible that those poor were derisively linked to Arnald of Brescia, the nonconformist canon who preached poverty and had been hanged four years earlier, in 1155? For a different interpretation, see Arsenio Frugoni, *Arnaldo di Brescia nelle fonti del secolo XII* (Turin, 1989), 157–58.

58. On the role of mercenaries, see Nicholas Morton, *The Crusader States and Their Neighbours: A Military History, 1099–1187* (Oxford, 2020), 144–51.

59. For details, see B. Z. Kedar, "The Fourth Crusade's Second Front," in *Urbs Capta: The Fourth Crusade and Its Consequences*, ed. Angeliki Laiou (Paris, 2005), 106.

60. *Odeoporicum et pericula Margarite Iherosolimitane*, ed. Paul Gerhardt Schmidt, "'Peregrinatio periculosa': Thomas von Froidmont über die Jerusalemfahrten seiner Schwester Margareta," in *Kontinuität und Wandel: Lateinische Poesie von Naevius bis Baudelaire. Franco Munari zum 65. Geburtstag*, ed. Ulrich Justus Stache, Wolfgang Maaz, and Fritz Wagner (Hildesheim, 1986), 478. For analysis, see Christoph T. Maier, "Über die Rolle der Frauen in der Krezzugsbewegung," in *Päpste, Pilger, Pönitentiarie: Festschrift für Ludwig Schmugge zum 65. Geburtstag*, ed. Andreas Meyer, Constanze Rendtel, and Maria Wittmer-Butsch (Tübingen, 2004), 258–65; Anthony Bale, "Reading and Writing in Outremer," in *The Cambridge Companion to the Literature of the Crusades* (Cambridge, 2019), 85–86. On a woman who assisted in the crusader siege of Acre in 1191, see Krijnie N. Ciggaar, "Glimpses of Life in Outremer in *Exempla* and *Miracula*," in *EWCS*, 2:136–38, 149–50. On Frankish women warriors in Muslim sources, see Carole Hillenbrand, *The Crusades: Islamic Perspectives* (Edinburgh, 1999), 348–49.

61. On the Angevin influx, see Hans Eberhard Mayer, "Angevins *versus* Normans: The New Men of King Fulk of Jerusalem," *Proceedings of the American Philosophical Society* 133 (1989): 1–25; Mayer, "Einwanderer in der Kanzlei und am Hof der Kreuzfahrerkönige von Jerusalem," in *Kreuzfahrerstaaten*, 25–26. For the argument that few of these Angevins were noblemen and the rest of modest social status, see Bruno Lemesle, "Foulques V, de l'Occident à l'Orient: Les réseaux du comte d'Anjou," in *D'Orient en Occident*, 128–31. On kinsmen of Baldwin II who arrived in the East after his accession to the throne, see Murray, *Baldwin of Bourcq*, 94, 113, 133–34, 195.

62. "artifices et agricolae, qui de laboribus suis sibi possint acquirere necessaria, et terrae subsidia ministrare: quamvis non multi talium, propter brevitatem possessionum et paucitatem inhabitantium ibi sunt opportuni." X 3.34.8, in *Corpus iuris canonici*, ed. Friedberg, 2:593.

63. For the text, see now *Projets de croisade (v. 1290–v. 1330)*, ed. Jacques Paviot (Paris, 2008), 46. On Amaurry de la Roche, see Jochen Burgtorf, *The Central Convent of Hospitallers and Templars: History, Organization, and Personnel (1099/1120–1310)* (Leiden, 2008), 425, 470–74, 709–10, and passim. For other instances of opposition to the poor moving East, see *Cronica Reinhardsbrunnensis*, ed. Oswald Holder-Egger, in MGH SS 30.1:555–56; X 3.34.8, in *Corpus iuris canonici*, ed. Friedberg, 2:593.

64. Al-Qāḍī al-Fāḍil in Ibn Khallikān, *RHC Or*, 3:421; *Ibn Khallikan's Biographical Dictionary*, trans. William MacGuckin de Slane, 4 vols. (Paris, 1843–71), 4:526. Translation: Elon Harvey.

65. *Der Ludus de Antichristo*, ed. Wilhelm Meyer (Munich, 1892), 17–40.

66. Joshua Prawer, *Crusader Institutions* (Oxford, 1980), 20–47; Jonathan Riley-Smith, *The Feudal Nobility and the Kingdom of Jerusalem, 1174–1277* (London, 1973).

67. For a discussion of Frankish social stratification and mobility, see Joshua Prawer, "Social Classes in the Latin Kingdom: The Franks," in *Crusades*, ed. Setton, 5:117–92.

68. Rainer C. Schwinges, "Regionale Identität und Begegnung der Kulturen in Stadt und 'Kreuzfahrerkönigreich' Jerusalem," in Meyer, Rendtel, and Wittmer-Butsch, *Päpste, Pilger, Pönitentiarie*, 242.

69. See, for instance, the description of women providing drinking water to the First Crusaders and encouraging them during the Battle of Dorylaeum in 1097: *Gesta Francorum et aliorum Hierosolymitanorum*, ed. Roger Mynors, trans. Rosalind Hill (Oxford, 1962), 19; Keren Caspi-Reisfeld, "Women Warriors during the Crusades, 1095–1254," in *Gendering the Crusades*, ed. Susan B. Edgington and Sarah Lambert (Cardiff, 2001), 97; Geldsetzer, *Frauen*, 129, 258 n. 31.

70. My calculations are based on Riley-Smith, *The First Crusaders*, app. I, 197–226; see also 107–8 with n. 19. In addition to the seven spouses, six other women appear in the list as having wished to participate in the expedition or as having done so. Geldsetzer lists three further women who went East with their husbands: Geldsetzer, *Frauen*, 184–85, nos. 3–5; also, five women who went there on their own: Geldsetzer, *Frauen*, 184, 186, nos. 1–2, 13–15.

71. Jaspert lists eight Catalan couples who left for Jerusalem in the years 1101–68 and quotes a testament of 1137 that states, "Si autem in Iherosolimitanis partibus remanserimus aut proprium reliquerimus": Nikolas Jaspert, "Penitencia y apocalipsis en tiempos de la primera cruzada: Una investigación documental," in *Memoria y fuentes de la guerra santa peninsular (siglos X–XV)*, ed. Carlos de Ayala Martínez et al. (Gijón, 2021), 472.

72. Kedar, "The Passenger List," esp. 272–74. For discussion, see Geldsetzer, *Frauen*, 196–98.

73. JdV 73 (276–77). As Ruth Morgan aptly put it, the legend "has no evidence of any kind to support it, and must be dismissed as one of those shots in the dark so characteristic of popular etymology": Morgan, "The Meanings of Old French *polain*, Latin *pullanus*," *Medium Aevum* 48 (1979): 43. For attempts to explain the name's origin, see Prawer, "Social Classes in the Latin Kingdom," 120 n. 1.

74. "Canons of the Council of Nablus," nos. 17–18, ed. B. Z. Kedar, *Speculum* 74 (1999): 334.

75. "Assises des Bourgeois," c. 162 (2:111–12). The law has no counterpart in *Lo Codi*, the apparent source of the *Assises*: see Prawer, *Crusader Institutions*, 364, 394.

76. FC 3.37 (748).

77. On the curb of rape, see "Canons of the Council of Nablus," 333, nos. 12–14; on the willingness to recognize forcible baptisms, see B. Z. Kedar, *Crusade and Mission: European Approaches toward the Muslims* (Princeton, NJ, 1984), 72–74.

78. Riso: *Cart St Sép*, 175, no. 75; "Barutellus et uxor sua Sarracena," *Cart Hosp*, 1:144, no. 183; also 1:224–25, no. 311.

79. Usama ibn Munqidh, *The Book of Contemplation: Islam and the Crusades*, trans. Paul M. Cobb (London, 2008), 152. For an insightful analysis of Usāma's writings and motivation, see Robert Irwin, "Usamah ibn Munqidh: An Arab-Syrian Gentleman at the Time of the Crusades Reconsidered," in *Crusade Sources*, 71–87.

80. Celestine III's letter, "Laudabilem pontificalis officii," which made its way into the Decretals of Gregory IX (X 3.33.1), has been reedited and translated by Anne J. Duggan, "*Manu sollicitudinis*: Celestine III and Canon Law," in *Pope Celestine III (1191–1198): Diplomat and Pastor*, ed. John Doran and Damian J. Smith (Farnham, 2008), 223–31; for the instruction in question, see 225 (text), 229 (translation).

81. For the prohibitions, see "Canons of the Council of Nablus," 333–34, nos. 12–15.

82. Runciman, *A History of the Crusades*, 2:101. Surprisingly, Runciman's assertion was adopted by David Jacoby, "Intercultural Encounters in a Conquered Land: The Latin Kingdom of Jerusalem in the Twelfth and Thirteenth Centuries," in *Europa im Geflecht der Welt: Mittelalterliche Migrationen in globalen Bezügen*, ed. Michael Borgolte et al. (Berlin, 2012), 143.

83. According to the summary, Arnulf was accused of having been polluted "immixtione cum Girardi uxore et quadam Sarracena": *RRH*, no. 83.

84. *Cart St Sép*, 208, no. 91.

85. For a sensitive appraisal of Runciman's crusades trilogy, see Minoo Dinshaw, *Outlandish Knight: The Byzantine Life of Steven Runciman* (London, 2016), 378–405.

86. Amaurry's letter is edited in Paul Riant, "Six lettres relatives aux croisades," *AOL* 1 (1881): 386–87, repr. in *Cart Hosp*, 1:280, no. 404. The date has been convincingly established by Jonathan Phillips, *Defenders of the Holy Land: Relations between the Latin East and the West, 1119–1187* (Oxford, 1996), 151 n. 54.

87. Of the 107 men who vowed in 1158 to fight for three years "for the defense of the Christian faith" and went East under the leadership of Geoffroy of Mayenne, only 35 returned in November 1162; the rest fell in battle in the Sinai Desert. The account containing the list of the 107 crusaders was printed by Gilles Ménage, *Histoire de Sablé* (Paris, 1683), 179–81; repr. in *Recueil des Historiens des Gaules et de la France*, vol. 12 (Paris, 1877), 556–57. Probably they fell under Amaurry, then count of Jaffa and Ascalon, who raided Egypt in 1161 or 1162. On the raid's date, see Michael S. Fulton, *Contest for Egypt: The Collapse of the Fatimid Caliphate, the Ebb of Crusader Influence, and the Rise of Saladin* (Leiden, 2022), 28–31.

88. James A. Brundage, "Marriage Law in the Latin Kingdom of Jerusalem," in *Outremer*, 269–71.

89. For data pointing to a predominance of newcomers in certain groups and sectors, see Amnon Linder, "'Like Purest Gold Resplendent': The Fiftieth Anniversary of the Liberation of Jerusalem," *Crusades* 8 (2009): 49.

90. On Le Petit Gerin, which appears to have been fortified, see Pringle, *Churches*, 1:276–79; for the analysis, see Piers D. Mitchell and Andrew R. Millard, "Approaches to the Study of Migration during the Crusades," *Crusades* 12 (2013): 5–12.

91. Marc Haber et al., "A Transient Pulse of Genetic Admixture from the Crusaders in the Near East Identified from Ancient Genome Sequences," *American Journal of Human Genetics* 104, no. 5 (2019): 977–84.

92. For a promising way to ascertain the health of different groups by comparing their children's age at death, see Piers Mitchell, "A Comparison of Health at a Village and Castle in the Kingdom of Jerusalem in the Twelfth Century," in *The Military Orders*, vol. 4: *On Land and by Sea*, ed. Judi Upton-Ward (Aldershot, 2008), 23–28.

93. On the Muslim population under Frankish rule in general, see Hans Eberhard Mayer, "Latins, Muslims and Greeks in the Latin Kingdom of Jerusalem," *History* 63 (1978): 175–87; B. Z. Kedar, "The Subjected Muslims of the Frankish Levant," in *Muslims under Latin Rule, 1100–1300*, ed. James M. Powell (Princeton, NJ, 1990), 135–74; and the spirited discussion by Brian A. Catlos, *Muslims of Medieval Latin Christendom, c.1050–1614* (Cambridge, 2014), 128–62.

94. B. Z. Kedar, "The Jerusalem Massacre of July 1099 in the Western Historiography of the Crusades," *Crusades* 3 (2004): 15–75, and see appendix 2, below.

95. David Cook, "Al-Samʿānī's Travels in Syria during the Summer of 535/1141," *Crusades* 22, no. 1 (2023): 53.

96. For a discussion of these modes of conquest (which discards the older view that massacre was the rule until 1110 and moderation thereafter; in reality, Bilbays, conquered in 1168, provides the last example of a massacre upon the taking of a city by assault), see Kedar, "The Subjected Muslims," 143–47. For the modes' similarity to those in Iberia, see Joseph F. O'Callaghan, "The Mudejars of Castile and Portugal in the Twelfth and Thirteenth Centuries," in Powell, *Muslims under Latin Rule*, 13–18.

97. On Islamic studies in pre-1099 Jerusalem, see Joseph Drory, "Some Observations during a Visit to Palestine by Ibn al-ʿArabī of Seville in 1092–1095," *Crusades* 3 (2004): 121, excerpt 21.

98. Nāser-e Khosraw, *Book of Travels (Safarnāma)*, trans. W. M. Thackston Jr. (Albany, NY, 1986), 16, 19; Drory, "Some Observations," 119, 121–24, excerpts 19, 21–24.

99. Etan Kohlberg, "The Development of the Imāmī Shiʿī Doctrine of *jihād*," *Zeitschrift der Deutschen Morgenländischen Gesellschaft* 126 (1976): 69–70; Hannes Möhring, "Die Kreuzfahrer, ihre muslimischen Untertanen und die heiligen Stätten des Islam," in *Toleranz im Mittelalter*, ed. Alexander Patschovsky and Harald Zimmermann (Sigmaringen, 1998), 141–42.

100. *The Travels of Ibn Jubayr*, trans. R. J. C. Broadhurst (London, 1952), 317. For evaluations of this testimony, see Kedar, "The Subjected Muslims," 167–68.

101. Gautier the Chancellor, *Bella Antiochena* 1, pr. 6, ed. Heinrich Hagenmeyer (Innsbruck, 1896), 62–63. Thomas Asbridge and Susan B. Edgington translate *intolerabilior* as "irresistible": *Walter the Chancellor's "The Antiochene Wars": A Translation and Commentary* (Aldershot, 1999), 68, 80. However, the other instances in which Gautier uses this term tend to vindicate Hagenmeyer's assumption that he means here "more intolerable."

102. "Quant les Templiers furent saisiz de l'isle de Chypre, il vostrent justiser les gens de l'isle de Chypre a la maniere qu'il meneient les gens d'un casal qui est en la terre de Jerusalem. Il les voleient raembre, batter et maumener." WT Cont. Lyon, 135. Cf. Louis de Mas Latrie, *Histoire de l'île de Chypre sous le règne des princes de la Maison de Lusignan*, 4 vols. (Paris, 1861), 1:32; Angel Nicolaou-Konnari, "The Conquest of Cyprus by Richard the Lionheart and Its Aftermath: A Study of Sources and Legend, Politics and Attitudes in the Year 1191–1192," *Επετηρίδα* 26 (2000): 65.

103. *La Règle du Temple*, ed. Henri de Curzon (Paris, 1886), 193–94, §336; cf. Marie-Luise Favreau-Lilie, "'Multikulturelle Gesellschaft' oder 'Persecuting Society'? 'Franken' und 'Einheimische' im Königreich Jerusalem," in *Jerusalem im Hoch- und Spätmittelalter: Konflikte und Konfliktbewältigung—Vorstellungen und Vergegenwärtigungen*, ed. Dieter Bauer, Klaus Hebers, and Nikolas Jaspert (Frankfurt am Main, 2001), 83–84.

104. This is the conclusion of David E. P. Jackson, "Some Considerations Relating to the History of the Muslims in the Crusader States," in *EWCS*, 1:26. He points out that the Muslim peasant had no choice but to live under an oppressive conqueror, whether a Frank, a Turk, or a Kurd.

105. *Cart St Sép*, 247, no. 122.

106. Emmanuel Sivan, "Refugiés syro-palestiniens au temps des croisades," *Revue des études islamiques* 35 (1967): 137–39; Joseph Drory, "Hanbalīs of the Nablus Region in the Eleventh and Twelfth Centuries," *Asian and African Studies* 22 (1988): 93–99; B. Z. Kedar and Muhammad al-Hajjūj, "Muslim Villagers of the Frankish Kingdom of Jerusalem: Some Demographic and Onomastic Data," in *Itinéraires d'Orient: Hommages à Claude Cahen*, ed. Raoul Curiel and Rika Gyselen, Res Orientales 6 (Bures-sur-Yvette, 1994), 145–56; Daniella Talmon-Heller and B. Z. Kedar, "Did Muslim Survivors of the 1099 Massacre of Jerusalem Settle in Damascus? The True Origins of the al-Ṣāliḥiyya Suburb," *Al-Masāq* 17 (2005): 165–69. Yet at least one refugee from Jerusalem, Riḍwān al-Maqdisī, fled to Damascus: Cook, "Al-Samʿānī's Travels," 49. On the wish of the Muslim villagers of Bayt Āhūn—in the Frankish lordship of Toron—to settle in Ayyubid Bāniyās, possibly in the late 1170s, see Jean-Michel Mouton and Janine Sourdel-Thomine, "Nouveau témoignage sur les mouvements des populations rurales à l'époque des croisades," *Journal Asiatique* 308, no. 2 (2020): 145–50.

107. Drory, "Hanbalīs of the Nablus Region," 102–3.

108. Daniella Talmon-Heller, "The Shaykh and the Community: Popular Hanbalite Islam in 12th–13th Century Jabal Nablus and Jabal Qasyūn," *Studia Islamica* 79 (1994): 108–16.

109. On the *ra'īs*, see Kedar, "The Subjected Muslims," 170; Kevin J. Lewis, "Medieval Diglossia: The Diversity of the Latin Christian Encounter with Written and Spoken Arabic in the 'Crusader' County of Tripoli, with a Hitherto Unpublished Arabic Note from the Principality of Antioch," *Al-Masāq* 27 (2015): 126–30.

110. Al-Maqdisī, "*The Cited Tales*," 138–39 (the Arabic text appears on 121–22), © The Society for the Study of the Crusades and the Latin East, reprinted by permission of Taylor & Francis Ltd, https://www.tandfonline.com, on behalf of the Society for the Study of the Crusades and the Latin East. In another instance the *ra'īs* instructs a friend to roast a head of cattle and bring it to the shaykh: al-Maqdisī, "*The Cited Tales*," 124 (text), 144 (translation).

111. B. Z. Kedar, "Some New Sources on Palestinian Muslims before and during the Crusades," in *Kreuzfahrerstaaten*, 136.

112. Text translated by Drory, "Hanbalīs of the Nablus Region," 96.

113. Al-Maqdisī, "*The Cited Tales*," 121 (text), 136 (translation).

114. Donald S. Richards, "A Text of 'Imād al-Dīn on 12th-Century Frankish-Arabic Relations," *Arabica* 25 (1978): 203; al-Bundarī, *Sanā al-Barq al-Shāmi*, ed. Fathiyya al-Nabarāwī (Cairo, 1979), 302. The Muslim shrines of the Prophet Yūnus (Jonah) in Ḥalḥūl near Hebron and of the Prophet Shu'ayb (Jethro) in Ḥīṭṭīn near Tiberias—not venerated by Christians—were tended by Muslim caretakers: Cook, "Al-Sam'ānī's Travels," 48, 51–52.

115. For the quotation, see 'Imād al-Dīn, *El-Barq el-Shāmī*, ed. Ramazan Şeşen (Istanbul, 1979), 151. Translation: Etan Kohlberg.

116. B. Z. Kedar, "Muslim Conversion in Canon Law," in *Proceedings of the Sixth International Conference of Medieval Canon Law, Berkeley 1980*, ed. Stephan Kuttner and Kenneth Pennington (Vatican City, 1985), 321–32; Kedar, "Multidirectional Conversion in the Frankish Levant," in *Varieties of Religious Conversion in the Middle Ages*, ed. James Muldoon (Gainesville, 1997), 190–93. On a multilingual Turk whom Bohemond raised from the font and gave him his name, see *Le "Liber" de Raymond d'Aguilers*, 158–59.

117. Kedar, "Multidirectional Conversion," 194.

118. "Assises des Bourgeois," c. 235 (2:170); Prawer, *Crusader Institutions*, 439–57. For the attribution of this law to King Baldwin II, see Jonathan Riley-Smith, "Further Thoughts on Baldwin II's *établissement* on the Confiscation of Fiefs," in *CS*, 176–80.

119. *Decretales Ineditae saeculi XII*, ed. Stanley Chodorow and Charles Duggan (Vatican City, 1982), 166–67, no. 94.

120. *Le Livre au Roi*, c. 23, ed. Myriam Greilsammer, DRHC 17 (Paris, 1995), 203–4; also, 183, c. 16. *Le Livre au Roi*, literally "The Book [dedicated] to the King" (Peter Edbury's suggestion, pers. comm., 18 March 2024).

121. On cultural commuting, see Thomas F. Glick, *Islamic and Christian Spain in the Early Middle Ages* (Princeton, NJ, 1979), 167.

122. Usama ibn Munqidh, *The Book of Contemplation*, 143.

123. Celestine III, "Laudabilem pontificalis officii," ed. Duggan, 225 (text), 229–30 (translation). On the impossibility, from a Roman Catholic standpoint, of an interreligious marriage, see Martin Aurell, "Joan of England and al-'Âdil's

Harem: The Impossible Marriage between Christians and Muslims (Eleventh-Twelfth Centuries)," *Anglo-Norman Studies* 43 (2021): 1–14.

124. X 4.19.7, in *Corpus iuris canonici*, ed. Friedberg, 2:722–23. Kedar, "Muslim Conversion in Canon Law," 325 n. 20; Juraj Kamas, *The Separation of the Spouses with the Bond Remaining* (Rome, 1997), 107–9.

125. Kedar, "The Subjected Muslims," 148–49.

126. On Bethlehem and Thecua, see WT 1.6 (114); also 8.7 (394). An Ottoman census reveals that at the end of the sixteenth century Bethlehem had 239 Christian and only six Muslim family heads, whereas Taqūʿ (Thecua) was predominantly Muslim, with only five out of sixty-seven family heads being Christian: Wolf-Dieter Hütteroth and Kamal Abulfattah, *Historical Geography of Palestine, Transjordan and Southern Syria in the Late 16th Century* (Göttingen, 1977), 114 (Taqūʿ), 121 (Bayt Lahm).

127. Ronnie Ellenblum, *Frankish Rural Settlement in the Latin Kingdom of Jerusalem* (Cambridge, 1998), 231–52, 282–84. Ellenblum's conclusion has been contested by Smarandache, who argues that Frankish settlements often existed in close proximity to Muslim ones: Bogdan C. Smarandache, "A Reassessment of Frankish Settlement Patterns in the Latin Kingdom of Jerusalem, 493–583 AH/1099–1187 AD," in *Minorities in Contact in the Medieval Mediterranean*, ed. Clara Almagro Vidal, Jessica Tearney-Pearce, and Luke Yarbrough (Turnhout, 2020), 285–335. But the argument should be read with caution; for instance, the claim (297) that "a charter of the *Regesta*" confirms that Muslim townspeople inhabited Vallis Moysis as late as 1161 is unfounded: see *Tabulae ordinis Theutonici*, ed. Ernst Strehlke (Berlin, 1869), 3–5, no. 3, and *RRH*, no. 366.

128. GN 7.45 (347).

129. WT 11.27 (535–36); Ibn al-Qifṭī, *Ta'rīkh al-ḥukamā'*, ed. Julius Lippert (Leipzig, 1903), 378–78; translation in Etan Kohlberg and B. Z. Kedar, "A Melkite Physician in Frankish Jerusalem and Ayyubid Damascus: Muwaffaq al-Dīn Yaʿqūb b. Siqlāb," *Asian and African Studies* 22 (1988): 121.

130. Calculations based on vol. 3 of Pringle, *Churches*.

131. On the *Syri/Suriani*, see Johannes Pahlitzsch, *Graeci und Suriani im Palästina der Kreuzfahrerzeit: Beiträge und Quellen zur Geschichte des griechisch-orthodoxen Patriarchats von Jerusalem* (Berlin, 2001), 14–15. On the marginal position of the native Arabic-speaking Orthodox, see Andrew Jotischky, "Ethnographic Attitudes in the Crusader States: The Franks and the Indigenous Orthodox People," in *EWCS*, 3:3–8. For the view that especially in the Principality of Antioch the term *Suriani* referred also to Jacobites, see Andrew D. Buck, *The Principality of Antioch and Its Frontiers in the Twelfth Century* (Woodbridge, 2017), 168–71.

132. On intermarriage, see below, chap. 9; on Petrus Armenus, see *Cart Hosp*, 1:226, no. 312. He is probably identical with Pierre l'Ermin, whose son Simon, a Jerusalemite, owed the service of two knights: John of Ibelin, *Le Livre des Assises*, ed. Peter W. Edbury (Leiden, 2003), 609, c. 238. On Jacobus Surianus, see Christiane Tischler, *Die Burgenses von Jerusalem im 12. Jahrhundert: Eine Prosographie über die nichtadligen Einwohner Jerusalems von 1120 bis 1187* (Frankfurt am Main, 2000), 281, no. 187.

133. The inscription reads: "O homines qui transitis per viam, in caritate rogo vos orare pro anima mei, magistri Ebuli Fazle, hujus ecclesie edificatoris." Camille Enlart, *Les monuments des croisés dans le royaume de Jérusalem: Architecture religieuse et civile*, 2 vols. (Paris, 1925–28), 2:30–33. Enlart established that the inscription's letters are typical of the twelfth century; Estelle Ingrand-Varenne adds that so is the formula "O homines qui transitis" (pers. comm., 7 November 2022). For the decipherment of the benefactor's name, see Claude Cahen, "Une inscription mal comprise concernant le rapprochement entre Maronites et Croisés," in *Medieval and Middle Eastern Studies in Honour of Aziz Suryal Atiya*, ed. Sami A. Hanna (Leiden, 1972), 62–63. Cahen believed that Ebu'l Fazl was probably a Maronite; his hypothesis has been adopted by Pierre-Vincent Claverie, "Notes sur l'onomastique franque durant les croisades et quelques énigmes prosopographiques," in *Egypt and Syria in the Fatimid, Ayyubid and Mamluk Eras*, vol. 8, ed. Urbain Vermeulen, Kristof D'hulster, and Jo Van Steenbergen (Leuven, 2016), 146–47. But see Denys Pringle, "Notes on Some Inscriptions from Crusader Acre," in *In Laudem Hierosolymitani: Studies in Crusades and Medieval Culture in Honour of Benjamin Z. Kedar*, ed. Iris Shagrir, Ronnie Ellenblum, and Jonathan Riley-Smith (Aldershot, 2007), 202–3.

134. On the Eastern Christians, see Joshua Prawer, "Social Classes in the Crusader States: The 'Minorities,'" in *Crusades*, ed. Setton, 5:59–94; Mayer, "Latins, Muslims and Greeks," 187–92; B. Z. Kedar, "Latins and Oriental Christians in the Frankish Levant, 1099–1291," in *Sharing the Sacred: Contacts and Conflicts in the Religious History of the Holy Land. First–Fifteenth Centuries*, ed. Arieh Kofsky and Guy G. Stroumsa (Jerusalem, 1998), 209–22; Kedar, "The Eastern Christians in the Frankish Kingdom of Jerusalem: An Overview," in *Eastern Christianity, Judaism and Islam between the Deaths of Muhammad and Tamerlane (632–1405)*, ed. Marián Gálik and Martin Slobodník (Bratislava, 2011), 143–53. For contrasting views on Frankish/Eastern Christian relations, see Ellenblum, *Frankish Rural Settlement*, 119–28, 250–52; Pahlitzsch, *Graeci und Suriani*, 209–12.

135. Andrew Jotischky, "The Frankish Encounter with the Greek Orthodox in the Crusader States: The Case of Gerard of Nazareth and Mary Magdalene," in *Tolerance and Intolerance*, ed. Michael Gervers and James M. Powell (Syracuse, NY, 2001), 102. For the identification of the locality in question with ʿAyn Kārim, see Jotischky, *The Perfection of Solitude*, 90 n. 70; Johannes Pahlitzsch, "Die Bedeutung der Azymenfrage für die Beziehungen zwischen griechisch-orthodoxer und lateinischer Kirche in den Kreuzfahrerstaaten," in *Die Folgen der Kreuzzüge für die orientalische Religionsgemeinschaft*, ed. Walter Beltz (Halle, 1996), 84–86; Pahlitzsch, *Graeci und Suriani*, 203–4.

136. *Chartes Josaphat*, 87–88, no. 40.

137. For this interpretation, see Ellenblum, *Frankish Rural Settlement*, 119–20; see also Christopher MacEvitt, *The Crusades and the Christian World of the East: Rough Tolerance* (Philadelphia, 2008), 126–28 (but the 1178 accord does not stipulate that henceforward *Suriani* were not to be baptized in the Church of St. George). For a critique of the "rough tolerance" thesis, see Dorothea Weltecke in *Le Muséon* 123 (2010): 252–57.

138. Greek Orthodox institution: Pringle, *Churches*, 2:356.

139. Attracting Frankish parishioners: This is the interpretation of Hamilton, *The Latin Church*, 100. On the fees, see Hamilton, *The Latin Church*, 150; on Odo of Châteauroux's attempt, at the Council of Acre of 1254, to suppress them, see *The Synodicum Nicosiense and Other Documents of the Latin Church of Cyprus, 1196–1373*, ed. and trans. Christopher Schabel (Nicosia, 2001), 176–83.

140. *Cart Hosp*, 1:503, no. 808.

141. WT Cont. Lyon, 62; see also 86. The detail does not appear in *Ernoul*, 317–18.

142. *Cart Hosp*, 3:91–92, no. 3105. On Saliba, see Richard, *The Latin Kingdom*, 358; Riley-Smith, *The Feudal Nobility*, 79–80; Iris Shagrir, *Naming Patterns in the Latin Kingdom of Jerusalem* (Oxford, 2003), 77; Pringle, *Churches*, 4:23 and passim; and esp. Florian Besson, "Les rencontres entre communautés dans l'Acre latine du XIIIe siècle: L'exemple de Saliba, marchand et bourgeois," *Bulletin du Centre d'études médiévales d'Auxerre* 26, no. 2 (2016), DOI: 10.4000/cem.14523.

143. For a Catalan parallel of 1074 for the order to become Christian, see Charles Verlinden, *L'esclavage dans l'Europe médiévale*, 2 vols. (Brugge, 1955–77), 1:133 n. 82.

144. Richard, followed by Riley-Smith and Besson (see note 142 above) assumed that Saliba of the 1264 testament is identical with *Salibbi habitatoris Acconis* who in 1268 appealed—together with twenty-one other Easterners—to the podestà of Genoa for compensation for goods that the Genoese Lucchetto Grimaldi seized from a ship at Corycos, Cilicia. But Grimaldi was not a privateer, as Richard assumed, and the seizure did not take place "some five years before" the appeal of 1268, as Riley-Smith hypothesized. The *Annales Januenses* (MGH SS 18:260–61) state that the goods were seized in 1267 by a Genoese fleet commanded by Grimaldi. See Mas Latrie, *Histoire de l'île de Chypre*, 1:74–79; Cornelio Desimoni, "Actes passés en 1271, 1274 et 1279 à l'Aïas (Petite Arménie) et à Beyrouth," *AOL* 1 (1881): 434, 441–42.

145. Etienne of Meses is attested as Grand Preceptor in the years 1264–66: Burgtorf, *The Central Convent*, 661 and passim.

146. Richard (*The Latin Kingdom*, 358) believed that Saliba's bequest of two bezants *hospitali S. Kateline* was to a Greek institution; however, Pringle shows that the bequest went to the Latin Hospital of St. Catherine of the Battlefield: Pringle, *Churches*, 4:23, 73.

147. *Cart Hosp*, 3:159, no. 3263. However, Röhricht, *RRH*, no. 1349[a], and Burgtorf, *The Central Convent*, 661, assume that Haternia is identical with Saliba's daughter Katelina, who appears in the 1264 will as the recipient of 150 bezants.

148. "Annales de Terre Sainte," ed. Reinhold Röhricht and Gaston Raynaud, *AOL* 2, no. 2 (1884): 453 (Version B).

149. On this ranking, see Alan V. Murray, "Franks and Indigenous Communities in Palestine and Syria (1099–1187): A Hierarchical Model of Social Interaction in the Principalities of Outremer," in *East Meets West in the Middle Ages and Early Modern Times: Transcultural Experiences in the Premodern World*, ed. Albrecht Classen (Berlin, 2013), 291–309. There is, however, no evidence that Jews and Samaritans occupied a higher position, in Frankish eyes, than the Muslims (303). The ban on Jewish settlement was reimposed in 1229: see Shelomo

Dov Goitein, "Geniza Sources for the Crusader Period: A Survey," in *Outremer*, 320–21. On the "pecking order of confessions" in the Frankish East, see Peter W. Edbury, "Cultural Encounters in the Latin East: John of Jaffa and Philip of Novara," in *Cultural Encounters during the Crusades*, ed. Kurt Villads Jensen, Kirsi Salonen, and Helle Vogt (Odense, 2013), 235.

150. Title of Frankish kings: in 1115 and 1120, the formula used was *Latinitatis Iherosolimorum rex*: *UKJ*, 1:197, 226, nos. 64, 85. From 1125 onward, *rex Ierusalem Latinorum*: *UKJ*, 1:244, 248, 263, nos. 93, 94, 105, and passim; Mayer, "Latins, Muslims and Greeks," 175–76. Title of Alfonso VI: Angus MacKay and M'hammad Benaboud, "Alfonso VI of León and Castile, 'al-Imbratūr dhū-l-Millatayn,'" *Bulletin of Hispanic Studies* 56 (1979): 95–102, and Norman Roth's exchanges with them, *Bulletin of Hispanic Studies* 61 (1984): 165–69, 171–81, and 62 (1985): 179–84.

2. Everyday Life in the Kingdom of Jerusalem

1. For a critical edition and German translation, see Rudolf Simek, *Altnordische Kosmographie* (Berlin, 1990), 478–90; on Nikulás's biography, see 264–67. For his description of the Kingdom of Jerusalem, in Old Icelandic and in English translation, see B. Z. Kedar and Christian Westergård-Nielsen, "Icelanders in the Crusader Kingdom of Jerusalem: A Twelfth-Century Account," *Mediaeval Scandinavia* 11 (1978–79): 203–6.

2. *Cart St Sép*, 84, 310–12, 353–54, nos. 24, 159–60, app. 4; see also Denys Pringle, *Secular Buildings in the Crusader Kingdom of Jerusalem: An Archaeological Gazetteer* (Cambridge, 1997), 95; Pringle, *Churches*, 2:329–32.

3. See esp. *Cart St Sép*, 237–40, no. 117. Cf. Denys Pringle, "Magna Mahumeria (al-Bīra): The Archaeology of a Frankish New Town in Palestine," in *CS*, 147–68; Pringle, *Churches*, 1:161–65, 4:259–66.

4. For this corpus, see Reinhold Röhricht, *Bibliotheca geographica Palaestinae*, ed. David H. K. Amiran (London, 1989; originally published Berlin, 1890).

5. Simek, *Altnordische Kosmographie*, 481 (text), 486 (translation).

6. On Nikulás as the only source on the Varangian presence in Paphos, see George Hill, *A History of Cyprus*, 4 vols. (Cambridge, 1940–52), 1:266.

7. Roberto S. Lopez, "Sul Medioevo ed i medievisti," *Quaderni medievali* 2.4 (1977): 126.

8. William of Newburgh, *Historia rerum Anglicarum*, 3.19 (262); WT Cont. Lyon, 60. On the Frankish use of bells and its cultural significance, see Iris Shagrir, "Urban Soundscape: Defining Space and Community in Twelfth-Century Jerusalem," in *Communicating the Middle Ages: Essays in Honour of Sophia Menache*, ed. Iris Shagrir, B. Z. Kedar, and Michel Balard (Abingdon, 2018), 103–20; on a bell cast in Acre in 1266 by artisans from Messina and Pisa, see Geneviève Bresc-Bautier and Henri Bresc, "La cloche de Šibenik qui sonne pour la libération de la patrie (Acre, 1266)," in Montesano, *"Come l'orco della fiaba,"* 49–71.

9. See *King Harald's Saga*, trans. Magnus Magnusson and Hermann Pálsson (Harmondsworth, 1966), 63.

10. On Acre's chain, originally installed in 880, see B. Z. Kedar, "Prolegomena to a World History of Harbour and River Chains," in *Shipping, Trade and*

Crusade in the Medieval Mediterranean: Studies in Honour of John Pryor, ed. Ruthy Gertwagen and Elizabeth Jeffreys (Farnham, 2012), 8–9. The Franks conquered Acre in 1104; on the chain's role during the Egyptian attack of 1110, see AA 9.29 (802–3).

11. On Lordemer, see David Jacoby, "Three Notes on Crusader Acre," *Zeitschrift des Deutschen Palästina-Vereins* 109 (1993): 88–91; Jacoby, "Aspects of Everyday Life in Frankish Acre," *Crusades* 4 (2005): 82–83, quoting the Granadan traveler Ibn Jubayr and the Greek pilgrim Joannes Phocas. Cf. Holmes, "Life among the Europeans in Palestine," 6. The account of Joannes Phocas is now attributed to Joannes Doukas, who undertook a diplomatic mission to the Kingdom of Jerusalem in 1177: see Charis Messis, "Littérature, voyage et politique au XIIe siècle: L'*Ekphrasis des lieux saints* de Jean 'Phokas,'" *Byzantinoslavica* 69 (2011): 146–66.

12. The German pilgrim Theoderich describes the roofs of Jerusalem: "tecta non nostro more culminibus sublimata sed plano scemate habent equalia." Theoderich in *Peregrinationes tres: Saewulf, Iohannes Wirziburgensis, Theodericus*, ed. Robert B. C. Huygens, CCCM 139 (Turnhout, 1994), 146.

13. See, for instance, Adrian Boas, *Crusader Archaeology: The Material Culture of the Latin East* (Abingdon, 1999), 124, 132.

14. Ranieri of Pisa stayed in Jerusalem in the house of a *religiosa matrona*, Joachim of Fiore in that of a Christian widow, Ibn Jubayr—in Acre—in the house of a Christian woman, while Thietmar enjoyed the hospitality of a *muliercula graeca* near Karak and of a *vidua gallica* in Shobak: Rudolf Hiestand, "Ein Zimmer mit Blick auf das Meer: Einige wenig beachtete Aspekte der Pilgerreisen ins Hl. Land im 12. und 13. Jahrhundert," in *EWCS*, 3:139–64.

15. On the defrauding of pilgrims, see, for example, Rostagnus Cluniacensis (fl. 1202) in Paul Riant, *Exuviae sacrae Constantinopolitanae*, 2 vols. (Geneva, 1878–79), 1:130; JdV 73, 83 (292, 334); Burchard of Mount Sion, *Descriptio Terræ Sanctæ*, 190–92, c. 111. Discussed already by Prutz, *Kulturgeschichte*, 119.

16. The area was still vacant in the 1230s: Jacoby, "Aspects of Everyday Life," 78–79.

17. For a plan of such house, see fig. 1; also Adrian J. Boas, "The Acclimatisation of the Frankish Population to Life in the Latin East: Some Examples from Daily Life," in *Transferts*, 364–65.

18. On the high incidence of the name Petrus among Franks in 1130–89, particularly among burgesses, see Shagrir, *Naming Patterns*, 24, 26; on the frequency of the name Fāṭima among Muslim women, see Kedar and al-Hajjūj, "Muslim Villagers," 153–54.

19. On the prominence of textiles among the furnishings of the Eastern home, see *AMS*, 4:107–29.

20. Cf. *AMS*, 4:105. Apologies to my late friend Shelomo Dov Goitein for placing his assertion in Ragnvald's mouth.

21. *Laws of Early Iceland*, trans. Andrew Dennis et al., 2 vols. (Winnipeg, 2006; originally published 1980), 2:66; Jenny Jochens, *Women in Old Norse Society* (Ithaca, NY, 1995), 117.

22. Cf. "Lettres de Jacques de Vitry," 2.221–25 (567): "Erat autem prostibulis civitas passim repleta, nam quia meretrices carius quam alii conducebant, non

solum laici sed persone ecclesiastice et quidam regulares in publicis scortis hospitia sua per totam civitatem locabant."

23. The tomb in question is that of the prophet Ṣāliḥ: see *The Travels of Ibn Jubayr*, trans. Broadhurst, 318.

24. Early in the tenth century, when the Scandinavian Rus' made peace with Byzantium, they stipulated that baths should be prepared for their countrymen in Constantinople: *The Russian Primary Chronicle: Laurentian Text*, trans. Samuel Hazzard Cross and Olgerd P. Sherbowitz-Wetzor (Cambridge, MA, 1953), 64–65.

25. Jacques of Vitry mentions a knight of Acre "dum more orientalium iret ad publica balnea": *Die Exempla des Jacob von Vitry: Ein Beitrag zur Geschichte der Erzählungsliteratur des Mittelalters*, ed. Goswin Frenken (Munich, 1914), 133, no. 72. The *Pactum Warmundi* of 1124 granted the Venetians the right to construct a bathhouse in their quarter in Acre: *UKJ*, 3:1334, no. 764.

26. On nuisance caused by bathhouse furnaces, see *AMS*, 5:96.

27. A charter issued by King Baldwin III in 1153 lays down that this is the sum the Frankish settlers in the village of Casal Imbert, north of Acre, have to pay each time they use the local bathhouse: *UKJ*, 1:421, no. 228.

28. See plans in B. Z. Kedar, "Frankish Bathhouses: *Balneum* and *furnus*—A Functional Dyad?," in Shagrir, Kedar, and Balard, *Communicating the Middle Ages*, 127–28.

29. Cf. Usama ibn Munqidh, *The Book of Contemplation*, 149.

30. Howard Smithline, Edna J. Stern, and Eliezer Stern, "A Crusader-Period Bathhouse in ʿAkko (Acre)," *ʿAtiqot* 73 (2013): 84, 101.

31. See the reconstruction by Yael Gorin-Rosen, "Glass Finds from the Crusader-Period Bathhouse in ʿAkko (Acre)," *ʿAtiqot* 73 (2013): 111–13.

32. Cf. Philip of Tripoli, *Secretum Secretorum cum glossis et notulis: Tractatus brevis et utilis ad declarandum quedam obscure dicta Fratris Rogeri*, ed. Robert Steele (Oxford, 1920), 97; for an English translation of the Arabic original, see 210–11.

33. Al-Shayzarī, *The Book of the Market Inspector: Nihāyat al-Rutba fī Talab al-Hisba (The Utmost Authority in the Pursuit of Hisba) by Abd al-Rahmān b. Nasr al-Shayzarī*, trans. Ronald P. Buckley (Oxford, 1999), 106.

34. See the account of Archbishop Askil's beard attesting to his pilgrimage: Saxo Grammaticus, *Gesta Danorum*, 14.45 (1366).

35. *The Travels of Ibn Jubayr*, trans. Broadhurst, 320–21. I transposed the nuptial procession from Tyre to Acre.

36. For the carpet-covered stone bench and ebony inkstand, see *The Travels of Ibn Jubayr*, trans. Broadhurst, 317.

37. On the use of paper by notaries of Genoa, attested from 1154 onward, and by a Genoese notary in Tyre, see B. Z. Kedar, "The Use of Paper in the Frankish Levant: A Comparative Study," in *Crusading and Trading between East and West: Essays in Honour of David Jacoby*, ed. Sophia Menache, B. Z. Kedar, and Michel Balard (Abingdon, 2019), 6–8.

38. Boas, *Crusader Archaeology*, 76–83.

39. This type of sugar is listed in the customs tariffs of Frankish Acre: "Assises des Bourgeois," c. 242, no. 40 (2:176).

40. *Tahine* (present-day vernacular Arabic: *ṭaḥīne*) appears, too, in these tariffs: see below, note 170.

41. The story of the Muslim merchant who comes to Frankish Acre to sell linen from Upper Egypt and becomes infatuated with a Frankish woman is told in Night 894 in *The Book of the Thousand Nights and a Night*, trans. Richard F. Burton, 12 vols. (London, 1894–97), 7:99–104. For a different version, without the 1001-Nights frame, see Jean-Georges Varsy, "Anecdote des croisades," *Journal Asiatique* 4, no. 16 (1850): 75–92.

42. "Experimento itaque discunt, sed mirantur, quod tantam possit humane fragilitatis condicio sufferre penuriam, inconsueti uidelicet ardoris, intemperiei sitisque ariditatem propter aque potabilis raritatem, eo quod magno exigua stilla pretio mutuatur." "Historia de profectione Danorum in Hierosolymam," c. 25, in *Scriptores minores Historiae Danicae medii aevi*, ed. Martin C. Geertz, 2 vols. (Copenhagen, 1917–20), 2:489. Likewise, a Byzantine envoy who passed through Acre in 1161, complained: "when a man is shrivelled up by fiery thirst, / he finds no drink but ill-smelling and full of mire, / for which he has to pay much, too (oh, lack of wet!)." Konstantinos Manasses, *Hodoiporikon*, First Poem, vv. 324–26, ed. and trans. Willem J. Aerts, "A Byzantine Traveller to One of the Crusader States," in *EWCS*, 3:192–93.

43. See the animals listed in *Tractatus*, 128. On *lonca* meaning hyena, see Kedar, "A Second Incarnation," 83–84.

44. See, for instance, Vulgate, Ionas 1:3. For twelfth-century sources, see, for example, *Le "Liber" de Raymond d'Aguilers*, 142–43; Saewulf in *Peregrinationes tres*, 61, 63, 72, 75–76, Johann of Würzburg in *Peregrinationes tres*, 85, 108, 133; Fretellus, 39; *Cart St Sép*, 76, 82, 118, 266, nos. 20, 23, 42, 135, and passim.

45. "in Ioppen, que nunc uulgo Iaffa nuncupatur." Benincasa, *Vita sancti Rainerii*, 157–38, c. 59.

46. Denys Pringle, trans., *Saewulf, John of Würzburg, Theoderic: Three Pilgrimages to the Holy Land* (Turnhout, 2022), introduction, 12.

47. "Sur et Saegete, quae sunt Tyrus et Sydon." Saewulf in *Peregrinationes tres*, 75.

48. On the names of Sidon in Western sources, see Pringle, *Churches*, 2:317; *Gesta regis Henrici secundi*, ed. William Stubbs, RS 49, 2 vols. (London, 1867), 2:23.

49. *Gesta Francorum*, 86.

50. *Le "Liber" de Raymond d'Aguilers*, 129.

51. FC 1.25 (274).

52. Sur: AA 9.32 (680), 10.36 (750), 11.11 (782), 12.10 (838—six times), 12.17 (848), 12.32 (880—twice). "Tyrum quam nunc Sur vocant," "Sur que est Tyrus," etc.: AA 5.41 (394), 7.34 (538), 7.51 (560), 9.18 (640), 10.9 (726), 11.31 (804), 12.17 (850). Tyrus: AA 6.54 (474), 12.1 (826), 12.7 (832–34—twice).

53. In a Venetian act of 1157, drawn up in Tyre, both "in Tyro" and "in Suro" appear: *Documenti del commercio veneziano nei secoli XI–XIII*, ed. Raimondo Morozzo della Rocca and Antonino Lombardo, 2 vols. (Turin, 1940), 1:126–27. Similarly, the Genoese notary Manuele Loco, drawing up acts in Tyre on 14 July 1265, makes a merchant state in one act, "in galea . . . quam in *Tyro* armavi," and in the following one, "in galea . . . quam armavi in *Sur*": Laura Balletto,

"Fonti notarili genovesi del secondo Duecento per la Storia del Regno Latino di Gerusalemme," in *I comuni italiani*, 263–64, nos. 15a–b; see also 267, no. 17 (emphases added).

54. "Here lies messire Berthelme Chayn, knight of Tyre." Denys Pringle, "Crusader Inscriptions from Southern Lebanon," *Crusades* 3 (2004): 139–40; Cécile Treffort, "Les inscriptions latines et françaises des XIIe et XIIIe siècles découvertes à Tyr," in *Sources de l'histoire de Tyr: Textes de l'Antiquité et du Moyen Age*, ed. Pierre-Louis Gatier, Julien Aliquot, and Lévon Nordiguian (Beirut, 2011), 230–32, where the date of the knight's death is corrected to 1 January 1267.

55. AA 7.16 (506-8—thrice), 7.20 (514), 7.45 (552–54—twice), 9.13 (652), 10.4 (722), 10.5 (722), 10.8 (726—twice), 10.16 (732), 10. 18 (734), 10.25 (742—twice), 10. 31 (748), 10. 54 (768—twice), 10.55 (768), 10.56 (770), 11.12 (782), 12.9 (838), 12.30 (874), 12.31 (874).

56. If, as present-day consensus has it, Albert gathered his information from returning crusaders, he may not have comprehended that the Tabaria they were mentioning was identical with the Tiberias of the New Testament. This is, however, hardly possible, because he writes: "Arx autem hec Tabaria sita est iuxta lacum quem appellant mare Tyberiadis": AA 7.16 (508). I intend to reexamine the consensus view; in the meantime, see Claude Cahen, "A propos d'Albert d'Aix et de Richard le Pèlerin," *Le Moyen Age* 96 (1990): 31–33.

57. See, for example, WT OF, index, s.v. Saiete, Sur, Tabarie ou Tabarié; *Ernoul*, index, s.v. Sidon, Saiete; Tiberias, Tabarie; Tyre, Sur; John of Ibelin, *Le Livre des Assises*, 591–616, cc. 226–39.

58. Cyril Aslanov, *Le français au Levant, jadis et naguère: A la recherche d'une langue perdue* (Paris, 2006), 83–89; Aslanov, "The Historical Formation of a Macro-ecology: The Case of the Levant," in *Linguistic Ecology and Language Contact*, ed. Ralph Ludwig, Peter Mühlhäusler, and Steve Pagel (Cambridge, 2019), 137.

59. *UKJ*, 1:272, no. 111; *Cart St Sép*, 309, no. 158.

60. For Aramaic Ṭūr Karma that was to become in Arabic Ṭūlkarm, see *UKJ*, 1:369, no. 184; Félix-Marie Abel, "La liste de donations de Baïbars en Palestine d'après la charte de 663H (1265)," *Journal of the Palestine Oriental Society* 19 (1939–40): 40. For further instances, see Meron Benvenisti, "Bovaria-Babriyya: A Frankish Residue on the Map of Palestine," in *Outremer*, 131; Ellenblum, *Frankish Rural Settlement*, 73–74. The village east of Lydda later known in Arabic as Barfīliyyā appears in Latin documents of 1136–71 as Porphiria or Porfilia: *Cart St Sép*, 82, 118, 125, 154, 264, 309, nos. 23, 42, 45, 61, 135, 158. The last document mentions the church "built or to be built" in the village.

61. B. Z. Kedar and Denys Pringle, "La Fève: A Crusader Castle in the Jezreel Valley," *Israel Exploration Journal* 35 (1985): 164–79; Aslanov, *Le français au Levant*, 85. Aslanov points also to the translation of the Arabic hydronym Nahr al-Kalb as Fluvium Canis / Fleuve du Chien, and to the reference to Hebron as St. Abraham, possibly influenced by the town's Arabic name al-Khalīl (the Friend [of God], i.e., Abraham).

62. WT 15.21 (703), 20.26 (950), 22.5 (1012), 22.29 (1055). In its turn, the Arabic *Karak* originates in the Aramaic *Karka* (fortress): Charles Clermont-Ganneau, "Les trois Karak de Syrie," in Clermont-Ganneau, *Recueil d'archéologie*

orientale, vol. 4 (Paris, 1901), 60–66. For examples in the County of Tripoli, see Lewis, "Medieval Diglossia."

63. WT 14.22 (660–61). For a discussion of the location's names, and for the probability that it was known also as *al-Sabʿ* and therefore identified with Beersheba, see Moshe Sharon, "Bayt Jibrīn," in *Corpus inscriptionum arabicarum Palaestinae*, ed. Sharon, 2:109–20.

64. See *The Works of Ibn Wāḍih al-Yaʿqūbī*, trans. Matthew S. Gordon et al., 3 vols. (Leiden, 2018), 1:166; al-Muqaddasī, *The Best Divisions for Knowledge of the Regions*, trans. Anthony Collins (Reading, 1994), 157. Also Guy Le Strange, *Palestine under the Moslems* (London, 1890), 412–13.

65. WT 20.19 (937). For reservations about this etymology, see Pringle, *Churches*, 1:194.

66. On the question of William's knowledge of literary Arabic, see below, chaps. 5 and 6. Kevin Lewis argues persuasively that the Franks lacked knowledge of written Arabic yet acquired some familiarity with the spoken language: Lewis, "Medieval Diglossia."

67. WT 22.17 in BAV, Vat. lat. 2002, fol. 221rb: "Salahadinus . . . ad eum locum accessit qui dicitur lingua eorum ras elme. quod interpretatur caput aque."

68. Raseline: in *Gesta Dei per Francos*, ed. Jacques Bongars (Hanau, 1611), 1027, and in *RHC Oc*, 1:1093. Ras el Ine: WT 22.17 (1030), ed. Huygens (see also 2, n. 9, for Huygens's attempt to correct William, maintaining that *Ine* should have been translated as *Fontis* and not as *Aque*). Yet BAV, Vat. lat. 2002, on which Huygens based his edition, has indisputably: "ras elme" (see previous note). See also "et castra metati sunt in loco qui dicitur Rasseleme, quod interpretatur capud aque": *Libellus*, 112. For the location of Rās al-Māʾ, see map 20 in Prawer, *Histoire*, 1:603.

69. Prawer, *The Latin Kingdom*, 521–22; Laura Minervini, "Les emprunts arabes et grecs dans le lexique français d'Orient (XIIIe–XIVe siècles)," *Revue de linguistique romane* 76 (2012): 99–198 (in my count I skipped the derivations from Arabic attested solely for Cyprus).

70. Kedar, "Latins and Oriental Christians in the Frankish Levant," 216. On Persian *rawshan* as "window balcony," see *AMS*, 4:61. For a different explanation, see Cyril Aslanov, *Evidence of Francophony in Mediaeval Levant: Decipherment and Interpretation—MS Paris BnF copte 43* (Jerusalem, 2006), 101–2, 162–63.

71. *La Bible d'Acre, Genèse et Exode*, ed. Pierre Nobel (Besançon, 2006), 37, 64, 142; cf. Minervini, "Les emprunts arabes," 124.

72. Pierre Nobel, "Écrire dans le Royame franc: La scripta de deux manuscrits copiés à Acre au XIIIe siècle," in *Variations linguistiques: Koinè, dialectes, français régionaux*, ed. Pierre Nobel (Besançon, 2003), 41.

73. Prawer was aware of this possibility; see *The Latin Kingdom*, 522.

74. For *arabismos* in modern parlance, see the list in Federico Corriente, *Dictionary of Arabic and Allied Loanwords: Spanish, Portuguese, Catalan, Galician and Kindred Dialects* (Leiden, 2008), 1–480, which, however, contains modern loans, too.

75. Cf. the lists in Minervini, "Les emprunts arabes," 175, and Eero K. Neuvonen, *Los arabismos del español en el siglo XIII* (Helsinki, 1941), 258–59.

76. Neuvonen, *Los arabismos del español*, 301.

77. Aslanov, *Evidence of Francophony*, 133–52; Aslanov, *Le français au Levant*, 43–76; Aslanov, "The Historical Formation of a Macro-ecology," 132–34. See Jean Richard's enthusiastic review in *Comptes rendus des séances de l'Académie des Inscriptions et Belles-Lettres* 151, no. 1 (2007): 281–82.

78. Alan Murray, "The Origins of the Frankish Nobility of the Kingdom of Jerusalem, 1100–1118," *Mediterranean Historical Review* 4 (1989): 281–300.

79. Cf. Mayer, "Angevins *versus* Normans"; Mayer, "Einwanderer in der Kanzlei," 25–26; Rudolf Hiestand, "Der lateinische Klerus der Kreuzfahrerstaaten: Geographische Herkunft und politische Rolle," in *Kreuzfahrerstaaten*, 43–68; Bernard Hamilton, "King Consorts of Jerusalem and Their Entourages from the West from 1186 to 1250," in *Kreuzfahrerstaaten*, 13–24.

80. According to a recent analysis of Frankish toponymic surnames, 44 percent of the Franks who originated in present-day France came from the country's central part, 32 percent from the south, and 26 percent from the north. The predominance of central France correlates with the prevalence of coins from that region found in controlled excavations: Robert Kool, "Finding French Deniers in the Latin Kingdom of Jerusalem: The Archaeological and Cultural Perspective," in *Transferts*, 126–28.

81. Aslanov, *Evidence of Francophony*, 162–79; Aslanov, *Le français au Levant*, 77–108. On the impact of Occitan, Arabic, and esp. the langue d'oïl, see also Nobel, "Écrire dans le Royame franc," 35–47.

82. *La Rectorique de Cyceron tradotta da Jean d'Antioche: Edizione e glossario*, ed. Elisa Guadagnini (Pisa, 2009). 303. Johan may have had in mind native Arabic speakers who learned the French vernacular. On the p-to-b shift, see Rubin, *Learning in a Crusader City*, 79.

83. See the glossary in *Cronaca del Templare di Tiro (1243–1314): La caduta degli Stati Crociati nel racconto di un testimone oculare*, ed. Laura Minervini (Naples, 2000), 389–90, 415, 428; Minervini, "Gli orientalismi nel francese d'Oltremare," in *Sprachkontakte in der Romania: Zum 75. Geburtstag von Gustav Ineichen*, ed. Volker Noll and Sylvia Thiele (Tübingen, 2004), 123; Aslanov, *Le français au Levant*, 91.

84. For the characterization of the French spoken in the Kingdom of Jerusalem as "une variété particulière du français médiéval," see Laura Minervini, "Le français dans l'Orient latin: Eléments pour la caractérisation d'une *scripta* du Levant," *Revue de linguistique romane* 74 (2010): 119, 140. More recently she characterized it as "an Old French dialect used in the Latin East": Laura Minervini, "What We Know and Don't Yet Know about Outremer French," in *The French of Outremer*, 15. Minervini believes (21–22) that this dialect bore especially the imprint of western French dialects, but provides also examples of Walloon and Lotharingian impact.

85. Hartwig Derenbourg, "Note sur quelques mots de la langue des Francs au douzième siècle d'après le texte arabe de l'autobiographie d'Ousâma ibn Mounkidh," in *Mélanges Renier: Recueil de travaux publiés par l'Ècole pratique des hautes études en mémoire de son président Léon Renier* (Paris, 1887), 462–64. For the hypothesis that Usāma depended on interpreters, see Stefan Wild, "Open Questions, New Light: Usama Ibn Munqidh's Account of His Battles against Muslims and Franks," in *The Frankish Wars and Their Influence on Palestine*, ed. Khalil

Athamina and Roger Heacock (Birzeit, 1994), 17–19. For the view that Usāma had a working knowledge of the Frankish dialect, see Bogdan C. Smarandache, "Re-Examining Usama ibn Munqidh's Knowledge of 'Frankish': A Case Study of Medieval Bilingualism during the Crusades," *Medieval Globe* 3 (2017): 61–70.

86. Shelomo Dov Goitein, *Palestinian Jewry in Early Islamic and Crusader Times in the Light of the Geniza Documents*, ed. Joseph Hacker (Jerusalem, 1980), 259–60 (introduction), 266 (edition and modern Hebrew translation); Goitein, "Geniza Sources for the Crusader Period," 318.

87. B. Z. Kedar, "Religion in Catholic-Muslim Correspondence and Treaties," in *Diplomatics in the Eastern Mediterranean, 1000–1500. Aspects of Cross-Cultural Communication*, ed. Alexander D. Beihammer, Maria G. Parani, and Christopher D. Schabel (Leiden, 2008), 418–19.

88. Cedric Norman Johns, *Guide to 'Atlit: The Crusader Castle, Town and Surroundings* (Jerusalem, 1947), 94–98, repr. in Johns, *Pilgrims' Castle ('Atlit), David's Tower (Jerusalem) and Qal'at ar-Rabad ('Ajlun): Three Middle Eastern Castles from the Time of the Crusades*, ed. Denys Pringle (Aldershot, 1997), Study I, 94–98; Johns, "Excavations at Pilgrims' Castle ('Atlit): The Faubourg and Its Defences," Study II in Johns, *Pilgrims' Castle ('Atlit)*, ed. Pringle, 111–13; also, François Gilet, "La Tour de Détroit et les débuts de l'ordre du Temple," in *D'Orient en Occident*, 311–16.

89. However, attention has been drawn to the Arabic name's probable existence before the crusader conquest: Milka Levy-Rubin, *The "Continuatio" of the Samaritan Chronicle of Abū l-Fath al-Sāmirī al-Danafī* (Princeton, NJ, 2002), 71 with n. 202, 89, and Arabic text, 140, 155.

90. Cahen, *Orient et Occident*, 170; Moshe Sharon, "Vassal and Faṣal: The Evidence of the Farkhah Inscription from 608/1210," *Crusades* 4 (2005): 117–30; B. Z. Kedar and Cyril Aslanov, "Problems in the Study of Trans-Cultural Borrowing in the Frankish Levant," in *Hybride Kulturen im mittelalterlichen Europa*, ed. Michael Borgolte and Bernd Schneidmüller (Berlin, 2010), 278–79.

91. Balász Major, "*Anklīs*—A Possible Trace of European Presence in the Medieval Syrian Vocabulary," in *More Modoque: Die Wurzeln der europäischen Kultur und deren Rezeption im Orient und Okzident. Festschrift für Miklós Maróth zum siebzigsten Geburtstag*, ed. Pál Fodor et al. (Budapest, 2013), 377–84.

92. Johns, "Excavations at Pilgrims' Castle," 128.

93. Benvenisti, "Bovaria-Babriyya," 132–52.

94. "[Gentiles] qui quoniam sapientiores filiis lucis in generatione sua sunt, multa excogitant, que nostrates non noverunt, nisi forte ab eis didicerint." Arnold of Lübeck, *Chronica Slavorum*, 5.27, ed. Johann Martin Lappenberg, MGH SS 21:206–7. Cf. Luke 16:8. On the use of carrier pigeons, see Prutz, *Kulturgeschichte*, 415, 565; Holmes, "Life among the Europeans in Palestine," 31–32; Susan B. Edgington, "The Doves of War: The Part Played by Carrier Pigeons in the Crusades," in *Autour*, 167–75; Dietrich Lohrmann, "Echanges techniques entre Orient et Occident au temps des Croisades," in *Occident et Proche-Orient*, 117, 130–33.

95. For a detailed, annotated discussion, see Kedar, "Frankish Bathhouses," 121–40.

96. For the bath in the palace of Antioch, see WT 15.3 (677), 18.25 (848); Krijnie N. Ciggaar, "Adaptation to Oriental Life by Rulers in and around

Antioch: Examples and Exempla," in *EWMEM*, 263–68. For the other places, see Kedar, "Frankish Bathhouses," 122.

97. For some use of—or acquaintance with—gold in western European areas close to the Islamicate realm, see Oren Tal, Robert Kool, and Issa Baidoun, "A Hoard Twice Buried? Fatimid Gold from Thirteenth Century Crusader Arsur (Apollonia—Arsuf)," *Numismatic Chronicle* 173 (2013): 272 n. 27.

98. This predominance has been confirmed by excavation finds of numerous hoards of high-grade Fatimid gold dīnārs: Robert Kool, Issa Baidoun, and Jacob Sharvit, "The Fatimid Gold Treasure from Caesarea Maritima Harbor (2015): Preliminary Results," in *5th Simone Assemani Symposium on Islamic Coins: Rome, 29–30 September 2017*, ed. Bruno Callegher and Arianna D'Ottone Rambach, Polymnia: Numismatica antica e medievale, Studi 12 (Trieste, 2018), 129–30. In Frankish documentation, the term "bezant" appears as early as 1102–3, evidently referring to Fatimid gold coins: *Cart St Sép*, 73, no. 19.

99. First appearance in the Kingdom of Jerusalem: in the *Pactum Warmundi* of 1124: see *UKJ*, 3:1334, no. 764, and Mayer's observation on 1332; this requires the modification of statements like that by Prawer, *The Latin Kingdom*, 385. Venetian references to genuine Fatimid dīnārs: *Documenti del commercio veneziano*, 1:77 (a. 1139), 308 (a. 1179), nos. 74, 312.

100. "bizancios saracenatos bonos auri de rege illius terrae de pesa secundum consuetudinem illius terrae." *Documenti del commercio veneziano*, 1:84, no. 81; see Michael L. Bates and D. M. Metcalf, "Crusader Coinage with Arabic Inscriptions," in *Crusades*, ed. Setton, 6:441–42. On the imitation gold coins minted in the County of Tripoli, see the observations by Lewis, "Medieval Diglossia," 141–44.

101. *Documenti del commercio veneziano*, 1:152 (a. 1161), 164 (a. 1165), 182 (a. 1167), 306–7 (a. 1179), 369 (a. 1190), 402–3 (a. 1192), 2:40 (a. 1208), 48 (a. 1209), 54 (a. 1209), 69–70 (a. 1211), nos. 154, 167, 182, 309–10, 376, 411–12, 500, 509, 514, 529.

102. For data on the rates of exchange of the Frankish imitation dīnār and its buying power, see Adrian J. Boas, *Domestic Settings: Sources on Domestic Architecture and Day-to-Day Activities in the Crusader States* (Leiden, 2010), 223–24, 232–39.

103. Cahen (*Orient et Occident*, 142) pointed out that, in the twelfth century, the only Europeans to strike gold coins were the Franks and the Normans of Sicily, both in contact with the realm of Islam. Also Sébastien Gasc, "Les monnayages méditerranéens," in *Transferts*, 135–37.

104. Robert Kool, "Between *Moneta* and *Sikka*: Minters and Mints in the Frankish East (1099–1291)," in *EO*, 2:197–215.

105. On the widespread use of Byzantine *nomismata* in northern Syria, see Stefan Heidemann, *Die Renaissance der Städte in Nordsyrien und Nordmesopotamien* (Leiden, 2002), 383–87.

106. See, for example, the coins and inscriptions reproduced in Henry Lavoix, *Monnaies à légendes arabes frappées en Syrie par les Croisés* (Paris, 1877), 34–39; Gasc, "Les monnayages méditerranéens," 139.

107. For silver deniers, see John Porteous, "Crusader Coinage with Greek or Latin Inscriptions," in *Crusades*, ed. Setton, 6:369–74. (The Fatimid caliphate used some petty silver currencies. Coin finds attest to the circulation of dirham

cuttings that served for small day-to-day transactions: Kool, Baidoun, and Sharvit, "The Fatimid Gold Treasure from Caesarea," 129–30.) For comparison of French and Jerusalemite *deniers*, see Alan M. Stahl, "The *Denier* Outremer," in *The French of Outremer*, 33–34. For evidence on the widespread use of petty cash in new Frankish villages, see Robert Kool, "Coin Circulation in the *villeneuves* of the Latin Kingdom of Jerusalem: The Cases of Parva Mahumeria and Bethgibelin," in *Archaeology and the Crusades*, ed. Peter Edbury and Sophia Kalopissi-Verti (Athens, 2007), 133–56. On French *deniers* constituting only 9 percent of coin finds in a very large number of controlled excavations, see Kool, "Finding French Deniers," 120–25. Some Frankish silver coins appear to have percolated to Muslim territory: al-Shayzarī, *The Book of the Market Inspector*, 96; see Robert Irwin, "The Supply of Money and the Direction of Trade in Thirteenth-Century Syria," in *Coinage in the Latin East*, ed. Peter W. Edbury and D. M. Metcalf, BAR International Series 77 (Oxford, 1980), 93–94.

108. Bates and Metcalf, "Crusader Coinage," 429–30 with n. 25; Sharon, "Vassal and Faṣal," 122–24. Back in 1877, Lavoix drew attention to the statement of al-Qazwīnī (d. 1283) that the dīnārs of Tyre served the inhabitants of Syria and Iraq: Lavoix, *Monnaies*, 33. On a 2:3 exchange rate of Egyptian dīnārs to Frankish imitations, see Kool, "Finding French Deniers," 110.

109. For the argument that the Frankish imitations hurt the international reputation of the Fatimid gold currency, see Andrew S. Ehrenkreutz, "Arabic *Dīnārs* Struck by the Crusaders: A Case of Ignorance or of Economic Subversion?," *Journal of the Economic and Social History of the Orient* 7 (1964): 167–82; Ehrenkreutz, "Crusader Imitation *Dīnārs*—Once Again," in Curiel and Gyselen, *Itinéraires d'Orient*, 111–17. For a comparison between the coinages of Norman Sicily and the Frankish East, see D. Michael Metcalf, "Islamic, Byzantine and Latin Influences in the Iconography of Crusader Coins and Seals," in *EWCS*, 2:163–75.

110. Al-Shayzarī, *The Book of the Market Inspector*, 94; see Irwin, "The Supply of Money," 91–92.

111. Robert Kool, Nikolaus Schindel, and Issa Baidoun, "A New Assemblage of Cut Gold Fragments from the Crusader Period," *Israel Numismatic Research* 14 (2019), 169–92.

112. Robert Kool, "Lead Token Money in the Kingdom of Jerusalem," *Numismatic Chronicle* 173 (2013): 299–339; Kool, "'Coins, Purses and Pigs': The Medieval Coins of Vadum Iacob," in *The Excavation of the Templar Fortress at Jacob's Ford (1993–2009): In Memory of Professor Ronnie Ellenblum*, ed. Kate Raphael, Annual of the Nelson Glueck School of Biblical Archaeology 13 (Jerusalem, 2023), 298–300.

113. On the Ayyubid introduction of silver dirhams, see Stefan Heidemann, "Economic Growth and Currency in Ayyūbid Palestine," in *Ayyubid Jerusalem: The Holy City in Context, 1187–1250*, ed. Robert Hillenbrand and Sylvia Auld (London, 2009), 284, 289, 291.

114. On the Frankish imitation silver issues, see Bates and Metcalf, "Crusader Coinage," 435–36, 457–73.

115. D. Michael Metcalf, Robert Kool, and Ariel Berman, "Coins from the Excavations at 'Atlit (Pilgrims' Castle) and Its *Faubourg*," *'Atiqot* 37 (1999), *107;

Kool, "Coin Circulation," 147; Robert Kool and Uzi ʿAd, "A Late Twelfth-Century Silver Purse Hoard from Ibelin," *Israel Numismatic Research* 11 (2016): 171.

116. On the circulation in Ayyubid Palestine, see Kool, "Coin Circulation," 147–49, 156. The Fayyūm hoard is said to have consisted of about five thousand coins, yet most were melted down. The residual 346 coins, all of them silver dirhams, were discussed by Paul Balog, "La trouvaille de Fayoum: Dirhems ayoubites, du premier roi mamelouk Aybek et d'imitation arabe des Croisés," *Bulletin de l'Institut d'Egypte* 34 (1951–52): 17–55.

117. Eudes's letter to Innocent IV has not survived. It is mentioned in the pope's answer: *Les registres d'Innocent IV*, ed. Elie Berger, 4 vols (Paris, 1881–1921), 3:176, no. 6336. On Louis IX's probable role, see Lavoix, *Monnaies*, 60–62; Gustave Schlumberger, *Numismatique de l'Orient latin* (Paris, 1878), 142.

118. Muslim counterparts to this move were (a) the Sālimī dīnār struck in 1401 by Yalbughā al-Sālimī, major-domo of the Mamluk Sultan Faraj, that aimed at replacing the "figured" ducat and florin; and (b) the Ashrafī dīnār introduced in 1425 to replace the "coinage of the Firanj bearing the insignia of their infidelity, hence not permitted by Muslim religious law." Yet Italian gold coins continued to be in use in Cairo at least until 1457: see William Popper, *Egypt and Syria under the Circassian Sultans, 1382–1468 A.D.: Systematic Notes to Ibn Taghri Birdi's Chronicles of Egypt* (Berkeley, 1957), 45–48.

119. Translation by Bates and Metcalf, "Crusader Coinage," 447.

120. Balog, "La trouvaille de Fayoum," 17–19, 45–48; the author comments that the Christian character of these coins was progressively diluted. Similarly, Metcalf states that the coins with conspicuous crosses were rejected by the Franks' Muslim neighbors, and therefore in 1253 the Acre mint "reverted to more deceptive imitations": D. Michael Metcalf, *Coinage of the Crusades and the Latin East in the Ashmolean Museum, Oxford*, 2nd ed. (London, 1995), 103. On the problems the Frankish imitation dirhams caused in Damascene markets in 1259/60, see Irwin, "The Supply of Money," 94–96.

121. "Ceste vile [Acre] vaut a sun segnur chescun an cinquante mile livres d'argent." "Légendes de l'itinéraire de Londres à Jérusalem," in *Itinéraires á Jérusalem et descriptions de la Terre Sainte rédigés en français aux XIe, XIIe, & XIIIe siècles*, ed. Henri Michelant and Gaston Raynaud (Geneva, 1882), 137.

122. On the English Crown's annual cash income, see David A. Carpenter, *The Struggle for Mastery: Britain 1066–1284* (London, 2004), 312. For an appraisal by a crusade historian, see Tyerman, *God's War*, 717, 970 n. 9.

123. "Ceste cité . . . vaut chascun iur au seignur de la vile cinc cenz livre de esterlings." "Légendes de l'itinéraire de Londres à Jérusalem," 127.

124. On the minting of the *januinus*, see Robert S. Lopez, "Back to Gold, 1252," *Economic History Review*, n.s. 9.2 (1956): 219–40; on Sicilian and Frankish coinage as possible models for Genoa's gold coin, see 226–28.

125. For a detailed, annotated discussion, see Kedar, "The Use of Paper in the Frankish Levant."

126. Boas, *Domestic Settings*, 243; for a description of the house in question, see 271–74. Boas's conclusion ties in with the analysis of the no longer extant palace hall in Beirut, visited in 1211 by the German envoy Wilbrand of Oldenburg: see Lucy-Anne Hunt, "John of Ibelin's Audience Hall in

Beirut: A Crusader Palace Building between Byzantine and Islamic Art in Its Mediterranean Context," in *The Emperor's House: Palaces from Augustus to the Age of Absolutism*, ed. Michael Featherstone et al. (Boston, 2015), 257–91.

127. "Wilbrand of Oldenburg's Journey to Syria, Lesser Armenia, Cyprus and the Holy Land (1211–1212): A New Edition," ed. Denys Pringle, *Crusades* 11 (2012): 123.

128. Boas, *Domestic Settings*, 79–81, 244–45. For a description of a Genoese palazzo in Acre, see 267–70, with fig. 67. On Western-type piazzas in Acre's Genoese and Venetian quarters, see Tomasz Borowski, "Public Squares in the Latin East: Designing Piazzas in New and Old Urban Centres," in *EO*, 1:96–100.

129. Danny Sion, Eliezer Stern, and Piers D. Mitchell, "Water Installation in Crusader Acre," in *'Akko III, the 1991–1998 Excavations: The Late Periods*, ed. Eliezer Stern, Danny Syon, and Ayelet Tatcher (in press); George T. Scanlon, "Housing and Sanitation: Some Aspects of Medieval Islamic Public Services," in *The Islamic City*, ed. Albert Habib Hourani and Samuel M. Stern (Oxford, 1970), 187–94.

130. Boas, *Domestic Settings*, 90–93, 321–32. On the street-village unearthed in 2016 at al-Rām, north of Jerusalem, see Boas, "The Acclimatisation of the Frankish Population," 366. On chimneys, see Boas, *Domestic Settings*, 164–71; "The Acclimatisation," 380–82.

131. See the plan of Parva Mahumeria (al-Qubayba) in Pringle, *Secular Buildings*, 86, and the plan of the village excavated northwest of Jerusalem in Adrian J. Boas, "A Recently Discovered Frankish Village at Ramot Allon, Jerusalem," in *Autour*, 589.

132. For a brief discussion of the kingdom's indigenous villages, see Boas, *Domestic Settings*, 203–6.

133. Boas, *Domestic Settings*, 162.

134. *Ernoul*, 179.

135. See, for example, the Arsenal Bible, fol. 364v, upper right scene, available at Gallica: https://gallica.bnf.fr/ark:/12148/btv1b550071673/f732.image.r=arsenal%20bible.

136. *Tractatus*, 125–26.

137. Joinville, *Vie de saint Louis*, ed. and trans. Jacques Monfrin, 6th ed. (Paris, 2020), 444, §504.

138. Hannah Rose Buckingham, "Identity and Archaeology in Daily Life: The Material Culture of the Crusader States" (PhD diss., Cardiff University, 2016), 86.

139. On Theoderich's pilgrimage having taken place between 1171 and 1174, see Pringle, *Saewulf, John of Würzburg, Theoderic*, 28–30. For his description of the Hospital, see Theoderich in *Peregrinationes tres*, 157–58.

140. B. Z. Kedar, ed., "A Twelfth-Century Description of the Jerusalem Hospital," in Kedar, *Franks, Muslims*, Study X, 19, 24.

141. *Papsturkunden für Templer und Johanniter*, ed. Rudolf Hiestand (Göttingen, 1984), 262–63, no. 45.

142. Malcolm C. Lyons and D. E. P. Jackson, *Saladin: The Politics of the Holy War* (Cambridge, 1982), 274–75. Usāma's story about a Frank of Nablus who comes home and discovers a man in bed with his wife—*The Book of Contemplation*, 148—does not prove that the Franks used bedsteads, because the term Usāma

uses, *firāsh*, refers to a "furnishing on which one rested in stretched-out position" (*AMS*, 4:108–9), yet that lacked a frame (Elon Harvey, pers. comm.).

143. *Le Livre au Roi*, 197, c. 21.

144. Joinville, *Vie de saint Louis*, 386, 388, 444, §§410, 416, 502.

145. Guillaume de St-Pathus, *Vie de Saint Louis*, ed. Henri-François Delaborde (Paris, 1899), 46–47.

146. Filippo da Novara, *Guerra di Federico II in Oriente (1223–1242)*, ed. Silvio Melani (Naples, 1994), 110, c. 46. For the dates, see Philip of Novara, *Le Livre de Forme de Plait*, ed. and trans. Peter W. Edbury (Nicosia, 2009), 15–16, 322 n. 325.

147. See Boas, *Domestic Settings*, 164 n. 17. On the issue of the extent to which material culture is realistically depicted in religious iconography, see Maria G. Parani, *Reconstructing the Reality of Images* (Leiden, 2003), esp. 1–5, 118, 218–23; also Sharon E. J. Gerstel, "Art and Identity in the Medieval Morea," in *The Crusades from the Perspective of Byzantium and the Muslim World*, ed. Angeliki E. Laiou and Roy Parviz Mottahedeh (Washington, DC, 2001), 276–78.

148. *AMS*, 4:107–29, 314–17.

149. For a trousseau list of Tyre, 1079, that includes three cushions and a pair of mats, together worth one dīnār, see Mordechai Akiva Friedman, *Jewish Marriage in Palestine*, 2 vols. (Tel Aviv, 1980–81), 2:132–34 (text), 134–36 (translation). The one Frankish trousseau I have come across—that of Melisende of Tripoli in 1161: WT 18.31 (856)—is irrelevant for the present purpose.

150. For a similar assumption, see Hadia Dajani-Shakeel, "Natives and Franks in Palestine: Perceptions and Interactions," in *Conversion and Continuity: Indigenous Christian Communities in Islamic Lands, Eighth to Eighteenth Centuries*, ed. Michael Gervers and Ramzi Jibran Bikhazi (Toronto, 1990), 175.

151. For an overview, see Edna J. Stern, "Franks, Locals and Merchants: Ceramic Production in the Latin East," in *EO*, 2:156–80.

152. Edna J. Stern, *'Akko I, the 1991–1998 Excavations: The Crusader Period Pottery*, Part 1: *Text* (Jerusalem, 2012), 40–47; Edna J. Stern, Sylvie Yona Waksman, and Anastasia Shapiro, "The Impact of the Crusades on Ceramic Production and Use in the Southern Levant: Continuity or Change?," in *Multidisciplinary Approaches to Food and Foodways in the Medieval Eastern Mediterranean*, ed. Sylvie Yona Waksman (Lyon, 2020), 99–100. Back in 1986, long before Beirut's role came to be known, Denys Pringle wrote of these glazed cooking vessels that they appear to "represent an indigenous Palestinian type that was adopted by the Franks," and added that "such a conclusion is not only unexpected, but also of some interest in terms of economic and cultural history": Denys Pringle, "Pottery as Evidence for Trade in the Crusader States," in *I comuni italiani*, 465. On the export of red and white Beirut glasses to Egypt (and thence to Aden) in the 1130s, see S. D. Goitein and Mordechai Akiva Friedman, *India Traders of the Middle Ages: Documents from the Cairo Geniza* (Leiden, 2008), 429.

153. Tasha Vorderstrasse, *Al-Mina: A Port of Antioch from Late Antiquity to the End of the Ottomans* (Leiden, 2005), 118–22; Stern, *'Akko I*, Part 1: *Text*, 55–58, Part 2: *Plates*, 72–86.

154. Stern, *'Akko I*, Part 1: *Text*, 58–91. On local and imported pottery at Jaffa, see Katherine S. Burke and Edna J. Stern, "Crusader Pottery," in *Excavations at the Ottoman Military Compound in Jaffa, 2007, 2009*, ed. Yoav Arbel (Münster,

2021), 75–126. On pottery produced in Tiberias, and on imported ware from Beirut and the Aegean, see Edna J. Stern, "Tiberias, Aviv Hotel: Domestic and Industrial Pottery from the Abbasid and Crusader Periods," *'Atiqot* 92 (2018): 199–206.

155. Denys Pringle, "Some More Proto-Maiolica from 'Athlit (Pilgrims' Castle) and a Discussion of Its Distribution in the Levant," *Levant* 14 (1982): 104–17.

156. Stern, *'Akko I*, Part 1: *Text*, 52–54.

157. "poterie c'on aporte de Paienime en Acre": "Assises des Bourgeois," c. 243, no. 7 (2:179); cf. Pringle, "Pottery as Evidence for Trade," 453.

158. Stern, *'Akko I*, Part 1: *Text*, 34–38; Stern, Waksman, and Shapiro, "The Impact of the Crusades," 101–3.

159. AA 5.37 (388–89) (my translation differs slightly); for a less detailed account, see FC 1.33 (329–30). In 1111 the Genoese, having won a naval battle off Damietta, took possession of four thousand cases of sugar laden on the Egyptian ships: Anne-Marie Eddé, "Francs et musulmans de Syrie au début du XIIe siècle d'après l'historien Ibn Abī Tayyi'," in *Dei gesta per Francos: Etudes sur les croisades dédiées à Jean Richard*, ed. Michel Balard, B. Z. Kedar, and Jonathan Riley-Smith (Aldershot, 2001), 168. On the name by which the product came to be known by Westerners, see Bruno Laurioux, "Quelques remarques sur la découverte du sucre par les premiers croisés d'Orient," in *Chemins d'outre-mer: Etudes sur la Mediterranée médiévale offertes à Michel Balard*, ed. Damien Coulon et al., 2 vols. (Paris, 2004), 2:534–36.

160. AA 10.36 (752).

161. Charter edited by Jean Richard in his "Le chartrier de Sainte-Marie-Latine et l'établissement de Raymond de Saint-Gilles à Mont-Pèlerin," in *Mélanges d'histoire du Moyen Age dédiés à la mémoire de Louis Halphen* (Paris, 1951), 612; for the possibility that this charter, and an earlier one of 1103, refer to a mill at which the reeds were crushed, see 610 n. 1, 611 n. 1.

162. *RRR*, *s.v.* sugar.

163. Hamdan Taha, "The Sugarcane Industry in Jericho, Jordan Valley," in *The Origins of the Sugar Industry and the Transmission of Ancient Greek and Medieval Arab Science and Technology from the Near East to Europe*, ed. Konstantinos D. Politis (Athens, 2015), 51–77; Edna J. Stern et al., "Sugar Production in the 'Akko Plain from the Fatimid to the Early Ottoman Periods," in Politis, *The Origins of the Sugar Industry*, 87–94. For evidence on sugar production at Tiberias, see Stern, "Tiberias, Aviv Hotel," 208–10.

164. See the pathbreaking study of Philip Slavin, "'With a Grain of Sugar': Native Agriculture and Colonial Capitalism in the Frankish Levant, 1100–1300," *Crusades* 22, no. 1 (2023): 1–38; also David Jacoby, "The Economic Function of the Crusader States of the Levant: A New Approach," in *Relazioni economiche tra Europa e mondo islamico secc. XIII–XVIII*, ed. Simonetta Cavaciocchi (Florence, 2007), 170–72; Mohamed Ouerfelli, *Le sucre* (Leiden, 2008), 37–53; Anat Peled, *Sugar in the Kingdom of Jerusalem* (Jerusalem, 2009) [in Hebrew]. For the possible impact of sugar production on social relations, see Judith Bronstein, Edna J. Stern, and Elisabeth Yehuda, "Franks, Locals and Sugar Cane: A Case Study of Cultural Interaction in the Latin Kingdom of Jerusalem," *Journal of Medieval*

History 45 (2019): 316–30; also Lohrmann, "Echanges techniques entre Orient et Occident," 127–30.

165. *The Itinerary of Benjamin of Tudela*, ed. and trans. Marcus Nathan Adler (London, 1907), 20–21 (text), 19 (translation); WT 13.3 (589–90). Cf. Peled, *Sugar in the Kingdom of Jerusalem*, 271–73.

166. *UKJ*, 3:1179, no. 690a. A *fontica de çucaro* in Tyre is mentioned in an act drawn up in Acre in 1209: *Documenti del commercio veneziano*, 2:52, no. 513.

167. *Tractatus*, 128–29. For the visit's date, see B. Z. Kedar and Paolo Trovato, "New Perspectives on *Tractatus de locis et statu sancte terre ierosolimitane*," *Storie e Linguaggi* 4, no. 2 (2018): 1–32. On cotton, see Jacoby, "The Economic Function," 172–73.

168. See also Lewis, "Medieval Diglossia," 148.

169. JdV 86 (342–47). For the date at which Jacques was writing, see Donnadieu's introduction to JdV, 10–12.

170. *Tahine*: "Assises des Bourgeois," c. 243, no. 38 (2:181 and n. 1). The provision regarding *tahine* belongs to a group whose enactment has been attributed to the years 1191–1229: see David Jacoby, "The *fonde* of Crusader Acre and Its Tariff: Some New Considerations," in Balard, Kedar, and Riley-Smith, *Dei gesta per Francos*, 292–93.

171. Eliyahu Ashtor, "Il regno dei crociati e il commercio di Levante," in *I comuni italiani*, 37–43; on the trade of Acre, see Michel Balard, *Histoire des épices au Moyen Âge* (Paris, 2023), 114, 124–25.

172. See the groundbreaking study of Judith Bronstein, Edna J. Stern, and Elisabeth Yehuda, "Viticulture in the Latin Kingdom of Jerusalem in the Light of Historical and Archaeological Evidence," *Journal of Mediterranean Archaeology* 33, no. 1 (2020): 55–78. On the possible import of wine-press technologies from Sicily and Europe's rainy regions, see Rabei G. Khamisy, "Frankish Viticulture, Wine Presses, and Wine Production in the Levant: New Evidence from Castellum Regis (Miʿilyā)," *Palestine Exploration Quarterly* 153 (2021): 191–221.

173. Frankish documentation: "Administrative Regulations for the Hospital of St John in Jerusalem Dating from the 1180s," ed. Susan B. Edgington, *Crusades* 4 (2005): 26 (also, 24: *char de porc*); *Der Bericht des Marsilio Zorzi: Codex Querini-Stampalia IV3 (1064)*, ed. Oliver Berggötz (Frankfurt am Main, 1991), 141 (*tuazo* tax), 152, 165 (*ara* = *hara*, that is, hog-sty); *La Règle du Temple*, 141, 339, §§196, 662; *Cart Hosp*, 3:227, no. 3396, §8; Joinville, *Vie de saint Louis*, 444, §502. Norman and Angevin documentation: Walther Holtzmann, "Papst-, Kaiser- und Normannenurkunden aus Unteritalien, I: San Filippo—S. Maria Latina in Agira," *Quellen und Forschungen aus italienischen Archiven und Bibliotheken* 35 (1955): 70–71, no. 7; John H. Pryor, "*In subsidium Terrae Sanctae*: Exports of Foodstuffs and War Materials from the Kingdom of Sicily to the Kingdom of Jerusalem, 1265–1284," *Asian and African Studies* 22 (1988): 137–40, 144.

174. For instance, the percentage of pig bones out of all bones excavated at Turris Rubea was 86 percent; at Caymont, 4.2 percent; at Krak des Chevaliers, AD 1110–70, 34.8 percent and AD 1170–1271, 19.4 percent; at Arsur, in everyday diet, 3.7 percent and in siege diet, 60.8 percent; at Vadum Iacob (AD 1178–79), 32.9 percent. The total number of bones excavated was 57, 452, 621, 680, 374, 880, and 2,784, respectively: Judith Cartledge, "Faunal

Remains," in Denys Pringle, *The Red Tower (al-Burj al-Ahmar): Settlement in the Plain of Sharon at the Time of the Crusaders and Mamluks, A.D. 1099–1516* (London, 1986), 177 (table 12, column C); Liora Kolska-Horwitz and Edna Dahan, "Animal Husbandry Practices during the Historic Periods," in *Yoqne'am I: The Historic Periods*, ed. Amnon Ben-Tor et al., Qedem Reports 3 (Jerusalem, 1996), 247 (table XXII.1); Benoît Clavel and Alessio Bandelli, "Die Tierreste," in John Zimmer, Werner Meyer, and Letizia Boscardin, *Krak des Chevaliers in Syrien: Archäologie und Bauforschung 2003 bis 2007* (Koblenz, 2011), 157; Miriam Pines, Lidar Sapir-Hen, and Oren Tal, "Crusader Diet in Times of War and Peace: Arsur (Israel) as a Case Study," *Oxford Journal of Archaeology* 36 (2017): 313; Ron Kehati, "The Faunal Remains from the Templar Fortress and the Mamluk Hamlet," in Raphael, *The Excavation of the Templar Fortress at Jacob's Ford*, 174–76.

175. Usama ibn Munqidh, *The Book of Contemplation*, 153.

176. Maxime Rodinson, "Recherches sur les documents arabes relatifs à la cuisine," *Revue des études islamiques* 17 (1949): 152; for the date, see 128. See also *Scents and Flavors: A Syrian Cookbook*, ed. and trans. Charles Perry (New York, 2017), 190–91. This edition, based on a different manuscript, does not contain the concluding remark; it presents, however (80–81), a recipe for "Frankish roast." On conservatism and innovation in Frankish bread making, see Elisabeth Yehuda et al., "Frankish Bread and Baking Ovens in the Latin Kingdom of Jerusalem," *Medieval Archaeology* 66 (2022): 400–430.

177. On the spread of shaving beards in Europe at that time, see Giles Constable, "Introduction on Beards in the Middle Ages," in *Apologiae duae*, ed. Robert B. C. Huygens, CCCM 62 (Turnhout, 1985), 95–102. On the importance of beards for Orientals, see WT 11.11 (511). For the view that long hair and beardedness signified, for Westerners, effeminacy and lack of military competence, see Andrew Jotischky, "The Image of the Greek: Western Pilgrims' Views of Eastern Monks and Monasteries in the Holy Land, c.1200–1500," *Speculum* 94 (2019): 689–90.

178. GN 5.6 (206).

179. *Tractatus*, 124.

180. Bahā' al-Dīn ibn Shaddād, *The Rare and Excellent History of Saladin*, trans. D. S. Richards (Aldershot, 2001), 123–24.

181. Bahā' al-Dīn, *History of Saladin*, 173. (My translation differs slightly).

182. "uiri duo crinibus et barbis concreti, calamistrati non ex industria, sed, ut apparebat, ex incuria." *Papsturkunden für Kirchen*, 120, no. 15; Hiestand, "Der lateinische Klerus," 49. The names and titles of the envoys are spelled out in a papal bull in favor of Monte Cassino: Erasmus Gattola, *Ad historiam abbatiae Cassinensis accessiones*, 2 vols. (Venice 1734), 2:715; in another version Pons, too, appears as legate: PL 163:314. Cf. John G. Rowe, "Paschal II and the Relations between the Spiritual and Temporal Powers in the Kingdom of Jerusalem," *Speculum* 32 (1957): 494.

183. On the ecclesiastical legislation on clerics' beards, see Constable, "Introduction on Beards," 103–12.

184. On the beards of the first three Baldwins: WT 10.2 (454), 12.4 (551), 16.1 (715), 19.3 (867). "Most rulers in the twelfth century had either no beard

or only a short beard": Constable, "Introduction on Beards," 98. On Geoffroy, see Marie-Madeleine Gauthier, "Art, savoir-faire médiéval et laboratoire moderne, à propos de l'effigie funéraire de Geoffroy Plantagenêt," *Comptes rendus des séances de l'Académie des Inscriptions et Belles-Lettres* 123, no. 1 (1979): 105–31; *Corpus des inscriptions de la France médiévale*, vol. 24: *Maine-et-Loire, Mayenne, Sarthe*, ed. Vincent Debiais (Paris, 2010), 227–29.

185. Herbertus: *Cart St Sép*, 216, no. 98. Humbertus: *Cart St Sép*, 100, no. 34 (the editor assumes an identity), 383, 385; also *UKJ*, 1:321, no. 138.

186. *Cart St Sép*, 238–39, no. 117. I disagree with Prawer's contention that beards disappeared by the mid-twelfth century and that the designation *cum barba* pointed to an exception: Prawer, *The Latin Kingdom*, 520. The burgess *Robertus sine barba* witnessed a charter in Jerusalem in 1125 (*Cart St Sép*, 213, no. 95); as we have just seen, in 1130/33 another burgess is called *Humbertus cum barba*. It is improbable that "beardless" was an exception in 1125 and five or eight years later "bearded" had so become. The designations may have aimed at distinguishing between individuals bearing the same name: *Robertus sine barba* appears in proximity to *Robertus janitor porte David*, and *Arnaldus cum barba* to *Arnaldus Tardi*.

187. WT Cont. Lyon, 53. On a bearded knight of Acre tricked into losing his beard in a bathhouse, see *Die Exempla des Jacob von Vitry*, 133, no. 72.

188. Significantly, Egyptian guidelines of 1280 stipulated that the beards of Frankish prisoners of war must be shaved: Léonor Fernandes, "On Conducting the Affairs of State: A Guideline of the Fourteenth [recte: Thirteenth] Century," *Annales Islamologiques* 24 (1989): 84; Hillenbrand, *The Crusades*, 555–56; Ciggaar, "Adaptation to Oriental Life," 278.

189. John H. Pryor, "The *Eracles* and William of Tyre," in *Horns*, 270–93; Bernard Hamilton, "The Old French Translation of William of Tyre as an Historical Source," in *EC*, 93–112. More recently, the work was dated to 1219–23: Philip Handyside, *The Old French William of Tyre* (Leiden, 2015), 114–19.

190. Describing King Baldwin II, the adapter writes, "La barbe ne fu pas espesse, mès ele fu longue jusqu'en piz, selon la costume qui lors coroit en cele terre," and with regard to King Amaurry he notes that "Les joes et le menton ot bien vestues de barbe, à la costume qui lors coroit." WT OF 12.4, 19.3 (1:438, 2:255). See Frankwalt Möhren, "Kreuzzugsvokabular: Exotisches Dekorum oder kulturelle Übernahme?," in *Kulturelle und sprachliche Entlehnung*, ed. Mechtild Bierbach and Barbara von Gemmingen (Bonn, 1999), 116.

191. *La Règle du Temple*, 140, §195. Magdalena Satora, "Mantle and Beard as Symbols of the Templars in the Records of the Paris Proceedings against the Order (1309–1311)," in *Studies in the Military Orders, Prussia, and Urban History: Essays in Honour of Roman Czaja on the Occasion of his Sixtieth Birthday*, ed. Jürgen Sarnowsky et al. (Debrecen, 2020), 105–15.

192. WT *C-F Cont*, 157; WT Cont. Lyon, 88.

193. Jacques of Vitry, *The Exempla or Illustrative Stories from the Sermones Vulgares of Jacques de Vitry*, ed. Thomas Frederick Crane (London, 1890), 39, no. 87. For a discussion of Templar beards, see Simonetta Cerrini, *L'Apocalisse dei Templari: Missione e destino dell'ordine religioso e cavalleresco più misterioso del Medioevo*

(Milan, 2012), 84–89; Cerrini, *La rivoluzione dei Templari: Una storia perduta del dodicesimo secolo* (Milan, 2014), 113–14; also Ciggaar, "Adaptation to Oriental Life," 278, 282.

194. For the broader argument about the order's nonclerical nature, see Cerrini's books quoted in the previous note.

195. Bearded Tancred: Metcalf, *Coinage of the Crusades*, 25 (no. 4), 27 (no. 4), plate 4 (nos. 63–70); Ciggaar, "Adaptation to Oriental Life," 268–70, 272. Allegedly wearing a turban: see for instance R. C. Smail, *Crusading Warfare (1097–1193)* (Cambridge, 1956), 41 n. 1. Figment of imagination: Metcalf, *Coinage of the Crusades*, 27.

196. Nurith Kenaan-Kedar, "A Neglected Series of Crusader Sculpture: The Ninety-Six Corbels of the Church of the Holy Sepulchre," *Israel Exploration Journal* 42 (1992): 109–11. Cf. Kenaan[-Kedar], "Local Christian Art in Twelfth-Century Jerusalem," *Israel Exploration Journal* 23 (1973): 167–75, 221–29. On the interpretation of heads on Romanesque corbels—situated next to such that depict masons' tools—as self-representations of sculptors, see Kenaan-Kedar, *Marginal Sculpture in Medieval France: Towards the Deciphering of an Enigmatic Pictorial Language* (Aldershot, 1995), 36–46.

197. Ibn al-Athīr in *RHC Or*, 2A:59; for explanations of the Arabic terms, see Francesco Gabrieli, *Arab Historians of the Crusades*, trans. E. J. Costello (Berkeley, 1969), 242 n. 1.

198. Buckingham, "Identity and Archaeology in Daily Life," 48–63, 67–68.

199. Prawer, *The Latin Kingdom*, 519–20; David Jacoby, "Society, Culture and the Arts in Crusader Acre," in *France and the Holy Land*, 107.

200. JdV 73 (290–91).

201. Ralph Niger, *De re militari*, 3.83 (193–94); see also 3.65 (186–87).

202. "Canons of the Council of Nablus," no. 16: "Si Sarracenus aut Sarracena francigeno more se induant, infiscentur." I see no reason for assuming that this decision also forbade Franks to wear Muslim dress (Yolles, *Making the East Latin*, 20, 70).

203. Ibn Khaldūn, *The Muqaddima: An Introduction to History*, trans. Franz Rosenthal, 2nd ed., 3 vols. (Princeton, NJ, 1967), 1:299. The oft-repeated hypothesis that the ban against wearing Frankish dress was influenced by the Muslim imposition of a distinctive code dress on Christians and Jews cannot be ruled out, but it is conceivable that similar situations independently elicited similar solutions, which, however, operated differently: to forbid subjected people to wear the attire of the dominant group differs from coercing them to add some differentiating apparel to their clothing.

204. Ibn Abī Usaybi'a, *A Literary History of Medicine: The 'Uyūn al-anba' fī tabaqāt al-atibbā'*, ed. and trans. Emilie Savage-Smith, Sion Swain, and Geert Jan van Gelder, 3 vols. (Leiden, 2020), 2.2:1242 (text), 3.2:1408–9 (translation). See Kohlberg and Kedar, "A Melkite Physician," 113–26; Johannes Pahlitzsch, "Ärzte ohne Grenzen: Melkitische, jüdische und samaritanische Ärzte in Ägypten und Syrien zur Zeit der Kreuzzüge," in *Gesundheit—Krankheit: Kulturtransfer medizinischen Wissens von der Spätantike bis in die frühe Neuzeit*, ed. Florian Steger and Kay Peter Jankrift (Cologne, 2004), 110–12.

205. Saʿdī, *Badāyiʿ: The Odes of Sheikh Muslihud Din Saʿdi Shirazi*, trans. Lucas W. King (Berlin, ca. 1926), 27, no. 24. Possibly, "Frankish" means here European. On Saʿdī's imprisonment in Tripoli, see Kedar, "Some New Sources," 140.

206. Cf. Krijnie Ciggaar, "Cultural Identities in Antioch (969–1268): Integration and Disintegration—New Texts and Images," in Borgolte and Schneidemüller, *Hybride Kulturen im mittelalterlichen Europa*, 115. A presentation of the Franks' achievement as a mere "acculturation de façade," arrives nevertheless at the conclusion: "Aussi superficielle fût-elle, cette hybridation leur donnait une identité spécifique dont ils avaient pleinement conscience": Aurell, "De l'acculturation à l'ethnotype," 337, 358.

207. On innovativeness, hybridity, and stigmatization in general, see Chan Kwok-bun, ed., *Cultural Hybridity: Contradictions and Dilemmas* (Abingdon, 2012).

208. See above, note 15; also Joaquim Miret I Sans, *Itinerari de Jaume I "El Conqueridor"* (Barcelona, 1918), 447, 464.

209. William of Newburgh, *Historia rerum Anglicarum*, 3.15 (254). The gradual estrangement between Franks and Westerners is discussed by Florian Besson, "Devenir étranger: Des anti-transferts culturels en Orient latin," in *Transferts*, 307–25.

210. "ceaus d'Ybelin, les desleaus d'Outremer, qui plus aiment les Sarazins que les Crestiens." Filippo da Novara, *Guerra di Federico II*, 90, §31. Somewhat later Phelippe has him say that all Christendom would exclaim: "Li traïtour d'Outremer ont ocis lor seignor l'empereor," 94, §33.

211. Glick, *Islamic and Christian Spain*, 165–66.

212. Usama ibn Munqidh, *The Book of Contemplation*, 151–52. On the considerable overlap between Usāma's description of the duel and Frankish thirteenth-century assizes, see Adam M. Bishop, "Usāma ibn Munqidh and Crusader Law in the Twelfth Century," *Crusades* 12 (2013): 56–61. On al-Qarāfī, see Erdmann Fritsch, *Islam und Christentum im Mittelalter: Beiträge zur Geschichte der muslimischen Polemik gegen das Christentum in arabischer Sprache* (Breslau, 1930), 147; Diego R. Sarrió Cucarella, *Muslim-Christian Polemics across the Mediterranean: The "Splendid Replies" of Shihāb al-Dīn al-Qarāfī (d. 684/1285)* (Leiden, 2015), 103–4. On dueling in Frankish law, see "Assises des Bourgeois," c. 275 (2:207–8).

213. Philippe de Novare, *Mémoires (1218–1243)*, ed. Charles Kohler (Paris, 1913), 4. Cf. WT Prologue (99): "natalis soli magis tracti dulcedine."

214. JdV 51–52 (218–20).

3. An Intellectual Backwater?

1. Hamilton, *The Latin Church*, 134.

2. Prawer, *The Latin Kingdom*, 529; Riley-Smith, *The Crusades: A Short History*, 56; the second statement is not repeated in Riley-Smith, *The Crusades: A History*, 75.

3. Tyerman, *God's War*, 235–36.

4. "magister scolasticus": *Cart St Sép*, 74, no. 19. See Hamilton, *The Latin Church*, 134 n. 3; Riley-Smith, *The Crusades: A Short History*, 56; Riley-Smith, *The Crusades: A History*, 75.

5. *Cart St Sép*, 223, no. 103. For his later career, see below, chap. 6.

6. These data were assembled and discussed by Mayer, *Die Kanzlei*, 1:388–90. For the names of the Antioch masters, see *Cart Hosp*, 1:447, no. 665. For an overview of the evidence for schools and libraries, see Yolles, *Making the East Latin*, 23–31.

7. FC 2.57 (598 n. g to first apparatus; the remark appears only in the chronicle's first redaction). See also Verena Epp, *Fulcher von Chartres: Studien zur Geschichtsschreibung des ersten Kreuzzuges* (Düsseldorf, 1990), 26.

8. "Chartes de l'abbaye de Notre-Dame de la Vallée de Josaphat en Terre-Sainte (1108–1291)," ed. Charles Kohler, *ROL* 7 (1899): 127, no. 17. The title *bibliotecarius* was unusual: see James A. Brundage, "Latin Jurists in the Levant: The Legal Elite of the Crusader States," in *Crusaders and Muslims in Twelfth-Century Syria*, ed. Maya Shatzmiller (Leiden, 1993), 30 n. 57.

9. WT 21.25 (998), 12.13 (563).

10. See appendix 3, below.

11. My totals of volumes (100) and titles (72) are based on the catalog's indications that twenty-one works were available in more than one copy, and that in six cases a volume contained two or more works. Cf. Robert B. C. Huygens, *Latijn in "Outremer": Een blik op de latijnse letterkunde der kruisvaarderstaten in het Nabije Oosten* (Leiden, 1964), 13. For art historical reflections on the catalog, see Folda, *Crusader Art in the Holy Land*, 92–93, 402.

12. For the volume's content, see Wilhelm Schum, *Beschreibendes Verzeichniss der amplonianischen Handschriften-Sammlung zu Erfurt* (Berlin, 1887), 360–62, no. 102. The two titles appear in the catalog as *Scintilarius; Pastoralis Gregorii*, with no indication that they form part of the same volume. In fact, they take up about four-fifths of it.

13. James S. Beddie, "Libraries in the Twelfth Century: Their Catalogues and Contents," in *Anniversary Essays in Mediaeval History by Students of Charles Homer Haskins* (Boston, 1929), 2; Jean-Philippe Genet, "Essai de bibliométrie médiévale," *Revue française d'histoire du livre* 46 (1977): 535.

14. In the West, the number of bequeathed books could be considerable. In about 1148 Chancellor Thierry gave fifty-nine volumes to the library of Chartres, but only four titles are spelled out; in 1180 John of Salisbury, the town's bishop, gave it twenty-six volumes: *Obituaires de la Province de Sens*, vol. 2: *Diocèse de Chartres*, ed. Auguste Molinier (Paris, 1906), 107–8; Clement C. J. Webb, "Note on Books Bequeathed by John of Salisbury to the Cathedral Library of Chartres," *Mediaeval and Renaissance Studies* 1 (1941): 128. The proportion of biblical or liturgical books in a bequest could be high; for instance, one half of the books Pope Celestine II (d. 1144) gave to Città di Castello were biblical: André Wilmart, "Les livres légués par Célestin II a Città di Castello," *Revue Bénédictine* 35 (1923): 98–102.

15. **Novara**: Albert Werminghoff, "Reise nach Italien im Jahre 1901," *Neues Archiv der Gesellschaft für ältere deutsche Geschichtskunde* 27 (1902): 601–3. Werminghoff was able to decipher words no longer legible later; cf. Paul Liebaert, "Inventaire inédit de la bibliothèque capitulaire de Novare dressé en 1175," *Revue des Bibliothèques* 21 (1911): 107–8; Gabriella de Ferrari, "I più antichi codici della biblioteca capitolare di Santa Maria di Novara," *Bollettino storico per la provincia*

di Novara 46 (1956): 55–57. **Rouen** and **Durham**: Gustavus Becker, *Catalogi bibliothecarum antiqui* (Bonn, 1885), 224–25, no. 106 (Rouen), 239–45, no. 117 (Durham). **Lincoln**: Reginald M. Woolley, *Catalogue of the Manuscripts of Lincoln Cathedral Chapter Library* (Oxford, 1927), v–ix. For the catalogs' dates, see Birger Munk Olsen, *L'étude des auteurs classiques latins aux XI*[e] *et XII*[e] *siècles*, vol. 3.1: *Les classiques dans les bibliothèques médiévales* (Paris, 1987), 95 (Durham), 139 (Lincoln), 175 (Novara), 214 (Rouen).

16. For a comparison of the Nazareth library with the much larger private libraries in the contemporary Islamicate realm, see B. Z. Kedar, "On Books and Hermits in Nazareth's Short Twelfth Century," in *Nazareth: Archaeology, History and Cultural Heritage*, ed. Mahmoud Yazbak and Sharif Sharif (Nazareth, 2012), 50–51; also Max Meyerhof, "Über einige Privatbibliotheken im fatimidischen Ägypten," *Rivista degli studi orientali* 12 (1930): 286–90. For studies of Islamicate libraries, see Etan Kohlberg, *A Medieval Muslim Scholar at Work: Ibn Ṭawūs and His Library* (Leiden, 1992); Konrad Hirschler, *The Written Word in the Medieval Arabic Lands: A Social and Cultural History of Reading Practices* (Edinburgh, 2012), 124–63.

17. Isidore's *Etymologies* and *x libri de phisica*. Originally the Nazareth cleric wrote *ix libri de phisica*, then corrected the number; apparently, he found another copy at a chest's bottom (Malcolm Parkes, pers. comm., 8 February 1998).

18. Huygens, who counts titles, not volumes, concludes that the catalog lists forty-six theological and twenty-six profane titles: Huygens, *Latijn in "Outremer,"* 13. My count of titles results in a slightly different proportion, 44:28. The number of nontheological *volumes* exceeds that of the theological ones because of the considerable number of profane works available in two or more copies.

19. For the observation that "in most libraries the non-ecclesiastical content did not reach one third of the total," see Beddie, "Libraries in the Twelfth Century," 9.

20. Julian Yolles, "Latin Literature and Frankish Culture in the Crusader States (1098–1187)" (PhD diss., Harvard University, 2015), 188. For Konrad's canon see *Accessus ad auctores: Bernard d'Utrecht, Conrad d'Hirsau. Dialogus super auctores*, ed. Robert B. C. Huygens (Leiden, 1970).

21. The cleric who drew up the catalog does not appear to have enjoyed a rigorous Latin schooling, for he writes *Spropiri* instead of *Prosperi*, *stristium* instead of *tristium*. Perhaps he was dyslectic.

22. The biography of Rorgo Fretellus has been pieced together by Rudolf Hiestand, "Un centre intellectuel en Syrie du Nord? Notes sur la personnalité d'Aimeri d'Antioche, Albert de Tarse et *Rorgo Fretellus*," *Le Moyen Age* 100 (1994): 19–26, 35. Hiestand's reconstruction supersedes that by Boeren in Fretellus, viii–xii. But Hiestand's claim (20), that Fretellus was chaplain of the church of Nazareth in 1121, repeats Boeren's unfounded assertion (ix); the charter of 1121 has merely *R. capellano Sancte Nazarene ecclesie: Chartes Josaphat*, 35, no. 9. On Gerard, see above, chap. 1.

23. Long passages from the *Panormia*, commonly attributed to Ivo of Chartres, appear in the Ordinals of the Frankish Church of the Holy Sepulcher: Iris Shagrir, "Adventus in Jerusalem: The Palm Sunday Celebration in Latin Jerusalem," *Journal of Medieval History* 41 (2015): 15; Sebastián Salvadó, "The

Augustinian Reform, the *Panormia* Glosses and Reading the Bible in the Medieval Latin Liturgy of Jerusalem," *Revue d'études augustiniennes et patristiques* 62 (2016): 1–29.

24. For this view, see Tyerman, *God's War*, 236. It has recently been asserted that the Nazareth library possessed the *Sentences* of Petrus Lombardus: Hamilton in Bernard Hamilton and Andrew Jotischky, *Latin and Greek Monasticism in the Crusader States* (Cambridge, 2020), 123. In fact, the catalog lists "VII libri de sententiis" (see below, appendix 3, no. [42]). Yet it is implausible that the library owned no less than seven copies of Petrus Lombardus's *Libri quatuor sententiarum*, while the libraries of Lincoln and Durham owned just one copy each; also, the catalogs of these libraries (see note 15, above) list those copies as "sententie Magistri Petri Lumbardi" and "sentenciarum Petri Lumbardi," respectively. The "VII libri de sententiis" of the Nazareth catalog were probably copies of the *Liber Sententiarum*, a collection of passages from Augustine assembled by Prosper of Aquitaine that enjoyed considerable diffusion: *Sancti Prosperi Aquitani Liber Sententiarum*, ed. M. Gastaldo, Corpus Christianorum Series Latina 68A (Turnhout, 1972), 215, 254–55.

25. Beddie, "Libraries in the Twelfth Century," 22–23.

26. A list dated to 1165–83 enumerates among the gifts of Hugues's successor, Rotrou, "liber Hugonis archiepiscopi ad Albanensem episcopum" and "libellus eiusdem de expositione fidei catholicae et orationis Dominice": Becker, *Catalogi bibliothecarum antiqui*, 224, no. 104. On Archbishop Hugues, see Ryan P. Freeman, *Hugh of Amiens and the Twelfth-Century Renaissance* (Farnham, 2011).

27. For his biography, see Ludwig Schmugge in Ralph Niger, *De re militari*, 3–10.

28. Runciman, *A History of the Crusades*, 2:425.

29. *Lettres d'Étienne de Tournai*, ed. Jules Desilve (Valenciennes, 1893), 92–93, no. 78; *Cart St Sép*, 289, 291, nos. 147–48. Runciman's error probably stemmed from a literal reading of the claim by a continuator of William of Tyre that Eraclius "po savoit de letres": WT *C-F Cont*, 116. On Eraclius's career, see B. Z. Kedar, "The Patriarch Eraclius," in *Outremer*, 177–81.

30. One in 1126, one in 1134, four in 1140–49, four in 1150–59, twelve in 1160–69, twelve in 1170–79, and eight in 1180–85. Brundage, "Latin Jurists in the Levant," 34–35, and Mayer, *Die Kanzlei*, 1:241, 387–88, 2:168. See also *Cart Hosp*, 1:417, no. 613 of 1181, that mentions a *magister Georgius* in addition to the *magister Morellus* noted by Brundage. I removed Stephan of Nablus from Brundage's list, since Mayer has shown (*Die Kanzlei*, 1:832 n. 83) that he was *magister castelli Neapolis*, the lay commander of the local castle.

31. In the eastern regions of the empire masters appear later and less frequently. See Manfred Groten, "Der Magistertitel und seine Verbreitung im Deutschen Reich des 12. Jahrhunderts," *Historisches Jahrbuch* 113 (1993): 21–40. For examples from Chartres (1133–45), Norwich (1146–50), and Canterbury (1150–53), see Richard W. Southern, "The Schools of Paris and the School of Chartres," in *Renaissance and Renewal in the Twelfth Century*, ed. Robert L. Benson and Giles Constable (Cambridge, MA, 1982), 134–35. For data from 1134–58 on seven masters at Montpellier, four of whom engaged in law, see Laurent Mayali, "Les *magistri* dans l'ancienne Septimanie au XIIe siècle," in *Recueil de mémoires et*

travaux de la Société d'histoire du droit et des institutions des anciens pays de droit écrit, vol. 10 (Montpellier, 1979), 94–97. On the steady growth of university-trained masters in the twelfth-century diocese of Liège from one in the decade 1120–29 to fifteen in 1180–89, see Christine Renardy, *Les maîtres universitaires du diocèse de Liège: Repertoire biographique, 1140–1350* (Paris, 1981), 103–64. When Hubert Walter served as archbishop of Canterbury in the years 1193–1205, of the thirty-eight clerics who usually witnessed his deeds, twenty were masters: see Christopher R. Cheney, *English Bishops' Chanceries, 1100–1250* (Manchester, 1950), 11–15.

32. Mayer, *Die Kanzlei*, 2:828. A systematic comparison of Jerusalemite and Western *arengae* remains a desideratum.

33. Mayer, *Die Kanzlei*, 2:842.

34. Raoul of Caen, *Gesta Tancredi*, in *RHC Oc*, 3:604; see also the introduction to *The Gesta Tancredi of Ralph of Caen*, trans. Bernard S. Bachrach and David S. Bachrach (Farnham, 2010), 1–5. For an even-handed portrayal, see Raymonde Foreville, "Un chef de le Première Croisade: Arnoul Malecouronne," *Bulletin philologique et historique du Comité des travaux historiques et scientifiques*, 1953–54, 377–90; see also Jean Richard, "Quelques textes sur les premiers temps de l'Eglise latine de Jérusalem," in *Recueil de travaux offerts à M. Clovis Brunel*, 2 vols. (Paris, 1955), 2:420–23.

35. GN 7.15 (290–91); OV 9.16 (5:176–77).

36. GN 7.23 (329); see also 7.34 (332); Epp, *Fulcher von Chartres*, esp. 25, 45–63, 104–68, 376–80.

37. The identity of Acardus, *magister scholarum* at Arras, with Acardus, the archdeacon of Thérouanne who later went to Jerusalem, is highly probable. See Daniel Haigneré, "Les hommes illustres du diocèse de Thérouanne qui après la première Croisade furent au nombre des dignitaires de la Terre-Sainte," *Bulletin historique trimestriel de la Société des antiquaires de la Morinie* 8 (1887–91): 476–77; Ludo Milis, *L'ordre des chanoines reguliers d'Arrouaise*, 2 vols. (Brugge, 1969), 1:100, 103, 107, 124.

38. Anseau, "Letters," in *Cartulaire général de Paris*, vol. 1: *528–1180*, ed. Robert de Lasteyre (Paris, 1887), 171, no. 151. The letter has been dated to 1120 by Geneviève [Bresc-] Bautier, "L'envoi de la relique de la Vraie Croix à Notre-Dame de Paris en 1120," *Bibliothèque de l'École des chartes* 129 (1971): 387–97. For a similar scene, in which Patriarch William of Jerusalem (1130–45) asks a former fellow-hermit in the Touraine and a pilgrim to Jerusalem about the well-being of his erstwhile confrères, see "Historia monasterii Beatae Mariae de Fontanis Albis," in *Recueil de chroniques de Touraine*, ed. André Salmon (Tours, 1854), 261. For a reconstruction of Anseau's career, see Cara Aspesi, "The Cantors of the Holy Sepulchre and Their Contribution to Crusade History and Frankish Identity," in *Medieval Cantors and their Craft: Music, Liturgy and the Shaping of History, 800–1500*, ed. Katie Ann-Marie Bugyis, Andrew B. Kraebel, and Margot E. Fassler (Woodbridge, 2017), 280–81, 295–96.

39. See the remarks of Jonathan Riley-Smith at the symposium "The Crusading Kingdom of Jerusalem: The First European Colonial Society?," printed in *Horns*, 353–54. Similarly, Hamilton likened the intellectual activities in the Frankish East to those in nineteenth-century Australia and New Zealand: Hamilton, *The Latin Church*, 134.

40. *Íslendingabók. Landnámabók*, ed. Jakob Benediktsson (Reykjavík, 1986), 25; *The Letters of John of Salisbury*, ed. and trans. W. J. Millor and C. N. L. Brooke, 2 vols. (Oxford, 1979–86), 2:692–94, no. 298.

41. See the early sources on Joachim's life edited by Herbert Grundmann, "Zur Biographie Joachims von Fiore und Rainers von Ponza," in his *Ausgewählte Schriften*, vol. 2: *Joachim von Fiore*, MGH Schriften 25.2 (Stuttgart, 1977), 342–43, 354–55. Joachim briefly mentions his pilgrimage in the *Tractatus super Quatuor Evangelia*, ed. Ernesto Buonaiuti (Rome, 1930), 92.

42. Hiestand, "Der lateinische Klerus," 60–62. On clerics from Iberia, see Kedar, "Iberia y el reino franco," 45, 49.

43. Hiestand, "Der lateinische Klerus," 53–54. These figures pertain to the Kingdom of Jerusalem, the County of Tripoli, and the Principality of Antioch.

4. The Clergy and the Establishment of Cores of Devotion

1. Photographs of this page appear in "Un rituel et un bréviaire du Saint-Sépulcre de Jérusalem (XIIe–XIIIe siècle)," ed. Charles Kohler, *ROL* 8 (1900–1), opposite 394, and in *Codice diplomatico barlettano*, ed. Salvatore Santeramo, vol. 1 (Barletta, 1924), plate 2. For Kohler's edition and discussion of this *petite chronique*, see "Un rituel," 400–401, 456–58; for Santeramo's edition, see *Codice diplomatico barlettano*, 57–58 (I follow Kohler).

2. William, who writes that the king took along the Holy Cross, mentions neither that it was left behind in Tiberias nor that it was brought to the battlefield: WT 21.27–28 (1000–1002).

3. The term "True Cross," habitually used in the secondary literature, rarely appears in the sources. It has been argued that the term *vera crux* is an innovation that emerged in the West to designate fragments of the wood on which Jesus was crucified as authentic: Gia Toussaint, "Die Kreuzzüge und die Erfindung des Wahren Kreuzes," in Borgolte and Schneidmüller, *Hybride Kulturen im mittelalterlichen Europa*, 153–56. But a lament right after Ḥaṭṭīn refers to the Franks' True Cross: "Qar presa es la vera crotz e-l reis." *L'amour et la guerre: L'oeuvre de Bertran de Born*, ed. Gérard Gouiran, 2 vols. (Aix-en-Provence, 1985), 2:666. See also below, note 41.

4. On the pre-1099 stages of this process, see Erdmann, *Die Entstehung des Kreuzzugsgedankens*, 30–50. On this exceptional historian of the crusade idea, see Folker Reichert, *Fackel in der Finsternis: Der Historiker Carl Erdmann und das "Dritte Reich,"* 2 vols. (Darmstadt, 2022).

5. The story is told by the fifth-century Socrates Scholasticus, *Historia ecclesiastica* 1.17, in PG 67:119–20.

6. For the date, 21 March 631, see Venance Grumel, "La reposition de la Vraie Croix à Jérusalem par Héraclius: Le jour et l'année," *Byzantinische Forschungen* 1 (1966): 139–49.

7. *Le "Liber" de Raymond d'Aguilers*, 154. For the date, see Heinrich Hagenmeyer, "Chronologie de la première croisade (1094–1100)," *ROL* 7 (1899): 485–86. For discussion, see Kirschberger, *Erster Kreuzzug*, 315–23. On the difference between the accounts of Raymond and Foucher, see Yolles, *Making the East Latin*, 63.

8. On Arnoul's skepticism, see *Le "Liber" de Raymond d'Aguilers*, 114, and Raoul of Caen, *Gesta Tancredi*, cc. 102, 109, in *RHC Oc*, 3:678, 682. On the episode in general, see Colin Morris, "Policy and Visions: The Case of the Holy Lance at Antioch," in *War and Government in the Middle Ages: Essays in Honour of J. O. Prestwich*, ed. John Gillingham and J. C. Holt (Woodbridge, 1984), 33–45; see also John France, *Victory in the East: A Military History of the First Crusade* (Cambridge, 1994), 278–80, 294, 322.

9. On the golden image, see Raoul of Caen, *Gesta Tancredi*, c. 110, in *RHC Oc*, 3:683. Arnoul's wish to supplant the Holy Lance with the True Cross was discerned by Mayer, *Geschichte*, 79.

10. AA 6.41 (456). Pierre Tudebode relates that Arnoul brought the True Cross and Count Raymond IV of Toulouse's chaplain the Holy Lance: Petrus Tudebodus, *Historia de hierosolymitano itinere*, ed. John H. Hill and Laurita L. Hill, DRHC 12 (Paris, 1977), 145–46. On Petrus the Hermit as Pedron, see appendix 1, below.

11. AA 6.43 (458–60).

12. AA 7.65–68 (576–80). For a parallel, less dramatic account, see FC 2.11 (411, 414).

13. FC 2.21 (453–54). Epp, in her comparison of Foucher's two redactions, has shown that in the later redaction the True Cross is exalted more emphatically: Epp, *Fulcher von Chartres*, 27–28, 47–48.

14. FC 2.32 (495). Likewise, Theoderich writes that "salutare lignum adversus paganos in bello, cum necessitas exigit, gestare solent Christiani." Theoderich in *Peregrinationes tres*, 153.

15. Murray, in his study of the military employment of the True Cross, lists thirty-one instances: Alan V. Murray, "'Mighty against the Enemies of Christ': The Relic of the True Cross in the Armies of the Kingdom of Jerusalem," in *Crusade Sources*, 232–38. To these should be added Albert of Aachen's account about the presence of the Holy Cross in a battle of 1111 (AA 11.42 [818]) and King Fulk's act of 2 August 1135, in which he mentions having conveyed the Holy Cross to Antioch: *Cart St Sép*, 173, no. 74 (Fulk probably refers to his expedition of 1133–34, described in WT 14.6–7 [637–39]). Murray rightly remarks (222) that the actual number of instances may have been higher. The act of 1135 was first noted by Deborah Gerish, "The True Cross and the Kings of Jerusalem," *Haskins Society Journal* 8 (1996): 152. On the True Cross during an advance on Tripoli, see FC 3.11 (648).

16. This is the plausible hypothesis of Steve Tibble, *The Crusader Armies, 1099–1187* (New Haven, CT, 2018), 144.

17. For such an uplifting, see WT 16.11 (731).

18. Gautier the Chancellor, *Bella Antiochena*, 2.12 (104); Hagenmeyer's comment at 282.

19. Thus, in 1158, 1171, and 1177 the True Cross was carried by the archbishop of Tyre or the bishop of Bethlehem: WT 18.21 (842), 20.26 (950), 21.21 (990). For the Battle of Ḥaṭṭīn, in which the relic was carried by the bishops of Lydda and Acre, see Kedar, "The Patriarch Eraclius," 181–82. Hamilton claims that "unlike earlier patriarchs, there is no record that Heraclius carried the Holy Cross relic on campaign when the king went to war": Hamilton in Hamilton

and Jotischky, *Latin and Greek Monasticism*, 41. However, William mentions the presence of King Baldwin IV, Eraclius, and the Cross in the army at the Fountain of Saforie in 1182, and of Eraclius and the Cross during the raid into southern Syria later that year: WT 22.16 (1030), 22.21 (1038).

20. *La Règle du Temple*, 101, §122.

21. FC 3.6 (632–33), 3.19 (668), 3.36 (746), a. 1119, 1123, 1124; Kirschberger, *Erster Kreuzzug*, 340–42, speaks of a "Kreuzes-Adventus."

22. *Voyage de Charlemagne*, 34, v. 70.

23. *Die Urkunden Konrads III. und seines Sohnes Heinrich*, ed. Friedrich Hausmann, MGH Diplomata regum et imperatorum Germaniae 9 (Vienna, 1969), 358, 362, nos. 198, 200.

24. *Cart St Sép*, 76, no. 20; for confirmations in the years 1138–55, see 61, 69, 81, 118, nos. 15, 17, 23, 42. "On a military expedition"—*Cart St Sép*, 294, no. 150; Alexander III's confirmation of 1170 appears in 298, no. 151.

25. *Cart St Sép*, 280, no. 144 (a. 1168).

26. FC 3.9 (639). On the probability that Foucher became a canon of the Sepulcher in 1114, see Epp, *Fulcher von Chartres*, 27–34, and the remarks of Mayer in *Deutsches Archiv* 47 (1991): 630.

27. FC 3.5 (630), 3.9 (638–40).

28. Gaufridus, *S. Bernardi Vita prima*, in PL 185:367. It has been argued that the Cross did not accompany the army "on purely offensive long-distance expeditions where there were no Latin settlements to defend": Murray, "'Mighty against the Enemies of Christ,'" 225; however, the Cross did accompany the army that marched to Bosra in 1147: WT 16.11 (730).

29. AA 7.48 (556).

30. Anatole Frolow, *La relique de la vraie croix* (Paris, 1961), 308–45, esp. nos. 291, 297, 298, 311, 319, 320, 324, 329, 334, 337, 346, 349, 354, 363, 364, 365, 368, 369, 370, 372.

31. See above, chap. 1, note 39.

32. *Actus pontificum Cenomannis in urbe degentium*, ed. Gustave Busson and Ambroise Ledru (Le Mans, 1901), 407.

33. Anseau, "Letters," 171–73, nos. 151–52. On the veneration of the relic in Paris and the evolution of the liturgy commemorating its reception, see Miriam Rita Tessera, "La croce del legato: Conone di Preneste, il papato, e riflessi della missione in Oriente," in *Legati, delegati e l'impresa d'Oltremare (secoli XII–XIII): Atti del Convegno Internazionale di Studi, Milano, 9–11 marzo 2011*, ed. Maria Pia Alberzoni and Pascal Montaubin (Turnhout, 2014), 139, 154–60; M. Cecilia Gaposchkin, "Notre Dame of Paris, the True Cross of 1120, and the Power of Relic Narratives," *Journal of Ecclesiastical History* (in press).

34. *Die Urkunden und die ältesten Urbare des Klosters Scheyern*, ed. Michael Stephan (Munich, 1988), 28–33, nos. 10, 12.

35. Heribert Meurer, "Kreuzreliquiare aus Jerusalem," *Jahrbuch der Staatlichen Kunstsammlungen in Baden-Württemberg* 13 (1976): 7–18; Meurer, "Zu den Staurotheken der Kreuzfahrer," *Zeitschrift für Kunstgeschichte* 48 (1985): 65–76; Bianca Kühnel, *Crusader Art of the Twelfth Century: A Geographical, an Historical, or an Art Historical Notion?* (Berlin, 1994), 141–53; Folda, *The Art of the Crusaders*, 97–100, 166–69, 290–94, 480; Nikolas Jaspert, "The True Cross of Jerusalem in the Latin

West: Mediterranean Connections and Institutional Agency," in *Visual Constructs of Jerusalem*, ed. Bianca Kühnel, Galit Noga-Banai, and Hanna Vorholt (Turnhout, 2014), 207–21.

36. WT 1.1 (105). On the True Cross as having come close to a "Staatssymbol," see Verena Epp, "Die Entstehung eines 'Nationalbewußtseins' in den Kreuzfahrerstaaten," *Deutsches Archiv* 45 (1989): 600; on the cross, the True Cross, and the Church of the Holy Sepulcher as Frankish "Staatssymbole" whose common shortcoming as a symbol of the Kingdom of Jerusalem was their relevance for all Christendom, see Rudolf Hiestand, "*Nam qui fuimus Occidentales, nunc facti sumus Orientales*: Siedlung und Siedleridentität in den Kreuzfahrerstaaten," in *Siedleridentität: Neun Fallstudien von der Antike bis zur Gegenwart*, ed. Christof Dipper and Rudolf Hiestand (Frankfurt am Main, 1995), 70.

37. ʿImād al-Dīn al-Isfahānī, *Conquête de la Syrie et de la Palestine par Saladin*, trans. Henri Massé, DRHC 10 (Paris, 1972), 17–18, 29–30.

38. Letter edited in B. Z. Kedar, "Ein Hilferuf aus Jerusalem vom September 1187," *Deutsches Archiv* 38 (1982): 120–21.

39. "Un rituel," ed. Kohler, 401. In reality, the eclipse took place on the day Ascalon surrendered, 4 September 1187: Peter W. Edbury, "Making Sense of the *Annales de Terre Sainte*: Thirteenth-Century Vernacular Narratives from the Latin East," in *Crusader Landscapes in the Medieval Levant: The Archaeology and History of the Latin East*, ed. Micaela Sinibaldi et al. (Cardiff, 2016), 410.

40. Pierre of Blois, "Passio Raginaldi principis Antiochie," in *Petri Blesensis Tractatus duo*, ed. Robert B. C. Huygens, CCCM 194 (Turnhout, 2002), 50–51. Murray has drawn attention to William of Malmesbury's report that in a battle of 1113 the Cross was temporarily lost; Foucher of Chartres, who must have known about this, chose to ignore the presence of the Cross in this encounter: Murray, "'Mighty against the Enemies of Christ,'" 227, 233.

41. "Vera crux sancta, et sepulcrum resurrectionis Iesu Christi, protege civitatem Ierusalem cum habitatoribus suis." *Libellus*, 198–99.

42. For a detailed, annotated discussion of the miracle, see B. Z. Kedar, "Le miracle du Feu sacré à Jérusalem: Des origines à la suppression papale," in *Bourgogne/Orient*, 519–29.

43. *Carmina Burana*, ed. Alfons Hilka and Otto Schumann, 2 vols. (Heidelberg, 1930), 1.1:105, no. 52. Huygens did not believe that the first stanza ("Nomen a solemnibus . . . reus apud Eacum") forms part of the poem (pers. comm.).

44. Petrus Venerabilis, *Sermo domni Petri abbatis Cluniacensis de laude Dominici Sepulchri*, ed. Giles Constable, in "Petri Venerabilis sermones tres," *Revue Bénédictine* 64 (1954): 247–53.

45. Petrus Venerabilis, *Adversus Iudeorum inveteratam duritiem* c. 4, ed. Yvonne Friedman, CCCM 58 (Turnhout, 1985), 123–24. Petrus's attitude, by no means idiosyncratic, requires a revision of the view that the Fire "was regarded as miraculous by the more simple-minded pilgrims": Bernard Hamilton, "The Impact of Crusader Jerusalem on Western Christendom," *Catholic Historical Review* 80 (1994): 709.

46. ʿAlī al-Harawī, *A Lonely Wayfarer's Guide to Pilgrimage: ʿAlī ibn Bakr al-Harawī's Kitāb al-Ishārāt ilā Ma'rifat al-Ziyārāt*, ed. and trans. Josef W. Meri (Princeton, NJ, 2004), 76–77.

47. "quia inter vos multos fidei Christiane inbecilles et incredulos esse credimus." Caffaro, *Annales Ianuenses*, in *Annali genovesi di Caffaro e de' suoi continuatori*, ed. Luigi T. Belgrano (Rome, 1890), 1:8.

48. FC 2.8 (394–97); WT 10.13 (468).

49. *L'amour et la guerre: L'oeuvre de Bertran de Born*, 2:666. Text reprinted by permission of Presses Universitaires de Provence.

50. Ambroise, *L'Estoire de la Guerre Sainte: Histoire en vers de la Troisième Croisade (1190–1192)*, vv. 8381–8428, ed. Gaston Paris (Paris, 1897), cols. 224–25.

51. Marius Canard, "La destruction de l'Eglise de la Résurrection par le calife Hākim et l'histoire de la descente du feu sacré," *Byzantion* 35 (1965): 31 n. 3. Cf. Ignatij Kratchkovsky, "Le 'Feu béni' d'après le récit d'al-Bīrūnī et d'autres écrivains musulmans du Xe au XIIIe siècle," *Proche-Orient Chrétien* 49 (1999): 269–70 [appeared in Russian in 1914].

52. Sibṭ probably preached in Jerusalem during the years 1229–36 in which he was based in Karak: Joseph Drory, "Al-Nāsir Dāwūd: A Much Frustrated Ayyūbid Prince," *Al-Masāq* 15 (2003): 176. For his testimony about the Fire, see Kratchkovsky, "Le 'Feu béni,'" 270–71; Canard, "La destruction," 39–40. Nowadays the Holy Fire is transported by aircraft to Greece and other countries in which the Eastern Orthodox Church is dominant.

53. Of thirty Catalans who drew up their testaments in the years 1096–1105 before leaving for Jerusalem, eighteen mentioned the Holy Sepulcher as their goal: Jaspert, "Penitencia y apocalipsis," 476–79.

54. Mayer has argued that Godefrid and Baldwin I, and possibly Baldwin II, were buried below the hill of Calvary, then still outside the Church of the Holy Sepulcher; Fulk, in 1143, was buried at the same location, which formed, however, by that time part of the new Frankish Church of the Holy Resurrection; henceforward—resulting from what Mayer calls an unintended "Betriebsunfall"—Christ's tomb was no longer the only one to be seen in the sanctuary: Hans Eberhard Mayer, "Die Jerusalemer Grabeskirche als Begräbnisort in der Kreuzzugszeit," *Archiv für Kulturgeschichte* 103 (2021): 5–35. For alternative locations of the tombs within the church, and for the hypothesis that the remains of Godefrid, Baldwin I and II, as well as Fulk are still lying in unmarked pits under its present-day pavement, see Amit Re'em, Estelle Ingrand-Varenne, and Ilya Berkovich, "Surviving Three Cycles of Destruction: The Graves of the Crusader Kings in the Church of the Holy Sepulchre," *New Studies in the Archaeology of Jerusalem and Its Region* 15 (2022): 71–103.

55. The shift was discussed, though not contextualized, by Sylvia Schein, *Gateway to the Heavenly City: Crusader Jerusalem and the Catholic West (1099–1187)* (Aldershot, 2005), 66, 70–73. This posthumously published book should be used with caution: see my review in *Cahiers de civilisation médiévale* 37 (2014): 524–25.

56. *Cart St Sép*, 152, 170–71, 174–75, nos. 60, 72, 75.

57. *Cart St Sép*, 99, no. 34.

58. *Cart St Sép*, 75, 78, 79, nos. 20, 21, 22 (a. 1114, 1133–34, 1135–36); François Chandon de Briailles, "Sur deux bulles de l'Orient latin," in *Mélanges syriens offerts a Monsieur René Dussaud par ses amis et élèves*, 2 vols. (Paris, 1939), 1:139–40; Gustave Schlumberger, Ferdinand Chalandon, and Adrien Blanche, *Sigillographie de l'Orient latin* (Paris, 1943), 73–75 (a. 1123, 1136, 1137, 1139, 1143, 1142–45).

59. "Fragment d'un cartulaire de l'ordre de Saint-Lazare, en Terre Sainte," ed. Arthur de Marsy, *AOL* 2, no. 2 (1884): 127, no. 6 (a. 1148); *Cart St Sép*, 242, no. 119 (a. 1151–57); *Die Urkunden . . . des Klosters Scheyern*, 29, no. 10 (a. 1155–57); Chandon de Briailles, "Sur deux bulles," 140; Schlumberger, Chalandon, and Blanche, *Sigillographie*, 75–76.

60. Acts of Amaurry: *Cart St Sép*, 288, 290, 293, 314, nos. 147, 148, 150, 162 (a. 1167–68, 1168–69, 1177). Letter of Eraclius (a. 1187): ed. in Kedar, "Ein Hilferuf," 120. Seals: Schlumberger, Chalandon, and Blanchet, *Sigillographie*, 76–78. Also Rudolf Hiestand, "Die Urkunden der lateinischen Patriarchen von Jerusalem und Antiochia im 12. Jahrhundert," in *Die Diplomatik der Bischofsurkunde vor 1250* (Innsbruck, 1995), 88, who suggests that the new title might have been a riposte to the Antiochene formulation *sancte sedis apostolice*. For a list of the titles of the Jerusalemite patriarchs from 1103 to 1267, see Chandon de Briailles, "Sur deux bulles," 141–42.

61. E.g., *UKJ*, 1:395, no. 212 (a. 1144); 2:535, no. 308 (a. 1164); 2:656, no. 381 (a. 1174); 2:770, no. 451 (a. 1185); 2:798, no. 473 (a. 1186); 2:834, no. 488 (a. 1191).

62. Folda, *The Art of the Crusaders*, 203; also, 179.

63. Pre-1099 events: WT 1.4 (110), 1.5 (111), 1.6 (113), 1.12 (127), 7.23 (374); Clermont Address: WT 1.15 (133); description of Jerusalem: WT 8.3 (385).

64. WT 10.4 (456), 9.16 (441).

65. William's use of the new designation provides a clue for the dates at which he wrote or revised parts of his chronicle: see B. Z. Kedar, "Some New Light on the Composition Process of William of Tyre's *Historia*," in *Deeds Done beyond the Sea*, 5–9.

66. See for instance Le Strange, *Palestine under the Moslems*, 202.

67. Schlumberger, Chalandon, and Blanchet, *Sigillographie*, 75–78, plate 1:9; Hans Eberhard Mayer, *Das Siegelwesen in den Kreuzfahrerstaaten* (Munich, 1978), plate 1:2.

68. *Armenia and the Crusades, Tenth to Twelfth Centuries: The Chronicle of Matthew of Edessa*, trans. Ara Edmond Dostorian (Lanham, MD, 1993), 42, 60.

69. The seal was found in archaeological excavation in Winchester in 1963. See Vitalien Laurent, "Un sceau inédit du patriarche de Jérusalem Sophrone II trouvé à Winchester," *Numismatic Circular* 72 (1964): 49–50; Laurent, *Le corpus des sceaux de l'Empire byzantin*, vol. 5.2: *L'Église* (Paris, 1965), 393–98, nos. 1561–65; Philip Grierson, "Byzantine Seals," in *The Winchester Mint and Coins and Related Finds from the Excavations of 1961–71*, ed. Martin Biddle, Winchester Studies 8 (Oxford, 2012), 684–88. See also Robert Kool and Annette Landes-Nagar, "A Unique Crusader-Period Lead Seal from the Old City of Jerusalem," *'Atiqot* 110 (2023): 229–39. Schlumberger, Chalandon, and Blanchet (*Sigillographie*, 76) noted that the scene on the Frankish seals is "traitée à la manière byzantine," but were unaware of the antecedent Greek seals.

70. For this dating, see Pringle, *Saewulf, John of Würzburg, Theoderic*, 25–26.

71. Johann of Würzburg in *Peregrinationes tres*, 122; Theoderich in *Peregrinationes tres*, 151.

72. This discussion of the two connotations of the Resurrection and its pictorial representations is indebted to Anna D. Kartsonis, *Anastasis: The Making of an Image* (Princeton, NJ, 1986), 4–7, 19–24, 134, and passim. Alan Borg's cogent linkage between the seals, the mosaic, and the Melisende Psalter appears in his "The Lost Apse Mosaic of the Holy Sepulchre, Jerusalem," in *The Vanishing Past: Studies of Medieval Art, Liturgy and Metrology Presented to Christopher Hohler*, ed. Alan Borg and Andrew Martindale (Oxford, 1981), 7–12 and plates 1.1–3. Also Folda, *The Art of the Crusaders*, 230–31.

73. "Omnibus si pie deuocionis affectu dominicum sepulchrum pro instanti necessitate uisitare volentibus, tam in itinere morte preoccupatis quam ad nos usque peruenientibus, laborem itineris ad penitentiam et obedientiam atque remissionem omnium peccatorum suorum iniungimus uitam eternam." Bibliothèque Nationale de Luxembourg, MS 42, fols. 116v–117r. In his edition, inaccurate at two points, Riant inserts "[et]" before "vitam eternam": "Six lettres relatives aux croisades," 387, repr. in *Cart Hosp* 1:280, no. 404. For the date of Amaurry's call, see Phillips, *Defenders*, 151 and n. 54.

74. "auctoritate dominici [*sic*] passionis atque resurrectionis." Bibliothèque Nationale de Luxembourg, MS 42, fol. 116v.

75. Alexander III's bull is printed in PL 200:384–86; it is basically a reissue of the bull *Quantum praedecessores*, promulgated by Pope Eugenius III on 1 March 1146: Peter Rassow, "Text der Kreuzzugsbulle Eugens III.," *Neues Archiv der Gesellschaft für ältere deutsche Geschichtskunde* 45 (1924): 300–305; for analysis, see Giles Constable, "The Second Crusade as Seen by Contemporaries," *Traditio* 9 (1953): 248–53.

76. In a similar vein, Rudolf Hiestand regards the title *sancte resurrectionis ecclesie patriarcha* as a provocation of the papacy, as it juxtaposes Peter's tomb in Rome with Jerusalem's site of the Resurrection "or, to put it more sharply, the dead Apostle with the living God": Hiestand, "Die Urkunden der lateinischen Patriarchen," 88. This is exaggerated: the pope did not claim authority *only* because of being the successor of St. Peter. For instance, Eugenius III, in his bull of 1146, grants the crusade indulgence "*omnipotentis Dei* et beati Petri apostolorum principis auctoritate nobis *a Deo* concessa."

77. For a discussion of these precedents, see B. Z. Kedar, "Raising Funds for a Frankish Cathedral: The Appeal of Bishop Radulph of Sebaste," in *Entrepreneurship and the Transformation of the Economy (10th–20th Centuries): Essays in Honour of Herman Van der Wee*, ed. Paul Klep and Eddy van Cauwenberghe (Leuven, 1994), 449–50.

78. Patriarch Amaurry may have also had in mind Franks who contemplated a pilgrimage to Compostela. In 1169 Hue of Ibelin mentioned his vow to take the *via sancti Jacobi*: "Fragment d'un cartulaire de l'ordre de Saint-Lazare," 143, no. 25. A story about a blacksmith from Acre who made a pilgrimage to Compostela and Rocamadour appears in *Les miracles de Notre-Dame de Roc-Amadour au XIIe siècle*, 1.4, ed. and trans. Edmond Albe (Paris, 1907), 77–79. The collection dates from 1172–73: see the editor's introduction, 12–13, and Marcus Bull, *The Miracles of Our Lady of Rocamadour: Analysis and Translation* (Woodbridge,

1999), 3, 39–90. A pilgrim's badge to Compostela—a pierced scallop shell—was excavated in Tiberias: Stern, "Tiberias, Aviv Hotel," 210.

79. For Raoul's letter, see Kedar, "Raising Funds," 454–55.

80. "pater fidei et Christianorum et vicarius Jhesu Christi." *Tractatus*, 126. Under Innocent III *vicarius Christi* became the pope's foremost title: Michele Maccarrone, *Vicarius Christi: Storia del titolo papale* (Rome, 1952), 109–18.

81. *Die Texte des normannischen Anonymus*, ed. Karl Pellens (Wiesbaden, 1966), 84–90; G. H. Williams, *The Norman Anonymous of 1100 A.D.* (Cambridge, MA, 1951), 141–43; Karl Pellens, *Das Kirchendenken des normannischen Anonymus* (Wiesbaden, 1973), 173–83; Jannis Spiteris, *La critica bizantina del primato romano nel secolo XII* (Rome, 1979), 71–72, 187–88. See also the view of Joannes VIII, Greek patriarch of Jerusalem early in the twelfth century: Pahlitzsch, *Graeci und Suriani*, 125–26.

82. Michele Maccarrone, "'Fundamentum apostolicarum sedium': Persistenze e sviluppi dell'ecclesiologia di Pelagio I nell'Occidente latino tra i secoli XI e XII," in *La chiesa greca in Italia dal'VIII al XVI secolo* (Padua, 1973), 629–48; also Ferdinand R. Gahbauer, *Die Pentarchietheorie* (Frankfurt am Main, 1993), 365–69.

83. For Gilo's letter, see *Papsturkunden für Kirchen*, 137–40, no. 29; also 140, no. 30. William merely mentions that Gilo sent "most famous letters" to the Antiochenes: WT 13.23 (617–18).

84. WT 15.13 (692–93); *Papsturkunden für Kirchen*, 160–64, no. 46; Bernard Hamilton, "Ralph of Domfront, Patriarch of Antioch (1135–1140)," *Nottingham Medieval Studies* 28 (1984): 1–21; Rudolf Hiestand, "Ein neuer Bericht über das Konzil von Antiochia 1140," *Annuarium Historiae Conciliorum* 19 (1987): 314–50.

85. Mansi, *Concilia*, 21:1146.

86. Alexander III's bull was discovered and edited by Rudolf Hiestand in his *Papsturkunden für Templer und Johanniter: Archivberichte und Texte* (Göttingen, 1972), 251–53, no. 53. Alexander's dependence on Amaurry's letter has been pointed out by Phillips, *Defenders*, 153, with relevant passages of the texts juxtaposed in n. 62; his conclusion was adopted by Miriam Rita Tessera, *Orientalis ecclesia: Papato, Chiesa e regno latino di Gerusalemme (1099–1187)* (Milan, 2010), 332–34.

87. "Preterea omnibus dominicum sepulcrum pro instanti necessitate uisitare uolentibus tam in itinere morte preoccupatis quam usque illuc peruenientibus laborem itineris ad penitenciam, obedienciam et remissionem omnium peccatorum inungimus, ut post huius carnis ergastula uitam eternam consequi mereantur." *Papsturkunden für Templer und Johanniter*, 253. Cf. Amaurry's call above, note 73.

88. PL 200:601, 1296. Schwerin considered the words "dominicum sepulcrum visitare" of Alexander's bull as one of the infrequent appearances of the idea of pilgrimage in the vocabulary of crusade calls: Ursula Schwerin, *Die Aufrufe der Päpste zur Befreiung des Heiligen Landes von den Anfängen bis zum Ausgang Innozenz IV.: Ein Beitrag zur Geschichte der kurialen Kreuzzugspropaganda und der päpstlichen Epistolographie* (Berlin, 1937), 45. For a discussion of Alexander III's calls for help for the Kingdom of Jerusalem in 1165–74, see Tessera, *Orientalis ecclesia*, 328–51.

89. *Cart St Sép*, 275–87, 291–92, nos. 142–46, 149 (all of 1168). The term "Church of the Lord's Resurrection" appears only once, in a confirmation of the canons' possessions that copies a Jerusalemite act: 285, no. 146.

90. *Papsturkunden für Kirchen*, 231–32, no. 85. An 1138 letter of Pope Innocent II presents for the first time the patriarch of Jerusalem as a primate, that is, as subordinated to the pope similarly to the primates of Lyon and Reims: see Yael Katzir, "The Patriarch of Jerusalem, Primate of the Latin Kingdom," in *CS*, 169–75; Schein, *Gateway*, 52–53.

91. Germain Morin, "Le discours d'ouverture du concile général de Latran (1179) et l'oeuvre littéraire de maître Rufin, évêque d'Assise," *Atti della Pontificia Accademia Romana di Archeologia: Memorie* 2 (1928): 113–33. The address is edited on 116–20; the editor argues persuasively that Rufinus was its author. See also Gahbauer, *Die Pentarchietheorie*, 369–72; Tessera, *Orientalis ecclesia*, 370.

92. "Appendix ad Concilium Lateranense III," c. 26, in Mansi, *Concilia*, 22:372–73. Tessera, who drew attention to this decision, points out that, in a volume of the church of Sidon, the statement "Quod nullus episcopus incognitos homines in sua ecclesia ordinare debet" is commented on in the margins by "Contra usum istius terre." BAV, Vat. lat. 1345, fol. 148[r]. See Miriam Rita Tessera, "Dalla liturgia del Santo Sepolcro alla biblioteca di Sidone: Note sulla produzione libraria latina di Oltremare nel XII–XIII secolo," *Aevum* 79 (2005): 415.

93. *Papsturkunden für Kirchen*, 287–88, no. 114; see also 329, no. 152.

94. Peter W. Edbury and John G. Rowe, *William of Tyre: Historian of the Latin East* (Cambridge, 1988), 26–29, 170–71; Kedar, "Some New Light," 3–9.

95. AA 1.2–5 (2–6); WT 1.11–12 (124–27).

96. "suggerente Petro Heremita." WT 1.14 (130). Huygens's reediting at this point is one of his important emendations.

5. The Husbanding of Sanctity

1. For the argument against presenting such grants of access as a "sharing" of shrines, see B. Z. Kedar, "Studying the 'Shared Sacred Spaces' of the Medieval Levant: Where Historians May Meet Anthropologists," *Al-Masāq* 34 (2022): 111–26.

2. *Frutolfi et Ekkehardi Chronica necnon Anonymi Chronica Imperatorum*, ed. and trans. Franz-Joseph Schmale and Irene Schmale-Ott (Darmstadt, 1972), 178. Riley-Smith was the first to point out that the accounts of the descent of the Holy Fire in 1101 leave no doubt that Greek clerics participated in the liturgy: "The Latin Clergy and the Settlement in Palestine and Syria, 1098–1100," *Catholic Historical Review* 74 (1988): 553–54.

3. Theoderich in *Peregrinationes tres*, 151–53. As for his statement "Hee sunt professiones sive secte que in ecclesia Iherosolimitana divina peragunt officia, scilicet Latini, Suriani, Armenii, Greci, Iacobini, Nubiani" (152), Hamilton considers it more likely that this is "a parenthetical comment about the variety of Christian traditions found in the city of Jerusalem" and not about all these sects having altars within the Church of the Holy Sepulcher: Hamilton in Hamilton and Jotischky, *Latin and Greek Monasticism*, 37. But Theoderich explicitly

mentions, within the Church of the Holy Sepulcher, a main and several subsidiary altars of the Syrians and a chapel of the Armenians (151, 153, 157), Ranieri of Pisa miraculously comprehended the Armenian divine service he witnessed there (Benincasa, *Vita sancti Rainerii*, 127–28), and the officiating of Greeks in the shrine is known from various sources. Besides, Theoderich does not claim that all these sects have altars of their own in the church; he says that they "divina peragunt officia."

4. *Cart St Sép*, 257–58, no. 131. On the confrontation at Lombers, near Albi, in 1165, see Malcolm Barber, *The Cathars* (Harlow, 2000), 118–19.

5. Francis Wormald, "The Calendars of the Church of the Holy Sepulchre, Jerusalem," in Hugo Buchthal, *Miniature Painting in the Latin Kingdom of Jerusalem* (Oxford, 1957), 111, 114–15.

6. Mayer's argument that the political ties between Constantinople and Jerusalem led by 1164 to the admission of a chapter of Greek canons to the Church of the Holy Sepulcher (*Bistümer, Klöster und Stifte im Königreich Jerusalem*, MGH Schriften 26 [Stuttgart, 1977], 406–9), has to be modified on account of the evidence adduced by Pahlitzsch, *Graeci und Suriani*, 188–93.

7. For the Jacobites, this has been noted by MacEvitt, *The Crusades and the Christian World of the East*, 104.

8. *Ernoul*, 173; B. Z. Kedar, "The Frankish Period," in *The Samaritans*, ed. Alan D. Crown (Tübingen, 1989), 86.

9. **Sebaste**: Paul M. Cobb, "Usāma Ibn Munqidh's *Book of the Staff*: Autobiographical and Historical Excerpts," *Al-Masāq* 17 (2005): 119. **Acre**: *The Travels of Ibn Jubayr*, trans. Broadhurst, 318; he also relates that Muslims and Christians pray at the mosque at ʿAyn al-Baqar, in Frankish possession and with a Frankish-built eastern apse. **Lord's Temple**: Johann of Würzburg in *Peregrinationes tres*, 92; in about 1220 Jacques of Vitry wrote that even when Jerusalem was under Christian rule, Saracens came from afar to pray in the Lord's Temple, "which they call the Rock, or Temple of Solomon": JdV 6 (138). **Bethlehem**: Apparently Muslims were also able to visit the *miḥrāb* of Caliph ʿUmar in the Church of the Nativity: al-Harawī, *A Lonely Wayfarer's Guide*, 76, 246. See also Jonathan Riley-Smith, "Government and the Indigenous in the Latin Kingdom of Jerusalem," in *Medieval Frontiers: Concepts and Practices*, ed. David Abulafia and Nora Berend (Aldershot, 2002), 122–24. However, the notion that, under Frankish rule, Muslims built a new mosque in the village of ʿAjjūl north of Jerusalem in 1176–77—Riley-Smith, *The Crusades: A Short History*, 55; Pringle, *Secular Buildings*, 1—is based on a misreading of an inscription; the correct date is 1196 and the builder an Ayyubid official: see *Corpus inscriptionum arabicarum Palaestinae*, 1:17–19.

10. See appendix 4, below. On Shaykh Rabīʿ, see David Morray, *An Ayyubid Notable and His World: Ibn al-ʿAdīm and Aleppo as Portrayed in His Biographical Dictionary of People Associated with the City* (Leiden, 1994), 100–104; Yehoshua Frenkel, "Mardin and Jerusalem during the Ayyubid Age," in *First International Symposium of Mardin History Papers*, ed. Ibrahim Özcoşar and Hüseyin H. Güneş (Istanbul, 2006), 549–51. Catlos, who briefly summarizes the story of Rabīʿ (without giving its source), presents the fee as *baqshīsh*: Catlos, *Muslims of Medieval Latin Christendom*, 155.

11. See the autobiographical account in Maimonides, *Iggerot ha-Rambam* [The Letters of Maimonides], ed. Itzhak Shailat, 2 vols. (Maʿale Adumim, 1995), 1:225, 230. For an English translation based on an edition of 1866, see Prawer, *The History of the Jews*, 142 (but the date is 14 October, not 16). Prawer took "the Great and Holy House" to mean the Dome of the Rock: *The History of the Jews*, 143 n. 38; for a dissenting view, see Joel L. Kraemer, *Maimonides: The Life and World of One of Civilization's Greatest Minds* (New York, 2008), 138, 515 n. 34. Rabīʿ's account supports Prawer's interpretation.

12. On Sebaste, see ʿImād al-Dīn in Abū Shāma, *RHC Or*, 4:302. Benjamin of Tudela relates that a Jewish visitor would gain entrance to the Cave of the Patriarchs by paying a sum to the guardian: *The Itinerary of Benjamin of Tudela*, 27 (text), 25–26 (translation); cf. Petaḥya of Regensburg, *Die Rundreise des R. Petachjah aus Regensburg*, ed. and trans. Lazar Grünhut (Frankfurt am Main, 1905), 33–34 (text), 46 (translation). Al-Harawī relates that a Muslim descended into the Cave after ḥaving given its custodian a gift: *A Lonely Wayfarer's Guide*, 78–79.

13. Saewulf in *Peregrinationes tres*, 65 (twice), 67, 68, 70. Also, Johann of Würzburg in *Peregrinationes tres*, 102, 109, and Theoderich in *Peregrinationes tres*, 195.

14. "Inventio Patriarcharum," ed. Robert B. C. Huygens, *Crusades* 4 (2005): 135, 143.

15. Fretellus, 18, 34 (Version Zdík, cc. 25, 58).

16. JdV, 220–22.

17. Johann of Würzburg in *Peregrinationes tres*, 110–12; cf. Jotischky, "The Frankish Encounter," 106–9.

18. On the similarities between the Frankish canons of 1120 and clauses of Byzantine lawbooks of the eighth–tenth centuries, see B. Z. Kedar, "On the Origins of the Earliest Laws of the Frankish Kingdom of Jerusalem: The Canons of the Council of Nablus, 1120," *Speculum* 74 (1999): 313–23. A comparison of canon 4 with its Byzantine model suggests that the level of literacy among the Franks was lower than in Byzantium, 318–19. On the innovative nature of the Frankish canons, and their possible impact on the West, see Ruth Mazo Karras, "The Regulation of 'Sodomy' in the Latin East and West," *Speculum* 95 (2020): 969–86; for subtle arguments that the canons were not put into practice, see 973–74 (but the canons did not forbid "Franks from dressing in Saracen clothing," as claimed on 972).

19. WT 15.21 (703), 18.24 (846). Elsewhere, William emphasizes that the Franks "idiomatis Greci non habentes peritiam": WT 16.26 (753), and Huygens's notes on 703, 876.

20. On the vertical strokes, see Wormald, "Palaeographical Note," in Buchthal, *Miniature Painting*, 135. On the other hand, the twelfth-century redaction of the *typikon* of the Greek Orthodox monastery of Mār Sābā mentions the presence of groups of Franks, Georgians, and Syrians within the monastic community: Jotischky in Hamilton and Jotischky, *Latin and Greek Monasticism*, 366–67, 418.

21. FC 3.18 (665), 3.28 (697–98); also Petrus Tudebodus, *Historia de hierosolymitano itinere*, 144–45.

22. *Papsturkunden für Kirchen*, 105, no. 8.

23. The complaint appears in the first of two polemical treatises in which Joannes attacks the Latins for using unleavened bread: Pahlitzsch, *Graeci und Suriani*, 116. For a slightly earlier attack, written shortly after the crusader conquest of Antioch in 1098, which presents the Latins as heretics who use unleavened bread, see Milka Levi-Rubin, "'The Errors of the Franks' by Nikon of the Black Mountain," *Byzantion* 71 (2001): 422–37; also Daniel Galadza, "Greek Liturgy in Crusader Jerusalem: Witnesses of Liturgical Life at the Holy Sepulchre and St Sabas Lavra," *Journal of Medieval History* 43 (2017): 435–36.

24. *Tractatus*, 124–25. The account errs with regard to the beliefs of the Jacobites, claiming that one Jacob rendered them Nestorians.

25. WT 15.18 (699), 22.9 (1018–19); JdV 78 (314–18). Hamilton, *The Latin Church*, 204, 208, 332.

26. Gerard of Nazareth, *De conversacione*, c. 20 (73).

27. The discussion of this treatise appeared originally in Kedar, "Gerard of Nazareth," 63–64. My thanks to the Dumbarton Oaks Research Library and Collection, Trustees for Harvard University, for permitting me to reproduce it here.

28. Matthias Flacius Illyricus et al., *Ecclesiasticae historiae, integram Ecclesiae Christi ideam . . . secundum singulas centurias perspicuo ordine complectens*, vol. 6: *Duodecima Centuria* (Basel, 1569), cols. 1230–33; repr. in Kedar, "Gerard of Nazareth," 75–76.

29. Urban Holzmeister, "Die Magdalenenfrage in der kirchlichen Überlieferung," *Zeitschrift für katholische Theologie* 46 (1922): 402–22, 556–84.

30. For these and other feast days devoted to the two Marys, see Victor Saxer, "Les Saintes Marie Madeleine et Marie de Béthanie dans la tradition liturgique et homilétique orientale," *Revue des sciences religieuses* 32 (1958): 3–13.

31. One of Gerard's works is entitled, according to the Centuriators, "Ad ancillas Dei apud Bethaniam": *Duodecima Centuria*, cols. 1379–80; Kedar, "Gerard of Nazareth," 71.

32. Anselm Hufstader, "Lefèvre d'Étaples and the Magdalen," *Studies in the Renaissance* 16 (1969): 31–60. On Gerard's literary activity, see Yolles, *Making the East Latin*, 159–64.

33. *Duodecima Centuria*, col. 1233; Kedar, "Gerard of Nazareth," 77. On Sala being a Greek Orthodox priest and for an attempt to reconstruct his motivation, see Jotischky, "The Frankish Encounter," 109–14, who convincingly quashes my hypothesis, based on a statement by Josias Simmler in 1574, that Sala was a Templar. Gerard's learned treatise on the Magdalene issue may be compared with Johann of Würzburg's Gospel-based musings triggered by assertions of Jerusalemite Jacobites: see above, n. 17.

34. Unfounded is the view that Sala's name was Ṣalāḥ; that he may have been the son of a Zengid prince; and that, upon converting to Christianity, he became a Templar chaplain who defied Gerard's episcopal authority and attacked his treatise. For this view, see Pierre-Vincent Claverie, "L'influence des ordres militaires sur les techniques de combat des Fatimides et des Mamelouks," in *Entre Deus e o Rei: O Mundo das Ordens Militares*, ed. Isabel Cristina Ferreira Fernandes (Palmela, 2018), 286.

35. Jotischky, "The Frankish Encounter," 114.

36. For Aimery's letter, see Edmond Martène and Ursin Durand, *Thesaurus novus anecdotorum*, 5 vols. (Paris, 1717), 1:480–81, reprinted with some mistakes in PL 202:230.

37. For Petrus Comestor's answer, see Jean Leclercq, "Gratien, Pierre de Troyes et la seconde croisade," *Studia Gratiana* 2 (1954): 589–93.

38. For the text of the 1254 prohibition, see *The Synodicum Nicosiense*, 180, c. 17. On the custom's Eastern character, see B. Z. Kedar, "Ecclesiastical Legislation in the Kingdom of Jerusalem: The Statutes of Jaffa (1253) and Acre (1254)," in *CS*, 230.

39. See B. Z. Kedar, "A Commentary on the Book of Isaiah Ransomed from the Crusaders," in *Jerusalem in the Middle Ages*, ed. B. Z. Kedar (Jerusalem, 1979), 107–11 [in Hebrew]. On the ransom of 350 manuscripts, see Shelomo Dov Goitein, "Contemporary Letters on the Capture of Jerusalem by the Crusaders," *Journal of Jewish Studies* 3 (1952): 171–75.

40. The list is derived from the calendar of the Church of the Holy Sepulcher, BAV, Barb. lat. 659, copied after 1200; the *terminus ante quem* of the calendar is 1167 and of the breviary that follows it ca. 1170: see Bulst-Thiele, *Sacrae Domus Militiae Templi Hierosolymitani Magistri*, 12; Amnon Linder, "The Liturgy of the Liberation of Jerusalem," *Mediaeval Studies* 52 (1990): 122. For the saints' classification, see Paschalis Kallenberg, *Fontes liturgiae carmelitanae* (Rome, 1962), 84–89, 92–100, 285–300. For similar conclusions based on Barb. lat. 659 and five other Frankish manuscripts, see Wormald, "Calendars of the Church," in Buchthal, *Miniature Painting*, 107–8. The ten Palestinian saints appear also in the Sanctoral of a breviary of the Lord's Temple described by Victor Leroquais, *Les bréviaires manuscrits des bibliothèques publiques de France*, 5 vols. (Paris, 1934), 3:190–91, no. 594. On Frankish adoption of Eastern saints, see Hiestand, "*Nam qui fuimus Occidentales*," 69. A mid-thirteenth-century calendar from Antioch comprises about thirty Antiochene and Syrian entries, with more than twenty typical of various French regions: Victor Saxer, "Le calendrier de l'église latine d'Antioche à l'usage du patriarche Opizzo Ier Fieschi (1254–1255)," *Rivista di storia della chiesa in Italia* 26 (1972): 107–9, 112–21.

41. Hiestand, "Der lateinische Klerus," 51–55; the importance of the Iberian element was pointed out by Linder, "The Liturgy," 127 n. 54. Dondi, endeavoring to pinpoint the Western sources of the liturgy of the Frankish Holy Sepulcher, emphasized its many similarities to practices of the Norman diocese of Evreux: Cristina Dondi, *The Liturgy of the Canons Regular of the Holy Sepulchre of Jerusalem: A Study and a Catalogue of the Manuscript Sources* (Turnhout, 2004). But as the manuscripts recording the Evreux practices date from the thirteenth and fourteenth centuries, the flow of influence may have been inverse. On the influence of Saint-Ruf, Prémontré, and Saint-Jean-en-Vallée (Chartres) on the liturgy of the Church of the Holy Sepulcher, see Wolf Zöller, "The Regular Canons and the Liturgy of the Latin East," *Journal of Medieval History* 43 (2017): 374–79. For a groundbreaking study that reveals how Frankish clerics arrived at some liturgical sequences, see Salvadó, "The Augustinian Reform."

42. Amnon Linder, *Raising Arms: Liturgy in the Struggle to Liberate Jerusalem in the Late Middle Ages* (Turnhout, 2003), 116–18.

43. BAV, Barb. lat. 659, fol. 75[v], ed. Karl Young, "The Home of the Easter Play," *Speculum* 1 (1926): 75–76; Young, *The Drama of the Medieval Church*, 2 vols. (Oxford, 1933), 1:262. Barletta, Archivio della Chiesa del Santo Sepolcro, unnumbered MS, fols. 77[vb]–78[ra]: "Un rituel," ed. Kohler, 423; re-ed. Iris Shagrir, "The *Visitatio Sepulchri* in the Latin Church of the Holy Sepulchre in Jerusalem," *Al-Masāq* 22 (2010): 66–67.

44. "Quod dum cantatur, sint parati tres clerici iuvenes in modum mulierum retro altare iuxta cosuetudinem antiquorum, quod non facimus modo propter astantium peregrinorum multitudinem." "Un rituel," ed. Kohler, 423.

45. The latter possibility was suggested by Prawer, *The Latin Kingdom*, 181. Young assumed that the *Visitatio* enactment in its entirety was discontinued: "The Home of the Easter Play," 1–82; *The Drama of the Medieval Church*, 1:262–63. Shagrir has cogently argued that the enactment continued to be performed: Shagrir, "The *Visitatio Sepulchri*," 71–73 (but *modo* appears to mean here "now" or "lately," and the clerics impersonating the angels are said to wear amices on their heads). Gerhoch of Reichersberg sharply denounced clerics who "transform churches into theatres and fill them with mimes' performances of plays": *De Investigatione Antichristi*, c. 5, ed. Ernst Sackur, in MGH Libelli de lite (Hanover, 1897), 3: 315.

46. Theoderich in *Peregrinationes tres*, 147–48. See the discussion by Shagrir, "The 'Holy Women' in the Liturgy," 465–66. On the use of the Holy Women scene in early patriarchal seals as a Frankish innovation, on its appearance on pilgrim flasks produced in Frankish Jerusalem, as well as on a relic that Patriarch William (1130–45) sent to his erstwhile brethren at Fontaine-les-Blanches, all attesting to the motif's importance, see Shagrir, "The 'Holy Women' in the Liturgy," 466–74.

47. Description of the picture and rendition of the verses: Theoderich in *Peregrinationes tres*, 157. Johann of Würzburg (141) gives only the verses.

48. Marie-Luise Bulst-Thiele, "Die Mosaiken der 'Auferstehungskirche' in Jerusalem und die Bauten der 'Franken' im 12. Jahrhundert," *Frühmittelalterliche Studien* 13 (1979): 445–46; Kühnel, *Crusader Art*, 49–50; Folda, *The Art of the Crusaders*, 225. The authors differ in their appraisals of the scene's rarity.

49. On the versions containing this addition, see Young, *The Drama of the Medieval Church*, 1:369–410.

50. *Ernoul*, 256.

51. Jacques of Vitry explicitly emphasizes the event's uniqueness: "Cum autem per mundum universum a fidelibus dicatur: 'Surrexit Dominus de sepulchro qui pro nobis pependit in ligno,' soli canonici ecclesie Resurrectionis Dominice speciali gaudent prerogativa dicentes et ad oculum demonstrationem facientes: 'Surrexit Dominus de hoc sepulchro.' Similiter in evangelio paschali cum dicitur: '*Surrexit, non est hic!*' diaconus qui legit evangelium digito demonstrat dominicam sepulturam." JdV 61 (242–44).

52. Shagrir, who analyzed the part of the Barletta Ordinal dealing with the Palm Sunday ceremony and highlighted its similarity to *adventus* observances at a ruler's entry into a city, also drew attention to the absence of the Templars from the roster of Jerusalemite congregations and raised the possibility that the text may antedate their rise to prominence: Shagrir, "Adventus in Jerusalem," 7

n. 24. On the representations of Christ's Entry into Jerusalem as imitating the Roman imperial *adventus*, see Gertrud Schiller, *Iconography of Christian Art*, vol. 2: *The Passion of Jesus Christ*, trans. Janet Seligman (Greenwich, CT, 1972), 18–19.

53. For the hypothesis that the boys were the chapter's novices, see Zöller, "The Regular Canons," 381.

54. Kenneth G. Holum and Gary Vikan, "The Trier Ivory, *Adventus* Ceremonial, and the Relics of St. Stephen," *Dumbarton Oaks Papers* 33 (1979): 118, and fig. 4.

55. On this phenomenon in general, see Maurice Halbwachs, *La topographie légendaire des Évangiles en Terre Sainte*, 2nd ed. (Paris, 1971), 156–60.

56. For the Frankish Palm Sunday ceremony, see the part of the Barletta Ordinal reedited in Shagrir, "Adventus in Jerusalem," 18–20; BAV, Barb. lat. 659, fols. 65^{r}–66^{r}; Albert Schönfelder, "Die Prozessionen der Lateiner in Jerusalem zur Zeit der Kreuzzüge," *Historisches Jahrbuch* 32 (1911): 584–86. See also Johann of Würzburg in *Peregrinationes tres*, 96.

57. Johann of Würzburg in *Peregrinationes tres*, 94. Cf. Psalm 83:5.

58. Gregory Dix, *The Shape of the Liturgy* (Glasgow, 1945), esp. 348–53; Jonathan Z. Smith, *To Take Place: Toward Theory in Ritual* (Chicago, 1987), 86–95.

59. "Itinerarium Egeriae," c. 31, ed. A. Franceschini and R. Weber, in *Itineraria et alia geographica*, Corpus Christianorum. Series Latina 175 (Turnhout, 1965), 77.

60. The double procession is attested already in 1118: AA 12.29 (870).

61. On the probable influence of Chartres on the Frankish Palm Sunday ceremony, see Shagrir, "Adventus in Jerusalem," 11–15.

62. For Liberation Day as one of Jerusalem's major feasts, see *Cart St Sép*, 216, no. 98.

63. "Un sermon commémoratif de la prise de Jérusalem par les Croisés attribué à Foucher de Chartres," ed. Charles Kohler, *ROL* 8 (1900–1901): 158–64. Another sermon was identified by John France, "An Unknown Account of the Capture of Jerusalem," *English Historical Review* 87 (1972): 782–83, and edited and discussed by Linder, "A New Day, New Joy."

64. Simon John, "The 'Feast of the Liberation of Jerusalem': Remembering and Reconstructing the First Crusade in the Holy City, 1099–1187," *Journal of Medieval History* 41 (2015): 422–30.

65. For an ingenious attempt to reconstruct the original liturgy, see M. Cecilia Gaposchkin, "The Feast of the Liberation of Jerusalem in British Library Additional ms. 8927 Reconsidered," *Mediaeval Studies* 77 (2015): 127–81; it amounts to a revision of Linder, "The Liturgy." The discussion of Jerusalemite perceptions of the 1099 conquest may profit from analyzing the poem composed for the conquest's anniversary, which sings the praises of earthly Jerusalem: *Carmina Burana*, 1.1:104–5, no. 52.

66. "De hac liberatione secundum novam institutionem nichil facimus, preter processionem et missam matutinalem, propter dedicationem ecclesie. . . . Et eodem die dedicatio ecclesie dominici sepulcri, quam sollempniter celebramus iuxta voluntatem et preceptum domini Fulcherii patriarche. Missa matutinalis de captione tantum canitur, sed processio nunquam [MS: non quam] dimittitur, sed festive peragitur, ut prescriptum est." BAV, Barb. lat. 659, fols.

101v–102r, with *non quam* emended to *nunquam*, on the basis of two manuscripts, by Linder, "'Like Purest Gold Resplendent,'" 47 with n. 103. For the hypothesis that the feast underwent two or possibly three revisions and that the Sepulcher's cantors played a major role in their making, see Aspesi, "The Cantors," 283–96.

67. Sebastián Salvadó, "Rewriting the Latin Liturgy of the Holy Sepulchre: Text, Ritual and Devotion for 1149," *Journal of Medieval History* 43 (2017): 403–20.

68. For Bethlehem, see Johann of Würzburg in *Peregrinationes tres*, 85; Theoderich in *Peregrinationes tres*, 179.

69. On Zdík/Heinricus, see Jan Bistřický, "Studien zum Urkunden-, Brief- und Handschriftenwesen des Bischofs Heinrich Zdík von Olmütz," *Archiv für Diplomatik* 26 (1980): 229–31, no. 2. On the influence on the feasts in Autun, Bourges, and Laon, see M. Cecilia Gaposchkin, *Invisible Weapons: Liturgy and the Making of Crusade Ideology* (Ithaca, NY, 2017), 174–78. On the distych, see Estelle Ingrand-Varenne, "Transferts épigraphiques: Les inscriptions de l'abbaye du Val de Josaphat a Jérusalem," in *Transferts*, 88–92. On the Mass against the Pagans, see Linder, *Raising Arms*, 118–19, 137.

70. Dondi, *The Liturgy*, 32, 39; James Boyce, *Carmelite Liturgy and Spiritual Identity: The Choir Books of Kraków* (Turnhout, 2008), 70–74.

71. The four volumes of Pringle, *Churches*, discuss 489 edifices. According to my count, 338 of these were Latin (including churches whose existence may be merely assumed, like those of Barfīliyyā, Bir Mā'īn, Khirbat Kafr Rūt), 74 Greek Orthodox, 38 Eastern Christian, 26 unclassifiable, and 9 beyond the kingdom's borders.

72. For a survey of the building activity in and around Jerusalem, see Bernard Hamilton, "Rebuilding Zion: The Holy Places of Jerusalem in the Twelfth Century," in *Renaissance and Renewal in Christian History*, ed. Derek Baker (Oxford, 1977), 105–16.

73. Avraham Gross and Avraham Fraenkel, "The First Crusade and the Kingdom of Jerusalem in an Unpublished Hebrew Dirge," *Crusades* 11 (2012): 26 (lines 26–27). The poet claims (lines 41–42) that the Christians "have now been ruling the land for several years, dwelling quietly, fat and blooming."

74. Al-Qāḍī al-Fāḍil in Ibn Khallikan, *RHC Or*, 3:421–22; *Ibn Khallikan's Biographical Dictionary*, 4:526–27. Translation: Elon Harvey.

75. Oleg Grabar, "The Crusades and the Development of Islamic Art," in Laiou and Mottahedeh, *The Crusades from the Perspective of Byzantium and the Muslim World*, 244.

76. Melchior de Vogüé, *Les églises de la Terre Sainte* (Paris, 1860). For contemporary research, see esp. the monumental volumes by Jaroslav Folda, *The Art of the Crusaders* and *Crusader Art in the Holy Land*, as well as his *Crusader Art: The Art of the Crusaders in the Holy Land, 1099–1291* (Aldershot, 2008).

77. In 1979, Marie Luise Bulst-Thiele argued that the phrase "Kunst der fränkischen Kolonisten" is more correct than "Kreuzfahrerkunst," because Franks, not crusaders, produced the works of art: see her "Die Mosaiken der 'Auferstehungskirche' in Jerusalem," 442. In 1984, Valentino Pace coined the term "Frankish sculpture": see his "I capitelli di Nazareth e la scultura 'franca' del XII secolo a Gerusalemme," in *Scritti di storia del'arte in onore di Roberto Salvini*

(Florence, 1984), 87–95. In 2004, Jacoby ("Society, Culture and the Arts," 106, 120) expressed reservation about the term "crusader art" by placing the word "crusader" between inverted commas. For a valiant if problematic defense of the term "crusader art," see Gil Fishhof, *Shaping Identities in a Holy Land: Crusader Art in the Latin Kingdom of Jerusalem, Patrons and Viewers* (Abingdon, 2024), 7–9.

78. See the pioneering study by Kenaan, "Local Christian Art in Twelfth-Century Jerusalem." For a lucid overview of the subfield's evolution from 1860 to the present, see Fishhof, *Shaping Identities*, 12–28.

79. Folda, *The Art of the Crusaders*, 347–51; Bianca Kühnel and Gustav Kühnel, *The Church of the Nativity in Bethlehem: The Crusader Lining of an Early Christian Basilica* (Regensburg, 2019), 19–24 (Lamberz's reedition of the inscriptions appears on 148–51).

80. Folda, *The Art of the Crusaders*, 351–53; Kūhnel and Kühnel, *The Church of the Nativity*, 28–29. The Syriac inscription was discovered in 1983 by the late Gustav Kühnel: see his "Neue Feldarbeiten zur musivischen und malerischen Ausstattung der Geburts-Basilika in Bethlehem," *Kunstchronik* 37 (1984): 512.

81. Cf. Kühnel and Kühnel, *The Church of the Nativity*, 10, 43–44.

82. Prosper Viaud, *Nazareth et ses deux églises de l'Annonciation et de Saint-Joseph d'après les fouilles récentes* (Paris, 1910), 73–74 and figs. 10–11; Bellarmino Bagatti, *Gli scavi di Nazaret*, 2 vols. (Jerusalem, 1971–84), 2:77 (no. 22—Hagop, no. 23—Vardan [?]). Michael Stone and Kevork Hintlian deciphered the names for me.

83. Kenaan-Kedar, "A Neglected Series," esp. 110–11 and fig. 8.

84. Fishhof, *Shaping Identities*, 283–92.

85. John H. Elliott, *History in the Making* (New Haven, CT, 2012), 144–45.

86. See for instance the various interpretations of the Nazareth capitals: Gil Fishhof, "From Sepphoris to Nazareth: Aspects of Crusader Historiography and a New Reading of the Nazareth Sculpture," in *The Crusader World*, ed. Adrian J. Boas (Abingdon, 2016), 666–71; Fishhof, *Shaping Identities*, 181–82.

87. Kühnel, *Crusader Art*, 155–68; Nurith Kenaan-Kedar, "The Role and Meaning of Crusader Architectural Decoration: From Local Romanesque Traditions to Gothic Hegemony," in *Kreuzfahrerstaaten*, 165–78; Folda, *The Art of the Crusaders*, 13–15, 164–67.

88. Aslanov, *Le français au Levant*, 108; Folda, *Crusader Art*, 167–69; Folda, "Crusader Art and the West: Thoughts of Assessing the Impact of Art from the Crusader East on Medieval Art in Western Europe, Especially in Central Italy," in Boas, *The Crusader World*, 624–45.

89. Yolles, *Making the East Latin*, 86.

90. Kühnel, *Crusader Art*, 157.

91. On the relationship between the domes, see al-Muqaddasī, *The Best Divisions*, 146; for the Frankish period, see Nurith Kenaan-Kedar, "Symbolic Meaning in Crusader Architecture: The Twelfth-Century Dome of the Holy Sepulcher Church in Jerusalem," *Cahiers archéologiques* 34 (1986): 109–17. Yolles argues that Gaufridus, abbot of the Lord's Temple, presented his church as Jerusalem's spiritual center, and his variant of salvation history ignored the traditions linked to the Church of the Holy Sepulcher: Yolles, *Making the East Latin*, 107–8, 123.

92. On the role of the Lord's Temple in Frankish Jerusalem, see Schein, *Gateway*, 98–104.

93. *Gesta Francorum*, 92; *Le "Liber" de Raymond d'Aguilers*, 151.

94. FC 1.29 (305), 1.30 (310).

95. "Un rituel," ed. Kohler, 409–10, 412, 428–29.

96. On the coronation, see *Ernoul*, 179; John of Ibelin, *Le Livre des Assises*, 575, c. 220. See Prawer, *The Latin Kingdom*, 97–101; Sylvia Schein, "Between Mount Moriah and the Holy Sepulchre: The Changing Traditions of the Temple Mount in the Central Middle Ages," *Traditio* 40 (1984): 184–86.

97. Hans Eberhard Mayer and Claudia Sode, *Die Siegel der lateinischen Könige von Jerusalem*, MGH Schriften 66 (Wiesbaden, 2014). On the message of the seal's inscription and Baldwin I's possible role in its inception, see Robert Kool, "*Civitas regis regvm omnivm*: Inventing a Royal Seal in Jerusalem, 1100–1118," in *Crusading and Archaeology: Some Archaeological Approaches to the Crusades*, ed. Vardit Shotten-Hallel and Rosie Weetch (Abingdon, 2021), 244–62.

98. Acardus's poem was edited by Paul Lehmann, "Die mittellateinischen Dichtungen der Prioren des Tempels von Jerusalem Acardus und Gaufridus," in *Corona Quernea: Festgabe Karl Strecker*, MGH Schriften 6 (Leipzig, 1941), 307–30.

99. Lehmann, "Die mittellateinischen Dichtungen," 329–30. Albert of Aachen likewise writes that the Temple was rebuilt by Christians: AA 6.24 (432–34). See the commentary by Halbwachs, *La topographie légendaire*, 156.

100. Adso Dervensis, *De ortu et tempore Antichristi*, ed. D. Verhelst, CCCM 45 (Turnhout, 1976), 24.

101. Acardus, 308, 329–30, lines 15–32, 794–808. On Tancred's looting of the shrine immediately upon the conquest, see AA 6.23, 25 (432–36), FC 1.28 (302–3). Similarly, Fretellus remarks that the marble stone in front of Tyre on which Christ sat down remained there unharmed until the expulsion of the Gentiles—that is, the Muslims—from the town, but thereafter it was robbed by the Frankish and Venetian conquerors: Fretellus, 18 (Version Zdík, c. 25). Contrasting a considerate Muslim stewardship with the rapaciousness of Christian conquerors appears to have become a stock theme among some Frankish clerics.

102. For the quotation, see Acardus, 329, line 803; cf. 308, line 27.

103. WT 15.18 (699).

104. Gaufridus, "Super libros Machabeorum," ed. Eyal Poleg, "On the Books of Maccabees: An Unpublished Poem by Geoffrey, Prior of the *Templum Domini*," *Crusades* 9 (2010): 39, 42, lines 558, 674; Gaufridus, "De septem libris Iosephi," ed. Julian Yolles, "Geoffrey, Prior of the *Templum Domini*: *On the Seven Books of Josephus*," *Crusades* 13 (2014): 93, 111, lines 160, 795; Yolles, *Making the East Latin*, 101–13. On Gaufridus, see Amnon Linder, "An Unpublished Charter of Geoffrey, Abbot of the Temple in Jerusalem," in *Outremer*, 119–29; Rudolf Hiestand, "Gaufridus abbas Templi Domini: An Underestimated Figure in the Early History of the Kingdom of Jerusalem," in *EC*, 48–59.

105. "Un diplome inédit d'Amaury I, roi de Jérusalem, en faveur de l'abbaye du Temple-Notre-Seigneur (Acre, 6–11 avril 1166)," ed. Ferdinand Chalandon, *ROL* 8 (1900–1901): 311–17; Linder, "An Unpublished Charter," 121–24; Mayer, *Bistümer*, 172–96, 222–29.

106. John of Ibelin, *Le Livre des Assises*, 615, c. 239; for the date, see Peter W. Edbury, *John of Ibelin and the Kingdom of Jerusalem* (Woodbridge, 1997), 129–31.

107. For discussion, see Pringle, *Churches*, 3:397–417, no. 367; also Folda, *The Art of the Crusaders*, 136–37, 249–74, and passim; yet he assumes that the iron grill was removed after Ṣalāḥ al-Dīn's reconquest in 1187: Folda, *Crusader Art in the Holy Land*, 25b. In reality, it remained in situ until ca. 1966; one part of it is in the Islamic Museum near the Aqṣā Mosque, another in the Armenian part of the Church of the Holy Sepulcher.

108. Möhring, "Die Kreuzfahrer," 131–33.

109. The anti-Christian inscription on the northwestern side of the Dome of the Rock reads: "[Praise be] to Allah who hath not taken to Himself offspring, to Whom there has never been any partner in the sovereignty, nor any protector from abasement; magnify Him frequently [Qur'an 7:111]." *Corpus inscriptionum arabicarum Palaestinae*, 7:67. The Latin inscription had read: "Pax aeterna ab aeterno patre sit huic domui." Johann of Würzburg in *Peregrinationes tres*, 94; Theoderich in *Peregrinationes tres*, 160.

110. Saewulf in *Peregrinationes tres*, 67; Heribert Busse, "Vom Felsendom zum Templum Domini," in *Das Heilige Land im Mittelalter: Begegnungsraum zwischen Orient und Okzident*, ed. Wolfdietrich Fischer and Jürgen Schneider (Neustadt an der Aisch, 1982), 27–28. See also Iris Shagrir, "The Guide of MS Beinecke 481.77 and the Intertwining of Christian, Jewish and Muslim Traditions in Twelfth-Century Jerusalem," *Crusades* 10 (2011): 2, 4, 17–18.

111. Johann of Würzburg in *Peregrinationes tres*, 90; Busse, "Vom Felsendom," 30. Saewulf in *Peregrinationes tres* (68) reports that "ibidem adhuc apparent in rupe vestigia domini dum ipse abscondit se et exivit de templo."

112. Holy of Holies: Saewulf in *Peregrinationes tres*, 67; adulteress: Johann of Würzburg in *Peregrinationes tres*, 91.

113. The inscriptions appear, with some variations, in the itineraries of Johann of Würzburg in *Peregrinationes tres*, 94–95, and Theoderich in *Peregrinationes tres*, 160–61; for a discussion of their exact locations, see Folda, *The Art of the Crusaders*, 252.

114. Daniel the Abbot, "The Life and Journey of Daniel, Abbot of the Russian Land," in *Jerusalem Pilgrimage, 1099–1185*, trans. John Wilkinson, Joyce Hill, and W. F. Ryan (London, 1988), 132.

115. Fretellus, 32.

116. Fretellus, 58.

117. Johann of Würzburg in *Peregrinationes tres*, 88; but *quantum* in line 231 ought to be emended to *quartum*; cf. Fretellus, 32, 58.

118. Theoderich in *Peregrinationes tres*, 163–64.

119. WT 1.2 (107), 8.3 (386). Benjamin of Tudela, who visited Jerusalem about the same time, wrote likewise that it was ʿUmar b. al-Khaṭṭāb who built there "a large and very beautiful dome": *The Itinerary of Benjamin of Tudela*, 24 (text), 22 (translation).

120. On William's probable ignorance of literary Arabic, see Hannes Möhring, "Zu der Geschichte der orientalischen Herrscher des Wilhelm von Tyrus: Die Frage der Quellenabhängigkeiten," *Mittellateinisches Jahrbuch* 19 (1984): 173–74.

121. WT 1.15 (132).

122. Samer Akkach, "The Poetics of Concealment: al-Nabulusi's Encounter with the Dome of the Rock," *Muqarnas* 22 (2005): 114; also Oleg Grabar, *The Dome of the Rock* (Cambridge, MA, 2006), 201.

123. "Inventio Patriarcharum," 144. The account ascribes the pillaging to *Appamiensis episcopus*; this was Pierre of Narbonne, bishop of Albara and archbishop of Apamea: see Hamilton, *The Latin Church*, 10, 23, 114 n. 1, 130. For the probable date of pillage, see Drory, "Some Observations," 118, excerpt 17.

124. "Inventio Patriarcharum," 143–44; cf. Yolles, *Making the East Latin*, 118–19. The anonymous author mentions Patriarch Warmund of Jerusalem, who died in 1128, as *sanctae recordationis* ("Inventio Patriarcharum," 149) and relates that he learned about the discovery from Eudes, the oldest priest of the Hebron chapter, and Arnoul, the key figure in the search ("Inventio Patriarcharum," 144). Consequently, the account was written not too long after 1128.

125. "Inventio Patriarcharum," 138–43. Whalen has pointed out that the anonymous author aimed (a) to highlight the Latins' superiority over all earlier searchers for the remains, and (b) to refute the opinion that Hebron had not been a bishop's seat: Brett E. Whalen, "The Discovery of the Holy Patriarchs: Relics, Ecclesiastical Politics and Sacred History in Twelfth-Century Palestine," *Historical Reflections* 27 (2001): 143–52.

126. For the account, see "Inventio Patriarcharum," 144–49. For commentaries, see Louis-Hugues Vincent, Ernest J. H. Mackay, and Félix-Marie Abel, *Hébron, le Haram el-Khalil: Sépulture des Patriarches*, 2 vols. (Paris, 1923), 1:176–88; Kaspar Elm, "*Nec minori celebritate a catholicis cultoribus observatur et colitur*: Zwei Berichte über die 1119/20 erfolgte Auffindung und Erhebung der Gebeine der Patriarchen Abraham, Isaak und Jakob," *Zeitschrift für Religions- und Geistesgeschichte* 49 (1997): 319–44. For a lucid synthesis of the written and archaeological evidence, see Hervé Barbé, *Hébron 1119: L'invention du tombeau des patriarches* (Paris, 2017).

127. The anonymous author writes: "Anno igitur vicesimo primo regni Francorum" (144), which points to 1119/20, and gives 25 June and 6 October as the dates of the discovery and the translation, respectively; Muslim sources place the discovery in 513 AH (14 April 1119–1 April 1120); consequently, the year must be 1119. See Paul Riant, "Invention de la sépulture des patriarches Abraham, Isaac et Jacob à Hébron le 25 juin 1119," *AOL* 2, no. 1 (1884): 412–16; Vincent, Mackay, and Abel, *Hébron*, 177–78.

128. Measurements of the subterranean passage in 1981 and of the Herodian edifice in its entirety suggest that the canons' cubit amounted to 0.57 m: B. Z. Kedar and Hervé Barbé, "Dating the Subterranean Passage at the Patriarchs' Cave, Hebron," in *Israel's Land: Papers Presented to Israel Shatzman on His Jubilee*, ed. Joseph Geiger, Hannah M. Cotton, and Guy D. Stiebel (Ra'anana, 2009), 179–84. In 2017 Barbé argued for a slightly smaller cubit, measuring 0.56 m: Barbé, *Hébron 1119*, 96.

129. Text II in "Inventio Patriarcharum," 150–55.

130. In 1112 Rainier attests to a charter as Prior of St. Abraham [Hebron]: *Cart Hosp*, 1:26, no. 25. Since he closes the list of witnesses from among the clergy, he may have been appointed not much earlier: Hamilton in Hamilton and Jotischky, *Latin and Greek Monasticism*, 133.

131. See esp. Vincent, Mackay, and Abel, *Hébron*, 186, fig. 72.

132. For these measurements, see Ze'ev Yeivin, "The Machpela Cave Subterranean Complex," *Israel—People and Land: Haaretz Museum Yearbook*, n.s. 2–3 (1985–86), 53–62 [in Hebrew, with English summary]; Doron Chen, "Measuring the Cave of Abraham in Hebron," *Liber Annuus Studii Biblici Franciscani* 37 (1987): 291, 293; Barbé, *Hébron 1119*, 81–91.

133. "Inventio Patriarcharum," 148. The author does not divulge how the body was marked.

134. Benjamin of Tudela relates that in the Cave of Machpela there are "many jars full with bones of Israelites," because Jews used to deposit there their fathers' remains: *The Itinerary of Benjamin of Tudela*, 27 (text), 26 (translation).

135. Warmund's order and Rainier's compliance are mentioned only in the account's version that appears in Douai, Bibliothèque municipale, MS 851 that Huygens edited in "Inventio Patriarcharum." Al-Harawī relates that it was King Bardwīl (Baldwin II) who, upon the discovery of the patriarchs' remains, "renewed their shrouds, then sealed the place in the year 513 [*hijrī*]" (AD 1119): *A Lonely Wayfarer's Guide*, 80–81.

136. *Historia Compostellana* 2.28, ed. Emma Falque Rey, CCCM 70 (Turnhout, 1988), 272.

137. *The Itinerary of Benjamin of Tudela*, 27 (text), 26 (translation); al-Harawī, *A Lonely Wayfarer's Guide*, 78–79; Petaḥya of Regensburg, *Die Rundreise*, 33–34 (text), 46–47 (translation).

138. On the elevation of Hebron to a bishopric, see WT 20.3 (914); Mayer, *Bistümer*, 197–98.

139. "Henricus, Trecensis comes palatinus . . . tandem in optatam sanctorum patriarcharum Abrahae, Isaac et Jacob basilicam orandi gratia perveniens, R. venerabilis ejusdem ecclesiae Latinorum primi episcopi et canonicorum ibidem Deo devote servientium paupertati misericorditer compatiens." Henri d'Arbois de Jubainville, "Études sur les documents antérieurs à l'année 1285, conservés dans les archives de quatre petits hôpitaux de la ville de Troyes," *Mémoires de la société d'agriculture, des sciences, arts et belles-lettres du département de l'Aube* 2, no. 8 (1857): 109, no. 19. The count founded in the same year the priory of St. Abraham in Troyes, a daughter house of the church of Hebron: Wolf Zöller, "The Other Augustinian Consortium: The Templars and the Smaller Communities of Regular Canons of the Crusader States," in *D'Orient en Occident*, 187–88.

140. John of Ibelin, *Le Livre des Assises*, 615, c. 239.

141. **Church of the Holy Sepulcher**: Wormald, "Calendars of the Church," in Buchthal, *Miniature Painting*, 119; Kallenberg, *Fontes liturgiae carmelitanae*, 298. **Lord's Temple**: Leroquais, *Les bréviaires manuscrits*, 3:191. However, the feast goes unmentioned in Queen Melisende's Psalter and in the calendar from Antioch that dates from the mid-thirteenth century: Wormald, "Calendars of the Church," 126; Saxer, "Le calendrier," 119.

142. Frankish bishop attested from 1129: *Cart St Sép*, 93, no. 30. Usāma's remark appears in a passage of his *Kitāb al-ʿAṣā*, translated in Cobb, "Usāma Ibn Munqidh's *Book of the Staff*," 119.

143. Innocent II's grant is mentioned in Alexander III's letter of 1179: *Papsturkunden für Kirchen*, ed. Hiestand, 291, no. 117. The discovery is announced in

Patriarch William's letter, edited twice: (a) Antoine Le Roux de Lincy and Alexandre Bruel, "Notice historique et critique sur dom Jacques du Breul, prieur de Saint-Germain-des-Près," *Bibliothèque de l'École des chartes* 28 (1868): 492–93; (b) G. Estournet, "Les origines historiques de Nemours et sa charte de franchises," *Annales de la Société historique et archéologique du Gâtinais* 39 (1930): 240–42.

144. ʿImād al-Dīn in Abū Shāma, *RHC Or*, 4:302.

145. John of Ibelin, *Le Livre des Assises*, 615, c. 239.

146. "ecclesiam optimo coepimus lapidatu fabricare." Kedar, "Raising Funds," 454. Ronnie Ellenblum, "Construction Methods," in *Horns*, 170–71.

147. Raoul's appeal has been edited twice: (a) Estournet, "Les origines historiques," 242–44; (b) Kedar, "Raising Funds," 454–55.

148. Pierre Héliot and Marie-Laure Chastang, "Quêtes et voyages de reliques au profit des églises françaises du moyen âge," *Revue d'histoire ecclésiastique* 59 (1964): 796–98; Martin Warnke, *Bau und Überbau: Soziologie der mittelalterlichen Kultur nach den Schriftquellen* (Frankfurt am Main, 1976), 71; Patrick Geary, *Furta Sacra: Thefts of Relics in the Central Middle Ages*, 2nd ed. (Princeton, NJ, 1990), 63–65.

149. *Papsturkunden für Templer und Johanniter*, 253, no. 53.

150. Nurith Kenaan-Kedar, "The Cathedral of Sebaste: Its Western Donors and Models," in *Horns*, 99–120; Kenaan-Kedar, "Aspects des relations entre 'centre' et 'périphérie': Les cathédrales Saint-Étienne de Sens et Saint-Jean de Sébaste," in *Pèlerinages et croisades*, ed. Léon Pressouyre (Paris, 1995), 315–19—but see the reservations of Robert Ousterhout, "The French Connection? Construction of Vaults and Cultural Identity in Crusader Architecture," in *France and the Holy Land*, 82–83. On the sculptural program and architecture of Sebaste Cathedral, see Fishhof, *Shaping Identities*, 190–99, 204–9. An 1192 inventory of relics preserved at Sens Cathedral lists six items, some of which probably originated in Sebaste: "De sancto Johanne Baptista. De pulvere ejusdem. Item reliquie ipsius. Item reliquie ejus. De vestimentis ejusdem sancti Johannis Baptiste. Item de veste ejus." An extant label indicates that the cathedral also owned a fragment "De sancto sepulchro Johannis Baptiste." Maurice Prou and Eugène Chartraire, "Authentiques de reliques conservées au trésor de la cathédrale de Sens," *Mémoires de la Société nationale des antiquaires de France* 59 (1898): 136, 152, plate 12, no. 67.

151. Gerard of Nazareth, *De conversacione*, cc. 36–37 (74).

152. "Les chemins et les pelerinages de la Terre Sainte. Texte B," in *Itinéraires a Jérusalem*, 199. The text is dated to before 1268.

153. WT 20.25 (947–48). Jonathan Riley-Smith, "The Death and Burial of Latin Christian Pilgrims to Jerusalem and Acre, 1099–1291," *Crusades* 7 (2008): 177. Sick believers who visited the tomb of Count Eudes of Nevers, buried in Acre in 1266, were miraculously cured: *Cronaca del Templare di Tiro*, 104, §103.

154. On pilgrimage to tombs of Muslims who fell fighting the *jihād*, see Daniella Talmon-Heller, *Islamic Piety in Medieval Syria* (Leiden, 2008), 192.

155. The letter is printed in Martène and Durand, *Thesaurus novus anecdotorum*, 1:351–52. See also Hamilton, *The Latin Church*, 15.

156. "Istud est vere de illo precioso ligno sancte Crucis, quod dominus patriarcha Villalinus [Willelmus] coram me de illa sanctissima Cruce, que est

Jerosolimis et quam ipse in processione et contra paganos manibus suis portat, istam videlicet particulam accepit cum magno timore et mihi indigno dedit. Et ego rogo succcessores meos ut eam bene custodiant." Bistřický, "Studien," 229, no. 1; see also 141, 167, 179. Zdík's first pilgrimage took place in 1123. The authentication document, discovered in 1954, has not yet been utilized by crusade historians.

157. Cahen, *Orient et Occident*, 218; for discussion, see William J. Purkis, "'Holy Christendom's New Colony': The Extraction of Sacred Matter and the Colonial Status of the Latin Kingdom of Jerusalem," *Haskins Society Journal* 30 (2020): 177–211.

158. For Frederic's career and the letter's date, see Hans Eberhard Mayer, "Frederick of Laroche, Bishop of Acre and Archbishop of Tyre," *Tel Aviver Jahrbuch für deutsche Geschichte* 22 (1993): 59–72.

159. The letter is edited and discussed by Ursmer Berlière, "Frédéric de Laroche, évêque d'Acre et archevêque de Tyr: Envoi de reliques à l'abbaye de Florennes (1153–1161)," *Annales de l'Institut archéologique de Luxembourg* 43 (1908): 67–79; see also Berlière's earlier article, bearing the same title, in *Revue Bénédictine* 23 (1906): 501–13, and Berlière, "Une lettre de Frédéric de Laroche, évêque de S. Jean d'Acre (1153–1161)," *Revue Bénédictine* 24 (1907): 123–25.

160. Berlière, "Frédéric," 68, and, in general for Acre, Schlumberger, Chalandon, and Blanchet, *Sigillographie*, 101–4.

161. Berlière, "Frédéric," 78.

162. The letters are edited in Arthur Bertrand de Brousillon, *La maison de Craon (1050–1480): Étude historique accompagnée du Cartulaire de Craon*, 2 vols. (Paris, 1893), 1:100–5.

163. On the vow made in Egypt, see Bertrand de Brousillon, *La maison de Craon*, 1:117.

164. For the quotation, see Bertrand de Brousillon, *La maison de Craon*, 1:102.

165. Gui's letter is edited in "Documents inédits concernant l'Orient latin et les croisades (XIIe–XIVe siècle)," ed. Charles Kohler, *ROL* 7 (1899): 1–9. The letter's *terminus a quo* is 1161–66: see Hiestand, "Gaufridus abbas Templi Domini," 57. Since Gui mentions the prior, not the bishop of Hebron, the *terminus ad quem* should be 1168. On the relics given to Gui, see also Miriam Rita Tessera, "Le donne e la traslazione delle reliquie di Oltremare in Occidente nel secolo XII," *Reti Medievali Rivista* 21, no. 2 (2020): 120–23, 127–33.

166. *Actus pontificum Cenomannis*, 407.

167. *Die Urkunden . . . des Klosters Scheyern*, 29, no. 10.

168. Charles Clermont-Ganneau, "Un reliquaire des croisades," in Clermont-Ganneau, *Recueil d'archéologie orientale* 2:234–39; Fishhof, *Shaping Identities*, 70. For a letter of 1272 authenticating a composite relic prepared in Acre, see Pierre Battifol, "Authentique de reliques du XIIIe siècle," *Bulletin de la Société Nationale des Antiquaires de France*, 1891, 238.

169. *Les miracles de Notre-Dame de Roc-Amadour* 3.11 (289).

170. *Les miracles de Notre-Dame de Roc-Amadour* 2.19 (212–13).

171. I follow here the argument of Benedicta Ward, *Miracles and the Medieval Mind*, 2nd ed. (Philadelphia, 1987), 123–25.

172. Hiestand, "*Nam qui fuimus Occidentales*," 70–71.

173. Pierre of Blois, "Passio Raginaldi principis Antiochie," esp. 51, 57, 61–62, lines 519–20, 656–57, 776–77. Similarly, Ralph Niger wrote: "Occisus est etiam beatus Reinaldus, princeps Antiochiae, protestans se non redditurum Sarracenis vestigium unius pedis Sanctae Terrae pro redemptione vitae suae." *The Chronicles of Ralph Niger*, ed. Robert Anstruther (London, 1851), 94.

174. For Evremar's gift, see PL 162:677, ep. 77; Étienne of Tournai, *Lettres*, 147–48, no. 135.

175. AA 8.46 (636).

176. Jack Goody, *Renaissances: The One or the Many?* (Cambridge, 2010), 241–43.

177. Schlumberger, Chalandon, and Blanchet, *Sigillographie*, 94–95 (Caesarea), 96–98 (Nazareth), 106–7 (Bethlehem), 112–13 (Hebron), 116–17 (Tiberias), 122 (Bethany), 127 (Mount Tabor). For Caesarea, see also Harry W. Hazard, "The Sigillography of Crusader Caesarea," in *Near Eastern Numismatics, Iconography, Epigraphy and History: Studies in Honor of George C. Miles*, ed. Dickran K. Kouymjian (Beirut, 1974), 361–65; Arnold Spaer, "Archbishop Baldwin II of Caesarea," *Numismatic Chronicle* 140 (1980): 193–94, plate 25B; Spaer, "A Seal of Archbishop Ernesius (Hernes) of Caesarea," *Numismatic Chronicle* 165 (2005): 285–86, plate 27B. Bertrand de Brousillon, *La maison de Craon*, 1:103 n. 4.

178. The description survives in two slightly differing versions, the first dedicated to Bishop Zdík/Heinricus of Olomouc, the second to Count Rodrigo González de Lara; both datable to 1137–38. It was highly influential: Johann of Würzburg derived about 45 percent of his narrative from it, and Theoderich used it in about one-quarter of his work: Huygens, Introduction to *Peregrinationes tres*, 19.

179. Fretellus, 7 (Version Zdík, c. 3), 54 (Version González, cc. 2–7); Fretellus, 18 (Version Zdík, c. 24), 56 (Version González, *Descripcio Arabie*).

180. He presents Godefrid of Bouillon as "sperans Deo preeunte gratia restituere regnum David": Fretellus, 44 (Version Zdík, c. 77). Similarly, Orderic Vitalis claims that Godefrid was elevated to the throne *regni David regis*: OV 9.16 (5:174); cf. 10.21 (5:342). The Franks presented by Fretellus as second Israel: Fretellus, 6 (Version Zdík, c. 2), 53 (Version González, cc. 2–7).

181. On earlier emphasis on New Testament sites, see, for instance, the itineraries of Bernard the Monk in ca. 868 and of Saewulf in 1102–3: *Itinera hierosolymitana et descriptiones*, ed. Titus Tobler and Auguste Molinier (Geneva, 1879), 314–18; Saewulf in *Peregrinationes tres*, 63–75.

182. Fretellus, 26 (Version Zdík, c. 40): Beth Shean; 27 (c. 41): Ger (the Gur of the Hebrew Bible, Gaver of the Vulgate); 40 (c. 70): Beth Horon; 41 (c. 72): Jericho.

183. Fretellus, 26 (Version Zdík, c. 40): Jezebel; 42 (c. 73): Cain. On the legend about Cain's death at the hands of Lamech, see Ruth Mellinkoff, *The Mark of Cain* (Berkeley, 1981), 29, 61–72.

184. He starts with Hebron, the place where Adam was created and buried, lists the forty-two stations at which the Israelites stopped during their wanderings in the desert, and concludes with their conquest of Jericho. Fretellus, 9–17

(Version Zdík, cc. 7–22). On biblical motifs in Frankish visual culture, see Fishhof, *Shaping Identities*, 37–49, 63–70.

185. This is the explanation of Schwerin, *Die Aufrufe der Päpste*, 50–51. She points out that Ekkehard, Foucher, and Emperor Henry IV are the earliest to use the term, and that only in 1173 does it appear for the first time in the papal correspondence concerning the crusade.

186. FC 2.6.7 (388), 2.8.2 (397), 2.31.1 (490), 2.44.2 (546); Ekkehard, *Hierosolymita*, c. 27, in *RHC Oc*, 5:33; Luc d'Achéry, *Spicilegium, sive Collectio veterum aliquot scriptorum qui in Galliae bibliothecis delituerant*, 3 vols. (Paris, 1723), 3:443b; Baudri of Bourgueil, *The "Historia Ierosolimitana" of Baldric of Bourgueil*, ed. Steven Biddlecombe (Martlesham, Suffolk, 2014), 8.

187. *UKJ*, 1:323, no. 139; *Balduini III Historia Nicaena vel Antiochena necnon Jerosolymitana*, c. 2, in *RHC Oc*, 5:142 (an insertion into a passage depending on Robert the Monk). See also c. 70 (5:180).

188. *Tractatus*, 127.

189. Ezekiel 5:5. Wilhelm Heinrich Roscher, *Der Omphalosgedanke bei verschiedenen Völkern, besonders den semitischen: Ein Beitrag zur vergleichenden Religionswissenschaft, Volkskunde und Archäologie* (Leipzig, 1918), 12–25, 53–57, 102–3.

190. Some crusade historians assume that Jerusalem was at the world's center already on pre-1099 maps, but historians of cartography demonstrate that this happened later: Konrad Miller, *Mappaemundi: Die ältesten Weltkarten*, 6 fasc. (Stuttgart, 1895–98), fasc. 1:30; John K. Wright, *The Geographical Lore of the Time of the Crusades* (New York, 1925), 259–61, 460–61; David Woodward, "Medieval Mappaemundi," in *The History of Cartography*, vol. 1: *Cartography in Prehistoric, Ancient and Medieval Europe and the Mediterranean*, ed. J. Brian Harley and David Woodward (Chicago, 1987), 340–42.

191. *Tractatus*, 123.

192. I owe the concept of the fragment to Louis Hartz, who coined it to characterize a society founded by emigrants, which amounts merely to a part of the entity from which they came: Louis Hartz et al., *The Founding of New Societies: Studies in the History of the United States, Latin America, South Africa, and Australia* (New York, 1964), esp. chap. 1. For an application of the concept to a medieval society see Richard F. Tomasson, *Iceland: The First New Society* (Reykjavík, 1980).

193. For the reprimands, see, for instance, the *Libellus de penitentia et de diversis temptationibus* by an anonymous German Benedictine, written in 1189/90 and partially edited as an appendix to *Petri Blesensis Tractatus duo*, ed. Robert B. C. Huygens, CCCM 194 (Turnhout, 2002), 101–6.

194. Abelard, Letter I (Historia calamitatum), c. 59, in *The Letter Collection of Peter Abelard and Heloise*, ed. and trans. David Luscombe (Oxford, 2013), 92–93.

195. Petrus Cantor, *Summa*, quoted and discussed by John Baldwin, *Masters, Princes, and Merchants: The Social Views of Peter the Chanter and His Circle*, 2 vols. (Princeton, NJ, 1970), 1:224, 2:160 n. 128; James A. Brundage, "The Limits of the War-Making Power: The Contribution of the Medieval Canonists," in *Peace in a Nuclear Age*, ed. Charles J. Reid Jr. (Washington, DC, 1986), 80. Both authors were puzzled by the bishop's title, with Brundage speaking of the "mysterious Bishop of St. George."

196. See, for instance, "Ego Rogerius Liddensis Sancti Georgii episcopus": WT 12.25 (581; a. 1123); "Constantinus Sancti Georgii episcopus": *UKJ*, 1:474, no. 258 (a. 1160). See also *Libellus*, 188: "episcopum sancti Georgii." The bishop mentioned by Petrus Cantor was probably Bernard, abbot of Mount Tabor, bishop of Lydda since 1168.

197. Richard A. Landes coined offhand the term "sancterranean" when, in conversation, I mentioned my need for a term tantamount to the nonexistent "holy-landish."

198. Rodney M. Thomson, "England and the Twelfth-Century Renaissance," *Past and Present* 101 (1983): 4; Thomson, "The Place of Germany in the Twelfth-Century Renaissance," in *Manuscripts and Monastic Culture: Reform and Renewal in Twelfth-Century Germany*, ed. Alison I. Beach (Turnhout, 2007), 19–42.

199. Yolles, *Making the East Latin*, 71–84; for a persuasive reconstruction of Foucher's development as writer and thinker, see 48–71.

200. Nikolas Jaspert, *Die Reconquista* (Munich, 2019), 26, quoting Sāʿid al-Andalusī (d. 1070). On Toledan mathematicians, geometers, astronomers, and physicians of his day, see Sāʿid al-Andalusī, *Science in the Medieval World: "Book of the Categories of Nations,"* trans. Semaan R. I. Salem and Alok Kumar (Austin, TX, 1996), 68, 74–78. For an overview of translations after the Castilian conquest, see Marie-Thérèse d'Alverny, "Translations and Translators," in Benson and Constable, *Renaissance and Renewal in the Twelfth Century*, 444–47, 452–57.

201. Cf. Cahen, *Orient et Occident*, 115, 215–16.

202. Drory, "Some Observations," 104–14, 120–22, excerpts 1–3, 5, 8–12, 20–22. For additional details, see Omar Abed Rabo, "Islamic Cultural-Religious Life in Jerusalem on the Eve of the First Crusade," in *EO*, 1:24–43.

203. Hamilton in Hamilton and Jotischky, *Latin and Greek Monasticism*, 216.

204. Burnett dedicated a series of articles to the study of Stephanus's works. For an overview, see Charles Burnett, "Stephen, the Disciple of Philosophy, and the Exchange of Medical Learning in Antioch," *Crusades* 5 (2006): 113–29. On Stephanus's penchant for rhetorical learning, and for the importance of rhetorical skill in the Antiochene literary scene, see Yolles, *Making the East Latin*, 135–45, 174–75.

205. Olivier Hanne, "Adélard de Bath et les Arabes: Le renouvellement des sciences en Syrie du Nord au XIIe siècle," in *Transferts*, 263–303. Hanne assumes that Adelard was in the Principality of Antioch between ca. 1109 and ca. 1116 and learned Arabic there: "Adélard de Bath," 270–77, 302.

206. Prologue edited and translated by Charles Burnett, "Antioch as a Link between Arabic and Latin Culture in the Twelfth and Thirteenth Centuries," in *Occident et Proche-Orient*, 28–29.

207. *Liber Mamonis*, ed. and trans. in Dirk Grupe, *Stephen of Pisa and Antioch: Liber Mamonis. An Introduction to Ptolemaic Cosmology and Astronomy from the Early Crusader States* (Cham, Switzerland, 2019), 90–91,174–75, 324–25. My translation differs on several points.

208. "Arabem quendam." *Liber Mamonis*, 324–25. Similarly, Adelard of Bath was reproached for extoling Saracen opinions, while accusing "our people of ignorance in a disparaging way." Adelard of Bath, *Questiones naturales*, in Adelard

of Bath, *Conversations with His Nephew: On the Same and the Different, Questions on Natural Science and On Birds*, ed. and trans. Charles Burnett (Cambridge, 1998), 90–91.

209. This is the argument of Yolles, *Making the East Latin*, 174–75; for the hypothesis that Antioch may have been the source for the Christian Arabic texts that King Amaurry placed at William's disposal, see 201–3.

210. See Prawer, *Histoire*; Riley-Smith, *The Crusades: A History*; Tyerman, *God's War*. Runciman writes that "a certain Stephen of Antioch seems to have translated a medical treatise from the Arabic in 1227 [*sic*]": Runciman, *A History of the Crusades*, 3:490. Richard mentions briefly—between parentheses—that "(à Antioche, Étienne de Pise a traduit le grand traité de médecine d'al-Majûsi)": Jean Richard, *Histoire des croisades* (Paris, 1996), 128.

6. A Candid Portrait of the Kingdom's Most Erudite Cleric

1. "Li archevesques de Sur ot a non Guillaumes, et fu nés en Jherusalem, et ne savoit on en Crestiienté mellour clerc de lui a son tans": *Ernoul*, 144. The Old French adapter of William's *Historia* is less emphatic; for him, William "biens s'entendoit en clergie" and "bons clers estoit et preudom": WT OF 2:255, 363. On *clerc* as a man of learning, see, for instance, Peter Classen, "Die Hohen Schulen und die Gesellschaft im 12. Jahrhundert," *Archiv für Kulturgeschichte* 48 (1966): 152–53.

2. Charles Homer Haskins, *The Renaissance of the Twelfth Century* (Cambridge, MA, 1927), 270; Max Manitius, *Geschichte der lateinischen Literatur des Mittelalters*, vol. 3 (Munich, 1931), 433–38; Runciman, *A History of the Crusades*, 2:477; Edbury and Rowe, *William of Tyre*, 174.

3. On William's use of Arabic chronicles, see Möhring, "Zu der Geschichte." William kept this innovation under wraps and merely mentioned his awareness of "Oriental traditions" (WT 1.1 [105]; for discussion, see Yolles, *Making the East Latin*, 193–97); yet William did announce that his other chronicle—the *History of the Oriental Rulers* that has not come down to us—is mostly based on the Arabic work of a Greek patriarch of Alexandria.

4. **Abstains from using the term "pagans"**: This has been established by Rainer Christoph Schwinges, *Kreuzzugsideologie und Toleranz: Studien zu Wilhelm von Tyrus* (Stuttgart, 1977), 121–27. For a succinct presentation of his theses, see Schwinges, "William of Tyre, the Muslim Enemy, and the Problem of Tolerance," in Gervers and Powell, *Tolerance and Intolerance*, 124–32. For a criticism of Schwinges's *Toleranz*-thesis, see Kristin Skottki, *Christen, Muslime und der Erste Kreuzzug: Die Macht der Beschreibung in der mittelalterlichen und modernen Historiographie* (Münster, 2015), 149–64. But it is not true (160) that Schwinges overlooked four instances in which William presented the Muslims as pagans. The term appears only in two documents that William quotes verbatim, WT 11.12 (513), 12.25 (578—twice). This was explicitly pointed out by Schwinges, *Kreuzzugsideologie*, 121. (The computer brings forth also four appearances of "Pagani" and "Paganis," but *humint* analysis reveals that these are personal names.) **Sunni and Shiʿi Muslims**: WT 1.4 (109–10), 19.21 (891). William believed that according to the Shiʿis God intended to entrust his message to ʿAlī, but the angel Gabriel

made a mistake and gave it to Muḥammad. Medieval Muslim heresiographers, from Ibn Qutayba (d. 889) onward, indeed mention an extremist Shiʿi group, the Ghurābiyya, that purportedly believes that Gabriel committed the error because Muḥammad and ʿAlī looked alike more closely than one crow (*ghurāb*) resembles another: Etan Kohlberg, "Western Studies of Shiʿa Islam," in *Shiʿism, Resistance, and Revolution*, ed. Martin Kramer (Boulder, CO, 1987), 31–32. Possibly William's knowledge about Shiʿi beliefs derived from contacts with Tyre's Shiʿis: cf. Möhring, "Die Kreuzfahrer," 142. **Commanders' ethnic origins**: Ann E. Zimo, "Us and Them: Identity in William of Tyre's *Chronicon*," *Crusades* 18 (2019): 6–13. **Ethnographer**: Jonathan Rubin, "Ethnographic Writing in the Kingdom of Jerusalem: In Search of a Neglected Intellectual Tradition," *Journal of Medieval History* 48 (2022): 323–46.

5. **Muslims**: WT 4.13 (253), 13.18 (609), 17.23 (792), 17.29 (802), 20.8 (921); **Franks**: WT 10.21 (481), 11.24 (531); **Byzantines**: WT 1.9 (120). Cf. Schwinges, *Kreuzzugsideologie*, 216–19, 231, 237; B. Z. Kedar, "Croisade et *Jihād* vus par l'ennemi: Une étude des perceptions mutuelles des motivations," in *Autour*, 350–51.

6. Wolfgang Giese, "Stadt- und Herrscherbeschreibungen bei Wilhelm von Tyrus," *Deutsches Archiv* 34 (1978): 396–408; for Shirkūh, see Schwinges, *Kreuzzugsideologie*, 183–87.

7. WT 17.7 (768–69), 19.4 (869–70), 20.17 (934), 20.25 (948), 21.4 (965), 22.20 (1038).

8. FC 2.2 (360), 2.13 (416).

9. WT 16.11 (730–31). I translated the phrase "que illi totis viribus procurabant" as if the verb were spelled "procurrabant." The English MSS B and W, characterized by Robert Huygens as "a veritable medieval edition of William's chronicle" (Huygens's introduction to WT, 22–31), omit the phrase, probably because "procurabant" did not make sense to the medieval "editor."

10. WT 21.7 (969–71); my interpretation differs from the customary one. For the notion of Muslims purportedly lacking military experience at the time of the First Crusade, see also WT 10.14 (470), 13.7 (594).

11. WT 21.23 (994).

12. WT 21.29 (1004). See also WT 13.26 (622).

13. WT 20.3 (914–15).

14. Mayer, "Einwanderer in der Kanzlei," 30–31.

15. This figure, as well as most subsequent ones, is taken from Brepols's Cross-Data Searchtool.

16. WT 21.22 (991). On these terms, see Hamilton A. R. Gibb, "The Armies of Saladin," *Cahiers d'histoire égyptienne* 3 (1951): 309; Gibb, *Studies on the Civilization of Islam* (Boston, 1962), 77, 87 nn. 31–32.

17. WT 13.16 (606). See the discussion in Schwinges, "Regionale Identität," 237–40.

18. WT 1.4 (108), 1.9 (120).

19. **Al-Sulamī**: Niall Christie, *The Book of the Jihad of ʿAli ibn Tahir al-Sulami (d. 1106): Text, Translation and Commentary* (Farnham, 2015), 43 (text), 207 (translation). **Al-Qāḍī al-Fāḍil**: Emmanuel Sivan, *L'Islam et la croisade: Idéologie et propagande dans les reactions musulmanes aux croisades* (Paris, 1968), 112–15; Sivan, "Islam

and the Crusades: Antagonism, Polemics, Dialogue," in *Religionsgespräche im Mittelalter*, ed. Bernard Lewis and Friedrich Niewöhner (Wiesbaden, 1992), 210–13; Kedar, "Croisade et *Jihād*," 346–50. **Yāqūt**: *Jacut's geographisches Wörterbuch*, ed. Ferdinand Wüstenfeld, 6 vols. (Leipzig, 1866–73), 2:276.

20. WT 20.31 (965); Yasser Tabbaa, "Monuments with a Message: Propagation of Jihād under Nūr A-Dīn," in *The Meeting of Two Worlds: Cultural Exchange between East and West during the Period of the Crusades*, ed. Vladimir P. Goss and Christine Verzár Bornstein (Kalamazoo, MI, 1986), 226; Hillenbrand, *The Crusades*, 122–32.

21. WT 17.20 (787–89). For a tentative identification of William's "Hiaroquin" Turks with the grandsons of al-Yārūq b. Ortoq, see René Grousset, "Sur un passage obscur de Guillaume de Tyr," in *Mélanges syriens offerts à Monsieur René Dussaud*, 2:937–39.

22. Johann of Würzburg in *Peregrinationes tres*, 92, 94.

23. Archbishop William: WT 13.1–14 (584–602), 21.8 (973–74). Ibn Jubayr on mosques: see Kedar, "The Subjected Muslims," 138–39 with n. 6.

24. Pope Innocent II's letters: WT 14.11–13 (644–49). Ṣalāḥ al-Dīn' letter: Elon Harvey, "Saladin Consoles Baldwin IV over the Death of His Father," *Crusades* 15 (2016): 27–33.

25. For the few exceptions, see WT 6.5 (312), 11.14 (518), 20.26 (949), 21.20 (988–89). Apparently just one of these conversions occurred in the Kingdom of Jerusalem.

26. AA 2.37 (126–29); cf. WT 3.12 (209–11). Similarly, William skips Albert's story about a Turkish warrior who married the captive widow of Folbert of Bouillon: AA 5.5–7 (344–47); WT 7.3 (345–46).

27. WT 11.26 (534–35). *Cart St Sép*, 207–8, no. 91; *Papsturkunden für Kirchen*, 124–26, no. 19.

28. WT 11.28 (537–41).

29. WT 5.17 (293–94).

30. Theoderich in *Peregrinationes tres*, 151–52.

31. WT 21.1 (961–62).

32. Ibn Abī Usaybi'a, *A Literary History of Medicine*, 2.2:1119 (text), 3.2:1264 (translation). See Claude Cahen, "Indigènes et Croisés: Quelques mots a propos d'un médecin d'Amaury et de Saladin," *Syria* 15 (1934): 352. Hamilton explains that Abū al-Khayr had to teach the virtually one-handed Baldwin to control his horse in battle with his knees only: Bernard Hamilton, *The Leper King and His Heirs: Baldwin IV and the Crusader Kingdom of Jerusalem* (Cambridge, 2000), 28.

33. *Ernoul*, 173.

34. WT 10.7 (461) and WT 1.1 (105). See Nicholas Morton, "William of Tyre's Attitudes towards Islam: Some Historiographical Reflections," in *Deeds Done beyond the Sea*, 19; Skottki, *Christen, Muslime und der Erste Kreuzzug*, 162.

35. WT 7.18 (366), 9.1 (421–22), 10.2 (454–55), 11.15 (519), 11.26 (534), 12.6 (553). Cf. *Le "Liber" de Raymond d'Aguilers*, 154.

36. WT 20.9 (921), 20.20 (938), 21.4 (964). For William's depiction of Milo, see David W. T. C. Vessey, "William of Tyre and the Art of Historiography," *Mediaeval Studies* 35 (1973): 446–50.

37. WT 22.9 (1019) and WT 16.27 (755).

38. The only source on the 1180 election, and Agnes's role in it, is *Ernoul*, 144–46.

39. Hans Prutz, "Studien über Wilhelm von Tyrus," *Neues Archiv der Gesellschaft für ältere deutsche Geschichtskunde* 8 (1883): 93–94. The act is edited in *Cart St Sép*, 311–12, no. 160.

40. WT 8.3 (385).

41. See above, chap. 3, note 4.

42. WT 16.17 (738–39), 18.8 (820–21).

43. The identity of the schoolmaster of 1136 with the later archdeacon and cardinal was first surmised by Buchthal, *Miniature Painting*, xxx n. 4; for a reconstruction of his career, see Mayer, "Guillaume de Tyr à l'école"; Mayer, *Die Kanzlei*, 1:173–74.

44. Robert B. C. Huygens, "Guillaume de Tyr étudiant: Un chapitre (XIX, 12) de son 'Histoire' retrouvé," *Latomus* 21 (1962): 811–29.

45. Cf. Classen, "Die Hohen Schulen," 163.

46. Cf. Mayer, "Guillaume de Tyr à l'école," 264–65.

47. Huygens, "Guillaume de Tyr étudiant," 812–13; Huygens's introduction to WT, 7; WT, 862 n. 12.

48. WT 19.12 (879–81). For information about William's teachers, see Huygens, "Guillaume de Tyr étudiant," 825–29.

49. See the cogent arguments of Southern, "The Schools of Paris," 130–31. For the less convincing view that William studied in Chartres, see Mayer, *Die Kanzlei*, 1:175–76.

50. Classen, "Die Hohen Schulen," 163.

51. For the hypothesis that William, not yet able to grasp the teachings of Thierry and Gilbert themselves, preferred to study under their disciples, see Schwinges, *Kreuzzugsideologie*, 27.

52. Cf. Gen. 1.16: "Fecitque Deus duo luminaria magna: luminare majus, ut præesset diei: et luminare minus, ut præesset nocti."

53. The phrasing implies that Hugolinus and Bulgarus were William's main teachers of law, Martinus and Jacobus the secondary ones. William calls his teachers in the liberal arts and theology *magistri*, and the four Bologna jurists *domini*. For the possible significance, see Johannes Fried, *Die Entstehung des Juristenstandes im 12. Jahrhundert* (Cologne, 1976), 20–23.

54. WT 19.2 (865), 21.1 (962).

55. Southern, "The Schools of Paris," 131, 133.

56. Ioannes Saresberiensis, *Metalogicon* 2.10, ed. John B. Hall with Katharine S. B. Keats-Rohan, CCCM 98 (Turnhout, 1991), 71–72 (Latin); John of Salisbury, *Metalogicon* 2.10, trans. John B. Hall with Katharine S. B. Keats-Rohan (Turnhout, 2013), 198–201 (English; my translation differs on some points).

57. Golias: "Mitteilungen aus Handschriften, III: Die Metamorphose des Golias," ed. Robert B. C. Huygens, *Studi Medievali* 3, no. 3 (1962): 771–72, lines 189–236; for discussion, see John F. Benton, "Philology's Search for Abelard in the *Metamorphosis Goliae*," *Speculum* 50 (1975): 206–12; for the poem's date, see 216–17.

58. For a comparison of the accounts in John of Salisbury, William of Tyre, and the *Metamorphosis* that underscores the preeminence of Paris, see Southern, "The Schools of Paris," 128–33.

59. On the date of the revision: Edbury and Rowe, *William of Tyre*, 2–3, 26–29, 170–71; Kedar, "Some New Light." On the date of the autobiographical chapter: Huygens, "Guillaume de Tyr étudiant," 819–20.

60. WT 21.25 (998).

61. Edbury and Rowe, *William of Tyre*, 32–38, quotation on 35. Earlier (34) they state that "normally [William] introduced classical quotations simply to embellish the text rather than to furnish information."

62. On this problem in general, see Yolanda Plumley, Giuliano Di Bacco, and Stefano Jossa, preface to their *Citation, Intertextuality and Memory in the Middle Ages*, vol. 1 (Exeter, 2011), ix–x. Specifically, see Alan V. Murray, "Biblical Quotations and Formulaic Language in the Chronicle of William of Tyre," in *Deeds Done beyond the Sea*, 25–34, one of the conclusions being that apparently "William did not always think through the appropriateness of such [biblical] quotations."

63. Edbury and Rowe, *William of Tyre*, 33–34 with n. 7.

64. Cf. "difficile est enim ut bono claudantur exitu que malo sunt inchoata principio": WT 11.21 (527); "difficile est ut bono claudantur fine que malo sunt inchoata principio": WT 14.10 (642); "et difficile est ut bono peragantur exitu, quae malo sunt inchoate principio": *S. Leonis Magni epistolae*, ep. XII, in PL 54:647A. The slight differences between William's renderings suggest that he was quoting from memory.

65. WT 14.14 (651); Joseph Morawski, *Proverbes français antérieurs au XVe siècle* (Paris, 1925), 43, no. 1178; Arpad Steiner, "The Vernacular Proverb in Mediaeval Latin Prose," *American Journal of Philology* 65 (1944): 55 n. 108.

66. WT 2.2 (163), 19.7 (873), 20.2 (914), 22.13 (1024). For Huygens's comments on William's use of similes and on other twelfth-century instances of the simile concerning the maltreated host, see his introduction and apparatus, 43, 63. Huygens, who dedicated several years to the study of William's chronicle, often complained that historians use his critical edition but ignore his introduction. For a trenchant critique of William's language and style, see his introduction to WT, 39–72.

67. See Chrysogonus Waddell, "*Epitalamica*: An Easter Sequence by Peter Abelard," *Musical Quarterly* 72 (1986): 239–71; Peter Dronke, *Sources of Inspiration: Studies in Literary Transformations, 400–1500* (Rome, 1997), 375–95. WT 7.24 (377), 14.28 (669).

68. WT 3.13 (212), 7.20 (369), 14.24 (662–63).

69. "Iniquum est enim ei qui contra fidem fecit fidem seruari sibi." *Summa Codicis des Irnerius*, ed. Hermann Fitting (Berlin, 1894), 2.3 (De pactis), 26. (Fitting's attribution of the work to Irnerius was not accepted; it is referred to in the literature as the *Summa Trecensis*.) Jonathan Rubin drew my attention to the similarity between the formulations in the *Historia* and the *Summa*.

70. For this hypothesis, see André Gouron, "L'auteur et la patrie de la *Summa Trecensis*," *Ius Commune: Veröffentlichungen des Max-Planck-Instituts für Rechtsgeschichte* 12 (1984): 1–38. The recourse of William, who studied law in Bologna, to a

legal treatise presumably composed in the Midi is surprising. John of Salisbury, too, used the treatise: Georg Miczka, "Zur Benutzung der Summa Codicis Trecensis bei Johannes von Salisbury," in *The World of John of Salisbury*, ed. Michael Wilks (Oxford, 1984), 381–99. The section "De pactis" of the *Summa Trecensis* and William of Tyre's three statements call for some modification of the argument by Peter Landau, "*Pacta sunt servanda*: Zu den kanonistischen Grundlagen der Privatautonomie," in Landau, *Europäische Rechtsgeschichte und kanonisches Recht im Mittelalter* (Badenweiler, 2013), 761–72.

71. WT 15.11 (689), 16.8 (724). See Adolf Berger, *Encyclopedic Dictionary of Roman Law* (Philadelphia, 1953), s.v. *Arbitrium (arbitratus) boni viri.*

72. See for example the following repetitions: *faciens/tes de necessitate virtutem*, WT 3.23 (225), 7.21 (370), 10.16 (473), 11.4 (501), 15.19 (701); *nulla enim pestis efficacior ad nocendum quam familiaris inimicus*, WT 9.19 (445), 11.19 (524); *male cuncta ministrat impetus*, WT 10.19 (477), 14.7 (639), 22.1 (1007); *nocuit diferre paratis*, WT 10.29 (490), 20.15 (929); *timeo Danaos et dona ferentes*, WT 11.6 (503), 20.2 (914); *tua res agitur, paries cum proximus ardet*, WT 14.6 (638), 17.11 (774); *quot homines tot sententie*, WT 15.5 (680), 22.26 (1050). There are also many recurrent quotations from the Vulgate.

73. WT 15.3 (676–77), 18.25 (848).

74. "spectaculum factus populis infidelibus"; "spectaculum facti sunt populis infidelibus." WT 18.28 (852), 19.9 (875).

75. See Zimo, "Us and Them," 13–19. For William reproducing a royal charter in which King Baldwin I figures first as *primus rex Francorum* and then as *rex Ierusalem Latinorum primus*, see WT 11.12 (513–14); *UKJ*, 1:162–63, no. 40 (a. 1110).

76. Mayer, *Die Kanzlei*, 1:402–3.

77. For the royal chancery, see WT 11.12 (513–14); *UKJ*, 1:162–63, no. 40 (a. 1110). For the chapter's charters, see *Cart St Sép*, 155, 167, 219, 222, nos. 61 (a. 1136), 62 (a. 1131/32), 70 (a. 1135), 100 (a. 1135), 102 (a. 1135); Hans Eberhard Mayer, *Von der Cour des Bourgeois zum öffentlichen Notariat: Die freiwillige Gerichtsbarkeit in den Kreuzfahrerstaaten*, MGH Schriften 70 (Wiesbaden, 2016), 238, no. 6 (a. 1137). For the Hospitaller charters, see *Cart Hosp*, 1:133, 272–73, 341–42, 318–19, 349–50, nos. 168 (a. 1146), 399 (a. 1168), 450 (a. 1173), 464 (a. 1174), 508 (a. 1177). On the usage outside the royal chancery in general, see Mayer, *Die Kanzlei*, 1:403.

78. This recourse finds a counterpart in the archaic tendencies discernible in Frankish architecture, recently discussed by Fishhof, *Shaping Identities*, 99–105, 127–30.

79. See for instance: "prima eius partium Mesopotamia est, que quia *inter duo flumina* sita est Mesopotamia dicitur, quasi que *inter duo flumina* iaceat." WT 13.2 (587) (my emphasis). For other examples, see Huygens's introduction to WT, 44–47.

80. Huygens's introduction to WT, 63–70.

81. Huygens's introduction to WT, 53–63.

82. Otto of Freising, *Chronica sive Historia de duabus civitatibus*, ed. Adolf Hofmeister and Walther Lammers, trans. Adolf Schmidt (Berlin, 1960), 2. In the epistle to Rainald of Dassel Otto styles himself "bishop of the church of

Freising": Otto of Freising, *Chronica*, 6. In his *Gesta Friderici*, Otto notes briefly that he was one of the three bishops who took the cross in 1147, one of the two bishops who accompanied King Konrad III in 1151 to the Lower Rhine region, and one of the recipients of a letter by Emperor Frederick: Otto of Freising and Rahewinus, *Gesta Friderici seu rectius Cronica*, 1.3, 1.69, 2.52, ed. Franz-Josef Schmale, trans. Adolf Schmidt (Berlin, 1965), 210, 276, 384–86.

83. WT Prol. (97), 19.12 (881), 20.1 (913), 21.8 (973–74). For further references to his own activities, see WT 19.3 (867–68), 20.4–5 (916–17), 20.13 (927), 20.17 (934), 21.1 (961), 21.5 (967), 21.10 (976), 21.12 (978), 21.13–17 (979–85), 21.25 (996–98), 21.29 (1003), 22.4 (1009–11), 22.5 (1012), 22.7 (1017), 22.22 (1043), 22.24 (1046).

84. WT 20.4 (915–17), 20.13 (927), 21.13–17 (980–85), 22.4 (1009–11).

85. WT 17.1 (760).

86. Neither does William's chronicle figure in a medieval catalog: Huygens's introduction to WT, 3, n. 12.

87. On this point, see Huygens's introduction to WT, 74.

88. For a discussion that stops short of unequivocally attributing the Frankish usage to Norman influence, see Mayer, *Die Kanzlei*, 1:38–45.

89. "villas . . . que Siculi casalia vocant." Hugo Falcandus, *La Historia o Liber de Regno Sicilie*, ed. Giovanni Battista Siragusa (Rome, 1897), 112; Mayer, *Die Kanzlei*, 1:40.

90. "et suburbanorum nostrorum, que casalia dicuntur"; "in suburbanis que vulgo casalia appellant"; "suburbanorum adiacentium, que nostri casalia dicunt"; "loca suburbana, que vulgo casalia dicuntur": WT 11.19 (524), 18.19 (898), 20.19 (937), 22.21 (1038). See also the glossary in *Cronaca del Templare di Tiro*, 398–99 s.v. *cazau*. For *casale* in documents issued by William as chancellor, see, for instance, *UKJ*, 2:656–57, 681, 690–91, nos. 381, 398, 405.

91. See, for example, WT 15.25 (708), 19.24 (898), 21.9 (974), 22.9 (1057).

92. WT 11.12 (514), 22.24 (1045). The anonymous author of the Old French adaptation of William's chronicle saw fit to explain the term. In the first instance he wrote, "un caseau, einsi claime l'en là les villes champestres," and in the second: "Cil qui auront les villes champestres que l'en apele casiaus." WT OF 11.12, 22.22 (1:398, 2:451). See also 18.19, 20.18 (2:224, 339).

93. WT 13.13 (601), 15.17 (698). See also 3.24 (227), 16.19 (742) and 16.26 (753: both referring to Louis VII's crusading expedition), 18.5 (816: referring to pre-1099 Jerusalem), 20.19 (936: referring to Ṣalāḥ al-Dīn's army). Schwinges, *Kreuzzugsideologie*, 23, correctly states that according to this categorization William's parents must have belonged to the *secunda classis*.

94. WT 11.12 (514), 12.25 (580).

95. For a similar attitude of an early thirteenth-century bishop of Gibeleth/Jubayl (north of Beirut), see "Wilbrand of Oldenburg's Journey," ed. Pringle, 119. Cf. Lewis, "Medieval Diglossia," 149.

96. See the widely used, yet highly problematic, translation into English: *A History of Deeds Done beyond the Sea by William, Archbishop of Tyre*, trans. and annotated by Emily A. Babcock and August C. Krey, 2 vols. (New York, 1943). For its negative impact on some research, see Zimo, "Us and Them," 1–2.

97. Place names originating in Arabic: WT 9.19 (446), 14.8 (640), 16.8 (724), 18.17 (835); see also 19.8 (873), 22.21 (1038). Originating in Romance vernacular: WT 15.25 (708), 22.27 (1052). Medieval Latin neologisms: WT 10.27 (486), 14.30 (671), 18.19 (898), 22.21 (1038), 22.24 (1046). Latin appellations: WT 2.7 (170), 14.24 (663), 15.13 (693), 16.6 (722), 18.32 (858), 20.22 (942).

98. Similarly, Foucher of Chartres distinguishes between *grammatice* (or *litteratorie*) and *vulgariter*: FC 2.45 (555); cf. Yolles, *Making the East Latin*, 65–66.

99. WT 7.15 (361), 7.17 (365), 10.12 (467), 10.26 (486); "hodie vero corrupta nuncupatione Tortosa appellatur": WT 22.3 (1009).

100. WT 11.30 (543).

101. The name Babilonia derived from the Roman fortress of Babylon, besieged and conquered by the Arabs in 641, and situated south of what was to become the country's capital, Fusṭāṭ. See the plan of Cairo in Ṣalāḥ al-Dīn's time in Stanley Lane-Poole, *Saladin and the Fall of the Kingdom of Jerusalem* (New York, 1898), opposite 114. Macer: "Nobilem et egregiam metropolim que vulgo Babilonia dicitur, lingua vero Arabica Macer appellatur." WT 19.15 (884).

102. Cf. Lane-Poole, *Saladin*, 171, asterisk note. Elon Harvey enlightened me on this point.

103. "Cesarea Philippi dicta est. Dicitur autem et Paneas, sed nostri Latini, corrumpentes nomen sicut pene omnium aliarum urbium, Belinas vocant." WT 19.10 (876). Likewise, speaking of Attalia, William observes: "Hanc nostri, idiomatis Greci non habentes periciam, corrupto vocabulo Sataliam appellant, unde et totus ille maris sinus . . . vulgari appellatione Gulfus Satalie nuncupatur." WT 16.26 (753). Similarly, the author of the Old French adaptation of William of Tyre points out that "la laie gent" call the Lord's Temple "le Temple Dominus": WT OF 8.3 (1:267); see Handyside, *The Old French William of Tyre*, 93.

104. William has been recently acclaimed as one of the greatest historians of the Middle Ages "despite his tendency to assess everything in terms of his personal culture and to blacken the illiteracy of the Latin clergy in the East": Pierre-Vincent Claverie, "Les représentations des origines du Temple dans la chronique de Guillaume de Tyr," in *D'Orient en Occident*, 20.

105. See Ralph V. Turner, "The *Miles Literatus* in Twelfth- and Thirteenth-Century England: How Rare a Phenomenon?," *American Historical Review* 83 (1978): 931; Martin Aurell, *Le chevalier lettré* (Paris, 2006), 21–24.

106. WT 15.18 (700).

107. WT 13.26 (622), 14.11 (643). Patriarch Amaurry is described at the time of his election as "vir commode litteratus sed simplex nimium et pene inutilis" and at his death as "vir simplex nimium et pene inutilis": WT 18.20 (840–41), 22.4 (1011–12).

108. Frederic: WT 19.6 (872); also 19.28 (903); on the conflict, see WT 20.17 (934); on its possible nature, see Mayer, *Die Kanzlei*, 1:182–94. On Raoul: WT 16.17 (738).

109. WT 22.7 (1017). Eck assumes that Eudes studied at one of Europe's nascent universities: Thomas Eck, *Die Kreuzfahrerbistümer Beirut und Sidon im 12. und 13. Jahrhundert auf prosopographischer Grundlage* (Kiel, 1999), 48.

110. On Aimery, see Kedar, "Gerard of Nazareth," 65, 69–71; Hiestand, "Un centre intellectuel," 8–16, 32–35; Bernard Hamilton, "Aimery of Limoges, Patriarch of Antioch: Ecumenist, Scholar and Patron of Hermits," in *The Joy of Learning and the Love of God: Studies in Honor of Jean Leclercq*, ed. E. Rozanne Elder (Kalamazoo, MI, 1995), 271. However, the *Fazienda de Ultra Mar* should not be ascribed to Aimery: see B. Z. Kedar, "Sobre la génesis de la Fazienda de Ultra Mar," *Anales de Historia Antigua y Medieval* 28 (1995): 131–36.

111. WT 22.7 (1017).

112. Daibert: WT 9.14 (439). Arnoul: WT 7.18 (366), 8.11 (400); cf. AA 6.8 (414). Étienne of Chartres: WT 13.25 (619).

113. Raoul: WT 15.17 (698); Arnulf and Lambert: WT 14.10 (642).

114. Thierry: WT 19.12 (880); Egidius: WT 13.23 (617), same formulation with regard to a later legate, Johannes: WT 18.29 (852); Guibert, Gelasius, and Otto: WT 1.13 (128), 12.8 (555), 17.1 (760).

115. WT 21.7 (969). William's "filii scelerati, fidei Christiane prevaricatores" possibly influenced Jacques of Vitry's characterization of the Pullani as "filii scelerati et degeneres, homines corrupti et legis divine prevaricatores": JdV 73 (288). For Morgan the influence was obvious: "The Meanings of Old French *polain*," 45–46.

116. WT 9.5 (425), 11.10 (509); his "novella plantatio" may be compared to Guibert of Nogent's "sanctae illius Christianitatis novae coloniae": GN 7.25 (318). Our Syria, etc.: WT 19.23 (894), 20.13 (927), 20.18 (936), 21.25 (996), 22.11 (1020), 23 prologue (1061); see Miriam Rita Tessera, "Tra Oriente ed Occidente: Guglielmo di Tiro, l'Europa e l'identità degli stati latini di oltremare," in *Studi sull'Europa medioevale: L'Europa di fronte all'Oriente Cristiano tra alto e pieno Medioevo*, ed. Annamaria Ambrosioni (Alessandria, 2001), 105–7. Our Mediterranean Sea: WT 2.7 (169), 3.2 (198).

117. "urgentissimus instat amor patrie," "natalis soli magis tracti dulcedine." WT Prologue (99); see also prologue to book 23 (1061). William's early patriotism, appearing in the Kingdom of Jerusalem "with its mixed population, its loose government and its dicey future," was highlighted by Beryl Smalley, *Historians of the Middle Ages* (London, 1974), 38–39; she wondered whether the kingdom's vulnerability intensified the Franks' feelings of possession. See also Schwinges, *Kreuzzugsideologie*, 239–40; Bunna Ebels-Hoving, "William of Tyre and His *patria*," in *Media Latinitas: A Collection of Essays to Mark the Occasion of the Retirement of L.J. Engels*, ed. R. I. A. Nip et al. (Turnhout, 1996), 211–16; Tessera, "Tra Oriente ed Occidente."

118. WT 1.15 (132). For the royal seals, see Mayer and Sode, *Die Siegel*; cf. Shagrir, "Urban Soundscape," 105.

119. See Beth C. Spacey, "Refocusing the First Crusade: Authorial Self-Fashioning and the Miraculous in William of Tyre's *Historia Ierosolymitana*," in *Remembering the Crusades in Medieval Texts and Songs*, ed. Andrew D. Buck and Thomas W. Smith (Cardiff, 2019), 55, 59–61.

120. *Civitas sancta*: WT 1.15 (134), 8.22 (415, three times), 8.23 (416), 9.9 (431), 9.16 (441), 11.12 (513, twice), 11.14 (517), 12.3 (548), 12.15 (565), 12.25 (578), 13.25 (619), 17.20 (787), 18.5 (816), 19.1 (864), 20.3 (914), 21.20 (989).

Urbs sancta: WT 1.2 (106), 1.4 (110), 1.6 (114), 1.10 (122), 1.15 (131), 6.14 (325), 7.25 (378), 8.1 (381, twice), 9.14 (438), 11.2 (497), 11.27 (535, twice), 17.22 (791), 21.24 (996).

121. "sicut in Nicena synodo legitur: *episcopus Helie ab omnibus honoretur* et cetera." WT 8.2 (383).

122. Otto of Freising, *Historia de duabus civitatibus* 3.2 (216–19). The ruling as quoted by Otto reads: "Episcopus Heliae ab omnibus honoretur, salvo iure sui metropolitani." This may have been the text William had before his eyes. However, the critical edition of the ruling reads: "Quia consuetudo praevaluit et antiqua traditio ut Heliae episcopus honoretur, habeat honoris consequentiam, salva metropolitani propria dignitate." *Conciliorum oecumenicorum decreta*, ed. Giuseppe Alberigo (Bologna, 1973), 9. Neither here nor in Gratian, D. 65 c.7, does the ruling lay down that the bishop of Jerusalem should be honored *ab omnibus*.

123. For an overview, see Horst Fuhrmann, "Studien zur Geschichte der mittelalterlichen Patriarchate: I," *Zeitschrift der Savigny-Stiftung für Rechtsgeschichte: Kanonistische Abteilung* 39 (1953): 127–28.

124. Presenting the dispute between the patriarchs of Antioch and Jerusalem, William abbreviated papal letters in a manner that made them support his position: see Hans Eberhard Mayer, *Die Kreuzfahrerherrschaften Beirut und Blanchegarde* (Wiesbaden, 2022), 45.

125. Edbury and Rowe, *William of Tyre*, 170–72.

126. FC 2.64 (612–13); WT 11.31 (544). The difference was noted by Tyerman, *God's War*, 935 n. 33.

127. FC 3.18 (665); WT 12.21 (571–73).

128. FC 3.28 (697); WT 13.8 (595).

129. Yolles, *Making the East Latin*, 203–5.

130. For the possibility that when the rule of the Franks stabilized, they no longer felt the need to dwell on Eastern Christian concord, see Christopher MacEvitt, "Processing Together, Celebrating Apart: Shared Processions in the Latin East," in *Liturgy and Devotion in the Crusader States*, ed. Iris Shagrir and [M.] Cecilia Gaposchkin (Abingdon, 2019), 99–100. Like William, the anonymous author of the "Secunda pars Historiae Iherosolimitanae" (*RHC Oc*, 3:549–85), apparently writing in France in the early 1150s, chose to skip Foucher's references to inter-Christian concord: see Andrew D. Buck, "Remembering Outremer in the West: The *Secunda pars Historiae Iherosolimitanae* and the Crisis of Crusading in Mid-Twelfth-Century France," *Speculum* 97 (2022): 393–95. For other omissions by William, see Pahlitzsch, *Graeci und Suriani*, 93.

131. WT 22.16 (1029); also WT 14.23 (661), 18.34 (859).

132. "Canons of the Council of Nablus," 331–34; for William's account of the council, see WT 12.13 (563–64).

133. WT 22.24 (1043–46).

134. See B. Z. Kedar, "The General Tax of 1183 in the Crusading Kingdom of Jerusalem: Innovation or Adaptation?," *English Historical Review* 89 (1974): 339–45. In this early article I still adhered to the view that the Franks lacked inventiveness.

7. A Twelfth-Century Renaissance Ruler

1. The only work focusing on Amaurry is Reinhold Röhricht, "Amalrich I., König von Jerusalem (1162–1174)," *Mittheilungen des Instituts für Österreichische Geschichtsforschung* 12 (1891): 432–81; but his career—though not his cultural pursuits—is dealt with in all standard histories of the crusades. On the five expeditions of 1163, 1164, 1167, 1168, and 1169, see Prawer, *Histoire*, 1:432–45; Steve Tibble, *The Crusader Strategy: Defending the Holy Land, 1099–1187* (New Haven, CT, 2020), 186–220; Fulton, *Contest for Egypt*, 31–33, 45–123. For an analysis of the political background, see Michael A. Köhler, *Alliances and Treaties between Frankish and Muslim Rulers in the Middle East: Cross-Cultural Diplomacy in the Period of the Crusades*, trans. Peter M. Holt, rev. Konrad Hirschler (Leiden, 2012), 185–202. For a different interpretation, see Michael S. Fulton, "Frankish Intervention in Egypt during the Reign of Amalric: Conquest or Extortion?", in *EO*, 1:191–206. As for Amaurry's legislation, Johan of Ibelin wrote in the mid-1260s that a king of Jerusalem must promise, at his coronation, to keep "les assises dou roi Amauri et dou roi Bauduin son fis" in addition to "les ancienes costumes dou reiaume de Jerusalem"—which points toward a legislative campaign started under Amaurry and continued under Baldwin IV: John of Ibelin, *Le Livre des Assises*, 571, c. 220; cf. Auguste Arthur Beugnot, "Introduction aux Assises de la Cour des Bourgeois," *RHC Lois*, 2:xxxix. According to *Le Livre au Roi* (195–99, c. 21), an *assise* of Amaurry stipulated that a heretic knight was to be burned on the stake.

2. "Assises des Bourgeois," c. 288 (2:218). For Amaurry's legislation on maritime issues, see "Assises des Bourgeois," cc. 43–49 (42–47). On his much-discussed *Assise sur la ligece*, see Riley-Smith, *The Feudal Nobility*, 34–37, 130–31, 145–84, and passim.

3. WT 19.2–3 (864–68). I rearranged the description's components in order to highlight its discords. For a discussion following the original order, see Giese, "Stadt- und Herrscherbeschreibungen," 404–6; on Amaury's "portrait assez contrasté" see Élisabeth Crouzet-Pavan, *Le mystère des rois de Jérusalem, 1099–1187* (Paris, 2013), 313, 318. On Amaurry's conviction that the subjects' wealth is secure only when the ruler is no longer needy, see Mayer, *Die Kreuzfahrerherrschaften Beirut und Blanchegarde*, 46. Entertainers: *mimicis*. The Old French adapter was to explicate: "n'avoit cure de la vanité de jugleeurs ne d'autres menestereus qui les vanitez content." WT OF 19.2 (2:253).

4. On Amaurry's visit to Constantinople, see WT 20.22–24 (940–46); Steven Runciman, "The Visit of King Amalric I to Constantinople in 1171," in *Outremer*, 153–58.

5. Liveliness of innate mind: "literatus modice, sed magis tamen naturali mentis vivacitate scripturarum intelligentiam, more domini Amalrici regis, nitebatur apprehendere." WT 21.5 (967). Here, too, the translation of Babcock and Krey is inaccurate: "He was fairly well lettered . . . aided greatly, however, by his natural keenness of mind. Like King Amaury, he eagerly sought the knowledge contained in written works." *A History of Deeds Done beyond the Sea*, 2:403–4. For William's use of *scripture* in the sense of scriptures, see WT 16.5 (721).

6. "rei militaris experientissimo sed modice fidei et deum prorsus ignoranti." WT 18.15 (832). Gui appears as lord of Scandalium in the years

1148–79: Marie-Luise Favreau[-Lilie], "Die Kreuzfahrerherrschaft Scandalion (Iskanderūne)," *Zeitschrift des Deutschen Palästina-Vereins* 93 (1977): 12–13; *UKJ*, 2:692. Babcock and Krey translate the sentence as "a man wide experienced in war, but of doubtful loyalty and one who feared not God." *A History of Deeds Done beyond the Sea*, 2:263. This translates the Old French adaptation, that has "mais petit avoit de loiauté, et pou dotoit Nostre Seigneur." WT OF 2:217.

7. For the exchange, see WT 19.3 (867–68). The novelty of Amaurry's question was emphasized by Hans Benary, *Über die säkularisierende Wirkung der Kreuzzüge* (Hamburg, 1937), 10, 32, and Crouzet-Pavan, *Le mystère des rois de Jérusalem*, 313. For discussion, see Schwinges, *Kreuzzugsideologie*, 54–64.

8. Weltecke emphasizes that William let the king pose his question while suffering from a protracted fever, his doubts thus being rooted also in weakness and illness: Dorothea Weltecke, *"Der Narr spricht: Es ist kein Gott": Atheismus, Unglauben und Glaubenszweifel vom 12. Jahrhundert bis zur Neuzeit* (Frankfurt am Main, 2010), 228–29.

9. "Resurrecturam tamen carnem omnium quicumque nati sunt atque nascentur, et mortui sunt et morientur, nullatenus ambigere debet Christianus." Petrus Lombardus, *Sententiae in IV libris distinctae* 4.43.1, ed. Collegium S. Bonaventurae, 2 vols. (Grottaferrata, 1971–81), 2:510. Augustine, *Enchiridion*, c. 84, ed. Ernest Evans, Corpus Christianorum 46 (Turnhout, 1969), 95: "Resurrecturam tamen carnem omnium quicumque nati sunt hominum atque nascentur, et mortui sunt atque morientur, nullo modo dubitare debet christianus."

10. Peter Abailard, *Sic et Non*, c. 87, ed. Blanche B. Boyer and Richard McKeon (Chicago, 1976), 307–10.

11. Caroline Walker Bynum, *The Resurrection of the Body in Western Christianity, 200–1336* (New York, 1995), 153–55, 215–20, 230.

12. On authors spiritualizing the resurrected body, see Bynum, *The Resurrection of the Body*, 137–53, 180–86.

13. Jean R. Michot, "L'Épître de la résurrection des Ikhwān as-Safā'," cc. 42, 48–50, *Bulletin de philosophie médiévale* 16–17 (1974–75): 128, 130–32; on the issue's importance in the Brethren's thought, see 143 n. 1. Also Joshua Finkel, "Maimonides' Treatise on Resurrection: A Comparative Study," in *Essays on Maimonides: An Octocentennial Volume*, ed. Salo W. Baron (New York, 1941), 102–3.

14. Paul E. Walker, *Early Philosophical Shiism: The Isma'ili Neoplatonism of Abū Ya'qūb al-Sijistānī* (Cambridge, 1993), 134–42; Walker, *Abu Ya'qub al-Sijistani* (London, 1996), esp. 77–83. For an earlier Ismā'īlī avowal that the resurrection should be understood allegorically, see Edward G. Browne, *A Literary History of Persia*, vol. 1 (London, 1902), 407–15.

15. Ibn Sīnā: Avicenna, *Epistola sulla vita futura*, ed. and trans. Francesca Lucchetta (Padua, 1969), esp. 62–63, 68–70, 82–83, 96–97, 200–205; see Georges C. Anawati, "Un cas typique de l'ésoterisme avicennien: Sa doctrine de résurrection des corps," *Revue du Caire* 27, no. 141 (1951): 83–94. On Avicenna's views on the hereafter in general, see esp. Jean R. Michot, *La destinée de l'homme selon Avicenne* (Louvain, 1986); Sarah Stroumsa, "'True Felicity': Paradise in the Thought of Avicenna and Maimonides," *Medieval Encounters* 4 (1998): 58–67. On the epistle's date, see Michot, *La destinée de l'homme*, 2 n. 10, 6, 23–24.

16. Shamsuddīn al-Kīlānī, "The Muslim Fascination with Jerusalem: The Case of the Sufis," *Islamic Studies* 40 (2001): 617–18; Frank Griffel, *Al-Ghazālī's Philosophical Theology* (Oxford, 2009), xii, 45.

17. Al-Ghazālī, *The Incoherence of the Philosophers: Tahāfut al-Falāsifa*, 20, ed. and trans. Michael E. Marmura (Provo, UT, 2000), 208–25, quotation on 219. For a less literal translation, see Al-Ghazali, *Tahafut al-Falasifa (Incoherence of the Philosophers)*, trans. Sabih Ahmad Kamali (Lahore, 1958), 229–50, quotation on 241. A leading thirteenth-century physician imagined that the imperishable soul remains with the decomposed body in the tomb; at resurrection, it feeds the residual matter and makes the body grow afresh. *The Theologus Autodidactus of Ibn al-Nafis*, ed. and trans. Max Meyerhof and Joseph Schacht (Oxford, 1968), 59 (translation), 109 (text).

18. Ibn Rushd: *Averroes' Tahafut al-Tahafut (The Incoherence of the Incoherence)*, trans. Simon Van Den Bergh, 2 vols. (London, 1954), 1:359–63, quotation on 362. I am indebted to the late Shelomo Pines, of the Hebrew University of Jerusalem, for having encouraged me to pursue the hunch that Amaurry's query may have echoed the views of Muslim philosophers, and for having directed me to Ibn Rushd's work. For an analysis of al-Ghazālī's and Ibn Rushd's thinking on the issue, see Iysa A. Bello, *The Medieval Controversy between Philosophy and Orthodoxy: Ijmā ʿ and Ta ʾwīl in the Conflict between al-Ghazālī and Ibn Rushd* (Leiden, 1989), 126–41.

19. Juvaini, *Genghis Khan: The History of the World Conqueror*, trans. John Andrew Boyle (Manchester, 1958), 686–97, quotations on 689, 695. See Farhad Daftary, *The Isma ʿilis: Their History and Doctrines* (Cambridge, 1990), 385–91.

20. Bernard Lewis, "Kamal al-Din's Biography of Rašid al-Din Sinan," *Arabica* 13 (1966): 230, 239–42; Daftary, *The Isma ʿilis*, 400–402.

21. Bahā' al-Dīn, *History of Saladin*, 20.

22. *Kitāb al-alwāḥ (The Book of the Tablets)* 4.9, French translation by Henry Corbin in Shihaboddin Yahya Sohravardi, *L'Archange empourpré: Quinze traités et récits mystiques traduits du persan et de l'arabe* (Paris, 1976), 107–8. See also Max Horten, trans., *Die Philosophie der Erleuchtung nach Suhrawardi (1191†)* (Halle, 1912), 61–71.

23. For some of the latest discussions of Maimonides's views on the resurrection, see Kraemer, *Maimonides*, 407–25; Sarah Stroumsa, *Maimonides in His World: Portrait of a Mediterranean Thinker* (Princeton, NJ, 2009), 165–83. On his refusal to become Amaurry's physician, see below.

24. Moshe ben Maymon, *Mishneh Torah*, vol. 1: *Sefer ha-Mada ʿ*, Hil. Teshuvah 8.2–3, ed. Saul Liebermann, Jacob Cohen, and Moshe H. Katzenelenbogen (Jerusalem, 1964), 326–27; *The Book of Knowledge from the Mishneh Torah of Maimonides*, trans. Helen M. Russell and J. Weinberg (New York, 1983), 129–30. On the work's date, see Isadore Twersky, *Introduction to the Code of Maimonides* (New Haven, CT, 1980), 14, 28.

25. Moshe ben Maymon, *Mishneh Torah*, 329 (Hil. Teshuvah 8.6); *The Book of Knowledge*, 130. On Ibn Sīnā and Maimonides, see Harry Blumberg, "The Problem of Immortality in Avicenna, Maimonides and St. Thomas Aquinas," in *Harry Austryn Wolfson Jubilee Volume* (Jerusalem, 1965), 165–85; Dov Schwartz,

"Avicenna and Maimonides on Immortality," in *Medieval and Modern Perspectives on Muslim–Jewish Relations*, ed. Ronald L. Nettler (Luxembourg, 1995), 185–97; Stroumsa, "'True Felicity,'" 58–75.

26. "The Epistle of Rabbi Shmuel ben ʿEli on the Resurrection of the Dead," ed. Y. Tzvi Langerman, *Kobez ʿal Yad*, n.s. 15 (2000): 39–94 [in Hebrew].

27. The Arabic original of the *Silencing Epistle* is only partially extant; the Hebrew translation, prepared in Spain in the fourteenth century, has been edited by Sarah Stroumsa, *The Beginnings of the Maimonidean Controversy in the East* (Jerusalem, 1999) [in Hebrew].

28. Stroumsa, *The Beginnings*, 54–58, §§8–24 (Medieval Hebrew), 89–94 (Modern Hebrew rendering). Stroumsa assumes that Maimonides knew Shmuel ben ʿEli's treatise only through Yosef's quotations from it, and that in his *Treatise on the Resurrection* he was also reacting to his disciple's epistle: Stroumsa, *The Beginnings*, 17; Stroumsa, *Maimonides in His World*, 172–77.

29. Ibn Abī Usaybiʿa, *A Literary History of Medicine*, 2.2:1303 (text), 3.2:1482 (translation).

30. Joshua Finkel, ed., "Maimonides' Treatise on Resurrection," *Proceedings of the American Academy for Jewish Research* 9 (1938–39): 16; for translation, see Abraham Halkin and David Hartman, *Crisis and Leadership: Epistles of Maimonides* (Philadelphia, 1985), 219–20.

31. Hartman in Halkin and Hartman, *Crisis and Leadership*, 259; also Ralph Lerner, "Maimonides' Treatise on Resurrection," *History of Religions* 23 (1983–84): 140–55.

32. For the similar view of Abraham ben ʿEzra (1092–1167), with which Maimonides was not acquainted when he wrote his *Treatise*, see Finkel, "Maimonides' Treatise on Resurrection: A Comparative Study," 98–101. For Muslim sectarians who believed in a return to life (and, according to some, once again to death) before the resurrection, see Etan Kohlberg, "Radjʿa," in *Encyclopaedia of Islam*, 2nd ed., 8:372; Kohlberg, "Rāfiḍa," in *Encyclopaedia of Islam*, 2nd ed., 8:387. Maimonides's scenario resembles one of the possibilities Abelard considered with regard to the dead who had arisen at the time of Christ's resurrection: namely, that they later died (and presumably were to rise again at the Second Coming): see at note 10 above.

33. See for instance Daniel J. Silver, *Maimonidean Criticism and the Maimonidean Controversy 1180–1240* (Leiden, 1965), esp. 109–35.

34. On his biography and works, see Peter Schreiner, "Glykas Sikidites, Michael," in *Lexikon des Mittelalters*, 9 vols. (Munich, 1980–98), 4:1519.

35. Yannis Papadogiannakis, "Michael Glykas and the Afterlife in Twelfth-Century Byzantium," in *The Church, the Afterlife and the Fate of the Soul*, ed. Peter Clarke and Tony Claydon (Woodbridge, 2009), 135–37. Niketas Choniates ascribed to Sikidites a still more radical view, according to which the resurrected beings, lacking human form and senses, will resemble bodiless ghosts. See Alexander P. Kazhdan and Ann W. Epstein, *Change in Byzantine Culture in the Eleventh and Twelfth Century* (Berkeley, 1985), 161; Alicia Simpson, *Niketas Choniates: A Historiographical Study* (Oxford, 2013), 48–49.

36. Without giving his reasons, Waas assumed that Amaurry's query about the resurrection resulted from relations with Muslims: Waas, *Geschichte der*

Kreuzzüge, 2:244. His book, which had little impact on subsequent research, stands out for many insights and the utilization of neglected sources.

37. See Cahen, "Indigènes et Croisés." Friendship with emir: Abū Shāma in *RHC Or*, 4:135–36.

38. WT 20.29–30 (953–54); see Jerzy Hauziński, "On Alleged Attempts at Converting the Assassins to Christianity in the Light of William of Tyre's Account," *Folia Orientalia* 15 (1974): 232–46.

39. In the sentence that precedes the discussion about the resurrection, William relates that the king liked to converse with men knowledgeable about distant countries and foreign customs: WT 19.3 (867). This may imply that a conversation with such a man led Amaurry to ask his question.

40. WT OF 2:256. The adapter's use of the term *genz mescréanz*, and its significance, was noted by Schwinges, *Kreuzzugsideologie*, 58; however, he was unaware of the controversy about bodily resurrection among Muslims and Jews.

41. WT 19.3 (868). Amaurry's eyes glittering: the words *oculis fulgentibus* appear in William's description of the king's physique, WT 1.9.3 (867).

42. "King Amalric I of Jerusalem told William of Tyre of what I suspect were his own difficulties in believing in the resurrection—though, like many people confessing to embarrassing problems, he presented them as not actually his own. William was able to set the king's mind at rest, but then that is what one would expect in a story told by an archbishop about himself and the king he served." Susan Reynolds, "Social Mentalities and the Case of Medieval Scepticism," *Transactions of the Royal Historical Society* 5, no. 41 (1991): 33.

43. WT 8.22 (414–15). On William's revision of book 8 in the early 1180s, see Kedar, "Some New Light," 5–7. On Adhémar's various apparitions, see Conor Kostick, "The Afterlife of Bishop Adhémar of Le Puy," in Clarke and Claydon, *The Church, the Afterlife and the Fate of the Soul*, 120–29. William's source, Raymond of Aguilers, mentions only the appearance of Adhémar and does not regard it a proof of the future resurrection: *Le "Liber" de Raymond d'Aguilers*, 151.

44. *Tertullian's Treatise on the Resurrection*, c. 17, ed. and trans. Ernest Evans (London, 1960), 44–47. See Bynum, *The Resurrection of the Body*, esp. 35–36.

45. Anselm of Canterbury, *Monologion* 70–71, and *Cur Deus Homo* 2.3, ed. Franciscus S. Schmitt in *S. Anselmi Cantuariensis archiepiscopi Opera omnia*, 6 vols. (Stuttgart, 1968), 1:80–82, 2:98. On the similarity of the method and presuppositions of the Anselm/Bodo dialogue in *Cur Deus Homo* with those of the William/Amaurry dialogue, see Schwinges, *Kreuzzugsideologie*, 57–61. The similarity does not extend to the dialogues' contents.

46. Hugo of St.-Victor, *In Ecclesiasten homilia XIX*, in PL 175:247–48, 251–52.

47. Alain of Lille, *Contra haereticos* 1.24, in PL 210:324–25, 334. For the date, see Marie-Thérèse d'Alverny, *Alain de Lille: Textes inédits, avec une introduction sur sa vie et ses œuvres* (Paris, 1965), 156–60. The argument in the *De immortalitate animae* originally attributed to Domingo Gundisalvo (ca. 1100–ca. 1190), runs as follows: If the human *soul* were not to attain another life, that soul would have served God in vain, for in this life the cult of God often entails torment and affliction. Moreover, as neither the virtuous nor the wicked receive their due on earth, where would God's justice be if this life were not followed by a Judgement and another life? Except for the exclusive concentration on the soul, Part One

of the retribution argument is reproduced here. See *Des Dominicus Gundisssalinus Schrift von der Unsterblichkeit der Seele*, ed. Georg Bülow (Münster, 1897), 3–4. However, the *De immortalitate animae* is now regarded as the earlier of two versions, both written by William of Auvergne (ca. 1185–1249): see William of Auvergne, *The Immortality of the Soul*, trans. Roland J. Teske, Mediaeval Philosophical Texts in Translation 30 (Milwaukee, 1991), 1-6 (on the authorship), 25–27 (the retribution argument).

48. Athenagoras, *Legatio and De Resurrectione*, ed. and trans. William R. Schoedel (Oxford, 1972), 132–35 (retribution argument), 122–31 (primary reasoning); Leslie W. Barnard, *Athenagoras: A Study in Second-Century Christian Apologetic* (Paris, 1972), 126–34; Bynum, *The Resurrection of the Body*, 31–33.

49. Joannes the Damascene, *De fide orthodoxa* 4.27, in PG 94:1219–20. The similarity of William's reasoning to that of Joannes was pointed out by Schwinges, *Kreuzzugsideologie*, 57.

50. Michot, "L'Épître de la résurrection des Ikhwān as-Safā'," 131, c. 49.

51. Būlus of Antioch, bishop of Sidon, "Brief Letter on Reason," ed. and trans. Paul Khoury, in *Paul d'Antioche, évêque melkite de Sidon (XII*[e] *s.)* (Beirut, 1964), 25–33 (text), 142–46 (translation). See also Georg Graf, "Philosophisch-theologische Schriften des Paulus al-Râhib, Bischofs von Sidon," *Jahrbuch für Philosophie und spekulative Theologie* 20 (1906): 75–80. For the date, see below, chap. 10.

In the mid-eleventh century, the deacon ʿAbdallah ibn al-Fadl of Antioch, who translated some works of the Damascene into Arabic, restates solely Part One of the retribution argument in his "Essay Containing Ideas Useful for the Soul"; since he writes that "*souls* [my emphasis] have a world other than this one to which they go and receive recompense for their works, whether good or evil," he evidently does not subscribe to Part Two. See Samuel Noble, "ʿAbdallah ibn al-Fadl al-Antaki," in *The Orthodox Church in the Arab World, 700–1700*, ed. Samuel Noble and Alexander Treiger (De Kalb, IL, 2014), 180. I owe the latter reference to Yolles, *Making the East Latin*, 198–99. The belief in a noncorporeal retribution appears to have been widespread among Eastern Christians: Stroumsa, "'True Felicity,'" 53.

52. Hubert Koffler, *Die Lehre des Barhebräus von der Auferstehung der Leiber* (Rome, 1932), esp. 59–60, 64–65.

53. John Damascene, *De fide orthodoxa: Versions of Burgundio and Cerbanus*, ed. Eligius M. Buytaert (Louvain, 1955), xiv; for the dates of the translations into Old Slavonic, Arabic, and Georgian, see vi–vii.

54. Albertus Magnus, *Commentarii in IV. librum Sententiarum* 43.1, ed. Pierre Iammy in Albertus Magnus, *Opera Omnia*, 21 vols. (Lyon, 1651), 16:804a–b; Thomas Aquinas, *Summae contra Gentiles libri quatuor* 4.79, ed. and trans. Karl Albert et al., 5 vols. (Darmstadt, 1974–96), 4:474–75; Ramón Llull, "Dictatum Raimundi et eius commentum," 6.95, ed. Fernando Domínguez Reboiras, in *Raimundi Lulli Opera Latina*, CCCM 111 (Turnhout, 1993), 402–3; Ramón Llull, "Compendiosus tractatus de articulis fidei catholicae," 6.5, in *Raimundi Lulli Opera Latina*, 502. The similarity to Joannes the Damascene was first noted by Koffler, *Die Lehre*, 67–73.

55. Schwinges, *Kreuzzugsideologie*, 57. For the date, see Buytaert's discussion in the introduction to the Latin translation of *De fide orthodoxa*, ix–xv.

56. There is reason to believe that William was unable to read the work either in its Greek original or its Arabic translation: see Huygens's introduction to WT, 2.

57. Burgundio's translation runs as follows: "Si igitur non est resurrectio, neque Deus est, neque providentia: sponte autem omnia et aguntur et feruntur. Ecce enim videmus plurimos iustos quidem esurientes et iniuriam pat[i]entes, et nulla in praesenti vita potientes assumptione; peccatores autem et iniustos in divitiis et in omni voluptate exuberantes. Et quis unquam hoc iusti iudicii vel sapientis providentiae opus bene suspicabitur? Erit igitur, erit resurrectio. Iustus enim est Deus, et hiis qui sustinent ipsum mercedis retributor fit. Igitur, si quidem anima sola virtutibus certaminibus athletice pugnavit, ipsa sola et coronabitur. Et si sola voluptatibus involuta esset, sola iuste utique punietur. Sed quia neque existentiam separatam habuerunt, neque virtutem, neque malitiam anima pertransit sine corpore, recte ambo simul et retributionibus fruentur." John Damascene, *De fide orthodoxa*, 377–78.

58. Schwinges, the only historian to have discussed Amaurry's conversation with William in detail, is quite certain that William knew Joannes's argument. Consequently, he believes that William was insincere when reporting his discomfiture at Amaurry's question, and that he misrepresented the situation in order to highlight his learning: Schwinges, *Kreuzzugsideologie*, 54–63. The difficulties this construction entails have been discussed above.

59. "Abrahamic": For diverging views on the usefulness of this recently introduced term, see Guy G. Stroumsa, *The Making of the Abrahamic Religions in Late Antiquity* (Oxford, 2015), 7–8; Aaron W. Hughes, *Abrahamic Religions: On the Uses and Abuses of History* (New York, 2013).

60. The most ambitious of these are the studies of Koffler and Finkel, published in 1932 and 1941 respectively, with Finkel unaware of Koffler's work. Also, most studies on the resurrection have been written in a sanctimonial key. If one limited oneself to this literature, one would hardly suspect that the expression "la resurrezion della carne" could ever have been used to denote the male erection. But Boccaccio does use it in this manner (*Decameron* 3.10), and Auerbach assures us that such expressions formed part of the medieval repertory of droll stories: Erich Auerbach, *Mimesis: Dargestellte Wirklichkeit in der abendländischen Literatur* (Bern, 1946), 217.

61. Avicenna, *Epistola sulla vita futura*, 94–95; also xxix–xxx.

62. See more generally Kedar and Aslanov, "Problems in the Study of Trans-Cultural Borrowing."

63. *The Churches and Monasteries of Egypt and Some Neighbouring Countries, attributed to Abū Sālih, the Armenian*, ed. and trans. Basil T. A. Evetts (Oxford, 1895), 95–96 (text), 217–19 (trans.). The event is dated to AH 563 / AD 1167–68. The text is now believed to have been composed between 1160 and 1220 and goes under the name of the Coptic priest Abū al-Makārim, one of its compilers: see Clara Ten Hacken, "The Description of Antioch in Abū al-Makārim's History of the Churches and Monasteries of Egypt and some Neighbouring Countries," in *EWMEM*, 185–92.

64. The account has been critically edited by Miriam Rita Tessera, "Il sogno del re Amalrico, Bernardo di Clairvaux e la reliquia della Vera Croce," *Aevum* 87

(2013): 367–70; for discussion, see 343–66. (Account previously quoted from *S. Bernardi vita prima, liber V, auctore Gaufrido*, c. 26, in PL 185:366–68.) In 1174 Amaurry sent to Grandmont a fragment of the True Cross he had received in 1171 in Constantinople: Frolow, *La relique de la vraie croix*, 341–42, no. 365; also 320–22, no. 319. Salvatio was a Cistercian house, established in 1161; Pringle proposes to identify it with the complex of ruins near the village Maṭṭaʿ, twelve miles southwest of Jerusalem: Pringle, *Churches*, 1:47–51; Hamilton in Hamilton and Jotischky, *Latin and Greek Monasticism*, 251–52.

65. WT 19.25 (898–901); Prawer, *Histoire*, 1:435. Runciman, who read the account in *S. Bernardi vita prima* (PL 185:366–68), offers an idiosyncratic reconstruction: Amaurry hesitated whether to give battle; "Saint Bernard then made one of his unfortunate interventions into crusading history," blessing the relic's fragment; the king went on an attack that ended badly. Runciman, *A History of the Crusades*, 2:374.

66. WT 20.17 (933).

67. Reto R. Bezzola, *Les origines et la formation de la littérature courtoise en Occident (500–1200)*, 3 vols. (Paris, 1944–63), 3.2:446–53; Marc-René Jung, "Satirische, komische und realistische Literatur der Romania," in *Europäisches Hochmittelalter*, ed. Henning Krauss (Wiesbaden, 1981), 400–401.

68. *La Bible*, lines 311–475, in *Les oeuvres de Guiot de Provins, poète lyrique et satirique*, ed. John Orr (Manchester, 1915), 19–24.

69. *La Bible*, 20, lines 346–48. *Molt vi* and *molt revi* recur in the roll in the meaning of "much I saw": 23–24, lines 438, 458. Langlois reads: "quel prince ot ou [that is, dans le] roi Amauri!" Charles-Victor Langlois, *La vie en France au Moyen Age de la fin du XII*e *au milieu du XV*e *siècle*, 3 vols. (Paris, 1926–28), 1:64. For the text and a versified German translation, see Johann Friedrich Wolfart and San-Marte [Albert Schulz], *Des Guiot von Provins bis jetzt bekannte Dichtungen, altfranzösisch und in deutscher metrischen Übersetzung* (Halle, 1861), 41. The text has here "ot où," and the translation reads: "Welch ein Fürst war König Amalrich? / Ich sah, wie in Ruhm sein Leben stand / In Syrien, dem reichen Land." An alternative translation, proposed by Cyril Aslanov (pers. comm.): "What a prince it [Syria] had in the person of King Amaurry! The rich land of Syria saw his life as very glorious."

70. *La Bible*, 21, lines 378–79 and introduction, xiii; Langlois, *La vie*, 1:48. For his appraisal of the Knights Templar, see *La Bible*, 62–65, lines 1695–1788; for his negative view of the Knights Hospitaller, see 65–69, lines 1789–1926.

71. See Arthur Baudler, *Guiot von Provins, seine Gönner, die "Suite de la Bible" und seine lyrischen Dichtungen* (Halle, 1902), 19–49, 53.

72. *Voyage de Charlemagne*, 42, vv. 209–12. See Richard, "Sur un passage," 552–55; he dates the description to 1125–50.

73. Peire Vidal, "Ajostar e lassar," vv. 80–85, 99–102, in Peire Vidal, *Poesie*, ed. D'Arco Silvio Avalle, 2 vols. (Milan, 1960), 1:40–43. Lewis and Paterson date the poem to shortly before the Battle of Ḥaṭṭīn: Kevin J. Lewis, *The Counts of Tripoli and Lebanon in the Twelfth Century: Sons of Saint-Gilles* (Abingdon, 2017), 260–63, 301; Linda M. Paterson, *Singing the Crusades: French and Occitan Lyric Responses to the Crusading Movements, 1137–1336* (Woodbridge, 2018), 43–45. On Jaufre Rudel's

stay in the East, probably during the Second Crusade, see Paterson, *Singing the Crusades*, 32–34.

74. WT 20.4 (915–17).

75. *Carmina Burana*, 1.1:104, no. 51a. Text reprinted by permission of Universitätsverlag Winter GmbH.

76. *Carmina Burana*, 2.1:112. For a more positive appraisal, see Goswin Spreckelmayer, *Das Kreuzlied des lateinischen Mittelalters* (Munich, 1974), 76–80.

77. Ibn al-Athīr in *RHC Or*, 1:537; Abū Shāma in *RHC Or*, 4:121. Ibn al-Athīr claims that the verses refer to Amaurry's expedition of 1164; according to Abū Shāma, they refer to that of 1169. Translation: Elon Harvey.

78. WT Prologue (99), 19.12 (882), 20.31 (957).

79. WT 20.5 (917–18), 20.9–10 (921–25). See Edbury and Rowe, *William of Tyre*, 75–76, 90, 157.

80. WT 18.34 (860–61; Baldwin III's death), 20.31 (956), with Huygens's note at the page's bottom.

81. "Rex Almaricus, custos virtutis, amicus largus, honestatis comes, hostis et impietatis, iusticie cultor pietatis, criminis ultor." Erich Lamberz, "The Bilingual Inscription in the Bema and the Conciliar Inscriptions in the Nave," in Kühnel and Kühnel, *The Church of the Nativity*, 148–49.

82. WT Prologue (99–100) and 19.21 (892).

83. "Manet tamen adhuc perfida Iudeorum et gentilium civitas, sed . . . vix aliqua ab eis gesta stilo digna vel posteris commendanda inveniuntur." Otto of Freising, *Historia de duabus civitatibus*, Prologus libri quinti, 374.

84. "Roderici archiepiscopi Toletani Historia Arabum," in Rodericus Ximenius de Rada, *Opera* (Valencia, 1968), 242–83.

85. WT 1.2 (107), 8.3 (386); Möhring, "Zu der Geschichte," 173–74; Möhring, "Die Kreuzfahrer," 133–34. Yolles argues (*Making the East Latin*, 196) that William's error did not necessarily stem from an inability to read Arabic and may have resulted instead from Saʿīd ibn Baṭrīq's claim that ʿUmar b. al-Khaṭṭāb founded the Dome of the Rock, as well as from the foundation narrative of the canons of the Templum Domini. However, Saʿīd most probably ascribes to ʿUmar the erection of the early Aqṣā Mosque, not the Dome: see Eutichio Patriarcha di Alessandria, *Gli annali*, trans. Bartolomeo Pirone (Cairo, 1987), 337; also, 361, 364; cf. Amikam Elad, *Medieval Jerusalem & Islamic Worship* (Leiden, 1995), 24–25, 31. Besides, William erroneously claims that Arabic inscriptions mention the cost of erecting the shrine and the dates on which the work began and ended; see above, chap. 5, at n. 119. Yolles rightly notes (202) that the erroneous conflation of the roots *h-d-y* with *m-h-d* (WT 19.21 [891]) implies some knowledge of written Arabic. But whose knowledge—William's or his assistant's? William's transcriptions that replicate vernacular forms—*Mehedi, Mehemeth, Macer*, etc.—point toward the second possibility.

86. WT Prologue (100). See also WT 1.3 (109), where 1182 is given as the year in which William was writing the book, and WT 19.21 (892), where the year given is 1181. Möhring's question ("Zu der Geschichte," 183) whether the book also covered Sassanid history, finds its answer in WT 19.21 (892), where William announces that the book covers the period from the times of *Mehemeth* onward.

87. WT Prologue (100). I wonder how much William could have learned about the Oriental rulers from Saʿīd's chronicle, which focuses on ecclesiastical history. For instance, all Saʿīd has to say about the attainments of Hārūn al-Rashīd is that he went nine times on pilgrimage to Mecca, invaded Byzantium eight times, in AH 187 (AD 803) fell out with the [Iranian] Barmakids, appointed two governors in Egypt, and died while attempting to subdue a rebellion in Khurāsān. The bulk of the entry deals with the caliph's concubine who fell ill and was cured by a Melkite patriarch of Alexandria, and provides information about the three churchmen who succeeded him during the caliph's reign. See Eutichio, *Gli annali*, 397–98. Saʿīd, who mentions the physical traits of almost all caliphs, may have influenced William's portrayals of the kings of Jerusalem and of Shīrkūh.

88. Möhring, "Zu der Geschichte," 175–80. Also, William knows from "old histories" that the Arabs founded Ramla: WT 10.16 (472). He could not have learned this from Saʿīd, who believed that Ramla existed already at the time of Herod the Great: Eutichio, *Gli annali*, 148–49; also 304.

89. Eulogius, *Liber apologeticus martyrum*, in *Corpus scriptorum muzarabicorum*, ed. Juan Gil, 2 vols. (Madrid, 1973), 2:483–86; M. C. Díaz y Díaz, "Los textos anti-mahometanos más antiguos en codices españoles," *Archives d'histoire doctrinale et littéraire du Moyen Age* 37 (1970): 157–59.

90. Lamberz, "The Bilingual Inscription," 145–51.

91. Felix Fabri, *Evagatorium in Terrae Sanctae, Arabiae et Egypti peregrinationem*, ed. Conrad D. Hassler, 3 vols. (Stuttgart, 1843–49), 1:469.

92. The literature on the artwork, and on the balance between its Western and Eastern elements, is considerable. See esp. the works of Manuel Castiñeiras, Anthony Cutler, Jaroslav Folda, Andrew Jotischky, Gustav Kühnel, Johannes Pahlitzsch, Henri Stern, and Louis-Hugues Vincent/Félix-Marie Abel, listed in the bibliography of Kühnel and Kühnel, *The Church of the Nativity*. To these may be added Lucy-Anne Hunt, "Art and Colonialism: The Mosaics of the Church of the Nativity in Bethlehem (1169) and the Problem of 'Crusader' Art," *Dumbarton Oaks Papers* 45 (1991): 69–85; Maria Raffaella Menna, "Immagini e scritture nei mosaici della chiesa della Natività a Betlemme," in *Il cammino di Gerusalemme*, ed. Maria Stella Calò Mariani (Bari, 2002), 647–58; Messis, "Littérature, voyage et politique au XIIe siècle," 163; Hamilton in Hamilton and Jotischky, *Latin and Greek Monasticism*, 99–100; Katharina Palmberger, *Das unverrückbar Heilige—Jerusalems Loca Sancta in der Kreuzfahrerzeit* (Wiesbaden, 2020), 142–55; Fishhof, *Shaping Identities*, 299–320. If we accept Lamberz's reading of the summary of the decisions of the Second Council of Nicaea (787) that rejects the previous inclusion of the anathematization of three Byzantine emperors (Lamberz, "The Bilingual Inscription," 164–65), a considerable part of the earlier discussions becomes obsolete.

93. "in strenuissimi regis Amalrici sortibus." See Charles S. F. Burnett, "What Is the *Experimentarius* of Bernardus Silvestris? A Preliminary Survey of the Material," *Archives d'histoire doctrinale et littéraire du Moyen Age* 44 (1977): 117.

94. The part of the tract's introduction mentioning these events was first edited by Haskins, *Studies*, 136. A version containing accretions was edited by Mirella Brini Savorelli, "Un manuale di geomanzia presentato da Bernardo

Silvestre da Tours (XII secolo): L'*Experimentarius*," *Rivista critica di storia della filosofia* 14 (1959): 283–342; the reference to Amaurry's victory on 313–14. Burnett, who analyzed the material she published, demonstrated that only a part may be considered as the *Sortes regis Amalrici*: Burnett, "What Is the *Experimentarius*," 79–125.

95. WT 19.7 (872–73) 19.18 (887). Charles Burnett, "The *Sortes Regis Amalrici*: An Arabic Divinatory Work in the Latin Kingdom of Jerusalem?," *Scripta Mediterranea* 19–20 (1998–99): 231–33.

96. On the rare mention of Kurds in Latin accounts and their prominence in an account edited in 1997, see B. Z. Kedar, "A Western Survey of Saladin's Forces at the Siege of Acre," in *Montjoie*, 116–17.

97. "regi domino Francorum quinto in Ierusalem feliciter Deo protegente regnanti." Haskins, *Studies*, 136; Brini Savorelli, "Un manuale," 314; Burnett, "What Is the *Experimentarius*," 117. Hospitaller analogues: a charter of 1168 has "glorioso Amalrico rege Francorum quinto regnante," while one of 1173 has "regnante Amalrico Francorum rege quinto": *Cart Hosp*, 1:273, 342, nos. 399, 450. In another Hospitaller deed the king is said to declare, "ego Amalricus sancte civitatis Ierhusalem [*sic*] Francorum rex quintus": *UKJ*, 1:631, no. 363. In charters issued by the royal chancery the king figures as "Latinorum rex quintus."

98. Burnett, "The *Sortes Regis Amalrici*," 233.

99. Haskins, *Studies*, 136; Brini Savorelli, "Un manuale," 285–87. For an early assertion that the tract originated in an Arabic work, see Johannes Bolte, "Zur Geschichte der Losbücher," in *Georg Wickrams Werke*, vol. 4: *Losbuch* (Tübingen, 1903), 298–99.

100. Burnett, "The *Sortes Regis Amalrici*," 234–37. He mentions the possibility that an original, flawless version was distorted in the West, but discounts it. See also Burnett, "What Is the *Experimentarius*," 87.

101. See Alban Dold, "Die Orakelsprüche im St. Galler Palimpsestcodex 908 (die sogenannten 'Sortes Sangallenses')," *Sitzungsberichte der Österreichischen Akademie der Wissenschaften. Philos.-hist. Klasse* 225, no. 4 (1948): 11–15; Richard Meister, "Die Orakelsprüche im St. Galler Palimpsestcodex 908: Erläuterungen," *Sitzungsberichte der Österreichischen Akademie der Wissenschaften. Philos.-hist. Klasse*, 225, no. 5 (1951): esp. 100–102. For a comparison of the St. Gallen *Sortes* and several *Lunaria*, see Emanuel Svenberg, "Quelques remarques sur les 'Sortes Sangallenses,'" *Eranos: Acta Philologica Suecana* 38 (1940): 68–78. See also Svenberg, *Lunaria et zodiologia latina* (Göteborg, 1963).

102. See Meister, "Die Orakelsprüche," 101.

103. "Mens tua, mens stulta, meditatur friuola multa": André Boutemy, "Notice sur le recueil poétique du manuscript Cotton Vitellius A xii, du British Museum," *Latomus* 1 (1937): 301, line 53; "Desipis, insanis, tua mens est dedita uanis," 303, line 105. For the tract's date, see Theodore C. Skeat, "An Early Medieval 'Book of Fate': The *Sortes XII Patriarcharum*," *Mediaeval and Renaissance Studies* 3 (1954): 50.

104. For the list of the twenty-eight themes, see Brini Savorelli, "Un manuale," 318–19; Burnett, "What Is the *Experimentarius*," 103, 105–6. The responses are edited from a fourteenth-century manuscript—Oxford, Bodleian Library,

Digby 46—in Brini Savorelli, "Un manuale," 321–42. Burnett's edition of the responses in the first lunar mansion on the basis of six manuscripts ("What Is the *Experimentarius*," 108–9) and my comparison of Brini Savorelli's responses in all twenty-eight mansions with Munich, Bayerische Staatsbibliothek, Clm 677 (13th c.), fols. 4v–18r, suggest that a critical edition is a desideratum.

105. War: "Hostes tui fugiunt et bella parare timent," Mansion VIII, line 23, Brini Savorelli, "Un manuale," 327; "Pugnabunt pariter, sed tuis victoria datur," XIII, line 18, 331; "Pugnabunt tui maiora dampna passuri," XIV, line 17, 331; "Gladius et ignis vastabunt menia tua," XXV, line 6, 340. Enemy: "Est cum inimicis pax et concordia data," Mansion VI, line 28, Brini Savorelli, "Un manuale," 326; "Et tibi et tuis hostium caterva nocebit," XXV, line 9, 340.

106. Abū Maʿšar, *The Abbreviation of the Introduction to Astrology, together with the Medieval Latin Translation of Adelard of Bath*, ed. and trans. Charles Burnett, Keiji Yamamoto, and Michio Yano (Leiden, 1994), 78–79; Adelard translated: "cehem regni et imperii," 134–35. George Saliba, "The Role of the Astrologer in Medieval Islamic Society," *Bulletin d'études orientales* 44 (1992): 55, 58.

107. "Languet peregrinus, et nequit cito venire," Mansion II, line 16, Brini Savorelli, "Un manuale," 322; "Pausat peregrinus: prebent infortunia moram," Mansion VII, line 11, 326; "Captus peregrinus non venit ideo cito," Mansion XVI, line 2, 333 (*cito* according to a note in the margin of the Oxford manuscript, and Clm 677, fol. 12); "Valde infirmatur, et mortuus [Clm 677, fol. 16v: "vel moriturus"] est peregrinus," Mansion XXIII. line 23, 339.

108. "Quem prestolares veniet in tempore brevi," Mansion XI, line 7, Brini Savorelli, "Un manuale," 329; "Venit peregrinus, iam fere liminia tenet," Mansion XIII, line 5, 330. "Venit peregrinus, set multo tempore manet," Mansion I, line 17, ed. Burnett in "What Is the *Experimentarius*," 109; Clm 677, fol. 4v, has "Veniet peregrinus, sed tempore lungo manebit," and Brini Savorelli, "Un manuale," 321, "Venit peregrinus, set multo tempore languet," with a note in the margin of the Oxford manuscript: "vel manet."

109. "Venit cum leticia et lucrum fit peregrinus," Mansion V, line 13, Brini Savorelli, "Un manuale," 324; "Venit et portat gaudium prestantia lucra," Mansion XXVI, line 20, 341.

110. On the calls for help, see Phillips, *Defenders*, 13, 140–224.

111. Renaud of Châtillon: WT 18.29 (852), 21.10 (976). Raymond III of Tripoli: WT 19.9 (875), 20.28 (952).

112. Vernacular poetry, see Foulet, *Le Roman de Renard*, 104–6.

113. "Melius est in carcere maneat, quam exeat inde," Mansion IX, line 23, Brini Savorelli, "Un manuale," 328. Clm 677, fol. 8v, has "quod" instead of "in." On Muslim astrologers forecasting the liberation of jailed prisoners, see Saliba, "The Role of the Astrologer," 55, 62.

114. WT 18.34 (859); see Edbury and Rowe, *William of Tyre*, 56–57. William's contemptuous attitude toward Eastern medicine may be contrasted with that of Orderic Vitalis, who relates that when in about 1100 the heir to the French throne fell gravely ill and the chief physicians of the realm could not heal him, a doctor who sojourned in Barbary and learned there the secrets of medicine succeeded to do so: OV 9.9 (6:52–53).

115. "medicos Grecos Syros et illarum nationum homines." WT 20.31 (957); apparently an oblique reference to Muslim, Jewish, or Samaritan doctors. Cf. his account of Baldwin II's decree of 1120: "Dedit etiam Surianis, Grecis, Armenis et harum cuiuslibet nationum hominum, Sarracenis etiam nichilominus." WT 12.15 (565).

116. WT 20.31 (956–57).

117. Ibn al-Qiftī, *Ta'rīkh al-ḥukamā'*, 318; Bernard Lewis, "Maimonides, Lionheart, and Saladin," in *Eretz-Israel*, vol. 7 (Jerusalem, 1964), 70–75.

118. Ibn Abī Usaybi'a, *A Literary History of Medicine*, 2.2:1117–18 (text), 3.2:1261–62 (translation).

119. When we collapse the episodes, Abū Sulaymān Dāwūd—having arrived in Jerusalem, according to this reconstruction, in 1167—cannot be identical with the *medicus* of King Amaurry who compiled the *Sortes regis Amalrici*, since the introduction to this tract, as Burnett demonstrated, celebrates the Egyptian expedition of 1164. But if the two episodes are unrelated, Abū Sulaymān Dāwūd—who, according to Ibn Abī Uṣaybiʿa, acquired in Egypt "an extensive knowledge of astrology"—may have arrived in Jerusalem in 1164 and compiled the tract. For translation and discussion of the texts, see Françoise Michaud, "Les médecins orientaux au service des princes latins," in *Occident et Proche-Orient*, 96–103.

120. On the forecast, see Ibn Abī Usaybi'a, *A Literary History of Medicine*, 2.2:1119 (text), 3.2:1264 (translation). See Pahlitzsch, "Ärzte ohne Grenzen," 109–10.

121. On the salary of Ṣalāḥ al-Dīn's astrologer, which was identical to that of his physician, see Saliba, "The Role of the Astrologer," 64; on astrologers serving Muslim rulers, see 51, 52, 54, and passim.

122. "fist venir meges de Domas & fist veïr l'enfant, & y mirent lor curre, mais il ne le porent guarir dou tout." *Les Gestes des Chiprois: Recueil de chroniques françaises écrites en Orient aux XIII*[e] *et XIV*[e] *siècles*, ed. Gaston Raynaud (Geneva, 1887), 8, no. 31. The statement appears in the truncated chronicle—largely neglected in research—that forms the first part of the present-day MS Varia 433 of the Biblioteca Reale di Torino.

123. See Lawrence I. Conrad, "Usama ibn Munqidh and Other Witnesses to Frankish and Islamic Medicine in the Era of the Crusades," in *Medicine in Jerusalem throughout the Ages*, ed. Zohar Amar, Efraim Lev, and Joshua Schwartz (Tel Aviv, 1999), esp. xliv–lii; Piers D. Mitchell, *Medicine in the Crusades: Warfare, Wounds and the Medieval Surgeon* (Cambridge, 2004), 212–16, 220–31, 239; Susan B. Edgington, "Medicine and Surgery in the *Livre des Assises de la Cour des Bourgeois de Jérusalem*," *Al-Masāq* 17 (2005): 87–97; Thomas Gregor Wagner, *Die Seuchen der Kreuzzüge: Krankheit und Krankenpflege auf den bewaffneten Pilgerfahten ins Heilige Land* (Würzburg, 2009), 59–94. To Mitchell's list of medical practitioners in the Frankish states (17–40) one should add *Johannes medicus*, who was in Acre in 1222: "Liber magistri Salmonis, sacri Palatii notarii (1222–1226)," ed. Arturo Ferretto, *Atti della Società Ligure di Storia Patria* 36 (1906): 209–10, no. 533.

124. Ian Short, "Literary Culture at the Court of Henry II," in *Henry II: New Interpretations*, ed. Christopher Harper-Bill and Nicholas Vincent (Woodbridge,

2007), 359, n. 2, that refers to the main studies from Haskins onward; for Stubbs, see his *Seventeen Lectures on the Study of Mediaeval and Modern History* (Oxford, 1900), 132–78.

125. For skepticism, see esp. Karen M. Broadhurst, "Henry II of England and Eleanor of Aquitaine: Patrons of Literature in French?," *Viator* 27 (1996): 53–84; John Gillingham, "The Cultivation of History, Legend, and Courtesy at the Court of Henry II," in *Writers of the Reign of Henry II: Twelve Essays*, ed. Ruth Kennedy and Simon Meecham-Jones (New York, 2006), 25–52; Short, "Literary Culture." On the lack of interest in contemporary history, see Gillingham, "The Cultivation of History," 28–35.

126. Gillingham, "The Cultivation of History," 30. It is instructive to compare this list to that by Charles Homer Haskins, "Henry II as Patron of Literature," in *Essays in Medieval History Presented to Thomas Frederick Tout*, ed. A. G. Little and F. M. Powicke (Manchester, 1925), 74–76. See also Gillingham, "The Cultivation of History," 28–29, 36.

127. Gillingham, "The Cultivation of History," 26–27.

128. Gillingham, "The Cultivation of History," 42 n. 12; Short, "Literary Culture," 359. Also, Guiot of Provins places Henry II high on his list of patrons: *La Bible*, 19, line 318.

129. "From the French Sea to the Jordan": Walter Map, *De nugis curialium* 5.6, ed. and trans. M. R. James, rev. C. N. L. Brooke and R. A. B. Mynors (Oxford, 1983), 476–77.

130. See Hubert Houben, *Roger II of Sicily*, trans. Graham A. Loud and Diane Milburn (Cambridge, 2002), 100–13; William Tronzo, *The Cultures of His Kingdom: Roger II and the Cappella Palatina in Palermo* (Princeton, NJ, 1997). For a more skeptical appraisal that emphasizes "the lack of real contact between cultures" at Roger II's court, see David S. H. Abulafia, "The End of Muslim Sicily," in Powell, *Muslims under Latin Rule*, 121–25. For a general assessment, see Antonino De Stefano, *La cultura in Sicilia nel periodo normanno* (Bologna, 1954), 81–86; also Theo Kölzer, "Kanzlei und Kultur im Königreich Sizilien, 1130–1198," *Quellen und Forschungen aus italienischen Archiven und Bibliotheken* 66 (1986): 32–34.

131. "in sancta civitate Ierusalem Latinorum rex quintus." *UKJ*, 2:534, 538, 544, 546, 634, nos. 308, 310–12, 364, and passim.

132. See B. Z. Kedar and Merry Wiesner-Hanks, "Introduction," in *The Cambridge World History*, vol. 5: *Expanding Webs of Exchange and Conflict, 500 CE–1500 CE*, ed. Kedar and Wiesner-Hanks (Cambridge, 2015), 1–15.

133. Kedar, *Crusade and Mission*, 95; Craig L. Hanson, "Manuel I Comnenus and the 'God of Muhammad': A Study in Byzantine Ecclesiastical Politics," in *Medieval Christian Perceptions of Islam*, ed. John V. Tolan (New York, 1996), 55–82.

134. Resembling a bishop: WT 10.2 (454).

135. See Kool, "*Civitas regis regvm omnivm*," 245–62.

136. Kühnel, *Crusader Art*, 66–125; Folda, *The Art of the Crusaders*, 137–59.

137. WT 15.27 (711).

138. Cf. the description, nowadays attributed to Foucher of Chartres, of the Greeks and Syrians during the Holy Fire debacle of 1101: "prae nimio dolore genas suas et capillos suos ululando decerbebant." FC, Appendix, 833. The

description made its way to the West: see William of Malmesbury, *Gesta regum Anglorum* 4.379 (674–75).

139. WT 16.2 (715–16).

140. *Balduini III Historia*, in *RHC Oc*, 5:139–85. According to the rhymed prologue, "Balduinus tertius . . . compilavit simul et conscribere fecit hoc opus" (140). The prologue is reedited in Yolles, *Making the East Latin*, 243–45.

141. For a comparison of the compilation and its sources, and a discussion of its date and transmission, see Deborah Gerish, "Remembering Kings in Jerusalem: The *Historia Nicaena vel Antiochena*, and Royal Identity around the Time of the Second Crusade," in *The Second Crusade: Holy War on the Periphery of Latin Christendom*, ed. Jason T. Roche and Janus Møller Jensen (Turnhout, 2015), 53–65; see also Giulia Usberti, "Storie di Gerusalemme, Antiochia e altre terre crociate: Fulcherio di Chartres e Baldovino III a confronto" (master's thesis, Università degli Studi di Parma, 2009–10). My thanks to Deborah Gerish for placing at my disposal her copy of *Balduini III Historia* on which she marked words identical with those of Foucher or Robert. **Misunderstanding**: Foucher highlights the small number of crusaders who remained in the kingdom after most participants in the First Crusade had returned home: "non enim tunc habebamus plusquam CCC^{os} milites et tantum de peditibus, qui Hierusalem et Ioppem et Ramulam, Caypham etiam castrum custodiebant." FC 2.6 (389). The compiler thought that the sentence refers to reinforcements from the West: "Illo tempore, in terram Jerusalem venerant plus quam CCC equites et totidem pedites, qui Jerusalem, et Joppen, et Ramulam, et castrum Caypham custodierunt." *Balduini III Historia*, 177, c. 63.

142. "paulo minus quam iaciat arcus sagittam": FC 1.26 (284); "quantum est jactus lapidis": *Balduini III Historia*, 175, c. 59. William follows Foucher: WT 8.5 (391).

143. *Balduini III Historia*, 177–78, 182–83, cc. 64, 76.

144. FC 1.25 (280); *Balduini III Historia*, 174, c. 58. A few lines earlier Foucher relates that the "Graeci videlicet et Syri" of Bethlehem welcomed the Franks: FC 1.25 (278); the compiler reverses the order and writes: "videlicet Syri et Graeci." *Balduini III Historia*, 174, c. 58. See discussion by Kirschberger, *Erster Kreuzzug*, 242–47.

145. Compare Robert the Monk, *Historia Iherosolimitana*, ed. Damien Kempf and Marcus G. Bull (Woodbridge, 2013), 6, and *Balduini III Historia*, 142, c. 2.

146. "Regnat pro socero Volco, comes Andegavensis." *Balduini III Historia*, prologue, 140. Duke William IX of Aquitaine uses the cognate form "Folcos d'Angieus": see "Pos de chantar m'es pres talenz," line 13, in *Les Chansons de Guillaume IX*, 27.

147. On the work's aims, see the diverging hypotheses of Deborah Gerish that the emphasis is on crusading and holy war, "with royal identity trailing far behind in importance," and Julian Yolles that the aim is "to reclaim the crusade narrative for the crown": see Gerish, "Remembering Kings in Jerusalem," 79–90; Yolles, *Making the East Latin*, 78–83. In any case, the prologue's reference to the Kingdom of Jerusalem as *imperium* is not exceptional: Genoa's Golden Inscription of 1104 states that the Genoese "CESAREAM UERO ET ASSUR IEROSOLIMITANO IMPERIO ADDIDERUNT," whereas Foucher of Chartres

writes that Baldwin I "terras Arabum . . . addidit imperio": *UKJ*, 1:136, no. 28; FC 2.64 (614).

148. WT 21.1 (962).

149. The reconstruction was proposed and carried out by Zehava Jacoby in preparation for the second conference of the Society for the Study of the Crusades and the Latin East, Jerusalem and Acre, 2–6 July 1987: Zehava Jacoby, *A Display of Crusader Sculpture at the Archaeological Museum (Rockefeller)* (Jerusalem, 1987), 11–12; Zehava Jacoby, "The Tomb of Baldwin V, King of Jerusalem (1185–1186) and the Workshop of the Temple Area," *Gesta* 18 (1979): 3–14; Folda, *The Art of the Crusaders*, 467–69.

150. See Louis Halphen, "Etude sur l'authenticité du fragment de chronique attribué a Foulque le Réchin," in *Mélanges d'histoire du moyen âge*, ed. Achille Luchaire (Paris, 1901), 47–48; Bezzola, *Les origines*, 2:337–40; Aurell, *Le chevalier lettré*, 31.

151. "Fragmentum historiae Andegavensis," in *Chroniques des comtes d'Anjou et des seigneurs d'Amboise*, ed. Louis Halphen and René Poupardin (Paris, 1913), 232–38; Haskins, *The Renaissance of the Twelfth Century*, 248–49; Josèphe Chartrou, *L'Anjou de 1109 à 1151: Foulque de Jérusalem et Geoffroi Plantegenet* (Paris, 1928), 221; Bezzola, *Les origines*, 2.2:330; Jim Bradbury, "Fulk le Réchin and the Origin of the Plantagenets," in *Studies in Medieval History Presented to R. Allen Brown*, ed. Christopher Harper-Bill, Christopher J. Holdsworth, and Janet L. Nelson (Woodbridge, 1989), 27–41; Jane Martindale, "Secular Propaganda and Aristocratic Values: The Autobiographies of Count Fulk le Réchin of Anjou and Count William of Poitou, Duke of Aquitaine," in *Writing Medieval Biography, 750–1250: Essays in Honour of Professor Frank Barlow*, ed. David Bates et al. (Woodbridge, 2006), 143–59; Nicholas L. Paul, "The Chronicle of Fulk le Réchin: A Reassessment," *Haskins Society Journal* 18 (2007): 19–35. Aurell assumes that the count dictated a vernacular account to a cleric who translated it into Latin: Aurell, *Le chevalier lettré*, 164–65.

152. For Fulk's attendance at the consecration of Hildebert's new cathedral at Le Mans in 1120, see *Actus pontificum Cenomannis*, 415–17. A few years later Hildebert counseled Fulk to abstain from going on pilgrimage to Compostela: PL 171:181–83. For a discussion of literary activities and schools in Anjou in Fulk's times, see Chartrou, *L'Anjou*, 163–222.

153. For the charter, see "Cartulaire de Ronceray," ed. Paul Marchegay in *Archives d'Anjou: Recueil de documents et mémoires inédits sur cette province*, vol. 3 (Angers, 1854), 279–80; for discussion, see Léon Maitre, *Les écoles épiscopaux et monastiques en Occident avant les Universités (768–1180)* (Ligugé, 1924), 86; Chartrou, *L'Anjou*, 220, 275. As for the charter's date, Chartrou vacillates between 1066, 1106, 1116, and 1126, but since Fulk appears in it as "Andegavie et Cenomannie comes," the first two dates must be ruled out, as he became count of Maine in 1110.

154. "Chronica de gestis consulum Andegavensium," in Halphen and Poupardin, *Chroniques des comtes d'Anjou*, 71.

155. "Historia Gaufredi ducis Normannorum," in Halphen and Poupardin, *Chroniques des comtes d'Anjou*, 172–231, esp. 176, 212–13, 218; see Jim Bradbury,

"Geoffrey V of Anjou, Count and Knight," in *The Ideals and Practice of Medieval Knighthood*, vol. 3, ed. Christopher Harper-Bill and Ruth Harvey (Woodbridge, 1990), 21–38; Aurell, *Le chevalier lettré*, 31–32.

156. Bezzola, *Les origines*, 2.2:363–64; Philippe Contamine, *La guerre au moyen âge* (Paris, 1980), 355; Bernard S. Bachrach, "The Practical Use of Vegetius' *De Re Militari* during the Early Middle Ages," *The Historian* 47 (1985): 242–44, 250. For the Jerusalem hypothesis, see Jim Bradbury, "Greek Fire in the West," *History Today* 29 (1979): 326–31. For a doubt about the incident's likelihood, see Christopher Allmand, *The "De Re Militari" of Vegetius* (Cambridge, 2011), 67.

157. Guillaume de Conches, *Dragmaticon philosophiae*, ed. Italo Ronca, CCCM 152 (Turnhout, 1997), xi–xx (title, author, and date), 5 (imbuing sons with the study of letters), 11–13 (*confessio fidei*).

158. "Chronica de gestis consulum Andegavensium," 70–71; *Actus pontificum Cenomannis*, 436; also 431–32.

159. "Chronicon Turonense magnum," in Salmon, *Recueil de chroniques de Touraine*, 134. In reality, Fulk did not die on St. Martin's summer feast (4 July); the hunting accident occurred a day before St. Martin's main feast (11 November) and Fulk died two days later: WT 15.27 (711).

160. WT 14.1 (631–33), erroneously presenting Geoffroi IV Martel and Ermenjart as Fulk V's uterine siblings.

161. Paul, "The Chronicle of Fulk le Réchin," 30–34.

162. See B. Z. Kedar, "Bertrada von Montfort, verschmähte Königin der Franzosen: Blicke aus Okzident und Orient" (in press).

163. Mayer and Sode, *Die Siegel*, 60, 111, 113.

8. The Inventiveness of the Kingdom's Knights and Military-Religious Orders

1. *UKJ*, 1:315–21, no. 138.

2. Mayer, *Bistümer*, 375–81.

3. Such a unique appearance is rare. In Shagrir's database of Frankish names, only about 35 out of about 1,400 nobles of the period 1100–1189 are mentioned just once (pers. comm.).

4. For an overview of the knightly class and its stratification, see Prawer, "Social Classes in the Latin Kingdom," 123–44; for his dim view of the knights' culture, see 142. On the stratification of the knightly class, see also Jean Richard, "La noblesse de Terre Sainte (1097–1187)," *Arquivos do Centro Cultural Português* 26 (1989): 321–36; repr. in Richard, *Croisades et états latins d'Orient: Points de vue et documents* (Aldershot, 1992), Study IX.

5. On the age of majority, see John of Ibelin, *Le Livre des Assises*, 421, c. 169.

6. Aebischer, who assembled these and further data (but was unaware of the Jerusalem brothers), believed that the Roland-Olivier pairs reflect the impact of the *Song of Roland*, whereas the Olivier-Roland pairs, attested from 999/1030 to 1115, reflect the influence of an earlier work: Paul Aebischer, *Rollandiana et Oliveriana* (Geneva, 1967), 62–80, 152–73; Aebischer, *Préhistoire et protohistoire du "Roland" d'Oxford* (Bern, 1972), 157–62. My thanks to Ian Short for bringing these studies to my attention.

7. Short, "Literary Culture," 357.

8. *Les Chétifs*, vv. 1665–78, 1778–80, ed. Geoffrey M. Myers (University, AL, 1981), 40, 42; Geoffrey M. Myers, "*Les Chétifs*: Étude sur le développement de la chanson," *Romania* 105 (1984): 64–73; *The Chanson des Chétifs and Chanson de Jérusalem*, trans. Carol Sweetenham (Farnham, 2016), introduction, 9–16. For the view that the part of the *Chétifs* written under Raymond's patronage was not limited to the Sathanas episode, see *La Chanson d'Antioche*, ed. Suzanne Duparc-Quioc, 2 vols. (Paris, 1977–78), 2:126. For the hypothesis that the author of the Sathanas episode was born in the Principality of Antioch or resided there for a long time, see David Jacoby, "La littérature française dans les états latins de la Méditerranée orientale à l'époque des croisades: Diffusion et création," in *Essor et fortune de la chanson de geste dans l'Europe et l'Orient latin* (Modena, 1984), 640. On the *Chétifs* having no counterpart in the Frankish East, and for the view that it should be linked to the literature of the Poitiers dynasty, see Claude Cahen, *La Syrie du Nord à l'époque des croisades et la principauté franque d'Antioche* (Paris, 1940), 569–78; Cahen, *Orient et Occident*, 209.

Having asked whether the *Chanson des Chétifs* was an isolated phenomenon in Antioch, Paterson answers boldly that "it is possible, though not proven, that the *Chétifs* was the tip of an epic iceberg": Linda M. Paterson, "Occitan Literature and the Holy Land," in *The World of Eleanor of Aquitaine: Literature and Society in Southern France between the Eleventh and Thirteenth Centuries*, ed. Marcus Bull and Catherine Léglu (Woodbridge, 2005), 89. On the *Chétifs* as basically Western, with some local color, see Bale, "Reading," 92–93.

9. *Ernoul*, 101. In the description of the *Tiere de Promission* that may be a later interpolation, the men of Alexander the Great are said to have gone foraging, according to the *Fuerre de Gadres*, to *Val de Josafas*: *Ernoul*, 121 n. 66. See *Le Roman de Fuerre de Gadres d'Eustache*, ed. Edward C. Armstrong and Alfred Foulet (Princeton, NJ, 1942), 89–90. Eustache's work is dated to 1139–65.

10. See Simonetta Cerrini, "Une expérience neuve au sein de la spiritualité médiévale: L'ordre du Temple (1120–1314). Etude et édition des règles latine et française" (PhD thesis, Université de Paris-Sorbonne (Paris IV), 1997), 551; Cerrini, *La rivoluzione dei Templari*, 142–43, 177.

11. Peter [W.] Edbury, "Ernoul, *Eracles*, and the Collapse of the Kingdom of Jerusalem," in *The French of Outremer*, 46–56; Massimiliano Gaggero, "Western Eyes on the Latin East: The *Chronique d'Ernoul et de Bernard le Trésorier* and Robert de Clari's *Conquête de Constantinople*," in *The French of Outremer*, 88. While ruling the Kingdom of Acre in 1192–97, Henri of Champagne struck bronze coins with the reverse legend PUGES D'ACCON in French; in France, such a legend has a counterpart only in Le Puy: Stahl, "The *Denier* Outremer," 34. On somewhat later prose chroniclers who wrote in Old French, see Gabrielle M. Spiegel, *Romancing the Past: The Rise of Vernacular Prose Historiography in Thirteenth-Century France* (Berkeley, 1993), 214–313; Gillette Labory, "Les débuts de la chronique en français (XIIe et XIIIe siècles)," in *The Medieval Chronicle*, vol. 3, ed. Erik Kooper (Leiden, 2004), 11–20. Neither Spiegel nor Labory mentions Ernoul.

12. *Ernoul*, 147–48, 162. In reality, King Baldwin IV was absent; Gui of Lusignan, the regent, was in charge. For a detailed account of this "campaign without battle" of 1183, see R. C. "Otto" Smail, "The Predicaments of Guy of Lusignan,

1183–87," in *Outremer*, 160–73. On Ernoul's stature as chronicler, see Smail, "The Predicaments," 162–63; Hamilton, *The Leper King*, 8–9.

13. A rather loose translation of the biblical book of Judges into Old French, made for the benefit of Templars *sanz letreure*, was prepared in about 1173–74 for two masters of the Templar order in England, *Maistre Richard et frere Othon*; for a survey of the research literature, see Jaroslav Folda, *Crusader Manuscript Illumination at Saint-Jean d'Acre, 1275–1291* (Princeton, NJ, 1976), 60–65; Folda, *Crusader Art in the Holy Land*, 286. It has not yet been noted that the manuscript comprising that translation, BnF, nouv. acq. fr. 1404, copied in about 1280–81 in Acre, offers place-names—Saphet, Escalone, Acre, Gadre, Rames—that were current among contemporary Franks: see *Le livre des Juges: Les cinq textes de la version française faite au XIIe pour les chevaliers du Temple*, ed. Guigue A. M. J. A. Marquis d'Albon (Lyon, 1913), 5, 7, 37. Thus, Paul Meyer, probably the first to draw attention to this translation, must not have been totally wrong when he asked: "A-t-elle éte écrite en Terre Sainte?" See his review in *Romania* 17 (1888): 133.

14. "et quod in hostium <vinculis> summo labore collegerat, literatus modice." WT 21.5 (967).

15. Hiestand, "Der lateinische Klerus," 55.

16. Aurell, *Le chevalier lettré*, 49–70.

17. Ibn Abī Usaybi'a, *A Literary History of Medicine*, 2.2:1304 (text), 2.3:1484 (translation). For the text of the inscription mentioning Ṣalāḥ al-Dīn's order to construct a moat in Jerusalem in AH 587/AD 1191–92, see *Muslim Sources of the Crusader Period: An Anthology*, trans. James E. Lindsay and Suleiman A. Mourad (Indianapolis, 2021), 206–7. In both instances I translate خندق as "moat," not "trench."

18. The two parts of the treatise were published by Claude Cahen, ed. and trans., "Un traité d'armurerie composé pour Saladin," *Bulletin d'études orientales* 12 (1947–48): 103–63, and Antoine Boudot-Lamotte, ed. and trans., *Contribution à l'étude de l'archerie musulmane* (Damascus, 1968). See the discussion by Maya Shatzmiller, "The Crusades and Islamic Warfare," *Der Islam* 69 (1992): 261–64.

19. FC Prologue 4 (116–17).

20. FC 2.11.8 (411–12). The knights' purported wish to relocate to France ties in with Foucher's sentiment when in danger: "Ego quidem vel Carnoti vel Aurelianis mallem esse; alii quoque." FC 2.2 (360).

21. Lynn T. White, Jr., "The Crusades and the Technological Thrust of the West," in *War, Technology and Society in the Middle East*, ed. Vernon J. Parry and Malcolm E. Yapp (London, 1975), 99–100; John France, "Crusading Warfare and Its Adaptation to Eastern Conditions in the Twelfth Century," *Mediterranean Historical Review* 15 (2000): 59–62. On adaptation rather than innovation in Frankish/Muslim warfare, see Morton, *The Crusader States*, 218–41.

22. WT 5.2 (272), 6.17 (330), 6.18 (332), 10.21 (480), 11.25 (533), 12.9 (557), 12.12 (561), 18.18 (836), 21.21 (991), 22.17 (1031), 22.27 (1051); similarly, WT 3.14 (214).

23. WT 19.9 (875), 21.28 (1001).

24. WT 16.12 (732, term used twice). Of the seven other instances in which William mentions *disciplina militaris*, two concern camp vigilance or its absence (9.12 [435], 18.13 [829]), one the division of spoils (10.16 [474]), and one the

lack of discipline during a siege (21.24 [994]). *Disciplina militaris* is a characteristic of Baldwin I and his brothers (10.2 [454]) as well as of an unnamed Arab prince (9.22 [449]); it is inculcated in the Mamluks (21.22 [991]); see Smail, *Crusading Warfare*, 124–25. For discussions of the Frankish marching column and its Byzantine counterparts, see Matthew Bennett, "The Crusaders' 'Fighting March' Revisited," *War in History* 8 (2001): 1–18; Morton, *The Crusader States*, 237–39.

25. Yuval [N.] Harari, "The Military Role of the Frankish Turcopoles: A Reassessment," *Mediterranean Historical Review* 12 (1997): 75–116 [the future author of *Sapiens*, *Homo Deus*, and *Nexus*, submitted this paper while an undergraduate at the Hebrew University of Jerusalem]; France, "Crusading Warfare and Its Adaptation to Eastern Conditions," 58–60. Tibble, who relies heavily on Harari's article, nevertheless presents the Turcopoles as of native origin: Tibble, *The Crusader Armies*, 35, 41, 85 (but see 119). He also believes that in many Frankish armies the Franks were in a minority: Tibble, *The Crusader Armies*, 6, 98.

26. Claverie, "L'influence des ordres militaires," 288, quoting the chronicler Ibn al-Ṭuwayr (1130–1220); also *Ibn Khallikan's Biographical Dictionary*, 2:352, where the elite unit is likened to the Knights Templar and Hospitaller. The notion that al-Afḍal, murdered in December 1121, was aware of the Knights Templar is chronologically problematic. Ibn al-Ṭuwayr was writing in Ṣalāḥ al-Dīn's times; Ibn Khallikān started his dictionary in 1256.

27. "When arranging the ranks in a compact battle formation, it may be necessary to set up the troops in separate detachments [*karādis*] and to organize the horsemen according to banner [*ʿalam*] and corps [*khamīs*], because the enemy, when he storms, is wont to attack with all his forces and to engage our units [*katāʾib*] from up close with all his troops, as is the case with the accursed Franks and the brigands who resemble them. For that compact battle formation [in which all forces form a single mass] is favorable to them [the enemy], but this compact battle formation [in which the forces are split into detachments] confuses and stuns them. This is because, when they aim for one of our units and approach it in their attack, banners from every direction rise up against them and surround them. They are then engaged in combat and in struggle from every angle and every remaining direction. This will be the cause of achieving [our] objectives and having a powerful impact against them. The way to weaken and break them is through the excellence of the organization [of the army]." Mardī b. ʿAlī al-Tarsūsī, *Tabṣīra fī al-ḥurūb*, Oxford, Bodleian Library, Huntingdon 264, fol. 205a–b. Translation: Elon Harvey. For a partial translation of the above passage, based on Cahen's text, see David Nicolle, *Crusader Warfare*, 2 vols. (London, 2007), 2:130. See also Claverie, "L'influence des ordres militaires," 291.

28. France presents Belvoir as "a remarkable intellectual concept": John France, *Perilous Glory: The Rise of Western Military Power* (New Haven, CT, 2011), 125. For a distinction between two phases in the construction of Belvoir—the first in 1168–72, the second before 1187—and a detailed analysis of its defenses, see Rabei G. Khamisy and Moshe Bram, "Belvoir Castle Revisited: History and Development," in *EO*, 2:310–28.

29. Hugh Kennedy, *Crusader Castles* (Cambridge, 1994), 98–119; Ellenblum, *Crusader Castles*, 187–304, quotation on 304. For a different view, see John France, "Fortifications East and West," in *Muslim Military Architecture in Greater Syria: From the Coming of Islam to the Ottoman Period*, ed. Hugh Kennedy (Leiden, 2006), 281–94. But France, too, writes that "what is impressive about Belvoir is its intellectual achievement—this is a conception carried through almost perfectly" (290). When the Muslim counterweight trebuchets rendered concentric castles vulnerable, the Franks countered by constructing new castles on hills with steep slopes, out of range for the new ballistic weapons: Adrian J. Boas, *The Crusades Uncovered* (Leeds, 2022), 38–39. For an attempt to reconstruct the Franks' military thinking on the basis of their activities, see Tibble, *The Crusader Strategy*.

30. AA 6.42–44 (456–63).

31. For details, see Harari, "The Military Role," 102–3.

32. AA 12.13 (842–45). The Arrabits have been regarded as members of a Frankish knightly family of native origin: see Riley-Smith, *The Feudal Nobility*, 10; Prawer, *Crusader Institutions*, 208. For evidence that "seems to lessen the probability of Muslim origin," see Shagrir, *Naming Patterns*, 76–77. Mayer forwarded the hypothesis that they were Spaniards, their name derived from *rābit/rápita*: *UKJ*, 2:509. An Apulian origin is more plausible: *Simon f. Benedicti Arrabiti* appears in 1139 as the owner of a vineyard in Barletta, and *Maio miles f. Arrabiti* appears in acts drawn up at Canne in 1179, 1182, 1197, and about 1200: *Codice diplomatico Barese*, vol. 8, ed. Francesco Nitti di Vito (Bari, 1914), 75, 179, 181, 224, 232, nos. 45, 135, 137, 176, 181.

33. See Gary La Viere Leiser, "The Crusader Raid in the Red Sea, 578/1182–83," *Journal of the American Research Center in Egypt* 14 (1977): 91, 93, 94, quoting al-Qāḍī al-Fāḍil, al-Dhahabī, and al-Maqrīzī.

34. AA 9.48 (706); the Arabic sources are summarized by Köhler, *Alliances*, 83–84.

35. WT 15.7–11 (684–90), quotation on 686–87. See Köhler, *Alliances*, 143–45. On the prominent role of siege towers in Frankish, but not in Muslim, warfare, see Ellenblum, *Crusader Castles*, 203–30. For a discussion of their utilization, see Michael S. Fulton, *Siege Warfare during the Crusades* (Barnsley, Yorkshire, 2019), 143–54.

36. WT 19.23 (895–96) and 19.25 (898). For the background, see Prawer, *Histoire*, 1:434–37; Köhler, *Alliances*, 189–92.

37. WT 17.5–6 (765–68).

38. AA 6.4–5 (409–11). The princes tried to induce him to convert to Christianity; upon his refusal, he was beheaded in full view of the city's defenders.

39. WT 13.14 (602). Cf. WT 19.31 (907: conclusion of Amaurry's siege of Alexandria, 1167).

40. WT 15.11 (689–90).

41. WT 16.8 (725).

42. Usama ibn Munqidh, *The Book of Contemplation*, 147–48, 205–6.

43. Usama ibn Munqidh, *The Book of Contemplation*, 150.

44. Usama ibn Munqidh, *The Book of Contemplation*, 147.

45. Usama ibn Munqidh, *The Book of Contemplation*, 144. For doubts about the story's veracity, see Hillenbrand, *The Crusades*, 355.

46. WT 19.18–19 (887–89).

47. WT 17.17 (784). Twenty-five years later, Onfroi was accused of having unsatisfactorily presented the Frankish cause because of his "too great a friendship" with Ṣalāḥ al-Dīn. Four years later he died of wounds sustained in battle with Ṣalāḥ al-Dīn's men: WT 21.8 (973), 21.26 (999).

48. Jochen Burgtorf, "'Blood-Brothers' in the Thirteenth-Century Latin East? The Mamluk Sultan Baybars and the Templar Matthew Sauvage," in Shagrir, Kedar, and Balard, *Communicating the Middle Ages*, 3–14.

49. Robert of Auxerre, *Chronicon*, ed. Oswald Holder-Egger, in MGH SS 26:249.

50. Jean Richard, "An Account of the Battle of Hattin Referring to the Frankish Mercenaries in Oriental Moslem States," *Speculum* 27 (1952): 170–71. For a reappraisal of the Battle of Ḥaṭṭīn, see Morton, *The Crusader States*, 184–89.

51. *Ernoul*, 319–20; WT Cont. Lyon, 58–59, 87. See Helen J. Nicholson, *Templars, Hospitallers and Teutonic Knights: Images of the Military Orders, 1128–1291* (Leicester, 1993), 83–84; Jean Richard, "The Adventure of John Gale, Knight of Tyre," in *EC*, 189–95. Richard assumed that the knight Johannes of the Battle of Ḥaṭṭīn was identical with Johan Gale. But neither Ernoul nor the Continuator of William of Tyre mention Johan Gale's presence at Ḥaṭṭīn, nor do they claim that he used to fight in the Turkish ranks; and Raymond of Tripoli does not denounce the knight Johannes as a vassal who killed his lord. For doubt about the historicity of the Johan Gale story, see Peter W. Edbury, "The Lyon *Eracles* and the Continuations of William of Tyre," in *Montjoie*, 148. For an analysis of Johan Gale's story that also utilizes ʿImād al-Dīn's account, see Uri Zvi Shachar, *A Pious Belligerence: Dialogical Warfare and the Rhetoric of Righteousness in the Crusading Near East* (Philadelphia, 2021), 52–55.

52. *Ernoul*, 119. See Richard, "The Adventure of John Gale," 195 n. 26; Richard, "Les mercenaires francs dans les armées musulmanes au temps des croisades," in *Regards croisés sur le Moyen Age arabe: Mélanges à la mémoire de Louis Pouget s.j. (1928–2002)*, ed. Anne-Marie Eddé and Emma Gannage (Beirut, 2005), 232 n. 20. Benibrac: Ibn Ibreiq, the Mishnaic-Talmudic Bené Beraq, a village east of Jaffa (Palestine Grid, 133/160).

53. The story is still more fanciful in Howden's first version, written before his stay in Acre: cf. "Benedict of Peterborough" [=Howden's first version], *Gesta regis Henrici secundi*, 1:341–42; Roger of Howden, *Chronica*, 2:307.

54. Reinhold Röhricht, *Geschichte des Königreichs Jerusalem, 1100–1291* (Innsbruck, 1898), 411 n. 5. Röhricht, summarizing correctly Howden's account, states that Robert's army was *zurückgeschlagen*. This requires a correction of Richard, "The Adventure of John Gale," 195 n. 26, who claims, on the basis of Röhricht's summary, that Robert was killed. Howden expressly writes (*Chronica*, 2:307): "Robertus tamen vix evasit."

55. *Le Livre au Roi*, 200–204, c. 22–23. Cf. 182, c. 16 (ninth reason), and "Assises des Bourgeois," c. 240, seventh reason (2:170). The last two laws are attributed to King Baldwin II. See also Philip of Novara, *Le Livre de Forme de Plait*, 80 (text), 236 (translation); John of Ibelin, *Le Livre des Assises*, 167, c. 58; "Livre de Geoffroy Le Tort," in *RHC Lois*, 1:443, c. 32.

56. For the view that the law covers knights who entered Muslim service, see Richard, "Les mercenaires francs," 232–33. On mercenaries serving in Muslim armies, see also Morton, *The Crusader States*, 146–47. For a survey of much of the evidence on rapprochement between Frankish knights and their Muslim counterparts, see Pierre-Vincent Claverie, "La place de la chevalerie comme vecteur du rapprochement interconfessionel dans l'Orient des croisades," in *Através do olhar do Outro: Reflexões acerca da sociedade medieval europeia (séculos XII–XV)*, ed. José Albuquerque Carreiras, Giulia Rossi Vairo, and Kristjan Toomaspoeg (Tomar, 2018), 113–34.

57. *La Règle du Temple*, 154, 157, 244, 296, 309, §§230, 240, 455, 568, 596.

58. Usama ibn Munqidh, *The Book of Contemplation*, 147, 153.

59. See Yvonne Friedman, *Encounter between Enemies: Captivity and Ransom in the Latin Kingdom of Jerusalem* (Leiden, 2002), 117–18; the author assumes that former captives may have preferred to conceal the knowledge of Arabic acquired in captivity and claims that "evidently it was *bon ton* not to know Arabic," but does not substantiate these assertions.

60. On the torture of Patriarch Aimery, see WT 18.1 (809).

61. Carole Hillenbrand, "The Imprisonment of Reynald of Châtillon," in *Texts, Documents and Artefacts: Islamic Studies in Honour of D.S. Richards*, ed. Chase F. Robinson (Leiden, 2003), 79–102.

62. See Richard W. Southern, "Peter of Blois and the Third Crusade," in *Studies in Medieval History Presented to R.H.C. Davis*, ed. Henry Mayr-Herting and R. I. Moore (London, 1985), 212–16, with corrections by Robert B. C. Huygens in the introduction to his edition of *Petri Blesensis Tractatus duo*, 19–22. For an attempt to explain why Pierre of Blois's *Passio Raginaldi* failed to bring about Renaud's canonization, see Bernard Hamilton, "Why Did the Crusader States Produce So Few Saints?," in *Saints and Sanctity*, ed. Peter Clarke and Tony Claydon (Cambridge, 2011), 109–11.

63. Pierre of Blois, "Passio Raginaldi principis Antiochie," 52. Huygens believed (in his introduction to his edition of the "Passio Raginaldi," 15) that "cum in iuventute sua captivatus fuisset" refers to an otherwise unknown, short captivity of Renaud among the Muslims that took place in his youth. But Pierre, speaking of Renaud's fifteen-year-long imprisonment, relates that when ransomed, he was a young man whom captivity rendered prematurely old: "Passio Raginaldi principis Antiochie," 45.

64. Jacoby wrote that Renaud, in Muslim captivity from 1260 to 1276 (*sic*), knew classical Arabic, yet was helped by an interpreter since he had difficulty expressing himself in the vernacular: Jacoby, "Intercultural Encounters in a Conquered Land," 146 n. 80. He relies for this statement on Laura Minervini, "Les contacts entre indigènes et croisés dans l'Orient latin: Le rôle des drogmans," in *Romania arabica: Festschrift für Reinhold Kontzi zum 70. Geburtstag*, ed. Jens Lüdtke (Tübingen, 1996), 59; however, Renaud of Châtillon appears there erroneously instead of Renaud of Sidon.

65. Al-ʿUmarī, "Condizioni degli Stati cristiani dell'Occidente secondo una relazione di Domenichino Doria da Genova," ed. and trans. Michele Amari, *Atti della R. Accademia dei Lincei: Memorie dellla classe di scienze morali, storiche e filologiche* 11 (1883): 67–103, 306–8; Antonio Musarra, "Alcune note sulla descrizione

dell'Italia politica nel *Masālik al-absār fī mamālik al-amsār* di al-'Umarī (1340 ca.)," *Archivio Storico Italiano* 180, no. 3 (2022): 477–503. The exchange took place in 1339–40.

66. *The Travels of Ibn Jubayr*, trans. Broadhurst, 52.

67. Disregard: Runciman, *A History of the Crusades*, 2:437; Prawer, "Crusader Security and the Red Sea," in his *Crusader Institutions*, 482; Richard, *Histoire des croisades*, 206. Hamilton, who did refer to Ibn Jubayr's statement, claimed in 1978 that he "relates the rumour that Reynald's men intended to steal the prophet's body," and gave the view that this was possible, since the body could serve the Franks as a bargaining counter: Bernard Hamilton, "The Elephant of Christ: Reynald of Châtillon," in *Religious Motivation: Biographical and Sociological Problems for the Church Historian*, ed. Derek Baker (Oxford, 1978), 104 n. 52. In 2000 he wrote that Ibn Jubayr was told that the Franks "intended to destroy the tomb of the prophet," and gave the view that it was unlikely, since "the Franks had no horses and could not raid far inland": Hamilton, *The Leper King*, 182. In both publications Ayla is erroneously identified with present-day Eilat.

68. Al-Dhahabī and al-Maqrīzī are summarized by Leiser, "The Crusader Raid in the Red Sea," 93; for the reference to Mujīr al-Dīn, see 99 n. 26. Schlumberger mentioned Mujīr al-Dīn's account but, unaware of the other sources, dismissed it as fanciful: Gustave Schlumberger, *Renaud de Châtillon, prince d'Antioche, seigneur de la terre d'Outre-Jourdain*, 2nd ed. (Paris, 1923), 212 n. 2. For a translation of Mujīr al-Dīn's account, see "L'Histoire d'Alep de Kamal ad-Dîn," trans. Edgar Blochet, *ROL* 4 (1896): 160 n. 1. Mallett, who does not take ʿAbd al-Laṭīf al-Baghdādī's statement into account, considers the story implausible: Alex Mallett, "A Trip Down the Red Sea with Reynald of Châtillon," *Journal of the Royal Asiatic Society* 3, no. 18 (2008): 146–49.

69. Jean-Michel Mouton and Jacques Paviot, "Un témoignage inédit sur la bataille de Hattīn (4 juillet 1187) et les relations entre Saladin et Renaud de Châtillon," in *Bourgogne/Orient*, 485.

70. *Magistri Thietmari peregrinatio*, c. 20, ed. J. C. M. Laurent (Hamburg, 1857), 44. On the landed property, see Denys Pringle, *Pilgrimage to Jerusalem and the Holy Land, 1187–1291* (Farnham, 2012), 127 n. 218.

71. For the hypothesis that the nobleman was Phelippe of Nablus, lord of Transjordan and Master of the Templars who, presumably in the early 1160s, went on pilgrimage to the monastery of St. Catherine, see Jotischky in Hamilton and Jotischky, *Latin and Greek Monasticism*, 449.

72. Pierre of Blois, "Passio Raginaldi principis Antiochie," 51–52. The adapter of William's chronicle into Old French exhibits a more positive view toward Renaud than does William: Handyside, *The Old French William of Tyre*, 75–82, 222–23.

73. *Lignages d'Outremer*, ed. Marie-Adélaïde Nielen, DRHC 18 (Paris, 2003), 70; for the date, see 32–33.

74. Bahā' al-Dīn, *History of Saladin*, 90.

75. Bahā' al-Dīn, *History of Saladin*, 91.

76. Bahā' al-Dīn, *History of Saladin*, 95–96, 108; WT Cont. Lyon, 79–81. Shachar offers a "thick description" of the event, based on the Old French and

Arabic accounts: *A Pious Belligerence*, 55–59 (but Renaud was lord of Beaufort, not Montfort).

77. Bahā᾽ al-Dīn, *History of Saladin*, 191–92, 194.

78. Bahā᾽ al-Dīn, *History of Saladin*, 173, 196; ʿImād al-Dīn al-Isfahānī, *Conquête*, 340.

79. Prawer, *The Latin Kingdom*, 522–23; William S. Murrell, "Interpreters in Franco-Muslim Negotiations," *Crusades* 20 (2021): 131–50.

80. WT 16.12 (731).

81. See Joinville, *Vie de saint Louis*, 352, 356, 406, §§354, 361, 444.

82. *Cronaca del Templare di Tiro*, 204–7, §§250–51.

83. Al-Qalqashandī's statement is translated in Peter M. Holt, *Early Mamluk Diplomacy (1260–1290): Treaties of Baybars and Qalāwūn with Christian Rulers* (Leiden, 1995), 7. See Kedar, "Religion in Catholic-Muslim Correspondence and Treaties," 416–17.

84. WT 18.9 (822–23). Usāma, who played a role in the events and managed to reach Damascus, does not mention Nāṣr al-Dīn's attempt to convert: Usama ibn Munqidh, *The Book of Contemplation*, 26–36. Walter Map writes that he was close to Christianity while still in Egypt and does not mention that he learned Latin letters in captivity: *De nugis curialium*, 1.21 (62–67).

85. Research on the Knights Templar and the other military orders is intensively expanding, with conferences on the subject regularly taking place at London, Toruń, and Palmela, and their proceedings published in the three series *The Military Orders*; *Ordines Militares: Colloquia Torunensia Historica*; and *Ordens militares*.

86. On the Aragonese confraternities of Belchite and Monreal del Campo, virtually contemporary with the early Templars, see Alain Demurger, "Belchite, le Temple et Montjoie: La couronne d'Aragon et le Temple au XIIe siècle," in *Knighthoods of Christ: Essays on the History of the Crusades and the Knights Templar Presented to Malcolm Barber*, ed. Norman Housley (Aldershot, 2007), 124–29. Demurger cogently argues that Iberia was not the cradle of the military orders.

87. See the critical edition of the Rule in Cerrini, "Une expérience neuve au sein de la spiritualité médiévale" [hereafter quoted as *Templar Rule*, ed. Cerrini], c. 48 (135). For an English translation of this edition, see Malcolm Barber and Keith Bate, *The Templars: Selected Sources* (Manchester, 2002), 31–54 [hereafter quoted as *Templar Rule (English)*], with c. 48 on 47 (here and below my translation differs on some points).

88. Bernard of Clairvaux, *Éloge de la Nouvelle Chevalerie*, 54–55.

89. *Cart Tem*, 23–24, no. 31. See Kaspar Elm, "Die Spiritualität der geistlichen Ritterorden im Mittelalter," in *"Militia Christi" e Crociata nei secoli XI–XIII* (Milan, 1992), 517–18. The preamble does not present the Templars as combining features of those who pray and those who fight; for such a presentation, see Cerrini, *La rivoluzione dei Templari*, 6–8, 18, 38–40. For a critique of her view, see Karl Borchardt, "Historiography and Memory: What Was New and Unique about the Templars?," in *Ordens militares: Freires, Guerreiros, Cavaleiros*, ed. Isabel Cristina Ferreira Fernandes (Palmela, 2012), 53–57.

90. See Riley-Smith, *Templars and Hospitallers*, esp. 13, 35–38, 61–62. See also Christian Vogel, *Das Recht der Templer* (Berlin, 2007), 173.

91. "Precipimus ut omnes fratres tam futuri quam presentes, simbolum et dominicam orationem nescientes, latinis verbis aut romanis, prout melius poterint, discant." The rule, issued at the chapter of *Villa Mausonii*, is edited from Munich, Bayerische Staatsbibliothek, Clm 2649 in Alois Knöpfler, "Die Ordensregel der Tempelherren," *Historisches Jahrbuch* 8 (1887): 692. Cerrini established that Clm 2649 dates from 1150–75; this ties in with the subsequent ruling that mentions the dispatch of income to Jerusalem (Knöpfler, 694), which must have taken place before 1187. She tentatively identified *Villa Mausonii* with Masone, northwest of Genoa: Simonetta Cerrini, "La tradition manuscrite de la Règle du Temple: Etudes pour une nouvelle édition des versions latine et française," in *Autour*, 209–10. For a general survey that focuses on later periods, see Alan Forey, "Literacy and Learning in the Military Orders during the Twelfth and Thirteenth Centuries," in Nicholson, *The Military Orders*, 2:185–206.

92. See Vogel, *Das Recht der Templer*, 229–34. For a discussion of contemporary and present-day views of the place of the Templars and other military orders within medieval society, see Giles Constable, *Crusaders and Crusading in the Twelfth Century* (Farnham, 2008), 169–79.

93. Point made already by Gustav Schnürer, *Die ursprüngliche Templerregel, kritisch untersucht und herausgegeben* (Freiburg im Breisgau, 1903), 100–101.

94. "Canons of the Council of Nablus," no. 20: "Si clericus causa defensionis [*sic*] arma detulerit, culpa non teneatur." For a discussion of the place of canon 20 in canon law, see Kedar, "On the Origins of the Earliest Laws," 324–25; also Murray, *Baldwin of Bourcq*, 130–31. On clerics who participated in warfare while on crusade, see Thomas Haas, *Geistliche als Kreuzfahrer: Der Klerus im Konflikt zwischen Orient und Okzident, 1095–1221* (Heidelberg, 2012), 273–75. Riley-Smith assumed that canon 20 "was probably agreed in order to ease the way to the Church's recognition of the Templars, who were clerics, but were not priests": *The Knights Hospitallers in the Levant, c. 1070–1309* (Houndmills, 2012), 28; Riley-Smith, *Templars and Hospitallers*, 10. Yet "the Templars, as *religiosi laici* who were not clerics, faced no canonical bar to their bearing arms": Anthony Luttrell, "The Earliest Templars," in *Autour*, 199. On the lay status of the Knights Templar, see also Riley-Smith, *Templars and Hospitallers*, 38.

95. This hypothesis, first put forward by Rudolf Hiestand, "Kardinalbischof Matthäus von Albano, das Konzil von Troyes und die Entstehung des Templerordens," *Zeitschrift für Kirchengeschichte* 99 (1988): 317–19, 323, has become generally accepted as if factual. For a grant of 31 January 1120 to the Josaphat Valley Monastery, agreed upon sixteen days earlier in the margins of the Council of Nablus of 16 January 1120, see *UKJ*, 1:225–30, no. 85.

96. See *Templar Rule*, ed. Cerrini, Prologus (106), Prologues (161); *Templar Rule (English)*, 31–34.

97. See the reconstruction of Luttrell, "The Earliest Templars." The escorting of pilgrims *ad sacrosancta loca* and back is mentioned in an act dated ca. 1125: *Cart Tem*, 3, no. 6.

98. The phrase "servir Deu devotement" is attested in the mid-twelfth century, "tres devote creance" in about 1172: *Dictionnaire Étymologique de l'Ancien Français (DEAF)*, https://www.hadw-bw.de/fr/recherche/centre-de-recherche/dictionnaire-etymologique-de-lancien-francais-deaf, s.v. *devot*. Gratian quotes

Jerome's statement that the *conversi* are *Deo devoti*: C. 12 q. 1 c. 7, in *Corpus iuris canonici*, ed. Friedberg, 1:678. William of Tyre characterizes the earliest Templars as *deo devoti*: WT 12.7 (553).

99. R. Stephen Humphreys, "*Dāwiyya* and *Isbitāriyya*," in *Encyclopaedia of Islam*, 2nd ed., *s.v.* The first mention of the Templars as *dāwiyya* is in Ibn al-Qalānisī's description of a battle in AH 552/AD 1157. Michael the Syrian asserts that the *frēr* (Templars) "call themselves *dawyh* [*dāwiyya*], which is *alōhōyē*": *Chronique de Michel le Syrien, patriarche jacobite d'Antioche (1166–1199)*, ed. and trans. Jean-Baptiste Chabot, 4 vols. (Paris, 1899–1910), 3:207 (translation), 4:598 (text). Weltecke cogently argues that *alōhōyē* does not mean here "divine" (as Chabot translated), but "belonging to God, sacred," thus supporting the derivation of *dāwiyya* from *devot*: Dorothea Weltecke, "Contacts between Syriac Orthodox and Latin Military Orders," in *EWCS*, 3:62–63. Constable claims that *dāwayya* (*sic*) "refers to someone who takes a vow and lives in a community," and refers to an article by Pierre-Vincent Claverie, where the claim does not, however, appear: Constable, *Crusaders and Crusading*, 179 n. 61. Claverie himself proposed to see in *dāwiyya* a corruption of the dialectal form *tāwiyyé*, "in which it is easy to recognize a reminiscence of the word 'Templar'": Pierre-Vincent Claverie, *L'ordre du Temple dans l'Orient des Croisades* (Brussels, 2014), 17.

100. Hugo of Saint-Victor, "Sermo ad milites Templi," ed. Dominique Poirel, "Les Templiers, le diable et le chanoine: Le *Sermo ad Milites Templi* réattribué à Hugues de Saint-Victor," in *Amicorum Societas: Mélanges offerts à François Dolbeau pour son 65ᵉ anniversaire*, ed. Jacques Elfassi, Cécile Lanéry, and Anne-Marie Turcan-Verkerk (Florence, 2013), 659–63. Wolf Zöller (whose understanding of the letter's closing section differs from mine) doubts the attribution to Hugo of St.-Victor because, as he sees it, the letter divulges a striking familiarity with the complexities of professed religious life in the patriarchate of Jerusalem: Wolf Zöller, "The Religious Environment of the Nascent Military Orders: The Augustinian Consortium Revisited," in *Ordens militares: Identitade e Mudança*, ed. Isabel Cristina Ferreira Fernandes, vol. 1 (Palmela, 2021), 154–56.

101. *Templar Rule*, ed. Cerrini, c. 2 (115); *Templar Rule (English)*, 35. On the early Templars' boundless donations to the poor, see *Chronique de Michel le Syrien*, 3:207–8.

102. *Templar Rule*, ed. Cerrini, c. 6 (116-17); *Templar Rule (English)*, 36.

103. Gerard of Nazareth, *De conversacione*, c. 3 (72).

104. *Templar Rule*, ed. Cerrini, c. 17 (121-22); *Templar Rule (English)*, 39.

105. For the color differentiation, see *Templar Rule*, ed. Cerrini, c. 20 (123); *Templar Rule (English)*, 40–41.

106. *Templar Rule*, ed. Cerrini, c. 56 (138); *Templar Rule (English)*, 49–50. Cerrini (*La rivoluzione dei Templari*, 206 n. 16) rightly includes this ruling among those that altered the pre-1129 situation.

107. *Templar Rule*, ed. Cerrini, c. 53 (137); *Templar Rule (English)*, 49. Some Templar convents in the West disregarded the ban on sisters: see Alan Forey, "Women and the Military Orders in the Twelfth and Thirteenth Centuries," *Studia monastica* 29 (1987): 65–66; Helen Nicholson, "Templar Attitudes towards Women," *Medieval History* 1 (1991): 74–80; Vogel, *Das Recht der Templer*, 184–86; Myra Miranda Bom, *Women in the Military Orders of the Crusades* (New York,

2012), 23–27. Also, when Ernoul entered the Templar castle of La Fève on 1 May 1187 to find out where the knights had gone, "ne vit homme ne feme qui li peust dire noveles": *Ernoul*, 211.

108. On this phenomenon, see Erich Auerbach, *Literary Language & Its Public in Late Latin Antiquity and in the Middle Ages*, trans. Ralph Manheim (London, 1965), 284–86.

109. *Templar Rule*, ed. Cerrini, cc. 17, 32, 49, 54 (121, 127, 135, 137); *Templar Rule (Old French)*, ed. Cerrini, cc. 20, 26, 45, 3 (178, 181, 191, 167). For a comparison of the Latin and Old French texts, see Cerrini, *La rivoluzione dei Templari*, 141–56.

110. *Templar Rule*, ed. Cerrini, cc. 8, 15 (118, 120); *Templar Rule (Old French)*, ed. Cerrini, cc. 11, 18 173, 176). *Signum* in the Rule of Benedict (c. 38) and elsewhere means "ringing of the bell," but while a Benedictine monk would immediately comprehend the term, a Knight Templar evidently needed an explication.

111. *Templar Rule*, ed. Cerrini, c. 5 (116); *Templar Rule (Old French)*, ed. Cerrini, c. 46 (192). The gap between *imitabor* and *vengerai* was first noted and commented on by Cerrini, *La rivoluzione dei Templari*, 153–54. On the disparity between the Latin and French versions on consorting with the excommunicated, see the views of Bulst-Thiele, *Sacrae Domus Militiae Templi Hierosolymitani Magistri*, 46–47; Cerrini, *La rivoluzione dei Templari*, 145–47.

112. On the kingdom's feudal nature, see the diverging views of Susan Reynolds, "Fiefs and Vassals in Twelfth-Century Jerusalem: A View from the West," *Crusades* 1 (2002): 29–48, vs. Peter W. Edbury, "Fiefs and Vassals in the Kingdom of Jerusalem: From the Twelfth Century to the Thirteenth," *Crusades* 1 (2002): 49–71, and Jonathan Rubin, "The Debate on Twelfth-Century Feudalism: Additional Evidence from William of Tyre's *Chronicon*," *Crusades* 8 (2009): 53–62. For a comparative study that exposes the emphasis on military service in Frankish feudal charters, see Rudolf Schieffer, "Das Lehnswesen in den Urkunden der Kaiserin Konstanze, in den frühen Königsurkunden Friedrichs II. und in den Urkunden der Könige von Jerusalem," in *Ausbildung und Verbreitung des Lehnswesens im Reich und in Italien im 12. und 13. Jahrhundert*, ed. Karl-Heinz Spieß (Ostfildern, 2013), 221–38.

113. Jan Frans Verbruggen, *The Art of Warfare in Western Europe during the Middle Ages from the Eighth Century to 1340*, trans. Sumner Willard and S. C. M. Southern (Amsterdam, 1977), 76–79, 87–88, 92–93; Matthew Bennett, "*La Règle du Temple* as a Military Manual, or How to Deliver a Cavalry Charge," in Harper-Bill, Holdsworth, and Nelson, *Studies in Medieval History Presented to R. Allen Brown*, 7–19; Alain Demurger, "Gli ordini religioso-militari e la guerra tra il XII e il XIII secolo," in *I Templari, la guerra e la santità*, ed. Simonetta Cerrini (Rimini, 2000), 63–67.

114. *Tractatus*, 125.

115. See Konrad Hirschler, "Ibn Wāsil: An Ayyūbid Perspective on Frankish Lordships and Crusades," in *Medieval Muslim Historians and the Franks in the Levant*, ed. Alex Mallett (Leiden, 2014), 136–60.

116. *Die Chronik des ibn Wāsil: Ǧamāl ad-Dīn Muhammad ibn Wāsil, Mufarriǧ al-Kurūb fī Ahbār Banī Ayyūb, Kritische Edition des letzten Teils (646/1248–659/1261) mit Kommentar*, ed. Mohamed Rahim (Wiesbaden, 2010), 70 n. 2.

117. On the work's branches, and on the problematic nature of BnF, arabe 1702, in which the comment appears, see Rahim's discussion in *Die Chronik des ibn Wāsil*, xxxviii–xlv. Francesco Gabrieli, who considered this manuscript to contain Ibn Wāṣil's genuine work, presented the comment as a part of it: Gabrieli, *Arab Historians of the Crusades*, 294. Jackson ascribed the comment to Ibn Wāṣil's reviser and continuator, Ibn ʿAbd al-Raḥīm: Peter Jackson, *The Seventh Crusade, 1244–1254: Sources and Documents* (Farnham, 2009), 148 n. 93.

118. *Tractatus*, 130.

119. Mamuka Tsurtsumia, "Commemoration of Crusaders in the Manuscripts of the Monastery of the Holy Cross in Jerusalem," *Journal of Medieval History* 38 (2012): 318–34. The numbers in parentheses refer to Tsurtsumia's list of commemorations. Templars: *tadzrelta*, from *tadzari* (temple).

120. Tsurtsumia, "Commemoration of Crusaders," 321–22, 325–26. On Gaufridus Fulcherii, see Burgtorf, *The Central Convent*, 532–34.

121. Tsurtsumia, "Commemoration of Crusaders," 323–25; see Malcolm Barber, "The Career of Philip of Nablus in the Kingdom of Jerusalem," in *EC*, 60–75. In addition to Phelippe and his family, Tsurtsumia identified the families of two Frankish noblemen, Eustache II Garnier (no. 22) and—less definitely—Baldwin, viscount of Nablus (no. 29).

122. Paul Devos, "Les premières versions occidentales de la légende de Saïdnaia," *Analecta Bollandiana* 65 (1947): 272–76.

123. For details, see B. Z. Kedar, "Convergences of Oriental Christian, Muslim and Frankish Worshippers: The Case of Saydnaya and the Knights Templar," in *The Crusades and the Military Orders: Expanding the Frontiers of Medieval Latin Christianity*, ed. Zsolt Hunyadi and József Laszlovszky (Budapest, 2001), 89–100; Bernard Hamilton, "Our Lady of Saidnaiya: An Orthodox Shrine Revered by Muslims and Knights Templar at the Time of the Crusades," in *The Holy Land, Holy Lands, and Christian History*, ed. Robert N. Swanson (Woodbridge, 2000), 207–15.

124. Gerard of Nazareth, *De conversacione*, c. 12 (72).

125. *RHGF*, 15:540–41. For the date, see Burgtorf, *The Central Convent*, 249, 482.

126. For details of his career, see Bulst-Thiele, *Sacrae Domus Militiae Templi Hierosolymitani Magistri*, 41–52. On the Templar Humbert III of Beaujeu, a contemporary of Everard who left the order and reverted to secular life, see Bulst-Thiele, *Sacrae Domus Militiae Templi Hierosolymitani Magistri*, 48. On Julian, lord of Sidon (d. 1275), who joined the Knights Templar late in his life and then switched to the Trinitarians or Premonstratensians, see Hans Eberhard Mayer, "The Life and Afterlife of Julian of Sidon," *Crusades* 18 (2019): 87, 90. See also Vogel, *Das Recht der Templer*, 199–200.

127. For Bernard's assurance, see Bernard of Clairvaux, *Éloge de la Nouvelle Chevalerie*, 58–61.

128. Isaac of l'Étoile, *Sermons*, ed. and trans. Anselm Hoste, Gaston Salet, and Gaetano Raciti, vol. 3, Sources Chrétiennes 339 (Paris, 1987), 158–61, Sermo 48.8; Poirel, "Les Templiers," 660.

129. Cf. Matt. 26:52.

130. "Omnes leges et omnia iura vim vi repellere permittunt." Cf. Paulus in Digesta 9.2.45.4: "uim enim ui defendere omnes leges omniaque iura

permittunt." See *Digesta Iustiniani Augusti*, ed. Theodor Mommsen, in *Corpus iuris civilis*, ed. Paul Krueger et al., 3 vols. (Berlin, 1868–70), 1:291.

131. Walter Map, *De nugis curialium* 1.20 (60). For discussion, see Kedar, *Crusade and Mission*, 106–8; Aurell, *Des chrétiens contre les croisades*, 206–11.

132. Walter Map, *De nugis curialium* 1.24 (80).

133. The anecdote, which does not figure in most works on Saint Bernard, has been noted in other contexts. See Giuseppe Candela, *L'offerta letteraria del "De nugis curialium" di Walter Map* (Palermo, 2019), 52–53; Massimo Oldoni, *La famiglia di Arlecchino: Il demonio prima della maschera* (Rome, 2021), 188, 306.

134. Riley-Smith, *Templars and Hospitallers*, 36, 42, 61–63.

135. WT 14.22 (659–61).

136. *Cart Hosp*, 4:247–48, no. 310 *bis*.

137. *Tractatus*, 126. For attempts to reconstruct the militarization process, see Rudolf Hiestand, "Die Anfänge der Johanniter," in *Die geistlichen Ritterorden Europas*, ed. Josef Fleckenstein and Manfred Hellmann (Sigmaringen, 1980), 64–80; Alan Forey, "The Militarization of the Hospital of St. John," *Studia monastica* 26 (1984): 75–89. Crucial for their reconstructions is Pope Innocent II's statement of 1139/43, which they interpret to mean that the brothers of the Hospital hired armed *servientes* to protect pilgrims on their way to the holy places. But when read in context, the statement "ut ipsi [infirmi] ad sacrosancta loca . . . securius valeant proficisci, servientes, quos fratres ejusdem domus ad hoc officium specialiter deputatos propriis sumptibus retinent, cum oportunitas exigit" (*Cart Hosp*, 1:107, no. 130) means rather that, when necessary, the brothers employed *servientes* to assist the recovered sick to go forth more safely to Jerusalem's Holy Places. See also Jonathan Phillips, "Archbishop Henry of Reims and the Militarization of the Hospitallers," in Nicholson, *The Military Orders*, 2:83–88.

138. For variants of the legend and the approximate date of its lost Latin original, see *Les Légendes de l'Hôpital de Saint-Jean de Jérusalem*, ed. and trans. Antoine Calvet (Paris, 2000). On its later diffusion, see Karl Borchardt, "Spendenaufrufe der Johanniter aus dem 13. Jahrhundert," *Zeitschrift für bayerische Landesgeschichte* 56 (1993): 1–5, 19–32.

139. For the hypothesis that the mural cycle of the Hospitaller church at Abū Ghosh, dated to the 1160s or 1170s, aimed at highlighting the order's history as depicted in the legend, see Fishhof, *Shaping Identities*, 59–78.

140. I prefer the term "medicalized hospital" to that of "true hospital," propounded by Timothy Miller, "The Knights of Saint John and the Hospitals of the Latin West," *Speculum* 53 (1978): 710. The latter term and its likes are "skewed towards a modernity defined by medicalization": see Peregrine Horden, *Cultures of Healing, Medieval and After* (Abingdon, 2019), 14.

141. Miller, "The Knights of Saint John," 720–23; Wagner, *Die Seuchen der Kreuzzüge*, 108. On the care of the sick at Genoa's San Giovanni di Prè in the thirteenth century and on the inquiry of 1343 according to which the hospital had around forty beds and paid two *medici*, one *cerogio*, and one *phisicus* to work there, see Elena Bellomo, "Convergences of Interdisciplinary Paths: The Hospitaller Convent of San Giovanni di Prè in Genoa through Historical

and Archaeological Evidence," in Shotten-Hallel and Weetch, *Crusading and Archaeology*, 57–58.

142. These Hospitaller statutes are usually dated to 1182, although both the Latin and the Old French versions have: Year of incarnation 1181, March, the Sunday of *Laetare Jerusalem*. Klement, who drew attention to this discrepancy, ascribed it to a misprint in Delaville Le Roulx's edition: Katja Klement, *Gottes Gastgeber: Die Ritter des Hospitals von Jerusalem. Die vatikanische Handschrift Vat. Lat. 4852* (Norderstedt, 2010), 40. In fact, in 1887 Delaville Le Roulx dated the statutes to 1181: Joseph Delaville Le Roulx, "Les statuts de l'Ordre de l'Hôpital de Saint-Jean de Jérusalem," *Bibliothèque de l'École des chartes* 48 (1887): 349. But later, editing them in *Cart Hosp*, 1:425–28, he apparently assumed that the Style of the Incarnation (according to which the year starts with the Annunciation on 25 March) was being used, and therefore gave the date 14 March 1182. In 1182 *Laetare Jerusalem* was celebrated on 7 March, equivalent to 14 March of the Gregorian calendar. See his remark that the kings and patriarchs of Jerusalem apparently followed "the Style of the Nativity or of 1 January," an assumption only partially corroborated by Mayer's painstaking study: *Cart Hosp*, 1:113 n. 6; Mayer, *Die Kanzlei*, 2:845–86. On the four wise *medici*, see *Cart Hosp*, 1:426, no. 627. The centrality of urines is highlighted by the law that laid down that no foreign doctor should "meger d'orine nuluy" before he passed an examination by four leading doctors and the local bishop: "Assises des Bourgeois," c. 238 (2:169).

143. "ubi summo cum honore receptus fuit ab Amalphitanis, qui Hierosolymis paucis ante annis duo extruxerant hospitalia ad homines et mulieres recipiendos, in quibus et alebantur, et infirmi curabantur, defendentes eos a Saracenis, et ut facilius id exequuntur vitam religiosam fere instituerant." *Italia sacra*, ed. Ferdinando Ughelli and Nicola Coleti, 10 vols. (Venice, 1717–22), 7:198. The phrase *infirmos curare* is biblical (see Matt. 10:8) and means "to heal the sick."

144. See Danielle Jacquart, "Le sens donné par Constantin l'Africain à son oeuvre: Les chapitres introductifs en arabe et en latin," in *Constantine the African and 'Alī ibn al-'Abbās al-Maǧūsī: The "Pantegni" and Related Texts*, ed. Charles Burnett and Danielle Jacquart (Leiden, 1994), 79.

145. *AMS*, 2:241, 254–56.

146. Bruno Figliuolo, "Amalfi e il Levante nel Medioevo," in *I comuni italiani*, 581–91; David Jacoby, "Amalfi nell'XI secolo: Commercio e navigazione nei documenti della Ghenizà del Cairo," *Rassegna del Centro di cultura e storia amalfitana* 28 (2008): 81–90; Jacoby, "Commercio e navigazione degli Amalfitani nel Mediterraneo orientale: Sviluppo e declino," in *Interscambi socio-culturali ed economici fra le città marinare d'Italia e l'Occidente dagli osservatori mediterranei*, ed. Bruno Figliuolo and Pinuccia F. Simbula (Amalfi, 2014), 89–128.

147. *Sefer Nameh: Relation du voyage de Nassiri Khosrau en Syrie, en Palestine, en Égypte, en Arabie et en Perse pendant les années de l'hégire 437–444*, ed. and trans. Charles Schefer (Paris, 1881), 21; translation: Reuven Amitai. Thackston's translation locates the *bīmāristān* in Jerusalem's eastern part: *Nāser-e Khosraw's Book of Travels*, 23. It appears to be based on an edition defective at this point.

148. Al-Muqaddasī, *The Best Divisions*, 153. In Syria of the years 1193–1260, seventeen out of fifty-six physicians were Christians, Jews, or Samaritans: Anne-Marie Eddé, "Les médecins dans la société syrienne du VIIe / XIIIe siècle," *Annales Islamologiques* 29 (1995): 92. For the hypothesis, see B. Z. Kedar, "A Note on Jerusalem's Bīmāristān and Jerusalem's Hospital," in *The Hospitallers, the Mediterranean and Europe: Festschrift for Anthony Luttrell*, ed. Karl Borchardt, Nikolas Jaspert, and Helen Nicholson (Aldershot, 2007), 7–11.

149. Nikulás in Kedar and Westergård-Nielsen, "Icelanders," 205; Johann of Würzburg in *Peregrinationes tres*, 131; Theoderich in *Peregrinationes tres*, 157–58; *The Itinerary of Benjamin of Tudela*, 23 (text), 22 (translation).

150. *Cart Hosp*, 1:63, no. 70.

151. "les seignors malades," in the Old French version: *Cart Hosp*, 1:67.

152. Ilya Berkovich and Amit Re'em, "The Location of the Crusader Hospital in the Muristan—A Reassessment," in *The Ancient Remains below the Church of the Redeemer, the Muristan and Its Surroundings*, ed. Dietrich Vieweger and Shimon Gibson (Oxford, 2016), 193–220. While the authors identify the excavated structures with the Hospital's wards, Pringle assumes that the wards may have been located on the now nonexistent first floor above them: Denys Pringle, "The Layout of the Jerusalem Hospital in the Twelfth Century: Further Thoughts and Suggestions," in Upton-Ward, *The Military Orders*, 4:91–110.

153. The regulations were first edited in the unpublished doctoral thesis of Katja Klement (Salzburg, 1996) and then in 2005 by Susan B. Edgington as "Administrative Regulations" (Old French text with English translation). For a slightly revised version of her unpublished thesis, see Klement, *Gottes Gastgeber*, where the regulations, with reproductions of the manuscript's folios and with a German translation, appear on 198–263; on the manuscript's date, see 140–42.

154. Munich, Bayerische Staatsbibliothek, Clm 4620. The account was first utilized by Berthold Waldstein-Wartenberg, *Die Vasallen Christi: Kulturgeschichte des Johanniterordens im Mittelalter* (Vienna, 1988), 110–18, 145–35, 357–60. I edited the text in an article published in 1998; when this article was about to be reprinted, I emended the text with the gracious help of Robert Huygens. See Kedar, "A Twelfth-Century Description of the Jerusalem Hospital," 13–26 (Latin text). On the deficiencies of Alain Beltjens's edition of 2004, see Robert B. C. Huygens, "Editorisch Verfehltes zum Hospital von Jerusalem," *Deutsches Archiv für Erforschung des Mittelalters* 61 (2005): 165–67.

155. Kedar, "A Twelfth-Century Description of the Jerusalem Hospital," 4. My call for caution was not heeded: for instance, the author is presented as a German priest who visited the Hospital in the 1180s: Riley-Smith, *Templars and Hospitallers*, 18–19; or as a German pilgrim who described his experience in the Hospital in the 1170s: Susan B. Edgington, "Oriental and Occidental Medicine in the Crusader States," in *The Crusades and the Near East: Cultural Histories*, ed. Conor Kostick (Abingdon, 2011), 206. Klement, without giving her reasons, dates the account to ca. 1165: *Gottes Gastgeber*, 25, 29.

156. Kedar, "A Twelfth-Century Description of the Jerusalem Hospital," 18, 22–23. For a discussion of the visitor's account, see Wagner, *Die Seuchen der Kreuzzüge*, 95–106.

157. Kedar, "A Twelfth-Century Description of the Jerusalem Hospital," 20–21. The visitor does not specify the number of surgeons. In a confirmation of the Hospitaller rule by Pope Lucius III, issued in eight different instances in 1184–85, the number of surgeons oscillates between three (five times) and four (three times); the number of doctors, between five (five times) and four (three times): Hiestand, *Papsturkunden für Templer und Johanniter*, 361, no. 172.

158. "Administrative Regulations," 32–33; Susan B. Edgington, "Medical Care in the Hospital of St John in Jerusalem," in Nicholson, *The Military Orders*, 2:27–28; Klement, *Gottes Gastgeber*, 238–41.

159. Kedar, "A Twelfth-Century Description of the Jerusalem Hospital," 18.

160. For a succinct overview of the *bīmāristān*s that stresses their secularity, see Peter E. Pormann and Emilie Savage-Smith, *Medieval Islamic Medicine* (Edinburgh, 2007), 96–101.

161. Shelomo D. Goitein, "The Medical Profession in the Light of the Cairo Geniza Documents," *Hebrew Union College Annual* 34 (1963): 187; *AMS*, 2:251. See also Horden, *Cultures of Healing*, 73.

162. Kedar, "A Twelfth-Century Description of the Jerusalem Hospital," 19; "Administrative Regulations," 26–27, 34–35; Klement, *Gottes Gastgeber*, 216–17, 248–55. Sami Hamarneh, "Development of Hospitals in Islam," *Journal of the History of Medicine and Allied Sciences* 17 (1962): 373–74.

163. Kedar, "A Twelfth-Century Description of the Jerusalem Hospital," 21; *The Travels of Ibn Jubayr*, trans. Broadhurst, 234–35, 286. The construction of Nūr al-Dīn's hospital was financed by ransom money of a Frankish captive: Yaacov Lev, "Saladin's Economic Policies and the Economy of Ayyubid Egypt," in *Egypt and Syria in the Fatimid, Ayyubid and Mamluk Eras*, vol. 5, ed. Urbain Vermeulen and Kristof D'hulster (Leuven, 2007), 337.

164. Ibn Abī Usaybi'a, *A Literary History of Medicine*, 2.2:1194–95 (text), 3.2:1351–52 (translation). Translation quoted by permission of Brill Academic Publishers.

165. Apparently at some point in the thirteenth century, a Frankish reader added Latin annotations to a fully vocalized manuscript, copied in 1196, of the widely used *Hundred Books on the Medical Art* by the Christian physician Abū Sahl al-Masīhī (d. 1010): Emilie Savage-Smith, "New Evidence for the Frankish Study of Arabic Medical Texts in the Crusader Period," *Crusades* 5 (2006): 99–112.

166. R. C. "Otto" Smail, *The Crusaders in Syria and the Holy Land* (London, 1973), 78. For an appreciation of Ibn Jubayr's account, see Georges Peyronnet, "Coexistence islamo-chrétienne en Sicile et au Moyen-Orient à travers le récit de voyage d'Ibn Jubayr," *Islamochristiana* 19 (1993): 55–73.

167. Ibn Jubayr, *The Travels*, ed. William Wright and Michael Jan de Goeje (Leiden, 1907), 330; translation: Etan Kohlberg. For a slightly different translation (but leading to the same conclusion), see Pormann and Savage-Smith, *Medieval Islamic Medicine*, 168. The passage was partially utilized by Robert Frédéric Bridgman, "Évolution comparée de l'organisation hospitalière en Europe et en pays d'Islam: Influences mutuelles au Moyen Age et à la Renaissance," in *Atti del primo congresso europeo di storia ospitaliera* (Reggio Emilia, 1962), 234.

168. *Cart Hosp*, 1:339–40, no. 494; "Administrative Regulations," 28–29; Klement, *Gottes Gastgeber*, 224–25; Kedar, "A Twelfth-Century Description of the Jerusalem Hospital," 19. On the use of spices, see Balard, *Histoire des épices*, 264.

169. Paul Gautier, "Le Typikon du Christ Sauveur Pantocrator," *Revue des études byzantines* 32 (1974): 52–53; *Byzantine Monastic Foundation Documents: A Complete Translation of the Surviving Typika and Testaments*, ed. John Philip Thomas and Angela Constantinides Hero, 5 vols. (Washington, DC, 2000), 2:745.

170. Ibn Riḍwān: Michael W. Dols and Adil S. Gamal, *Medieval Islamic Medicine: Ibn Ridwān's Treatise "On the Prevention of Bodily Ills in Egypt"* (Berkeley, 1984), 19 (text), 136–37 (translation); Ibn Zuhr: Abū Marwān ʿAbd al-Malik b. Zuhr, *Kitāb al-Agdiya (Tratado de los Alimentos)*, ed. and trans. Expiración García Sánchez (Madrid, 1992), 10 (text), 46 (translation); Maimonides, *On the Regimen of Health: A New Parallel Arabic-English Translation*, ed. and trans. Gerrit Bos (Leiden, 2019), 50–53. For Ibn Jumayʿ, see Eliyahu Ashtor, "Essai sur l'alimentation des diverses classes sociales dans l'Orient médiéval," *Annales E.S.C.* 23 (1968): 1020.

171. Kedar, "A Twelfth-Century Description of the Jerusalem Hospital," 21. The regulations of 1181/83 make the same provision without giving an explanation: "des chars femeles de beste a .iiii. pies li malade ne manicent en nul tems." "Administrative Regulations," 24–25; Klement, *Gottes Gastgeber*, 202–3.

172. Maimonides, *On Asthma: A Parallel Arabic-English Text*, ed. and trans. Gerrit Bos (Provo, UT, 2002), 15. I am indebted for this argument to my student Shulamit Schneidermann, "The Hospitallers' Hospital in Twelfth-Century Jerusalem in the Mirror of East and West" (master's thesis, Hebrew University of Jerusalem, 2000), 62, 73–74 [in Hebrew]. Ibn Zuhr, on the other hand, prefers in most cases the meat of female animals to that of males: *Kitāb al-Agdiya (Tratado de los Alimentos)*, 21–23 (text), 56–57 (translation).

173. Kedar, "A Twelfth-Century Description of the Jerusalem Hospital," 20. Without mentioning the two kitchens, the regulations of 1181/83 stress the choice—on Sunday, Tuesday, and Thursday—between pork and mutton as against hen and chicken, and the possibility to receive two deniers and a cooked dish instead of either kind of meat; also, the choice on the other days between four cooked eggs and one denier: "Administrative Regulations," 28–31; Klement, *Gottes Gastgeber*, 224–27, 230–31. Poultry market: "un grandisme place la u on vent les oes et les fromages et les poules et les aves." *Ernoul*, 254. See Prawer, *The Latin Kingdom*, 409.

174. Ibn Zuhr, *Kitāb al-Agdiya (Tratado de los Alimentos)*, 15, 18 (text), 51, 53 (translation).

175. Maimonides, *On the Regimen of Health*, 50–53, 58–59, 84–85. See also Maimonides, *On Asthma*, 14. For a recommendation to consume young chicken, see Ibn Ridwān, 137.

176. Riley-Smith, *Templars and Hospitallers*, 20. See also Klement, *Gottes Gastgeber*, 45–46.

177. "Des iii jors de la semaine soloient avoir les malades char fresche de porc ou de moton; et qui n'en pooit mangier si avoit geline": *Cart Hosp*, 1:428, no. 627. "Et qui ne vodra de la char de porc ou de moton, si doit avoir de la geline": "Administrative Regulations," 28–29; Klement, *Gottes Gastgeber*, 226–27.

Elsewhere Riley-Smith correctly writes that "pork, mutton or goat, or, if the sick could not stomach these, chicken . . . were served": Riley-Smith, *Templars and Hospitallers*, 46.

178. Mitchell, who prepared a comparative table of other proscribed and recommended foods in the statutes of the military orders on the one hand and in Western and Eastern medical texts on the other hand, concluded that the results "might suggest that it was local Eastern medical ideas, rather than those popular in Europe at that time, that were more dominant in determining diet in the [orders'] hospitals." Mitchell, *Medicine in the Crusades*, 68, 99–103. For the earlier view that medical knowledge in the Frankish East was mainly based on Salernitan lore, see Indrikis Sterns, "Care of the Sick Brothers by the Crusader Orders in the Holy Land," *Bulletin of the History of Medicine* 57 (1983): 53–55, 60–61; also Edgington, "Medical Care in the Hospital of St John," 31.

179. For this view, see Edgington, "Medical Care in the Hospital of St John," 33. For a more moderate formulation, see Edgington, "Oriental and Occidental Medicine in the Crusader States," 207–8.

180. Maimonides, *On the Regimen of Health*, 85–86. Translation quoted by permission of Brill Academic Publishers.

181. Here, too, I follow Schneidermann, "The Hospitallers' Hospital," 67–70.

182. "Administrative Regulations," 24–25; Klement, *Gottes Gastgeber*, 198–205. The anonymous visitor, too, mentions the diets the doctor prescribes during his visit of the sick: Kedar, "A Twelfth-Century Description of the Jerusalem Hospital," 21.

183. For the estimated size of the Palace of the Sick, see Berkovich and Re'em, "The Location of the Crusader Hospital in the Muristan," 202. For Nūr al-Dīn's hospital, see Ernst Herzfeld, "Damascus: Studies in Architecture—I," *Ars Islamica* 9 (1942): 5–6 (text and plan); Yasser Tabbaa, "Geometry and Memory in the Design of the Madrasat al-Firdows in Aleppo," in *Theories and Principles of Design in the Architecture of Islamic Societies*, ed. Margaret Bentley Sevcenko (Cambridge, MA, 1988), 28 (plan).

184. Horden, *Cultures of Healing*, 5, 16.

185. Kedar, "A Twelfth-Century Description of the Jerusalem Hospital," 24.

186. *Cart Hosp*, 1:426, no. 627. See Klement, *Gottes Gastgeber*, 43.

187. *Les miracles de Notre-Dame de Roc-Amadour* 2.19 (212–13).

188. *Cart Hosp*, 1:428, no. 627. In the same clause, the Hospital promises to provide needy couples with food for their weddings.

189. Kedar, "A Twelfth-Century Description of the Jerusalem Hospital," 24.

190. John Boswell, *The Kindness of Strangers: The Abandonment of Children in Western Europe from Late Antiquity to the Renaissance* (London, 1988), 275–95.

191. Kedar, "A Twelfth-Century Description of the Jerusalem Hospital," 21–22.

192. The innovation might have been influenced by Muslim field hospitals, one of the earliest of which is attested in Iraq in about 1120: see Reuben Levy, *A Baghdad Chronicle* (Cambridge, 1929), 212.

193. Gautier, "Le Typikon," 82–85; *Byzantine Monastic Foundation Documents*, 2:757. For Kosmosoteira, see *Byzantine Monastic Foundation Documents*, 2:830. Jerusalem: *Cart Hosp*, 1:426, no. 627; Kedar, "A Twelfth-Century Description

of the Jerusalem Hospital," 19; "Administrative Regulations," 26–29; Klement, *Gottes Gastgeber*, 216–17.

194. Gautier, "Le Typikon," 94–95; *Byzantine Monastic Foundation Documents*, 2:761; *Cart Hosp*, 1:427, no. 627.

195. Night duty and lamps: Kedar, "A Twelfth-Century Description of the Jerusalem Hospital," 22; "Administrative Regulations," 26–27; Klement, *Gottes Gastgeber*, 208–9; Gautier, "Le Typikon," 84–85, 92–93; *Byzantine Monastic Foundation Documents*, 2:757, 761. Chief physician: Gautier, "Le Typikon," 86–87; *Byzantine Monastic Foundation Documents*, 2:758.

196. Cyril Elgood, *A Medical History of Persia and the Eastern Caliphate from the Earliest Times until the Year 1932* (Cambridge, 1951), 177–78; Hamarneh, "Development of Hospitals in Islam," 373; Michael Dols, "Insanity in Byzantine and Islamic Medicine," *Dumbarton Oaks Papers* 38 (1984): 142; Pormann and Savage-Smith, *Medieval Islamic Medicine*, 100.

197. Elgood, *A Medical History*, 160–71; Hamarneh, "Development of Hospitals in Islam," 369–70; Gautier, "Le Typikon," 84–87.

198. Observation made already by Ernest Wickersheimer, "Organisation et législation sanitaires au Royaume franc de Jérusalem (1099–1291)," *Archives internationales d'histoire des sciences* 4 (1951): 699. For the contrary view, according to which the "établissements chrétiens latins" may have impressed the creators of the *bīmāristāns* of Damascus (1154) and Cairo (1182, 1284), and the "modèles hierosolymitains" stimulated the initiatives of Alexios Komnenos and his son Joannes in Constantinople, see François-Olivier Touati, "La Terre sainte: Un laboratoire hospitalier au Moyen Âge?," in *Sozialgeschichte mittelalterlicher Hospitäler*, ed. Neithard Bulst and Karl-Heinz Spieß (Ostfildern, 2007), 190–91.

199. Karl Borchardt, "The Military-Religious Orders: A Medieval 'School of Administrators'?," in Edbury, *The Military Orders*, 5:3–20.

200. Karl Borchardt, "The Military-Religious Orders of the Twelfth and Thirteenth Centuries as an Innovative Step for Western Religious Life," in Ferreira Fernandes, *Ordens militares*, 1:172–73.

9. Burgesses, Urban and Rural

1. For an overview of the burgess class, see Prawer, "Social Classes in the Latin Kingdom," 145–70; for specific studies, Prawer, *Crusader Institutions*, chaps. 9–13, 15. For later works, see Marwan Nader, *Burgesses and Burgess Law in the Latin Kingdoms of Jerusalem and Cyprus (1099–1325)* (Aldershot, 2006) [to be used with some caution; see Hans Eberhard Mayer, "Ex Cantabrigia lux? Zur Arbeitsweise von Marwan Nader," in *Rund um die Meere des Nordens: Festschrift für Hain Rebas*, ed. Michael Engelbrecht et al. (Heide, 2008), 203–8]; Mayer, *Von der Cour des Bourgeois*, 1–65, 218–340.

2. "Car por ce a non la terre des Crestiens et tels gens, *la terre des Frans*, et por ce si i devent estre toutes franchises de tous biens." "Assises des Bourgeois," c. 255 (2:191). Riley-Smith, like Beugnot before him, believed that this may be a later addition: *The Feudal Nobility*, 258 n. 10. However, in 1237 Gregory IX stated explicitly that a converted slave gained freedom *secundum terre consuetudinem*; see letter edited in Kedar, *Crusade and Mission*, 212, app. 2/a.

3. *Ernoul*, 280–82 (*menu peuple*), 282–85, 289–92 (*povres gens*). William differentiates at one point between the *secunda classis* and the *populus*: WT 13.13 (601).

4. FC 3.28 (697); WT 13.8 (595). On Jerusalemite burgesses who owned vineyards not far from the city walls, see Tischler, *Die Burgenses von Jerusalem*, 269, 289, 294, 306, nos. 117, 233, 267, 342.

5. WT 20.19 (937). William's *tenuiores homines* match Ernoul's *menu peuple*. See also Kostick, *The Social Structure of the First Crusade*, 156.

6. Ellenblum, *Frankish Rural Settlement*, esp. 54–63, 179–81, 213–87. The book is an expanded version of a Hebrew-written PhD dissertation submitted in 1991 at the Hebrew University of Jerusalem.

7. Denys Pringle, "Churches and Settlement in Crusader Palestine," in *EC*, 173–77.

8. WT 18.1 (810).

9. For Bethgibelin, see *Cart Hosp*, 1:272–73, no. 399. One of the burgesses of Bethgibelin is named Ugo Latro. For Balduinus Latro, presumably a burgess of Ramla, see "Fragment d'un cartulaire de l'ordre de Saint-Lazare," 126, no. 5; Mayer, *Die Kanzlei*, 2:899, no. 7. For Ibelin, see B. Z. Kedar, "In Search of Ibelin Castle: Experimenting with Non-Destructive Archaeology," in *EO*, 2:5–8.

10. *Libellus*, 176.

11. La Hadia: Pringle, *Secular Buildings*, 24, no. 23. Zoenite: *UKJ*, 3:1050, no. 639 (a. 1220), 1088, no. 654 (a. 1226), 1122, no. 666 (a. 1229). See also Pringle, *Secular Buildings*, 110, no. 238.

12. Edna J. Stern, "Pottery and Identity in the Latin Kingdom of Jerusalem: A Case Study of Acre and Western Galilee," in *Medieval and Post-Medieval Ceramics in the Eastern Mediterranean: Fact and Fiction*, ed. Joanita Vroom (Turnhout, 2015), 295–96, 315 (fig. 20).

13. Similarly, French coins constitute around 20 percent of all coins excavated in large towns and castles along main pilgrim routes, and "substantially" less in towns of the interior and smaller settlements: Kool, "Finding French Deniers," 124.

14. Shagrir, *Naming Patterns*, 23–32, 42–56.

15. For the names, see *Cart St Sép*, 237–40, no. 117, and Tischler, *Die Burgenses von Jerusalem*, 250–319.

16. See appendix 5, below. Lev mentions that Christians captured during a Fatimid raid were sent to the palace workshops and that the use of prisoners in its stores and mills continued under the Ayyubids: Yaacov Lev, "Prisoners of War during the Fatimid-Ayyubid Wars with the Crusaders," in Gervers and Powell, *Tolerance and Intolerance*, 16–17. Similarly, Friedman observes that commoner captives "remain nameless and were often employed as artisans or craftsmen: of their ultimate fate little is known": Friedman, *Encounter between Enemies*, 104. A monograph on Frankish captives deals exclusively with captive kings, princes, and knights: Philippe Goridis, *Gefangen im Heiligen Land: Verarbeitung und Bewältigung christlicher Gefangenschaft zur Zeit der Kreuzzüge* (Ostfildern, 2015).

17. "de captivis Christianis omnibus liberandis ex Aegypto." *RHGF*, 16:61, no. 196.

18. Kool, "Lead Token Money in the Kingdom of Jerusalem," 293–339, plates 49–54; also Robert Kool and Oren Tal, "'Underground' Money in an

Outremer Estate: Token Molds and Lead Tokens from Crusader Arsur," *Israel Numismatic Research* 10 (2015): 215–35; Kool and Tal, "Another Token Mold and Lead Token from Crusader Arsur (Apollonia)," *Schweizerische Numismatische Rundschau* 98 (2020): 215–22.

19. Otto of Freising, *Historia de duabus civitatibus* 8.18 (622); Theoderich in *Peregrinationes tres*, 179. Is it possible that by the time of Theoderich's pilgrimage the Valley of Josaphat became too congested with stone heaps and believers were constrained to place their markings elsewhere?

20. *Usāmah's Memoirs, Entitled Kitāb al-i'tibār*, ed. Philip K. Hitti (Princeton, NJ, 1930), 141; Usama ibn Munqidh, *The Book of Contemplation*, 154.

21. For the list, see Tischler, *Die Burgenses von Jerusalem*, 250–319; for bynames that may designate occupations, 224.

22. Aimo Stacionarius, Bernardus Mercator, Willelmus Mercerius.

23. *Cart St Sép*, 237–40, no. 117; cf. Ellenblum, *Frankish Rural Settlement*, 82–85.

24. Vardit Shotten-Hallel and Estelle Ingrand-Varenne, "William of Belvoir(?): A Short Note on an Even Shorter Inscription," *Crusades* 18 (2019): 21–24.

25. Viaud, *Nazareth et ses deux églises*, 73–82; Bagatti, *Gli scavi di Nazaret*, 2:74–84. On the marks' function, see Denys Pringle, "Some Approaches to the Study of Crusader Masonry Marks in Palestine," *Levant* 13 (1981): 173–99; Nicolas Reveyron, "'Marques lapidaires': The State of the Question," *Gesta* 42 (2003): 161–70; Yves Esquieu, Andreas Hartmann-Winrich, and Anne Baud, "Les signes lapidaires dans la construction médiévale: Études de cas et problèmes de méthode," *Bulletin Monumental* 165 (2007): 331–58.

26. Cf. *La Chanson de Roland*, laisses 12, 218, 256–57, 279, 287, ed. and trans. Ian Short (Paris, 1990), 40, 218, 248, 268, 272; "cuardise n'out unkes"—laisse 256.

27. "Chartes de Terre Sainte," ed. Joseph Delaville Le Roulx, *ROL* 11 (1905–8): 181–82, no. 1.

28. Calculation of interest rate by Mayer, *Von der Cour des Bourgeois*, 6–7.

29. Vincent of Prague, "Annales Bohemorum," ed. and trans. (into Czech) by Josef Emler in *Fontes rerum Bohemicarum*, vol. 2 (Prague, 1874), 447–48. The Jerusalemite expert is mentioned briefly, and without reference to a medieval source, by Prutz, *Kulturgeschichte*, 206, 413; he relies on the slightly longer statement, equally lacking reference to a source, by Wilhelm von Giesebrecht, *Geschichte der deutschen Kaiserzeit*, vol. 5.1 (Braunschweig, 1880), 201. Fastening sticks: *fustes*. Emler translates: *provazy* (ropes), apparently assuming that Vincent mistakenly wrote *fustes* instead of *funes*.

30. Both Wilhelm Wattenbach (MGH SS 17:677 n. 8) and Josef Emler ("Annales Bohemorum," 447 n. 9) assume that the anonymous Jerusalemite expert was identical with the master artisan Marchese/Marchisius/Marchexius who, according to Otto Morena, worked first in the service of Crema and then switched over to the emperor's side: see Otto Morena, "Historia," 87–91. But Vincent of Prague relates (447) that the Cremonese enthusiastically helped the Jerusalemite expert to construct the tower, and in Otto Morena's account (73) the extraordinary Cremonese tower appears much earlier than Marchese's switch. On the artisans at Ascalon, see WT 17.24 (794); also 17.27 (798).

31. 1099: AA 6.11 (416–19); France, *Victory in the East*, 352. 1124: WT 13.10 (598). 1159: Otto Morena, "Historia," 73.

32. "Plus sot de fust que nus clers de latin / Sou ciel n'a tor ne chastel si garni / Recet ne voute ne mur ne plaisseiz / Se il puet converser .xv. diz / Qu'il ne l'ait ars ou abatu ou pris." *Gerbert de Mez: Chanson de geste du XII*[e] *siècle*, vv. 2724–28, ed. Pauline Taylor (Namur, 1952), 72. Partially utilized by Holmes, "Life among the Europeans in Palestine," 30. For the meaning of *engigneor*, see *Dictionnaire Étymologique de l'Ancien Français*, s.v.

33. The text is edited in Malgorzata Hanna Malewicz, "Libellus de efficatia artis astrologice: Traité astrologique d'Eudes de Champagne, XIIe siècle," *Mediaevalia Philosophica Polonorum* 20 (1974): 69–70. On Eudes and his treatise, partially quoted in the chronicle of Hélinand of Froidmont (ca. 1160–ca. 1229), see Marie-Thérèse d'Alverny, "Astrologues et théologiens au XIIe siècle," in *Mélanges offerts à M.D. Chenu* (Paris, 1967), esp. 48–49; Mitchell, *Medicine in the Crusades*, 18.

34. For a list of localities possessing burgess courts, compiled in about 1265, see John of Ibelin, *Le Livre des Assises*, 603–6, c. 236. On the list's problems, see Edbury, *John of Ibelin*, 155–62. On the courts' jurisdiction, see Mayer, *Von der Cour des Bourgeois*, 3–6; for data on viscounts and burgess courts, see 260–340.

35. "sage borgois": "Abrégé du Livre des Assises de la Cour des Bourgeois," c. 28, in *RHC Lois*, 2:339. In 1193/94, Raimundus Antelme attested to a charter drawn up in Acre: *UKJ*, 2:948, no. 573.

36. Philip of Novara, *Le Livre de Forme de Plait*, 120 (text), 260 (translation) (my translation differs on one point). Raoul of Tiberias—a participant in the Battle of Ḥaṭṭīn—was born around 1170 and is last mentioned in May 1220. On his checkered career, see Martin Rheinheimer, *Das Kreuzfahrerfürstentum Galiläa* (Frankfurt am Main, 1990), esp. 236–38. On French and Frankish knights treating Italians—no matter how rich or brave—with contempt and regarding them as *vilains* (peasants; commoners of low standing), see WT Cont. Lyon, 46; cf. David Jacoby, "Knightly Values and Class Consciousness in the Crusader States of the Eastern Mediterranean," *Mediterranean Historical Review* 1 (1986): 176.

37. Prawer, *Crusader Institutions*, 289–90; Riley-Smith, *The Feudal Nobility*, 124. In 1226 Nicole attests as Nicolaus Antelmi and in 1231 as domnus Nicholaus Antelmi: *UKJ*, 2:1092, 1361, nos. 654, 783. In 1236, in Acre, he appears as one *de hominibus imperatoris*: *Tabulae ordinis Theutonici*, 66–67, no. 84. In 1249 the Genoese take possession of a house that belonged to him: "Quatre titres des propriétés des Génois à Acre et à Tyr," ed. Cornelio Desimoni, *AOL* 2, no. 2 (1884): 214, no. 1. For the June 1260/66 epitaph of Nico[laus] Antianme [read: Antiaume], found in Acre in 1923, see Félix-Marie Abel, "Une inscription médiévale de Saint-Jean d'Acre," *Revue Biblique* 33 (1924): 388–90, and Pringle, "Notes on Some Inscriptions from Crusader Acre," 195–96, no. 5; also Claverie, "Notes sur l'onomastique franque," 150.

38. FC 2.11 (408–9). See Richard, "La noblesse de Terre Sainte," 325–26.

39. Tischler, *Die Burgenses von Jerusalem*, 284, no. 207. Tischler's contention (254–55, no. 024) that Ansaldus de Brie, in 1167 a burgess, became a knight by 1175, hinges on the assumption that Anselmus de Brie of the 1175 deed is identical with Ansaldus de Brie. However, Anselmus de Brie appears among the knights already in 1164: *Cart St Sép*, 266, no. 135.

40. Tischler, *Die Burgenses von Jerusalem*, 255, no. 025, and discussion on 35–46.

41. Tischler, *Die Burgenses von Jerusalem*, 134–40, 149, 214.

42. Tischler, *Die Burgenses von Jerusalem*, 218–21.

43. See above, chap. 6.

44. WT 19.13 (882), 22.24 (1044).

45. For Ernoul's lost account probably having dealt with the period from the mid-1170s to 1187, see Peter Edbury and Massimiliano Gaggero, *The Chronique d'Ernoul and the Colbert-Fontainebleau Continuation of William of Tyre*, 2 vols. (Leiden, 2023), 1:6–19.

46. *Ernoul*, 98–102. Runciman and Prawer did not make use of this story, and Hamilton, who did, refrained from spelling out that the captives were burgesses: Hamilton, *The Leper King*, 134–35.

47. *Ernoul*, 179. Cf. John of Ibelin, *Le Livre des Assises*, 575–76, c. 220: "et les borgeis de Jerusalem servent cel jor les tables."

48. *Ernoul*, 180–82; for translation, see Pringle, *Pilgrimage to Jerusalem and the Holy Land*, 148–49. See also WT *C-F Cont*, 83–84. For the approximate location of the marble basins, see "L'Estat de la cité de Iherusalem," c. 6, in *Itinéraires a Jérusalem*, 26.

49. Surprisingly, Ernoul does not allude here to the Pool of Germain, in the Hinnom Valley just west of Mount Sion (nowadays the Sultan's Pool). This pool was constructed in the 1170s "at the foot of Mount Sion under the house of Germain," and earmarked for "the common use of the Christians": *Cart St Sép*, 313, no. 161 (a. 1176). See Mayer, *Von der Cour des Bourgeois*, 228, no. 3 (a. 1173); *UKJ*, 2:641, no. 373 (a. 1174); *UKJ*, 2:675, no. 393 (a. 1177). The description of Jerusalem, apparently interpolated into Ernoul's account, which appears also in the Rothelin Continuation, claims that Germain constructed the pool: *Ernoul*, 264; "L'Estoire de Eracles Empereur: Continuation dite du manuscrit de Rothelin," in *RHC Oc*, 2:502. See Catherine Croisy-Naquet, "La description de Jérusalem dans la Chronique d'Ernoul," *Romania* 115 (1997): esp. 70; Pringle, *Pilgrimage to Jerusalem and the Holy Land*, 30. See also Pringle, *Churches*, 3:153; Adrian J. Boas, *Jerusalem in the Time of the Crusades* (Abingdon, 2001), 173–74, with a correction of "German" to "Germain" in Boas, *The Crusades Uncovered*, 82–86.

50. See John 9:6–7.

51. *Ernoul*, 184; basically, I use Pringle's translation in *Pilgrimage to Jerusalem and the Holy Land*, 150.

52. *Ernoul*, 246; for a later reworking, see WT Cont. Lyon, 62. For a more detailed account, whose protagonists are *Ascalonite* and not *bourgois*, see *Libellus*, 186–91.

53. *Ernoul*, 247–49; cf. WT Cont. Lyon, 62–63.

54. See *Ernoul*, 100, 115, 143, 213, 237, 358, 363.

55. *Ernoul*, 237–38, 249; cf. WT Cont. Lyon, 57, 63, where the knighting of the *bourgois* sons goes unmentioned. On King Baldwin IV knighting Abū al-Khayr, his tutor in horsemanship, and King Richard of England knighting some of Ṣalāḥ al-Dīn's officers, see Ibn Abī Usaybi'a, *A Literary History of*

Medicine, 2.2:1119 (text), 2.3:1264 (translation), and Bahā' al-Dīn, *History of Saladin*, 223.

56. *Ernoul*, 275; cf. WT Cont. Lyon, 66.

57. *Ernoul*, 281–83; cf. WT Cont. Lyon, 68.

58. *Ernoul*, 287; cf. WT Cont. Lyon, 70.

59. *Ernoul*, 288–89; cf. WT Cont. Lyon, 70.

60. *Ernoul*, 296; a more detailed account in WT Cont. Lyon, 73–74.

10. The Non-Franks

1. Meron Benvenisti, *The Crusaders in the Holy Land* (Jerusalem, 1970), 17–20, 26–27 (140,000 Franks, 500,000 indigenous; Jerusalem: 30,000 inhabitants); Prawer, *Histoire*, 1:498, 568–72 (120,000 Franks, 360,000 indigenous; Jerusalem: 20,000); Josiah C. Russell, "The Population of the Crusader States," in *Crusades*, ed. Setton, 5:306 (Jerusalem: 10,000).

2. *Tractatus*, 130.

3. *The Itinerary of Benjamin of Tudela*, 21, 22, 29, 31 (text), 20, 28, 30 (translation).

4. For Gaza and Acre, see below; for Egypt, *Ernoul*, 173; *AMS*, 2:8, 250.

5. See Kedar, "The Frankish Period," 82–83.

6. *Abulfathi Annales Samaritani*, ed. Eduard Vilmar (Gotha, 1865), 132; *The Kitāb al-Tarīkh of Abu l'Fath*, trans. Paul Stenhouse (Sydney, 1985), 182–83.

7. On the raid of 1137, see WT 14.27 (666–67; William gives the name as "Bezzeuge"); on that of 1184, see Ibn Jubayr, *The Travels*, ed. Wright and de Goeje, 299. Translation: Eliyahu Ashtor.

8. For favorable New Testament references, see especially the parable of the good Samaritan (Luke 10:30–35), and Jesus's encounter with the Samaritan woman at Jacob's Well (John 4:7–42).

9. Ze'ev Ben-Hayyim, *The Literary and Oral Tradition of Hebrew and Aramaic among the Samaritans*, 5 vols. (Jerusalem, 1957–79); 2:318–21 [in Hebrew]; Abraham Tal, "Samaritan Literature," in Crown, *The Samaritans*, 419.

10. *The Tulida: A Samaritan Chronicle*, ed. and trans. (into modern Hebrew) Moshe Florentin (Jerusalem, 1999), 98.

11. *The Tulida*, 100–101.

12. *The Tulida*, 104–5; *Une nouvelle chronique samaritaine*, ed. and trans. Elkan-Nathan Adler and Max Seligsohn (Paris, 1903), 27. On the question whether Ab Gillūga is identical with the homonymous writer of a liturgical poem and a prayer, see the diverging views of Arthur E. Cowley, *The Samaritan Liturgy*, 2 vols. (Oxford, 1909), 2:xxiii; Ben-Hayyim, *The Literary and Oral Tradition*, 3.2:17; Alan D. Crown, "Samaritan Literature and Its Manuscripts," *Bulletin of the John Rylands Library* 76 (1994): 39.

13. On the grammar book, see Tal, "Samaritan Literature," 419–20. *The Book of Inheritance: Kitāb al-Mirāt: Das Buch der Erbschaft des Samaritaners Abū Ishāq Ibrāhīm*, ed. and trans. Heinz Pohl (Berlin, 1974). Ze'ev Ben-Hayyim's meticulous review of Pohl's edition appeared in *Orientalistische Literaturzeitung* 74 (1979): 130–38.

14. I. R. M. Bóid, "The Samaritan Halachah," in Crown, *The Samaritans*, 628; Crown, "Samaritan Literature and Its Manuscripts," 46.

15. August Frh. von Gall, *Der hebräische Pentateuch der Samaritaner*, 5 vols. (Giessen, 1914–18), 1:li, 5:lxxxvi. Were these *sheqel*s Saracenate bezants?

16. Gall, *Der hebräische Pentateuch*, 1:li. After the British Museum declined in 1907 to buy the codex, Moses Gaster made some photos of it. These are now kept in the John Rylands Library: see Edward Robertson, *Catalogue of the Samaritan Manuscripts in the John Rylands Library, Manchester*, vol. 2: *The Gaster Manuscripts* (Manchester, 1962), 40–42, no. 88 (1868).

17. "quoddam casale Samaritanorum." *UKJ*, 1:240, no. 92.

18. Gall, *Der hebräische Pentateuch*, 1:vi.

19. Gall, *Der hebräische Pentateuch*, 1:xxxiv. For further details on scrolls, see Kedar, "The Frankish Period," 89–90.

20. Usama ibn Munqidh, *The Book of Contemplation*, 63–64.

21. WT 18.34 (859).

22. Ibn Abī Usaybi'a, *A Literary History of Medicine*, 2.2:1365 (text), 3.2:1553 (translation). For the identification, see Tal, "Samaritan Literature," 419; Lutz Richter-Bernburg, "St. John of Acre-Nablus-Damascus: The Samaritan Minority under Crusaders and Muslims," in Beltz, *Die Folgen der Kreuzzüge für die orientalische Religionsgemeinschaft*, 122–23.

23. Ibn Abī Usaybi'a, *A Literary History of Medicine*, 2.2:1364–67 (text), 3.2:1553–56 (translation).

24. Ibn Abī Usaybi'a, *A Literary History of Medicine*, 2.2:1358–64 (text), 2.3: 1546–53 (translation). The importance of Ibn Abī Uṣaybiʿa for Samaritan history was pointed out by Richter-Bernburg, "St. John of Acre-Nablus-Damascus," 124–25.

25. Ibn Wāṣil, *Mufarrij al-kurūb fī akhbār Banī Ayyūb*, ed. J. al-Shayyal, Hassanein Rabie, and Said Ashour, 5 vols. (Cairo, 1953–77), 5:236–37; translation: Elon Harvey. On Amīn al-Dawla, see also Ibn Abī Usaybi'a, *A Literary History of Medicine*, 2.2:1368–69 (text), 3.2:1556–57 (translation).

26. Saved from apostasy: "nitzaltī min ha-shemad." Maimonides, *Iggerot ha-Rambam*, 1:225. On reverting Frankish converts to Islam, see above, chap. 1.

27. Fretellus, 28, c. 44. Similarly, Joannes Phocas (or Doukas) dismissed the Samaritans' claim that Abraham spoke with God on Mount Gerizim and intended to sacrifice Isaac there: *Jerusalem Pilgrimage, 1099–1185*, trans. John Wilkinson, Joyce Hill, and W. F. Ryan (London, 1988), 322–23.

28. See above, chap. 1.

29. For Haifa, see Prawer, *The History of the Jews*, 35–40.

30. On the flight from Ramla, see *Gesta Francorum*, 87.

31. The details appear in an Arabic-written letter from Acre to Egypt, edited and translated into modern Hebrew by Goitein, *Palestinian Jewry*, 302–5; see Prawer, *The History of the Jews*, 61.

32. Maimonides, *Responsa*, ed. and trans. into modern Hebrew Jehoshua Blau, 4 vols. (Jerusalem, 2014), 2:627–28. The responsum mentions also a Jewish trader of Acre who used to go on business in the neighboring villages and was murdered while traveling.

33. WT 11.27 (536).

34. *The Itinerary of Benjamin of Tudela*, 19–30 (text), 18–29 (translation).

35. *The Itinerary of Benjamin of Tudela*, 20 (text), 18 (translation).

36. *The Itinerary of Benjamin of Tudela*, 26 (text), 24–25 (translation); cf. Prawer, *The History of the Jews*, 138–40.

37. *The Itinerary of Benjamin of Tudela*, 23 (text), 22 (translation). Shachar (*A Pious Belligerence*, 100) presents them as painters.

38. Moshe Gil, *A History of Palestine, 634–1099*, trans. Ethel Broido (Cambridge, 1992), 744–45, 775–76.

39. Maimonides, *Responsa*, 1:204–86 (thirty-two queries); 2:627–28 (responsum to Acre); Maimonides. *Iggerot ha-Rambam*, 1:224–41 (letters to Rabbi Yefet and the convert).

40. Maimonides, *Responsa*, queries 6, 7, 9, 13.

41. Maimonides, *Responsa*, query 30.

42. On the enactment attributed to Baldwin II, see above chap. 1.

43. Maimonides, *Responsa*, query 31.

44. Maimonides, *Iggerot ha-Rambam*, 1:238–41.

45. Maimonides, *Iggerot ha-Rambam*, 1:193; Maimonides, *Responsa*, 1:204.

46. Maimonides, *Mishnah with the Commentary of Moshe b. Maymon, Order "Holy Things,"* ed. David Qafah (Jerusalem, 1967), Tractate "Firstborns," 163, chapter 4:4 [in Hebrew].

47. Maimonides, *Iggerot ha-Rambam*, 2:559.

48. "One of civilization's greatest minds": Kraemer, *Maimonides* (book's subtitle).

49. Gross and Fraenkel, "The First Crusade," 24–29.

50. Sidon: Ibn al-Athīr in *RHC Or*, 1:276; FC 2.44 (548). Tyre: Ibn al-Qalānisī, *Damas de 1075 à 1154: Traduction annotée de l'Histoire d'Ibn al-Qalānisī*, trans. Roger Le Tourneau (Damascus, 1952), 162; Ibn al-Athīr in *RHC Or*, 1:359. Ascalon: Ibn al-Qalānisī, 333. ʿImād al-Dīn, in Abū Shāma, *RHC Or*, 4:409, refers to the subjected Muslims of Sidon, Beirut, and Jubayl as poor people.

51. Al-Harawī, *A Lonely Wayfarer's Guide*, 74–75, 82–83; *Histoire de Jérusalem et d'Hébron: Fragments de la Chronique de Moudjir ed-Dyn*, trans. Henri Sauvaire (Paris, 1874), 45–46, 63.

52. Al-Maqdisī, "*The Cited Tales*," 119 (text), 132 (translation).

53. On Ḥamdān I follow the persuasive reconstruction by Paul M. Cobb, "Hamdan al-Atharibi's *History of the Franks* Revisited, Again," in *Syria in Crusader Times: Conflict and Coexistence*, ed. Carole Hillenbrand (Edinburgh, 2020), 3–20. For a translation of Ibn al-ʿAdīm's account of Ḥamdān's reward for healing the lord of Athārib, see *Muslim Sources of the Crusader Period*, 76–77.

54. See the pioneering if brief discussion by Sivan, "Refugiés," 142–43. For Ibn al-Qaysarānī's biography and anti-Frankish poems, see Nizar F. Hermes, "The Poet(ry) of Frankish Enchantment: The *Ifranjiyyāt* of Ibn Qaysarānī," *Middle Eastern Literatures* 20 (2017): 267–74. On Ibn Munīr lauding Nūr al-Dīn for ritually cleansing land recovered from the Franks and on Ibn al-Qaysarānī calling on him to purify Jerusalem by shedding the Franks' blood, see Shachar, *A Pious Belligerence*, 173–74, 176–77. Al-Samʿānī writes that Ibn al-Qaysarānī fled from Caesarea to Aleppo, where he met him, apparently in 1141: Cook, "Al-Samʿānī's Travels," 44.

55. For his poems about these women, see Ibn al-Qaysarānī, *Shiʿr Ibn al-Qaysarānī*, ed. Adel Jaber Saleh Muhammad (Zarqa, 1991), esp. 215, 254–55, 297, 310. For discussion, see Aleya Khattab, *Das Bild der Franken in der arabischen Literatur des Mittelalters: Ein Beitrag zum Dialog über die Kreuzzüge* (Göppingen, 1989), 33–43, 75–82; Hermes, "The Poet(ry) of Frankish Enchantment," 275–82; Osman Latiff, *The Cutting Edge of the Poet's Sword: Muslim Poetic Responses to the Crusades* (Leiden, 2018), 183–91; Jason Ng, "Women of the Crusades: The Constructedness of the Female Other, 1100–1200," *Al-Masāq* 31 (2019): 306–12. On the possibility that the poems' subtext warns against the dangers of Frankish temptation, see Latiff, 189–91, and the response by Ng, 315.

56. Konstantinos Manasses, *Hodoiporikon*, First Poem, 180–85, vv. 158–202.

57. For an overview, see Stefan Leder, "Charismatic Scripturalism: The Ḥanbalī Maqdisīs of Damascus," *Der Islam* 74 (1997): 279–304.

58. On his life and works, as well as of those of his close relatives, see the introduction to Muwaffaq al-Dīn ibn Qudāma, *Le précis de droit d'Ibn Qudāma, jurisconsulte musulman d'école hanbalite*, trans. Henri Laoust (Beirut, 1950), ix–lviii. For another of his works, see *Ibn Qudāma's Censure of Speculative Theology*, ed. and trans. George Makdisi (London, 1962). For a genealogical table of the early Banū Qudāma, see Kedar and al-Hajjūj, "Muslim Villagers," 148–49.

59. Muwaffaq al-Dīn, *Le précis de droit*, xviii; Sivan, "Refugiés," 143–44.

60. *RHC Or*, 4:286–87; identified as his work in B. Z. Kedar, "The Battle of Hattīn Revisited," in *Horns*, 192.

61. On these buildings, and the quarter's early history, see Toru Miura, *Dynamism in the Urban Society of Damascus: The Ṣāliḥiyya Quarter from the Twelfth to the Twentieth Centuries* (Leiden, 2016), 50–82.

62. On the Frankish spolia, see Jean Sauvaget, *Les monuments historiques de Damas* (Beirut, 1932), 94–96; Ernst Herzfeld, "Damascus: Studies in Architecture—IV," *Ars Islamica* 13–14 (1948): 123b.

63. Herzfeld, "Damascus—IV," 120a, fig. 4, and 123a. On the possibility that the capital originated in Sebaste Cathedral or its vicinity, see T. S. R. Boase, "Ecclesiastical Art in the Crusader States in Palestine and Syria," in *Crusades*, ed. Setton 4:101–2; Folda, *The Art of the Crusaders*, 564 n. 110. For a bold attempt to discern, in Frankish art, references to Muslims that different viewers may have perceived as negative or positive, see Fishhof, *Shaping Identities*, 245–58.

64. Rashīd al-Dīn al-Nabulusī, whose toponymic surname points to his, or his family's, origin in Nablus, wrote an anti-Frankish poem, either after Ṣalāḥ al-Dīn's conquest of Jerusalem or during the Third Crusade. See *Muslim Sources of the Crusader Period*, 97–98; Latiff, *The Cutting Edge*, 91.

65. For an overview, see Johannes Pahlitzsch, "The Greek Orthodox Church in the First Kingdom of Jerusalem (1099–1187)," in *Patterns of the Past, Prospects for the Future: The Christian Heritage in the Holy Land*, ed. Thomas Hummel, Kevork Hintlian, and Ulf Carmesund (London, 1999), 195–212.

66. This is the plausible hypothesis of Pahlitzsch, *Graeci und Suriani*, 106–9.

67. For an analysis of the tract, see Pahlitzsch, *Graeci und Suriani*, 111–19.

68. Pahlitzsch, *Graeci und Suriani*, 120–31, quotation on 125. Translation: Guy Stroumsa and Isidoros Katsos.

69. Pahlitzsch, *Graeci und Suriani*, 52–60.

70. Theodosios Goudeles, *The Life of Leontios, Patriarch of Jerusalem*, ed. and trans. Dimitris Tsougarakis (Leiden, 1993), 106–7, §63. In 1177, Leontios endeavored to establish himself as Greek patriarch in Jerusalem, probably in conjunction with a short-lived alliance between Byzantium and the Frankish Kingdom, but the hostility of the Frankish clergy brought his attempt to naught: Theodosios Goudeles, *The Life of Leontios*, 108–11, 126–39, §§67, 80–88. See Pahlitzsch, *Graeci und Suriani*, 161–74; Hamilton, *The Leper King*, 113–14, 127, 138–39. On Leontios II's treatises, see Goudeles, *The Life of Leontios*, introduction, 9–11.

71. Letter of Theorianos: Raymond J. Loenertz, ed. and trans., "L'épître de Théorien le Philosophe aux prêtres d'Oreiné," in *Mémorial Louis Petit: Mélanges d'histoire et d'archéologie byzantine* (Bucarest, 1948), 317–35. Loenertz (321) believed that Oreiné was Beth Zechariah, southwest of Jerusalem; Jotischky proved its identity with ʿAyn Kārim: Jotischky, *The Perfection of Solitude*, 90 n. 70; Pahlitzsch, *Graeci und Suriani*, 203–4.

72. For the eight dated manuscripts, see Pahlitzsch, *Graeci und Suriani*, List 1, 330–34, nos. 5, 11–14, 16–18; for the manuscripts of 1163 and 1186, see 332, 334, nos. 15, 19; the thirty-eight undated manuscripts ascribable to the twelfth century are designated as such in List 2, 336–50.

73. Pahlitzsch, *Graeci und Suriani*, 213–34.

74. Pahlitzsch, *Graeci und Suriani*, 191–93, 208, 333.

75. Pahlitzsch, *Graeci und Suriani*, 231, 333.

76. Panayotis L. Vocotopoulos, *Byzantine Illuminated Manuscripts of the Patriarchate of Jerusalem*, trans. Deborah M. Whitehouse (Athens, 2002), 38. On Greek bishops serving—contrary to Western canon law—alongside Latin ones in nine or more cities of the Kingdom of Jerusalem, see Hiestand, "Der lateinische Klerus," 49–50.

77. On the possibility of a Greek Orthodox elevation of Tiberias to archiepiscopal status after 1099, see Jotischky in Hamilton and Jotischky, *Latin and Greek Monasticism*, 326. On the move to Nazareth, see Mayer, *Bistümer*, 90–93.

78. Vocotopoulos, *Byzantine Illuminated Manuscripts*, 38; for a reproduction of the TIBEPIAΔIOTHCCA miniature, see 39. For the assumption that it was made in Tiberias, see Annemarie Weyl Carr, "A Group of Provincial Manuscripts from the Twelfth Century," *Dumbarton Oaks Papers* 36 (1982): 45, 51.

79. Jotischky in Hamilton and Jotischky, *Latin and Greek Monasticism*, 466–67, 470.

80. Jotischky in Hamilton and Jotischky, *Latin and Greek Monasticism*, 512.

81. See chap. 7 above.

82. Būlus of Antioch, bishop of Sidon, "On the Christian Sects," in Khoury, *Paul d'Antioche*, 84–97 (text), 188–99 (translation). Khoury attempts to explain the absence of the Latins by claiming that from the viewpoint of Christological doctrine they could have been considered as belonging to the Melkite faction: Khoury, *Paul d'Antioche*, 15.

83. Būlus of Antioch, "Letter to One of His Muslim Friends in Sidon," in Khoury, *Paul d'Antioche*, 59–83 (text), 169–87 (translation).

84. David Thomas, "Paul of Antioch's *Letter to a Muslim Friend* and the Letter from Cyprus," in *Syrian Christians under Islam: The First Thousand Years*, ed. David Thomas (Leiden, 2001), 203–21.

85. See chap. 2, note 212, above.

86. David Thomas, "Paul of Antioch," in *Christian–Muslim Relations: A Bibliographical History*, vol. 4: *1200–1350*, ed. David Thomas and Alex Mallett (Leiden, 2012), 78–82. Griffith opts for the first half of the thirteenth century, erroneously assuming that there was no Frankish presence in Sidon at that time: Sidney Griffith, "Paul of Antioch," in Noble and Treiger, *The Orthodox Church in the Arab World*, 217.

87. Khoury, *Paul d'Antioche*, 18; Jotischky in Hamilton and Jotischky, *Latin and Greek Monasticism*, 353–54, 486.

88. Cahen, *Orient et Occident*, 215, 273 n. 7; Pahlitzsch, *Graeci und Suriani*, 195 n. 409. Būlus's trip to Rome via Constantinople and Amalfi ties in with what is known about Amalfitan shipping in the eleventh century: cf. Jacoby, "Commercio e navigazione degli Amalfitani." For the view that Būlus was probably active in the second half of the eleventh century or in the early years of the twelfth, see Herman Teule, "Paul of Antioch's Attitude towards the Jews and the Muslims: His *Letter to the Nations and the Jews*," in *The Three Rings*, ed. Barbara Roggema et al. (Leuven, 2005), 94–95.

89. Thomas has argued that it is unlikely that the "Letter to a Muslim Friend," with its provocative contents, had lain unnoticed by Muslims for very long after its composition, and therefore a date around 1200 may be assumed: Thomas, "Paul of Antioch's *Letter to a Muslim Friend*," 204; Thomas, "Paul of Antioch," 81. But the major Muslim responses were not to Būlus's treatise but to its Cypriot revision, which triggered an immediate reaction. And medieval works sometimes lay unnoticed for a very long time: Gerard of Nazareth's "De conversacione virorum Dei" was first quoted, as far as we know, in 1370.

90. Joannes Phocas (or Doukas) in *Jerusalem Pilgrimage, 1099–1185*, 324, 329, 332–33; Andrew Jotischky, "Greek Orthodox and Latin Monasticism around Mar Saba under Crusader Rule," in *The Sabaite Heritage in the Orthodox Church from the Fifth Century to the Present*, ed. Joseph Patrich (Leuven, 2001), 85–86.

91. The vestiges, accessible only with much difficulty, were documented by Gustav Kühnel, *Wall Paintings in the Latin Kingdom of Jerusalem* (Berlin, 1988), 185–91, plates LXIII–LXXI. The fragmentary mural of the Greek Orthodox Church of St.-Nicholas, discovered in Jerusalem's Old City and datable to the twelfth century, exhibits Byzantine characteristics, yet the armor of one of the figures is made of chain mail, suggesting Western influence: Gil Fishhof, Amit Re'em, and David Yeger, "Two Recently Discovered Mural Paintings and the Development of Monumental Painting in Twelfth-Century Jerusalem," in *EO*, 2:133–47; Fishhof, *Shaping Identities*, 279–81.

92. Claude R. Conder and Horatio H. Kitchener, *The Survey of Western Palestine: Memoirs of the Topography, Orography, Hydrography and Archaeology*, vol. 3: *Judaea* (London, 1883), 192–98; Pringle, *Churches*, 1:189–91. On Jifnā/Jafenia, see Ellenblum, *Frankish Rural Settlement*, 135–36, 239.

93. On Yaʿqūb ibn Siqlāb, see Ibn Abī Usaybi'a, *A Literary History of Medicine*, 2.2:1326–29 (text), 3.2:1509–13 (translation); Kohlberg and Kedar, "A Melkite Physician." St. Sabas Monastery: the text has "the Sīq Monastery," but Pahlitzsch (*Graeci und Suriani*, 283) has adduced evidence that Dayr al-Sīq is identical with Mār Sābā.

94. See Yana Tchekhanovets, *The Caucasian Archaeology of the Holy Land: Armenian, Georgian and Albanian Communities between the Fourth and Eleventh Centuries CE* (Leiden, 2018); for archaeological evidence on the Georgians, esp. in Jerusalem and the Judean foothills, see 136–200.

95. For a brief overview, see Prawer, "Social Classes in the Crusader States," 87–89 (but Shota Rustaveli did not write *The Knight in the Panther's Skin* in Jerusalem); for longitudinal studies of Georgian presence, see Gotcha Japaridze, *The Georgian Monasteries and Monastic Community in the Holy Land in the 11th–18th Centuries according to the Arabic Narratives and Documentary Sources* (Tbilisi, 2018) [in Georgian, with English summary on 290–343]; Giorgi Gagoshidze et al., *Georgian Christian Community in the Holy Land* (Tbilisi, 2022) [in Georgian and English].

96. While the military qualities of Eastern Christian groups are disparaged, the *Georgiani* are characterized as "armis plurimum exerci[ta]ti": *Tractatus*, 124. For an overview of Frankish/Georgian relations, see Bernard Hamilton, "Latins and Georgians and the Crusader Kingdom," *Al-Masāq* 23 (2011): 117–24.

97. Anseau, "Letters," 172, no. 151. See Johannes Pahlitzsch, "Georgians and Greeks in Jerusalem (1099–1310)," in *EWCS*, 3:35–37. For attempts at identifying the Georgian queen, see Tessera, "Le donne," 113–14.

98. See above, chap. 8.

99. *Georgian Manuscripts Copied Abroad, in Libraries and Museums of Georgia: Illustrated Catalogue*, ed. Thamar Otkhmezuri, trans. Menana Odisheli (Tbilisi, 2018), 48; for the correct date, 1155, see Tsurtsumia, "Commemoration of Crusaders," 318. The manuscript is in Tbilisi, National Centre of Manuscripts, shelfmark H-1661.

100. *The Georgian Manuscript Book Abroad*, ed. Nestan Chkhikvadze, trans. Lado Mirianashvili (Tbilisi, 2018), 221. This manuscript is Paris, BnF, géorgien 28.

101. *The Georgian Manuscript Book Abroad*, 139 (Jer.Geo.63).

102. *The Georgian Manuscript Book Abroad*, 50 (Tbilisi, NCM, A-1347), 101 (Sin.Geo.O.69), 119 (Jer.Geo.102), 134 (Jer.Geo.59), 136–37 (Jer.Geo.143), 142 (Jer.Geo.71).

103. *The Georgian Manuscript Book Abroad*, 52 (Tbilisi, NCM, H-1664).

104. The contract was discovered, edited, and translated by Pahlitzsch, *Graeci und Suriani*, 314–24.

105. Cf. the "good golden *bizancii saracenati* of the king of that country," of the Venetian act of 1142: see chap. 2.

106. For the Greek text, see the note of Eduard Kurtz in *Byzantinische Zeitschrift* 3 (1894): 168–70. For English translation by Leah Di Segni, see Joseph Patrich, *Sabas, Leader of Palestinian Monasticism: A Comparative Study in Eastern Monasticism, Fourth to Seventh Centuries* (Washington, DC, 1995), 274–75.

107. Joannes Phocas (or Doukas) in *Jerusalem Pilgrimage, 1099–1185*, 326, 330–31.

108. Catia Galatariotou, *The Making of a Saint: The Life, Times and Sanctification of Neophytos the Recluse* (Cambridge, 1991), 14.

109. "Narratio de monacho palaestinensi," ed. Hyppolite Delehaye, "Saints de Chypre," *Analecta Bollandiana* 26 (1907): 162–75. Translation: Shay Eshel. See also Jotischky in Hamilton and Jotischky, *Latin and Greek Monasticism*, 426–28.

110. Mentioned in a marginal note edited by Delehaye, "Saints de Chypre," 281–82.

111. *Tractatus*, 124, where "circa ecclesiastica instituta" must be corrected to "contra ecclesiastica instituta." See Paolo Trovato, *Everything You Always Wanted to Know about Lachmann's Method* (Padua, 2017), 282.

112. MacEvitt, *The Crusades and the Christian World of the East*, 162–63.

113. Joachim of Fiore, *Tractatus super Quatuor Evangelia*, 93. When Ranieri of Pisa was irritated by his inability to understand the Armenians' divine service in the Church of the Holy Sepulcher, God opened his ear and henceforth he comprehended it better than the Latin one: Benincasa, *Vita sancti Rainerii*, 127–28.

114. For a discussion of Frankish-Armenian relations in the ecclesiastical sphere, see Hamilton, *The Latin Church*, 201–7. On Frankish-Armenian rapport in the twelfth century, see Gérard Dédéyan, "Un projet de colonisation arménienne dans le royaume latin de Jérusalem sous Amaury Ier (1162–1174)," in *Le partage du monde: Échanges et colonisation dans la Méditerranée médiévale*, ed. Michel Balard and Alain Ducellier (Paris, 1998), 101–40; Camille Rouxpetel, "Les Arméniens, la 'nation' préférée des Latins partis pour la Terre sainte entre XIIe et XIIIe siècles?," *Mélanges de l'Ecole française de Rome—Moyen Âge* 130 (2018): 41–51.

115. Michael E. Stone, "The Manuscript Library of the Armenian Patriarchate in Jerusalem," *Israel Exploration Journal* 19 (1969): 26–30. On 1215 as the date of the earliest manuscript (and not 1314, as Stone supposed), see Abraham Terian, "Armenian Writers in Medieval Jerusalem," in Hummel, Hintlian, and Carmesund, *Patterns of the Past*, 151, 156.

116. *The Churches and Monasteries of Egypt and Some Neighbouring Countries, attributed to Abū Sālih, the Armenian*, 4–6 (text), 2–8 (trans.); see chap. 7, note 63 above. The location of the Monastery of St. Sarkis is not known: Pringle, *Churches*, 3:358.

117. Prawer, "Social Classes in the Crusader States," 86.

118. On the church-turned-mosque, see Kedar, "In Search of Ibelin Castle," 14–15.

119. The last two paragraphs are based on the posthumously published article by Nurith Kenaan-Kedar, "Decorative Architectural Sculpture in Crusader Jerusalem: The Eastern, Western and Armenian Sources of a Local Visual Culture," in Boas, *The Crusader World*, 609–23. For discussions of the Church of the Holy Archangels, the Armenian cathedral, and Melisende's tomb, see Pringle, *Churches*, 3:112–17, 168–82, 298–300; Folda, *The Art of the Crusaders*, 247–49, 324–28. For the views that the goudron frieze is an Islamic motif, or that different observers could recognize it as either Armenian or Islamic, see Fishhof, *Shaping Identities*, 283–87.

120. Theo Maarten van Lint, "The *Poem of Lamentation over the Capture of Jerusalem* Written in 1189 by Grigor Tłay, Catholicos of All Armenians," in *The Armenians in Jerusalem and the Holy Land*, ed. Michael E. Stone, Roberta R. Ervine, and Nira Stone (Leuven, 2002), 121–42.

121. L. M. Alishan, *Sissouan ou l'Armeno-Cilicie* (Venice, 1899), 517; Paul Peeters, "Traductions et traducteurs dans l'hagiographie orientale à l'epoque byzantine," *Analecta Bollandiana* 40 (1922): 271–72; Cahen, *La Syrie du Nord*, 565; Jos J. S. Weitenberg, "Literary Contacts in Cilician Armenia," in *EWCS*, 1:68–69.

122. Beth 'Arīf: see *Tabula Imperii Romani: Iudaea. Palaestina, Maps and Gazetteer*, ed. Yoram Tsafrir, Leah Di Segni, and Judith Green (Jerusalem, 1994), 80. 'Adse, identified with Khirbat 'Adasa, three miles north of Jerusalem: *Tabula Imperii Romani*, ed. Tsafrir, Di Segni, and Green, 57 [Adasa I]; Pringle, *Secular Buildings*, 17–18, no. 6.

123. The first two colophons were edited and translated by Jean-Pierre Hippolyte Martin, "Les premiers princes croisés et les Syriens jacobites de Jérusalem," *Journal Asiatique* 8, no. 12 (1888): 471–90, and 8, no. 13 (1889): 33–79; for a partial English translation based on an unpublished reedition, see Andrew Palmer, "The History of the Syrian Orthodox in Jerusalem. Part Two: Queen Melisende and the Jacobite Estates," *Oriens Christianus* 76 (1992): 77–80, 82–84. See also François Nau, "Le croisé lorrain Godefroy d'Ascha, d'après deux documents syriaques du XIIe siècle," *Journal Asiatique* 9, no. 14 (1899): 21–31. For a summary of the dispute, see Mayer in *UKJ*, 1:208–10, 308–9, 314–15, nos. 75, 133, 136–37. Gonfré has been identified with Gunfridus, castellan of the Tower of David, captured by the Fatimids in 1106 (AA 10.14 [732]), and with Gonfroy II of Marquise: Pierre-Vincent Claverie, "Les tribulations orientales du seigneur Gonfroy II de Marquise (1098–1138)," in Vermeulen, D'hulster, and Van Steenbergen, *Egypt and Syria in the Fatimid, Ayyubid and Mamluk Eras*, 8:163–85. For the date of Ignatius II Hesnūn's death, see Andrew Palmer and Geert Jan van Gelder, "Syriac and Arabic Inscriptions at the Monastery of St. Mark's in Jerusalem," *Oriens Christianus* 78 (1994): 37–38.

124. Dayr Dakariyya should be probably sought at Tell Zakariyya, sixteen miles southwest of Jerusalem: Pringle, *Churches*, 1:204. Jacobite presence in the village of 'Abūd (eleven miles northwest of Ramallah) is attested by a Syriac inscription of 1058 in the local church; according to a colophon, a Syriac monk from the village copied in 1104 the Gospels at Mount Sinai; two other monks appear in colophons of the eleventh and thirteenth centuries: Pringle, *Churches*, 1:17–20; Ellenblum, *Frankish Rural Settlement*, 128–34.

125. The colophon was edited and translated by William R. Taylor, "A New Syriac Fragment Dealing with Incidents in the Second Crusade," *Annual of the American Schools of Oriental Research* 11 (1931): 120–30; corrected but partial translation by Palmer, "The History of the Syrian Orthodox in Jerusalem. Part Two," 85–87 (I use Palmer's translation). For a summary, see Mayer in *UKJ*, 1:406, no. 219.

126. François Nau, "Sur quelques autographes de Michel le Syrien, patriarche d'Antioche de 1166 à 1199," *Revue de l'Orient chrétien* 19 (1914): 379; cf. Palmer,

"The History of the Syrian Orthodox in Jerusalem. Part Two," 93 n. 70. Michael the Syrian was in Jerusalem in 1179: *Chronique de Michel le Syrien*, 3:379.

127. Pringle, *Churches*, 3:327–35; the 1915 demolition is mentioned by Enlart, *Les monuments des croisés*, 2:237. On the 1978 excavation, see Dan Bahat, "Recently Discovered Crusader Churches in Jerusalem," in *Ancient Churches Revealed*, ed. Yoram Tsafrir (Jerusalem, 1993), 126–27. The Western character is highlighted by Johannes Pahlitzsch, "St. Maria Magdalena, St. Thomas und St. Markus: Tradition und Geschichte dreier syrisch-orthodoxer Kirchen in Jerusalem," *Oriens Christianus* 81 (1997): 82–96.

128. Dionysius Bar Salībī, *Expositio liturgiae*, ed. and trans. Jérôme Labourt, Corpus Scriptorum Christianorum Orientalium. Scriptores Syri, 2nd series, 93 (Paris, 1903), 1 (text), 33 (trans.). On Dionysius, see the introduction to *Dionysius Bar Salībī's Treatise against the Jews*, ed. and trans. Rifaat Y. Ebied, Malatius M. Malki, and Lionel R. Wickham (Leiden, 2020). Dionysius writes that Ignatius asked for an exposition allowing to answer "the Romans, that is, the Franks," and then goes on to state that the Byzantines call themselves Romans fraudulently.

129. *Chronique de Michel le Syrien*, 3:201–3, 377–78; Bernard Hamilton, "Aimery of Limoges, Latin Patriarch of Antioch (c. 1142–c. 1196) and the Unity of the Churches," in *EWCS*, 2:6.

11. Cultural Activities in the Kingdom of Acre (1191–1291)

1. On the stages of the French presence, see Jonathan Riley-Smith, "The Crown of France and Acre, 1254–1291," in *France and the Holy Land*, 45–62.

2. For details, see B. Z. Kedar, "On Some Characteristics of the Second Kingdom of Jerusalem, 1191–1291," in *Settlement and Crusade in the Thirteenth Century: Multidisciplinary Studies of the Latin East*, ed. Gil Fishhof, Judith Bronstein, and Vardit Shotten-Hallel (Abingdon, 2021), 3–8.

3. *Cart Hosp*, 2:673–74, no. 2482. Two charters of 1261 envisage the possibility "que la crestiente perdist la cite d'Accre" as well as the prospect that "deu rendist Acre as crestiens": *Tabulae ordinis Theutonici*, 108, 113, nos. 119, 121. See also the anonymous Latin text of 1273 quoted by Rubin, *Learning in a Crusader City*, 7.

4. Letter edited in Kedar, "Le miracle du Feu sacré," 529. Gregory's ruling ties in with his insistence that only authenticated miracles should count in canonization proceedings: see André Vauchez, "La papauté et l'importance des miracles dans l'appréciation de la sainteté dans la première moitié du XIIIe siècle," in *Bourgogne/Orient*, 721–26.

5. Schlumberger, Chalandon, and Blanchet, *Sigillographie*, 73–81. Already in 1201, King Aimery of Jerusalem and Cyprus granted "Monacho, venerabili Domini Sepulcri patriarche," a *casale* in Cyprus: *Cart St Sép*, 331, no. 174. In 1207, Albert of Vercelli styled himself "dei gracia sancte resurrectionis vocatus patriarcha": *Tabulae ordinis Theutonici*, 34, no. 42; Gérold, in 1229, addressed the pope and all Christians simply as "patriarcha Hierosolymitanus": *Historia diplomatica Friderici Secundi*, ed. Jean-Louis-Alphonse Huillard-Bréholles, 7 vols. (Paris, 1852–61), 3:102, 135.

6. Mansi, *Concilia*, 22:989–92.

7. For the confusion with Accaron, see FC 2.25 (464).

8. *I Pelrinages communes, i Pardouns de Acre e la crisi del Regno Crociato: Storia e testi*, ed. Fabio Romanini and Beatrice Saletti (Padua, 2012), 155; Debra J. Birch, *Pilgrimage to Rome in the Middle Ages: Continuity and Change* (Woodbridge, 1998), 196. Pringle proposed that the *Pardouns* were written between 1258 and 1263: *Pilgrimage to Jerusalem and the Holy Land*, 45.

9. *Les registres de Nicolas IV*, ed. Ernest Langlois, 9 vols. (Paris, 1886–93), 1:64, no. 334; *I Pelrinages communes*, 151. Compare also Alexander IV's promise, in 1255, of one hundred days to visitors of the Franciscan church in Acre within the octaves of three feasts, with the much more generous promise in the *Pardouns*: Pringle, *Pilgrimage to Jerusalem and the Holy Land*, 15–16, tables 1–2; Kedar, "On Some Characteristics," 12.

10. *I Pelrinages communes*, 143. Romanini and Saletti, who point out the exceptionality of the list, raise the possibility of a forgery (90–93). The indulgences recorded by pilgrims between 1347 and 1418 never exceed seven years and 280 days: see Niccolò da Poggibonsi, *Libro d'Oltramare (1345–1350)*, ed. Bellarmino Bagatti (Jerusalem, 1945), introduction, xlvi–xlviii, l–li.

11. David Jacoby, "Pilgrimage in Crusader Acre: The *Pardouns dAcre* [*sic*]," in *De Sion exibit lex et verbum domini de Hierusalem: Essays on Medieval Law, Liturgy, and Literature in Honour of Amnon Linder*, ed. Yitzhak Hen (Turnhout, 2001), 107–17. His view was adopted by Folda, *Crusader Art in the Holy Land*, 399; see also Shlomo Lotan, "Pilgrimage Processions, Religious Sensibilities and Piety in the City of Acre in the Latin Kingdom of Jerusalem," *Mirabilia/MedTrans* 10 (2019): 254–60; Danny Sion, "The Archaeology of the *Pardouns de Acre*," in *EO*, 2:107–16. In a later article, Jacoby dwelt on the difference between the indulgence rates of the *Pardouns* and those promised by the popes and raised the possibility that the English copyist of the single manuscript that contains the *Pardouns* inflated the original, lost figures: David Jacoby, "Ports of Pilgrimage to the Holy Land, Eleventh–Fourteenth Century: Jaffa, Acre, Alexandria," in *The Holy Portolano: The Sacred Geography of Navigation in the Middle Ages*, ed. Michele Bacci and Martin Rohde (Berlin, 2014), 56–64.

12. See the projection of the itinerary on a plan of Acre in Pringle, *Pilgrimage to Jerusalem and the Holy Land*, fig. 7. For the erratic course, see esp. points 9–12, 36–39.

13. "Les chemins et les pelerinages de la Terre Sainte. Texte B," 190. Burchard of Mount Sion, *Descriptio Terrae Sanctae*, 230–31. This was already the view of Jacques of Vitry: See "Lettres de Jacques de Vitry," 2.275–56 (569).

14. "Lettres de Jacques de Vitry," 2.204–6 (567).

15. Joinville, *Vie de saint Louis*, 510, §613.

16. ʿImmanuel of Rome, *Maḥbarot ʿImmanuel ha-Romī* [The Cantos of Manuello Romano], 6.401, ed. Dov Yarden, 2 vols. (Jerusalem, 1957), 1:122.

17. For the appellation "Saint-Jean d'Acre," see Folda, *Crusader Manuscript Illumination at Saint-Jean d'Acre*; Folda, *Crusader Art in the Holy Land*, 399a–b, with partial reservation at 653 n. 305. The appellation also appears elsewhere in the research literature; see, for instance, Bale, "Reading," 91.

18. See Aryeh Graboïs, "Les pèlerins occidentaux en Terre Sainte et Acre: D'Accon des croisés à Saint-Jean d'Acre," *Studi Medievali* 24 (1983): 263–64. He claims that the term originated with French pilgrims of the fifteenth century, but refers only to Greffin Affagart, *Relation de Terre Sainte (1533–34)*, ed. Jules Chavanon (Paris, 1902)—where the term does not occur. Michel Nau, who visited Acre in 1667–68, devotes a chapter to "la ville de saint Jean d'Acre": Michel Nau, *Voyage nouveau de la Terre-Sainte* (Paris, 1679), 649–53, and the report of Etienne Gravier d'Ortières's expedition of 1685–87 contains the "Veue de St Jean D'Acre": https://gallica.bnf.fr/ark:/12148/btv1b55000061m/f6.item. Danny Sion brought Nau's description to my attention.

19. For details, see Kedar, "On Some Characteristics," 9, table 1.1.

20. Kenneth Pennington, *Pope and Bishops: The Papal Monarchy in the Twelfth and Thirteenth Centuries* (Philadelphia, 1984), esp. chaps. 3–4, quotation on 99.

21. Calculation based on the data of Hiestand, "Der lateinische Klerus," 53–54. Phenomenon noted by Cahen, *Orient et Occident*, 180.

22. Authority based mainly on legatine status: Hiestand, "Der lateinische Klerus," 57–59, 63–64, 66; Klaus-Peter Kirstein, *Die lateinischen Patriarchen von Jerusalem: Von der Eroberung der Heiligen Stadt durch die Kreuzfahrer bis zum Ende der Kreuzfahrerstaaten 1291* (Berlin, 2002), 448–54, 468.

23. *RRR*, nos. 2317, 2319–22, 2324–27.

24. On Jacques Pantaléon as patriarch and his tense relations with the bishops of Acre and Bethlehem, see Hamilton, *The Latin Church*, 267–71.

25. *Les registres de Grégoire X (1272–1276)*, ed. Jean Guiraud (Paris, 1892), 54, no. 160 (31 March 1272). See Philip B. Baldwin, *Pope Gregory X and the Crusades* (Woodbridge, 2014), 52–57.

26. Hamilton, *The Latin Church*, 280–81.

27. Rubin, *Learning in a Crusader City*, 17.

28. On his career, see Kirstein, *Die lateinischen Patriarchen*, 411–46. Mayer (*Die Kanzlei*, 1:309) observes that Albert was the only Latin patriarch of Jerusalem to attain sainthood. For a critical edition, see *The Rule of Saint Albert*, ed. and trans. Bede Edwards (Aylesford, 1973), 75–93.

29. See Christine Caldwell, "Peter Martyr: The Inquisitor as Saint," *Comitatus* 31 (2000): 146–47 and passim.

30. Thomas Kaeppeli, *Scriptores Ordinis Praedicatorum Medii Aevi*, 4 vols. (Rome, 1970–93), 3:168–71. The copy of *Liber de exemplis sacre scripture* preserved in Brugge, Openbare Bibliotheek, MS 270 (a. 1399) can be consulted at the Mmmonk digital library, https://www.mmmonk.be/nl/, under B_OB_MS270. The attribution to Patriarch Haymarus Monachus (1197–1202) of a poem about the siege of Acre is unwarranted: *Der "Rithmus de expeditione Ierosolimitana" des sogenannten Haymarus Monachus Florentinus: Ein Augenzeugenbericht über die Belagerung Akkons (1189–1191) während des dritten Kreuzzugs*, ed. and German prose translation by Sascha Falk, Italian verse translation by Antonio Placanica (Florence, 2006), lvii–lxvii. Falk's arguments against Haymarus Monachus's authorship are cogent; the decision to subscribe, in the absence of a more convincing alternative, to the traditional attribution, is not.

31. *Tractatus super erroribus quos citra et ultra mare invenimus*. See Rubin, *Learning in a Crusader City*, 151–55, 185–86.

32. Reinhold Röhricht, "Die Kreuzzüge des Grafen Theobald von Navarra und Richard von Cornwallis," *Forschungen zur deutschen Geschichte* 26 (1886): 72 n. 7; Paul-Antonin Amargier, "Benoît d'Alignan, évêque de Marseille (1229–1268)," *Le Moyen Age* 72 (1966): 445–46; Michael Lower, *The Barons' Crusade: A Call to Arms and Its Consequences* (Philadelphia, 2005), 54.

33. *De constructione castri Saphet: Construction et fonctions d'un château fort franc en Terre Sainte*, ed. Robert B. C. Huygens (Amsterdam, 1981), 34–38.

34. See Jonathan Rubin, "Benoît d'Alignan and Thomas Agni: Two Frankish Intellectuals and the Study of Oriental Christianity in Thirteenth-Century Kingdom of Jerusalem," *Viator* 44 (2013): 190–93.

35. Rome, Biblioteca Alessandrina, MS 141, fols. 1ra, 1va, 2rb. On the treatise's contents, see Martin Grabmann, "Der Franziskanerbischof Benedictus de Alignano (†1268) und seine Summa zum Caput Firmiter des. 4. Laterankonzils," in *Kirchengeschichtliche Studien P. Michael Bihl dargeboten*, ed. Ignatius Maria Freudenreich (Kolmar, 1941), 55–59.

36. "ubi olim cum primo pro subsidio Terre Sancte huc venimus opus incepimus." "Hoc opus incepimus olim quando primo transfretavimus pro subsidio Terre Sancte." Biblioteca Alessandrina, MS 141, fols. 1va, 2rb. The first sentence is missing from the transcription in Étienne Baluze, *Miscellanea*, ed. Giovanni Domenico Mansi, 4 vols. (Lucca, 1761–64), 2:242–43.

37. On Tommaso's probable status as *legatus missus*, see Mayer in *UKJ*, 3:1412.

38. On Tommaso's career, see Abele L. Redigonda, "Agni, Tommaso," in *Dizionario biografico degli Italiani*, vol. 1 (Rome, 1960), 445–47. Rubin, "Benoît d'Alignan and Thomas Agni," 195–98; Rubin, *Learning in a Crusader City*, 148–61.

39. Biblioteca Alessandrina, MS 141, fol. 1rb–va; Baluze, *Miscellanea*, 2:242–43.

40. On William of Agen, see Hamilton, *The Latin Church*, 271–75; for the date of his arrival in Acre, see *Cronaca del Templare di Tiro*, 92, §84; "Annales de Terre Sainte," 451. While Urban IV translated Willliam from Agen to Acre, he transferred the bishop of Lydda to Agen and Jean of Troyes to Lydda: Hamilton, *The Latin Church*, 271.

41. Filippo Lotta, "Del Cassero Martino (Martino da Fano)," in *Dizionario Biografico degli Italiani* 36 (1988): https://www.treccani.it/enciclopedia/martino-del-cassero_%28Dizionario-Biografico%29/.

42. See Martin Bertram, "Johannes de Ancona: Ein Jurist des 13. Jahrhunderts in den Kreuzfahrerstaaten," *Bulletin of Medieval Canon Law* 7 (1977): 49–64 (quotation on 59); Jonathan Rubin, "John of Ancona's *Summae*: A Neglected Source for the Juridical History of the Latin Kingdom of Jerusalem," *Bulletin of Medieval Canon Law*, n.s. 29 (2012): 183–218; Rubin, *Learning in a Crusader City*, 92–113. The treatise on feudal law is entitled *Summa super usibus feudorum*.

43. The Sidonese books were identified and briefly discussed by Anneliese Maier in three articles published in *Manuscripta* 11 (1967): 39–45, and 12 (1968): 22–25, 106–7, and repr. in *Anneliese Maier, Ausgehendes Mittelalter: Gesammelte Aufsätze zur Geistesgeschichte des 14. Jahrhunderts*, vol. 3, ed. Agostino Paravicini-Bagliani (Rome, 1977), 281–94. See also Pierre Gasnault, "L'homéliaire de l'*ecclesia Sydonensis*," *Bulletin de la Société Nationale des Antiquaires de France*, 1967, 276–82.

44. For discussions of the pre-Gratian collection, contained in BAV, Vat. lat. 3831, see Paul Fournier, "Une collection canonique italienne du commencement du XIIe siècle," *Annales de l'enseignement supérieur de Grenoble* 6 (1894): 343–441; Giuseppe Motta, "Osservazioni intorno alla Collezione Canonica in tre libri," in *Proceedings of the Fifth International Congress of Medieval Canon Law*, ed. Stephan Kuttner and Kenneth Pennington (Vatican City, 1980), 51–65. For the text, see *Collectio Canonum Trium Librorum*, ed. Joseph [Giuseppe] Motta, 2 vols. (Vatican City, 2005–8). The Nablus decisions, preserved only in BAV, Vat. lat. 1345, were reedited in "Canons of the Council of Nablus," 331–34. For discussion of other works contained in this codex, see Tessera, "Dalla liturgia," 414–15.

45. On the Seneca works, see Jeannine Fohlen, "Un nouveau manuscrit de l'église de Sidon à la Bibliothèque Vaticane (Vat. lat. 2220)," *Scriptorium* 38 (1984): 302–4.

46. BnF, lat. 1794, fols. 46r–165v; a modern hand added in the margins: "Ordinarium canonicorum regularium s. Johannis Carnotensis." On its influence, see Zöller, "The Regular Canons," 378–79.

47. Bav. Vat. Borgh. 287; see Anneliese Maier, *Codices Burghesiani Bibliothecae Vaticanae* (Vatican City, 1952), 328–30. The codex also contains four short canon law texts; a fifth mentions persons active in Bologna in about 1160.

48. BAV, Vat. Borgh. 6; Maier, *Codices Burghesiani*, 10–11.

49. BAV, Vat. Borgh. 141, fols. 3r–4v; Maier, *Codices Burghesiani*, 189–91.

50. See *Algazel's Metaphysics, a Medieval Translation*, ed. Joseph T. Muckle (Toronto, 1933). Maier established that the Sidonese fragment appears on 108, line 11 to 127, line 12.

51. Anthony H. Minnema, "Algazel Latinus: The Audience of the 'Summa Theoricae Philosophiae,' 1150–1600," *Traditio* 69 (2014): 166–67.

52. General Chapter of Paris: *Acta capitulorum generalium Ordinis Praedicatorum*, vol. 1: *Ab anno 1220 ad annum 1303*, ed. Benedikt Maria Reichert (Rome, 1898), 9. The letter of Prior Philip appears in two slightly diverging versions in Albericus Trium Fontium, *Chronica*, ed. Paul Scheffer-Boichorst, in MGH SS 23:941–42, and in Matthew Paris, *Chronica Majora*, 3:398. But "et eas [sc. linguas] ad studium in singulis conventibus statuimus" of the first version, and "et studium linguarum in singulis conventibus statuimus" of the second, do not refer to the establishment of a language *studium*.

53. Letter edited in Kedar, *Crusade and Mission*, 213.

54. Two orders originated in the Kingdom of Acre: the Teutonic Knights and the Carmelite order.

55. The 1287 decision lays down "quod nullus minister scienter mittat fratres insolentes ad provinciam Terre Sancte." Franz Ehrle, "Die ältesten Redactionen der Generalconstitutionen des Franziskanerordens," *Archiv für Literatur- und Kirchengeschichte des Mittelalters* 6 (1892): 58.

56. François Balme, "La province dominicaine de Terre-Sainte de janvier 1277 à octobre 1280," *ROL* 1 (1893): 531–34, no. 2. Other friars, debarred from voting because of too short a service in the order or in its Holy Land Province, may have resided in the convent. Balme estimates (535 n. 2) that the province (with its convents of Nicosia, Acre, and Tripoli) had about eighty friars. He also assumes (530 n. 4) that the six electors mentioned in the proceedings must

have been either masters of theology or general preachers, because each of them owned a personal seal.

57. For details, see Rubin, *Learning in a Crusader City*, 48–52.

58. William of Rubrouck, *Itinerarium*, in *Sinica Franciscana*, vol. 1: *Itinera et relationes Fratrum Minorum saeculi XIII et XIV*, ed. Anastasius van den Wyngaert (Quaracchi, 1929), 329–30. On the religious disputation in which William participated, see B. Z. Kedar, "The Multilateral Disputation at the Court of the Grand Qan Möngke, 1254," in *The Majlis: Interreligious Encounters in Medieval Islam*, ed. Hava Lazarus-Yafeh et al. (Wiesbaden, 1999), 162–83. For a partial list of thirteenth-century Westerners who played important roles in European culture and visited Acre, see Bale, "Reading," 91.

59. See Jonathan Rubin, "The Beginnings of the Study of Foreign Languages in the Dominican Order: Regulation, Implementation, and Impact," in *Making and Breaking the Rules: Discussion, Implementation, and Consequences of Dominican Legislation*, ed. Cornelia Linde (Oxford, 2018), 257–65.

60. Joinville, *Vie de saint Louis*, 406, §§444–45; also, 414–18, §§458–63. Marie-Thérèse d'Alverny, "La connaissance de l'Islam au temps de saint Louis," in *Septième centenaire de la mort de saint Louis* (Paris, 1976), 238; Annemarie Schimmel, introduction to Margaret Smith, *Rābiʿa the Mystic and her Fellow Saints in Islam* (Cambridge, 1984), xxvii, 98–99. The story was recorded in Persian in 1318 by Shams al-Dīn Aflākī; see Clement Huart, *Les saints derviches tourneurs: Récits traduits du persan et annotés*, 2 vols. (Paris, 1918), 1:310–11.

61. Jacques of Vitry on the Prophet: JdV 3–7 (104–42). The ostrich fable: *Die Exempla des Jacob von Vitry*, 137, no. 79b.

62. *Aesop's Fables*, trans. Laura Gibbs (Oxford, 2002), 171, no. 362. Abū al-Faḍl al-Maydānī: see Frenken's introduction to Jacques de Vitry, *Die Exempla*, 66, and *Amthāl al-ʿArab: Arabum proverbia*, ed. and trans. Georg Wilhelm Friedrich Freytag, 3 vols. (Bonn, 1838–43), 3.1:514, no. 3088.

63. See Engels's introduction to William of Tripoli, *Notitia de Machometo*, 26–32. Engels doubts that William was to accompany the Polos. Also B. Z. Kedar, "Marco Polo in Frankish Acre and Mamluk Jerusalem, 1271" (in press)

64. Report edited in William of Tripoli, *Notitia de Machometo*, 191–261.

65. Errors: see Engels's introduction and notes to William of Tripoli, *Notitia de Machometo*, 55, 87–89, 382 n. 44, 384 n. 54, 385 n. 61, 387 n. 74, and passim. The assumption that William lacked command of the written language is based on his translation of the Qur'anic سورة (*sūrah*, chapter) by *ymago* and *forma*, which indicates that he mixed up سورة (*sūrah*, chapter) with صورة (*ṣūrah*, form, shape), a mix-up possible when one hears the two words but not when one reads them, since the letters *sīn* and *ṣād* differ markedly. Engels supposes (88) that the relatively exact translations from the Qur'an in chaps. 7 and 10 were prepared by somebody else. Wooden Latin style: Engels's introduction to *Notitia de Machometo*, 59.

66. Engels (*Notitia de Machometo*, 79–80) draws attention to a similarity to a detail in the story of Muḥammad and Baḥīrā as told in a Latin account that, according to Bischoff, originated in the Frankish East before the mid-twelfth century: see Bernhard Bischoff, "Ein Leben Mohammeds (Adelphus?) (Zwölftes Jahrhundert)," in Bischoff, *Anecdota Novissima: Texte des vierten bis sechzehnten*

Jahrhunderts (Stuttgart, 1984), 106–22. For a discussion of this account, see Yolles, *Making the East Latin*, 156–59.

67. William of Tripoli, *Notitia de Machometo*, 222.

68. William of Tripoli, *Notitia de Machometo*, 260 (on the end of Islam).

69. Engels's introduction to *Notitia de Machometo*, 100–103. For a discussion of the *Notitia* in a broader framework, see Rubin, *Learning in a Crusader City*, 115–28, 133–37.

70. On the possible connection between the Flagellant pilgrimages and the Mongol advances in eastern Europe and Syria, see Gary Dickson, "The Flagellants of 1260 and the Crusades," *Journal of Medieval History* 15 (1989): 248–51 (but Dickson was unaware of the Flagellants in Acre).

71. Al-Makīn ibn al-ʿAmīd, *Chronique des Ayyoubides (602–658/1205–6–1259–60)*, trans. Anne-Marie Eddé and Françoise Micheau, DRHC 16 (Paris, 1994), 114.

72. B. Z. Kedar, *Merchants in Crisis: Genoese and Venetian Men of Affairs and the Fourteenth-Century Depression* (New Haven, CT, 1976), 114.

73. "Ordinationes seu Institutiones domini Odonis Tusculani episcopi, apostolicae sedis legati in regno Cypri, anno MCCXLVIII," c. 2, in *The Synodicum Nicosiense*, 162–63.

74. *Les registres d'Innocent IV*, 1:89, no. 509. For earlier evidence, see Brundage, "Latin Jurists in the Levant," 29.

75. "Petro canonico Acconensi nato nobilis viri Roggerii de Savignone. . . . Hinc est quod nos tuis supplicationibus inclinati ut fructus prebende tue quam in Acconensi ecclesia obtines, in scolis cum ea integritate percipere valeas—distributionibus cotidianis dumtaxat exceptis—qua illos perciperes si ipsa ecclesia personaliter resideres." Archivio Segreto Vaticano, Reg. Vat. 23, fol. 177r–v, no. 230. Summary in *Les registres d'Innocent IV*, 3:515, no. 8059.

76. *Chartularium studii Bononiensis: Documenti per la storia dell'Università di Bologna dalle origini fino al secolo XV*, 13 vols. (Quaracchi, 1907–40), 10:23, nos. 45–46; 11:12, no. 23. *Dominus Petrus de Canis Achonensis, filius domini Petri*, also presented as *scolaris Bononie* (11:46, no. 110), may be the same person if *de Canis* is a misreading of *decanus*.

77. *Chartularium studii Bononiensis*, 8:92–93, no. 180. In 1266 at Bologna, Simon bought a glossed copy of Gratian's *Decretum* for a sizable sum: Brundage, "Latin Jurists in the Levant," 29.

78. *Chartularium studii Bononiensis*, 8:211, no. 428.

79. *Chartularium studii Bononiensis*, 8:137, no. 275.

80. "Die Statuten der Juristen-Universität Padua vom Jahre 1331," ed. Heinrich Denifle, *Archiv für Literatur- und Kirchengeschichte des Mittelalters* 6 (1892): 399 (Liber 1, §13).

81. See Pearl Kibre, *The Nations in the Medieval Universities* (Cambridge, MA, 1948), 117 with n. 7.

82. "Rogant diffinitores magistrum ordinis, quod studentes provinciarum Grecie et Terre Sancte missos ad studia generalia, aliis provinciis non assignet, quousque per aliquot annos in eisdem provinciis exercuerint officium lectorie." *Acta capitulorum generalium Ordinis Praedicatorum*, 1:245.

83. Prologue edited and translated in Steven J. Williams, *The Secret of Secrets: The Scholarly Career of a Pseudo-Aristotelian Text in the Latin Middle Ages* (Ann Arbor, 2003), 359–65.

84. This biographical sketch is based on the widely dispersed documentation assembled by Agostino Paravicini-Bagliani, "La scienza araba nella Roma del Duecento: Prospettive di ricerca," in *La diffusione delle scienze islamiche nel medio evo europeo* (Rome, 1987), 130–38, and, independently of him, by Wolfgang Antweiler, *Das Bistum Tripolis im 12. und 13. Jahrhundert: Personengeschichtliche und strukturelle Probleme* (Düsseldorf, 1991), 279–92. For an attempt to reconstruct Filippo's career in detail, see Williams, *The Secret of Secrets*, 68–90.

85. Philip of Tripoli, *Secretum Secretorum*, 40–41; translation of the Arabic original, 178–79. For the date of the translation, see Williams, *The Secret of Secrets*, 108–9.

86. Text edited by Hermann Suchier, *Denkmäler provenzalischer Literatur und Sprache*, vol. 1 (Halle, 1883), 473–80. For a discussion of Johannes's authorship of the translation, see Williams, *The Secret of Secrets*, 30–59; for an edition and translation of Johannes's prologue, see 353–58.

87. Pointed out by Steele in his introduction to Philip of Tripoli, *Secretum Secretorum*, xxi.

88. See Mahmoud A. Manzalaoui, "Philip of Tripoli and His Textual Methods," in *Pseudo-Aristotle, The Secret of Secrets: Sources and Influences*, ed. William F. Ryan and Charles B. Schmitt (London, 1982), 57–63. On Filippo's misrepresentation of Islamic political theory, see Mario Grignaschi, "La diffusion du 'Secretum Secretorum' (Sirr al-asrār) dans l'Europe occidentale," *Archives d'histoire doctrinale et littéraire du Moyen Age* 47 (1980): 27–45.

89. Philip of Tripoli, *Secretum Secretorum*, 66; translation of the Arabic original, 194.

90. See chap. 2 above. Remarkably, Filippo follows the Arabic original in advising a man who suffers pain in the stomach or abdomen that "tunc necessaria tibi est amplecti puellam calidam et speciosam": Philip of Tripoli, *Secretum Secretorum*, 73; translation of the Arabic original, 198. Perhaps the Davidic precedent (1 Kings 1:1–4) allowed him to include this advice. Steele—a member of the Fabian Society—recaps it as a recommendation of "animal heat."

91. For instance, where Johannes elegantly translates the statement "Man becomes old and his body grows weak from two causes" with "Nam duobus modis inveteratur homo ac deficit," Filippo offers the cumbersome "Sciendum est in hoc loco quod destruccio et corrupcio corporis provenit ex duabus causis." See the English translation of the Arabic original in Philip of Tripoli, *Secretum Secretorum*, 204; Latin translation by Johannes Hispalensis: Suchier, *Denkmäler*, 479 line 145, and quoted by Filippo in *Secretum Secretorum*, 81 lines 24–25; Latin translation by Filippo of Tripoli: *Secretum Secretorum*, 89 lines 4–5.

92. For the date, see Williams, *The Secret of Secrets*, 180–81.

93. Bacon on skeptics: Philip of Tripoli, *Secretum Secretorum*, 93 n. 3; see also 39, n. 4. Oresme and Ibn Khaldūn: Jacques Monfrin, "La place du *Secret des Secrets* dans la littérature française médiévale," in Ryan and Schmitt, *Pseudo-Aristotle, The Secret of Secrets*, 99; Mario Grignaschi, "L'origine et les

métamorphoses du 'Sir al-asrār,'" *Archives d'histoire doctrinale et littéraire du Moyen Age* 43 (1976): 61–62.

94. Manzalaoui, "Philip of Tripoli," 62. Similarly, Grignaschi ("L'origine," 10) characterizes the Arabic original as addressing the "demi-savants." On the scholarly reception of Filippo's translation and its limits, see Williams, *The Secret of Secrets*, 190–350.

95. My counts, based on appendices 3.2 and 3.3 in Williams, *The Secret of Secrets*, 388–413.

96. However, Manzalaoui's conjecture ("Philip of Tripoli," 67) that the saying "Custom is second nature" entered general usage via Filippo's translation (Philip of Tripoli, *Secretum Secretorum*, 75) is unlikely: see Steven Shapin, "Why Was 'Custom a Second Nature' in Early Modern Medicine?," *Bulletin of the History of Medicine* 93 (2019): 1–26.

97. For a discussion of this genre in medieval times, see William Eamon, *Science and the Secrets of Nature: Books of Secrets in Medieval and Early Modern Culture* (Princeton, NJ, 1994), 39–90.

98. See *Le Livre au Roi*, introduction, 117–19. Possibly the "assises dou roi Amauri et dou roi Bauduin son fis" (see chap. 7, note 1, above), which antedate the *Livre* by two or three decades, were composed in the vernacular. Recently, it has been contended that the *Livre* dates from the years 1285–1306: Louis-Marie Audrerie, *Le droit hiérosolymitain dans l'Orient latin du XI*[e] *au XVI*[e] *siècle: Les "Assises de Jérusalem"* (Paris, 2023), 209–22. But the argument is not cogent; for instance, it ignores the mention of Nablus in the *Livre au Roi*, 239, c. 36.

99. Rudolf Hiestand, "La langue vulgaire dans les chartes de Terre Sainte avec un regard sur la chancellerie royale française," in *Von Outremer bis Flandern: Miscellanea zur Gallia Pontificia und zur Diplomatik*, ed. Klaus Herbers and Waldemar Könighaus (Berlin, 2013), 269–304. See also Laura K. Morreale, "French-Language Documents Produced by the Hospitallers, 1231–1310," *Journal of Medieval History* 40 (2014): 439–57; she points out (443 with n. 16) that the earliest evidence for the use of Old French in official documents of the Teutonic Knights, Templars, and Hospitallers dates from 1228, 1229, and 1231, respectively. On the mid-thirteenth-century transition to the vernacular in Frankish epigraphy, see Estelle Ingrand-Varenne, "French Inscriptions in the Latin Kingdom of Jerusalem: From the Written Word to the Museum," *'Atiqot* 110 (2023), 241–62.

100. Donnadieu's introduction to JdV, 7–8.

101. Jacoby, "La littérature française," 644; Jacoby, "Knightly Values," 175.

102. Filippo da Novara, *Guerra di Federico II*. For the argument that the *Estoires d'Outremer et de la naissance Salehadin*, which exhibits a pro-Ibelin bias, is of Oriental provenance, with its compiler "exposed to sources that circulated only in the Holy Land," see Shachar, *A Pious Belligerence*, 71–77.

103. Minervini's introduction to the *Cronaca del Templare di Tiro*, 1.

104. See Peter Edbury, "The Colbert-Fontainebleau Continuation of William of Tyre, 1184–1247: Structure and Composition," in *Chronicle, Crusade, and the Latin East: Essays in Honour of Susan B. Edgington*, ed. Andrew D. Buck and Thomas W. Smith (Turnhout, 2022), 203–22; Edbury emphasizes inter alia the author's endeavor to free Balian of Ibelin and Renaud of Sidon from blame.

And see most recently Edbury and Gaggero, *The Chronique d'Ernoul*, 2:29–35. Also Guy Perry, *John of Brienne, King of Jerusalem, Emperor of Constantinople, c.1175–1237* (Cambridge, 2013), 14–15.

105. Written by a cleric: Edbury, "The Lyon *Eracles*," 148. Knightly disdain for burgesses: WT Cont. Lyon, 104–5, para. 103; noted by Jacoby, "Knightly Values," 175–76.

106. Clerical authorship: Edbury, "Making Sense." Knightly outlook: For the original Latin entries, preserved in a Barletta manuscript, see above, chap. 4, note 1.

107. In Filippo da Novara, *Guerra di Federico II*, 110–11, c. 46, Phelippe spells out the adversaries' real names and their Renartesque equivalents. For discussion, see Jacoby, "La littérature française," 625–26. For the view that the poems Phelippe inserted into the chronicle were essentially parodic, see Cyrille [Cyril] Aslanoff [Aslanov], "Récit historique et discours poétique dans l'*Estoire de la guerre des Ibelins contre les Impériaux* de Philippe de Novare," *Le Moyen Age* 103 (1997): 67–81.

108. Philippe of Novara, *Mémoires (1218–1243)*, 7, §VI (112).

109. *Cronaca del Templare di Tiro*, 170–71, c. 203. For discussion, see Jacoby, "La littérature française," 630–33; Jacoby, "Knightly Values," 166–68, 177. While Minervini translates *bendoient* as "si bendavano," Jacoby, presenting the scene as a satire on the clergy's sexual mores, proposes the translation "se seraient liés" (633) or "embraced [?]" (167). On Montmusard's *Herberge* or *Auberge*, see Pringle, *Churches*, 4:115–16.

110. Philip of Novara, *Le Livre de Forme de Plait*, 122, c. 48 (text), 261 (translation). Jacoby, "La littérature française," 617.

111. *Cart Hosp*, 3:52, no. 3039, cc. 39, 42.

112. On the now untraceable non-Islamic works that made their way from Damascus to Berlin, where they were photographed before being sent back to Damascus, see Hermann von Soden, "Ein Weihnachtsgeschenk des Sultans an die deutsche Wissenschaft," *Die Christliche Welt: Evangelisches Gemeindeblatt für Gebildete aller Stände* 15 (1901): 1247–49; von Soden, "Bericht über die in der Kubbet in Damaskus gefundenen Handschriftenfragmente," *Sitzungsberichte der Königlich Preussischen Akademie der Wissenschaften, Philosophisch-historische Classe* 43 (1903): 825–30. Three Old French fragments were edited by Adolf Tobler, "Bruchstücke altfranzösischer Dichtung aus den in der Kubbet in Damaskus gefundenen Handschriften," *Sitzungsberichte der Königlich Preussischen Akademie der Wissenschaften, Philosophisch-historische Classe* 43 (1903): 960–76. These fragments are discussed in detail by Giannini and Minervini, who also offer the first edition of the fragments of the *Enfances Godefroi* that never left Damascus but were photographed there by Bruno Violet in 1900: Gabriele Giannini and Laura Minervini, "The Old French Texts of the Damascus Qubba," in *The Damascus Fragments: Towards a History of the Qubbbat al-khazna Corpus of Manuscripts*, ed. Arianna D'Ottone Rambach, Konrad Hirschler, and Ronny Vollandt (Beirut, 2020), 331–64; Gabriele Giannini and Laura Minervini, "Retour à Damas: Des charmes et une épave des *Enfances Godefroi*," *Romania* 138 (2020): 276–304. In an earlier discussion of literary activities in Outremer, Minervini subscribed to the view that the fragments were part of war booty: Laura Minervini, "Outremer,"

in *Lo spazio letterario del Medioevo*, 2: *Il Medioevo volgare*, vol. 1.2: *La produzione del testo*, ed. Piero Boitani, Mario Mancini, and Alberto Vàrvaro (Rome, 2001), 619. In the above articles, however, more peaceful scenarios are highlighted. On the Latin fragments that made their way into the Qubbbat al-khazna, see Yolles, *Making the East Latin*, 40–42.

113. Hiram Peri, "Episodes inédits du Roman de Tristan (manuscrit de Jérusalem) avec deux nouveaux 'lais de Tristan,'" *Scripta hierosolymitana* 2 (1955): 1-24; Jacoby, "La littérature française," 628–29.

114. Martial-Alphonse Chazaud, "Inventaire et comptes de la succession d'Eudes, comte de Nevers (Acre 1266)," *Mémoires de la Société nationale des antiquaires de France* 32 (1871): 188. The editor claims (166), without giving his reasons, that the *Chançoners* "undoubtedly" contained the works of Thibaud, king of Navarra. For an attempt to reconstruct the library of a Frankish noble of that time, see Aryeh Graboïs, "La bibliothèque du noble d'*Outremer* à Acre dans la seconde moitié du XIII[e] siècle," *Le Moyen Age* 103 (1997): 53–66.

115. "Por c et lv gelines vendues, xxxi[b]." Chazaud, "Inventaire," 202. On Eudes's books, see Jacoby, "La littérature française," 620–23; Jacoby, "Knightly Values," 165.

116. *La Règle du Temple*, 75-350, §§77–686. "Ir' e dolors s'es dins mon cor asseza," ed. Giulio Bertoni, in "Il serventese di Ricaut Bonomel (1265)," *Zeitschrift für romanische Philologie* 34 (1910): 701–7. Translation: Linda Paterson, http://www.rialto.unina.it/Templ/439.1(Paterson).htm. See also the poem of 1250 that urges King Louis IX to stay in the East and claims that "Dieus a pou d'amis": "La chanson composée à Acre en juin 1250," ed. G[aston] P[aris], *Romania* 22 (1893): 541–47.

117. "La prière des malades dans les hôpitaux de l'Ordre de Saint-Jean de Jérusalem," ed. Léon Le Grand, *Bibliothèque de l'École des chartes* 57 (1896): 325–38; Keith V. Sinclair, "The French Prayer for the Sick in the Hospital of the Knights of Saint John of Jerusalem at Acre," *Mediaeval Studies* 40 (1978): 484–88.

118. *La Rectorique de Cyceron*. The treatise that *maistre* Johan translated consists of Cicero's *De Inventione* and the *Rhetorica ad Herennium* of unknown authorship.

119. Mistakes: L[éopold] D[elisle], "Maître Jean d'Antioche, traducteur, et frère Guillaume de Saint-Étienne, Hospitalier," in *Histoire littéraire de la France*, vol. 33 (Paris, 1906), 13–17; Guadagnini's introduction to *La Rectorique de Cyceron*, 13–25. Remarkable insinuation: Rubin, *Learning in a Crusader City*, 72–80.

120. Anthony Luttrell, "The Hospitallers' Early Written Records," in *Crusade Sources*, 135–54; Klement, *Gottes Gastgeber*, 138–40, who argues convincingly that Johan translated the records for William of St. Estiene. For a reappraisal of William's activities, see Klement, *Gottes Gastgeber*, 130–37.

121. William of Saint Estiene, "Comment la sainte maison de l'Hospital de S. Johan de Jerusalem commença," in *RHC Oc*, 5:422–27; see Riley-Smith, *The Knights Hospitallers in the Levant*, 16–17.

122. Lewis Thorpe, "Mastre Richard, a Thirteenth-Century Translator of the 'De re militari' of Vegetius," *Scriptorium* 6 (1952): 39–50; Thorpe, "Mastre Richard at the Skirmish of Kenilworth?," *Scriptorium* 7 (1953): 120–21; M. Dominica

Legge, "The Lord Edward's Vegetius," *Scriptorium* 7 (1953): 262–65; Rubin, *Learning in a Crusader City*, 71–72.

123. "me sire Willame li Pulains, chevalier and mestre Jaques Sarasin le ypoticaires, noveau crestien." See "Il glossario arabo-francese di Messer Guglielmo e Maestro Giacomo," ed. Gustav Ineichen, *Atti dell'Istituto Veneto di Scienze, Lettere ed Arti: Classe di scienze morali, lettere ed arti* 130 (1971–72): 363 and tavola I.

124. See Nobel's introduction to *La Bible d'Acre: Genèse et Exode*, esp. xiv–xv, xxxi–xxxvi, lxxi–lxxviii. On the possibility that the translation was made for a member of a military order who did not know Latin, see Pierre Nobel, "Les translations bibliques et leur public: L'exemple de la *Bible d'Acre* et de la *Bible Anglo-normande*," *Revue de linguistique romane* 66 (2002): 454.

125. Adam "was formed in *Ebron* [Hebron] near *Naples*"; Abraham's father Terah died in *Aram* (Ḥaran, probably Ḥarrān, southeast Turkey) "in the land of *Naples*"; Jacob meets shepherds from *Aram*, "which is close to *Naples*"; Sichem "is the region of *Naples*"; "Canaan is the region of *Surie* with *Naples* and the land around it"; "Sychem is *Naples*." *La Bible d'Acre: Genèse et Exode*, 9, 14, 32, 36, 37, 38. The land of the Chaldeans is "Haman [Ḥamāh] et Maubec [Baalbek] et La Chamelle [Ḥomṣ]": *La Bible d'Acre: Genèse et Exode*, 17; cf. WT OF 21.5 (2:370).

126. *La Bible d'Acre: Genèse et Exode*, 18.

127. Isidore of Seville, *Etymologiarum sive originum libri XX*, ed. Wallace M. Lindsay (Oxford, 1911), 9.2.6, 57.

128. Riley-Smith, *The Feudal Nobility*, 121–44, quotation on 128.

129. John of Ibelin, *Le Livre des Assises*; the tract on the *bailliage* is edited on 804–8. On Johan and his oeuvre, see Edbury, *John of Ibelin*.

130. This is the cogent argument of Myriam Greilsammer, "Anatomie d'un mensonge: Le *Livre au Roi* et la révision de l'histoire du Royaume Latin par les juristes du XIIIe siècle," *Tijdschrift voor rechtsgeschiedenis / Revue d'histoire du droit* 67 (1999): 239–54.

131. See *UKJ*, 1:246, 263, nos. 93, 105.

132. "Livre de Geoffroy Le Tort," in *RHC Lois*, 1:433–50. See Peter W. Edbury, "The 'Livre' of Geoffrey Le Tor and the 'Assises' of Jerusalem," in *Historia administrativa y ciencia de la administración comparada: Trabajos en homaje a Ferran Valls i Taberner*, ed. Manuel J. Peláez, vol. 15 (Barcelona, 1990), 4291–98; Audrerie, *Le droit hiérosolymitain*, 184–86.

133. "Livre de Jacques d'Ibelin," in *RHC Lois*, 1:451–68; see Gilles Grivaud, "Literature," in *Cyprus: Society and Culture, 1191–1374*, ed. Angel Nicolaou-Konnari and Chris Schabel (Leiden, 2005), 252; Audrerie, *Le droit hiérosolymitain*, 186–88.

134. See the discussion by Rubin, *Learning in a Crusader City*, esp. 87–91, 96–97.

135. "et hec eadem constitutio obtinet ultra mare." *Historia diplomatica Friderici Secundi*, 5.1:252–53; cf. Hans Niese, *Die Gesetzgebung der normannischen Dynastie im Regnum Siciliae* (Halle a. S., 1910), 121–25.

136. "nule borgesies . . . ne peut estre doné a yglise ne a relegion, par dreit." *Livre au Roi*, 265, c. 43. The stipulation had little impact on reality: see Prawer, *Crusader Institutions*, 321–26; Nader, *Burgesses*, 116–26.

137. Phelippe of Novara, *Les quatre âges de l'homme: Traité moral de Philippe de Navarre*, ed. Marcel de Freville (Paris, 1888), 122, c. 233. Translation in Edbury's introduction to Philip of Novara, *Le Livre de Forme de Plait*, 14 (my translation differs slightly on some points). The original title is: *Des .iiii. tenz d'aage d'ome.*

138. I follow here the appraisal of Edbury in his introduction to Philip of Novara, *Le Livre de Forme de Plait*, 14.

139. On this argument, see chap. 7 above.

140. Phelippe of Novara, *Les quatre âges de l'homme*, 81–83, cc. 147–149, quotation on 82.

141. WT OF 19.3 (2:255–57). In both texts, God is *droituriers*, and while the adapter writes: "donques sera-il uns autres siecles où cil qui bien auront fet recevront bon loier, et li autre comparront leur mals oevres de cestui siecle," Phelippe has: "donc i a il autre siecle en quoi il fornist droiture et as bons et as maus, de ce dont ele n'est fornie en cest siecle."

142. Charles Burnett, "Master Theodore, Frederick II's Philosopher," in *Federico II e le nuove culture: Atti del XXXI Convegno storico internazionale, Todi, 9–12 ottobre 1994* (Spoleto, 1995), 252–53.

143. Decipherment: Moshe Sharon and Ami Schraeger, "Frederick II's Arabic Inscription from Jaffa (1229)," *Crusades* 11 (2012): 153.

144. Decipherment and translation: Sharon and Schraeger, "Frederick II's Arabic Inscription," 144–45.

145. Geoffroy of Beaulieu, "Vita Ludovici noni," in *RHGF*, 20:15, c. 23. The great sultan about whom Louis heard may have been Nūr al-Dīn, who established in Damascus the Dār al-ḥadīth al-Nūriyya: Youssef Eche, *Les bibliothèques arabes publiques et semi-publiques en Mésopotamie, en Syrie et en Égypte au Moyen Age* (Damascus, 1967), 211–14; Hillenbrand, *The Crusades*, 127. On Arnold of Lübeck, see above, chap. 2.

146. See above, chap. 9.

147. See esp. Prawer, *Crusader Institutions*, 54–67.

148. Filippo da Novara, *Guerra di Federico II*, 222–23, c. 125.

149. Philip of Novara, *Le Livre de Forme de Plait*, 107 (text), 252 (translation), c. 38. In the 1230s, Raymond appears as *jurat* of Acre's *Cour des bourgeois*: Philip of Novara, *Le Livre de Forme de Plait*, 334.

150. Filippo da Novara, *Guerra di Federico II*, 230–31, c. 129.

151. Philip of Novara, *Le Livre de Forme de Plait*, 122 (text), 261 (translation), c. 48; see also 332–33.

152. Raoul of Tiberias, Phelippe of Novara, Johan of Ibelin, Jofrey le Tor, Jacques of Ibelin (see above); Johan of Beirut, Balian of Sidon, Guillaume Vesconte, Harneis of Giblet, Guillaume of Rivet the Younger: Philip of Novara, *Le Livre de Forme de Plait*, 122 (text), 261 (translation), c. 48; Stephanus de Savegni and Jacobus Vitalis: Rubin, *Learning in a Crusader City*, 29, n. 29.

153. "Assises des Bourgeois," 2:1–226.

154. Prawer, *Crusader Institutions*, 372.

155. Maurice Grandclaude, *Etude critique sur les livres des Assises de Jérusalem* (Paris, 1923), 70; Prawer, *Crusader Institutions*, 366; Jacoby, "The *fonde* of Crusader Acre," 278 n. 5; Riley-Smith, *The Feudal Nobility*, 85, 87, 268 n. 186; Nader, *Burgesses*, 49–53.

156. Adam M. Bishop, "*Les Assises de la Cour des Bourgeois* de Jérusalem: La question de leurs sources," in *Autour des Assises de Jérusalem*, ed. Jerôme Devard and Bernard Ribemont (Paris, 2018), 113–25.

157. Charles Giraud, "Du droit français dans l'Orient au moyen âge et de la traduction en grecque des Assises de Jérusalem," *Revue de législation et de jurisprudence* 17 (1843): 30.

158. Joshua Prawer, "Étude préliminaire sur les sources et la composition du Livre des Assises des Bourgeois," *Revue historique de droit français et étranger* 31 (1954): 198–227, 358–82; Prawer, *Crusader Institutions*, 358–411; but see the reservations of Nader, *Burgesses*, 56–57; Bishop, "*Les Assises*," 118–19, 124.

159. Adam M. Bishop, "Adaptations of the Roman *Lex Aquilia* in the Burgess Assizes of Jerusalem," in *Crusading in Art, Thought and Will*, ed. Matthew E. Parker, Ben Halliburton, and Anne Romine (Leiden, 2019), 110–25. The study concludes with the assertion that "at least a few chapters [of the *Livre*] were written by one jurist who was trained in Roman and canon law in Europe" (123–24). This appraisal should be compared to those of Prutz, *Kulturgeschichte*, 344–51; Grandclaude, *Etude critique*, 123–25; and Prawer, *Crusader Institutions*, 366–68.

160. Private law treatise: Prawer, *Crusader Institutions*, 359, 377. Public law book: Nader, *Burgesses*, 49, 54; Bishop, "*Les Assises*," 125. Similarly, Mayer writes: "Um 1240 gab sich die Bourgeoisie in Jerusalem ihr eigenes Recht mit dem *Livre des Assises des Bourgeois*": Mayer, *Geschichte*, 212 (he refers to the kingdom, not the city).

161. See the example quoted by Rubin, *Learning in a Crusader City*, 92.

162. David Jacoby, "A Venetian Manual of Commercial Practice from Crusader Acre," in *I comuni italiani*, 403–28. Jacoby planned to edit the manual; the edition remains a desideratum. The portolan fragment was edited by Patrick Gautier Dalché, *Carte marine et portulan au XII*[e] *siècle: Le Liber de existencia riveriarum et forma maris nostri mediterranei* (Rome, 1995), app. I.

163. Brundage, "Latin Jurists in the Levant," 21–27 and table 3, to which should be added, under the year 1286, Petrus de Brundusio, *legum professor* in Tripoli: *RRH*, no. 1462.

164. For Sens, see chap. 5, note 150 above.

165. Folda, *Crusader Art in the Holy Land*, 178b–182b, 280b. See also Zehava Jacoby, "The Impact of Northern French Gothic on Crusader Sculpture in the Holy Land," in *Il Medio Oriente e l'Occidente nell'arte del XIII secolo*, ed. Hans Belting (Bologna, 1982), 123–27. On the "deep knowledge and awareness of French and German Gothic sculpture" by the artisans responsible for the architectural sculpture at Montfort, see Nurith Kenaan-Kedar, "The Architectural Sculpture of Montfort Castle Revisited," in *Montfort: History, Early Research and Recent Studies of the Principal Fortress of the Teutonic Order in the Latin East*, ed. Adrian J. Boas with Rabei G. Khamisy (Leiden, 2017), 273–81.

166. Jean Mesqui, *Césarée maritime: Ville fortifiée du Proche-Orient* (Paris, 2014), 158. On the capitals and consoles, see Kenaan-Kedar, "The Role and Meaning," 169–70 and figs. 9–17; Kenaan-Kedar, "Les chapiteaux des portes de l'enceinte de Césarée (1251–1252): De la tradition romane à l'art gothique," *Bulletin Monumental* 164 (2006): 95–98. On Louis IX's works in the city, see Mesqui, *Césarée maritime*, 110–11, 154–330. For further counterparts of the Caesarea capitals

in antecedent royal buildings in the Ile-de-France, see Vardit Shotten-Hallel, Jean Mesqui, and Uzi ʿAd, "Three Main Towers of Medieval Caesarea: Their Architecture and Function," in *The Art of Siege Warfare and Military Architecture from the Classical Age to the Middle Ages*, ed. Michael Eisenberg and Rabei Khamisy (Oxford, 2021), 202–4, 209.

167. St.-André: Pringle, *Churches*, 3:65. Doorway installed in Cairo: Pringle, *Churches*, 3:65–66, plates xx–xxi. Al-Maqrīzī: text translated in Keppel A. C. Creswell, *The Muslim Architecture of Egypt*, vol. 2: *Ayyūbids and Early Baḥrite Mamluks* (Oxford, 1959), 234.

168. Jacoby, "Society, Culture and the Arts," 117–18. See also his critique (115–16) of the ascription of several illuminated manuscripts to Acre, a critique developed by Jens T. Wollesen, *Acre or Cyprus? A New Approach to Crusader Painting around 1300* (Berlin, 2013); but see the view of Edbury and Gaggero, *The Chronique d'Ernoul*, 2:71–72.

169. For data on married Parisian illuminators, see Richard H. Rouse and Mary A. Rouse, *Manuscripts and Their Makers: Commercial Book Producers in Medieval Paris, 1200–1500*, 2 vols. (Turnhout, 2000), 1:32–34, 46–47, 127–40; 2:37–38, 54, 92–93, 125–27.

170. Folda, *Crusader Art in the Holy Land*, 283b–336a, 345a–350a, 436a–441b, quotation on 294b.

171. Folda, *Crusader Art in the Holy Land*, 404a.

172. Folda, *Crusader Art in the Holy Land*, 396b–397a, 411b–435b, 495b–502b, 512b, 519a–520a.

173. On this ratio, see Folda, *Crusader Art in the Holy Land*, 434b.

174. For details, see B. Z. Kedar, "Benvenutus Grapheus of Jerusalem, an Oculist in the Era of the Crusades," *Korot: The Israel Journal of the History of Medicine and Science* 11 (1995): 14–41; Laurence M. Eldredge, "A Thirteenth-Century Ophthalmologist, Benvenutus Grassus: His Treatise and Survival," *Journal of the Royal Society of Medicine* 91 (1998): 47–52. On the manuscripts, see Eldredge, "The Latin Manuscripts of Benvenutus Grassus' Treatise on Diseases and Injuries to the Eye," in *Benvenutus Grassus on the Well-Proven Art of the Eye: Practica oculorum & De probatissima arte oculorum. Synoptic Edition and Philological Studies*, ed. Antonio Miranda-García and Santiago González Fernández-Corugedo (Bern, 2011), 19–33. This volume presents (167–505) a synoptic edition of the Latin text, the Provençal translation, and four Middle English versions. On Benvenutus's impact on the leading surgeons Jehan Yperman (ca. 1260–ca. 1330) and Guy of Chauliac (ca. 1300–1368), see B. Z. Kedar, "Benvenuto Grapheo da Gerusalemme e la sua *Ars probatissima oculorum*," in *Le vie del Mediterraneo*, ed. Gabriella Airaldi (Genoa, 1997), 14. The only crusade historian aware of Benvenutus was Cahen, who mentioned "un certain Bienvenu de Jérusalem": *Orient et Occident*, 282 n. 32.

175. For the dating on the basis of the three Western medical treatises, see Jonathan Rubin and Cornelia Linde, "Western Medicine for the Masters of Damascus: Benvenutus Grapheus's *Experimenta*," *Al-Masāq* 26 (2014): 183–95.

176. Gilbertus Anglicus, *Compendium medicine* (Lyon, 1510), 137a. The names Hue and Bertram recur in the Genoese Embriaco family that ruled

Gibeleth: See *Lignages d'Outremer*, 114–16. On Gilbertus, see John Pearn, "Two Medieval Doctors: Gilbertus Anglicus (c. 1180–c. 1250) and John of Gaddesden (1280–1361)," *Journal of Medical Biography* 21 (2013): 3–4.

177. "frater episcopi Veronensis." Benvenutus, *Practica oculorum*, BAV, Vat. lat. 5373 (a. 1475), fol. 179v. The presence of a Saracen physician in thirteenth-century Verona is quite surprising. Possibly the scribe chose the familiar *Veronensis* instead of the *Valeniensis* or *Valaniensis* of the text he was copying, which would refer to Valenia (Bāniyās, north of Tortosa), a bishop's seat.

178. "Assises des Bourgeois," cc. 65, 241 (2:55–56, 171–72).

179. See, in general, Prawer, *The History of the Jews*, 149–68, 263–91; on apocalyptic expectations, see Israel Jacob Yuval, "Das Jahr 1240: Das Ende eines jüdischen Milleniums," in *Kulturtransfer und Hofgesellschaft im Mittelalter*, ed. Gundula Grebner and Johannes Fried (Berlin, 2008), 20–24; Shachar, *A Pious Belligerence*, 97–151, 186–89.

180. On R. Shimshon of Sens, see Henri Gross, "Etude sur Simson ben Abraham de Sens," *Revue des études juives* 7 (1883): 46–48.

181. For details, see Rubin, *Learning in a Crusader City*, 41–44, 57–61. R. Yitzḥaq of Acre was to become a leading Kabbalist and author of a lost chronicle that also dealt with the Mamluk conquest of Acre in 1291. For the edition of the chronicle's vestiges that deal with the conquest, see B. Z. Kedar, "Jews and Samaritans in the Crusading Kingdom of Jerusalem," *Tarbiz* 53 (1983/84): 405–6 [in Hebrew].

182. See Simcha Emanuel, "Halakhic Questions of Thirteenth-Century Acre Scholars as a Historical Source," *Crusades* 17 (2018): 115–30.

183. Prawer, *The History of the Jews*, 273.

184. For a reconstruction of the Acre confrontation, see Prawer, *The History of the Jews*, 282–90.

185. William of Tripoli, *Notitia de Machometo*, 242, and Engels's introduction and commentary, 89, 394; Rubin, *Learning in a Crusader City*, 135–37.

186. "Tear flows, joy drowns, woe sets in, the Sons of Esau are rolled up. How did God's finger [cf. Exodus 8:19] come upon them, and some perished / of hunger and others by drowning, for the River Nile swept them away, their remnant encircled in the desert; and the city of Acre was in confusion [cf. Esther 3:15]. / And they bewailed how the King's rage fell upon them, how he hurled from heaven his wrath, / how his jealousy came down on them [cf. Deuteronomy 29:20], until their spirit and innards were gone. Therefore, this country is mourning, and its inhabitants are weeping." The letter has been edited by Shmuel Glick, *Seride Teshuvot of the Ottoman Empire Sages from the Cairo Genizah* (Ramat Gan, 2016), 2:589–95; passage quoted on 590 (my translation). Later (594) the writer mentions a decision of "our Rabbi Shimshon [of Sens]." See also Emanuel, "Halakhic Questions," 119.

187. ʿEli Yassif, "Sephardic Memories: Legend and History in an Early 16th-Century Collection of Tales," *Sefunot*, n.s. 12, no. 27 (2022): 413–14 [in Hebrew].

188. Yassif, "Sephardic Memories," 408. Yassif assumes that the stories were written in about 1500 (415). The manuscript in which they appear was copied

in the first half of the sixteenth century (375), but the stories could have been composed much earlier: the same manuscript contains epistles by Maimonides and Naḥmanides, etc.

189. Lucien Leclerc, *Histoire de la médecine arabe*, 2 vols. (Paris, 1876), 2:171.

190. On Ibn al-Sūrī, see Ibn Abī Usaybi'a, *A Literary History of Medicine*, 2.2:1330–36 (text), 3.2: 1513–20 (translation); Zohar Amar and Yaron Serri, "Ibn al-Suri, Physician and Botanist of al-Sham," *Palestine Exploration Quarterly* 135 (2003): 124–30. ʿAlī of Tripoli completed in 1219/20 a book titled *The Wise Man's Ornament*, which deals with pharmacology, the Philosophers' Stone, and a method of divination: see Stefano Assemani, *Bibliothecae Medicae Lauerentianae et Palatinae codicum mss. Orientalium catalogus* (Florence, 1742), 362, no. 237; Emmanuel Rey, *Les colonies franques de Syrie aux XII*[me] *et XIII*[me] *siècles* (Paris, 1883), 183.

191. JdV 75 (298); "Lettres de Jacques de Vitry," 2.163–69, 352–54 (564–65, 572).

192. Andrew Jotischky, "The Fortunes of War: An Eleventh-Century Greek Liturgical Manuscript (Sinai gr 512) and Its History," *Crusades* 9 (2010): 173–84; Jotischky in Hamilton and Jotischky, *Latin and Greek Monasticism*, 438, 471–72.

193. Pahlitzsch, *Graeci und Suriani*, 228 n. 550, 350–51, no. 112; Rubin, *Learning in a Crusader City*, 12.

194. Burchard of Mount Sion, *Descriptio Terrae Sanctae*, 6.

195. Hamilton, *The Latin Church*, 347–60; Rubin, *Learning in a Crusader City*, 147–48.

196. "Relation de la conférence tenue entre le docteur Mĕkhithar de Daschir, envoyé du Catholicos Constantin Ier et le légat du pape, à Saint-Jean-d'Acre en 1262," in *RHC Documents arméniens*, 1:691–98. Cf. Hamilton, *The Latin Church*, 343–44; Rubin, *Learning in a Crusader City*, 155–56.

197. "Procès de Nicéphore," in *Dossier grec de l'Union de Lyon (1273–1277)*, ed. and trans. Vitalien Laurent and Jean Darrouzès (Paris, 1976), 82–88, 486–506; Rubin, *Learning in a Crusader City*, 156–60. Rubin has been the first to utilize this source.

198. "Relation," 693, 696; "Procès," 490.

199. For Theodore's career, see Burnett, "Master Theodore"; B. Z. Kedar and Etan Kohlberg, "The Intercultural Career of Theodore of Antioch," *Mediterranean Historical Review* 10 (1995): 164–76.

200. "Epistola Theodori phi[losoph]i ad imperatorem Fridericum," ed. and trans. in Burnett, "Master Theodore," 266–74.

201. For comments on the prologue's Latinity, see Burnett, "Master Theodore," 281.

202. See B. Z. Kedar, *From Genoa to Jerusalem and Beyond: Studies in Medieval and World History* (Padua, 2019), 552–53.

203. "magister meus theod[or]us medicus imperatoris." Petrus Hispanus, *Die Ophthalmologie des Petrus Hispanus*, ed. and trans. Albrecht Maria Berger (Munich, 1899), 4; Kedar and Kohlberg, "The Intercultural Career," 168 n. 15.

204. *Epistulae et chartae ad historiam primi belli sacri spectantes: Die Kreuzzugsbriefe aus den Jahren 1088–1100*, ed. Heinrich Hagenmeyer (Innsbruck, 1901), 164.

Conclusion

1. The subject deserves a comprehensive study. On the Frankish exodus in general, see Marie-Luise Favreau-Lilie, "The Military Orders and the Escape of the Christian Population from the Holy Land in 1291," *Journal of Medieval History* 19 (1993): 201–27.

2. *Paris sous Philippe-le-Bel d'après des documents originaux, et notamment d'après un manuscrit contenant le rôle de la taille imposée sur les habitants de Paris en 1292*, ed. Hercule Géraud (Paris, 1837), 21, 40, 62, 83, 91, 94, 116, 133, 135, 143; *Le rôle de la taille de Paris l'an 1296*, ed. Karl Michaëlson (Göteborg, 1958), 4, 29, 133–34, 172, 194–96, 202, 207, 262; *Le livre de la taille de Paris l'an 1297*, ed. Karl Michaëlson (Göteborg, 1962), 17, 29, 121, 157, 179–81, 188, 191, 249, 287; *Le livre de la taille de Paris l'an de grace 1313*, ed. Karl Michaëlson (Göteborg, 1951), 17, 19, 23, 34, 132, 199, 203, 226.

3. *Venetiarum Historia, vulgo Petro Iustiniano Iustiniani filio adiudicata*, ed. Roberto Cessi and Fanny Bennato (Venice, 1964), 205–6, 272–73. See Marie-Luise Favreau-Lilie, "The Fall of Acre (1291): Considerations of Annalists in Genoa, Pisa, and Venice (13th/14th–16th Centuries)," in *Acre and Its Falls: Studies in the History of a Crusader City*, ed. John France (Leiden, 2018), 176–77.

4. For written sources and a description of remains, see Camille Enlart, *Gothic Art and the Renaissance in Cyprus*, trans. and ed. David Hunt (London, 1987), 157–60.

5. Angel Nicolaou-Konnari, "Women in Medieval Famagusta: Law, Family, and Society," in *Famagusta*, vol. 2: *History and Society*, ed. Gilles Grivaud, Angel Nicolaou-Konnari, and Chris Schabel (Turnhout, 2020), 515.

6. See Anne Gilmour-Bryson, "The Fall of Acre, 1291, and Its Effect on Cyprus," in France, *Acre and Its Falls*, 116–29; Kedar, "On Some Characteristics," 7.

7. Gilles Grivaud, "Les minorités orientales à Chypre (époques médiévale et moderne)," in *Chypre et la Méditerranée orientale: Formations identitaires, perspectives historiques et enjeux contemporains*, ed. Yiannis Ioannou, Françoise Métral, and Marguerite Yon (Lyon, 2000), 43–70; on Jacobite and Nestorian bishops in thirteenth-century Cyprus, 51–52. On the Melkites, see Johannes Pahlitzsch, "The *Suriani* in Lusignan Cyprus until Peter I (1369): Terminology, Legal Status, and the *Curia Surianorum*," in *Crusading, Society, and Politics in the Eastern Mediterranean in the Age of King Peter I of Cyprus*, ed. Alexander D. Beihammer and Angel Nicolaou-Konnari (Turnhout, 2022), 361–82.

8. Julien Loiseau, "Frankish Captives in Mamlūk Cairo," *Al-Masāq* 23 (2011): 52.

9. B. Z. Kedar, "Muslime in den fränkischen Burgen des Königreichs Jerusalem," *Burgen und Schlösser* 52 (2011): 212–17. Regrettably, most archaeologists tend to remove the remains of the Muslim villages without studying them and focus exclusively on the Frankish structures.

10. For a list, see Röhricht, *Bibliotheca geographica Palaestinae*.

11. See Eliyahu Ashtor, *Levant Trade in the Later Middle Ages* (Princeton, NJ, 1983), 24, 43; Kedar, *Merchants in Crisis*, 29; Benjamin Arbel, "Venetian Trade in Fifteenth-Century Acre: The Letters of Francesco Bevilaqua (1471–1472)," *Asian and African Studies* 22 (1988): 227–88.

12. Jacob Burckhardt, *Weltgeschichtliche Betrachtungen* (Leipzig, 1955), 175.

13. Vespasiano da Bisticci, *Renaissance Princes, Popes and Prelates*, trans. William George and Emily Waters (New York, 1963; originally published 1926), 371–72.

14. Pryor, "The *Eracles* and William of Tyre," 273, 293; Hamilton, "The Old French Translation of William of Tyre as an Historical Source," 112, where the adaptation is presented as "a chivalresque epic."

15. The Arabic translation, published in 1959 in Damascus, does use the problematic term but adds an explication: *Crusade in Europe: The Allied Invasion of Europe during the Second World War*.

Selected Bibliography

This bibliography comprises mainly publications focusing on crusading and the Frankish East. It does not include the publications appearing in the list of abbreviations.

Primary Sources

"Abrégé du Livre des Assises de la Cour des Bourgeois." In *RHC Lois*, 2:227–352. Paris, 1843.

Acardus of Arrouaise. In *Corona Quernea: Festgabe Karl Strecker*, MGH Schriften 6, 307–30. Leipzig, 1941.

"Administrative Regulations for the Hospital of St John in Jerusalem Dating from the 1180s." Edited by Susan B. Edgington. *Crusades* 4 (2005): 21–37.

Ambroise. *L'Estoire de la Guerre Sainte: Histoire en vers de la Troisième Croisade (1190–1192)*. Edited by Gaston Paris. Paris, 1897.

Anna Comnena. *Alexias*. Edited by Diether R. Reinsch and Athanasios Kambylis. Corpus Fontium Historiae Byzantinae 40. Berlin, 2001.

Anseau. "Letters." In *Cartulaire général de Paris*, vol. 1: *528–1180*, ed. Robert de Lasteyre, 171–73, docs. 151–52. Paris, 1887.

Arnold of Lübeck. *Chronica*. Edited by Johann Martin Lappenberg. In MGH SS 21, 100–250. Hanover, 1869.

Bahā᾿ al-Dīn ibn Shaddād. *The Rare and Excellent History of Saladin*. Translated by D. S. Richards. Aldershot, 2001.

Balduini III Historia Nicaena vel Antiochena necnon Jerosolymitana. In *RHC Oc*, 5:139–85.

Baudri of Bourgueil. *The "Historia Ierosolimitana" of Baldric of Bourgueil*. Edited by Steven Biddlecombe. Martlesham (Suffolk), 2014.

Benincasa. *Vita sancti Rainerii confessoris de civitate pisana*. Edited by Réginald Grégoire. In his *San Ranieri di Pisa (1117–1160) in un ritratto agiografico inedito del secolo XIII*, 99–254. Ospedaletto, 1990.

Benjamin of Tudela. *The Itinerary of Benjamin of Tudela*. Edited and translated by Marcus Nathan Adler. London, 1907.

Benvenutus Grassus on the Well-Proven Art of the Eye: Practica oculorum & De probatissima arte oculorum. Synoptic Edition and Philological Studies, ed. Antonio Miranda-García and Santiago González Fernández-Corugedo. Bern, 2011.

Bernard of Clairvaux. *Éloge de la Nouvelle Chevalerie*. Edited and translated by Pierre-Yves Emery. Paris, 1990.

La Bible d'Acre: Genèse et Exode. Edited by Pierre Nobel. Besançon, 2006.

al-Bundarī. *Sanā al-Barq al-Shāmi*. Edited by Fathiyya al-Nabarāwī. Cairo, 1979.

Burchard of Mount Sion. *Descriptio Terrae Sanctae*. Edited and translated by John R. Bartlett. Oxford, 2019.

Caffaro. *Annales Ianuenses*. In *Annali genovesi di Caffaro e de' suoi continuatori*, edited by Luigi T. Belgrano, 1:1–75. Rome, 1890.

"Canons of the Council of Nablus." Edited by B. Z. Kedar. *Speculum* 74 (1999): 331–34. Repr. in Kedar, *Franks, Muslims*, Study I.

Celestine III. "Laudabilem pontificalis officii." Edited and translated by Anne J. Duggan, in "*Manu sollicitudinis*: Celestine III and Canon Law." In *Pope Celestine III (1191–1198): Diplomat and Pastor*, ed. John Doran and Damian J. Smith, 223–31. Farnham, 2008.

"La chanson composée à Acre en juin 1250." Edited by G[aston] P[aris]. *Romania* 22 (1893): 541–47.

La Chanson d'Antioche. Edited by Suzanne Duparc-Quioc. 2 vols. Paris, 1977–78.

La Chanson de Roland. Edited and translated by Ian Short. Paris, 1990.

"Chartes de l'abbaye de Notre-Dame de la Vallée de Josaphat en Terre-Sainte (1108–1291)." Edited by Charles Kohler, *ROL* 7 (1899): 108–222.

"Chartes de Terre Sainte." Edited by Joseph Delaville Le Roulx. *ROL* 11 (1905–8): 181–91.

"Les chemins et et les pelerinages de la Terre Sainte. Texte B." In *Itinéraires a Jérusalem et descriptions de la Terre Sainte rédigés en français aux XIe, XIIe & XIIIe siècles*, ed. Henri Michelant and Gaston Raynaud, 189–99. Geneva, 1882.

Les Chétifs. Edited by Geoffrey M. Myers. The Old French Crusade Cycle 5. University, AL, 1981.

Corpus inscriptionum arabicarum Palaestinae. Edited by Moshe Sharon. Leiden, 1997– [7 volumes to date].

Corpus inscriptionum Crucesignatorum Terrae Sanctae. Edited by Sabino De Sandoli. Jerusalem, 1974.

Cronaca del Templare di Tiro (1243–1314): La caduta degli Stati Crociati nel racconto di un testimone oculare. Edited by Laura Minervini. Naples, 2000.

Daniel the Abbot. "The Life and Journey of Daniel, Abbot of the Russian Land." In *Jerusalem Pilgrimage, 1099–1185*, translated by John Wilkinson, Joyce Hill, and W. F. Ryan, 120–71. London, 1988.

De constructione castri Saphet: Construction et fonctions d'un château fort franc en Terre Sainte. Edited by Robert B. C. Huygens. Amsterdam, 1981.

"Un diplome inédit d'Amaury I, roi de Jérusalem, en faveur de l'abbaye du Temple-Notre-Seigneur (Acre, 6–11 avril 1166)." Edited by Ferdinand Chalandon. *ROL* 8 (1900–1901): 311–17.

Documenti del commercio veneziano nei secoli XI–XIII. Edited by Raimondo Morozzo della Rocca and Antonino Lombardo. 2 vols. Turin, 1940.

"Documents inédits concernant l'Orient latin et les croisades (XIIe–XIVe siècle)." Edited by Charles Kohler. *ROL* 7 (1899): 1–37.

Ekkehard. *Hierosolymita*. *RHC Oc*, 5.

Epistulae et chartae ad historiam primi belli sacri spectantes: Die Kreuzzugsbriefe aus den Jahren 1088–1100. Edited by Heinrich Hagenmeyer. Innsbruck, 1901.

"L'Estoire de Eracles Empereur: Continuation dite du manuscrit de Rothelin," in *RHC Oc*, 2:483–639

Filippo da Novara [Phelippe of Novara]. *Guerra di Federico II in Oriente (1223–1242)*. Edited by Silvio Melani. Naples, 1994.

"Fragment d'un cartulaire de l'ordre de Saint-Lazare, en Terre Sainte." Edited by Arthur de Marsy. *AOL* 2, no. 2 (1884): 121–57.

Gaufridus. "De septem libris Iosephi." Edited by Julian Yolles, "Geoffrey, Prior of the *Templum Domini*: On the Seven Books of Josephus." *Crusades* 13 (2014): 77–118.

Gaufridus. "Super libros Machabeorum." Edited by Eyal Poleg, "On the Books of Maccabees: An Unpublished Poem by Geoffrey, Prior of the *Templum Domini*." *Crusades* 9 (2010): 11–56.

Gautier the Chancellor [Galterius Cancellarius]. *Bella Antiochena*. Edited by Heinrich Hagenmeyer. Innsbruck, 1896.

Geoffroy Le Tor. "Livre de Geoffroy Le Tort." In *RHC Lois*, 1:433–50.

Gerard of Nazareth. *De conversacione virorum Dei in Terra Sancta morantium*. Edited in B. Z. Kedar, "Gerard of Nazareth," 71–75.

Gesta Dei per Francos. Edited by Jacques Bongars. Hanau, 1611 [NB: Hanau, NOT Hanover].

Gesta Francorum et aliorum Hierosolymitanorum. Edited by Roger Mynors, translated by Rosalind Hill. Oxford, 1962.

"Il glossario arabo-francese di Messer Guglielmo e Maestro Giacomo." Edited by Gustav Ineichen. *Atti dell'Istituto Veneto di Scienze, Lettere ed Arti: Classe di scienze morali, lettere ed arti* 130 (1971–72): 353–407.

Guiot of Provins. *Les oeuvres de Guiot de Provins, poète lyrique et satirique*. Edited by John Orr. Manchester, 1915.

al-Harawī, ʿAlī. *A Lonely Wayfarer's Guide to Pilgrimage: ʿAlī ibn Bakr al-Harawī's Kitāb al-Ishārāt ilā Maʿrifat al-Ziyārāt*. Edited and translated by Josef W. Meri. Princeton, NJ, 2004.

Hebräische Berichte über die Judenverfolgungen während des Ersten Kreuzzugs. Edited and translated by Eva Haverkamp. MGH Hebräische Texte aus dem mittelalterlichen Deutschland 1. Hanover, 2005.

"Historia de profectione Danorum in Hierosolymam." In *Scriptores minores Historiae Danicae medii aevi*, ed. Martin C. Geertz, 2:457–92. Copenhagen, 1917–20.

Hugo of Saint-Victor. "Sermo ad milites Templi." Edited by Dominique Poirel, "Les Templiers, le diable et le chanoine: Le *Sermo ad Milites Templi* réattribué à Hugues de Saint-Victor." In *Amicorum Societas: Mélanges offerts à François Dolbeau pour son 65ᵉ anniversaire*, ed. Jacques Elfassi, Cécile Lanéry, and Anne-Marie Turcan-Verkerk, 659–63. Florence, 2013.

Ibn Abī Usaybiʾa. *A Literary History of Medicine: The ʿUyūn al-anbaʾ fī tabaqāt al-atibbāʾ*. Edited and translated by Emilie Savage-Smith, Sion Swain, and Geert Jan van Gelder. 3 vols. Leiden, 2020.

Ibn al-ʿArabī: Excerpts translated by Joseph Drory. "Some Observations during a Visit to Palestine by Ibn al-ʿArabī of Seville in 1092–1095." *Crusades* 3 (2004): 104–24.

Ibn al-Athīr. In *RHC Or*, 1 and *RHC Or*, 2A.

Ibn Jubayr. *The Travels*. Edited by William Wright and Michael Jan de Goeje. Leiden, 1907.

Ibn Jubayr. *The Travels of Ibn Jubayr*. Translated by R. J. C. Broadhurst. London, 1952.

Ibn al-Qalānisī. *Damas de 1075 à 1154: Traduction annotée de l'Histoire d'Ibn al-Qalānisī*. Translated by Roger Le Tourneau. Damascus, 1952.

Ibn al-Qaysarānī. *Shi'r Ibn al-Qaysarānī*. Edited by Adel Jaber Saleh Muhammad. Zarqa, 1991.

Ibn Wāsil. *Die Chronik des ibn Wāsil: Ğamāl ad-Dīn Muhammad ibn Wāsil, Mufarriğ al-Kurūb fī Ahbār Banī Ayyūb, Kritische Edition des letzten Teils (646/1248–659/1261) mit Kommentar*. Edited by Mohamed Rahim. Wiesbaden, 2010.

ʿImād al-Dīn al-Isfahānī in Abū Shāma. *RHC Or*, 4.

ʿImād al-Dīn al-Isfahānī. *Conquête de la Syrie et de la Palestine par Saladin*. Translated by Henri Massé. DRHC 10. Paris, 1972.

ʿImād al-Dīn al-Isfahānī. *El-Barq el-Shāmī*. Edited by Ramazan Şeşen. Istanbul, 1979.

ʿImmanuel of Rome. *Maḥbarot ʿImmanuel ha-Romī* [The Cantos of Manuello Romano]. Edited by Dov Yarden. 2 vols. Jerusalem, 1957.

"Inventio Patriarcharum." Edited by Robert B. C. Huygens. *Crusades* 4 (2005): 131–55.

"Ir' e dolors s'es dins mon cor asseza." Edited by Giulio Bertoni, in "Il serventese di Ricaut Bonomel (1265)." *Zeitschrift für romanische Philologie* 34 (1910): 701–7.

Itinéraires á Jérusalem et descriptions de la Terre Sainte rédigés en français aux XIe, XIIe, & XIIIe siècles. Edited by Henri Michelant and Gaston Raynaud. Geneva, 1882.

Itinerarium Peregrinorum et gesta regis Ricardi. Edited by William Stubbs. RS 38.1. London, 1864.

Jacques of Ibelin. "Livre de Jacques d'Ibelin." In *RHC Lois*, 1:451–68.

Jacques of Vitry. *The Exempla or Illustrative Stories from the Sermones Vulgares of Jacques de Vitry*. Edited by Thomas Frederick Crane. London, 1890.

Jacques of Vitry. *Die Exempla des Jacob von Vitry: Ein Beitrag zur Geschichte der Erzählungsliteratur des Mittelalters*. Edited by Goswin Frenken. Munich, 1914.

Jacques of Vitry. "Lettres." In *Serta Mediaevalia: Textus varii saeculorum X–XIII in unum collecti. Tractatus et epistulae*, edited by Robert B. C. Huygens, CCCM 171, 491–657. Turnhout, 2000.

Jerusalem Pilgrimage, 1099–1185. Translated by John Wilkinson, Joyce Hill, and W. F. Ryan. London, 1988.

Johann of Würzburg in *Peregrinationes tres: Saewulf, Iohannes Wirziburgensis, Theodericus*, edited by Robert B. C. Huygens, CCCM 139, 78–141. Turnhout, 1994.

John [Johan] of Ibelin. *Le Livre des Assises*. Edited by Peter W. Edbury. Leiden, 2003.

Joinville. *Vie de saint Louis*. Edited and translated by Jacques Monfrin. 6th ed. Paris, 2020; originally published 1995.

Konstantinos Manasses. *Hodoiporikon*. Edited and translated by Willem J. Aerts, "A Byzantine Traveller to One of the Crusader States." In *EWCS*, 3:165–221.

Les Légendes de l'Hôpital de Saint-Jean de Jérusalem. Edited and translated by Antoine Calvet. Paris, 2000.

Liber Mamonis. Edited and translated in Dirk Grupe, *Stephen of Pisa and Antioch: Liber Mamonis. An Introduction to Ptolemaic Cosmology and Astronomy from the Early Crusader States*. Cham, Switzerland, 2019.

Lignages d'Outremer. Edited by Marie-Adélaïde Nielen. DRHC 18. Paris, 2003.

Le Livre au Roi. Edited by Myriam Greilsammer. DRHC 17. Paris, 1995.

Le livre des Juges: Les cinq textes de la version française faite au XIIe *pour les chevaliers du Temple*. Edited by Guigue A. M. J. A. Marquis d'Albon. Lyon, 1913.

al-Maqdisī, Ḍiyāʾ al-Dīn. "*The Cited Tales of the Wondrous Doings of the Shaykhs of the Holy Land* by Ḍiyāʾ al-Dīn Abū ʿAbd Allāh Muhammad b. ʿAbd al-Wāhid al-Maqdisī (569/1173–643/1245): Text, Translation and Commentary," edited and translated by Daniella Talmon-Heller. *Crusades* 1 (2002): 111–54.

Mardī b. ʿAlī al-Tarsūsī. *Tabsīra fī al-hurūb*. Part I: "Un traité d'armurerie composé pour Saladin," edited and translated by Claude Cahen. *Bulletin d'études orientales* 12 (1947–48): 103–63.

Mardī b. ʿAlī al-Tarsūsī. *Tabsīra fī al-hurūb*. Part II: *Contribution à l'étude de l'archerie musulmane*. Edited and translated by Antoine Boudot-Lamotte. Damascus, 1968.

Marsilio Zorzi. *Der Bericht des Marsilio Zorzi: Codex Querini-Stampalia IV3 (1064)*. Edited by Oliver Berggötz. Frankfurt am Main, 1991.

Matthew of Edessa. *Armenia and the Crusades, Tenth to Twelfth Centuries: The Chronicle of Matthew of Edessa*. Translated by Ara Edmond Dostorian. Lanham, MD, 1993.

Matthew Paris. *Chronica majora*. Edited by Henry R. Luard. RS 57. 7 vols. London, 1872–80.

Muslim Sources of the Crusader Period: An Anthology. Translated by James E. Lindsay and Suleiman A. Mourad. Indianapolis, 2021.

Nāser-e Khosraw. *Book of Travels (Safarnāma)*. Translated by W. M. Thackston Jr. Persian Heritage Series 36. Albany, NY, 1986.

Odeoporicum et pericula Margarite Iherosolimitane. Edited by Paul Gerhardt Schmidt, as "'Peregrinatio periculosa': Thomas von Froidmont über die Jerusalemfahrten seiner Schwester Margareta." In *Kontinuität und Wandel: Lateinische Poesie von Naevius bis Baudelaire. Franco Munari zum 65. Geburtstag*, ed. Ulrich Justus Stache, Wolfgang Maaz, and Fritz Wagner, 472–85. Hildesheim, 1986.

Papsturkunden für Kirchen im Heiligen Lande. Edited by Rudolf Hiestand. Göttingen, 1985.

Papsturkunden für Templer und Johanniter. Edited by Rudolf Hiestand. Göttingen, 1984.

I Pelrinages communes, i Pardouns de Acre e la crisi del Regno Crociato: Storia e testi. Edited by Fabio Romanini and Beatrice Saletti. Padua, 2012.

Petaḥya of Regensburg. *Die Rundreise des R. Petachjah aus Regensburg.* Edited and translated by Lazar Grünhut. Frankfurt am Main, 1905.

Petrus Tudebodus. *Historia de hierosolymitano itinere.* Edited by John H. Hill and Laurita L. Hill. DRHC 12. Paris, 1977.

Petrus Venerabilis. *Adversus Iudeorum inveteratam duritiem.* Edited by Yvonne Friedman. CCCM 58. Turnhout, 1985.

Petrus Venerabilis. *De miraculis libri duo.* Edited by Denise Bouthiller. CCCM 83. Turnhout, 1988.

Petrus Venerabilis. *Sermo domni Petri abbatis Cluniacensis de laude Dominici Sepulchri.* Edited by Giles Constable. In "Petri Venerabilis sermones tres," *Revue Bénédictine* 64 (1954): 247–53.

Phelippe of Novara. *Les quatre âges de l'homme: Traité moral de Philippe de Navarre.* Edited by Marcel de Fréville. Paris, 1888.

Philip of Novara [Phelippe of Novara]. *Le Livre de Forme de Plait.* Edited and translated by Peter W. Edbury. Nicosia, 2009.

Philippe de Novare [Phelippe of Novara]. *Mémoires (1218–1243).* Edited by Charles Kohler. Paris, 1913.

Philip of Tripoli. *Secretum Secretorum cum glossis et notulis: Tractatus brevis et utilis ad declarandum quedam obscure dicta Fratris Rogeri.* Edited by Robert Steele. Opera hactenus inedita Rogeri Baconis 5. Oxford, 1920.

Pierre of Blois. "Passio Raginaldi principis Antiochie." In *Petri Blesensis Tractatus duo,* edited by Robert B. C. Huygens, CCCM 194, 31–73. Turnhout, 2002.

"La prière des malades dans les hôpitaux de l'Ordre de Saint-Jean de Jérusalem." Edited by Léon Le Grand. *Bibliothèque de l'École des chartes* 57 (1896): 325–38.

"Procès de Nicéphore." In *Dossier grec de l'Union de Lyon (1273–1277),* ed. and trans. Vitalien Laurent and Jean Darrouzès, 82–88, 486–506. Paris, 1976.

Al-Qāḍī al-Fāḍil in Ibn Khallikān. *RHC Or,* 3.

"Quatre titres des propriétés des Génois à Acre et à Tyr." Edited by Cornelio Desimoni, *AOL* 2, no. 2 (1884): 213–30.

Ralph Niger [Radulfus Niger]. *De re militari et triplici via peregrinationis ierosolimitanae (1187/88).* Edited by Ludwig Schmugge. Berlin, 1977.

Raoul of Caen. *Gesta Tancredi.* In *RHC Oc,* 3:587–716.

Raymond of Aguilers. *Le "Liber" de Raymond d'Aguilers.* Edited by John Hugh Hill and Laurita L. Hill. DRHC 9. Paris, 1969.

La Rectorique de Cyceron tradotta da Jean d'Antioche: Edizione e glossario. Edited by Elisa Guadagnini. Pisa, 2009.

La Règle du Temple. Edited by Henri de Curzon. Paris, 1886. Repr. Geneva, 1977.

"Relation de la conférence tenue entre le docteur Mĕkhithar de Daschir, envoyé du Catholicos Constantin Ier et le légat du pape, à Saint-Jean-d'Acre en 1262." In *RHC Documents arméniens,* 1:689–98.

Der "Rithmus de expeditione Ierosolimitana" des sogenannten Haymarus Monachus Florentinus: Ein Augenzeugenbericht über die Belagerung Akkons (1189–1191) während des dritten Kreuzzugs. Edited and German prose translation by Sascha Falk, Italian verse translation by Antonio Placanica. Florence, 2006.

"Un rituel et un bréviaire du Saint-Sépulcre de Jérusalem (XIIe-XIIIe siècle)." Edited by Charles Kohler. *ROL* 8 (1900–1): 383–500.

The Rule of Saint Albert. Edited and translated by Bede Edwards. Aylesford, 1973.

Saewulf in *Peregrinationes tres: Saewulf, Iohannes Wirziburgensis, Theodericus*, ed. Robert B. C. Huygens, CCCM 139, 58–77. Turnhout, 1994.

Scents and Flavors: A Syrian Cookbook. Edited and translated by Charles Perry. New York, 2017.

"Un sermon commémoratif de la prise de Jérusalem par les Croisés attribué à Foucher de Chartres." Edited by Charles Kohler. *ROL* 8 (1900–1901): 158–64.

al-Shayzarī. *The Book of the Market Inspector: Nihāyat al-Rutba fī Talab al-Hisba (The Utmost Authority in the Pursuit of Hisba) by Abd al-Rahmān b. Nasr al-Shayzarī*. Translated by Ronald P. Buckley. Oxford, 1999.

"Six lettres relatives aux croisades." Edited by Paul Riant. *AOL* 1 (1881): 383–92.

al-Sulamī: Niall Christie. *The Book of the Jihad of 'Ali ibn Tahir al-Sulami (d. 1106): Text, Translation and Commentary*. Farnham, 2015.

The Synodicum Nicosiense and Other Documents of the Latin Church of Cyprus, 1196–1373. Edited and translated by Christopher Schabel. Nicosia, 2001.

Tabulae ordinis Theutonici. Edited by Ernst Strehlke. Berlin, 1869. Repr. Jerusalem, 1975.

Templar Rule, ed. Cerrini: Simonetta Cerrini. "Une expérience neuve au sein de la spiritualité médiévale: L'ordre du Temple (1120–1314). Etude et édition des règles latine et française." PhD thesis, Université de Paris-Sorbonne (Paris IV), 1997. Latin text: 106–47; Old French text: 161–97.

Templar Rule (English): Malcolm Barber and Keith Bate. *The Templars: Selected Sources*, 31–54. Manchester, 2002.

Theoderich in *Peregrinationes tres: Saewulf, Iohannes Wirziburgensis, Theodericus*, ed. Robert B. C. Huygens, CCCM 139, 142–97. Turnhout, 1994.

Thietmar. *Magistri Thietmari peregrinatio*. Edited by J. C. M. Laurent. Hamburg, 1857.

"A Twelfth-Century Description of the Jerusalem Hospital." Edited by B. Z. Kedar. In Kedar, *Franks, Muslims*, Study X, 13–26 [Latin text].

Usama ibn Munqidh. *The Book of Contemplation: Islam and the Crusades*. Translated by Paul M. Cobb. London, 2008.

Usama ibn Munqidh. *Usāmah's Memoirs, Entitled Kitāb al-i'tibār*. Edited by Philip K. Hitti. Princeton, NJ, 1930.

Vincent of Prague. "Annales Bohemorum." Edited and translated (into Czech) by Josef Emler. In *Fontes rerum Bohemicarum*, 2:407–60. Prague, 1874.

"Wilbrand of Oldenburg's Journey to Syria, Lesser Armenia, Cyprus and the Holy Land (1211–1212): A New Edition." Edited by Denys Pringle, *Crusades* 11 (2012): 109–37.

William of Saint Estiene. "Comment la sainte maison de l'Hospital de S. Johan de Jerusalem commença." In *RHC Oc*, 5:422–27.

William of Tripoli [Wilhelm von Tripolis]. *Notitia de Machometo: De statu Sarracenorum.* Edited and translated by Peter Engels. Würzburg, 1992.

Secondary Literature

Abed Rabo, Omar. "Islamic Cultural-Religious Life in Jerusalem on the Eve of the First Crusade." In *EO*, 1:24–43.

Abel, Félix-Marie. "Une inscription médiévale de Saint-Jean d'Acre." *Revue Biblique* 33 (1924): 388–90.

Amar, Zohar, and Yaron Serri. "Ibn al-Suri, Physician and Botanist of al-Sham." *Palestine Exploration Quarterly* 135 (2003): 124–30.

Antweiler, Wolfgang. *Das Bistum Tripolis im 12. und 13. Jahrhundert: Personengeschichtliche und strukturelle Probleme.* Düsseldorf, 1991.

Ashtor, Eliyahu. "Il regno dei crociati e il commercio di Levante." In *I comuni italiani*, 15–56.

Aslanoff [Aslanov], Cyrille. "Récit historique et discours poétique dans l'*Estoire de la guerre des Ibelins contre les Impériaux* de Philippe de Novare." *Le Moyen Age* 103 (1997): 67–81.

Aslanov, Cyril. *Evidence of Francophony in Mediaeval Levant: Decipherment and Interpretation—MS Paris BnF copte 43.* Jerusalem, 2006.

Aslanov, Cyril. *Le français au Levant, jadis et naguère: A la recherche d'une langue perdue.* Paris, 2006.

Aslanov, Cyril. "The Historical Formation of a Macro-ecology: The Case of the Levant." In *Linguistic Ecology and Language Contact*, edited by Ralph Ludwig, Peter Mühlhäusler, and Steve Pagel, 131–46. Cambridge, 2019.

Aspesi, Cara. "The Cantors of the Holy Sepulchre and Their Contribution to Crusade History and Frankish Identity." In *Medieval Cantors and Their Craft: Music, Liturgy and the Shaping of History, 800–1500*, edited by Katie Ann-Marie Bugyis, Andrew B. Kraebel, and Margot E. Fassler, 278–96. Woodbridge, 2017.

Audrerie, Louis-Marie. *Le droit hiérosolymitain dans l'Orient latin du XI*[e] *au XVI*[e] *siècle: Les "Assises de Jérusalem."* Paris, 2023.

Aurell, Martin. *Des chrétiens contre les croisades, XII*[e]*–XIII*[e] *siècle.* Paris, 2013.

Aurell, Martin. "De l'acculturation à l'ethnotype: L'alterité du Latin d'Orient." In *Transferts*, 327–59.

Aurell, Martin. "Joan of England and al-ʿÂdil's Harem: The Impossible Marriage between Christians and Muslims (Eleventh-Twelfth Centuries)." *Anglo-Norman Studies* 43 (2021): 1–14.

Bagatti, Bellarmino. *Gli scavi di Nazaret.* 2 vols. Jerusalem, 1971–84.

Bahat, Dan. "Recently Discovered Crusader Churches in Jerusalem." In *Ancient Churches Revealed*, edited by Yoram Tsafrir, 123–27. Jerusalem, 1993.

Balard, Michel. *Histoire des épices au Moyen Âge.* Paris, 2023.

Baldwin, Philip B. *Pope Gregory X and the Crusades.* Woodbridge, 2014.

Bale, Anthony. "Reading and Writing in Outremer." In *The Cambridge Companion to the Literature of the Crusades*, edited by Anthony Bale, 85–101. Cambridge, 2019.

Balletto, Laura. "Fonti notarili genovesi del secondo Duecento per la Storia del Regno Latino di Gerusalemme." In *I comuni italiani*, 175–279.

Balme, François. "La province dominicaine de Terre-Sainte de janvier 1277 à octobre 1280." *ROL* 1 (1893): 526–36.

Barbé, Hervé. *Le château de Safed et son territoire depuis l'époque des croisades: Construction, organisation, fonctions et postérité d'une fortification franque de Terre Sainte (XIIe–XIIIe siècle)*. Mémoires et travaux du Centre de recherche français à Jérusalem, 12. Paris, 2022.

Barbé, Hervé. *Hébron 1119: L'invention du tombeau des patriarches*. Paris, 2017.

Barber, Malcolm. "The Career of Philip of Nablus in the Kingdom of Jerusalem." In *EC*, 60–75.

Barber, Malcolm. *The New Knighthood: A History of the Order of the Temple*. Cambridge, 1994.

Barthélemy, Anatole de. "Libre exercice de commerce octroyé à un pèlerin champenois (1153)." *AOL* 1 (1881): 535–36.

Bates, Michael L., and D. M. Metcalf. "Crusader Coinage with Arabic Inscriptions." In *Crusades*, ed. Setton, 6:421–82.

Bautier, Geneviève. "L'envoi de la relique de la Vraie Croix à Notre-Dame de Paris en 1120." *Bibliothèque de l'École des chartes* 129 (1971): 387–97.

Beddie, James S. "Some Notices of Books in the East in the Period of the Crusades." *Speculum* 8 (1933): 240–42.

Bennett, Matthew. "The Crusaders' 'Fighting March' Revisited." *War in History* 8 (2001): 1–18.

Bennett, Matthew. "*La Règle du Temple* as a Military Manual, or How to Deliver a Cavalry Charge." In *Studies in Medieval History Presented to R. Allen Brown*, edited by Christopher Harper-Bill, Christopher J. Holdsworth, and Janet L. Nelson, 7–19. Woodbridge, 1989. Repr. in *The Rule of the Templars: The French Text of the Rule of the Order of the Knights Templar*, translated by J. M. Upton-Ward, 175–88. Woodbridge,1992.

Benvenisti, Meron. "Bovaria-Babriyya: A Frankish Residue on the Map of Palestine." In *Outremer*, 130–52.

Benvenisti, Meron. *The Crusaders in the Holy Land*. Jerusalem, 1970.

Berkovich, Ilya, and Amit Re'em. "The Location of the Crusader Hospital in the Muristan—A Reassessment." In *The Ancient Remains below the Church of the Redeemer, the Muristan and Its Surroundings*, edited by Dietrich Vieweger and Shimon Gibson, 193–220. Oxford, 2016.

Berlière, Ursmer. "Frédéric de Laroche, évêque d'Acre et archevêque de Tyr: Envoi de reliques à l'abbaye de Florennes (1153–1161)." *Annales de l'Institut archéologique de Luxembourg* 43 (1908): 67–79.

Bertram, Martin. "Johannes de Ancona: Ein Jurist des 13. Jahrhunderts in den Kreuzfahrerstaaten." *Bulletin of Medieval Canon Law* 7 (1977): 49–64.

Besson, Florian. "Devenir étranger: Des anti-transferts culturels en Orient latin." In *Transferts*, 307–25.

Besson, Florian. "Les rencontres entre communautés dans l'Acre latine du XIIIe siècle: L'exemple de Saliba, marchand et bourgeois." *Bulletin du Centre d'études médiévales d'Auxerre* (*BUCEMA*) 26, no. 2 (2016), DOI: 10.4000/cem.14523.

Bishop, Adam M. "Adaptations of the Roman *Lex Aquilia* in the Burgess Assizes of Jerusalem." In *Crusading in Art, Thought and Will*, edited by Matthew E. Parker, Ben Halliburton, and Anne Romine, 110–25. Leiden, 2019.

Bishop, Adam M. "*Les Assises de la Cour des Bourgeois* de Jérusalem: La question de leurs Sources." In *Autour des Assises de Jérusalem*, edited by Jerôme Devard and Bernard Ribemont, 113–25. Paris, 2018.

Bishop, Adam M. "Usāma ibn Munqidh and Crusader Law in theTwelfth Century." *Crusades* 12 (2013): 53–65.

Boas, Adrian J. "The Acclimatisation of the Frankish Population to Life in the Latin East: Some Examples from Daily Life." In *Transferts*, 361–86.

Boas, Adrian J. *Crusader Archaeology: The Material Culture of the Latin East.* Abingdon, 1999.

Boas, Adrian J. *The Crusades Uncovered.* Leeds, 2022.

Boas, Adrian J. *Domestic Settings: Sources on Domestic Architecture and Day-to-Day Activities in the Crusader States.* Leiden, 2010.

Bom, Myra Miranda. *Women in the Military Orders of the Crusades.* New York, 2012.

Borchardt, Karl. "The Military-Religious Orders: A Medieval 'School of Administrators'?" In *The Military Orders*, vol. 5: *Politics and Power*, edited by Peter W. Edbury, 3–20. Farnham, 2012.

Borchardt, Karl. "The Military-Religious Orders of the Twelfth and Thirteenth Centuries as an Innovative Step for Western Religious Life." In *Ordens militares: Identitade e Mudança*, edited by Isabel Cristina Ferreira Fernandes, 1:163–76. Palmela, 2021.

Borg, Alan. "The Lost Apse Mosaic of the Holy Sepulchre, Jerusalem." In *The Vanishing Past: Studies of Medieval Art, Liturgy and Metrology Presented to Christopher Hohler*, edited by Alan Borg and Andrew Martindale, 7–12. Oxford, 1981.

Bresc-Bautier, Geneviève. "Les effectifs du chapitre du Saint-Sépulcre de Jérusalem (1112–1178)." In *Bourgogne/Orient*, 404–10.

Bresc-Bautier, Geneviève, and Henri Bresc, "La cloche de Šibenik qui sonne pour la libération de la patrie (Acre, 1266)." In *"Come l'orco della fiaba": Studi per Franco Cardini*, edited by Marina Montesano, 49–71. Florence, 2010.

Brini Savorelli, Mirella. "Un manuale di geomanzia presentato da Bernardo Silvestre da Tours (XII secolo): l'*Experimentarius*." *Rivista critica di storia della filosofia* 14 (1959): 283–342.

Bronstein, Judith, Edna J. Stern, and Elisabeth Yehuda. "Franks, Locals and Sugar Cane: A Case Study of Cultural Interaction in the Latin Kingdom of Jerusalem." *Journal of Medieval History* 45 (2019): 316–30.

Bronstein, Judith, Edna J. Stern, and Elisabeth Yehuda. "Viticulture in the Latin Kingdom of Jerusalem in the Light of Historical and Archaeological Evidence." *Journal of Mediterranean Archaeology* 33, no. 1 (2020): 55–78.

Brundage, James A. "Latin Jurists in the Levant: The Legal Elite of the Crusader States." In *Crusaders and Muslims in Twelfth-Century Syria*, edited by Maya Shatzmiller, 18–42. Leiden, 1993.

Brundage, James A. "Marriage Law in the Latin Kingdom of Jerusalem." In *Outremer*, 258–71.

Buchthal, Hugo. *Miniature Painting in the Latin Kingdom of Jerusalem*. Oxford, 1957.

Buck, Andrew D. *The Principality of Antioch and Its Frontiers in the Twelfth Century*. Woodbridge, 2017.

Buck, Andrew D. "Remembering Outremer in the West: The *Secunda pars Historiae Iherosolimitanae* and the Crisis of Crusading in Mid-Twelfth-Century France." *Speculum* 97 (2022): 377–414.

Buck, Andrew D. "Settlement, Identity and Memory in the Latin East: An Examination of the Term 'Crusader States.'" *English Historical Review* 135 (2020): 271–302.

Buckingham, Hannah Rose. "Identity and Archaeology in Daily Life: The Material Culture of the Crusader States." PhD dissertation, Cardiff University, 2016.

Bulst-Thiele, Marie Luise. "Die Mosaiken der 'Auferstehungskirche' in Jerusalem und die Bauten der 'Franken' im 12. Jahrhundert." *Frühmittelalterliche Studien* 13 (1979): 442–71.

Bulst-Thiele, Marie Luise. *Sacrae Domus Militiae Templi Hierosolymitani Magistri: Untersuchungen zur Geschichte des Templerordens 1118/19–1314*. Göttingen, 1974.

Burgtorf, Jochen. "'Blood-Brothers' in the Thirteenth-Century Latin East? The Mamluk Sultan Baybars and the Templar Matthew Sauvage." In *Communicating the Middle Ages: Essays in Honour of Sophia Menache*, edited by Iris Shagrir, B. Z. Kedar, and Michel Balard, 3–14. Abingdon, 2018.

Burgtorf, Jochen. *The Central Convent of Hospitallers and Templars: History, Organization, and Personnel (1099/1120–1310)*. Leiden, 2008.

Burnett, Charles. "Antioch as a Link between Arabic and Latin Culture in the Twelfth and Thirteenth Centuries." In *Occident et Proche-Orient*, 1–78.

Burnett, Charles. "Master Theodore, Frederick II's Philosopher." In *Federico II e le nuove culture: Atti del XXXI Convegno storico internazionale, Todi, 9–12 ottobre 1994*, 225–85. Spoleto, 1995.

Burnett, Charles. "The *Sortes Regis Amalrici*: An Arabic Divinatory Work in the Latin Kingdom of Jerusalem?" *Scripta Mediterranea* 19–20 (1998–99): 229–37.

Burnett, Charles. "Stephen, the Disciple of Philosophy, and the Exchange of Medical Learning in Antioch." *Crusades* 5 (2006): 113–29.

Busse, Heribert. "Vom Felsendom zum Templum Domini." In *Das Heilige Land im Mittelalter: Begegnungsraum zwischen Orient und Okzident*, edited by Wolfdietrich Fischer and Jürgen Schneider, 19–32. Neustadt an der Aisch, 1982.

Cahen, Claude. "Indigènes et Croisés: Quelques mots a propos d'un médecin d'Amaury et de Saladin." *Syria* 15 (1934): 351–60. Repr. in Cahen, *Turcobyzantina et Oriens Christianus*, Study F. London, 1974.

Cahen, Claude. "Une inscription mal comprise concernant le rapprochement entre Maronites et Croisés." In *Medieval and Middle Eastern Studies in Honour of Aziz Suryal Atiya*, edited by Sami A. Hanna, 62–63. Leiden, 1972.

Cahen, Claude. *Orient et Occident au temps des Croisades*. Paris, 1983.

Cahen, Claude. *La Syrie du Nord à l'époque des croisades et la principauté franque d'Antioche*. Paris, 1940.

Caspi-Reisfeld, Keren. "Women Warriors during the Crusades, 1095–1254." In *Gendering the Crusades*, edited by Susan B. Edgington and Sarah Lambert, 94–107. Cardiff, 2001.

Catlos, Brian A. *Muslims of Medieval Latin Christendom, c.1050–1614*. Cambridge, 2014.

Cerrini, Simonetta. *L'Apocalisse dei Templari: Missione e destino dell'ordine religioso e cavalleresco più misterioso del Medioevo*. Milan, 2012.

Cerrini, Simonetta. "Une expérience neuve au sein de la spiritualité médiévale: L'ordre du Temple (1120–1314). Etude et édition des règles latine et française." PhD thesis, Université de Paris-Sorbonne (Paris IV), 1997.

Cerrini, Simonetta. *La rivoluzione dei Templari: Una storia perduta del dodicesimo secolo*. Milan, 2014.

Chandon de Briailles, François. "Sur deux bulles de l'Orient latin." In *Mélanges syriens offerts a Monsieur René Dussaud par ses amis et élèves*, 2 vols., 1:139–50. Paris, 1939.

Chazaud, Martial-Alphonse. "Inventaire et comptes de la succession d'Eudes, comte de Nevers (Acre 1266)." *Mémoires de la Société nationale des antiquaires de France* 32 (1871): 164–206.

Chen, Doron. "Measuring the Cave of Abraham in Hebron." *Liber Annuus Studii Biblici Franciscani* 37 (1987): 291–94.

Ciggaar, Krijnie N. "Adaptation to Oriental Life by Rulers in and around Antioch: Examples and Exempla." In *EWMEM*, 261–82.

Ciggaar, Krijnie N. "Cultural Identities in Antioch (969–1268): Integration and Disintegration—New Texts and Images." In *Hybride Kulturen im mittelalterlichen Europa*, edited by Michael Borgolte and Bernd Schneidemüller, 105–22. Berlin, 2010.

Ciggaar, Krijnie N. "Glimpses of Life in Outremer in *Exempla* and *Miracula*." In *EWCS*, 2:131–52.

Claverie, Pierre-Vincent. "L'influence des ordres militaires sur les techniques de combat des Fatimides et des Mamelouks." In *Entre Deus e o Rei: O Mundo das Ordens Militares*, edited by Isabel Cristina Ferreira Fernandes, 283–95. Palmela, 2018.

Claverie, Pierre-Vincent. "Notes sur l'onomastique franque durant les croisades et quelques énigmes prosopographiques." In *Egypt and Syria in the Fatimid, Ayyubid and Mamluk Eras*, vol. 8, edited by Urbain Vermeulen, Kristof D'hulster, and Jo Van Steenbergen, 145–62. Leuven, 2016.

Claverie, Pierre-Vincent. *L'ordre du Temple dans l'Orient des Croisades*. Brussels, 2014.

Claverie, Pierre-Vincent. "La place de la chevalerie comme vecteur du rapprochement interconfessionel dans l'Orient des croisades." In *Através do olhar do*

Outro: Reflexões acerca da sociedade medieval europeia (séculos XII–XV), edited by José Albuquerque Carreiras, Giulia Rossi Vairo, and Kristjan Toomaspoeg, 113–34. Tomar, 2018.

Claverie, Pierre-Vincent. "Les représentations des origines du Temple dans la chronique de Guillaume de Tyr." In *D'Orient en Occident*, 20–26.

Claverie, Pierre-Vincent. "Les tribulations orientales du seigneur Gonfroy II de Marquise (1098–1138)." In *Egypt and Syria in the Fatimid, Ayyubid and Mamluk Eras*, vol. 8, edited by Urbain Vermeulen, Kristof D'hulster, and Jo Van Steenbergen, 163–85. Leuven, 2016.

Cobb, Paul M. "Hamdan al-Atharibi's *History of the Franks* Revisited, Again." In *Syria in Crusader Times: Conflict and Coexistence*, edited by Carole Hillenbrand, 3–20. Edinburgh, 2020.

Cobb, Paul M. "Usāma Ibn Munqidh's *Book of the Staff*: Autobiographical and Historical Excerpts." *Al-Masāq* 17 (2005): 109–23.

Conrad, Lawrence I. "Usama ibn Munqidh and Other Witnesses to Frankish and Islamic Medicine in the Era of the Crusades." In *Medicine in Jerusalem throughout the Ages*, edited by Zohar Amar, Efraim Lev, and Joshua Schwartz, xxvii–lii. Tel Aviv, 1999. Repr. in *Islamic Medical and Scientific Tradition: Critical Concepts in Islamic Studies*, edited by Peter E. Pormann, 2:260–82. Abingdon, 2011.

Constable, Giles. *Crusaders and Crusading in the Twelfth Century*. Farnham, 2008.

Cook, David. "Al-Samʿānī's Travels in Syria during the Summer of 535/1141." *Crusades* 22, no. 1 (2023): 39–61.

Croisy-Naquet, Catherine. "La description de Jérusalem dans la Chronique d'Ernoul." *Romania* 115 (1997): 69–89.

Crouzet-Pavan, Élisabeth. *Le mystère des rois de Jérusalem, 1099–1187*. Paris, 2013.

Dajani-Shakeel, Hadia. "Natives and Franks in Palestine: Perceptions and Interactions." In *Conversion and Continuity: Indigenous Christian Communities in Islamic Lands, Eighth to Eighteenth Centuries*, edited by Michael Gervers and Ramzi Jibran Bikhazi, 161–84. Toronto, 1990.

Dédéyan, Gérard. "Les colophons de manuscrits arméniens comme sources pour l'histoire des Croisades." In *Crusade Sources*, 89–110.

Dédéyan, Gérard. "Un projet de colonisation arménienne dans le royaume latin de Jérusalem sous Amaury Ier (1162–1174)." In *Le partage du monde: Échanges et colonisation dans la Méditerranée médiévale*, edited by Michel Balard and Alain Ducellier, 101–40. Paris, 1998.

D[elisle], L[éopold]. "Maître Jean d'Antioche, traducteur, et frère Guillaume de Saint-Étienne, Hospitalier." In *Histoire littéraire de la France*, 33:1–40. Paris, 1906.

Demurger, Alain. "Belchite, le Temple et Montjoie: La couronne d'Aragon et le Temple au XIIe siècle." In *Knighthoods of Christ: Essays on the History of the Crusades and the Knights Templar Presented to Malcolm Barber*, edited by Norman Housley, 123–35. Aldershot, 2007.

Demurger, Alain. "Gli ordini religioso-militari e la guerra tra il XII e il XIII secolo." In *I Templari, la guerra e la santità*, edited by Simonetta Cerrini, 49–68. Rimini, 2000.

Derenbourg, Hartwig. "Note sur quelques mots de la langue des Francs au douzième siècle d'après le texte arabe de l'autobiographie d'Ousâma ibn Mounkidh." In *Mélanges Renier: Recueil de travaux publiés par l'École pratique des hautes études en mémoire de son président Léon Renier*, 453–65. Paris, 1887.

Dondi, Cristina. *The Liturgy of the Canons Regular of the Holy Sepulchre of Jerusalem: A Study and a Catalogue of the Manuscript Sources*. Turnhout, 2004.

Drory, Joseph. "Early Muslim Reflections on the Crusaders." *Jerusalem Studies in Arabic and Islam* 25 (2001): 92–101.

Drory, Joseph. "Hanbalīs of the Nablus Region in the Eleventh and Twelfth Centuries." *Asian and African Studies* 22 (1988): 93–112.

Drory, Joseph. "Some Observations during a Visit to Palestine by Ibn al-ʿArabī of Seville in 1092–1095." *Crusades* 3 (2004): 104–24.

Ebels-Hoving, Bunna. "William of Tyre and His *patria*." In *Media Latinitas: A Collection of Essays to Mark the Occasion of the Retirement of L.J. Engels*, edited by R. I. A. Nip et al., 211–16. Turnhout, 1996.

Eck, Thomas. *Die Kreuzfahrerbistümer Beirut und Sidon im 12. und 13. Jahrhundert auf prosopographischer Grundlage*. Kiel, 1999.

Edbury, Peter W. "Cultural Encounters in the Latin East: John of Jaffa and Philip of Novara." In *Cultural Encounters during the Crusades*, edited by Kurt Villads Jensen, Kirsi Salonen, and Helle Vogt, 229–35. Odense, 2013. Repr. in Edbury, *Law and History in the Latin East*, Study VI. Farnham, 2014.

Edbury, Peter [W]. "Ernoul, *Eracles*, and the Collapse of the Kingdom of Jerusalem." In *The French of Outremer*, 44–67.

Edbury, Peter W. *John of Ibelin and the Kingdom of Jerusalem*. Woodbridge, 1997.

Edbury, Peter W. "The 'Livre' of Geoffrey Le Tor and the 'Assises' of Jerusalem." In *Historia administrativa y ciencia de la administración comparada: Trabajos en homaje a Ferran Valls i Taberner*, edited by Manuel J. Peláez, 15:4291–98. Barcelona, 1990. Repr. in Edbury, *Kingdoms of the Crusades: From Jerusalem to Cyprus*, Study X. Aldershot, 1999.

Edbury, Peter W. "The Lyon *Eracles* and the Continuations of William of Tyre." In *Montjoie*, 139–53.

Edbury, Peter W. "Making Sense of the *Annales de Terre Sainte*: Thirteenth-Century Vernacular Narratives from the Latin East." In *Crusader Landscapes in the Medieval Levant: The Archaeology and History of the Latin East*, edited by Micaela Sinibaldi et al., 403–13. Cardiff, 2016.

Edbury, Peter [W.], and Massimiliano Gaggero. *The Chronique d'Ernoul and the Colbert-Fontainebleau Continuation of William of Tyre*. 2 vols. Leiden, 2023.

Edbury, Peter W., and John G. Rowe. *William of Tyre: Historian of the Latin East*. Cambridge, 1988.

Eddé, Anne-Marie. "Francs et musulmans de Syrie au début du XIIe siècle d'après l'historien Ibn Abī Tayyi'." In *Dei gesta per Francos: Etudes sur les croisades dédiées à Jean Richard*, edited by Michel Balard, B. Z. Kedar, and Jonathan Riley-Smith, 159–69. Aldershot, 2001.

Edgington, Susan B. "The Doves of War: The Part Played by Carrier Pigeons in the Crusades." In *Autour*, 167–75.

Edgington, Susan B. "Medical Care in the Hospital of St John in Jerusalem." In *The Military Orders*, vol. 2: *Welfare and Warfare*, edited by Helen Nicholson, 27–33. Aldershot, 1998.

Edgington, Susan B. "Medicine and Surgery in the *Livre des Assises de la Cour des Bourgeois de Jérusalem*." *Al-Masāq* 17 (2005): 87–97.

Edgington, Susan B. "Oriental and Occidental Medicine in the Crusader States." In *The Crusades and the Near East: Cultural Histories*, edited by Conor Kostick, 189–215. Abingdon, 2011.

Ehrenkreutz, Andrew S. "Arabic *Dīnārs* Struck by the Crusaders: A Case of Ignorance or of Economic Subversion?" *Journal of the Economic and Social History of the Orient* 7 (1964): 167–82. Repr. in Ehrenkreutz, *Monetary Change and Economic History in the Medieval Muslim World*, edited by Jere L. Bachrach, Study XVII. Aldershot, 1992.

Eldredge, Laurence M. "The Latin Manuscripts of Benvenutus Grassus' Treatise on Diseases and Injuries to the Eye." In *Benvenutus Grassus on the Well-Proven Art of the Eye: Practica oculorum & De probatissima arte oculorum. Synoptic Edition and Philological Studies*, edited by Antonio Miranda-García and Santiago González Fernández Corugedo, 19–33. Bern, 2011.

Ellenblum, Ronnie. *Crusader Castles and Modern Histories*. Cambridge, 2007.

Ellenblum, Ronnie. *Frankish Rural Settlement in the Latin Kingdom of Jerusalem*. Cambridge, 1998.

Elm, Kaspar. "*Nec minori celebritate a catholicis cultoribus observatur et colitur*: Zwei Berichte über die 1119/20 erfolgte Auffindung und Erhebung der Gebeine der Patriarchen Abraham, Isaak und Jakob." *Zeitschrift für Religions- und Geistesgeschichte* 49 (1997): 319–44.

Emanuel, Simcha. "Halakhic Questions of Thirteenth-Century Acre Scholars as a Historical Source." *Crusades* 17 (2018): 115–30.

Enlart, Camille. *Les monuments des croisés dans le royaume de Jérusalem: Architecture religieuse et civile*. 2 vols. + 2 albums. Paris, 1925–28.

Epp, Verena. "Die Entstehung eines 'Nationalbewußtseins' in den Kreuzfahrerstaaten." *Deutsches Archiv* 45 (1989): 596–604.

Epp, Verena. *Fulcher von Chartres: Studien zur Geschichtsschreibung des ersten Kreuzzuges*. Düsseldorf, 1990.

Erdmann, Carl. *Die Entstehung des Kreuzzugsgedankens*. Stuttgart, 1935.

Favreau, Marie-Luise. "Die Kreuzfahrerherrschaft Scandalion (Iskanderūne)." *Zeitschrift des Deutschen Palästina-Vereins* 93 (1977): 12–29.

Favreau-Lilie, Marie-Luise. "'Multikulturelle Gesellschaft' oder 'Persecuting Society'? 'Franken' und 'Einheimische' im Königreich Jerusalem." In *Jerusalem im Hoch- und Spätmittelalter: Konflikte und Konfliktbewältigung—Vorstellungen und Vergegenwärtigungen*, edited by Dieter Bauer, Klaus Hebers, and Nikolas Jaspert, 55–93. Frankfurt am Main, 2001.

Figliuolo, Bruno. "Amalfi e il Levante nel Medioevo." In *I comuni italiani*, 571–677.

Fishhof, Gil. "From Sepphoris to Nazareth: Aspects of Crusader Historiography and a New Reading of the Nazareth Sculpture." In *The Crusader World*, edited by Adrian J. Boas, 663–74. Abingdon, 2016.

Fishhof, Gil. *Shaping Identities in a Holy Land: Crusader Art in the Latin Kingdom of Jerusalem, Patrons and Viewers*. Abingdon, 2024.

Fishhof, Gil, Amit Re'em, and David Yeger. "Two Recently Discovered Mural Paintings and the Development of Monumental Painting in Twelfth-Century Jerusalem." In *EO*, 2:132–55.

Folda, Jaroslav. *The Art of the Crusaders in the Holy Land, 1098–1187*. Cambridge, 1995.

Folda, Jaroslav. "Before Louis IX: Aspects of Crusader Art at St. Jean d'Acre, 1191–1244." In *France and the Holy Land*, 138–57.

Folda, Jaroslav. *Crusader Art: The Art of the Crusaders in the Holy Land, 1099–1291*. Aldershot, 2008.

Folda, Jaroslav. "Crusader Art and the West: Thoughts of Assessing the Impact of Art from the Crusader East on Medieval Art in Western Europe, Especially in Central Italy." In *The Crusader World*, edited by Adrian J. Boas, 624–45. Abingdon, 2016.

Folda, Jaroslav. *Crusader Art in the Holy Land from the Third Crusade to the Fall of Acre, 1187–1291*. Cambridge, 2005.

Folda, Jaroslav. *Crusader Manuscript Illumination at Saint-Jean d'Acre, 1275–1291*. Princeton, NJ, 1976.

Foreville, Raymonde. "Un chef de le Première Croisade: Arnoul Malecouronne." *Bulletin philologique et historique du Comité des travaux historiques et scientifiques*, 1953–54, 377–90.

Forey, Alan. "Literacy and Learning in the Military Orders during the Twelfth and Thirteenth Centuries." In *The Military Orders*, vol. 2: *Welfare and Warfare*, edited by Helen Nicholson, 185–206. Aldershot, 1998.

Forey, Alan. "The Militarization of the Hospital of St. John." *Studia monastica* 26 (1984): 75–89.

Forey, Alan. "Women and the Military Orders in the Twelfth and Thirteenth Centuries." *Studia monastica* 29 (1987): 63–92.

France, John. "Crusading Warfare and Its Adaptation to Eastern Conditions in the Twelfth Century." *Mediterranean Historical Review* 15 (2000): 49–66.

France, John. "Fortifications East and West." In *Muslim Military Architecture in Greater Syria: From the Coming of Islam to the Ottoman Period*, edited by Hugh Kennedy, 281–94. Leiden, 2006.

France, John. "An Unknown Account of the Capture of Jerusalem." *English Historical Review* 87 (1972): 771–83.

France, John. *Victory in the East: A Military History of the First Crusade*. Cambridge, 1994.

Friedman, Yvonne. *Encounter between Enemies: Captivity and Ransom in the Latin Kingdom of Jerusalem*. Leiden, 2002.

Fulton, Michael S. *Contest for Egypt: The Collapse of the Fatimid Caliphate, the Ebb of Crusader Influence, and the Rise of Saladin*. Leiden, 2022.

Fulton, Michael S. "Frankish Intervention in Egypt during the Reign of Amalric: Conquest or Extortion?" In *EO*, 1:191–206.

Fulton, Michael S. *Siege Warfare during the Crusades*. Barnsley, Yorkshire, 2019.

Gabrieli, Francesco. *Arab Historians of the Crusades*. Translated by E. J. Costello. Berkeley, 1969.

Gaggero, Massimiliano. "Western Eyes on the Latin East: The *Chronique d'Ernoul et de Bernard le Trésorier* and Robert de Clari's *Conquête de Constantinople*." In *The French of Outremer*, 86–109.

Gal, Zvi. "Saladin's Dome of Victory at the Horns of Ḥaṭṭīn." In *Horns*, 213–15.

Galadza, Daniel. "Greek Liturgy in Crusader Jerusalem: Witnesses of Liturgical Life at the Holy Sepulchre and St Sabas Lavra." *Journal of Medieval History* 43 (2017): 421–37 (the article also appears in Shagrir and Gaposchkin, *Liturgy and Devotion in the Crusader States*).

Gaposchkin, M. Cecilia. "The Feast of the Liberation of Jerusalem in British Library Additional ms. 8927 Reconsidered." *Mediaeval Studies* 77 (2015): 127–81.

Gaposchkin, M. Cecilia. *Invisible Weapons: Liturgy and the Making of Crusade Ideology*. Ithaca, NY, 2017.

Gaposchkin, M. Cecilia. "Notre Dame of Paris, the True Cross of 1120, and the Power of Relic Narratives." *Journal of Ecclesiastical History* (in press)

Geldsetzer, Sabine. *Frauen auf Kreuzzügen, 1096–1291*. Darmstadt, 2003.

Gerish, Deborah. "Remembering Kings in Jerusalem: The *Historia Nicaena vel Antiochena*, and Royal Identity around the Time of the Second Crusade." In *The Second Crusade: Holy War on the Periphery of Latin Christendom*, edited by Jason T. Roche and Janus Møller Jensen, 51–90. Turnhout, 2015.

Gerish, Deborah. "The True Cross and the Kings of Jerusalem." *Haskins Society Journal* 8 (1996): 137–55.

Giannini, Gabriele, and Laura Minervini. "The Old French Texts of the Damascus Qubba." In *The Damascus Fragments: Towards a History of the Qubbat al-khazna Corpus of Manuscripts*, edited by Arianna D'Ottone Rambach, Konrad Hirschler, and Ronny Vollandt, 331–64. Beirut, 2020.

Giannini, Gabriele, and Laura Minervini. "Retour à Damas: Des charmes et une épave des *Enfances Godefroi*." *Romania* 138 (2020): 276–304.

Giese, Wolfgang. "Stadt- und Herrscherbeschreibungen bei Wilhelm von Tyrus." *Deutsches Archiv* 34 (1978): 381–409.

Gilet, François. "La Tour de Détroit et les débuts de l'ordre du Temple." In *D'Orient en Occident*, 308–27.

Goitein, Shelomo Dov. "Contemporary Letters on the Capture of Jerusalem by the Crusaders." *Journal of Jewish Studies* 3 (1952): 162–77.

Goitein, Shelomo Dov. "Geniza Sources for the Crusader Period: A Survey." In *Outremer*, 306–22.

Goridis, Philippe. *Gefangen im Heiligen Land: Verarbeitung und Bewältigung christlicher Gefangenschaft zur Zeit der Kreuzzüge*. Ostfildern, 2015.

Graboïs, Aryeh. "La bibliothèque du noble d'*Outremer* à Acre dans la seconde moitié du XIIIe siècle." *Le Moyen Age* 103 (1997): 53–66.

Graboïs, Aryeh. "Les pèlerins occidentaux en Terre Sainte et Acre: D'Accon des croisés à Saint-Jean d'Acre." *Studi Medievali*, series 3, 24 (1983): 247–64.

Grandclaude, Maurice. *Etude critique sur les livres des Assises de Jérusalem*. Paris, 1923.

Greilsammer, Myriam. "Anatomie d'un mensonge: Le *Livre au Roi* et la révision de l'histoire du Royaume Latin par les juristes du XIIIe siècle." *Tijdschrift voor rechtsgeschiedenis / Revue d'histoire du droit* 67 (1999): 239–54.

Gross, Avraham, and Avraham Fraenkel. "The First Crusade and the Kingdom of Jerusalem in an Unpublished Hebrew Dirge." *Crusades* 11 (2012): 19–29.

Grousset, René. "Sur un passage obscur de Guillaume de Tyr." In *Mélanges syriens offerts à Monsieur René Dussaud par ses amis et élèves*, 2:937–39. Paris, 1939.

Haas, Thomas. *Geistliche als Kreuzfahrer: Der Klerus im Konflikt zwischen Orient und Okzident, 1095–1221*. Heidelberg, 2012.

Haber, Marc, et al., "A Transient Pulse of Genetic Admixture from the Crusaders in the Near East Identified from Ancient Genome Sequences." *American Journal of Human Genetics* 104, no. 5 (2019): 977–84.

Hamilton, Bernard. "Aimery of Limoges, Latin Patriarch of Antioch (c. 1142–c. 1196) and the Unity of the Churches." In *EWCS*, 2:1–12.

Hamilton, Bernard. "Aimery of Limoges, Patriarch of Antioch: Ecumenist, Scholar and Patron of Hermits." In *The Joy of Learning and the Love of God: Studies in Honor of Jean Leclercq*, edited by E. Rozanne Elder, 269–90. Kalamazoo, MI, 1995. Repr. in Hamilton, *Crusaders, Cathars and the Holy Places*, Study VIII. Aldershot, 1999.

Hamilton, Bernard. "The Elephant of Christ: Reynald of Châtillon." In *Religious Motivation: Biographical and Sociological Problems for the Church Historian*, edited by Derek Baker, 97–108. Oxford, 1978.

Hamilton, Bernard. "The Impact of Crusader Jerusalem on Western Christendom." *Catholic Historical Review* 80 (1994): 695–713.

Hamilton, Bernard. "King Consorts of Jerusalem and Their Entourages from the West from 1186 to 1250." In *Kreuzfahrerstaaten*, 13–24.

Hamilton, Bernard. *The Latin Church in the Crusader States: The Secular Church*. London, 1980.

Hamilton, Bernard. "Latins and Georgians and the Crusader Kingdom." *Al-Masāq* 23 (2011): 117–24.

Hamilton, Bernard. *The Leper King and His Heirs: Baldwin IV and the Crusader Kingdom of Jerusalem*. Cambridge, 2000.

Hamilton, Bernard. "The Old French Translation of William of Tyre as an Historical Source." In *EC*, 93–112.

Hamilton, Bernard. "Our Lady of Saidnaiya: An Orthodox Shrine Revered by Muslims and Knights Templar at the Time of the Crusades." In *The Holy Land, Holy Lands, and Christian History*, edited by Robert N. Swanson, 207–15. Woodbridge, 2000.

Hamilton, Bernard. "Ralph of Domfront, Patriarch of Antioch (1135–1140)." *Nottingham Medieval Studies* 28 (1984): 1–21.

Hamilton, Bernard. "Rebuilding Zion: The Holy Places of Jerusalem in the Twelfth Century." In *Renaissance and Renewal in Christian History*, edited by Derek Baker, 105–16. Oxford, 1977.

Hamilton, Bernard. "Why Did the Crusader States Produce So Few Saints?" In *Saints and Sanctity*, edited by Peter Clarke and Tony Claydon, 103–11. Cambridge, 2011.

Hamilton, Bernard, and Andrew Jotischky. *Latin and Greek Monasticism in the Crusader States*. Cambridge, 2020.

Handyside, Philip. *The Old French William of Tyre*. Leiden, 2015.

Harari, Yuval [N.]. "The Military Role of the Frankish Turcopoles: A Reassessment." *Mediterranean Historical Review* 12 (1997): 75–116.

Harvey, Elon. "Saladin Consoles Baldwin IV over the Death of His Father." *Crusades* 15 (2016): 27–33.

Haskins, Charles H. *The Renaissance of the Twelfth Century*. Cambridge, MA, 1927

Haskins, Charles H. *Studies in the History of Mediaeval Science*. Cambridge, MA, 1924

Hermes, Nizar F. "The Poet(ry) of Frankish Enchantment: The *Ifranjiyyāt* of Ibn Qaysarānī." *Middle Eastern Literatures* 20 (2017): 267–87.

Hiestand, Rudolf. "Die Anfänge der Johanniter." In *Die geistlichen Ritterorden Europas*, edited by Josef Fleckenstein and Manfred Hellmann, 31-80. Sigmaringen, 1980.

Hiestand, Rudolf. "Un centre intellectuel en Syrie du Nord? Notes sur la personnalité d'Aimeri d'Antioche, Albert de Tarse et *Rorgo Fretellus*." *Le Moyen Age* 100 (1994): 7–36.

Hiestand, Rudolf. "Gaufridus abbas Templi Domini: An Underestimated Figure in the Early History of the Kingdom of Jerusalem." In *EC*, 48–59.

Hiestand, Rudolf. "Kardinalbischof Matthäus von Albano, das Konzil von Troyes und die Entstehung des Templerordens." *Zeitschrift für Kirchengeschichte* 99 (1988): 295–323.

Hiestand, Rudolf. "La langue vulgaire dans les chartes de Terre Sainte avec un regard sur la chancellerie royale française." In *Von Outremer bis Flandern: Miscellanea zur Gallia Pontificia und zur Diplomatik*, edited by Klaus Herbers and Waldemar Könighaus, 269–304. Berlin, 2013.

Hiestand, Rudolf. "Der lateinische Klerus der Kreuzfahrerstaaten: Geographische Herkunft und politische Rolle." In *Kreuzfahrerstaaten*, 43–68.

Hiestand, Rudolf. "*Nam qui fuimus Occidentales, nunc facti sumus Orientales*: Siedlung und Siedleridentität in den Kreuzfahrerstaaten." In *Siedleridentität: Neun Fallstudien von der Antike bis zur Gegenwart*, edited by Christof Dipper and Rudolf Hiestand, 61–80. Frankfurt am Main, 1995.

Hiestand, Rudolf. "Ein neuer Bericht über das Konzil von Antiochia 1140." *Annuarium Historiae Conciliorum* 19 (1987): 314–50.

Hiestand, Rudolf. *Papsturkunden für Templer und Johanniter: Archivberichte und Texte*. Göttingen, 1972.

Hiestand, Rudolf. "Die Urkunden der lateinischen Patriarchen von Jerusalem und Antiochia im 12. Jahrhundert." In *Die Diplomatik der Bischofsurkunde vor 1250*, 85–95. Innsbruck, 1995.

Hiestand, Rudolf. "Ein Zimmer mit Blick auf das Meer: Einige wenig beachtete Aspekte der Pilgerreisen ins Hl. Land im 12. und 13. Jahrhundert." In *EWCS*, 3:139–64.

Hillenbrand, Carole. *The Crusades: Islamic Perspectives*. Edinburgh, 1999.

Hillenbrand, Carole. "The Imprisonment of Reynald of Châtillon." In *Texts, Documents and Artefacts: Islamic Studies in Honour of D.S. Richards*, edited by Chase F. Robinson, 79–102. Leiden, 2003.

Hirschler, Konrad. "Ibn Wāsil: An Ayyūbid Perspective on Frankish Lordships and Crusades." In *Medieval Muslim Historians and the Franks in the Levant*, edited by Alex Mallett, 136–60. Leiden, 2014.

Hirschler, Konrad. "The Jerusalem Conquest of 492/1099 in the Medieval Arabic Historiography of the Crusades: From Regional Plurality to Islamic Narrative." *Crusades* 13 (2014): 37–76.

Holmes, Urban Tignor. "Life among the Europeans in Palestine and Syria in the Twelfth and Thirteenth Centuries." In *Crusades*, ed. Setton, 4:3–35.

Holt, Peter M. *Early Mamluk Diplomacy (1260–1290): Treaties of Baybars and Qalāwūn with Christian Rulers*. Leiden, 1995.

Hunt, Lucy-Anne. "Art and Colonialism: The Mosaics of the Church of the Nativity in Bethlehem (1169) and the Problem of 'Crusader' Art." *Dumbarton Oaks Papers* 45 (1991): 69–85.

Hunt, Lucy-Anne. "John of Ibelin's Audience Hall in Beirut: A Crusader Palace Building between Byzantine and Islamic Art in Its Mediterranean Context." In *The Emperor's House: Palaces from Augustus to the Age of Absolutism*, edited by Michael Featherstone et al., 257–91. Boston, 2015.

Huygens, Robert B. C. "Guillaume de Tyr étudiant: Un chapitre (XIX, 12) de son 'Histoire' retrouvé." *Latomus* 21 (1962): 811–29.

Huygens, Robert B. C. *Latijn in "Outremer": Een blik op de latijnse letterkunde der kruisvaarderstaten in het Nabije Oosten*. Leiden, 1964.

Ingrand-Varenne, Estelle. "French Inscriptions in the Latin Kingdom of Jerusalem: From the Written Word to the Museum." *'Atiqot* 110 (2023): 241–62.

Ingrand-Varenne, Estelle. "Transferts épigraphiques: Les inscriptions de l'abbaye du Val de Josaphat a Jérusalem." In *Transferts*, 75–100.

Irwin, Robert. "Usamah ibn Munqidh: An Arab-Syrian Gentleman at the Time of the Crusades Reconsidered." In *Crusade Sources*, 71–87.

Jackson, David E. P. "Some Considerations Relating to the History of the Muslims in the Crusader States." In *EWCS*, 1:21–29.

Jackson, Peter. *The Seventh Crusade, 1244–1254: Sources and Documents*. Farnham, 2009.

Jacoby, David. "Aspects of Everyday Life in Frankish Acre." *Crusades* 4 (2005): 73–105.

Jacoby, David. "The Economic Function of the Crusader States of the Levant: A New Approach." In *Relazioni economiche tra Europa e mondo islamico secc. XIII–XVIII*, edited by Simonetta Cavaciocchi, 159–91. Florence, 2007. Repr. in Jacoby, *Medieval Trade in the Eastern Mediterranean and Beyond*, Study 4. Abingdon, 2018.

Jacoby, David. "The *fonde* of Crusader Acre and Its Tariff: Some New Considerations." In *Dei gesta per Francos: Etudes sur les croisades dédiées à Jean Richard*, edited by Michel Balard, B. Z. Kedar, and Jonathan Riley-Smith, 277–93. Aldershot, 2001.

Jacoby, David. "Intercultural Encounters in a Conquered Land: The Latin Kingdom of Jerusalem in the Twelfth and Thirteenth Centuries." In *Europa im Geflecht der Welt: Mittelalterliche Migrationen in globalen Bezügen*, edited by Michael Borgolte et al., 133–54. Berlin, 2012.

Jacoby, David. "Knightly Values and Class Consciousness in the Crusader States of the Eastern Mediterranean." *Mediterranean Historical Review* 1 (1986): 158–86. Repr. in Jacoby, *Studies on the Crusader States and on Venetian Expansion*, Study I. Northampton, 1989.

Jacoby, David. "La littérature française dans les états latins de la Méditerrannée orientale à l'époque des croisades: Diffusion et création." In *Essor et fortune de la chanson de geste dans l'Europe et l'Orient latin*, 617–46. Modena, 1984. Repr. in Jacoby, *Studies on the Crusader States and on Venetian Expansion*, Study II. Northampton, 1989.

Jacoby, David. "Pilgrimage in Crusader Acre: The *Pardouns dAcre* [*sic*]." In *De Sion exibit lex et verbum domini de Hierusalem: Essays on Medieval Law, Liturgy, and Literature in Honour of Amnon Linder*, edited by Yitzhak Hen, 105–17. Turnhout, 2001.

Jacoby, David. "Society, Culture and the Arts in Crusader Acre." In *France and the Holy Land*, 97–137.

Jacoby, Zehava. "The Impact of Northern French Gothic on Crusader Sculpture in the Holy Land." In *Il Medio Oriente e l'Occidente nell'arte del XIII secolo*, edited by Hans Belting, 123–27. Bologna, 1982.

Jacoby, Zehava. "The Tomb of Baldwin V, King of Jerusalem (1185–1186) and the Workshop of the Temple Area." *Gesta* 18 (1979): 3–14.

Jaspert, Nikolas. "The True Cross of Jerusalem in the Latin West: Mediterranean Connections and Institutional Agency." In *Visual Constructs of Jerusalem*, edited by Bianca Kühnel, Galit Noga-Banai, and Hanna Vorholt, 207–21. Turnhout, 2014.

John, Simon. "The 'Feast of the Liberation of Jerusalem': Remembering and Reconstructing the First Crusade in the Holy City, 1099–1187." *Journal of Medieval History* 41 (2015): 409–31.

John, Simon. *Godfrey of Bouillon, Duke of Lower Lotharingia, Ruler of Latin Jerusalem, c.1060–1100*. Abingdon, 2018.

Johns, Cedric Norman. "Excavations at Pilgrims' Castle ('Atlit): The Faubourg and Its Defences." *Quarterly of the Department of Antiquities in Palestine* 1 (1931): 111–29. Repr. in Johns, *Pilgrims' Castle ('Atlit), David's Tower (Jerusalem) and Qal'at ar-Rabad ('Ajlun): Three Middle Eastern Castles from the Time of the Crusades*, edited by Denys Pringle, Study II. Aldershot, 1997.

Johns, Cedric Norman. *Guide to 'Atlit: The Crusader Castle, Town and Surroundings* (Jerusalem, 1947). Repr. in Johns, *Pilgrims' Castle ('Atlit), David's Tower (Jerusalem) and Qal'at ar-Rabad ('Ajlun): Three Middle Eastern Castles from the Time of the Crusades*, edited by Denys Pringle, Study I. Aldershot, 1997.

Jotischky, Andrew. "Ethnographic Attitudes in the Crusader States: The Franks and the Indigenous Orthodox People." In *EWCS*, 3:1–19.

Jotischky, Andrew. "The Fortunes of War: An Eleventh-Century Greek Liturgical Manuscript (Sinai gr 512) and Its History." *Crusades* 9 (2010): 173–84.

Jotischky, Andrew. "The Frankish Encounter with the Greek Orthodox in the Crusader States: The Case of Gerard of Nazareth and Mary Magdalene." In *Tolerance and Intolerance: Social Conflict in the Age of the Crusades*, edited by Michael Gervers and James M. Powell, 100–114. Syracuse, NY, 2001.

Jotischky, Andrew. "Gerard of Nazareth, John Bale and the Origins of the Carmelite Order." *Journal of Ecclesiastical History* 46 (1995): 214–36.

Jotischky, Andrew. "Greek Orthodox and Latin Monasticism around Mar Saba under Crusader Rule." In *The Sabaite Heritage in the Orthodox Church from the Fifth Century to the Present*, edited by Joseph Patrich, 85–96. Leuven, 2001.

Jotischky, Andrew. "The Image of the Greek: Western Pilgrims' Views of Eastern Monks and Monasteries in the Holy Land, c.1200–1500." *Speculum* 94 (2019): 674–703.

Jotischky, Andrew. *The Perfection of Solitude: Hermits and Monks in the Crusader States.* University Park, PA, 1995.

Jotischky, Andrew. "Pilgrimage, Procession and Ritual Encounters between Christians and Muslims in the Crusader States." In *Cultural Encounters during the Crusades*, edited by Kurt Villads-Jensen, Kirsi Salonen, and Helle Vogt, 245–62. Odense, 2013.

Karras, Ruth Mazo. "The Regulation of 'Sodomy' in the Latin East and West." *Speculum* 95 (2020): 969–86.

Katzir, Yael. "The Patriarch of Jerusalem, Primate of the Latin Kingdom." In *CS*, 169–75.

Kedar, B. Z. "The Battle of Hattīn Revisited." In *Horns*, 190–207. Repr. in Kedar, *The Franks*, Study IX.

Kedar, B. Z. "Benvenutus Grapheus of Jerusalem, an Oculist in the Era of the Crusades." *Korot: The Israel Journal of the History of Medicine and Science* 11 (1995): 14–41. Repr. in Kedar, *Franks, Muslims*, Study XIV.

Kedar, B. Z. "Convergences of Oriental Christian, Muslim and Frankish Worshippers: The Case of Saydnaya and the Knights Templar." In *The Crusades and the Military Orders: Expanding the Frontiers of Medieval Latin Christianity*, edited by Zsolt Hunyadi and József Laszlovszky, 89–100. Budapest, 2001. Repr. in Kedar, *Crusaders*, Study XXI.

Kedar, B. Z. "Croisade et *Jihād* vus par l'ennemi: Une étude des perceptions mutuelles des motivations." In *Autour*, 345–55. Repr. in Kedar, *Franks, Muslims*, Study XVI.

Kedar, B. Z. *Crusade and Mission: European Approaches toward the Muslims.* Princeton, NJ, 1984.

Kedar, B. Z. "Ecclesiastical Legislation in the Kingdom of Jerusalem: The Statutes of Jaffa (1253) and Acre (1254)." In *CS*, 225–30.

Kedar, B. Z. "The Fourth Crusade's Second Front." In *Urbs Capta: The Fourth Crusade and Its Consequences*, edited by Angeliki Laiou, 89–110. Paris, 2005. Repr. in Kedar, *Crusaders*, Study XV.

Kedar, B. Z. "Frankish Bathhouses: *Balneum* and *furnus*—A Functional Dyad?" In *Communicating the Middle Ages: Essays in Honour of Sophia Menache*, edited by Iris Shagrir, B. Z. Kedar, and Michel Balard, 121–40. Abingdon, 2018.

Kedar, B. Z. "The General Tax of 1183 in the Crusading Kingdom of Jerusalem: Innovation or Adaptation?" *English Historical Review* 89 (1974): 339–45. Repr. in Kedar, *The Franks*, Study VII.

Kedar, B. Z. "Gerard of Nazareth: A Neglected Twelfth-Century Writer in the Latin East. A Contribution to the Intellectual and Monastic History of the Crusader States." *Dumbarton Oaks Papers* 37 (1983): 55–77. Repr. in Kedar, *The Franks*, Study IV.

Kedar, B. Z. "Ein Hilferuf aus Jerusalem vom September 1187." *Deutsches Archiv* 38 (1982): 112–22. Repr. in Kedar, *The Franks*, Study X.

Kedar, B. Z. "Holy Men in a Holy Land: Christian, Muslim and Jewish Religiosity in the Near East at the Time of the Crusades." Royal Holloway University of London. Hayes Robinson Lecture Series. Egham, Surrey, 2005.

Kedar, B. Z. "Iberia y el reino franco de Jerusalén." *Ad Limina* 8 (2017): 39–61.

Kedar, B. Z. "In Search of Ibelin Castle: Experimenting with Non-Destructive Archaeology." In *EO*, 2:5–28.

Kedar, B. Z. "The Jerusalem Massacre of July 1099 in the Western Historiography of the Crusades." *Crusades* 3 (2004): 15–75. Repr. in Kedar, *Crusaders*, Study VIII.

Kedar, B. Z. "The Latin Hermits of the Frankish Levant Revisited." In *"Come l'orco della fiaba": Studi per Franco Cardini*, edited by Marina Montesano, 185–202. Florence, 2010. Repr. in Kedar, *Crusaders*, Study XVIII.

Kedar, B. Z. *Merchants in Crisis: Genoese and Venetian Men of Affairs and the Fourteenth-Century Depression*. New Haven, CT, 1976.

Kedar, B. Z. "Le miracle du Feu sacré à Jérusalem: Des origines à la suppression papale." In *Bourgogne/Orient*, 519–29.

Kedar, B. Z. "Muslim Conversion in Canon Law." In *Proceedings of the Sixth International Conference of Medieval Canon Law, Berkeley 1980*, edited by Stephan Kuttner and Kenneth Pennington, 321–32. Vatican City, 1985. Repr. in Kedar, *The Franks*, Study XIV.

Kedar, B. Z. "Muslime in den fränkischen Burgen des Königreichs Jerusalem." *Burgen und Schlösser* 52 (2011): 210–18.

Kedar, B. Z. "A Note on Jerusalem's Bīmāristān and Jerusalem's Hospital." In *The Hospitallers, the Mediterranean and Europe: Festschrift for Anthony Luttrell*, edited by Karl Borchardt, Nikolas Jaspert, and Helen Nicholson, 7–11. Aldershot, 2007. Repr. in Kedar, *Crusaders*, Study II.

Kedar, B. Z. "On the Origins of the Earliest Laws of Frankish Jerusalem: The Canons of the Council of Nablus, 1120." *Speculum* 74 (1999): 310–35. Repr. in Kedar, *Franks, Muslims*, Study I.

Kedar, B. Z. "On Some Characteristics of the Second Kingdom of Jerusalem, 1191–1291." In *Settlement and Crusade in the Thirteenth Century: Multidisciplinary Studies of the Latin East*, edited by Gil Fishhof, Judith Bronstein, and Vardit Shotten-Hallel, 3–16. Abingdon, 2021.

Kedar, B. Z. "The Passenger List of a Crusader Ship, 1250: Toward the History of the Popular Element on the Seventh Crusade," *Studi Medievali*, series 3, 13 (1972): 267–79. Repr. in Kedar, *The Franks*, Study XVI.

Kedar, B. Z. "The Patriarch Eraclius." In *Outremer*, 177–204. Repr. in Kedar, *The Franks*, Study VIII.

Kedar, B. Z. "Raising Funds for a Frankish Cathedral: The Appeal of Bishop Radulph of Sebaste." In *Entrepreneurship and the Transformation of the Economy (10th–20th Centuries): Essays in Honour of Herman Van der Wee*, edited by Paul Klep and Eddy van Cauwenberghe, 443–55. Leuven, 1994. Repr. in Kedar, *Franks, Muslims*, Study XI.

Kedar, B. Z. "A Second Incarnation in Frankish Jerusalem." In *EC*, 79–92. Repr. in Kedar, *Franks, Muslims*, Study XIII.

Kedar, B. Z. "Some New Light on the Composition Process of William of Tyre's *Historia*." In *Deeds Done beyond the Sea*, 3–11. Repr. in Kedar, *Crusaders*, Study XIV.

Kedar, B. Z. "The Subjected Muslims of the Frankish Levant." In *Muslims under Latin Rule, 1100–1300*, edited by James M. Powell, 135–74. Princeton, NJ, 1990. Repr. in Kedar, *The Franks*, Study XVIII.

Kedar, B. Z. "The Use of Paper in the Frankish Levant: A Comparative Study." In *Crusading and Trading between East and West: Essays in Honour of David Jacoby*, edited by Sophia Menache, B. Z. Kedar, and Michel Balard, 3–16. Abingdon, 2019.

Kedar, B. Z., ed. "A Twelfth-Century Description of the Jerusalem Hospital." In Kedar, *Franks, Muslims*, Study X, 3–26.

Kedar, B. Z. "La *Via sancti sepulchri* come tramite di cultura araba in Occidente." In *Itinerari medievali e identità europea*, edited by Roberto Greci, 181–201. Bologna, 1999. Repr. in Kedar, *Franks, Muslims*, Study VIII.

Kedar, B. Z. "Vestiges of Templar Presence in the Aqsa Mosque." In *The Templars and Their Sources*, edited by Karl Borchardt et al., 3–24. Abingdon, 2017.

Kedar, B. Z. "A Western Survey of Saladin's Forces at the Siege of Acre." In *Montjoie*, 113–22. Repr. in Kedar, *Franks, Muslims*, Study VII.

Kedar, B. Z., and Cyril Aslanov. "Problems in the Study of Trans-Cultural Borrowing in the Frankish Levant." In *Hybride Kulturen im mittelalterlichen Europa*, edited by Michael Borgolte and Bernd Schneidmüller, 277–85. Berlin, 2010. Repr. in Kedar, *Crusaders*, Study XXII.

Kedar, B. Z., and Muhammad al-Hajjūj. "Muslim Villagers of the Frankish Kingdom of Jerusalem: Some Demographic and Onomastic Data." In *Itinéraires d'Orient: Hommages à Claude Cahen*, edited by Raoul Curiel and Rika Gyselen, Res Orientales 6, 145–56. Bures-sur-Yvette, 1994. Repr. in Kedar, *Franks, Muslims*, Study IV.

Kedar, B. Z., and Etan Kohlberg. "The Intercultural Career of Theodore of Antioch." *Mediterranean Historical Review* 10 (1995): 164–76. Repr. in Kedar, *Franks, Muslims*, Study XV.

Kedar, B. Z., and Denys Pringle. "La Fève: A Crusader Castle in the Jezreel Valley." *Israel Exploration Journal* 35 (1985): 164–79. Repr. in Kedar, *The Franks*, Study XI.

Kedar, B. Z., and Denys Pringle. "1099–1187: The Lord's Temple and the Temple of Salomon under Frankish Rule." In *Where Heaven and Earth Meet: Jerusalem's Sacred Esplanade*, edited by Oleg Grabar and B. Z. Kedar, 132–49. Jerusalem, 2009.

Kedar, B. Z., and Paolo Trovato. "New Perspectives on *Tractatus de locis et statu sancte terre ierosolimitane*." *Storie e Linguaggi* 4, no. 2 (2018): 1–32.

Kedar, B. Z., and Christian Westergård-Nielsen. "Icelanders in the Crusader Kingdom of Jerusalem: A Twelfth-Century Account." *Mediaeval Scandinavia* 11 (1978–79): 193–211. Repr. in Kedar, *The Franks*, Study V.

Kehati, Ron. "The Faunal Remains from the Templar Fortress and the Mamluk Hamlet." In *The Excavation of the Templar Fortress at Jacob's Ford (1993–2009): In Memory of Professor Ronnie Ellenblum*, edited by Kate

Raphael, Annual of the Nelson Glueck School of Biblical Archaeology 13, 171–93. Jerusalem, 2023.

Kenaan, Nurith. "Local Christian Art in Twelfth-Century Jerusalem." *Israel Exploration Journal* 23 (1973): 167–75, 221–29.

Kenaan-Kedar, Nurith. "Aspects des relations entre 'centre' et 'périphérie': Les cathédrales Saint-Étienne de Sens et Saint-Jean de Sébaste." In *Pèlerinages et croisades*, edited by Léon Pressouyre, 315–19. Paris, 1995.

Kenaan-Kedar, Nurith. "The Cathedral of Sebaste: Its Western Donors and Models." In *Horns*, 99–120.

Kenaan-Kedar, Nurith. "Decorative Architectural Sculpture in Crusader Jerusalem: The Eastern, Western and Armenian Sources of a Local Visual Culture." In *The Crusader World*, edited by Adrian J. Boas, 609–23. Abingdon, 2016.

Kenaan-Kedar, Nurith. "A Neglected Series of Crusader Sculpture: The Ninety-Six Corbels of the Church of the Holy Sepulchre." *Israel Exploration Journal* 42 (1992): 103–14.

Kenaan-Kedar, Nurith. "The Role and Meaning of Crusader Architectural Decoration: From Local Romanesque Traditions to Gothic Hegemony." In *Kreuzfahrerstaaten*, 165–78.

Kenaan-Kedar, Nurith. "Symbolic Meaning in Crusader Architecture: The Twelfth-Century Dome of the Holy Sepulcher Church in Jerusalem." *Cahiers archéologiques* 34 (1986): 109–17.

Kennedy, Hugh. *Crusader Castles*. Cambridge, 1994.

Khamisy, Rabei G. "Frankish Viticulture, Wine Presses, and Wine Production in the Levant: New Evidence from Castellum Regis (Mi'ilyā)." *Palestine Exploration Quarterly* 153 (2021): 191–221.

Khamisy, Rabei G., and Moshe Bram. "Belvoir Castle Revisited: History and Development." In *EO*, 2:310–28.

Khattab, Aleya. *Das Bild der Franken in der arabischen Literatur des Mittelalters: Ein Beitrag zum Dialog über die Kreuzzüge*. Göppingen, 1989.

Khoury, Paul. *Paul d'Antioche, évêque melkite de Sidon (XIIe s.)*. Beirut, 1964.

Kirschberger, Timo. *Erster Kreuzzug und Ethnogenese: In novam formam commutatus—Ethnogenetische Prozesse im Fürstentum Antiochia und im Königreich Jerusalem*. Göttingen, 2015.

Kirstein, Klaus-Peter. *Die lateinischen Patriarchen von Jerusalem: Von der Eroberung der Heiligen Stadt durch die Kreuzfahrer bis zum Ende der Kreuzfahrerstaaten 1291*. Berlin, 2002.

Klement, Katja. *Gottes Gastgeber: Die Ritter des Hospitals von Jerusalem. Die vatikanische Handschrift Vat. Lat. 4852*. Norderstedt, 2010.

Kohlberg, Etan, and B. Z. Kedar. "A Melkite Physician in Frankish Jerusalem and Ayyubid Damascus: Muwaffaq al-Dīn Yaʿqūb b. Siqlāb." *Asian and African Studies* 22 (1988): 113–26. Repr. in Kedar, *The Franks*, Study XII.

Köhler, Michael A. *Alliances and Treaties between Frankish and Muslim Rulers in the Middle East: Cross-Cultural Diplomacy in the Period of the Crusades*, translated by Peter M. Holt, revised by Konrad Hirschler. Leiden, 2012.

Kool, Robert. "Between *Moneta* and *Sikka*: Minters and Mints in the Frankish East (1099–1291)." In *EO*, 2:181–215.

Kool, Robert. "*Civitas regis regvm omnivm*: Inventing a Royal Seal in Jerusalem, 1100–1118." In *Crusading and Archaeology: Some Archaeological Approaches to the Crusades*, edited by Vardit Shotten-Hallel and Rosie Weetch, 244–62. Abingdon, 2021.

Kool, Robert. "Coin Circulation in the *villeneuves* of the Latin Kingdom of Jerusalem: The Cases of Parva Mahumeria and Bethgibelin." In *Archaeology and the Crusades*, edited by Peter Edbury and Sophia Kalopissi-Verti, 133–56. Athens, 2007.

Kool, Robert. "'Coins, Purses and Pigs': The Medieval Coins of Vadum Iacob." In *The Excavation of the Templar Fortress at Jacob's Ford (1993–2009): In Memory of Professor Ronnie Ellenblum*, edited by Kate Raphael, Annual of the Nelson Glueck School of Biblical Archaeology 13, 292–338. Jerusalem, 2023.

Kool, Robert. "Finding French Deniers in the Latin Kingdom of Jerusalem: The Archaeological and Cultural Perspective." In *Transferts*, 101–28.

Kool, Robert. "Lead Token Money in the Kingdom of Jerusalem." *Numismatic Chronicle* 173 (2013): 299–339.

Kool, Robert, Issa Baidoun, and Jacob Sharvit. "The Fatimid Gold Treasure from Caesarea Maritima Harbor (2015): Preliminary Results." In *5th Simone Assemani Symposium on Islamic Coins: Rome, 29–30 September 2017*, edited by Bruno Callegher and Arianna D'Ottone Rambach, Polymnia: Numismatica antica e medievale, Studi 12, 127–44. Trieste, 2018.

Kool, Robert, and Annette Landes-Nagar. "A Unique Crusader-Period Lead Seal from the Old City of Jerusalem." *ʿAtiqot* 110 (2023): 229–39.

Kool, Robert, Nikolaus Schindel, and Issa Baidoun. "A New Assemblage of Cut Gold Fragments from the Crusader Period." *Israel Numismatic Research* 14 (2019): 169–92.

Kool, Robert, and Oren Tal. "Another Token Mold and Lead Token from Crusader Arsur (Apollonia)." *Schweizerische Numismatische Rundschau* 98 (2020): 215–22.

Kool, Robert, and Oren Tal. "'Underground' Money in an Outremer Estate: Token Molds and Lead Tokens from Crusader Arsur." *Israel Numismatic Research* 10 (2015): 215–35.

Kostick, Conor. "The Afterlife of Bishop Adhémar of Le Puy." In *The Church, the Afterlife and the Fate of the Soul*, edited by Peter Clarke and Tony Claydon, 120–29. Woodbridge, 2009.

Kostick, Conor. *The Social Structure of the First Crusade*. Leiden, 2008.

Kühnel, Bianca. *Crusader Art of the Twelfth Century: A Geographical, an Historical, or an Art Historical Notion?* Berlin, 1994.

Kühnel, Bianca, and Gustav Kühnel. *The Church of the Nativity in Bethlehem: The Crusader Lining of an Early Christian Basilica*. Regensburg, 2019.

Kühnel, Gustav. *Wall Paintings in the Latin Kingdom of Jerusalem*. Frankfurter Forschungen zur Kunst 14. Berlin, 1988.

Lamberz, Erich. "The Bilingual Inscription in the Bema and the Conciliar Inscriptions in the Nave." In Kühnel and Kühnel, *The Church of the Nativity*, 145–65.

Latiff, Osman. *The Cutting Edge of the Poet's Sword: Muslim Poetic Responses to the Crusades*. Leiden, 2018.

Laurent, Vitalien. *Le corpus des sceaux de l'Empire byzantin*. Vol. 5.2: *L'Église*. Paris, 1965.

Laurent, Vitalien. "Un sceau inédit du patriarche de Jérusalem Sophrone II trouvé à Winchester." *Numismatic Circular* 72 (1964): 49–50.

Leclercq, Jean. "Gratien, Pierre de Troyes et la seconde croisade." *Studia Gratiana* 2 (1954): 589–93.

Leiser, Gary La Viere. "The Crusader Raid in the Red Sea, 578/1182–83." *Journal of the American Research Center in Egypt* 14 (1977): 87–100.

Lemesle, Bruno. "Foulques V, de l'Occident à l'Orient: Les réseaux du comte d'Anjou." In *D'Orient en Occident*, 122–34.

Lev, Yaacov. "Prisoners of War during the Fatimid-Ayyubid Wars with the Crusaders." In *Tolerance and Intolerance: Social Conflict in the Age of the Crusades*, edited by Michael Gervers and James M. Powell, 11–27. Syracuse, NY, 2001.

Lewis, Bernard. "Maimonides, Lionheart, and Saladin." In *Eretz-Israel*, 7:70–75. Jerusalem, 1964.

Lewis, Kevin J. *The Counts of Tripoli and Lebanon in the Twelfth Century: Sons of Saint-Gilles*. Abingdon, 2017.

Lewis, Kevin J. "Medieval Diglossia: The Diversity of the Latin Christian Encounter with Written and Spoken Arabic in the 'Crusader' County of Tripoli, with a Hitherto Unpublished Arabic Note from the Principality of Antioch." *Al-Masāq* 27 (2015): 119–52.

Linder, Amnon. "'Like Purest Gold Resplendent': The Fiftieth Anniversary of the Liberation of Jerusalem." *Crusades* 8 (2009): 31–51.

Linder, Amnon. "The Liturgy of the Liberation of Jerusalem." *Mediaeval Studies* 52 (1990): 110–31.

Linder, Amnon. "A New Day, New Joy: The Liberation of Jerusalem on 15 July 1099." In *L'idea di Gerusalemme nella spiritualità cristiana del Medioevo*, edited by Walter Brandmüller, 46–64. Vatican City, 2003.

Linder, Amnon. "An Unpublished Charter of Geoffrey, Abbot of the Temple in Jerusalem." In *Outremer*, 119–29.

Lower, Michael. *The Barons' Crusade: A Call to Arms and Its Consequences*. Philadelphia, 2005.

Luttrell, Anthony. "The Earliest Templars." In *Autour*, 193–202.

Lyons, Malcolm C., and D. E. P. Jackson. *Saladin: The Politics of the Holy War*. Cambridge, 1982.

MacEvitt, Christopher. *The Crusades and the Christian World of the East: Rough Tolerance*. Philadelphia, 2008.

MacEvitt, Christopher. "Processing Together, Celebrating Apart: Shared Processions in the Latin East." In *Liturgy and Devotion in the Crusader States*, edited by Iris Shagrir and [M.] Cecilia Gaposchkin (Abingdon, 2019), 95–109.

MacEvitt, Christopher. "What Was Crusader about the Crusader States?" *Al-Masāq* 30 (2018): 317–30.

Maier, Christoph T. "Über die Rolle der Frauen in der Krezzugsbewegung." In *Päpste, Pilger, Pönitentiarie: Festschrift für Ludwig Schmugge zum 65. Geburtstag*, edited by Andreas Meyer, Constanze Rendtel, and Maria Wittmer-Butsch, 253–81. Tübingen, 2004.

Mallett, Alex. "A Trip Down the Red Sea with Reynald of Châtillon." *Journal of the Royal Asiatic Society* 3, no. 18 (2008): 141–53.

Mayer, Hans Eberhard. "Angevins *versus* Normans: The New Men of King Fulk of Jerusalem." *Proceedings of the American Philosophical Society* 133 (1989): 1–25. Repr. in Mayer, *Kings and Lords in the Latin Kingdom of Jerusalem*, Study IV. Aldershot, 1994.

Mayer, Hans Eberhard. *Bistümer, Klöster und Stifte im Königreich Jerusalem*. MGH Schriften 26. Stuttgart, 1977.

Mayer, Hans Eberhard. "Einwanderer in der Kanzlei und am Hof der Kreuzfahrerkönige von Jerusalem." In *Kreuzfahrerstaaten*, 25–42.

Mayer, Hans Eberhard. "Frederick of Laroche, Bishop of Acre and Archbishop of Tyre." *Tel Aviver Jahrbuch für deutsche Geschichte* 22 (1993): 59–72.

Mayer, Hans Eberhard. *Geschichte der Kreuzzüge*. 10th ed. Stuttgart, 2005.

Mayer, Hans Eberhard. "Guillaume de Tyr à l'école." *Mémoires de l'Académie des sciences, arts et belles-lettres de Dijon* 127 (1988): 257–65. Repr. in Mayer, *Kings and Lords in the Latin Kingdom of Jerusalem*, Study V. Aldershot, 1994.

Mayer, Hans Eberhard. "Die Jerusalemer Grabeskirche als Begräbnisort in der Kreuzzugszeit." *Archiv für Kulturgeschichte* 103 (2021): 5–35.

Mayer, Hans Eberhard. *Die Kanzlei der lateinischen Könige von Jerusalem*. MGH Schriften 40. 2 vols. Hanover, 1996.

Mayer, Hans Eberhard. *Die Kreuzfahrerherrschaften Beirut und Blanchegarde*. Wiesbaden, 2022.

Mayer, Hans Eberhard. "Latins, Muslims and Greeks in the Latin Kingdom of Jerusalem." *History* 63 (1978): 175–92. Repr. in Mayer, *Probleme des lateinischen Königreichs Jerusalem*, Study VI. London, 1983.

Mayer, Hans Eberhard. "The Life and Afterlife of Julian of Sidon." *Crusades* 18 (2019): 67–92.

Mayer, Hans Eberhard. *Das Siegelwesen in den Kreuzfahrerstaaten*. Munich, 1978.

Mayer, Hans Eberhard. *Von der Cour des Bourgeois zum öffentlichen Notariat: Die freiwillige Gerichtsbarkeit in den Kreuzfahrerstaaten*. MGH Schriften 70. Wiesbaden, 2016.

Mayer, Hans Eberhard, and Claudia Sode. *Die Siegel der lateinischen Könige von Jerusalem*. MGH Schriften 66. Wiesbaden, 2014.

Mesqui, Jean. *Césarée maritime: Ville fortifiée du Proche-Orient*. Paris, 2014.

Messis, Charis. "Littérature, voyage et politique au XIIe siècle: L'*Ekphrasis des lieux saints* de Jean 'Phokas.'" *Byzantinoslavica* 69 (2011): 146–66.

Metcalf, D. Michael. *Coinage of the Crusades and the Latin East in the Ashmolean Museum, Oxford*. 2nd ed. London, 1995.

Metcalf, D. Michael. "Islamic, Byzantine and Latin Influences in the Iconography of Crusader Coins and Seals." In *EWCS*, 2:163–75.

Metcalf, D. Michael, Robert Kool, and Ariel Berman. "Coins from the Excavations at 'Atlit (Pilgrims' Castle) and Its *Faubourg*." *'Atiqot* 37 (1999): *89–*164.

Meurer, Heribert. "Kreuzreliquiare aus Jerusalem." *Jahrbuch der Staatlichen Kunstsammlungen in Baden-Württemberg* 13 (1976): 7–18.

Meurer, Heribert. "Zu den Staurotheken der Kreuzfahrer." *Zeitschrift für Kunstgeschichte* 48 (1985): 65–76.

Michaud, Françoise. "Les médecins orientaux au service des princes latins." In *Occident et Proche-Orient*, 96–103.

Miller, Timothy. "The Knights of Saint John and the Hospitals of the Latin West." *Speculum* 53 (1978): 709–33.

Minervini, Laura. "Les contacts entre indigènes et croisés dans l'Orient latin: Le rôle des drogmans." In *Romania arabica: Festschrift für Reinhold Kontzi zum 70. Geburtstag*, edited by Jens Lüdtke, 57–62. Tübingen, 1996.

Minervini, Laura. "Les emprunts arabes et grecs dans le lexique français d'Orient (XIIIe–XIVe siècles)." *Revue de linguistique romane* 76 (2012): 99–198.

Minervini, Laura. "Le français dans l'Orient latin: Eléments pour la caractérisation d'une *scripta* du Levant." *Revue de linguistique romane* 74 (2010): 119–98.

Minervini, Laura. "Gli orientalismi nel francese d'Oltremare." In *Sprachkontakte in der Romania: Zum 75. Geburtstag von Gustav Ineichen*, edited by Volker Noll and Sylvia Thiele, 123–33. Tübingen, 2004.

Minervini, Laura. "Outremer." In *Lo spazio letterario del Medioevo*, 2: *Il Medioevo volgare*, vol. 1.2: *La produzione del testo*, edited by Piero Boitani, Mario Mancini, and Alberto Vàrvaro, 611–48. Rome, 2001.

Minervini, Laura. "What We Know and Don't Yet Know about Outremer French." In *The French of Outremer*, 15–29.

Mitchell, Piers D. "A Comparison of Health at a Village and Castle in the Kingdom of Jerusalem in the Twelfth Century." In *The Military Orders*, vol. 4: *On Land and by Sea*, edited by Judi Upton-Ward, 23–28. Aldershot, 2008.

Mitchell, Piers D. *Medicine in the Crusades: Warfare, Wounds and the Medieval Surgeon*. Cambridge, 2004.

Mitchell, Piers D., and Andrew R. Millard. "Approaches to the Study of Migration during the Crusades." *Crusades* 12 (2013): 1–12.

Möhring, Hannes. "Die Kreuzfahrer, ihre muslimischen Untertanen und die heiligen Stätten des Islam." In *Toleranz im Mittelalter*, edited by Alexander Patschovsky and Harald Zimmermann, 129–57. Sigmaringen, 1998.

Möhring, Hannes. "Zu der Geschichte der orientalischen Herrscher des Wilhelm von Tyrus: Die Frage der Quellenabhängigkeiten." *Mittellateinisches Jahrbuch* 19 (1984): 170–83.

Morgan, M. Ruth. "The Meanings of Old French *polain*, Latin *pullanus*." *Medium Aevum* 48 (1979): 40–54.

Morreale, Laura K. "French-Language Documents Produced by the Hospitallers, 1231–1310." *Journal of Medieval History* 40 (2014): 439–57.

Morris, Colin. "Policy and Visions: The Case of the Holy Lance at Antioch." In *War and Government in the Middle Ages: Essays in Honour of J. O. Prestwich*, edited by John Gillingham and J. C. Holt, 33–45. Woodbridge, 1984.

Morton, Nicholas. *The Crusader States and Their Neighbours: A Military History, 1099–1187*. Oxford, 2020.

Morton, Nicholas. "William of Tyre's Attitudes towards Islam: Some Historiographical Reflections." In *Deeds Done beyond the Sea*, 13–23.

Mouton, Jean-Michel, and Jacques Paviot. "Un témoignage inédit sur la bataille de Hattīn (4 juillet 1187) et les relations entre Saladin et Renaud de Châtillon." In *Bourgogne/Orient*, 477–88.

Mouton, Jean-Michel, and Janine Sourdel-Thomine. "Nouveau témoignage sur les mouvements des populations rurales à l'époque des croisades," *Journal Asiatique* 308, no. 2 (2020): 145–50.

Murray, Alan V. *Baldwin of Bourcq, Count of Edessa and King of Jerusalem (1100–1131)*. Abingdon, 2022.

Murray, Alan V. "Biblical Quotations and Formulaic Language in the Chronicle of William of Tyre." In *Deeds Done beyond the Sea*, 25–34.

Murray, Alan V. "Ethnic Identity in the Crusader States: The Frankish Race and the Settlement of Outremer." In *Concepts of National Identity in the Middle Ages*, edited by Simon Forde, Lesley Johnson, and Alan V. Murray, 59–73. Leeds, 1995.

Murray, Alan V. "Franks and Indigenous Communities in Palestine and Syria (1099–1187): A Hierarchical Model of Social Interaction in the Principalities of Outremer." In *East Meets West in the Middle Ages and Early Modern Times: Transcultural Experiences in the Premodern World*, edited by Albrecht Classen, 291–309. Berlin, 2013.

Murray, Alan V. "'Mighty against the Enemies of Christ': The Relic of the True Cross in the Armies of the Kingdom of Jerusalem." In *Crusade Sources*, 217–38.

Murray, Alan V. "The Origins of the Frankish Nobility of the Kingdom of Jerusalem, 1100–1118." *Mediterranean Historical Review* 4 (1989): 281–300.

Murrell, William S. "Interpreters in Franco-Muslim Negotiations." *Crusades* 20 (2021): 131–50.

Myers, Geoffrey M. "*Les Chétifs*: Étude sur le développement de la chanson." *Romania* 105 (1984): 63–87.

Nader, Marwan. *Burgesses and Burgess Law in the Latin Kingdoms of Jerusalem and Cyprus (1099–1325)*. Aldershot, 2006.

Ng, Jeson. "Women of the Crusades: The Constructedness of the Female Other, 1100–1200." *Al-Masāq* 31 (2019): 303–22.

Nicholson, Helen J. "Templar Attitudes towards Women." *Medieval History* 1 (1991): 74–80.

Nicholson, Helen J. *Templars, Hospitallers and Teutonic Knights: Images of the Military Orders, 1128–1291*. Leicester, 1993.

Nicolle, David. *Crusader Warfare*. 2 vols. London, 2007.

Nobel, Pierre. "Écrire dans le Royame franc: La scripta de deux manuscrits copiés à Acre au XIIIe siècle." In *Variations linguistiques: Koinè, dialectes, français régionaux*, edited by Pierre Nobel, 33–52. Besançon, 2003.

Nobel, Pierre. "Les translations bibliques et leur public: L'exemple de la *Bible d'Acre* et de la *Bible Anglo-normande*." *Revue de linguistique romane* 66 (2002): 451–72.

Ousterhout, Robert. "The French Connection? Construction of Vaults and Cultural Identity in Crusader Architecture." In *France and the Holy Land*, 77–94.

Pace, Valentino. "I capitelli di Nazareth e la scultura 'franca' del XII secolo a Gerusalemme." In *Scritti di storia del'arte in onore di Roberto Salvini*, 87–95. Florence, 1984.

Pahlitzsch, Johannes. "Ärzte ohne Grenzen: Melkitische, jüdische und samaritanische Ärzte in Ägypten und Syrien zur Zeit der Kreuzzüge." In *Gesundheit—Krankheit: Kulturtransfer medizinischen Wissens von der Spätantike bis in die frühe Neuzeit*, edited by Florian Steger and Kay Peter Jankrift, 101–19. Cologne, 2004.

Pahlitzsch, Johannes. "Die Bedeutung der Azymenfrage für die Beziehngen zwischen griechisch-orthodoxer und lateinischer Kirche in den Kreuzfahrerstaaten." In *Die Folgen der Kreuzzüge für die orientalische Religionsgemeinschaft*, edited by Walter Beltz, 75-91. Halle, 1996.

Pahlitzsch, Johannes. "Georgians and Greeks in Jerusalem (1099-1310)." In *EWCS*, 3:35-51.

Pahlitzsch, Johannes. *Graeci und Suriani im Palästina der Kreuzfahrerzeit: Beiträge und Quellen zur Geschichte des griechisch-orthodoxen Patriarchats von Jerusalem*. Berlin, 2001.

Pahlitzsch, Johannes. "The Greek Orthodox Church in the First Kingdom of Jerusalem (1099-1187)." In *Patterns of the Past, Prospects for the Future: The Christian Heritage in the Holy Land*, edited by Thomas Hummel, Kevork Hintlian, and Ulf Carmesund, 195-212. London, 1999.

Pahlitzsch, Johannes. "St. Maria Magdalena, St. Thomas und St. Markus: Tradition und Geschichte dreier syrisch-orthodoxer Kirchen in Jerusalem." *Oriens Christianus* 81 (1997): 82–106.

Palmberger, Katharina. *Das unverrückbar Heilige—Jerusalems Loca Sancta in der Kreuzfahrerzeit*. Wiesbaden, 2020.

Palmer, Andrew. "The History of the Syrian Orthodox in Jerusalem. Part Two: Queen Melisende and the Jacobite Estates." *Oriens Christianus* 76 (1992): 74–94.

Paterson, Linda M. "Occitan Literature and the Holy Land." In *The World of Eleanor of Aquitaine: Literature and Society in Southern France between the Eleventh and Thirteenth Centuries*, edited by Marcus Bull and Catherine Léglu, 83–99. Woodbridge, 2005.

Paterson, Linda M. *Singing the Crusades: French and Occitan Lyric Responses to the Crusading Movements, 1137–1336*. Woodbridge, 2018.

Phillips, Jonathan. "Archbishop Henry of Reims and the Militarization of the Hospitallers." In *The Military Orders*, vol. 2: *Welfare and Warfare*, edited by Helen Nicholson, 83-88. Aldershot, 1998.

Phillips, Jonathan. *Defenders of the Holy Land: Relations between the Latin East and the West, 1119–1187*. Oxford, 1996.

Pines, Miriam, Lidar Sapir-Hen, and Oren Tal. "Crusader Diet in Times of War and Peace: Arsur (Israel) as a Case Study." *Oxford Journal of Archaeology* 36 (2017): 307–28.

Poirel, Dominique. "Les Templiers, le diable et le chanoine: Le *Sermo ad Milites Templi* réattribué à Hugues de Saint-Victor." In *Amicorum Societas: Mélanges offerts à François Dolbeau pour son 65e anniversaire*, edited by Jacques Elfassi, Cécile Lanéry, and Anne-Marie Turcan-Verkerk, 635-63. Florence, 2013.

Porteous, John. "Crusader Coinage with Greek or Latin Inscriptions." In *Crusades*, ed. Setton, 6:354–420.

Prawer, Joshua. *Crusader Institutions*. Oxford, 1980.

Prawer, Joshua. "Étude préliminaire sur les sources et la composition du Livre des Assises des Bourgeois." *Revue historique de droit français et étranger* 31 (1954): 198–227, 358–82.

Prawer, Joshua. *Histoire du Royaume latin de Jérusalem*. Translated by Gérard Nahon. 2 vols. Paris, 1969–71.

Prawer, Joshua. *The History of the Jews in the Latin Kingdom of Jerusalem*. Oxford, 1988.

Prawer, Joshua. *The Latin Kingdom of Jerusalem: European Colonialism in the Middle Ages*. London, 1972.

Prawer, Joshua. "Social Classes in the Crusader States: The 'Minorities.'" In *Crusades*, ed. Setton, 5:59–94.

Prawer, Joshua. "Social Classes in the Latin Kingdom: The Franks." In *Crusades*, ed. Setton, 5:117–92.

Pringle, Denys. "Churches and Settlement in Crusader Palestine." In *EC*, 161–78. Repr. in Pringle, *Churches, Castles and Landscape in the Frankish East*, Study II. Farnham, 2013.

Pringle, Denys. "Crusader Inscriptions from Southern Lebanon." *Crusades* 3 (2004): 131–51.

Pringle, Denys. "The Layout of the Jerusalem Hospital in the Twelfth Century: Further Thoughts and Suggestions." In *The Military Orders*, vol. 4: *On Land and by Sea*, edited by Judi Upton-Ward, 91–110. Aldershot, 2008.

Pringle, Denys. "Magna Mahumeria (al-Bīra): The Archaeology of a Frankish New Town in Palestine." In *CS*, 147–68. Repr. in Pringle, *Fortification and Settlement in Crusader Palestine*, Study VI. Aldershot, 2000.

Pringle, Denys. "Notes on Some Inscriptions from Crusader Acre." In *In Laudem Hierosolymitani: Studies in Crusades and Medieval Culture in Honour of Benjamin Z. Kedar*, edited by Iris Shagrir, Ronnie Ellenblum, and Jonathan Riley-Smith, 191–209. Aldershot, 2007.

Pringle, Denys. *Pilgrimage to Jerusalem and the Holy Land, 1187–1291*. Farnham, 2012.

Pringle, Denys. "Pottery as Evidence for Trade in the Crusader States." In *I comuni italiani*, 449–75.

Pringle, Denys. *The Red Tower (al-Burj al-Ahmar): Settlement in the Plain of Sharon at the Time of the Crusaders and Mamluks, A.D. 1099–1516*. London, 1986.

Pringle, Denys, trans. *Saewulf, John of Würzburg, Theoderic: Three Pilgrimages to the Holy Land*. Turnhout, 2022.

Pringle, Denys. *Secular Buildings in the Crusader Kingdom of Jerusalem: An Archaeological Gazetteer*. Cambridge, 1997.

Pringle, Denys. "Some Approaches to the Study of Crusader Masonry Marks in Palestine." *Levant* 13 (1981): 173–99.

Pringle, Denys. "Some More Proto-Maiolica from 'Athlit (Pilgrims' Castle) and a Discussion of Its Distribution in the Levant." *Levant* 14 (1982): 104–17.

Prutz, Hans. *Kulturgeschichte der Kreuzzüge*. Berlin, 1883. Repr. Hildesheim, 1994.

Prutz, Hans. "Studien über Wilhelm von Tyrus." *Neues Archiv der Gesellschaft für ältere deutsche Geschichtskunde* 8 (1883): 93–132.

Pryor, John H. "*In subsidium Terrae Sanctae*: Exports of Foodstuffs and War Materials from the Kingdom of Sicily to the Kingdom of Jerusalem, 1265–1284." *Asian and African Studies* 22 (1988): 127–46.

Purkis, William J. "'Holy Christendom's New Colony': The Extraction of Sacred Matter and the Colonial Status of the Latin Kingdom of Jerusalem." *Haskins Society Journal* 30 (2020): 177–211.

Re'em, Amit, Estelle Ingrand-Varenne, and Ilya Berkovich. "Surviving Three Cycles of Destruction: The Graves of the Crusader Kings in the Church of the Holy Sepulchre." *New Studies in the Archaeology of Jerusalem and Its Region* 15 (2022): 71–103.

Rey, Emmanuel. *Les colonies franques de Syrie aux XII*^me^ *et XIII*^me^ *siècles*. Paris, 1883.

Rheinheimer, Martin. *Das Kreuzfahrerfürstentum Galiläa*. Frankfurt am Main, 1990.

Richard, Jean. "An Account of the Battle of Hattin Referring to the Frankish Mercenaries in Oriental Moslem States." *Speculum* 27 (1952): 168–77.

Richard, Jean. "The Adventure of John Gale, Knight of Tyre." In *EC*, 189–95.

Richard, Jean. *L'esprit de la croisade*. Paris, 1969.

Richard, Jean. *Histoire des croisades*. Paris, 1996.

Richard, Jean. *The Latin Kingdom of Jerusalem*. Translated by Janet Shirley. 2 vols. Amsterdam, 1979.

Richard, Jean. "Les mercenaires francs dans les armées musulmanes au temps des croisades." In *Regards croisés sur le Moyen Age arabe: Mélanges à la mémoire de Louis Pouget s.j. (1928–2002)*, edited by Anne-Marie Eddé and Emma Gannage, 227–38. Beirut, 2005.

Richard, Jean. "La noblesse de Terre Sainte (1097–1187)." *Arquivos do Centro Cultural Português* 26 (1989): 321–36. Repr. in Richard, *Croisades et états latins d'Orient: Points de vue et documents*, Study IX. Aldershot, 1992.

Richards, Donald S. "A Text of ʿImād al-Dīn on 12th-Century Frankish-Arabic Relations." *Arabica* 25 (1978): 202–4.

Richter-Bernburg, Lutz. "St. John of Acre-Nablus-Damascus: The Samaritan Minority under Crusaders and Muslims." In *Die Folgen der Kreuzzüge für die orientalische Religionsgemeinschaft*, edited by Walter Beltz, 117–30. Halle, 1996.

Riley-Smith, Jonathan. "The Crown of France and Acre, 1254–1291." In *France and the Holy Land*, 45–62.

Riley-Smith, Jonathan. *The Crusades: A History*. 2nd ed. London, 2005.

Riley-Smith, Jonathan. *The Crusades: A Short History*. New Haven, CT, 1987.

Riley-Smith, Jonathan. "Crusading as an Act of Love." *History* 65 (1980): 177–92. Repr. in Riley-Smith, *Crusaders and Settlers in the Latin East*, Study VI. Farnham, 2008.

Riley-Smith, Jonathan. "The Death and Burial of Latin Christian Pilgrims to Jerusalem and Acre, 1099–1291." *Crusades* 7 (2008): 165–79.

Riley-Smith, Jonathan. *The Feudal Nobility and the Kingdom of Jerusalem, 1174–1277*. London, 1973.

Riley-Smith, Jonathan. *The First Crusade and the Idea of Crusading*. Philadelphia, 1986.

Riley-Smith, Jonathan. "The First Crusade and the Persecution of the Jews." In *Persecution and Toleration*, edited by William J. Sheils, 51–72. Cambridge, 1984.

Riley-Smith, Jonathan. *The First Crusaders, 1095–1131*. Cambridge, 1997.

Riley-Smith, Jonathan. "Government and the Indigenous in the Latin Kingdom of Jerusalem." In *Medieval Frontiers: Concepts and Practices*, edited by David Abulafia and Nora Berend, 121–31. Aldershot, 2002. Repr. in Riley-Smith, *Crusaders and Settlers in the Latin East*, Study XI. Farnham, 2008.

Riley-Smith, Jonathan. *The Knights Hospitallers in the Levant, c. 1070–1309*. Houndmills, 2012.

Riley-Smith, Jonathan. "The Latin Clergy and the Settlement in Palestine and Syria, 1098–1100." *Catholic Historical Review* 74 (1988): 539–57.

Riley-Smith, Jonathan. *Templars and Hospitallers as Professed Religious in the Holy Land*. Notre Dame, IN, 2010.

Röhricht, Reinhold. "Amalrich I., König von Jerusalem (1162–1174)." *Mittheilungen des Instituts für Österreichische Geschichtsforschung* 12 (1891): 432–81.

Röhricht, Reinhold. *Beiträge zur Geschichte der Kreuzzüge*. 2 vols. Berlin, 1874–78.

Röhricht, Reinhold. *Bibliotheca geographica Palaestinae*. Edited by David H. K. Amiran. London, 1989. Originally published Berlin, 1890.

Röhricht, Reinhold. *Geschichte des Königreichs Jerusalem, 1100–1291*. Innsbruck, 1898.

Rowe, John G. "Paschal II and the Relations between the Spiritual and Temporal Powers in the Kingdom of Jerusalem." *Speculum* 32 (1957): 470–501.

Rubin, Jonathan. "The Beginnings of the Study of Foreign Languages in the Dominican Order: Regulation, Implementation, and Impact." In *Making and Breaking the Rules: Discussion, Implementation, and Consequences of Dominican Legislation*, edited by Cornelia Linde, 253–72. Oxford, 2018.

Rubin, Jonathan. "Benoît d'Alignan and Thomas Agni: Two Frankish Intellectuals and the Study of Oriental Christianity in Thirteenth-Century Kingdom of Jerusalem." *Viator* 44 (2013): 189–99.

Rubin, Jonathan. "Burchard of Mount Sion's *Descriptio Terrae Sanctae*: A Newly Discovered Extended Version." *Crusades* 13 (2014): 173–90.

Rubin, Jonathan. "Ethnographic Writing in the Kingdom of Jerusalem: In Search of a Neglected Intellectual Tradition." *Journal of Medieval History* 48 (2022): 323–46.

Rubin, Jonathan. "John of Ancona's *Summae*: A Neglected Source for the Juridical History of the Latin Kingdom of Jerusalem." *Bulletin of Medieval Canon Law*, n.s. 29 (2012): 183–218.

Rubin, Jonathan. *Learning in a Crusader City: Intellectual Activity and Intercultural Exchange in Acre, 1191–1291*. Cambridge, 2018.

Rubin, Jonathan, and Cornelia Linde. "Western Medicine for the Masters of Damascus: Benvenutus Grapheus's *Experimenta*." *Al-Masāq* 26 (2014): 183–95.

Runciman, Steven. *A History of the Crusades*. 3 vols. Cambridge, 1951–54.

Runciman, Steven. "The Visit of King Amalric I to Constantinople in 1171." In *Outremer*, 153–58.

Russell, Josiah C. "The Population of the Crusader States." In *Crusades*, ed. Setton, 5:295–314 [to be read together with Robert Irwin's review in the *Times Literary Supplement*, March 7, 1986, page 237].

Salvadó, Sebastián. "The Augustinian Reform, the *Panormia* Glosses and Reading the Bible in the Medieval Latin Liturgy of Jerusalem." *Revue d'études augustiniennes et patristiques* 62 (2016): 1–29.

Salvadó, Sebastián. "Rewriting the Latin Liturgy of the Holy Sepulchre: Text, Ritual and Devotion for 1149." *Journal of Medieval History* 43 (2017): 403–20 (the article also appears in Shagrir and Gaposchkin, *Liturgy and Devotion in the Crusader States*).

Savage-Smith, Emilie. "New Evidence for the Frankish Study of Arabic Medical Texts in the Crusader Period." *Crusades* 5 (2006): 99–112.

Saxer, Victor. "Le calendrier de l'église latine d'Antioche à l'usage du patriarche Opizzo Ier Fieschi (1254–1255)." *Rivista di storia della chiesa in Italia* 26 (1972): 105–23.

Schein, Sylvia. "Between Mount Moriah and the Holy Sepulchre: The Changing Traditions of the Temple Mount in the Central Middle Ages." *Traditio* 40 (1984): 175–96.

Schein, Sylvia. *Gateway to the Heavenly City: Crusader Jerusalem and the Catholic West (1099–1187)*. Aldershot, 2005.

Schlumberger, Gustave. *Numismatique de l'Orient latin*. Paris, 1878. Repr. Graz, 1954.

Schlumberger, Gustave. *Renaud de Châtillon, prince d'Antioche, seigneur de la terre d'Outre-Jourdain*. 2nd ed. Paris, 1923.

Schlumberger, Gustave, Ferdinand Chalandon, and Adrien Blanchet. *Sigillographie de l'Orient latin*. Paris, 1943.

Schneidermann, Shulamit. "The Hospitallers' Hospital in Twelfth-Century Jerusalem in the Mirror of East and West." Master's thesis, Hebrew University of Jerusalem, 2000 [in Hebrew].

Schnürer, Gustav. *Die ursprüngliche Templerregel, kritisch untersucht und herausgegeben*. Freiburg im Breisgau, 1903.

Schwerin, Ursula. *Die Aufrufe der Päpste zur Befreiung des Heiligen Landes von den Anfängen bis zum Ausgang Innozenz IV.: Ein Beitrag zur Geschichte der kurialen Kreuzzugspropaganda und der päpstlichen Epistolographie*. Berlin, 1937.

Schwinges, Rainer Christoph. *Kreuzzugsideologie und Toleranz: Studien zu Wilhelm von Tyrus*. Stuttgart, 1977.

Schwinges, Rainer Christoph. "Regionale Identität und Begegnung der Kulturen in Stadt und 'Kreuzfahrerkönigreich' Jerusalem." In *Päpste, Pilger, Pönitentiarie: Festschrift für Ludwig Schmugge zum 65. Geburtstag*, edited by Andreas Meyer, Constanze Rendtel, and Maria Wittmer-Butsch, 237–51. Tübingen, 2004.

Shachar, Uri Zvi. *A Pious Belligerence: Dialogical Warfare and the Rhetoric of Righteousness in the Crusading Near East*. Philadelphia, 2021.

Shagrir, Iris. "Adventus in Jerusalem: The Palm Sunday Celebration in Latin Jerusalem." *Journal of Medieval History* 41 (2015): 1–20.

Shagrir, Iris. "The 'Holy Women' in the Liturgy and the Art of the Church of the Holy Sepulchre in Twelfth-Century Jerusalem." In *The Uses of the*

Bible in Crusader Sources, edited by Elizabeth Lapina and Nicholas Morton, 455–75. Leiden, 2017.

Shagrir, Iris. *Naming Patterns in the Latin Kingdom of Jerusalem*. Prosographica et Genealogica 12. Oxford, 2003.

Shagrir, Iris. "Urban Soundscape: Defining Space and Community in Twelfth-Century Jerusalem." In *Communicating the Middle Ages: Essays in Honour of Sophia Menache*, edited by Iris Shagrir, B. Z. Kedar, and Michel Balard, 103–20. Abingdon, 2018.

Shagrir, Iris. "The *Visitatio Sepulchri* in the Latin Church of the Holy Sepulchre in Jerusalem." *Al-Masāq* 22 (2010): 57–77.

Shagrir, Iris, and Cecilia Gaposchkin, eds. *Liturgy and Devotion in the Crusader States*. Abingdon, 2020.

Sharon, Moshe. "Vassal and Faṣal: The Evidence of the Farkhah Inscription from 608/1210." *Crusades* 4 (2005): 117–30.

Sharon, Moshe, with Ami Schrager. "Frederick II's Arabic Inscription from Jaffa (1229)." *Crusades* 11 (2012): 139–58.

Shatzmiller, Maya. "The Crusades and Islamic Warfare." *Der Islam* 69 (1992): 247–88.

Shotten-Hallel, Vardit, and Estelle Ingrand-Varenne. "William of Belvoir(?): A Short Note on an Even Shorter Inscription." *Crusades* 18 (2019): 21–24.

Shotten-Hallel, Vardit, Jean Mesqui, and Uzi ʿAd. "Three Main Towers of Medieval Caesarea: Their Architecture and Function." In *The Art of Siege Warfare and Military Architecture from the Classical Age to the Middle Ages*, edited by Michael Eisenberg and Rabei Khamisy, 189–211. Oxford, 2021.

Sinclair, Keith V. "The French Prayer for the Sick in the Hospital of the Knights of Saint John of Jerusalem at Acre." *Mediaeval Studies* 40 (1978): 484–88.

Sion, Danny, Eliezer Stern, and Piers D. Mitchell, "Water Installation in Crusader Acre," in *ʿAkko III, the 1991–1998 Excavations: The Late Periods*, edited by Eliezer Stern, Danny Syon, and Ayelet Tatcher, IAA Reports. Jerusalem (in press)

Sivan, Emmanuel. *L'Islam et la croisade: Idéologie et propagande dans les reactions musulmanes aux croisades*. Paris, 1968.

Sivan, Emmanuel. "Refugiés syro-palestiniens au temps des croisades." *Revue des études islamiques* 35 (1967): 135–47.

Skottki, Kristin. *Christen, Muslime und der Erste Kreuzzug: Die Macht der Beschreibung in der mittelalterlichen und modernen Historiographie*. Münster, 2015.

Slavin, Philip. "'With a Grain of Sugar': Native Agriculture and Colonial Capitalism in the Frankish Levant, 1100–1300." *Crusades* 22, no. 1 (2023): 1–38.

Smail, R. C. *The Crusaders in Syria and the Holy Land*. London, 1973.

Smail, R. C. *Crusading Warfare (1097–1193)*. Cambridge, 1956.

Smail, R. C. "The Predicaments of Guy of Lusignan, 1183–87." In *Outremer*, 159–76.

Smarandache, Bogdan C. "A Reassessment of Frankish Settlement Patterns in the Latin Kingdom of Jerusalem, 493–583 AH/1099–1187 AD."

In *Minorities in Contact in the Medieval Mediterranean*, edited by Clara Almagro Vidal, Jessica Tearney-Pearce, and Luke Yarbrough, 285–335. Turnhout, 2020.

Smarandache, Bogdan C. "Re-Examining Usama ibn Munqidh's Knowledge of 'Frankish': A Case Study of Medieval Bilingualism during the Crusades." *Medieval Globe* 3 (2017): 47–85.

Smithline, Howard, Edna J. Stern, and Eliezer Stern. "A Crusader-Period Bathhouse in ʿAkko (Acre)." *ʿAtiqot* 73 (2013): 71–108.

Southern, Richard W. "Peter of Blois and the Third Crusade." In *Studies in Medieval History Presented to R.H.C. Davis*, edited by Henry Mayr-Herting and R. I. Moore, 207–18. London, 1985.

Spacey, Beth C. "Refocusing the First Crusade: Authorial Self-Fashioning and the Miraculous in William of Tyre's *Historia Ierosolymitana*." In *Remembering the Crusades in Medieval Texts and Songs*, edited by Andrew D. Buck and Thomas W. Smith, 51–65. Cardiff, 2019.

Spreckelmayer, Goswin. *Das Kreuzlied des lateinischen Mittelalters*. Munich, 1974.

Stahl, Alan M. "The *Denier* Outremer." In *The French of Outremer*, 30–43.

Stern, Edna J. *ʿAkko I, the 1991–1998 Excavations: The Crusader Period Pottery*. Part 1: *Text*. Part 2: *Plates*. Jerusalem, 2012.

Stern, Edna J. "Franks, Locals and Merchants: Ceramic Production in the Latin East." In *EO*, 2:156–80.

Stern, Edna J. "Pottery and Identity in the Latin Kingdom of Jerusalem: A Case Study of Acre and Western Galilee." In *Medieval and Post-Medieval Ceramics in the Eastern Mediterranean: Fact and Fiction*, edited by Joanita Vroom, 287–315. Turnhout, 2015.

Stern, Edna J., et al. "Sugar Production in the ʿAkko Plain from the Fatimid to the Early Ottoman Periods." In *The Origins of the Sugar Industry and the Transmission of Ancient Greek and Medieval Arab Science and Technology from the Near East to Europe*, edited by Konstantinos D. Politis, 79–112. Athens, 2015.

Stern, Edna J., Sylvie Yona Waksman, and Anastasia Shapiro. "The Impact of the Crusades on Ceramic Production and Use in the Southern Levant: Continuity or Change?" In *Multidisciplinary Approaches to Food and Foodways in the Medieval Eastern Mediterranean*, edited by Sylvie Yona Waksman, 95–112. Lyon, 2020.

Tal, Oren, Robert Kool, and Issa Baidoun, "A Hoard Twice Buried? Fatimid Gold from Thirteenth Century Crusader Arsur (Apollonia—Arsuf)." *Numismatic Chronicle* 173 (2013): 261–92.

Talmon-Heller, Daniella. "The Shaykh and the Community: Popular Hanbalite Islam in 12th–13th Century Jabal Nablus and Jabal Qasyūn." *Studia Islamica* 79 (1994): 103–20.

Talmon-Heller, Daniella, and B. Z. Kedar. "Did Muslim Survivors of the 1099 Massacre of Jerusalem Settle in Damascus? The True Origins of the al-Ṣāliḥiyya Suburb." *Al-Masāq* 17 (2005): 165–69. Repr. in Kedar, *Crusaders*, Study IX.

Ten Hacken, Clara. "The Description of Antioch in Abū al-Makārim's History of the Churches and Monasteries of Egypt and some Neighbouring Countries." In *EWMEM*, 185–216.

Tessera, Miriam Rita. "Dalla liturgia del Santo Sepolcro alla biblioteca di Sidone: Note sulla produzione libraria latina di Oltremare nel XII–XIII secolo." *Aevum* 79 (2005): 407–15.

Tessera, Miriam Rita. "Le donne e la traslazione delle reliquie di Oltremare in Occidente nel secolo XII." *Reti Medievali Rivista* 21, no. 2 (2020): 105–45.

Tessera, Miriam Rita. *Orientalis ecclesia: Papato, Chiesa e regno latino di Gerusalemme (1099–1187)*. Milan, 2010.

Tessera, Miriam Rita. "Il sogno del re Amalrico, Bernardo di Clairvaux e la reliquia della Vera Croce." *Aevum* 87 (2013): 343–70.

Tessera, Miriam Rita. "Tra Oriente ed Occidente: Guglielmo di Tiro, l'Europa e l'identità degli stati latini di oltremare." In *Studi sull'Europa medioevale: L'Europa di fronte all'Oriente Cristiano tra alto e pieno Medioevo*, edited by Annamaria Ambrosioni, 95–115. Alessandria, 2001.

Tibble, Steve. *The Crusader Armies, 1099–1187*. New Haven, CT, 2018.

Tibble, Steve. *The Crusader Strategy: Defending the Holy Land, 1099–1187*. New Haven, CT, 2020.

Tischler, Christiane. *Die Burgenses von Jerusalem im 12. Jahrhundert: Eine Prosographie über die nichtadligen Einwohner Jerusalems von 1120 bis 1187*. Frankfurt am Main, 2000.

Touati, François-Olivier. "La Terre sainte: Un laboratoire hospitalier au Moyen Âge?" In *Sozialgeschichte mittelalterlicher Hospitäler*, edited by Neithard Bulst and Karl-Heinz Spieß, 169–211. Ostfildern, 2007.

Treffort, Cécile. "Les inscriptions latines et françaises des XIIe et XIIIe siècles découvertes à Tyr." In *Sources de l'histoire de Tyr: Textes de l'Antiquité et du Moyen Age*, edited by Pierre-Louis Gatier, Julien Aliquot, and Lévon Nordiguian, 221–51. Beirut, 2011.

Tsurtsumia, Mamuka. "Commemoration of Crusaders in the Manuscripts of the Monastery of the Holy Cross in Jerusalem." *Journal of Medieval History* 38 (2012): 318–34.

Tyerman, Christopher. *God's War: A New History of the Crusades*. London, 2006.

Varsy, Jean-Georges. "Anecdote des croisades." *Journal Asiatique* 4, no. 16 (1850): 75–92.

Vasselot de Régné, Clément de. "A Crusader Lineage from Spain to the Throne of Jerusalem: The Lusignans." *Crusades* 16 (2017): 95–114.

Vessey, David W. T. C. "William of Tyre and the Art of Historiography." *Mediaeval Studies* 35 (1973): 433–55.

Viaud, Prosper. *Nazareth et ses deux églises de l'Annonciation et de Saint-Joseph d'après les fouilles récentes*. Paris, 1910.

Vogel, Christian. *Das Recht der Templer*. Berlin, 2007.

Voltaire. *Histoire des croisades*. Berlin, 1751.

Vorderstrasse, Tasha. *Al-Mina: A Port of Antioch from Late Antiquity to the End of the Ottomans*. Leiden, 2005.

Waas, Adolf. *Geschichte der Kreuzzüge*. 2 vols. Freiburg im Breisgau, 1956.

Wagner, Thomas Gregor. *Die Seuchen der Kreuzzüge: Krankheit und Krankenpflege auf den bewaffneten Pilgerfahten ins Heilige Land*. Würzburg, 2009.

Waldstein-Wartenberg, Berthold. *Die Vasallen Christi: Kulturgeschichte des Johanniterordens im Mittelalter*. Vienna, 1988.

Weitzmann, Kurt. "Thirteenth Century Crusader Icons on Mount Sinai." *Art Bulletin* 45 (1963): 179–203.

Weltecke, Dorothea. "Contacts between Syriac Orthodox and Latin Military Orders." In *EWCS*, 3:54–77.

White, Lynn T., Jr. "The Crusades and the Technological Thrust of the West." In *War, Technology and Society in the Middle East*, edited by Vernon J. Parry and Malcolm E. Yapp, 97–112. London, 1975.

Wild, Stefan. "Open Questions, New Light: Usama Ibn Munqidh's Account of His Battles against Muslims and Franks." In *The Frankish Wars and Their Influence on Palestine*, edited by Khalil Athamina and Roger Heacock, 9–29. Birzeit, 1994.

Williams, Steven J. *The Secret of Secrets: The Scholarly Career of a Pseudo-Aristotelian Text in the Latin Middle Ages*. Ann Arbor, 2003.

Wormald, Francis. "The Calendars of the Church of the Holy Sepulchre, Jerusalem." In Hugo Buchthal, *Miniature Painting in the Latin Kingdom of Jerusalem*, 107–21. Oxford, 1957.

Yehuda, Elisabeth, Judith Bronstein, and Edna J. Stern. "Frankish Bread and Baking Ovens in the Latin Kingdom of Jerusalem: Between Conservatism and Adaptation." *Medieval Archaeology* 66 (2022): 400–430.

Yeivin, Ze'ev. "The Machpela Cave Subterranean Complex." *Israel—People and Land: Haaretz Museum Yearbook*, n.s. 2–3 (1985–86): 53–62 [in Hebrew, with English summary].

Yolles, Julian. *Making the East Latin: The Latin Literature of the Levant in the Era of the Crusades*. Washington, DC, 2022.

Zimmer, John, Werner Meyer, and Letizia Boscardin. *Krak des Chevaliers in Syrien: Archäologie und Bauforschung 2003 bis 2007*. Koblenz, 2011.

Zimo, Ann E. "Us and Them: Identity in William of Tyre's *Chronicon*." *Crusades* 18 (2019): 1–19.

Zöller, Wolf. "The Other Augustinian Consortium: The Templars and the Smaller Communities of Regular Canons of the Crusader States." In *D'Orient en Occident*, 180–93.

Zöller, Wolf. "The Regular Canons and the Liturgy of the Latin East," *Journal of Medieval History* 43 (2017): 367–83 (the article also appears in Shagrir and Gaposchkin, *Liturgy and Devotion in the Crusader States*).

Zöller, Wolf. "The Religious Environment of the Nascent Military Orders: The Augustinian Consortium Revisited." In *Ordens militares: Identitade e Mudança*, edited by Isabel Cristina Ferreira Fernandes, 1:149–61. Palmela, 2021.

Index